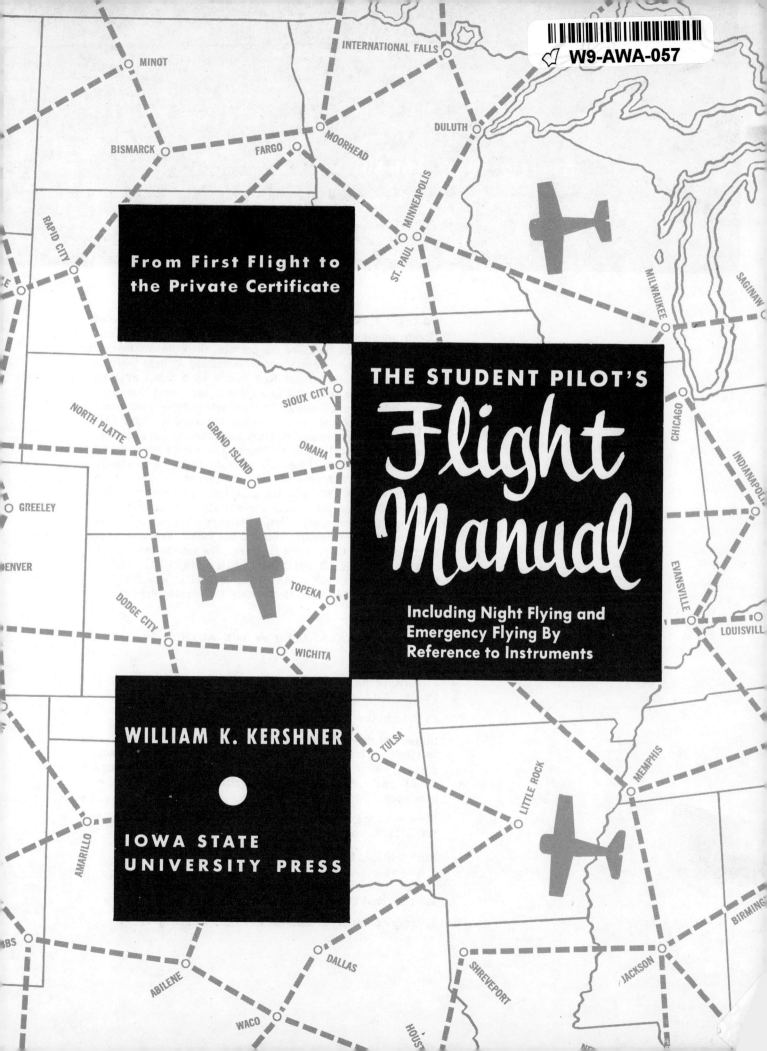

TO BETTY, CINDY, AND BILL

WILLIAM K. KERSHNER began flying in 1945 at the age of fifteen, washing and propping airplanes to earn flying time. By this method he obtained the private, then the commercial and flight instructor certificates, becoming a flight instructor at nineteen. He spent four years as a naval aviator; most of the time as a pilot in a night fighter squadron, both shore- and carrier-based. He flew nearly three years as a corporation pilot and for four years worked for Piper Aircraft Corporation, demonstrating airplanes to the military, doing experimental flight testing and acting as special assistant to William T. Piper, Sr., president of the company. Kershner holds a degree in technical journalism from Iowa State University. While at the university he took courses in aerodynamics, performance, and stability and control. He holds airline transport pilot, commercial, and flight and ground instructor certificates and has flown airplanes ranging from 40 HP Cubs to jet fighters. He also is the author of THE ADVANCED PILOT'S FLIGHT MANUAL, THE INSTRUMENT FLIGHT MANUAL, and THE FLIGHT INSTRUCTOR'S MANUAL (Iowa State University Press).

ILLUSTRATED by THE AUTHOR

© 1979, 1973, 1968, 1964, 1960 The Iowa State University Press. All rights reserved

Printed in the U.S.A.

First, second, third, and fourth editions, © 1960, 1964, 1968, 1973, carried through twenty-seven printings.

Fifth edition, 1979, revised fourth printing, 1984

International Standard Book Number: 0-8138-1610-6

Library of Congress Catalog Card Number: 78-71364

ATLANTA
SECTIONAL AERONAUTICAL CHART
SCALE 1:500,000

Lambert Conformal Conic Projection Standard Parallels 33°20' and 38°40'
Topographic data corrected to July 19

PUBLISHED IN ACCORDANCE WITH INTER-AGENCY AIR CARTOGRAPHIC COMMITTEE
SPECIFICATIONS AND AGREEMENTS. APPROVED BY:
DEPARTMENT OF DEFENSE ★ FEDERAL AVIATION ADMINISTRATION ★ DEPARTMENT OF COMMERCE

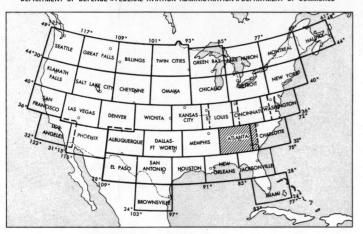

CONTOUR INTERVAL 500 feet
Intermediate contour 250 feet

HIGHEST TERRAIN elevation is 6684 feet
located at 35°46'N – 82°16'W

Critical elevation - - - - - - - - - - - - - ▲4254
Approximate elevation - - - - - - - - - - ×3200

Doubtful locations are indicated by omission
of the point locator (dot or "x")

MILITARY TRAINING ROUTES (MTRs)

All IR and VR MTRs are shown, and may extend from the surface upwards. Only the route centerline, direction of flight along the route and the route designator are depicted – route widths and altitudes are not shown.

Since these routes are subject to change every 56 days, and the charts are reissued every 6 months, you are cautioned and advised to contact the nearest FSS for route dimensions and current status for those routes effecting your flight.

Routes with a change in the alignment of the charted route centerline will be indicated in the Aeronautical Chart Bulletin of the Airport/Facility Directory. Also, the VFR Wall Planning Chart is issued every 56 days and displays current route configurations and a composite tabulation of altitudes along these routes. Military Pilots refer to Area Planning AP/1B Military Training Route North and South America for current routes.

CONVERSION OF ELEVATIONS

FEET (Thousands) 0 2 4 6 8 10 12 14 16 18 20 22 24 26 28 30
METERS (Thousands) 0 1 2 3 4 5 6 7 8 9

Published at Washington, D.C.
U.S. Department of Commerce
National Oceanic and Atmospheric Administration
National Ocean Survey

CONTROL TOWER FREQUENCIES ON ATLANTA SECTIONAL CHART

Airports which have control towers are indicated on this chart by the letters CT followed by the primary VHF local control frequency. Selected transmitting frequencies for each control tower are tabulated in the adjoining spaces, the low or medium transmitting frequency is listed first followed by a VHF local control frequency and the primary VHF and UHF military frequencies, when these frequencies are available. An asterisk (*) follows the part time tower frequency remoted to the collocated full time FSS for use as Airport Advisory Service (AAS) during hours tower is closed. Receiving frequencies are shown thus: 122.5R. Hours shown are local time.
Automatic Terminal Information Service (ATIS) frequencies, shown on the face of the chart are normal arriving frequencies, all ATIS frequencies available are tabulated below
ASR and/or PAR indicates Radar Instrument Approach available:

HUNTSVILLE-MADISON CO . . . . ATIS 121.25 . . . . 119.7 257.8 ASR
(Huntsville Twr)
    TRSA: 125.6 354.1 (359°-179°)
    118.05 239.0 (180°-239°)

KNOXVILLE DOWNTOWN ISLAND . . . . Opr 0730-2200 . . . . 126.6
(Downtown Twr)

LAWSON AAF . . . ATIS 111.4 . . . Opr 0700-2300 Mon-Fri . . . . 126.2 229.4 ASR/PAR
exc Hol

LOVELL (Chattanooga Twr) . . . . ATIS 119.85 . . . . 118.3 257.8 ASR
    TRSA: 125.1 379.1 (016°-195°)
    119.2 321.2 (196°-015°)

McGHEE TYSON (Knoxville Twr) . . . . . ATIS 128.35 . . . . 118.7 257.8 ASR
    TRSA: 123.9 353.6 (225°-044°)
    125.05 360.8 (045°-224°)

NASHVILLE METRO (Nashville Twr) . . . . ATIS 120.0 . . . . 119.1 257.8 ASR
    TRSA: 124.0 360.7 (016°-196°)
    120.6 388.0 (197°-015°)

ATLANTA
LEGEND

Airports having Control Towers (Airport Traffic Areas) are shown in blue, all others in magenta.
Consult Airport/Facility Directory for details involving airport lighting, facilities, and navigation aids.

AIRPORTS

- Civil – Public use
- Military – Without charting restrictions (identified by abbreviations AFB, NAS, AAF, etc.) (For complete airport information consult DOD–FLIP)
- (R) Private "(Pvt)" – Non-public use, having emergency use or landmark value
- (H) Heliport – Selected
- (U) Unverified – Emergency use only
- ⊗ Abandoned – Paved, having landmark value
- ⚓ Seaplane Base (SPB)

Airports with paved runways at least 1500 feet long are shown by pattern. All recognizable runways, including those closed are shown for visual identification.

AIRPORTS WITH SERVICES

Fuel available and field tended normal working times

Non-hard-surfaced Runways – turf, gravel, asphalt-treated, etc.

Hard-surfaced Runways – concrete/asphalt

Rotating light in operation Sunset to Sunrise

AIRPORTS WITH EMERGENCY OR NO SERVICES

AIRPORT DATA

FSS ◄— Indicates FSS on field
NAME CT –118.3*
ATIS 124.9
03 L 92 122.95 ◄— UNICOM
VFR Advsy 125 3
Airport of entry

FSS – Flight Service Station
CT – 118.3 – Control Tower (CT) – primary frequency
★ – Star indicates operation part time. See tower frequencies tabulation for hours of operation.
ATIS 124.9 – Automatic Terminal Information Service
UNICOM – Aeronautical advisory station.
VFR Advsy – VFR Advisory Service shown where ATIS not available and frequency is other than primary CT frequency.
03 – Elevation in feet
L – Lighting in operation Sunset to Sunrise
***L** – Lighting available Sunset to Sunrise only on request (by radio call, letter, phone, telegram).
(L) – Lighting in operation part of the night and on request, or not operating thereafter.
Ⓛ – Pilot-controlled lighting (PCL)
92 – Length of longest runway in hundreds of feet
S – Normally sheltered take-off area (SPB)
When facility or information is lacking, the respective character is replaced by a dash. All lighting codes refer to runway lights.
All times are local.
NFCT – Non Federal Control Tower

RADIO AIDS TO NAVIGATION AND COMMUNICATION BOXES

- ⊙ VHF OMNI RANGE (VOR)
- VORTAC
- VOR-DME
- Non-Directional Radiobeacon

RBn
POINT LOMA
302
H+00 & ev 6m
Marine Radiobeacon

○ Other facilities, i.e., Commercial Broadcast Stations, FSS Outlets– RCO, LRCO, SFO, SSFO, etc.

Triangles in corners of box indicate Enroute Flight Advisory Service (EFAS) on frequency 122.0, Voice Call "Oakdale Flight Watch".
122.1R 122.6 123.6

OAKDALE OAK
362 116.8 OAK

Underline indicates no voice on this freq

122.1R
MIAMI
Controlling FSS.

Square indicates Transcribed Weather Broadcast (TWEB) available at this NAVAID.

LOS ANGELES FLIGHT WATCH
Remoted EFAS on frequency 122.0

CHICAGO CHI

Heavy line box indicates Flight Service Station (FSS). Freqs 121.5, 122.2, 243.0 and 255.4 are normally available at all FSS s and are not shown above boxes. All other freqs are shown.

For Airport Advisory Service use FSS freq 123.6

Frequencies above thin line box are remoted to NAVAID site. Other freqs at controlling FSS may be available determined by altitude and terrain. Consult Airport/Facility Directory for complete information.
In Canada all available FSS frequencies are shown.

R – receive only   T – transmit only

AIRPORT TRAFFIC SERVICE AND AIRSPACE INFORMATION

AIRSPACE INFORMATION

Only the controlled and reserved airspace effective below 18,000 ft MSL are shown on this chart. All times are local.

092→ V 3

Low Altitude Federal Airways are indicated by center line.

The limits of controlled airspace are shown by tint bands (Vignette) and are color-coded in blue and magenta.

magenta Floor 700 feet above surface
blue Floor 1200 feet above surface

2000
2000 MSL Floors other than 700 feet or 1200 feet above surface

TA – Transition Area   CZ – Control Zone

Prohibited, Restricted, Warning and Alert Area
MOA – Military Operations Area
CZ extends upwards from the surface. For part time hours see Airport/Facility Directory.
TTTTT CZ within which fixed-wing special VFR Flight is prohibited
Positive CZ (Canada)
Parachute Jumping Area - See Airport/facility Directory
Intersection
Arrows are directed toward facilities which establish intersection.
NAME (Red, Blue, or Black)
Visual Check Point
TCA – Terminal Control Area
TRSA – Terminal Radar Service Area
IR292 MTR-Military Training Route

AIRPORT TRAFFIC AREA

Tower Controlled Airport
DAYTON CT – 119.9
1008 L 70

Special Airport Traffic Areas

Special Air Traffic Rules
(See F.A.R. Part 93 for details.)

NON-TOWER AIRPORTS
MARTIN
556 L 70

OBSTRUCTIONS

1000 ft and higher AGL
below 1000 ft AGL
Group Obstruction
Obstruction with hi-intensity lights
1520 – Elevation of the top above mean sea level
(1210) – Height above ground
UC – Under Construction or reported: position and elevation unverified

CAUTION: Guy wires may extend outward from structures.

MISCELLANEOUS

–2°W– Isogonic Line (1975 VALUE)
FI☆ Flashing Light   ● Marine Light
Light Ship   Glider Operating Area

TOPOGRAPHICAL INFORMATION

- Roads
- Road Markers
- Railroad
- Bridges And Viaducts
- Power Transmission Lines
- Aerial Cable
- Mines And Quarries
- Lookout Tower P-17 (Site Number) 618 (Elevation Base Of Tower)
- CG Coast Guard Station
- Race Track
- Tank – water, oil or gas
- Oil Well   Water Well
- Mountain Pass 11823 (Elevation of Pass)
- Outdoor Theater   Rocks
- Shipwreck   Pier
- Perennial Lake
- Non-Perennial Lake
- Dams

PROHIBITED, RESTRICTED, WARNING, AND ALERT AREAS ON ATLANTA SECTIONAL CHART

NO.	NAME	ALTITUDE	TIME	APPROPRIATE AUTHORITY
P-77	Plains, Ga.	To 1500	Continuous	Admin., FAA, Washington, D.C.
R-2101	Anniston Army Depot, Ala.	To 5000	0700 to 1800 Mon. thru Fri.	C.O. Anniston Army Depot
R-2102	Fort McClellan, Ala.	Subarea A - To 8000 Subarea B - From 8000 to 14,000 Subarea C - From 14,000 to 24,000	Continuous	† FAA, Atlanta ARTC Center * Area FSS. C.O. Fort McClellan, Ala.
R-2104A	Huntsville, Ala.	FL 300	Continuous	† FAA, Memphis ARTC Center * Area FSS. C.G., U.S. Army Missile Command, Redstone Arsenal, Ala.
R-2104B	Huntsville, Ala.	To 2400	Continuous	† FAA, Memphis ARTC Center * Area FSS. C.G. U.S. Army Missile Command, Redstone Arsenal, Ala.
R-2104C	Huntsville, Ala.	To FL 300	Continuous	† FAA, Memphis ARTC Center * Area FSS. C.G., U.S. Army Missile Command, Redstone Arsenal, Ala.

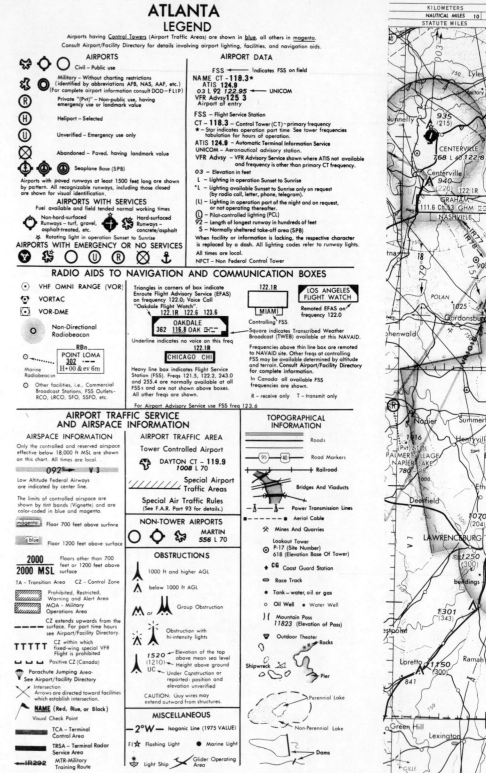

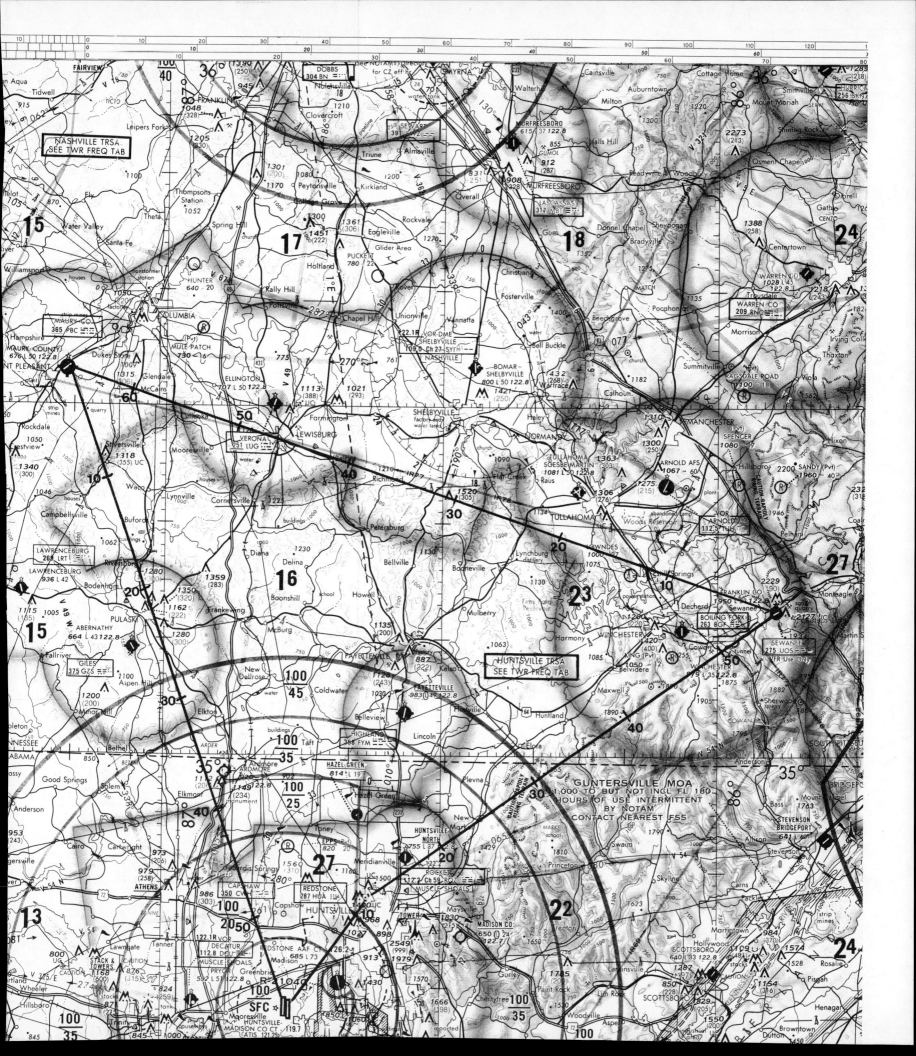

A NOTE FOR PRIVATE PILOTS PREPARING FOR THE BIENNIAL FLIGHT REVIEW

This book was basically written as a step-by-step ground and flight reference for the person starting to fly and working toward the private certificate, but also, with additions, is intended for use as a reference for the Biennial Flight Review for the private pilot (single-engine land airplane) who does not hold an instrument rating.

FAR 61.57 in the back of the book describes the general requirements for the Biennial Review and notes that it consists of a review of the current general operating and flight rules of FAR 91 (selected sections also included there) plus a review of those maneuvers and procedures which, in the discretion of the person giving the Review, are necessary to demonstrate that you can safely exercise the privileges of your pilot certificate.

Probably your biggest concern will be that of finding out just what may be expected of you on the Biennial Review, so it's suggested that you start with Chapters 27 and 28 to get an overall look at the knowledge required on the *initial* written and flight tests for a private certificate.

Chapter 27 can be used as a general reference for the oral part of the Review. Subject areas and chapter references are listed for points you feel should be looked at again. Then read the suggested chapter or chapters to get up to date on *details* of a particular maneuver or procedure. (In reading Chapter 27 substitute "review oral" for "written test.") Also a good look at FAR Part 91 — *General Operating and Flight Rules* — and a recheck of the included Part 61 — *Certification of Pilots and Flight Instructors* — would be in order, to note your responsibilities and limitations. It's suggested that you take the sample written test at the end of the chapter as a check of your knowledge after reviewing the reference chapters.

After you've had a good review of your general knowledge, use *Chapter 28* as an initial quick reference for maneuvers and then also go back to the chapters recommended for more detailed study of the theory and procedures. Chapter 28 covers the knowledge and skill requirements for the private pilot *flight test* and in some instances may repeat areas of knowledge covered in Chapter 27 (such as certificates and documents, weight and balance, and weather information), but will likely bring up some new ideas for you to use on the oral part of the review as well.

Consult the *Pilot's Operating Handbook* for the airplane you're flying to check and fill in the numbers in the form at the end of Chapter 28. If there is a question, procedures recommended by the *Pilot's Operating Handbook* and your instructor for your airplane will naturally take precedence over those in this book, since as a text it must take a general look at maneuvers and operational procedures.

Remember that you'll be taking a *review*, not a flight test and you can't "fail" it. If you're more rusty than you thought, the flight instructor won't make any notations in your logbook or send anything to the **Flight Standards District Office**; he might recommend some practice or more dual and then, when you've done this and straightened out any problems, will fly with you and endorse your logbook to the effect that the Biennial Flight Review is completed.

One problem you may face is "checkitis" as described in Chapter 28. It may have been several years since you had someone overseeing your procedures and flying technique or asking questions about FAR 91, so you can expect to be a little tense. Give yourself a good review at home and be familiar with the various maneuvers as listed in Chapter 28 and you'll do fine.

One question that came to mind when adapting this book to be used also as a Biennial Flight Review guide was whether the name "Student Pilot's Flight Manual" would turn off a private pilot who is "beyond all that." The answer is, of course, that if the needed material is available the name matters not and every pilot, whatever certificates or ratings he holds, as long as he flies, will be a student pilot, in the broad sense of the term. That's the appeal of flying; the fact that you'll never learn it all and are constantly challenged to improve.

After thirty-five years of flying this writer is still a "student pilot" and hopefully will remain so. So, forgive the title.

WILLIAM K. KERSHNER

Preface

This manual was written to give the student a reference for study between flights and also to save some of the flight instructor's preflight and postflight briefing time. It is intended both for students who are working for the private certificate "on their own" and for those who are a part of ROTC flight programs. Certain maneuvers required especially for ROTC programs are included.

Various background items have been added, particularly elementary aerodynamics and certain navigational theory. This was done with the realization that the average student who goes out to the airport to buy flight time does not always have the chance to attend formal ground school as members of the ROTC programs do. The lift equation and other mathematics were added for those who are interested.

This is a gathering of material used in preflight and postflight briefings and in-flight instruction. The maneuvers are written in the probable order of introduction to the student. The spin was included because the writer felt that the student should have some idea of just what this maneuver entailed, even if he* would never be required to practice one. No attempt was made to set up a rigid schedule of maneuvers, because such a schedule is precluded by variation in student ability.

I would like to thank the following for help on this manual:

Colonel E. F. Quinn, Professor of Air Science at Iowa State University, whose encouragement and backing got the book started.

Major J. W. Carothers and Captain H. E. Fischer also of the Iowa State University Air Science Department, who reviewed the manuscript and made suggestions and comments.

Dr. M. L. Millett of the Department of Aeronautical Engineering at Iowa State University, who reviewed both the first and final drafts of the manuscript, with particular attention to the aerodynamics and instrument theory, and who made comments and suggestions which improved the book.

The Army Aviation School personnel at Fort Rucker, Ala., who reviewed the manuscript and made many valuable suggestions.

The Air Force ROTC Headquarters personnel at Maxwell Field, Ala., who reviewed and encouraged the completion of the manual.

A. J. Prokop, who checked the first manuscript; Eugene Anderson, also of the Des Moines Aviation Safety District Office, who checked the manuscript with particular emphasis on emergency recovery by instruments; and Glen Bower, flight instructor of Ames, Iowa, who reviewed and commented on the manual.

The FAA General Operations Branch Office personnel in Washington, D.C., who made several pertinent corrections and suggestions.

J. M. Bennett of Morgantown, W.Va., who furnished reports on the instrument training program at the University of West Virginia.

Particular thanks must go to K. R. Marvin, former head of the Department of Technical Journalism at Iowa State University, who backed the effort.

John Murray, of the Weather Bureau Airport Station at Williamsport, Pa., for his review and suggestions for revision of the chapter on weather.

Jerome Bosworth and John Leck of the Williamsport, Pa., Flight Service Station for their help in obtaining the latest material about the functions of the FSS.

---

*Throughout the book, the student pilot and flight instructor are referred to as "he," avoiding the "he/she" hassle. I recognize that many women are pilots (or studying to be) and instructors and the members of the *Ninety Nines* are my favorite people.

Delbert W. Robertson of the Chattanooga, Tenn., Weather Bureau Airport Station for answering questions and furnishing weather data for the third printing of the second edition.

James D. Lee of the Crossville, Tenn., Flight Service Station for furnishing late FSS information for the third printing of the second edition.

Col. Leslie McLaurin, flight instructor and manager of the airport here at Sewanee, for suggestions and ideas which were used in the book.

W. D. Thompson, chief, Flight Test and Aerodynamics, Commercial Aircraft Division of Cessna Aircraft Company, for furnishing data on Cessna airplanes.

I've had many good suggestions for improving the book from student and private pilots and flight instructors. I would especially like to mention Allen Hayes of Chartair, Inc., Ithaca, New York, and Robert S. Woodbury of Massachusetts Institute of Technology.

This edition was prepared in order to bring the manual up to the requirements of the current Federal Aviation Regulations (Part 61 — Certification of Pilots and Flight Instructors) and to also include new material which I felt would help the student or private pilot cope with the actual requirements of flight. Based on this latter idea, I have attempted to give more than the minimum required to pass the written or flight test for the private certificate. New material on flying by reference to instruments, wind drift correction maneuvers, weather, cross-country flying, and night flying have been added with this in mind.

During the writing and updating of this edition, weather reporting procedures and communications frequencies were changed. As a subscriber to government publications, I see that even they are sometimes out of date in this regard. A text that requires six to ten months from writing to the readers' hands cannot hope to cope with all changes. Look to those publications or your local facilities for the latest frequencies and changes in weather presentation.

Again, I've been lucky in having the help of knowledgeable individuals preparing this edition. Any errors are mine, though. I would especially like to thank the following people:

William Thompson, who, as with other editions, sent me data on Cessna airplanes with dispatch, and with valuable personal comments on the aerodynamics of flight.

Thanks must also go to Cessna and Grumman for allowing me to use information on their airplanes as examples.

Appreciation is expressed to Dr. A. V. Ray of Burlington, Ontario, for suggestions on improving the section in Chapter 26 on the physiology of the eye.

Special thanks must go to Elizabeth Motlow, who flew the example cross-country with me and took pictures of the checkpoints.

The people at the Chattanooga Weather Service Office, as always, were most cooperative and this time came through with actual material, and, more importantly, simple explanations for the new computerized methods of weather reporting and forecasting. In particular, I would mention Ed Higdon and W. R. Wright. Others who helped are, Ray R. Casada, Hugh Pritchard, Jr., Delbert Robertson, M. H. Smith, Jack Phillips, and Sam DeLay.

Thanks to Jules Bernard of Tullahoma, Tenn., for help on this 5th edition.

David F. Shaw, of Penn Yan, N.Y., gave good suggestions for later printings.

Thanks to Larry Crawford, of the Nashville Flight Service Station, for furnishing actual weather information for this edition.

Kermit Anderson of the FAA at OKC gave much appreciated and valuable help for later printings.

My wife encouraged me, as always, and gave practical help by typing the rough copies of the manuscript. Mrs. Barbara Hart typed the smooth copy.

As a textbook, a general approach must be taken here in discussing maneuvers and other flight areas. Some airplanes may require specific techniques in, for instance, use of flaps, carburetor heat, or recommended spin entries and recoveries. The procedures for a particular airplane as outlined in the *Pilot's Operating Handbook* or Airplane Flight Manual will naturally be the final guide for operations. And, as is noted in Chapter 3, your flight instructor will also have suggestions for your airplane and operating conditions.

WILLIAM K. KERSHNER

Sewanee, Tennessee

Contents

1. Starting to Fly

There are many reasons why people want to start flying. Maybe you are a younger person who wants to make it a lifetime career or maybe you are a slightly more senior citizen who always wanted to fly but until now haven't had the money. Whether a man or woman, young or old, you still may have a few butterflies in your stomach while worrying about how you will like it or whether you can do it. That's a natural reaction.

What can you expect as you go through the private pilot training course? You can expect on most flights to work hard and to come down from some flights very tired and wet with perspiration, but with a feeling of having done something worthwhile. After others, you may consider forgetting the whole idea.

Okay, so there will be flights that don't go so well, no matter how well you get along with your instructor. The airplane will seem to have decided that it doesn't want to do what you want it to. The situation gets worse as the flight progresses and you end the session with a feeling that maybe you just aren't cut out to be a pilot. If you have a couple of these in a row you should consider changing your schedule to early morning instead of later afternoon flights, or vice versa. You may have the idea that everybody but you is going through the course with no strain at all, but every person who's gone through a pilot training course has suffered some "learning plateaus" or has setbacks that can be discouraging.

After you start flying you may at some point decide that it would be better for your learning process if you changed instructors. This happens with some people and is usually a no-fault situation, so don't worry about a change or two.

It's best if you get your FAA (Federal Aviation Administration) medical examination out of the way very shortly after you begin to fly or, if you think that you might have a problem, get it done before you start the lessons. The local flight instructors can give you names of nearby FAA Aviation Medical Examiners. You also should fill out and mail the FCC (Federal Communications Commission) application for a radiotelephone license; these forms are usually available at flight schools.

How do you choose a flight school? You might visit a few in your area and see which one suits you best. Watch the instructors and students come and go to the airplanes. Are the instructors friendly, showing real interest in the students? There should be pre- and postflight briefings of students. You may not hear any of the details but can see that such briefings are happening. Talk to students currently flying at the various schools and get their opinions of the learning situation. One good hint about the quality of maintenance of the training airplanes is how clean they are. Usually an airplane that is clean externally is maintained well internally, though certainly there are exceptions to this.

What about the cost? It's a good idea to have money ahead so that you don't have to lay off and require a lot of reviewing from time to time. Some flight schools give a discount if you pay for several hours ahead of time.

You are about to set out on one of the most rewarding of experiences; for an overall look at flight training and future flying you might read the following:

THE BIG THREE

As you go through any flight program, particularly in a military flight program, you will hear three terms used many times: *Headwork, Air Discipline,* and *Attitude toward Flying.*

You may be the smoothest pilot since airplanes were invented, but without having a good grip on the above requirements, you'll last about as long as Simon Legree at an Abolitionist meeting.

HEADWORK

For any pilot, private or professional, the most important thing is good headwork. Nobody cares if you slip or skid a little or maybe every once in a while land a mite harder than usual. But if you don't use your head—if you fly into bad weather, or

Fig. 1-1. Headwork is remembering to put the landing gear down.

forget to check the gas and have to land in a plowed field—you'll find people avoiding you. Later, as you progress in aviation and lead flights or fly passengers, it's a lot more comfortable for all concerned if they know you are a person who uses his head in flying. So as the sign says—THILK, er, think.

AIR DISCIPLINE

This is a broad term but generally means having control of the aircraft and of yourself at all times. Are you a precise pilot or do you wander around during maneuvers? Do you see a sports car and decide to buzz it? Air discipline is difficult at times. It's mighty tough not to fly over that good-looking member of the opposite sex who happens to be sunbathing right where you are doing S-turns across the road—but be firm!

More seriously, air discipline is knowing, and flying by, your own limitations. This means, for instance, holding down for bad weather, and not risking your and your passengers' lives. It also means honestly analyzing your flying faults and doing something about them. In short, air discipline means a mature approach to flying.

ATTITUDE

A good attitude toward flying is important. Most instructors will go all out to help a guy who's really trying, even if he's a complete bungler. Many an instructor's favorite story is about ol' Joe Blow who was pretty terrible at first, but who kept at it until he got the word, and who is now flying rockets for Trans-Galaxy Airlines. With a good attitude you will get plenty of help from everybody. More students have failed in flying because of poor headwork and attitude than for any other reason. This doesn't imply "apple polishing." It does mean that you are interested in flying and study more about it than is required by law.

2. The Airplane and How It Flies

THE FOUR FORCES

Four forces act on an airplane in flight: *Lift*, *Thrust*, *Drag*, and *Weight* (Fig. 2-1).

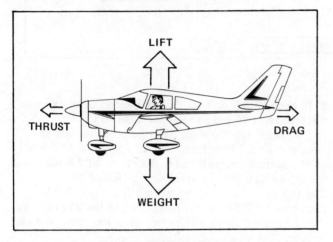

Fig. 2-1. The Four Forces.

LIFT

Lift is a force exerted by the wings. (Lift may also be exerted by the fuselage or other components, but at this point it would be best just to discuss the major source of the airplane's lift, the wings.) It is a force created by the "airfoil," the cross-sectional shape of the wing being moved through the air or, as in a wind tunnel, the air being moved past the wing. The result is the same in both cases. The

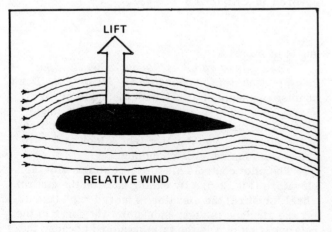

Fig. 2-2. The airfoil.

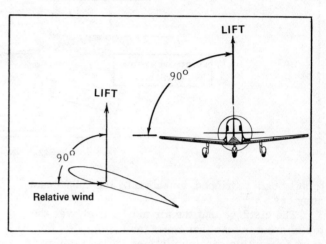

Fig. 2-3.

"relative wind" (wind moving in relation to the wing and airplane) is a big factor in producing lift, although not the only one (Fig. 2-2).

Lift is always considered to be acting perpendicularly both to the wingspan and to the relative wind (Fig. 2-3). The reason for this consideration will be shown later as you are introduced to the various maneuvers.

As the wing moves through the air, either in gliding or powered flight, lift is produced. How lift is produced can probably be explained most simply by Bernoulli's theorem, which briefly puts it this way: "The faster a fluid moves past an object the less sidewise pressure is exerted on the body by the fluid." The fluid in this case is air; the body is an airfoil. Take a look at Figure 2-4, which shows the relative wind approaching an airfoil, all neatly lined up in position (1). As it moves past the airfoil (or as the airfoil moves past it — take your choice),

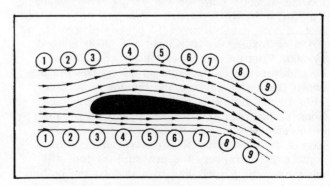

Fig. 2-4.

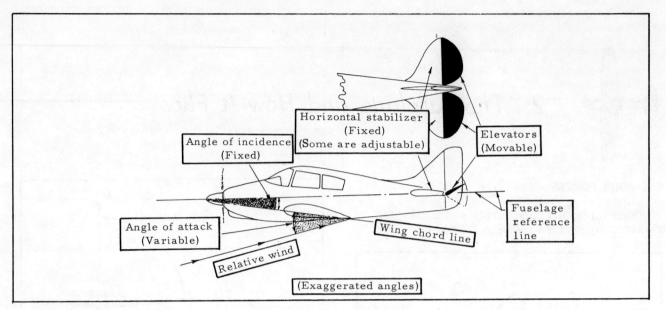

Fig. 2-5. Nomenclature.

things begin to happen, as shown by the subsequent numbers.

The distance that the air must travel over the top is greater than that under the bottom. As the air moves over this greater distance it speeds up in an apparent attempt to reestablish equilibrium at the rear (trailing edge) of the airfoil. (Don't worry, equilibrium *won't* be established.) Because of this extra speed, the air exerts less sidewise pressure on the top surface of the airfoil than on the bottom, and lift is produced. The pressure on the bottom of the airfoil is normally increased also and you can think that, as an average, this contributes about 25 percent of the lift; this percentage varies with "angle of attack" (Fig. 2-5).

Some people say, "Sure, I understand what makes a plane fly. There's a vacuum on top of the wing that holds the airplane up." Let's see about that statement:

The standard sea level air pressure is 14.7 pounds per square inch (psi), or 2116 pounds per square foot (psf). As an example, suppose an airplane weighs 2000 pounds, has a wing area of 200 square feet, and is in level flight at sea level. (The wing area is that area you would see by looking directly down on the wing.) This means that for it to fly level (lift = weight), each square foot of wing must support 10 pounds of weight, or the wing loading is 10 pounds psf (2000 divided by 200). Better expressed; there would have to be a difference in pressure of 10 pounds psf between the upper surface and the lower surface. This 10 psf figure is an average; on some portions of the wing the difference will be greater, on others, less. Both surfaces of the wing can have a reduced sidewise pressure under certain conditions. However, the pressure on top still must average 10 psf less than that on the bottom to meet our requirements of level flight for the airplane mentioned. The sea level pressure is

2116 pounds psf, and all that is needed is an average difference of 10 psf for the airplane to fly.

Assume for the sake of argument that in this case the 10 psf is obtained by an *increase* of 2.5 psf on the bottom surface and a *decrease* of 7.5 psf on the top (which gives a total difference of 10 psf). The top surface pressure varies from sea level pressure by 7.5 psf, and compared to the 2116 psf of the air around it, this is certainly a long way from a vacuum, but it produces flight!

Note in Figures 2-2 and 2-4 that the airflow is deflected downward as it passes the wing. Newton's Law: "For every action there is an equal and opposite reaction," also applies here. The wing deflects the airflow downward with a reaction of the airplane being sustained in flight. This can be easily seen by examining how a helicopter flies. Some engineers prefer Newton's theory over the Bernoulli theory. But the air *does* increase its velocity over the top of the wing (lowering the pressure), and the downwash also occurs. The downwash idea and how it affects the forces on the horizontal tail will be covered in Chapters 9 and 23.

Angle of Attack

The angle of attack is the angle between the relative wind and the chord line of the airfoil. Don't confuse the angle of attack with the angle of *incidence*. The angle of *incidence* is the *fixed* angle between the wing chord line and the reference line of the fuselage. You'd better take a look at Figure 2-5 before this gets too confusing.

The pilot controls his angle of attack with the elevators (Fig. 2-5). By easing back on the control wheel (or stick) the elevator is moved "up" (assuming the airplane is right-side-up). The force of the relative wind moves the tail down, and because the wings are rigidly attached to the fuselage (you hope),

4

they are rotated to a new angle with respect to the relative wind, or new *angle of attack*. At this new angle of attack the apparent curvature of the airfoil is greater, and for a very short period lift is increased. But because of the higher angle of attack more drag is produced, the airplane **slows, and equilibrium exists again.** (More about drag later.)

If the pilot gets too eager to climb and *mistakenly* believes that the reason an airplane climbs is because of an "excess" of lift (and so keeps increasing the angle of attack), he could find that he's made a mistake. He finds that as he increases the angle of attack the airplane slows and attempts to reestablish equilibrium, so he continues to increase it in hopes of getting an "excess" of lift for more climb. He may make the angle of attack so great that the air can no

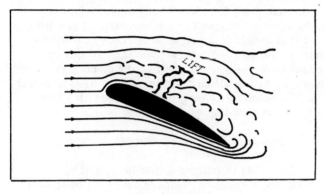

Fig. 2-6. The stall.

longer flow smoothly over the wing, and the airplane "stalls" (Fig. 2-6).

It's not like a car stalling, in which case the engine stops; the airplane stall is a situation where the lift has broken down and the wing, in effect, is no longer doing its job of supporting the airplane in the usual manner. (The engine may be humming like a top throughout the stall.) There is still some lift, but not enough to support the airplane. The pilot has forced the airplane away from the balanced situation he wants it to maintain. For the airplane to recover from a stall, the pilot must decrease the angle of attack so that smooth flow again occurs. In other words, point the plane where it's going! This is done with the elevators, the angle of attack (and speed) control (Fig. 2-5). For most lightplane airfoils the stalling angle of attack is in the neighborhood of 18°. Stalls will be covered more thoroughly in Chapters 12 and 14.

At first, the student is also confused concerning the *angle of attack* and airplane *attitude*. The attitude is how the plane looks in relation to the horizon. In Figure 2-7 the plane's attitude is 15° nose up, but it's climbing at an angle of 5° so the angle of attack is only 10°.

In a slow glide the nose attitude may be approximately level and the angle of attack close to that of the stall. Later in your flying you'll be introduced to the attitude of the wings (wing-down attitude, etc.), but for now only nose attitudes are of interest.

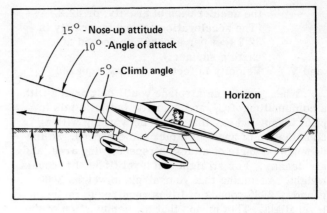

Fig. 2-7.

The coefficient of lift is a term used to denote the relative amounts of lift at various angles of attack for an airfoil. The plot of the coefficient of lift versus the angle of attack is a straight line, increasing with an increase in the angle of attack untill the stalling angle is reached (Fig. 2-8).

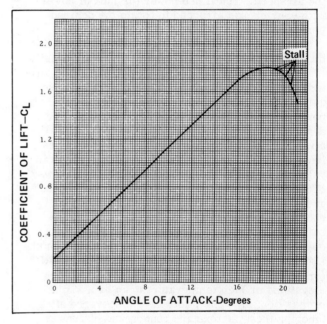

Fig. 2-8.

Lift depends on a combination of several factors. The equation for lift is:

$$L = C_L S \frac{\rho}{2} V^2 \text{ or } L = C_L \text{ x } S \text{ x} \frac{\rho}{2} \text{ x } V^2$$

Where L = Lift, in pounds.

C_L = Coefficient of lift. (Varies with the type of airfoil used and the angle of attack.)

S = Wing area in square feet.

$\frac{\rho}{2}$ = The air density (ρ) divided by 2. Rho (ρ) is air density, which for standard sea level conditions, is 0.002378 slugs per cubic foot. If you want to know the mass of an object in slugs divide the weight by the acceleration of gravity, or 32.2. (The acceleration caused by gravity is 32.2 feet per second per second at earth's surface.)

and V^2 = Velocity in feet per second squared.

When you fly an airplane you'll be working with a combination of C_L and velocity; but let's talk in pilot terms and say that you'll be working with a combination of angle of attack and airspeed. So lift depends on angle of attack, airspeed, wing **area**, and air density. For straight and level flight, lift equals weight. Assuming that your airplane weighs 2000 pounds, 2000 pounds of lift is required to maintain level flight. This means that the combination of the above factors must equal that value. The wing area (S) is fixed, and the air density (ρ) is fixed for any one time and altitude. Then C_L (angle of attack) and velocity (airspeed) can be worked in various combinations to maintain the 2000 pounds of lift required. Flying at a low airspeed requires a high angle of attack, and vice versa. As a pilot you will control angle of attack and, by doing so, control the airspeed. You'll use power (or lack of power) with your chosen airspeed to obtain the desired performance.

While the factors of lift are being discussed it might be well to say a little more about air density (ρ). The air density decreases with increased altitude and/or temperature increase. Airplanes require more runway to take off on hot days or at airports of high elevation because of decreased air density. You can see in the lift equation that if the air is less dense the airplane will have to move faster through the air in order to get the required value of lift for flight—and this takes more runway. (The airspeed mentioned is called "true airspeed" and will be discussed in more detail in the next chapter.) Not only is the lift of the wing affected, but the less dense air results in less power developed within the engine and, as the propeller is nothing more than a rotating airfoil, it also loses "lift" (or, more properly, "thrust"). Taking off at high elevations or high temperatures can be a losing proposition, as some pilots have discovered after ignoring these factors and running out of runway.

Interestingly enough, you will find that lift tends to remain at a constant value during climbs, glides, or straight and level flight. *Don't* start off by thinking that the airplane glides because of decreased lift or climbs because of excess lift. *It just isn't so.*

THRUST

Thrust is the second of the four forces and is furnished by a propeller or jet. The propeller is of principal interest to you at this point, however.

The theory of propellers is quite complicated, but Newton's "equal and opposite reaction" idea can be stated here. *The propeller takes a large mass of air and accelerates it rearward, resulting in the equal and opposite reaction of the plane moving forward.*

Maybe it's time a few terms such as "force" and "power" should be cleared up. Thrust is a *force* and like the other three forces is measured in pounds. A *force* can be defined as a tension, pressure, or weight. You don't necessarily have to move anything; you can exert force against a very heavy object and nothing moves. Or you can exert a force against a smaller object and it moves. When an object having force exerted upon it moves, *work* has been done.

Work, from an engineering point of view, is simply a measure of *force* times *distance*. And while at the end of a day of pushing against a brick wall, or trying to lift a safe that won't budge, you feel tired, actually you've done no *work* at all. If you pick up a 550-pound **safe** 1 foot off the floor you'll have done 550 foot-pounds of *work* (and no doubt strained yourself in the bargain). If you lift a 50-pound weight to a height of 11 feet you'll have done the same *work* whether you take all day or 1 second to do it—but you won't be developing as much *power* by taking all day. So the *power* used in lifting that 50 pounds up 11 feet, or 550 pounds up 1 foot, in 1 second would be expressed as:

$$Power = 550 \text{ foot-pounds per second}$$

Obviously, this is leading somewhere, and you know that the most common measurement for power is the term "horsepower." One horsepower is equal to a power of 550 foot-pounds per second, or 33,000 foot-pounds per minute (60 seconds x 550). Whether the average horse of today can actually do this is not known, and unfortunately nobody really seems to care.

The airplane engine develops horsepower within its cylinders and, by rotating a propeller, exerts thrust. In straight and level, unaccelerated, cruising flight, the thrust exerted (pounds) is considered to equal the drag (pounds) of the airplane.

You will hear a couple of terms concerning horsepower:

Brake horsepower—the horsepower developed at the crankshaft. In earlier times this was measured at the crankshaft by a braking system or absorption dynamometer known as a "prony brake." *Shaft horsepower* means the same thing. Your airplane engine is always rated in brake horsepower, or the power produced at the crankshaft. Brake horsepower and engine ratings will be covered more thoroughly in Chapter 23.

Thrust horsepower—the horsepower developed by the propeller in moving the airplane through the air. Some power is lost because the propeller is not 100 percent efficient, and for round figures you can say that the propeller is *at best* about 85 percent efficient (the efficiency of the fixed-pitch propeller varies with airspeed). The thrust horsepower developed, for instance, will be only up to about 85 percent of the brake horsepower.

If you are mathematically minded you might be interested in knowing that the equation for thrust horsepower (THP) is: THP = TV/550, where T is thrust (pounds) and V is velocity (feet per second) of the airplane. Remember that a *force* times a *distance* equals *work* and, when divided by time, *power* is found. In the equation above, *thrust* is the force, and velocity can be considered as being distance divided by time, so that TV (T x V) is power in foot-pounds per second. Knowing that 1 horsepower is 550 foot-pounds per second, the power (TV) is divided by 550 and the result would give the horsepower being developed; in this case, *thrust horsepower*.

For light trainers with **fixed-pitch propellers** a measure of the power (brake horsepower) being used is indicated on the airplane's tachometer in rpm's (revolutions per minute). The engine power is controlled by the throttle. For more power the throttle is pushed forward; for less power it is moved back. Since the airplane throttle moves opposite to that of the hand throttle of some automobiles or tractors, it may be a little confusing for the first couple of minutes. You'll use the throttle to establish certain rpm (power) settings for cruise, climb, and other flight requirements.

Torque

Because the propeller is a rotating airfoil, certain side effects are encountered. The "lift" force of the propeller is the thrust used by the airplane. The propeller also has a drag force. This force acts in a sidewise direction (parallel to the wing span or perpendicular to the fuselage reference line).

The propeller rotates clockwise as seen from the cockpit, causing a rotating mass of air to be accelerated toward the tail of the airplane. This air mass strikes the left side of the vertical stabilizer and rudder. This air mass, called "slipstream" or "propwash," causes the airplane to veer or "yaw" to the left. Right rudder must therefore be applied to hold the airplane on a straight track (Fig. 2-9). This reaction increases with power, so it is most critical during the take-off portion of the flight. The

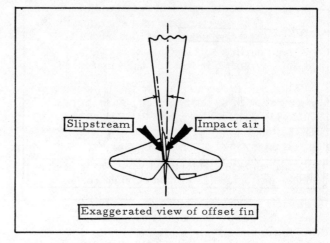

Fig. 2-10.

slipstream effect is the biggest factor of torque for the single-engine airplane.

An offset fin may be used to counteract this reaction. The fin setting is usually built in for maximum effectiveness at the rated cruising speed of the airplane, since the airplane will be flying most of the time at cruising speed (Fig. 2-10).

The balance of forces at this point results in no yawing force at all, and the plane flies straight with no right rudder being held.

Sometimes the fin may not be offset correctly due to tolerances of manufacturing, and a slight left yaw is present at cruising speed, making necessary a constant use of right rudder to hold the airplane straight. To take care of this, a small metal tab is attached to the trailing edge of the rudder and is bent to the left. The relative air pressure against the tab forces the rudder to the right (Fig. 2-11).

On many lightplanes this adjustment can be accomplished only on the ground. The tab is bent and the plane is test flown. This is done until the plane has no tendency to yaw in either direction at cruising speed.

Assuming that you have the tab bent correctly and the plane is balanced directionally, what happens

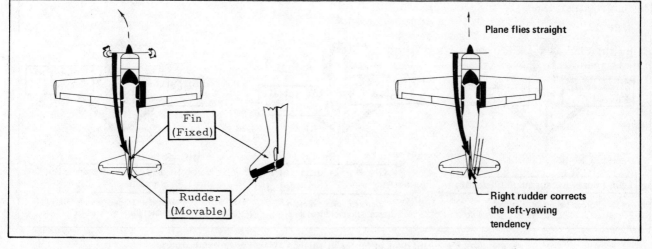

Fig. 2-9.

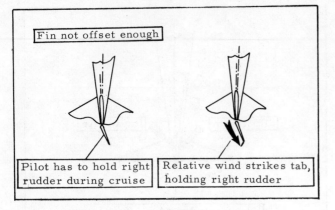

Fin not offset enough

Pilot has to hold right rudder during cruise

Relative wind strikes tab, holding right rudder

Fig. 2-11.

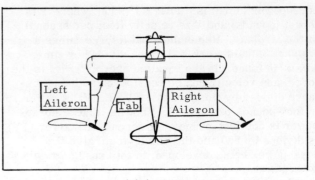

Left Aileron

Tab

Right Aileron

Fig. 2-13.

if you vary from cruising speed? If the same power setting of 2400 rpm, for instance, is used, the arrows in Figure 2-12 show a simplified approach to the relative forces at various airspeeds.

In a climb, right rudder is necessary to keep the plane straight. In a dive, left rudder is necessary to keep it straight.

In a glide there is considered to be no yawing effect. Although the engine is at idle and the torque effect is less, the airspeed is lower and the effect of the offset fin is also less.

Some manufacturers use the idea of "canting" the engine slightly so that the thrust line of the propeller (or crankshaft) is pointing slightly to the right. The correction for a left yawing tendency at cruise is taken care of in this way rather than by offsetting the fin. In such installations, however, right rudder is still necessary in the climb and left rudder in a dive, under the conditions shown in Figure 2-12.

Another less important contributor to the "torque effect" is the tendency of the airplane to rotate in an opposite direction to that of the propeller (for every action there is an opposite and equal reaction). The manufacturer flies each airplane and "rigs" it, making sure that any such rolling tendency

is minimized. They may "wash in" the left wing so that it has a greater angle of incidence (which results in a higher angle of attack for a particular nose attitude) than that of the right wing. This is the usual procedure for fabric-covered airplanes, resulting in more lift and more drag on that side. This may also contribute very slightly to the left yaw effect. In the case of metal airplanes, a small metal tab on one or both of the ailerons can be bent to deflect the ailerons as necessary, using the same principle as was described for the rudder tab (the tab makes the control surface move). The controls and their effects will be discussed in Chapter 8, and you may want to review this section again after reading that chapter. Figure 2-13 shows the ailerons and aileron tab.

Two additional factors that under certain conditions can contribute to the torque effect are gyroscopic precession and what is termed "propeller disk asymmetric loading" or "P-factor." Gyro precession acts *during* attitude changes of the plane, such as those that occur in moving the nose up or down or yawing it from side to side. Gyro precession will be discussed in Chapters 3 and 13. Asymmetric loading is a condition usually encountered when the plane is being flown at a constant, positive angle of attack, such as in a climb. The downward-moving blade, which is on the right side of the

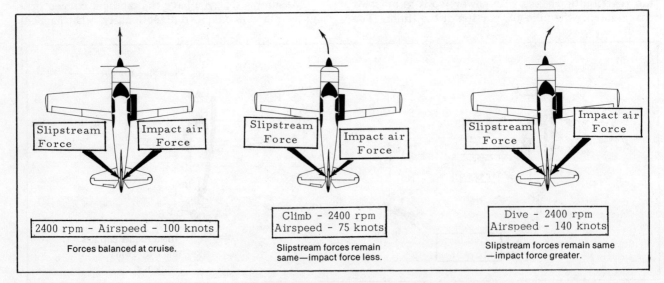

Slipstream Force

Impact air Force

2400 rpm - Airspeed - 100 knots

Forces balanced at cruise.

Slipstream Force

Impact air Force

Climb - 2400 rpm Airspeed - 75 knots

Slipstream forces remain same—impact force less.

Slipstream Force

Impact air Force

Dive - 2400 rpm Airspeed - 140 knots

Slipstream forces remain same—impact force greater.

Fig. 2-12. A comparison of forces at various airspeeds (constant rpm).

8

propeller arc as seen from the cockpit, has a higher angle of attack and higher thrust than the upward-moving blade on the left. This results in a left-turning moment.

Actually the problem is not so simple as it might at first appear. To be completely accurate, a vector system including the propeller angles and rotational velocity and the airplane's forward speed must be drawn to get a picture of the exact angle of attack difference for each blade. In other words, if the plane is flying at an angle of attack of 10° this *does not* mean that the downward-moving blade has an effective angle of attack 10° greater than normal, and the upward-moving blade has an effective angle 10° less than normal, as might be expected.

From a pilot's standpoint, you are only interested in what must be done to keep the plane straight. When the instructor speaks of "torque," he is including such things as the rotating slipstream, gyroscopic effects, asymmetric disk loading (P-factor), and any other power-induced forces or couples that tend to turn the plane to the left.

DRAG

Anytime a body is moved through a fluid (such as air), drag is produced. Drag acts parallel to, and in the same direction as, the relative wind. The "total" drag of an airplane is composed of two main types of drag, as is shown by Figure 2-14.

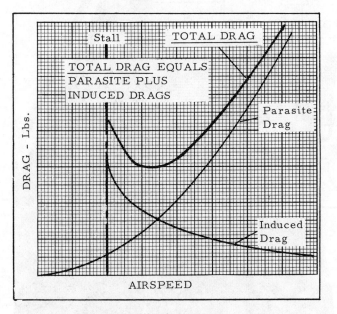

Fig. 2-14. The total drag of the airplane is made up of a combination of parasite and induced drag.

Parasite drag (Fig. 2-15) — the drag composed of (1) "form drag" (the landing gear and radio antennas, the shape of the wings, fuselage, etc.), (2) skin friction, and (3) airflow interference between components (such as would be found at the junction of the wing and fuselage, or fuselage and tail). As the word

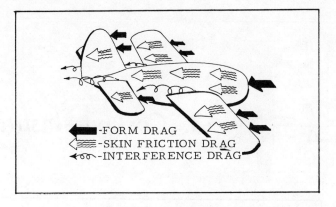

Fig. 2-15. Parasite drag.

"parasite" implies, this type of drag is of no use to anybody and is about as welcome as any other parasite. However, parasite drag exists and it's the engineers' problem to make it as small as possible. Parasite drag increases as the square of the airspeed. Double the airspeed and parasite drag increases *four* times. Triple the airspeed and parasite drag increases *nine* times.

Induced drag — the drag that results from lift being produced. The relative wind is deflected downward by the wing, giving a rearward component to the lift vector called induced drag (the lift vector is tilted rearward). A simple way to look at it is to realize that the air moves over each wing tip toward the low pressure on the top of the wing and vortices are formed that are proportional in strength to the amount of induced drag present. The strength of these vortices (and induced drag) increases radically at higher angles of attack so that the *slower* the airplane flies the *much greater* the induced drag (Figs. 2-14 and 2-16).

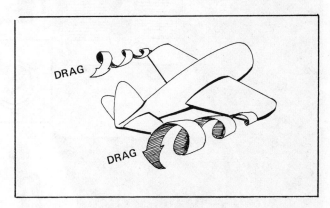

Fig. 2-16. Wing tip vortices.

WEIGHT

Gravity is like the common cold, always around and not much that can be done about it. This can be said, however: Gravity always acts "downward" (toward the center of the earth). Lift does not always act opposite to weight, as you will see in Chapter 9.

Fig. 3-1. The controls, radios, and instruments for a "composite" general aviation trainer.

Figure 3-1 shows controls and instruments for a "composite" airplane. The numbers are chapter references to indicate where more information may be found concerning each item. If there is no reference, the item is covered in this chapter. The seats and control wheels have been "removed" for clarity.

1. *Airspeed indicator* (ASI).
2. *Attitude indicator* (A/I).
3. *Altimeter*.
4. *Turn coordinator* (T/C).

5. *Heading indicator* (H/I).

6. *Vertical speed indicator* (VSI).

7. *Clock.*

8. *Magnetic compass.*

9. *Audio console.* This contains the transmitter selector (the black knob) that, in this installation, allows the pilot to select the number one transmitter (item 10) or the second transmitter (item 11). He can also choose whether he wants to listen to a selected set on the cabin speaker or through the earphones. (Also noted in item 37.) See Chapter 21.

10. *NAV/COMM* or *COMM/NAV set,* a combination of communications equipment and VHF omnirange (VOR) receiver and indicator. (Also called a "one-and-a-half" set.) The left side of the equipment, or the "one," is the communications *transceiver* (transmitter/receiver), and the right side is a navigation *receiver* (the "half"). See Chapter 21.

11. The second *NAV/COMM control* and *VOR indicator.*

12. *Transponder* (Chapter 21).

13. *Automatic Direction Finder* (ADF) control box and indicator (Chapter 21). It's unlikely that your "primary" trainer has all the aviation electronics (avionics) equipment shown here; it will more likely have a NAV/COMM plus maybe an ADF and/or transponder. You'll get familiar with more complex avionics as you progress to higher certificates and ratings.

14. *Tachometer* (indicates engine rpm).

15. *Ammeter.*

16. *Suction gage,* the instrument that indicates the inches-of-mercury drop created by the engine-driven vacuum pump. The vacuum pump provides the suction to operate the gyro horizon, directional gyro, and in some cases, the turn and slip indicator. (In most cases the turn coordinator or turn and slip is electrically driven as a backup.)

17. *Primer* (Chapter 5).

18. *Parking brake.*

19. *Rheostat* to control the brightness of the instrument panel and radio dial lights (Chapter 26).

20. *Engine instrument cluster,* which may include fuel quantity, fuel pressure, oil pressure, and oil temperature gages. High-wing trainers that depend on gravity for fuel feeding do not have a fuel pressure gage. Low-wing airplanes have an engine-driven fuel pump (something like that in your car) and must have an electrically driven pump as a standby. A fuel pressure gage is required (Chapters 5 and 7).

21. *Carburetor heat* (Chapter 4).

22. *Throttle* (Chapters 2, 5, and 7).

23. *Mixture control* (Chapter 5).

24. *Electric flap control.* You would move the handle down to indentations to preselect, for instance, 10°, 20°, or 30° of flap deflection (Chapter 13).

25. *Cabin heat control.*

26. *Cabin air control.* A combination of cabin air and cabin heat may be used to control temperature and flow rate in the cabin.

27. *Map compartment.* (Used to hold most everything except maps.)

28. *Master switch.* As will be discussed later in this chapter, it is a "split" switch to control both the alternator and battery.

29. *Electrically driven fuel pump* (low-wing airplanes) mentioned in item 20. This is turned ON as an aid in starting (for some airplanes) and as a safety standby for take-off and landings if the engine-driven fuel pump should fail (Chapter 7).

30. *Ignition switch.* The airplane has left (L) and right (R) magnetos to furnish ignition. The airplane is flown with the key in the "BOTH" position, using both magnetos. To start the airplane, the key is turned past the "BOTH" position to the spring-loaded "START." After starting, the key is released and moves back to "BOTH" (Chapter 4).

31. *Electrical switches.* These will be for navigation (position) lights, wing tip strobes and a red rotating beacon on the top of the fin. There will also be a taxi and landing light switch for most airplanes.

32. *Circuit breaker panel* for the items depending on the electrical system, such as radios and lights. These circuit breakers (fuses are used for various items in some airplanes) are designed to stop any overloading of circuits and are "safety cutoffs" to prevent fire or damage to the system.

33. *Aircraft papers.* The "Airworthiness Certificate" must be *displayed* (see end of chapter).

34. *Toe brake* (left) (Chapter 6).

35. *Rudder pedal* (Chapters 6 and 8).

36. *Elevator or stabilator trim wheel and indicator.*

37. *Microphone.* For receiving, the speaker (usually located on the cabin ceiling) is used in most cases; however, your trainer may have earphones. Many planes have both a speaker and earphones, and the pilot selects whichever method of receiving he prefers. See the right side of item 9.

38. *Fuel selector valve.* This example airplane has a tank in each wing and is selected to use fuel from the left wing tank. The "OFF" selection is very seldom used, but the selector valve should *always* be checked before starting to make sure the fuel is on an operating (and the fullest) tank.

39. An example of a *manual flap control.* The flap handle is operated in "notches," giving various preset flap settings. The button on the end of the handle is used to unlock the control from a previous setting. Your trainer will probably have one of the two types (items 24 and 39) shown here, but not both. Or your trainer may not have flaps (Chapter 13).

REQUIRED INSTRUMENTS

ALTIMETER

The altimeter is an aneroid barometer with the face calibrated in feet instead of inches of mercury. As the altitude increases, the pressure decreases at the rate of about one inch of mercury for each thousand feet altitude gain. The altimeter contains a sealed flexible diaphragm, correct only at sea level standard pressure (29.92 inches of mercury) and sea level standard temperature (59°F or 15°C). Indicating hands are connected to the diaphragm and geared so that a small change in the diaphragm results in the proper altitude indications. The altimeter has three hands. The longest indicates the hundreds of feet and the medium-sized hand, the thousands of feet. Another pointer indicates tens of thousands of feet, but it is doubtful if you will have a chance to use this one for a while.

A small window at the side of the face allows the altimeter to be set to the latest barometric pressure as corrected to sea level. As you know, the atmospheric pressure is continually changing and the altimeter, being a barometer, is affected by this.

Suppose that while you're flying, the pressure drops at the airport (maybe a low-pressure area is moving in). After you land, the altimeter will still be "in the air" because of the lower pressure. The instrument only measures the pressure and has no idea where the ground is unless you correct for pressure changes. The altimeter is usually set at field elevation so that a standard may be set among all planes. In other words, pilots fly their altitude with respect to sea level. The elevations of the airports around the country vary and if the altimeters were set at zero for each field, there would be no altitude standardization at all. The altitude you read when the altimeter has been set to the present corrected station barometric pressure is called "mean sea level" (MSL), or indicated, altitude. Remember that this does not tell you how high you are above the terrain at a particular time.

As an example, assume your field elevation is 720 feet. Set the altimeter at 720 feet with the setting knob, as shown in Figure 3-2.

If you want to fly at 2000 feet above the local terrain, your indicated altitude will be 2720, or 2720 feet above sea level (Fig. 3-3). If you were asked your altitude by a ground station (or another plane) you'd answer, "2720 feet MSL."

With the altimeter set to sea level you can call FAA Flight Service Stations or towers in the vicinity of the destination airport and get the altimeter setting. They'll give their barometric pressure in inches of mercury, corrected to sea level. You'll set this in the small barometric scale on the altimeter and this will correct for any pressure difference between your home field and the destination. The altimeter should read the destination field's elevation after you land. If not, there's an altimeter error.

Airplanes used for instrument flying must have had their altimeter(s) and static pressure system (see Fig. 3-4) tested and inspected to meet certain

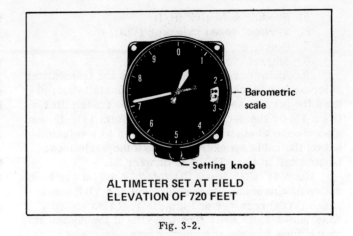

ALTIMETER SET AT FIELD
ELEVATION OF 720 FEET

Fig. 3-2.

minimums within the past 24 calendar months by the manufacturer or a certificated repair facility.

When you fly from a high- to a low-pressure area, the altimeter reads too high: H to L = H. When you fly from a low to a high the altimeter reads too low: L to H = L.

In other words, when you fly from a high-pressure region into one of lower pressure, the altimeter "thinks" the plane has climbed and registers accordingly, when actually your altitude above sea level may not have changed at all. As you will be flying in reference to the altimeter, this means that you will fly the plane down to what appears to be the correct altitude and will be low. If the outside temperature at a particular altitude is lower than standard, the altimeter will read higher than the airplane's actual altitude if not corrected. HALT (High Altimeter because of Low Temperature). Higher than standard temperature means a low reading altimeter.

Pressure altitude is that altitude shown on the altimeter when the pressure in the setting window is set at 29.92, meaning that this is your altitude as far as a standard pressure day is concerned. Unless the altimeter setting on the ground is exactly 29.92 and the pressure drop per thousand feet is standard, the pressure altitude and indicated altitude will be different. Pressure altitude computed with temperature gives the density altitude, or the standard altitude where the density of the air at your altitude is normally found.

Density altitude is used for computing aircraft performance. In your flying, you will use indicated altitude or the altitude as given by the actual barometric pressure corrected to sea level.

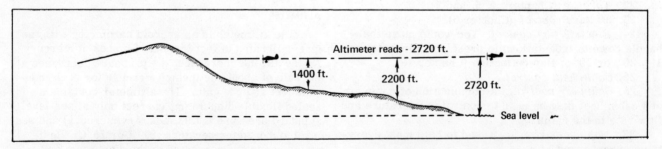
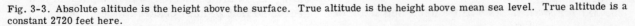

Fig. 3-3. Absolute altitude is the height above the surface. True altitude is the height above mean sea level. True altitude is a constant 2720 feet here.

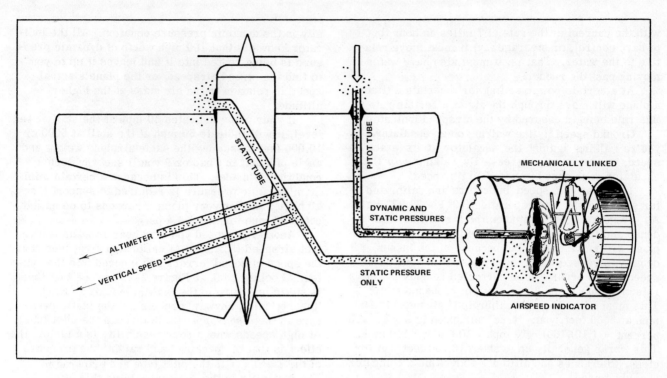

Fig. 3-4. Typical general aviation trainer airspeed indicator and pitot-static system.

AIRSPEED INDICATOR

The airspeed system is comprised of the pitot and static tubes and the airspeed indicator instrument. The pitot-static system measures the dynamic pressure of the air. As the airplane moves through the air the relative wind exerts a "ram" pressure in the pitot tube. This pressure expands a diaphragm which is geared to an indicating hand. This pressure is read as airspeed, in miles per hour or knots, rather than pressure. In short, the pitot-static system measures the pressure of the relative wind approaching the wings (and the entire plane, for that matter). A pitot tube alone would not tell the pilot how much of this pressure was the dynamic pressure giving the wings their lift. The static tube equalizes the static pressure within and without the system, leaving only the dynamic pressure or airspeed being measured. You will check the pitot tube and static vent openings during the preflight inspection, as will be covered in Chapter 4.

About *airspeed* and *ground speed* while we're on the subject. Once a plane is airborne, it is a part of the air. The airplane moves through the air, but the air itself may move over the ground. The plane's performance is not affected by the fact that the entire mass is moving. It is only affected by its relative motion to the mass. A boat may drift downstream

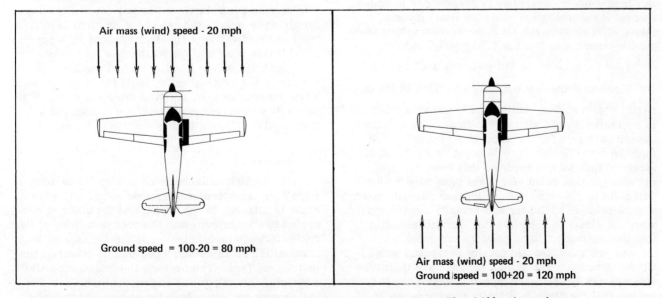

Fig. 3-5. The airplane's true airspeed is 100 mph; its ground speeds are 80 and 120 mph, as shown.

with the current at the rate of 7 miles an hour, but to have control, or steerageway, it must move relative to the water. That is, it must also have water moving past the rudder.

At a certain power setting for a certain attitude, a plane will move through the air at a certain rate, this rate being measured by the airspeed indicator.

Ground speed is like walking on an escalator. If you're walking against the escalator at its exact speed, you make no progress. By walking *with* the escalator your speed is *added* to its speed.

Lightplane airspeed indicators are calibrated for standard sea level operation (59°F - 29.92″ Hg). As you go to higher altitudes, the air will be less dense and therefore there will be less drag. The plane will move faster, but because of the lesser density, airspeed will register less than your actual speed. This error can be corrected roughly by the rule of thumb: "Add 2 per cent per thousand feet." This means that if your "calibrated" airspeed is 100 mph at 5000 feet, your "true" airspeed is 5 x 2 = +10 percent = (.10)(100) = 10 mph + 100 mph = 110 mph. This works generally up to about 10,000 feet, but for closer tolerances and altitudes above this a computer should be used.

The computer takes into consideration any deviation of temperature and pressure from the "normal lapse rate." The standard temperature at sea level is 59°F or 15°C. The "normal lapse rate," or temperature drop, is 3 1/2°F or 2°C per thousand feet. The "2 percent per thousand feet" rule of thumb uses this fact and does not take into consideration any change from the normal lapse rate, or from standard conditions.

The calibrated airspeed mentioned above is the corrected indicated airspeed, so in order to find the true airspeed the following steps would apply:

1. *Indicated airspeed (I.A.S.) + instrument and position error = calibrated airspeed (C.A.S.).*
2. *Calibrated airspeed plus pressure altitude and temperature correction (2 percent per thousand feet or use a computer) gives the true airspeed.* (Most light planes have I.A.S. correction information, but for others, assume I.A.S. to equal C.A.S.)

Looking back at the lift equation in Chapter 2 you'll see in it the expression $\frac{\rho}{2} V^2$. This is the dynamic pressure that contributes to the wing's lift and is measured by the airspeed indicator, as was discussed earlier. For instance, at an indicated 100 mph the dynamic pressure is about 25.7 psf. Your airspeed indicator is made so that when dynamic pressure of that value enters the pitot tube the hand will point to 100 mph. At sea level air density your motion relative to the air will actually *be* 100 mph when the airspeed indicates this amount (assuming that the instrument is completely accurate).

As you know, the air density decreases with altitude. When you are at 5000 feet and are indicating 100 mph (25.7 psf) the airspeed indicator doesn't reason that the plane is actually moving faster in relation to the air and making up for the lower den-

sity in the dynamic pressure equation. All the indicator knows is that 100 mph worth of dynamic pressure is being routed into it and leaves it up to you to find the "true" airspeed, or the plane's actual speed in relation to the air mass at the higher altitude.

If your plane indicates 50 mph at the stall at sea level, it will indicate 50 mph at the stall at 5000 or 10,000 feet (assuming the same airplane weight and angle of bank; in Chapter 9 you'll see why such a condition is made). This is because a certain minimum dynamic pressure is required to support the airplane, and for your plane it happens to be an indicated 50 mph (or about 6.4 psf).

Another airspeed you may hear about is equivalent airspeed (E.A.S.). At calibrated airspeeds near the speed of sound, errors are induced into the system. Looking back at Figure 3-4, you see that there is static pressure in the *instrument case*, which (theoretically, anyway) cancels out the static pressure in the *diaphragm* (let in through the pitot tube). At high speeds where compressibility is a factor, the effect is that of "packing" and raising the pressure of the *static* air in the pitot tube and diaphragm. The static air in the *case* doesn't get this effect, so that indicated (and calibrated) airspeeds are shown as *higher* than the actual value. A correction is made to obtain the "correct" calibrated airspeed; this is called the *equivalent* airspeed. E.A.S. would then be used to find the true airspeed. For high-speed airplanes the correction would be:

1. I.A.S. plus (or minus) instrument and position error = C.A.S.
2. C.A.S. minus compressibility error = E.A.S.
3. E.A.S. corrected for pressure altitude and temperature = T.A.S.

You won't have to cope with compressibility errors in the airplane you are training in, but you should be aware that such factors do exist.

You'll note that examples of true airspeed in this section used statute miles per hour. The trend for flying is toward the use of the nautical mile (6080 feet) and knots (1 knot equals 1 nautical mile per hour). This book will follow the data as produced in the *Pilot's Operating Handbook*s and use knots (K) for speed and nautical miles (NM) for distance, with a few exceptions to be noted in later chapters. While this will seem strange at first, you'll soon get accustomed to thinking in these terms in flying.

TACHOMETER

The lightplane tachometer is similar in many ways to a car speedometer. One end of a flexible cable is attached to the engine and the other is connected to the instrument. The rate of turning of the cable, through mechanical or magnetic means, is transmitted as revolutions per minute (rpm) on the instrument face. The average lightplane propeller is connected directly to the engine crankshaft so that the tachometer registers both the engine and propeller rpm. The propeller is usually geared down in larger planes, and in that case the ratio of engine speed to propeller speed can be found in the Airplane Flight Manual. At any rate, you always use the engine rpm for setting power because this is what is indicated on the tachometer in the geared engine.

Most tachometers have a method of recording flight hours, based on a particular rpm setting (say, 2300 rpm). This means that the engine is not "building up time" as fast when it's at idle, or at lower power settings. The time indicated on the recording tachometer is used as a basis for required inspections and overhauls, and the reading is noted in the logbooks whenever such work is done on the airplane and/or engine.

OIL PRESSURE GAGE

Every airplane is equipped with an oil pressure gage (Fig. 3-6), and to the majority of pilots it is the most important engine instrument (the fuel gage runs a close second). Some oil pressure gages have a curved Bourdon tube in the instrument. Oil pressure tends to straighten the tube, and, through mechanical linkage, a hand registers the pressure in pounds per

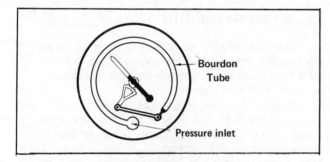

Fig. 3-6. Oil pressure gage.

square inch. The move now is toward using electrical transmitters and indicators, particularly for more complex engine installations.

Oil pressure should reach the normal operating value within 30 seconds after the engine starts. The instrument should be checked about every 5 minutes in flight as it is one of the first indicators of oil starvation, which means engine failure and a forced landing. If the oil pressure starts dropping, land as soon as is safely possible.

There have been many cases of the instrument itself giving bum information. After you notice the falling (or low) oil pressure, keep an eye on the oil temperature gage for a rising temperature as you turn toward an airport or good landing area. Pilots have depended solely on the oil pressure gage and landed in bad places when the engine was getting plenty of oil (and the oil temperature stayed normal).

OIL TEMPERATURE GAGE

The vapor-type temperature gage is commonly used for lightplanes. The indicating head or instrument contains a Bourdon tube and is connected by a fine tube to a bulb which contains a volatile liquid.

Vapor expansion exerts pressure which is read as temperature on the instrument. Most trainers do not have a cylinder head temperature gage, so the oil temperature gage is the only means of telling if the engine is running hot. Other models of airplanes use the principle of electrical resistance change for measuring oil temperature.

COMPASS

The airplane compass is a magnet with an attached face or "card" that enables you to read directions from 0° to 360°.

The magnet aligns itself with the Magnetic North Pole and the plane turns around it.

Every 30°, the compass has the number of that heading minus the 0. For instance, 60° is 6 and 240° is 24 on the compass card. It's broken down further into 10° and 5° increments. The compass card appears to be backward in the diagram, but as the plane actually turns around the compass, the correct reading will be given.

In a shallow turn, the compass is reasonably accurate on headings of East and West but leads ahead of the turn as the plane's heading approaches South and lags behind as it approaches North. If you are on a heading of *North* and make a turn in either direction, the compass will initially roll to a heading *opposite* to the bank. On a heading of *South* when the turn is started, the compass will initially roll to a heading indication *exceeding* that actually turned (North-Opposite, South-Exceeds, or NOSE). The amount of lead or lag depends on the amount of bank and other factors. Knowing the amount of lead or lag in the compass you are using will be helpful in rolling out on a heading.

Figure 3-7 is a simplified drawing of the magnetic compass. The magnets tend to point parallel to the earth's lines of magnetic force. As the compass is brought nearer to the Magnetic North Pole the magnets will have a tendency to point toward the earth's surface.

If directly over the Magnetic North Pole, the compass would theoretically point straight down, causing a great deal of confusion to all concerned. The magnetic compass is of little use close to the

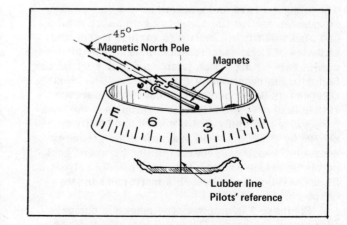

Fig. 3-7. Magnetic compass.

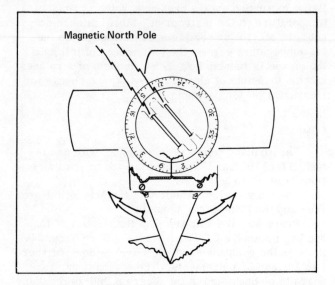

Fig. 3-8. The lubber line and instrument case are fastened to the aircraft, which turns around the free-floating compass card and magnets.

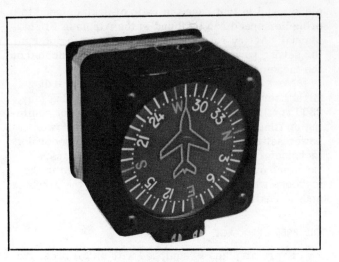

Fig. 3-9. Vertical card magnetic compass. (*Hamilton Instruments, Inc.*)

pole, so other methods of navigation are used in this area.

The suspension of the compass card causes certain problems. For instance, if you are flying on a generally easterly heading and accelerate, the compass will turn toward a northerly heading even though the plane has not turned. This occurs on a westerly heading as well.

If on these headings the plane decelerates, a southerly indication is given under these conditions, as can be seen by referring to Figure 3-7. The following can be noted:

Acceleration — The compass indicates a more
                northerly heading.
Deceleration -- The compass indicates a more
                southerly heading.

When the plane is climbed, dived, or banked (particularly a bank of more than $15°$-$20°$) inaccuracies result. Notice in a climb or glide (on an east or west heading) that the compass inches off its original indication because of the airplane's attitude (assuming that you have kept the nose from wandering). The compass card and magnets have a one-point suspension so that the assembly acts as a pendulum and also will tilt in reaction to various forces and attitudes of flight (acceleration, banks, nose attitudes, etc.). This tilting action is also a major contributing factor to the reactions of the compass. The "float" compass as described here is used for reference rather than precision flying. In turbulence the compass swings so badly that it's very hard to fly a course by it. It's a good instrument for getting on course or keeping a general heading between checkpoints on cross-country, but never blindly rely on it. There will be more about this instrument in later chapters.

Figure 3-9 is a newer type magnetic compass with a vertical card. The small airplane is fixed and the card turns in a more easily readable way

and is like the new faces on the heading indicator in Figure 3-21.

ADDITIONAL INSTRUMENTS

The instruments discussed in the earlier part of the chapter are all that are required for daytime VFR flight, but the following instruments will also be used in your training:

Federal Aviation Regulations require that emergency recovery from a loss of visual references (such as accidentally flying into clouds or fog) be demonstrated on the private flight test. There have been a large number of fatal accidents caused by pilots overestimating their abilities and flying into marginal weather. It can be easily demonstrated that flying by the seat of the pants when you have lost visual references is a one-way proposition — *Down.*

The instruments discussed earlier are those used for your day to day flying under Visual Flight Rules type of flying; for instrument flying (and your instruction in emergency flying using the instruments) more equipment is needed. The FAA requires that on the flight test the airplane be equipped with "appropriate flight instruments" for checking the pilot's ability to control the airplane by the use of the instruments. It's very likely that your trainer will be equipped with all of the instruments covered in this chapter, but in Chapter 15 techniques are given for using the turn coordinator or turn and slip (plus airspeed and altimeter) to maintain control of the airplane under simulated or actual instrument conditions.

GYRO INSTRUMENTS IN GENERAL

Gyro instruments work because of the gyroscopic properties of "rigidity in space" and "precession."

If you owned a toy gyroscope or top in your younger days, the property of "rigidity in space" is well known to you. While the top was spinning, it

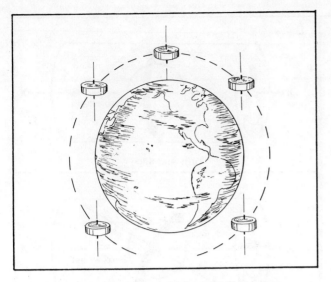

Fig. 3-10. The gyro maintains rigidity in space.

could not be pushed over but would move parallel to its plane of rotation (on the floor) in answer to such a nudge. The gyroscope resists any effort to tilt its axis (or its plane of rotation) (Fig. 3-10). This property is used in the attitude indicator and heading indicator.

The property of "precession" is used in the turn and slip indicator. If a force is exerted against the side of a rotating gyro, the gyro reacts as if the force were exerted at a point 90° around the wheel (in the direction of rotation) from the actual place of application (Fig. 3-11).

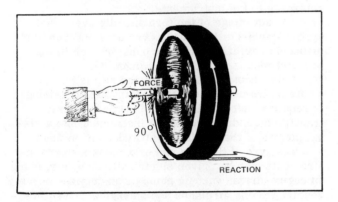

Fig. 3-11. Precession.

TURN AND SLIP (T/S) INDICATOR (NEEDLE AND BALL)

The turn and slip indicator is actually two instruments. The slip indicator is merely a liquid-filled, curved glass tube containing an agate or steel ball. The liquid acts as a shock dampener. In a balanced turn the ball will remain in the center since centrifugal force offsets the pull of gravity (Fig. 3-12).

In a slip, there is not enough rate of turn for the amount of bank. The centrifugal force will be weak and this imbalance will be shown by the ball's falling down toward the inside of the turn (Fig. 3-13). (You experience centrifugal force any time you turn a

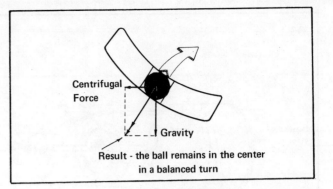

Fig. 3-12. A balanced right turn.

car — particularly in an abrupt turn at high speed as you tend to move to the outside of the turn.)

The skid is a condition in which there is too high a rate of turn for the amount of bank. The centrifugal force is too strong, and this is indicated by the ball's sliding toward the outside of the turn (Fig. 3-14). Usually a turn in an airplane is considered to be balanced if more than one-half of the ball is within the indicator marks.

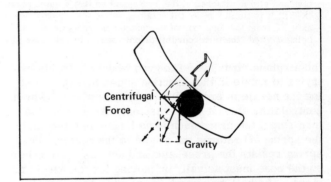

Fig. 3-13. A slipping right turn.

The slip and skid will be discussed further in "The Turn," in Chapter 9.

The turn part of the turn and slip indicator, or "needle" as it is sometimes called, uses precession to indicate the direction and approximate rate of turn of the airplane.

Figure 3-15 shows the reaction of the turn and slip indicator to a right turn. Naturally the case is rigidly attached to the instrument panel and turns as

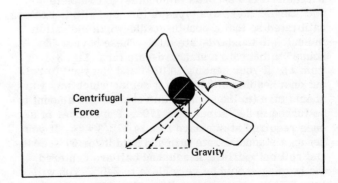

Fig. 3-14. A skidding right turn.

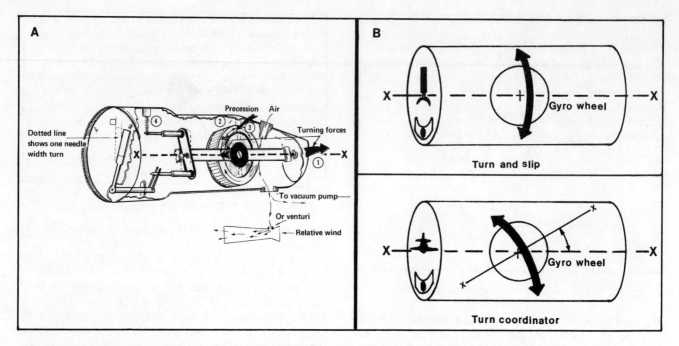

Fig. 3-15. (A) Turn and slip indicator (vacuum-driven). Newer instruments are electrically driven. (B) The gyro wheel in the turn and slip is attached in the instrument so that when it reacts to yaw it can only tilt around the long axis of the instrument (X-X). It is limited in its tilt action by stops. The gyro wheel in the turn coordinator moves (in reaction to precession) around an axis 30° from the long axis of the instrument and so reacts to both roll and yaw inputs. Since precession acts while a force is being *applied*, the turn coordinator only reacts to yaw (rate of turn) once the bank is established.

the airplane turns (1). The gyro wheel (2) reacts by trying to rotate in the direction shown by (3), moving the needle in proportion to the rate of turn (which controls the amount of precession). As soon as the turn stops, the precession is no longer in effect and the spring (4) returns the needle to the center. The spring resists the precession and acts as a dampener so the nose must actually be moving for the needle to move. The ball may be off to one side even though the needle is centered. For instance, in a side or forward slip (to be covered later) the airplane may be in a bank with the pilot holding opposite rudder. The ball will be in a more extreme position than that shown in Figure 3-13.

Some turn and slip indicators are calibrated so that a "standard-rate turn" of 3° per second will be indicated by the needle's being off center by one needle width (Fig. 3-15). This means that by setting up a standard-rate turn it is possible to roll out on a predetermined heading by the use of a watch or clock. It requires 120 seconds (2 minutes) to complete a 360° turn. There are types of turn and slip indicators calibrated so that a double-needle-width indication indicates a standard-rate turn. These have a "dog-house" to indicate a standard-rate turn (Fig. 3-1, item 2). If your heading is 070° and you want to roll out on a heading of 240°, first decide which way you should turn (to the right in this case). The amount to be turned is 240 minus 70 = 170°. The number of seconds required at standard rate is 170/3 = 57. If you set up a standard-rate turn and hold it for 57 seconds and roll out until the needle and ball are centered, the heading should be very close to 240°. You will have a chance to practice these timed turns "under the hood" (by instruments alone) during your training.

One of the most valuable maneuvers in coping with bad weather is the 180° turn, or "getting the hell out of there." It is always best to do the turn *before* you lose visual contact, but if visual references are lost inadvertently, the 180° turn may be done by reference to the instruments.

The advantage of the turn and slip over other gyro instruments is that the gyro does not "tumble" or become erratic as certain bank or pitch limits are exceeded (see *"Attitude Indicator"*).

A disadvantage of the turn and slip is that it is a rate instrument, and a certain amount of training is required before the student is able to quickly transfer the indications of the instrument into a visual picture of the airplane's attitudes and actions.

The gyro of the turn and slip and other gyro instruments may be driven electrically or by air, using an engine-driven vacuum pump or an outside-mounted venturi. (Some airplanes use an engine-driven *pressure* pump.) The venturi is generally used on older lightplanes because of its simplicity; it is nothing more than a venturi tube causing a drop in pressure and drawing air through the instrument past the vanes on the gyro wheel as the plane moves through the air (Fig. 3-15).

THE TURN COORDINATOR (T/C)

The turn coordinator is similar to the turn and slip in that a standard rate may be set up but, unlike that instrument, is designed to respond to *roll*, as well.

Note that the gyro wheel in the turn and slip (Fig. 3-15) is vertical and lined up with the axis of the instrument case when yaw forces aren't acting on it. In the turn coordinator the gyro wheel is set at approximately 30° from the instrument's long axis, allowing it to precess in response to both yaw and roll forces (Fig. 3-15). After the roll-in (or roll-out) is complete, the instrument indicates the rate of turn. Figure 3-16 compares the indications of the two instruments in a balanced standard-rate turn (3° per second) to the left. Note that the turn coordinator also makes use of a slip indicator (ball).

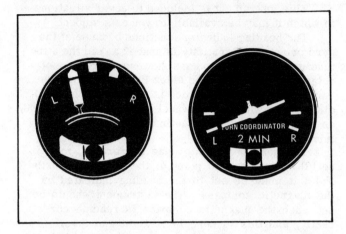

Fig. 3-16. A comparison of a standard-rate turn as indicated by the turn and slip and the turn coordinator. The "2 MIN" indicates that if the wing of the miniature airplane is placed on the reference mark, it will take 2 minutes to complete a 360° turn (3° per second).

ATTITUDE INDICATOR (A/I)

The attitude indicator (Fig. 3-17) or gyro horizon (artificial horizon) depends on the "rigidity in space" idea and is a true attitude instrument. The gyro plane of rotation is horizontal and remains in this position with the aircraft (and instrument case)

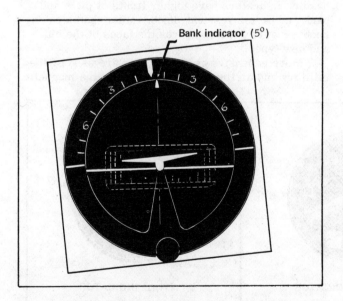

Fig. 3-17. Attitude indicator. Shown is a nose-up, left-wing-down (5° bank) attitude. Although it appears to indicate a shallow climbing turn to the left, a check with other instruments is needed to confirm this.

being moved about it. Attached to the gyro is a face with a white horizon line and other reference lines on it. When the instrument is operating correctly, this line will always represent the actual horizon. A miniature airplane, attached to the case, moves with respect to this artificial horizon precisely as the real airplane moves with respect to the real horizon. This instrument is particularly easy for the student to use because he is able to "fly" the small airplane as he would the large airplane itself.

There are limits of operation on the less expensive attitude indicators and these are, in most cases, 70° of pitch (nose up or down) and 100° of bank. The gyro will "tumble" above these limit stops and will give false information as the gyro is forced from its rotational plane. The instrument also will give false information during the several minutes required for it to return to the normal position after resuming straight and level flight.

"Caging" is done by a knob located on the instrument front and is useful in locking the instrument before doing acrobatics, which include the spin demonstration discussed later. Because it is possible to damage the instrument through repeated tumbling, this caging is a must before you do deliberate acrobatics. Most of the later attitude indicators do not have a caging knob. Figure 3-18 compares two types of attitude indicators.

The more expensive attitude indicators have no limits of pitch or bank, and acrobatics such as rolls or loops can be done by reference to the instrument. These are used in jet fighters and are generally electrically driven rather than air driven, as in the case of the older type gyros, because of the loss of efficiency of the air-driven type at high altitudes.

Most attitude indicators have a knob that allows you to move the miniature airplane up or down to compensate for small deviations in the horizontal-line position.

The attitude indicator is more expensive than the turn and slip but allows the pilot to get an immediate picture of the plane's attitude. It can be used to establish a standard-rate turn, if necessary, without reference to the turn coordinator or turn and slip indicator, as will be shown.

An airplane's rate of turn depends on its velocity

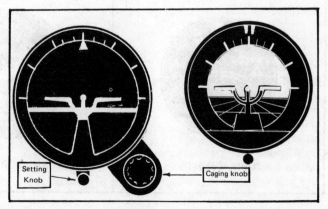

Fig. 3-18. Attitude indicators (caging and noncaging types).

19

V mph	V knots	Degrees Angle of Bank φ
60	52	8
70	61	9.5
80	69	11
90	78	12
100	87	13.5
110	96	14.6
120	104	16
130	113	17
140	122	18.5
150	130	20
160	139	21
170	148	22
180	156	23
190	165	24.5
200	174	25.5
250	188	31

Fig. 3-19.

and amount of bank. For any airplane, the slower the velocity and the greater the angle of bank, the greater the rate of turn. This will be evident as soon as you begin flying and is probably so even now.

A good rule of thumb to find the amount of bank needed for a standard-rate turn at various airspeeds is to divide your airspeed by 10 and add 5 to the answer. For instance, airspeed = 150/10 = 15; 15 + 5 = 20° bank required. This thumb rule is particularly accurate in the 100 to 200 mph range, as you can see by checking Figure 3-19, and is as close as you'll be able to hold the bank at any speed range.

Figure 3-20 compares the indications of the turn and slip, turn coordinator, and attitude indicator in a standard-rate turn to the right at 110 mph (96 K) *true airspeed*. (True airspeed would be the proper one to use in the table above or the rule of thumb, but indicated or calibrated airspeed is OK for a quick result.)

A rule of thumb for finding the required bank for a standard-rate turn when you are working with knots is to divide the airspeed by 10 and multiply the result by 1 1/2. As an example, at an airspeed of 156 K you'd get 15.6° (call it 16°). One and one-half times 16 is 24° required. (Figure 3-19 says 23° of bank for 156 K, but the thumb rule is close enough for practical purposes.)

HEADING INDICATOR (H/I)

This instrument is included to cover situations in which it may be available to you as a student.

The heading indicator functions because of the gyro principle of "rigidity in space" as did the attitude indicator. In this case, however, the plane of rotation is vertical. The older H/I has a compass card or azimuth scale which is attached to the gyro gimbal and wheel. The wheel and card are fixed and, as in the case of the magnetic compass, the plane turns about them.

The heading indicator has no "brain" (magnet) that causes it to point to the Magnetic North Pole; it must be set to the heading indicated by the magnetic compass. The instrument should be set when the magnetic compass is reading correctly, and this is done in straight and level flight when the magnetic compass has "settled down."

The advantage of the heading indicator is that it does not oscillate in rough weather and it gives a true reading during turns when the magnetic compass is erratic. A setting knob is used to cage the instrument for acrobatics or to set the proper heading.

A disadvantage of the older types of heading indicators is that they tumble when the limits of 55° nose up or down or 55° bank are reached. The instrument creeps and must be reset with the magnetic compass about every 15 minutes. Newer heading indicators have higher limits of pitch and bank and have a resetting knob, rather than a caging knob. Figure 3-21 compares the faces of the old and new types.

More expensive gyros, such as are used by the military and airlines, are connected with a magnetic

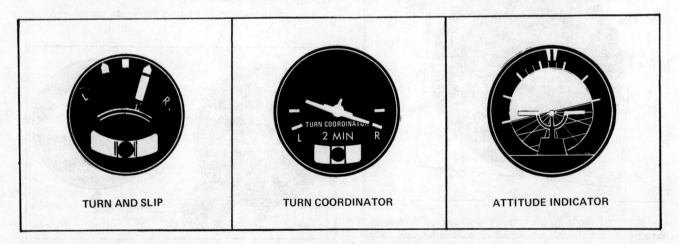

TURN AND SLIP   TURN COORDINATOR   ATTITUDE INDICATOR

Fig. 3-20. The turn and slip, turn coordinator, and attitude indicator indications in a standard-rate turn at 96 knots. Setting up the thumb rule for the bank angle only works for the balanced turn (no slip or skid).

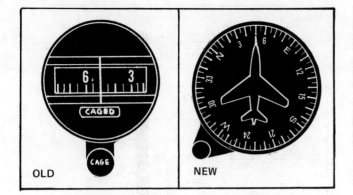

Fig. 3-21. Two types of heading indicators.

compass in such a way that this creep is automatically compensated for.

The greatest advantage of the heading indicator is that it allows you to turn directly to a heading without the allowance for lead or lag which is necessary with a magnetic compass.

Figure 3-22 shows the schematic of the engine-driven vacuum system of a popular trainer. The air filter is on the firewall under the instrument panel.

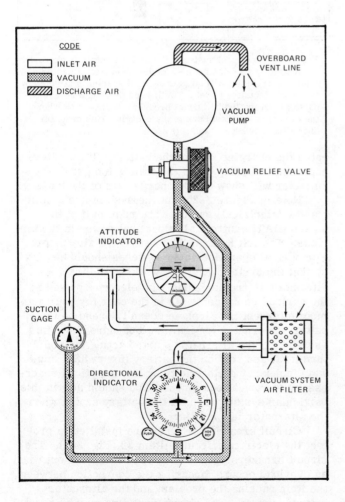

Fig. 3-22. Engine-driven vacuum pump system.

VERTICAL SPEED INDICATOR

This is an instrument that is useful in maintaining a constant rate of climb or glide.

It is a "rate" instrument and depends on a diaphragm for its operation, as does the altimeter. In the rate of climb indicator, the diaphragm measures the change of pressure rather than the pressure itself, as does the diaphragm in the altimeter.

The diaphragm has a tube connecting it to the static port (see Fig. 3-4), or the tube may just have access to the outside air pressure in the case of cheaper or lighter installations. This means that the inside of the diaphragm has the same pressure as the air surrounding the plane. Opening into the otherwise sealed instrument case is a capillary, or very small tube. This difference in the diaphragm and capillary tube sizes means a lag in the equalization of pressure in the air within the instrument case as the altitude (outside pressure) changes.

Figure 3-23 is a schematic diagram of a vertical speed indicator. As an example, suppose the plane is flying at a constant altitude. The pressure

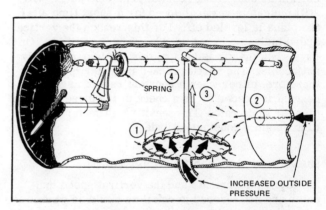

Fig. 3-23. A simplified view of a vertical speed indicator. As plane descends, outside pressure increases. The diaphragm expands immediately (1). Because of the small size of the capillary tube (2), pressure in the case is not increased at the same rate. The link pushes upward (3) rotating the shaft (4) which causes needle to indicate 400 fpm down as shown. The spring helps return needle to zero when pressures are equal and also acts as a dampener. The instrument here is shown proportionally longer than the actual rate of climb indicator so that the mechanism may be clearly seen.

within the diaphragm is the same as that of the air surrounding it in the instrument case. The rate of climb is indicated as zero.

The plane is put into a glide or dive. Air pressure inside the diaphragm increases at the same rate as that of the surrounding air. However, because of the small size of the capillary tube, the pressure in the instrument case does not change at the same rate. In the case of a glide or dive, the diaphragm would expand -- the amount of expansion depending on the difference of pressures. The diaphragm is mechanically linked to a hand, and the appropriate rate of descent, in hundreds (or thousands) of feet per minute, is read on the instrument face.

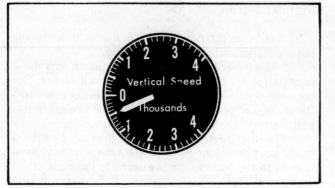

Fig. 3-24. Standard rate of descent.

In a climb the pressure in the diaphragm decreases faster than that within the instrument case, and the needle will indicate an appropriate rate of climb. The standard rate of descent in instrument work is 500 fpm (Fig. 3-24).

Because in a climb or dive the pressure in the case is always "behind" the diaphragm pressure, a certain amount of lag results. The instrument will still indicate a vertical speed for a short time after the plane is leveled off. For this reason the vertical speed indicator is not used to maintain altitude. On days when the air is bumpy, this lag is particularly noticeable. The vertical speed indicator is used, therefore, either when a constant rate of ascent or descent is needed or as a check of the plane's climb, dive, or glide rate. The sensitive altimeter is used to maintain a constant altitude.

SUMMARY OF THE ADDITIONAL INSTRUMENTS

Gyro instruments and the vertical speed indicator are not covered in detail as would be done in a training manual for an instrument rating. The calibrations and procedures used by instrument pilots are not covered for obvious reasons. For the noninstrument-qualified private pilot or the student, these instruments are to be used in an emergency only — as a means of survival. Even the most expensive instruments cannot compensate for lack of preflight planning — or poor headwork in flight.

ELECTRICAL SYSTEM

Since most trainers these days have electrical systems for starting and for lights and radios, Figure 3-25 is included to give an idea of a simple system.

The battery stores electrical energy, and the engine-driven alternator (or generator) creates current and replenishes the battery, as necessary, as directed by the voltage regulator.

The ammeter (item 15, Fig. 3-1) indicates the flow of current, in amperes, from the alternator to the battery or from the battery to the electrical system. When the engine is operating and the master switch (item 28, Fig. 3-1) is "ON" the ammeter indi-

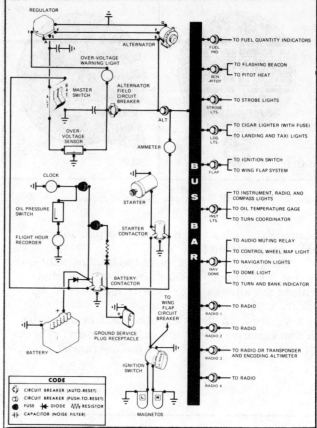

Fig. 3-25. Electrical system. If you don't have a background in electricity these diagrams can seem very complicated. Your job as a pilot will be to know what system is affected by a loss of electrical power. You'll need to know what components are protected by circuit breakers or fuses and where the breakers (or fuses) are in the cockpit. This diagram shows the electrical items. (*Cessna*)

cates the charging rate of the battery. If the alternator isn't working, or if the load is too great, the ammeter will show the discharge rate of the battery.

Note in Figure 3-25 that the system has a split master (electrical) switch. The right half of the switch (BAT) controls all electrical power in the airplane. The left half (ALT) controls the alternator. For normal operations both switches should be "ON" so that the system (BAT) is working and the alternator is "replenishing" the electricity used by the various components, as is the case for your automobile (except the airplane doesn't depend on the battery/alternator for ignition, but more about this shortly). If the alternator started acting up, you'd turn it off and rely on the battery (for awhile, anyway), conserving electricity by turning off all unnecessary electrical equipment. You should not, in this particular system, turn off the battery switch when the alternator is operating.

Circuit breakers or fuses are installed to protect the electrical circuits (item 32, Fig. 3-1). The circuit breakers "pop out" or the fuses burn out when an overload occurs, breaking the connection between the item causing the problem and the alternator-battery system. The circuit breakers may be reset, but a 2-minute cooling period is usually recommended. Most pilots figure that if a breaker pops three times in a row, it's best to leave it out. In the case of a system using fuses, spare fuses are sometimes carried in clips in the map compartment.

The ignition system is shown in Figure 3-25, but it is self-sustaining and independent of the alternator-battery system. An airplane engine does *not* need an alternator-battery system to operate. In fact, for many years most did not have one — the engine was started by hand. The magnetos are run by the engine and in turn furnish the spark for combustion — a sort of "you rub my back and I'll rub yours" arrangement that works very well. The magnetos will be covered again in following chapters.

AIRCRAFT DOCUMENTS

Every aircraft must have three documents at all times in flight: (1) Certificate of Registration or ownership, (2) Certificate of Airworthiness (this must be displayed), and (3) Airplane Flight Manual or equivalent form containing an equipment list and limitations. Look in your plane and know where these documents are.

CERTIFICATE OF REGISTRATION

The Certificate of Registration contains the name and address of the owner, the aircraft manufacturer, model, registration number, and the manufacturer's serial number. When a plane changes owners, a new registration certificate must be obtained.

CERTIFICATE OF AIRWORTHINESS

The Certificate of Airworthiness is a document showing that the airplane has met the safety requirements of the Federal Aviation Administration and is "airworthy." It remains in effect as long as the aircraft is maintained in accordance with the Federal Aviation Regulations. This means that required inspections or repairs are done and notice of this is in the aircraft and/or engine logbook.

AIRPLANE FLIGHT MANUAL OR PILOT'S OPERATING HANDBOOK

The *Pilot's Operating Handbooks* for general aviation airplanes are laid out as follows for standardization purposes:

Section 1 — General

This is a general section and contains a three-view of the airplane and descriptive data on engine, propeller, fuel and oil, dimensions, and weights. It contains symbols, abbreviations, and terminology used in airplane performance.

Section 2 — Limitations

This section includes airspeed limitations such as shown in Figure 3-27.

The primary airspeed limitations are given in knots and in both indicated and calibrated airspeeds (although some manufacturers furnish mph data as well) and the markings are in knots and indicated airspeeds.

The maneuvering speed, which is the maximum indicated airspeed at which the controls may be abruptly and fully deflected without overstressing the airplane, depends on the stall speed, which decreases as the airplane gets lighter. More about this in Chapter 23. Figure 3-28 shows some markings for a fictitious airplane.

Included here also are power plant limitations (engine rpm limits, maximum and minimum oil pressures, and maximum oil temperature and rpm range to be used (Fig. 3-29). Weight and center of gravity limits are included for the particular airplane.

Maneuver and flight load factor limits (also to be discussed in Chapter 23) are listed, and operations limits (day and night, VFR, and IFR) are found here. Fuel limitations (usable and unusable fuel) and minimum fuel grades are covered in this section. An airplane may not be able to use some of the fuel in flight and this is listed as "unusable fuel." For ex-

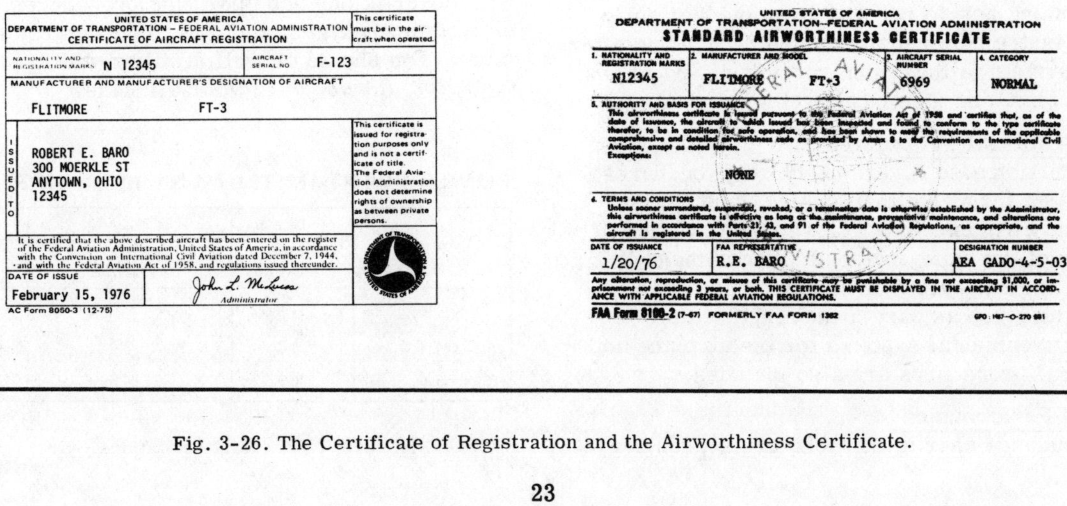
UNITED STATES OF AMERICA
DEPARTMENT OF TRANSPORTATION – FEDERAL AVIATION ADMINISTRATION
CERTIFICATE OF AIRCRAFT REGISTRATION
This certificate must be in the aircraft when operated.
NATIONALITY AND REGISTRATION MARKS N 12345 | AIRCRAFT SERIAL NO F-123
MANUFACTURER AND MANUFACTURER'S DESIGNATION OF AIRCRAFT
FLITMORE FT-3
ISSUED TO
ROBERT E. BARO
300 MOERKLE ST
ANYTOWN, OHIO
12345
This certificate is issued for registration purposes only and is not a certificate of title. The Federal Aviation Administration does not determine rights of ownership as between private persons.
It is certified that the above described aircraft has been entered on the register of the Federal Aviation Administration, United States of America, in accordance with the Convention on International Civil Aviation dated December 7, 1944, and with the Federal Aviation Act of 1958, and regulations issued thereunder.
DATE OF ISSUE February 15, 1976
John L. McLucas
Administrator
AC Form 8050-3 (12-75)

UNITED STATES OF AMERICA
DEPARTMENT OF TRANSPORTATION—FEDERAL AVIATION ADMINISTRATION
STANDARD AIRWORTHINESS CERTIFICATE
1. NATIONALITY AND REGISTRATION MARKS N12345 | 2. MANUFACTURER AND MODEL FLITMORE FT-3 | 3. AIRCRAFT SERIAL NUMBER 6969 | 4. CATEGORY NORMAL
5. AUTHORITY AND BASIS FOR ISSUANCE
This airworthiness certificate is issued pursuant to the Federal Aviation Act of 1958 and certifies that, as of the date of issuance, the aircraft to which issued has been inspected and found to conform to the type certificate therefor, to be in condition for safe operation, and has been shown to meet the requirements of the applicable comprehensive and detailed airworthiness code as provided by Annex 8 to the Convention on International Civil Aviation, except as noted herein.
Exceptions:
NONE
6. TERMS AND CONDITIONS
Unless sooner surrendered, suspended, revoked, or a termination date is otherwise established by the Administrator, this airworthiness certificate is effective as long as the maintenance, preventative maintenance, and alterations are performed in accordance with Parts 21, 43, and 91 of the Federal Aviation Regulations, as appropriate, and the aircraft is registered in the United States.
DATE OF ISSUANCE 1/20/76 | FAA REPRESENTATIVE R.E. BARO | DESIGNATION NUMBER AEA GADO-4-5-03
Any alteration, reproduction, or misuse of this certificate may be punishable by a fine not exceeding $1,000, or imprisonment not exceeding 3 years, or both. THIS CERTIFICATE MUST BE DISPLAYED IN THE AIRCRAFT IN ACCORDANCE WITH APPLICABLE FEDERAL AVIATION REGULATIONS.
FAA Form 8100-2 (7-67) FORMERLY FAA FORM 1362

Fig. 3-26. The Certificate of Registration and the Airworthiness Certificate.

AIRSPEED LIMITATIONS

	SPEED	KCAS	KIAS	REMARKS
V$_{NE}$	Never Exceed Speed	141	141	Do not exceed this speed in any operation.
V$_{NO}$	Maximum Structural Cruising Speed	104	107	Do not exceed this speed except in smooth air, and then only with caution.
V$_A$	Maneuvering Speed: 1600 Pounds 1450 Pounds 1300 Pounds	95 90 85	97 93 88	Do not make full or abrupt control movements above this speed.
V$_{FE}$	Maximum Flap Extended Speed	89	85	Do not exceed this speed with flaps down.
	Maximum Window Open Speed	141	141	Do not exceed this speed with windows open.

AIRSPEED INDICATOR MARKINGS

MARKING	KIAS VALUE OR RANGE	SIGNIFICANCE
White Arc	42 - 85	Full Flap Operating Range. Lower limit is maximum weight V$_{SO}$ in landing configuration. Upper limit is maximum speed permissible with flaps extended.
Green Arc	47 - 107	Normal Operating Range. Lower limit is maximum weight V$_S$ at most forward C.G. with flaps retracted. Upper limit is maximum structural cruising speed.
Yellow Arc	107 - 141	Operations must be conducted with caution and only in smooth air.
Red Line	141	Maximum speed for all operations.

Fig. 3-27. Airspeed limitations and airspeed markings as given in a *Pilot's Operating Handbook*. Note that the stall speeds (V$_s$ for flaps up, and V$_{so}$ for landing configuration) are given for maximum certificated weight. Compare the airspeed limitations with the indicator markings here. V$_{NO}$ is the maximum structural cruising speed (or max speed for *Normal Operations*). (*Cessna*)

ample, one airplane has a total fuel capacity of 24 U.S. gallons with 22 U.S. gallons being available in flight (2 gallons unusable).

Section 3 — Emergency Procedures

Here are checklists for such things as engine failures at various portions of the flight; forced landings, including ditching; fires during start and in flight; icing; electrical power supply malfunctions; and airspeeds for safe operations.

There are amplified procedures for these "problems" including how to recover from inadvertently flying into instrument conditions and recovering after a vacuum system failure, spin recoveries, rough engine operations, and electrical problems.

Section 4 — Normal Procedures

This section also covers checklist procedures from preflight through climb, cruise, landing, and securing the airplane. It's followed by amplified procedures of the same material. Recommended speeds for normal operation are summarized, as well as being given as part of the amplified procedures. Environmental systems for the airplane and other normal procedures are also included.

Section 5 — Performance

Performance charts (take-off, cruise, landing)

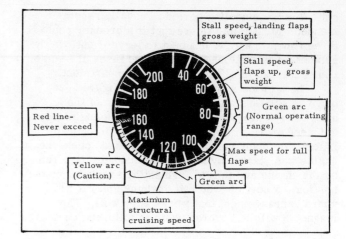

Fig. 3-28. Important airspeed markings. For most airplanes manufactured before the 1976 models the values were given in miles per hour and calibrated airspeed; 1976 and later models will have the airspeed markings as *indicated* airspeed in knots. (1 K = 1.152 statute mph — see Chapter 19.) Your instructor will give you the word about this for the airplane you are using.

with sample problems are included with range and endurance information, airspeed calibration, and stall speed charts.

Section 6 — Weight and Balance and Equipment List

Airplane weighing procedures are given here, with a loading graph and an equipment list with weights and arms of the various airplane components.

Section 7 — Airplane and Systems Descriptions

The airframe, with its control systems, is described and diagrammed. The landing gear, engine and engine controls, etc., are covered in this section. Also, fuel, brake, electrical, hydraulic, and instrument systems are laid out in detail. Additional systems such as oxygen, antiicing, ventilation, heating, and avionics are covered here.

Section 8 — Airplane Handling, Service, and Maintenance

Here is the information you need for preventive maintenance, ground handling, servicing and cleaning, and care for that particular airplane.

Section 9 — Supplements

This is devoted to covering optional systems with descriptions and operating procedures of the electronics, oxygen, and other nonrequired equipment. You should be well familiar with the *Pilot's Operating Handbook* of your airplane.

POWER PLANT INSTRUMENT MARKINGS

INSTRUMENT	RED LINE	GREEN ARC	RED LINE
	MINIMUM LIMIT	NORMAL OPERATING	MAXIMUM LIMIT
Tachometer	- - -	2000 - 2750 RPM	2750 RPM
Oil Temperature	- - -	100° - 240°F	240°F
Oil Pressure	10 psi	30 - 60 psi	100 psi

Fig. 3-29. Power plant limitations. (*Cessna*)

If your airplane has had any major repairs or alterations since its manufacture, a copy, or copies, of the *Major Repair and Alteration Form* must be aboard the airplane (normally it's attached to the Weight and Balance information for convenience). This lists the airplane make and model, registration number, manufacturer's serial number, and the owner's name and address, plus it may have that particular airplane's latest empty weight, the empty center of gravity location in inches from datum, and the useful load of the plane. The useful load includes the weight of usable fuel, occupants, and baggage. The maximum weight minus the empty weight equals the useful load. (Use actual passenger weights.) The gas weight is 6 pounds per gallon, and the oil, 7 1/2 pounds per gallon. When you are loading the baggage compartment, do not exceed the placard weight, even if you have plenty of weight left before reaching the maximum for the airplane. You may overstress the compartment as well as adversely affect the position of the center of gravity of the plane. (Chapter 23 covers this subject in more detail.) Any major repairs or additions of equipment such as radios, etc., that would affect the position of the center of gravity are noted on this form.

On the back of the *Major Repair and Alteration Form* is a description of the work accomplished. The person authorized for such work signs the form and gives the date that the repair or alteration was completed.

AIRCRAFT RADIO STATION LICENSE

Airplanes having transmitting equipment installed are required to have a radio station license on board at all times. The license is issued by the Federal Communications Commission for the particular airplane and lists its transmitting equipment.

LOGBOOKS

The Federal Aviation Regulations require that the registered owner or operator keep a maintenance record. (See FAR 91.173 and 91.174 in the back of this book.)

Airplanes have to have had an annual inspection within the preceding 12 calendar months to be legal. (There are some exceptions for special flight permits or a progressive (continuing) inspection procedure, but the vast majority of airplanes fall under the requirements of an annual inspection. You might check with your instructor about your airplane.) The annual inspection has to be done, even if the airplane has not been flown during that time.

In addition, if the airplane is operated carrying persons for hire (charter, rental, flight instruction, etc.), it must have had an inspection within the past 100 hours of flying (tachometer time or other approved method of noting the time). The 100-hour limitation may be exceeded by not more than 10 hours if necessary to reach a place at which the inspection can be done. The excess time must be included in the next 100 hours of time in service. (See FAR 91.169 in the back of this book.)

The 100-hour inspection can be completed and signed by a certificated Airframe and Powerplant mechanic, but the annual inspection must be supervised by an A and P mechanic or facility holding inspection authorization. If you get the 100 hours done by such mechanics or facilities, it can count as an annual inspection. If an annual inspection is done in, say, the month of May (which means that it is good until the end of the following May), and it's necessary to get a 100-hour inspection in August, this 100-hour inspection, if done by the same people who did the annual, can count as a new annual inspection — which means that the next annual is due the following *August,* not the next May. The inspectors will note the date and recorded tach time (or other flight time), and the type of inspection will be noted in the logbooks.

The logbooks are not required to be in the plane at all times, as are the first four documents discussed, but must be available to an FAA inspector if he should ask for them. This means that if you're flying away from the plane's normal base, it would be wise to take the logbooks with you.

RADIO EQUIPMENT

The instructor may explain the use of the radio equipment before the first flight, particularly if you are flying from an airport with a control tower or a Flight Service Station (FAA radio station). You will have a chance to watch and listen to the instructor for the first few flights and will soon be asking for taxi instructions and take-off and landing clearances yourself, under his supervision. A Federal Communications Commission (FCC) radiotelephone permit is required for pilots using an aircraft transmitter and you can apply for it using a pretyped form, as mentioned in the first chapter. If you are flying from an airport where a radio is required you might also look at Chapter 21 -- USING THE RADIO — soon after you start flying.

Most small airports have a "unicom" or aeronautical advisory station for use in giving traffic information and wind and runway conditions to pilots operating in the vicinity of the airport. You may get an early start in the use of radio while operating out of an airport so equipped.

SUMMARY

Don't expect to have all the information in this chapter and the following four chapters down cold before you start flying. Read them over and then use them for review purposes after you've been introduced to the various subjects (The Cockpit, Preflight Check, Starting, and Taxiing) by the instructor. This is a workbook and is intended to be used both before and *as* you fly. Remember, too, that your instructor and the *Pilot's Operating Handbook* will have recommendations as to what is best for your particular airplane and operating conditions.

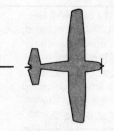

4. Preflight Check

An organized check is the best way to start a flight. The best way to proceed is to make a clockwise (or counterclockwise, if you like) check starting at the cockpit and getting each item as you come to it. Don't be like Henry Schmotz, student pilot, who checked things as he thought of them. He'd check the prop, then the tailwheel and run back up front to look at the oil, etc. One day Henry was so confused that he forgot to check the wings (they were gone -- the mechanic had taken them off for recovering) and tried to take off. He wound up in dire straits in the middle of a chicken farm right off the end of the runway. After he cleaned himself up the first thing he did was to set up an organized preflight check, and he's had no trouble since.

One of the biggest problems the new student (and

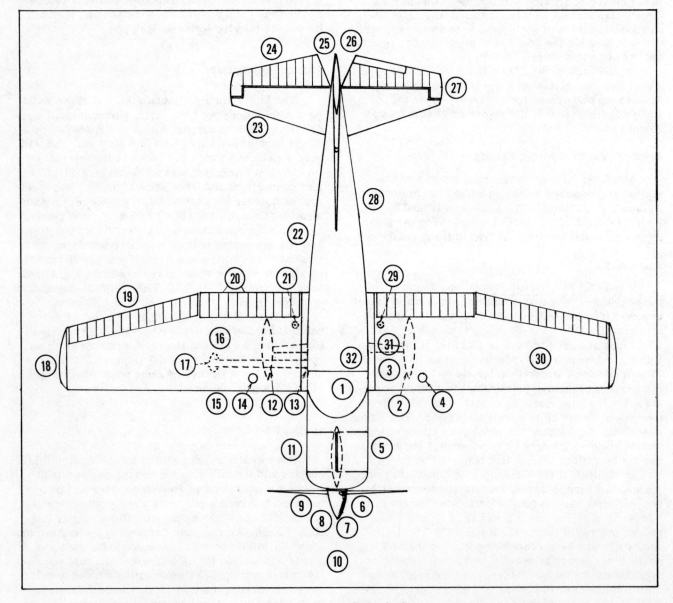

Fig. 4-1. The preflight check.

the more experienced pilot, too) has is knowing what to look for in the preflight check. The first few times you look into the engine compartment and see that maze of wires, pipes, plates, etc., it seems that you wouldn't know if anything is out of place or not. The airplane engine assembly is compact and sealed. What's meant by this is that: (1) There should be no evidence of excess *fluid leaks* (oil, brake fluid, or other fluids) in the compartment or on the engine. You may expect a certain small amount of oil, etc., present; but if in doubt about the "allowed amount," ask someone. (2) There should not be any loose wires or cables. Every wire or cable should be attached at both ends. If you find one dangling loosely, ask your instructor or a mechanic about it. Don't feel shy about asking questions.

Look at the inside of the bottom cowling to check for indications of fluid leaks. Some airplanes have cowlings that require a great deal of effort to remove — it's a bit impractical to remove what appears to be several hundred fine-threaded screws to check the engine before each flight. This is a bad design by the manufacturers, since the preflight check is definitely more than just the checking of the oil.

Discussed here (and shown in Fig. 4-1) is a clockwise check of a typical high-wing general aviation airplane with side-by-side seating. As you walk out to the plane, look at its general appearance; sometimes discrepancies can be seen better at a distance. Start the actual check at the cockpit.

Your instructor will point out the following items and note the things to look for on your particular airplane:

1. *Switch off.* You'll be checking the propeller so make sure the magneto switch is in the "OFF" position. This does not guarantee that the ignition is off, but you will double check the magnetos themselves later.

Lower the flaps so that the hinges and operating rods may be examined more closely. Remove control locks.

For some planes with an electric stall warning horn you may want to turn the master (electrical) switch on and move the tab on the wing to hear the horn. For other airplanes with a stall warning light (no horn) and the stall warning tab well out on the wing, have somebody else move it while you watch the light on the instrument panel. Make sure the master switch is off after either type of these checks is completed. Chapter 12 goes into more detail on the principle of stall warning devices.

Nearly every nut on the airplane is safetied by safety wire, an elastic stop nut, or a cotter pin; there *are* a few exceptions, so if in doubt about a particular item, ask your instructor.

2. *Tires and brakes.* The tires should be inspected for fabric showing or for deep cuts. Roll the airplane a foot or so to see all sides of the tire. (Obviously, if this were a jet airliner it would be quite a job to roll it back and forth, but this book was written for lightplanes.) Check the brakes and brake lines for evidences of hydraulic leaks. Check

the landing gear struts for damage and for proper inflation of the oleo strut, if the plane has this type of shock absorber.

3. *Look for wrinkles* or any signs of strain or fracture along the side of the fuselage near the landing gear. If the plane has been landed hard this will be the first place that will show it. Check for pulled or distorted rivets in a metal airplane.

4. If the aircraft has *wing tanks,* check the one on this side *visually* at this point — don't rely on tank gages. You should drain fuel from the tank into a clear container, such as a jar, to check for dirt and/or water. Hold the jar up to the light (or sun) to get a better look. If contaminants are found, the fuel should be repeatedly drained and checked until it is clear. As a student pilot, however, the presence of foreign matter in the fuel should call for a discussion with your instructor and an extra check before flying.

It's best to fill the fuel tanks in the evening after the last flight; this keeps moisture from condensing on the sides of the tank during the cooler night temperatures.

Some pilots make up a crude tank dipstick from a 12-inch wooden ruler or wooden dowel so that they can get a look at the relative amount of fuel in the tank and calibrate the sticks by filling the tanks a gallon or two at a time and marking them. One caution is that rubberized tanks may be punctured by a *sharp* stick.

5. *Engine compartment.* Open the cowling on the pilot's side and check:

   a. *Ignition lead wires* for looseness or fraying. There are two magnetos, each firing its own set of plugs (two separate leads and plugs for each cylinder). The dual ignition system is for safety, and each magneto will be checked during the pre-take-off check at the end of the runway. The magnetos are self-supporting ignition and have nothing to do with the battery. The battery-alternator system only furnishes power to the starter and other electrical equipment.

   b. *Each magneto* has a ground wire on it. When the ignition switch is turned to "RIGHT" or "LEFT," the ground wire is electrically disconnected on that magneto, and it is no longer "grounded out" but is "ON." You may do the same by a physical disconnection of the ground wire on a magneto. It may also vibrate loose and that magneto will be "ON" even though the switch inside says "OFF." It may vibrate off inside the magneto where it can't be seen, so it is best to always consider the prop as being "hot" even after checking the switch and ground wires. *Check both magneto ground wires at this point,* if possible.

   c. *Look at the carburetor heat and cabin heat muffs for cracks.* These are shrouds around the exhaust that collect the heated air to be routed to the carburetor or cabin heater. Carburetor heat is necessary because float type carburetors are very effective refrigerators. The temperature of the air entering the carburetor is lowered for two reasons: (1) The pressure of the mixture is lowered as it goes through the venturi (narrow part of the throat), which causes a drop in temperature. (2) The evaporation of the fuel causes a further drop in temperature. The result is that there may be a drop of up to 60° F below the outside temperature in the carburetor. If there is moisture in the air these droplets may form ice on the sides of the venturi and on the jets, resulting in loss of power. If the situation gets bad enough, this can cause complete stoppage of the engine. That's where carburetor heat comes in. In a plane with a fixed pitch prop (no manifold pressure gage) the usual indication of icing is a dropping back of rpm with no change in throttle setting. There may be only a small amount of ice in the venturi and the effects may not be noticeable at full or cruising throttle, but when the throttle is closed to the idle position, all outside air may be shut out and the engine literally strangles. *So . . . before you close the throttle in the air—pull the carburetor heat*—give it about 10 seconds to clear out any ice before pulling the throttle back. (See item 26, Fig. 3-1.)

Carburetor icing boils down to this: It isn't the heat, or the lack of it, it's the humidity. At very low temperatures—say about 0° F—the air is so dry that carburetor icing is no problem. A wet cloudy day with a temperature of 35-65° F is the best condition for carburetor icing to occur.

As you pull the carburetor heat control knob in the cockpit, a butterfly valve is opened, allowing the prewarmed air from around the exhaust to mix with the outside air coming into the carburetor; This prevents ice from forming or melts ice already formed. (Figure 4-2 shows a *full* hot setting.)

Here are some of the indications of carburetor icing. The rpm starts creeping back slowly. Being a normal pilot, you'll probably open the throttle more to keep a constant rpm setting. A few minutes later (or sooner if icing conditions are bad) you'll have to open the throttle farther. Finally, realizing there is ice about, you'll pull the carburetor heat and get a good shock. There'll be about a 100 rpm drop plus some soul-shaking reactions from the engine for a few seconds as the ice melts.

If there's a lot of ice, here's what happens. The ice melts and becomes a deluge of water into the engine. A little water helps compression—World War II fighters used water injection for bursts of

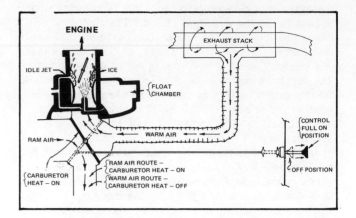

Fig. 4-2. Carburetor heat system.

power—but you can get too much of a good thing. Some pilots recommend partial heat in this situation, but the best answer is to use full heat as soon as signs of icing appear and continue using it as long as necessary, realizing that some power is lost because of the warmer air.

As part of the pretake-off check, pull on the carburetor heat with the engine running at 1800 rpm (or whatever rpm the manufacturer may ask for) and watch for a drop off of about 100 rpm. It'll vary from plane to plane, but this is about the average drop. The heated air going into the engine is less dense than an equal volume of the outside cold air and the engine will suffer a slight loss in power. In other words, if there's no drop off, you're not getting heat to the carburetor, and it would be wise to find out what's up before flying.

The air coming through the carburetor heat system is not filtered, as is the normal outside air coming to the carburetor (see item 8), so that it's possible to pick up dust and dirt when the carburetor heat is used on the ground. It's best to avoid extensive use of carburetor heat on the ground, particularly when taxiing which may "stir up the dust."

Carburetor heat richens the mixture (the warmer air is less dense for the same weight of fuel going to the engine) so that using carburetor heat with the mixture full rich at higher altitudes makes the engine run rough.

The fuel injection system is becoming more popular because of better fuel distribution to the cylinders, but the carburetor will still be used for quite a while.

Most lightplane cabin heaters operate on the same principle of using hot air from around the exhausts. Pulling the cabin heat control opens a valve and allows the hot air to come into the cockpit. The effectiveness of the carburetor (and cabin) heat depends on the temperature of the air in the shroud(s) and this depends on the power being produced. If on a cold day

28

you've been descending for some time at a low power setting with carb and cabin heats on and suddenly find that your feet are getting cold, you can be sure that the carburetor heat is becoming as ineffective as the cabin heat. Get power back on to assure effectiveness of the carb heat or you shortly may have trouble getting the engine to respond. Larger planes will have the more efficient and more expensive gasoline cabin heaters.

d. The fuel strainer drain (not just for the fuel tanks) is located at the bottom of the airplane near the firewall. (The firewall separates the engine compartment from the passenger compartment.) Drain the fuel into a clear container, as was noted in item 4, and check for contaminants.

e. While you're browsing in the engine compartment, your instructor will show you how the *engine accessories* should look. (Is that wire that's dangling there normal?) Since you probably don't have experience as an airplane mechanic, many things will just have to *look* right. Know the preflight check so thoroughly that anything not in its place will stick out like a sore thumb.

f. If the oil tank cap is on this side, *check the oil*. In most planes of this type, the oil is on the right, but don't count on it. The minimum allowable amount will vary from plane to plane. The instructor will give you this information. Most light-planes of the 100 hp range hold 6 quarts and have a minimum flyable level of 4 quarts. Make sure the cap is secured after you've checked the oil. If you add oil, be sure it is the recommended grade or viscosity for the season and your airplane. Know whether your airplane uses ashless dispersant or straight mineral oil.

g. *Check the alternator* for good wiring and connections (if you can see it; some airplanes have alternators that are pretty inaccessible without taking the cowling off). To repeat from Chapter 3, the alternator serves the same purpose as that one in your car; it keeps the system up for starting and operating the electrical accessories such as lights and radios and some engine and flight instruments as noted earlier. The battery box (and battery) is located in the engine compartment in some airplanes and should be checked for security here.

Figure 4-3 shows the components of a current trainer using a Lycoming 0-235 L2C engine that develops 110 brake horsepower at 2550 rpm. (You might review Chapter 2 about brake and thrust horsepower.) The propeller(s) has been removed.

Looking at the various parts: AB – alternator drive belt. AL – alternator. BB – battery box. CB – carburetor. CH – carburetor heat hose from the muffler shroud (CM). CS – carburetor intake screen. CX – the common exhaust outlet or stack. CY – one of the four cylinders. EP – external electric power plug (for use on those cold mornings when the battery is dead; this is optional equipment). FC – filler cap (oil). FS – fuel strainer. HT – hose from the muffler shroud for cabin heat. IM – intake manifold (route of the fuel-air mixture from the carburetor to the cylinder; there are four of them here). ML – magneto (left). MR – magneto (right). OB – oil breather line. This releases pressure created in the crankcase by the hot oil vapors (when you go out to the airplane after it has just come down, you may see a small patch of light brown froth of oil on the ground under the outlet pipe. You can trace the route here

Fig. 4-3. Components of the engine and systems of a current trainer as discussed in this chapter.

from the front of the crankcase to the outlet opening). OC — oil cooler. The oil is routed from the engine-driven oil pump through this small radiator to the engine and finally to the sump (it's slightly more complicated than that). OF — oil filter. OL — oil line from the oil cooler. OS — the oil sump or oil storage tank. SP — spark plugs. Each cylinder has two plugs. SW — spark plug (ignition) wire or lead. VV — vacuum system overboard vent line. (See Fig. 3-22.) XM — exhaust manifold.

It's unlikely that you'll get the cowlings this much off of your airplane during any preflight check, but you might quietly watch the mechanics working on an engine in the hangar or look at an engine in the process of being overhauled. (Don't move *any* propellers; the mechanic might not appreciate it and it could be dangerous.)

h. Make sure the *cowling* is secured.
i. On some trainers the *vent for the static system* is located on the left side of the fuselage just behind the cowling. The static system instruments are, as you recall, the altimeter, rate of climb indicator, and airspeed indicator (which also needs a source of ram pressure, the pitot tube). The designers have located the static pressure orifice at a point where the actual outside static pressure exists (without any ram or eddying effects), and the hole must be clear to insure accurate readings of the three instruments. Other locations for the static opening are on the pitot tube (which would then make it a *pitot-static tube*) and on the side (or sides) of the fuselage between the wing and the tail assembly. Check with your instructor about the particular system for your airplane. (See Fig. 3-4.)

6. *Check the propeller* for spinner security and for nicks. Propellers are bad about sucking up gravel and then batting it back against the tail. A sharp nick is called a "stress raiser" by engineers because stresses can be concentrated at the point of the nick, possibly causing structural failure and the loss of a propeller tip. (You may have used this same principle by notching a piece of wood to break it more easily.) Since the propeller is turning at 40 revolutions per second, an unbalanced propeller could literally pull the engine from its mount. If you have any doubts about prop damage when making the preflight check, you'd better have someone take a look at it. Figure 4-4 shows a method that mechanics use to eradicate comparatively small stress raisers. *Don't move the prop. The ground wire might be off inside the mag where you can't see it — or if the engine is hot, it may kick over if the prop is moved, even if the mags are working normally.*

7. *Look in the engine cooling openings* for objects that might hinder air flow. Planes have hit small birds, and these have been jammed into the engine fins causing a hot spot, followed by the ruin-

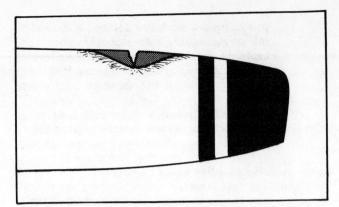

Fig. 4-4. An exaggerated view of a "stress raiser" and the method of "dressing" the nick to eliminate this problem. A nick of this relative size usually means that the propeller is sent back to the manufacturer or discarded. (Enough nicks — and dressing — on one blade could cause a balance problem.) The shaded area shows removed material.

ing of a cylinder. The fins are finely engineered and any obstruction cuts down the cooling efficiency.

8. *Look at the carburetor intake screen.* The screen is there to stop bugs, dirt, and other foreign matter from going into the carburetor. Check for security and see if the screen is clogged.

9. *Check the oil radiator* for obstructions or damage.

10. *Step back to check alignment of the landing gear.* You'll never make a hard landing, of course, but that character who just flew the plane might have. Look behind before you step back. (One student stepped back and sat in a 5-gallon can of freshly drained oil.) This would be the point where you'd check the nosewheel tire and oleo for signs of wear or damage.

11. *Open the right side of the cowling.*
    a. *Check the ignition leads and the right magneto.* If the leads are frayed bring this to the attention of the instructor.
    b. *Check the oil* if it's on this side — probably it will be.
    c. *Generally take a good look at the items that were hard to check from the other side.* Don't be like Oswald Zilch who checked only the side the oil was on. One day a mechanic took off two of the cylinders, and since Oswald never checked that side, he tried to take off and ran through the same chicken farm that Henry Schmotz, of no-wing fame, had recently vacated.
    d. *Secure the cowling.*

12. *Check the tire and landing gear strut. Check the brake assembly.*

13. *Check the strut fittings* at the fuselage for safetying, if they aren't covered by a fairing.

14. *Check the fuel quantity visually on this side.*

15. *Check the pitot-static tube,* if it's on this side, for obstructions.

16. *Look under the wing for tears or wrinkles* in the skin structure. A wrinkle means a strained member.

17. *Check the strut wing attachments* for safetying.

18. *Grasp the wing* in line with the two spars,

if it is a fabric-covered trainer, and give it a brisk shake. Make sure the instructor is not standing under the other wing or you may knock him cockeyed. This is a bad way to start a flight. (On the other hand you may *want* to knock him cockeyed. Use your own judgment.)

The reason for holding the wings in this manner is that you are putting a direct stress on the spars; if there has been any damage to these members or if there are broken drag wires, the damage will show up by sound and/or by wrinkling in the skin.

The metal trainers with plastic wingtips are somewhat harder to check for damage in this manner. The main wing structure may consist of a single box spar with the metal airfoil shape built around attached ribs (with the ailerons and flaps added) rather than a two-spar and rib system. You should try to move it to check for wrinkles, but you also should look at the rivets in the wing to check for signs of overstress. Sometimes, but not always, this will be indicated by the paint being cracked around the rivet, or it may appear that certain rivets have moved slightly or seem elongated.

19. *Check the ailerons* for excessive play or slackness between the two. Look at the aileron hinge assembly for security.

20. *Check the flap hinges* for cracks or excessive wear. Look at the general condition of the flaps (no stretched rivets or cracks).

21. *Drain some fuel* from the right tank drain to check for water or other contamination. Some flight school operators advocate the check for water once a day rather than every flight. However, it's better to drain them every flight so that *you* can see that it's clear, rather than taking someone's word for it. (A $25,000 airplane and your neck are a pretty high price to pay just to avoid draining 15 cents worth of gasoline.)

22. *Look alongside the fuselage for tears or wrinkles or pulled rivets.* If the static vent is in this area, make sure it's clear of dirt. (Look under the belly, also.)

23. If the *stabilizer* is externally braced, look at the brace wires or struts and check for slack wire or loose attachments. Most stabilizers now are of cantilever construction and have no external bracing. Grasp the tip of the stabilizer and check for internal damage by exerting up and down forces on it. *Don't try to pick the tail up by the stabilizer tip. It's quite possible that you might damage it.* Many lightplanes have signs painted on the stabilizers warning against lifting the tail this way, but you can get a pretty good idea if things aren't up to snuff by shaking it. Better to find out now than at 500 feet. Some planes have an adjustable stabilizer instead of a trim tab. Some trainers have a "stabilator" (stabilizer-elevator combination) and the entire horizontal tail surface acts as the elevator.

24. *Move the elevators* up and down to check for full movement. Note any binding of the hinges and check for safetying on all hinge bolts. Look under the elevator and stabilizer for tears and wrinkles. If your plane has a "stabilator," check its movement and condition.

25. *Check the rudder* for binding and limits of operation. Look for fraying of the cables and safetying of the cable attachments at the rudder horn.

26. *Tailwheel.* If your airplane is the tailwheel type, naturally this would be the place to check the tailwheel. The rudder is connected to the tailwheel by coiled springs which absorb ground shocks to the rudder and also make for smoother directional control on the ground. Check these springs. Check the tailwheel attachment bolts for signs of wear or shear breakage. The last student may have landed slightly sideways, and this puts a large shear stress on the attaching bolts.

27. *Check the other stabilizer and elevator, and look at the trim tab.* Is it set at nose up? Nose down? Neutral? Check the trim tab cables for wear if they are accessible.

28. *Check this side for tears or wrinkles.*

29. *Check this tank for water and other contamination.*

30. *Check this wing, aileron, flap, and strut. Check the pitot tube* if it is on this side.

31. *Check the strut fuselage attachments* for safety.

32. *You should now be back at the door, ready to get in.* If for some reason you are not back at the door, ask somebody how to get there.

A suggestion for the preflight check — make sure the switches are "OFF" and then check all of the fuel items at the same time. Note that there are *five* items that pertain to the fuel or fuel systems to be checked: the *two* tanks (should be checked visually) and the *three* drains (two wing tank drains and the main system drain). You might be less apt to overlook one of these items if you get them at the same time and then proceed with the clockwise check (starting from the cockpit as illustrated). If you use this system, make sure you don't pull a Henry Schmotz.

It's usually a good idea to drain the wing tank drains first to get water or other contaminants that have settled to the tank bottom, then drain the main (lowest) drain.

It could happen that draining the main drain first would pull contaminants down into the line between the tank and the carburetor and so not show up as in the wing tank draining. The garbage might only make itself known at a very bad spot just after lift-off.

Some systems require that each tank be drained through the fuel strainer (lowest) drain. Your instructor will issue you a *Pilot's Operating Handbook* shortly after you start to fly, and his discussions and your reading will make things much clearer about the systems of your airplane.

When you are flying solo, make sure that the other seat belt and shoulder harness is fastened so that there are no "loose ends" to hang out of the airplane. A seat belt and/or shoulder harness banging in the slipstream against the fuselage sounds like an engine malfunction. Pilots have put airplanes down in strange places and damaged them because it sounded as if the engine were blowing up.

After the complete check, the airplane is O.K. and you are ready to get in, fasten your belt and shoulder harness, and start the engine.

The plane with a starter has one disadvantage against it's many advantages. There is nobody out front cranking the prop and keeping people from getting hit by it. A dog or small child can easily get under the nose unseen and be killed or seriously injured when you start the engine. *Before you start the engine shout, "CLEAR?" and receive the acknowledgment, "CLEAR!" from the somebody on the ramp who is in a position to see.* If you don't get this reply but go ahead and push the starter button anyway, you may have reason to regret it the rest of your life.

Sure, if you holler, all of the airport personnel will get out of the way, but the visitors or kids won't know what the word means. Some pilots are criminal in their starting procedures -- they shout, "Clear!" and before the word is out of their mouths are starting the engine. This is as bad as saying nothing. Get set up to start, get acknowledgment of your shout, then start the engine. Don't check that everything is clear and then dawdle in the cockpit until somebody has a chance to stick a sawhorse or something under the prop.

PROCEDURE (Use *Pilot's Operating Handbook*)

1. *Preflight check complete.*
2. *Seat belts and shoulder harness fastened.*
3. *Controls move freely.*
4. *Fuel "ON" fullest tank.*
5. *Mixture rich.*
6. *Prime as needed.* (You may pump the throttle — this will be covered later.)
7. *Throttle cracked 1/4 of an inch.*
8. *Brakes "ON."*
9. *Radios and other unnecessary electrical equipment OFF.*
10. *Turn ON the master switch and the electrically driven fuel pump* (if the airplane is so equipped) before starting to see if it's working. You can hear it and see the fuel pressure come up. You'll turn the electric pump OFF after the engine starts to check that the engine-driven pump is working. (See Chapter 6.)
11. CLEAR? After receiving acknowledgment, ensure that the master switch is ON and engage the starter.

COLD WEATHER STARTING

When the mercury is nudging down toward zero the airplane's engine, like the automobile's, can get cantankerous to start at times. The principle for starting on a cold day is generally the same for both. In the car, you'll pump the accelerator, or the automatic choke will be helping. You want a rich mixture, or a high ratio of gasoline to air, during the start. The same thing applies to starting the plane. Prime the engine well and leave the primer out, so you can give it a shot if needed after the engine starts. It's possible that you may have to keep it running with the primer until the engine starts to warm up. Once the engine is running on its own, push the primer in and lock it, or the engine will run rough, particularly at low rpm, because raw gas will be pulled into the engine, making the mixture too rich.

One procedure for cold weather starting is to turn the fuel "ON," crack the throttle, make sure the mags are "OFF," and give it about five or six good shots of primer (pull the primer out, let it fill, and slowly push it in). Leave the plane tied down and chocked if there is no one to stay in the cockpit, pull the propeller through several times by hand, then untie the plane and use the starter. You've checked the mag ground wires and checked the ignition switch and *think* it's off — but it's best to have someone qualified in the cockpit anytime the prop is being pulled through. The reason for this pulling through by hand is to save the starter and battery. There will be a certain number of times for the propeller to turn before the engine starts. With the oil almost like grease and the battery weak because of the cold weather, this initial pulling through will ease the load considerably.

HOT WEATHER STARTING

The engine will run hot and stay hot a long time after being shut down in the summer. A hot engine has a tendency to "load up," or flood itself, and the fuel-air ratio should be comparatively low for best starting.

Suppose you come out to the plane just after it has come down on a hot day. You run a preflight check and the prestart check is completed. The guys on the ramp give you a thumbs up and you push the starter. The prop turns over, and over, and over. If you've done the prestart procedure correctly, the chances are that the engine is loaded. One way to clear it out is to turn off all the switches, open the throttle wide, and have somebody pull the prop through several times. Then close the throttle and start the prestart procedure again. The reason for the open throttle is that as the engine turns over, the added air through the carburetor helps to clear the cylinders of excess fuel.

Another procedure is to open the throttle at least halfway as soon as you realize the engine is loaded and then continue the start. The engine will clear itself out and start. Of course, you'll have to pull the throttle back as soon as it starts, or everybody in the hangar will hear the noise and figure that you'll be coming through there any second.

If the engine is obviously loaded you can open the throttle and have the mixture at idle cutoff as the start is continued. This is a more complicated approach for the inexperienced pilot, since the throttle must be retarded and the mixture control moved out of idle cutoff as the engine starts. This procedure is mentioned for later use.

Priming is needed only in cold weather starting. *Over*priming anytime can be asking for a fire.

Sometimes during a start the engine will backfire, causing the fuel in the carburetor to be ignited. *If you suspect that there is a fire in the carburetor intake, keep the engine turning over. The fire will be sucked into the cylinders where it belongs.* A fire extinguisher may have to be used outside the airplane in some conditions. You may put the mixture to idle cutoff, turn fuel off, and open throttle as you keep the engine turning over with the starter. Review the *Pilot's Operating Handbook* for specific procedures.

After the fire is out, shut down the engine and have a mechanic inspect the carburetor and engine compartment for damage.

ACCELERATING PUMP

While discussing the subject of starting, it might be well to mention that some trainers have an accelerating pump on the carburetor whereby a quick forward movement of the throttle results in an added spurt of fuel being injected into the carburetor throat. This is done so that should the pilot suddenly open the throttle, the engine gets enough fuel to accelerate quickly and smoothly. The accelerating pump is useful also in starting the airplane and can often be used in lieu of the primer. By pumping the throttle, raw fuel is injected into the carburetor throat and an extra rich mixture is pulled into the cylinders when the engine starts turning over. (You have a similar accelerating pump in your car.) The primer is normally set up to send fuel *directly* to the cylinders rather than injecting fuel into the carburetor throat, as does the accelerating pump.

When the temperature is very low, using the primer is the most effective means of assuring that sufficient fuel is available for starting. (Excessive priming tends to wash oil from the cylinder walls with resulting increased engine wear, but it's a necessary evil.) A method you may use in cold weather when you become more proficient is to use the primer as the engine is turning over. This tends to decrease the chances of loading up because the engine will usually start when conditions are "right" for it.

MIXTURE CONTROL

The purpose of the mixture control is to allow the pilot to set the ratio of fuel-to-air mixture going to the engine. As a quick and dirty figure, a mixture of 1 pound of fuel to 15 pounds of air is about right to support combustion.

Assume that your airplane doesn't have a mixture control but the carburetor has been set at sea level by a mechanic to give the amount of fuel to the engine to get this 1-to-15 ratio. As the airplane climbs, the air becomes less dense, weighs less. The carburetor, though, is sitting there fat, dumb, and happy, letting the engine get the same amount (weight) of fuel as it did at sea level, but now it is getting less than the correct amount (weight) of air. The mixture, which was just right for sea level, is now overly "rich" (too much fuel for the air available), combustion efficiency drops, and power is lost. You are also using more fuel than is necessary. You may have run into this problem in driving to high elevations in your car.

Now suppose you do all of your flying from an airport high in the Andes, where the air is "thin." There still being no mixture control in the cockpit, the mechanic has adjusted the carburetor to get the magic 1-to-15 ratio of fuel to air at that high elevation. When you fly down to a sea level airport you'll find that as you descend the engine starts to run rough, coughs a couple of times, and quits. Why? Because as you descend, the air becomes denser and the fuel that the carburetor had been metering to the engine at the high altitude is not enough to support a combustion mixture in the denser air. The engine is running too "lean" and, in fact, doesn't want to run at all.

Lest you think that the 1-to-15 ratio (or 15-to-1, whichever way you prefer to think of it) is the only mixture for an airplane to operate with, it might be added that combustion can occur in mixtures as widely divergent as 1 to 7 (very rich) to 1 to 20 (very lean), but these are the extremes. The mixture control in the airplane allows you to take care of such variations as necessary.

When the mixture control is full forward the setting is full rich. This full rich position is always set slightly richer than would give the best fuel-to-air ratio for full power. This is done to be on the safe side because a rich mixture aids in engine cooling and only a slight amount of power is lost. As the control is pulled out or moved aft, the mixture becomes progressively leaner, until the "idle cutoff" position is reached at the full aft or full out position. The fuel is cut off completely in idle cutoff position. This is the way the engine with a mixture control is shut down.

The mixture control is normally in the full rich position for take-off and other high-power conditions and for starting. However, you can see that for take-offs from airports at high elevations this could be too rich and power would be lost. Later you'll learn the techniques for leaning the mixture for take-offs under these conditions, but for now use full rich unless the instructor says otherwise. (You may never take off from an airport of an elevation — or density altitude — where this leaning is necessary.) In Chapter 23 more details will be given on cruise control (setting power and mixture) in flight.

STOPPING THE ENGINE

Occasionally in hot weather, the engine of older type trainers won't stop when the ignition is turned off (no mixture control). The engine is so hot that it's "preigniting," or setting off the fuel mixture without benefit of spark plugs. After you cut the switch, open the throttle wide as the engine runs down. This will send fuel and cool air into the cylinders, lowering the temperature and keeping preignition from occurring.

In some cases, the engine will kick backward after the switch is cut. This is a form of preignition, and opening the throttle will usually stop any tendencies toward this engine-punishing action.

The throttle is opened on the shutdown in the winter to send fuel into the cylinders to help the next start. This is particularly important if your primer isn't as good as it should be.

For airplanes equipped with mixture controls, the shutdown technique is to pull the throttle back to idle and pull the mixture all the way aft (to the idle cutoff position). The engine will quit smoothly. The beauty of using the mixture control rather than the ignition switch to shut down the engine is that the possibility of preignition is eliminated (there's no fuel left in the cylinders to be ignited). If the idle cutoff is improperly set, you might find that the engine tends to continue running at idle because some fuel is still getting through the carburetor. One method of shutting down in this case is to leave the control in idle cutoff and advance the throttle until the incoming air leans the mixture to a point where combustion can no longer be supported. (In extreme conditions you may have to turn the fuel selector off and wait it out.)

PROPPING THE PLANE

Nearly all planes have starters these days, but the following is presented for your possible use. If you plan on doing any propping, you should receive instruction from someone with experience; it's an extremely risky business. Another rule is to *never* prop an airplane without a competent pilot or mechanic, *who is familiar with the particular airplane,* at the controls. Propping a plane without a competent operator inside is asking for great excitement, tire tracks on your sports jacket, and loss of an airplane.

The idea of starting is the same as with an electric starter except you have manpower instead of electricity turning the prop. There'll be a little more conversation in this case.

Man out front: "OFF AND CRACKED!" (Meaning switch off and throttle cracked.)

You: (*After* checking to make sure that the fuel valve is "ON," the mags are "OFF," and the throttle is cracked) "OFF AND CRACKED."

Man out front: (After pulling the prop through several times to get the engine ready for start) "BRAKES AND CONTACT!"

You: Check the brakes and say, "BRAKES AND CONTACT," *before* turning the switch on. Notice that you're giving him the benefit of the doubt in all cases.

He pulls the prop again and the engine starts. If in hot weather the engine loads up and doesn't start, he will have to clear the cylinders of the excess fuel. If he trusts you he may say, "Keep it hot and give me half," meaning for you to leave the switch on and open the throttle halfway. He may add that you are expected to hold brakes firmly and pull the throttle back as soon as the engine starts. He may push against the prop hub to see if you are holding the brakes. He will then pull the prop through until the engine starts. He will be very, very unhappy if you forget to pull the throttle back and are not holding any brakes. One student chased a mechanic with an airplane for 50 yards one day. Of course, soon afterward the mechanic chased the student with a wrench.

In most cases with students, the man propping will say, "SWITCH OFF AND THROTTLE OPEN," and you will make sure the switch is off and the throttle is open. When he thinks the plane is ready to start, he'll say, "THROTTLE CLOSED, BRAKES AND CONTACT." You'll close the throttle (he can hear it close from outside), say, "THROTTLE CLOSED, BRAKES AND CONTACT," hold the brakes, and turn the switch on.

The whole idea in starting an airplane is safety. That prop is a meat cleaver just itching to go to work on somebody. Don't you be the man who causes it to happen, and don't be the one that it happens to.

WHEN YOU'RE SWINGING THE PROP

Always figure the switch is on, no matter what the guy in the cockpit says. Push against the prop hub to see if he's holding the brakes. He may be an old poker-playing buddy, but he can do you a lot of damage here so don't take any chances.

Before you start to prop the plane, look at the ground under the prop. Is there oil, grease, or gravel that might cause your feet to slip out from under you? If the ground doesn't look right, then move the plane — better a tired back than a broken one.

You: "OFF AND CRACKED."

Man in the cockpit: (After checking) "OFF AND CRACKED."

A lot of nonpilots think that the prop is turned backward and "wound up" and released, but this is wrong. You will turn the prop in its normal direction — that is, clockwise as seen from the cockpit, counterclockwise as seen by you when standing in

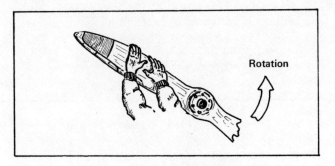

Fig. 5-1. Propping the airplane.

front of the plane. You're doing the same thing a starter does — turning the prop over until the engine starts. (Your car starter doesn't turn the engine backward and then let go to make it start.)

Put both hands close together on the prop about halfway between the hub and the tip (Fig. 5-1). Don't wrap your fingers around the trailing edge; just have enough of the tips there to pull the prop through, because if the engine should kick back, your fingers would suffer. (You may also be fired into orbit if you hang on tight enough.) Stand at about a 45-degree angle to the prop — this should have your right shoulder pointing in the general direction of the hub. Keep both feet on the ground but have most of your weight on the right foot. As you pull the propeller through, step back on the left foot. This moves you back away from the prop each

time. Listen for a sucking sound that tells you the engine is getting fuel. This will be learned from experience — an open or half-open throttle does not have this sound.

When you think the engine is ready, step back and say, "BRAKES AND CONTACT." After the acknowledgment from the cockpit, step forward and give the prop a sharp snap. Then step backward and to one side as the engine starts.

The starting problems you may encounter have already been discussed.

Don't stand too far from the prop. This causes you to lean into it each time you pull it through.

If the prop is not at the right position for you to get a good snap, have the man in the cockpit turn the switch off. Then move the prop carefully to the position required. *As far as you are concerned, the switch is always on.*

AFTER STARTING

The oil pressure should come up to normal within 30 seconds in warmer weather. Any undue delay should cause you to shut the engine down. Your instructor will have advice for cold weather starts.

After the engine is running well you should retract the flaps (they were down for the preflight) and, if electrically driven, you will want to wait until the alternator is in operation and helping the system.

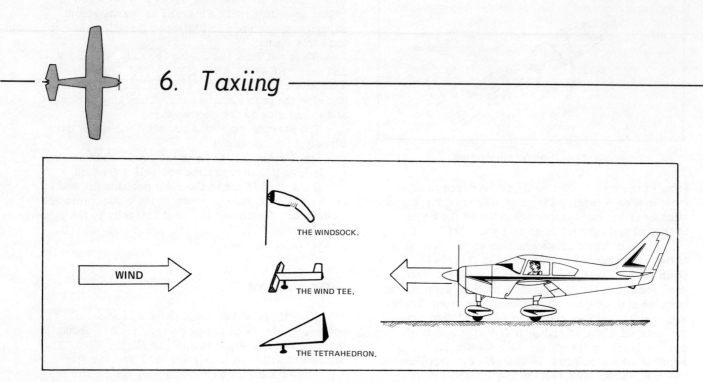

6. Taxiing

Fig. 6-1. Airport wind indicators.

COMMUNICATIONS

At uncontrolled airports you'll set one of the communications transceivers to the "Unicom" frequency to coordinate your take-off, pattern, and landing with other traffic in the area.

At some controlled airports (with a tower) you will listen to ATIS (Automatic Terminal Information Service) — a continual broadcast of recorded noncontrol information concerning winds, ceiling, visibility, and runway(s) in use — and when you contact ground control for taxi instructions you'll let them know that you have "Information Bravo" or "Charlie," the latest information (the recording is updated periodically and a new alphabet symbol assigned to it).

There's more detail on communications in Chapter 21.

WIND INDICATORS

Get in the habit of checking the wind indicators before getting into the plane so you'll know which runway is in use. There are three main types of wind indicators (Fig. 6-1): (1) the windsock, a cloth sleeve that has the advantage of telling both wind direction and velocity; (2) the wind tee, a free-swinging T-shaped marker that resembles an airplane; and (3) the tetrahedron (a Greek word meaning "four bases or sides"), a four-sided object that resembles an arrowhead when seen from the air.

Airplanes usually take off and land into the wind because the lower groundspeed shortens the ground run.

Some students remember the correct way to use the windsock at first by thinking of the plane as being blown from a trumpet. Think of the tee as an airplane. The way it's heading is the way you want to take off and land. The tetrahedron is an arrowhead pointing the way for you to take off and land.

SEGMENTED CIRCLE

Usually the wind indicator is in a segmented circle to draw the pilot's attention to it from the air (Fig. 6-2). The runways are shown as extensions from the circle. If one or more of the runways has a right-hand traffic pattern — the normal pattern is left-hand — this will be indicated by the extensions. Perhaps there is a hospital or town on one side of the airport and it's best to keep the air traffic away from that area.

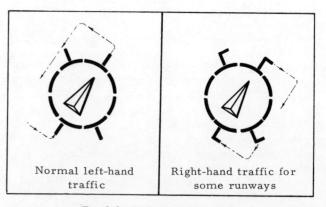

| Normal left-hand traffic | Right-hand traffic for some runways |

Fig. 6-2. The segmented circle.

Take off and land with the other traffic even though this does not agree with the wind indicator. However, remember one thing: When solo, *you* are the pilot in command of your airplane. If some character is trying to break his neck by landing downwind (with the wind) in strong wind, or other such foolishness, you'd be better off to continue to circle until he accomplishes his mission, and then you can land in the proper direction.

Incidentally, hard-surfaced runways are numbered by their magnetic headings to the nearest 10°. Runway 22 means that the plane's magnetic heading on this runway will be about 220° when taking off or landing. The actual heading may be 224°, but it is called 22. If the actual heading were 226°, then the runway would be 23, or considered to be 230°. The opposite direction on the same runway (22) would be called 4 (40°). (See Fig. 6-3.) These numbers are painted on the runways. This enables transient pilots to pick out the active runway more easily from the air after the tower has given them landing instructions.

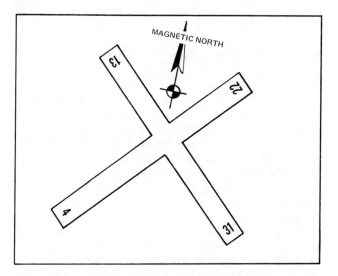

Fig. 6-3. Runway numbering system.

TAXIING

The majority of the trainers used today are of the tricycle-gear type which, if nothing else, has cut down on the number of taxiing accidents. In the older tailwheel types the nose was high and obscured the view of the pilot, so continual "S-turning" was required to keep the taxi area ahead in sight. Sometimes the nose was swung just in time for the pilot to realize that he was bearing down fast on a large, immovable and/or expensive object. The lower nose of the nosewheel type makes it easier to see ahead at all times.

Also, the nosewheel steering is usually more positive and gives better control in strong wind conditions.

The airplane on the ground is out of its element. It lumbers and shakes and moves awkwardly. But in order to fly, you first must taxi, and you'll find that

a certain degree of skill is required to move the airplane on the ground under varying wind conditions.

Most tricycle-gear airplanes are steered on the ground with the rudder pedals, which are connected to the nosewheel *and* rudder. Some airplanes have stiff connections between the rudder pedals and the nosewheel, while others have a softer feeling spring-loaded bungee to transmit the pedal pressure to the nosewheel. In any type, push the rudder pedal in the desired direction of turn. As will be noted later, brakes may be used in some cases to tighten the turn. Other types have a free-castering type of nosewheel (not connected to the rudder pedals), with brakes being the primary steering control at low speed taxiing.

Your probable tendency in the first taxiing session (and later ones, too) will be to grab that control wheel in front of you and use it to steer the airplane. Your past experience in driving cars can result here in what educators call "negative transfer"; turning the wheel does nothing but move those ailerons out on the wings, which are sometimes an aid in taxiing but won't help you avoid that million-dollar corporation jet you're headed for. The instructor may have you keep your hands off the wheel the first couple of taxi periods so that you can break the car habit.

The taxi speed, which is controlled with the throttle, should be a fast walk out on the taxiway and much slower in a congested area such as the apron. Use the throttle as necessary to maintain the taxi speed.

FLIGHT CONTROLS IN TAXIING

When taxiing downwind, and the wind is strong, hold the wheel forward so that the wind strikes the down elevator and keeps the tail from rising.

When taxiing upwind (into the wind) hold the wheel back so that the wind force and propwash hold the tail down. At any rate, always hold the wheel so that forces acting on the elevator will hold the tail down (Fig. 6-4).

As was noted earlier, the tricycle-gear airplane generally has more positive reactions in taxiing and doesn't tend to weathercock as easily as the tail-wheel type. One problem with the latter is that a too-fast taxi, moving downwind, can be a hazard if sudden braking is required. The airplane may tend to nose over and, if the wheel or stick is pulled back (which is a usual reaction to "keep the tail down"), the tail wind gets under the elevators and magnifies the problem, sometimes to the price of a propeller or worse.

Under certain wind conditions the ailerons are useful in taxiing.

In Figure 6-5 the wind, coming from the side and behind, wants to make the plane weathercock or turn into the wind and is also trying to push the plane over. The elevators are down, and opposite rudder is needed to keep the plane from weathercocking. By turning the wheel to the right, the right aileron is up and the left is down as shown. The impact of the wind on the down left aileron helps fight the

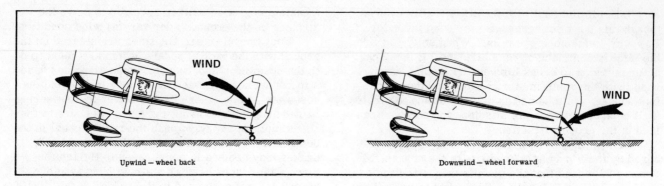

Fig. 6-4. Elevator handling — upwind and downwind taxiing (tailwheel type).

WIND FROM LEFT REAR
Right aileron
Right rudder as necessary
Down elevator

Fig. 6-5. This applies to tricycle-gear airplanes also.

overturning tendency, and the added area of the down aileron works against the weathercocking force. The aileron control (wheel or stick) is held away from the wind in a quartering tail wind.

When the plane is taxiing into a quartering head wind, the aileron is held into the wind, the wheel is back to keep the tail down, and opposite rudder is used as needed to stop any weathercocking tendency (Fig. 6-6).

If the wind is directly from the side, the ailerons are of no assistance unless your taxi speed is high enough to get a good relative wind against the ailerons, and if you are taxiing that fast — *slow down.*

In days of old, when men were bold and planes were light and ailerons large, ailerons were used opposite to the turn. The drag of the down aileron helped the plane to turn. The planes are now heavier and the ailerons smaller, so ailerons have a negligible effect unless you happen to be doing at least 25 K or so and, again, this is taxiing too fast.

If there is a strong, quartering tail wind it is possible to nose over a tricycle-gear airplane, especially if brakes are abruptly applied. What happens is that the plane "bows." The wind is able to get under the upwind wing and the stabilizer, and the plane may rotate around an imaginary line drawn between the nosewheel and the downwind main wheel. This reaction is aggravated if the elevators are in the *up* position. The same tendency is present, particularly in high-wing airplanes (where the center of gravity is farther above the wheels), when an abrupt turn is made while taxiing downwind in a strong wind. One memory aid is that when the wind is strong and behind the airplane (straight or quartering), hold the wheel as far away from the wind as possible. (Push and turn it away from the wind.)

Although the tricycle landing gear has made taxiing much safer and easier, you will still need to exercise caution at all times. Figures 6-5 and 6-6 show control deflections as they would apply to either landing gear type.

This matter of using controls in taxiing may be quite confusing at first, but just visualize what you want the wind to do when it strikes a particular control surface and go on from there. After a while it'll become second nature.

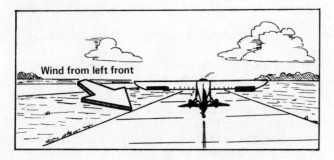

Wind from left front

Fig. 6-6.

BRAKES

Most airplanes have separately controlled brakes for each main wheel. Your plane may have either heel brakes or toe brakes, that is, the pedal is operated by your heel or toe. The *toe brake* is a

38

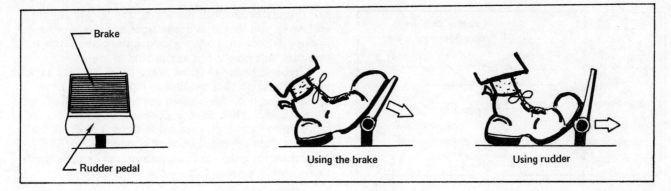

Fig. 6-7. The toe brakes.

part of each of the rudder pedals and is applied by bending your foot so that the ball of your foot or your toes apply the pressure (Fig. 6-7). You will taxi with your heels on the floor until the brake is needed. Then slide your foot up and apply brakes along with the rudder. Toe brakes are hydraulic brakes, similar in action to those in your car, except you aren't able to brake one wheel at a time in the car.

The *heel brake* is usually a cheaper, mechanical brake and is being phased out. The pedals are located under the rudder pedal and slightly toward the inside of the pedal. Instead of using hydraulic pressure to do the braking, the heel brake usually has a steel cable running from the pedal to its wheel. It is used by placing your heels on the pedals as shown in Figure 6-8 and applying pressure.

Don't use brakes for taxiing unless you have to. There will be days when you have to taxi crosswind in a tailwheel type for a long distance with the wind so strong that opposite rudder won't be enough. In many cases you can help steering by applying short bursts of power to help the rudder and tailwheel do the job. Obviously, any blasting of the rudder must be of short duration. You don't want to take off except on the runway. If none of these work, you may have to use downwind brake from time to time.

After continued usage, the brake may get hot and fade out completely, and you're worse off than when you started. If it's that windy, it would be best to use brakes or whatever else is needed to get back to the hangar and lock the plane in it.

The brakes are used for stopping the plane at slow speeds, holding it at a standstill, and making a tight turn.

If you have to make a tight turn, use full rudder and then apply brakes. Never lock a wheel to turn the plane. This is hard on tires. If you get in a spot requiring a locked-wheel turn, stop the engine, get out, and push the plane around. An easy way to lose friends is to start the engine on the ramp, jam on full throttle, and brake to make a jazzy turn. The guy whose plane is being blasted by your propwash and flying gravel is going to take a dim view of your taxi technique.

Don't jam on both brakes quickly at the same time! You don't have to be an aeronautical engineer to figure out what would happen if you did. You may get away with it in a tricycle-gear plane, but even on this it could throw a great stress on the nose-wheel assembly and slide the tires.

Don't depend on the brakes — they may fail when least expected. In a congested area, taxi so that the plane will slow down immediately when the throttle is closed. There's nothing more disconcerting than to come roaring up to somebody's $100,000 airplane at the gas pit, applying brakes, and feeling that sickening mushiness as they fail. This is a time when you wish you had a ceremonial sword to fall on — and as quickly as possible.

Don't taxi with a lot of power and use brakes to keep the speed down. The brakes will burn up very quickly. This seems to be one of the most common faults of students' taxiing. Many people flew for

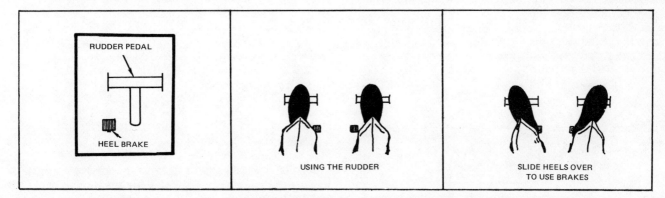

Fig. 6-8. The heel brakes are being phased out.

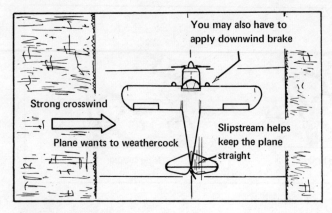

Fig. 6-9. Taxiing in a strong direct crosswind (tailwheel type).

years before brakes became universal for airplanes, so don't become dependent on them.

Your plane will probably have a parking brake and the instructor will show you how to use it. He will warn you that it is sometimes unreliable and it is best to chock the wheels or tie the plane down if you have to leave it for any period of time.

A type of brake used on some tricycle-gear airplanes consists of a handbrake that operates both brakes simultaneously when pressure is applied. This system, when used in conjunction with the steerable nosewheel, also allows turns of small radius. This system requires a short period of transition for pilots not accustomed to using a handbrake, but it proves to be quite satisfactory.

AN IMPORTANT NOTE

You should check the brake effectiveness immediately as power is added and the airplane starts to move out of the parking spot. You can see if they are working *before* picking up speed and boring into something expensive.

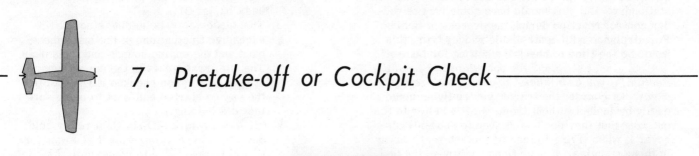

7. Pretake-off or Cockpit Check

Fig. 7-1. A thorough pretake-off check is vital to a safe flight. (Sounds rather pompous, eh?) Do it anyway!

This check is the last chance you'll have of finding something wrong with the airplane before the flight, so it should be a thorough one. In the preflight check on the line it was found that the airplane *looked* okay; here you will find out if the airplane *operates* okay. *Use a checklist for your particular airplane.*

PROCEDURE

1. *Taxi to the warm-up spot by the runway and turn the plane into the wind.* The modern air-cooled engine is designed to operate in the air, and the less it runs on the ground the better off it is. It's better to turn into the wind when you operate it on the ground. Don't have your tail pointed across the runway when you make the run-up. Your propwash could give landing planes some problems.

2. *Run the engine up to about 1000 rpm and leave it there while you check the controls.* This gives the engine a chance to be warming and smoothing while you run through the rest of the cockpit check. If you are flying a plane with an electrical system, it's a good idea to run the rpm up to where the alternator is effective, usually at about 1200-1300 rpm. The days are gone when a pilot sat on the end of the runway and took a lot of time warming the engine up. It's possible to damage an engine by prolonged ground runs. When you finish the cockpit check and the engine will take the throttle smoothly —take off.

3. *Check the ailerons by moving the wheel or

stick to the left and say to yourself, "Wheel to the left, left aileron up, right aileron down."* Move the wheel in the opposite direction and watch how the ailerons move. *DON'T JUST WIGGLE 'EM TO SEE IF THEY MOVE FREELY—MAKE SURE THEY MOVE IN THE RIGHT DIRECTION.* Aileron cable arrangements may have been reversed by mechanics who replaced them. If you take off with the ailerons reversed (turning the wheel to the left makes the plane bank to the right), a crash is almost certain to occur before you realize what's happening.

4. *Move the wheel through its full backward and forward range.* (Wheel back, elevator up, etc.) Look back at the elevators and check the elevator trim tab to see that it is neutral. Check the trim tab control setting in the cockpit to see that it coincides with the actual setting of the tab. If your plane has an adjustable stabilizer, look back to check its actual setting with the stabilizer indication in the cockpit. For future references (in case you are at a strange field and the indicator is broken) you might check the number of turns of the cockpit trim control from either full-up or full-down to get the neutral position. Obviously this technique should be necessary only on a temporary basis; the indicator should be repaired at the earliest possible time. It's considered good practice by many pilots to roll the elevator tab or adjustable stabilizer control through its full travel (up and down) to check for possible binding; at any rate make sure it's in the correct setting for take-off.

5. *You checked the rudder control while taxiing, but look back and move it again for full play.* In some

41

tricycle-gear airplanes you will not be able (and shouldn't try) to move the rudder while the plane is stationary. But you should have some idea of rudder control reaction during the process of taxiing. For airplanes with controllable rudder trim, this would be the time to check the setting for take-off.

6. *Check the flaps for operation and equal deflection, if you hadn't done so during the preflight check.* Of course, the trainer you're flying could easily be landed without them, but it's better to find out *now* that they don't work than to suddenly discover it when trying to land on the shortest runway in three counties. If your flaps don't pass the test, taxi back and get them fixed. If you wait to try them in the air for landing, you might find that only one will extend. (And no student pilot should be doing slow rolls on final approach.)

7. *Start on the left side of the instrument panel and check each instrument as you move from left to right.* There may be a slight variation of this order of checking for your particular airplane — and you may not have some of the instruments mentioned.

   a. The *airspeed indicator* should be reading zero, or well below the stalling speed.
   b. The *attitude indicator* small reference airplane should be set as close to the actual attitude of your airplane as possible.
   c. The *heading indicator* is set with the *magnetic compass*. (Check that the compass is reading right for your approximate heading.) Some instructors recommend setting the H/I after the airplane is lined up with the runway on known runway headings; this can give a double check of the magnetic compass.
   d. Set the *altimeter* and check *both hands* for proper field elevation setting. Too many pilots look only at the hundred-foot hand and set the altimeter wrong – particularly after a large change in atmospheric pressure. Notice that the short (thousand-foot) hand in Figure 3-2, on page 12, also registers approximately 720 feet. This gives you a double check.
   e. When taxiing you should have noted the reactions of the *needle in the turn and slip* (left turn, needle to the left, etc.) or turn coordinator. This naturally assumes that the instrument is powered by an engine-driven vacuum pump or is electrically powered. If it is venturi-driven it shouldn't be operating when you taxi, because if it does, you've been taxiing quite a few knots too fast.
   f. Check and set the *airplane clock*.
   g. The *vertical speed indicator* should be indicating a zero rate of climb.
   h. The instructor will show you how to check the *radio* if the plane has one and if you are in a position to receive. (In a controlled field you will have turned the radio transmitter-receiver on after start

and contacted ground control for taxi instructions to your present position — see Chapter 21.)

   i. The *tachometer* is holding steady. No excessive fluctuations of the instrument hand and the engine sounds and feels okay.
   j. The *oil pressure* is in the normal operating range. (You checked it right after the engine started and want to make sure that it's holding.)
   k. *Oil temperature* — O.K. On a really cold day you'll have a long wait if you wait for the oil temperature to come up to the operating range. Just look to see that it's not *too* high or whether it's beginning to *move* if the day isn't very cold.
   l. If the airplane is a low-wing type with wing tanks, check to see if the *engine-driven fuel pump* is working properly with the *electric boost pump off*. The fuel pressure should stay in the normal range. Turn the electric pump *on* again as an emergency standby for take-off unless the *Pilot's Operating Handbook* specifically says otherwise. Its job is to aid in starting (for some airplanes) and as an emergency standby for take-offs and landings in case the engine-driven pump fails (it, of course, would be turned on should the engine-driven pump fail anytime in flight). *After take-off* you will normally turn it off after reaching a safe altitude. Watch the fuel pressure as you turn it off; the engine-driven pump may have failed and the electric pump may have been carrying the load. If, after shutting it off, the fuel pressure falls and the engine starts cutting out, turn the pump on and enter the traffic pattern for landing.
   m. Check the *ammeter* for proper charge if the plane has an electrical system.
   n. Note the *suction gage* for normal value. (This instrument indicates the drop in atmospheric pressure — in inches of mercury — established for the vacuum-type gyro instruments by the engine-driven vacuum pump.) Most vacuum gages in normal operation will indicate a drop in pressure of between 4 and 5 inches, but the instructor and/or *Pilot's Operating Handbook* will furnish the specifics for your airplane.

8. *Gas* on fullest tank. Check the fuel gages to see if the indications jibe approximately with the fuel amount shown in your visual inspection of the fuel quantity.

9. Check *again* that you won't blast another plane behind you, then run the engine up to 1800 rpm or that recommended by the manufacturer and check *each magneto*. Turn the switch from "BOTH" to "R" (right magneto only). Watch the tachometer for an rpm drop. You are allowed a 75- to 125-rpm drop, depending on the airplane. (If the rpm drops more

than is allowable it's best to take the plane back to the hangar.) Turn the switch back to "BOTH" and watch it pick up. This gives you a double check on the rpm loss.

Turn the switch from "BOTH" to "L," or left, and watch for the drop. Now turn back to "BOTH" and watch the rise. Make sure the switch is on "BOTH" after you check the mags. Compare the rpm drops.

*Pilot's Operating Handbook*s give both a maximum allowable drop on each magneto and a maximum allowable difference between mag drops. For instance, one airplane cites a maximum drop of 150 rpm for each magneto or a maximum of 75-rpm drop differential between the two.

When you turn the switch to "LEFT," the right magneto is grounded out and the engine is running on the left magneto only. Since one spark plug does not give the smooth burning of the mixture in a cylinder as occurs with both plugs firing, a drop in rpm is expected (and the limits are given by the manufacturer). If you switch to one of the mags and the engine does as well (no drop) as it did on "BOTH," you are probably still running on both mags (a ground wire is off or the ignition switch is bad). Make sure this is reported so that no one can be hurt if they move the prop with the "hot" mag still in action. Remember, at these earlier stages anything unusual on the preflight or pretake-off check should be reported to an instructor or mechanic immediately. If you should inadvertently go to the "OFF" position while checking the mags, close the throttle before turning the switch back on. You'll usually have time to close the throttle *and* turn the switch on before the engine dies and won't get a backfire.

Occasionally you'll have an excessive drop in rpm that is caused by fouled spark plugs. On some makes of engines the left magneto is more susceptible to this problem than the right because it feeds the bottom plugs on *all* of the cylinders and the bottom plugs are more apt to be fouled by oil. (The right magneto fires all of the top plugs in these engines.) This plug problem is most likely to be present if the plane has been sitting idle for a long period or if the piston rings are worn. The scarcity of grade 80 fuel, necessitating the use of grade 100, has caused plug fouling by lead deposits. On other makes of engines, the right magneto fires the *left top* and *right bottom* plugs. (And, of course, the left magneto fires the *right top* and *left bottom*.) You might check with your instructor on the ignition setup for your particular airplane.

If your plane has a mixture control it is often possible to clear a fouled plug by leaning the mixture during the run-up. This causes the temperature in the cylinder to rise enough to "burn out" the trouble. Needless to say, this treatment can be overdone from the engine's viewpoint. You are better off at your point of experience to taxi back to have a mechanic look at the problem.

Don't make your run-up over loose gravel, because the propeller will pick it up and will be damaged. (If you doubt the "picking up" ability of a prop,

watch when an airplane is sitting over a puddle of water with the engine running — a minor waterspout will result.)

10. While at 1800 rpm, pull the *carburetor heat* "ON." Watch for a drop of about 100 rpm, showing that the warm air is getting into the engine, cutting down its power — and the carburetor heat is working. Leave the carburetor heat on for 10 seconds. If the rpm suddenly increases during that time it means that you picked up carb ice since starting up and warns you that icing conditions exist for this flight. (The heat cleared it up — temporarily.) Push the heat off for the take-off, as it will cut down on the power available. If carburetor icing conditions are bad, you can leave it on until the throttle is full open for the take-off. At fields of high elevation with the mixture in full rich and carburetor heat full on you'll find that take-off power is practically nonexistent. The actual high density altitude (the air is less dense), plus a full rich mixture setting, *plus* the even more lowered density of the warm air from the carburetor heat can cut down power drastically.

11. If the field is short or if you so desire, hold *brakes* and make a *full-power run-up*. With experience (and word from the instructor) you'll be able to see what is normal for a "static" rpm indication (no windmill effects because of forward speed).

12. Close the *throttle* and check the *idle rpm*. This should be between 500 and 700 and the engine should idle without loping. If you didn't lock the primer after starting, the engine will draw raw gas through the primer system and will tend to load up and quit at idle. Check primer for security.

13. *Make sure the door is closed and latched.* Quite a stir can be created by the sudden opening of a door just after lift-off. *Check with your instructor about possible procedures should this occur.* Assure yourself that your seat is latched securely — you don't want to slide away from the controls at a critical point during the take-off.

14. Switch to *tower frequency* and ask for *take-off clearance* and follow the tower's instructions when you are fully ready to go. Usually the tower will give one of three basic instructions in such a case:
    a. *Hold position* (or hold short), meaning you are not to go onto the runway.
    b. *Taxi into position and hold,* meaning taxi onto the runway and line up. But remember you are *not* cleared for take-off; this is done usually because of other traffic or possible wake turbulence.
    c. *Cleared for take-off.* Just what it says. If your condition was (a) above, you'd taxi right onto the runway and take off. In (b) this instruction would clear you to open the throttle and go. You would acknowledge the tower in each case to show that you understood. On uncontrolled fields, after the check is complete, turn the airplane, and if there is no landing traffic, taxi onto the runway for take-off. Read Chapter 21 for more details in this regard.

8. Effects of Controls

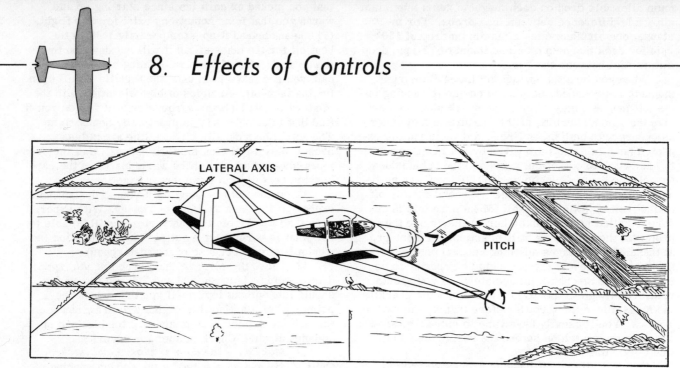

Fig. 8-1. Elevators control movement about the lateral axis (pitch).

FIRST FLIGHT

Most of your first flight will consist of finding out how the various controls affect the airplane. The instructor will climb the plane to a safe altitude — at least 1500 feet above the ground — and demonstrate the use of each of the flight controls. You will then use the controls until the plane's reaction to each becomes familiar to you.

The instructor will also trim the airplane for straight and level flight and show you how the plane flies by itself, demonstrating its natural stability. During the flight he will also show you the practice areas and point out outstanding landmarks and their reference to the airport.

Bumpy air on this first flight may cause you to be tense at first. The "bumps" are caused by uneven heating of the earth's surface. A plowed field reflects heat; a forest or water area absorbs it. As you fly over the terrain, the rising air currents are of different velocities, so the plane rises and drops slightly. As the air rises, it is cooled and soon becomes stable and smooth. The altitude at which this occurs varies from day to day, but on a hot summer day you may climb to 6000 or 8000 feet before finding smooth air.

ELEVATORS

The elevators control the pitching motion of the plane and are your airspeed control (Fig. 8-1). Under normal flying conditions (the plane is right side up), pressing back on the wheel moves the elevators "up." The relative wind forces the tail downward, the nose moves up, and *if you started with sufficient power and airspeed,* the plane starts to climb. Conversely, if the wheel is pressed forward, the nose goes down and the plane dives. If the plane is inverted and you press the wheel back, obviously the plane will not climb but will dive.

The best way to look at elevator movement, however, is to think of it as follows: wheel (or stick) back, the nose moves toward you; wheel forward, the nose moves away from you. This works for all attitudes.

At a low airspeed you might still think you can climb, or climb at a greater rate, by pulling the nose up, but you find that the up-elevators don't "elevate" the airplane but just decrease the airspeed. The nose moves up, *but* the increased drag causes the airplane to climb less or even start sinking! Power makes the airplane climb.

Let's take a situation such as the one you'll face when you're first introduced to the normal climb.

You're flying along at cruise power and airspeed and want to climb. Back pressure is exerted on the wheel until the nose moves to the normal climb position relative to the horizon, as shown by your instructor. (You will also open the throttle to climb power.)

Okay, when you applied back pressure on the wheel the elevators moved up. The relative wind moving past the elevators results in the tail moving downward (Fig. 8-2). Since the wings are rigidly attached to the fuselage they are rotated as well. This results in an increase in angle of attack (and drag), the plane starts slowing up to the speed for best rate of climb, you apply climbing power, and the plane climbs. *This is the technique for a steady climb.* You'll find you can "zoom" the airplane; that is, get a short-term climb by trading airspeed for altitude, using the momentum of cruise speed. In fact, because of this excess energy available at cruise speed, the airplane will start to climb as soon as you start to ease the nose up. (You will see that the airspeed will start decreasing immediately.)

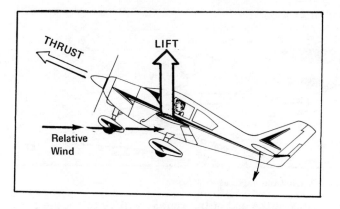

Fig. 8-2. Relative wind at instant of plane's rotation.

The job of the elevators in the climb is that of airspeed control — to get to that speed at which the greatest excess horsepower is available, which is the speed for best rate of climb. As a rule of thumb for most trainers, this will be found at about 1.4-1.5 times the flaps-up, power-off stall speed. (This is for calibrated airspeed, or CAS. You might review this in Chapter 3.)

To repeat: The elevators control the angle of attack (and indirectly the airspeed) of the airplane. Because most lightplanes don't have angle of attack indicators, you'll be watching the airspeed indicator for the plane's reactions to your use of the elevators. Therefore, the elevators are considered to directly control the airspeed.

Power (or lack of it) gives the required performance. Suppose a light trainer uses the same airspeed for best rate of climb speed and recommended glide speed. You would maintain with the elevators the same airspeed for both maneuvers; the difference in performance (climb or glide) would be in the amount of power used (climb power or idle). Or, you could fly straight and level at that same speed by using *some* power. So, one of the things

you'll learn is that the "elevators" are really misnamed; everybody uses the term, though, so it's a little late to change it. Probably it started back in the early days of flying when it was believed that this was their function — to "elevate" the airplane.

The trainer you will be flying may have a "stabilator" or "flying tail" instead of a stabilizer-elevator combination. The entire horizontal tail of the plane moves and acts as a stabilizer or elevators, as required. The principle of operation is the same — the "stabilator" is an angle of attack and airspeed control and, like the elevator, has a trim tab to help the pilot correct for various airplane loadings and airspeeds.

ELEVATOR TRIM TAB

Elevator or stabilator trim tabs are used to hold elevator or stabilator pressure for the pilot. If an unusually heavy load were placed in a back baggage compartment the tail would be heavy, the nose would want to rise, and you would have to hold forward pressure on the wheel to keep from slowing up. The trim tab is controlled from the cockpit, and during flight the plane can be trimmed for climb, glide, or straight and level. Some planes use an adjustable stabilizer for this purpose.

Larger planes require use of trim tab or adjustable stabilizer when speed or power is changed, but your instructor probably will have you fly all maneuvers *at first* with the plane trimmed for straight and level so that the varying control pressures can be felt. Some students get in the habit of trimming the plane full nose-up for landing but this can lead to difficulties if a go-around is required. The application of power may cause the nose to rise so sharply that the plane is stalled before the nose can be lowered. This will be discussed further in Chapter 14.

Returning to the example of a heavy load in the baggage compartment (Fig. 8-3):

The nose wants to go up; the pilot holds the nose at the proper position and trims the plane "nose down" until there is no pressure against the wheel. When the tab control is moved to the "nose-down" position, the tab on the elevator moves up. The relative wind strikes the tab, forcing the elevator down for the pilot. (This is strictly an example; you'll read later that the baggage compartment is *not* to be overloaded.)

RUDDER

The rudder controls the yawing motion of the airplane (Fig. 8-4). Push the left rudder pedal and the nose yaws to the left — push the right and the opposite occurs. The prime purpose of the rudder is to overcome the adverse yaw of the aileron. In certain maneuvers such as the slip and crosswind landing, ailerons and rudder are used opposite to each other, but 99.99 percent of the time they are used together in the air.

On tailwheel type airplanes the rudder is connected to the tailwheel by coil springs, and this is

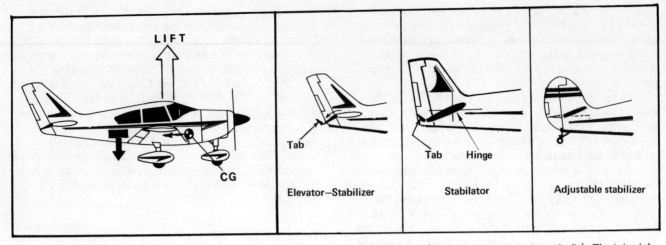

Fig. 8-3. Pilot has to hold wheel forward because the plane wants to nose upward. (Center of gravity is moved aft.) The trim tab or the adjustable stabilizer does it for him. "Nose-down" trim is set in all cases here.

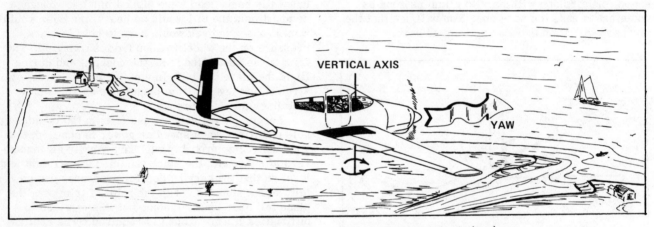

Fig. 8-4. The rudder controls movement about the vertical axis (yaw).

the main factor in ground steering. The tricycle-gear types have a mechanical linkage between the rudder pedals and the nosewheel so that ground steering depends even less on the rudder. (In the tailwheel airplane, sometimes a blast of slipstream striking the rudder can help in turning; for tricycle-gear types it has little effect.) "Rudder" is another term that is misleading. A rudder of a boat is the main tool for turning. An airplane's rudder is not the primary control used for turning; in normal flight it is an auxiliary to the ailerons.

However, you'll find that by application of rudder in the air it is possible to turn. By pushing rudder you skid the airplane, causing one wing to move faster than the other (Fig. 8-5). This added lift causes the airplane to bank and the rest of the turn is normal. It can be rolled out in the same manner, as will be demonstrated to you.

RUDDER TRIM

In Chapter 2 the "bendable" rudder tab was discussed; some of the later model trainers have a rudder bungee or tab that is controllable from the cockpit. You can adjust the rudder trim as necessary in flight to get the desired reaction. In these airplanes, one of your jobs during the pretake-off

check at the end of the runway will be to set the trim properly. (It's set to a "nose-right" indication to help you on that right rudder to overcome "torque" on take-off and climb.)

AILERONS

The ailerons roll the airplane. If the stick is moved to the left (or in an airplane with a wheel, the wheel is turned to the left), the left aileron moves

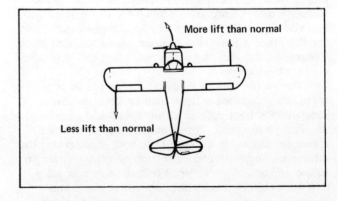

Fig. 8-5.

46

Fig. 8-6. The ailerons control movement about the longitudinal axis (roll).

up and the right aileron moves down. The relative wind strikes the control surfaces as shown and the airplane rolls to the left (Fig. 8-6).

The plane will continue to roll as long as the ailerons are deflected. In fact, this generally would be the way you'd do a slow roll — plus the use of other controls to aid the process.

Ailerons are used to bank the airplane. The airplane banks in order to turn. There's nothing in the world that gives less traction than air. When a rudder pedal is pushed, the nose yaws around, but the plane tries to continue in a straight line. True, it would gradually turn, but at best it would be a slow and distance-eating process. When the airplane is banked, the lift force acts as a centripetal, or holding, force as well and can be considered to be broken down into two parts — this is a legal assumption according to engineering mechanics (Fig. 8-7).

The centripetal force then helps the plane to stay in the turn. It is the force acting against the centrifugal force set up by the turn. *So, in order to turn properly, the airplane must be banked.*

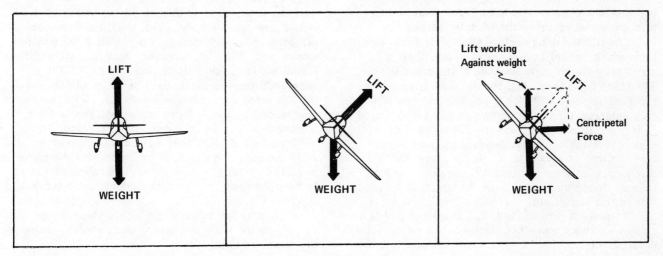

Fig. 8-7.

9. The Four Fundamentals

During the first flight, after you are familiar with the effects of the controls, the instructor will introduce you to one or more of the Four Fundamentals: the turn, the normal climb, the normal glide and straight and level. These are the basic maneuvers of flying, and you'll be using them or a combination of them for the rest of your flying career, so get them down pat now.

THE TURN

In the discussion of ailerons it was found that the plane must be banked in order to turn in the air. Fine — all you have to do is jam the wheel over in the direction you want and you turn that way. *Not so fast!* There's more to it than that. Let's see what happens when you give it left aileron (that is, you turn the wheel or move the stick to the left).

The lift and drag vectors (Fig. 9-1) show that although the wheel is turned to the left, there's more drag on the right because of the down aileron. The plane rolls to the left but the nose yaws to the right. The plane will slip to the left and finally set up a balanced turn. The right yaw you got is called "adverse aileron yaw," and the rudder is used to correct for this. *The rudder is used any time the ailerons are used in a turn.* Newer planes have a differential aileron movement (aileron moves farther up than down) and aileron designs that decrease this initial yaw effect.

To make a turn to the left, left aileron and left rudder are used smoothly together. As soon as the desired amount of bank is reached, the controls are neutralized. The wheel is moved smoothly back to

the neutral position, the pressure on the control wheel is eased off, and rudder pressure is no longer needed. This is called "neutralizing" the controls — the relaxing of exerted pressure on them: This term will be used throughout this chapter. Air pressure should streamline the control surfaces when the control wheel and rudder pedal pressures are relaxed. If the controls are not neutralized, the turn will become steeper and steeper.

You're in the turn. If you let go of the controls the plane will turn indefinitely — or at least as long as the fuel lasts — *except for one small detail.*

Lift is considered to act perpendicularly to the wingspan. Consider an airplane in straight and level flight where lift equals weight. Assume the airplane's weight to be 2000 lbs.

In Figure 9-2A everything's great — lift equals weight. If the plane is banked 60° as in Figure 9-2B, things are not so rosy. The weight's value or direction does not change. It's still 2000 pounds downward. The lift, however, is acting at a different angle. The vertical component of lift is only 1000 pounds since the cosine of 60° is 0.500 (60° is used for convenience here). With such an unbalance the plane loses altitude. The answer, Figure 9-2C, is to increase the lift vector to 4000 pounds so that the vertical component is 2000 pounds. This is done by increasing the angle of attack. Back pressure is applied to the elevators to keep the nose up. To establish a turn to the left:

1. Apply left aileron and left rudder, smoothly.
2. As the bank increases, start applying back pressure, smoothly.
3. When the desired amount of bank is reached, the ailerons and rudder are neutralized, but the back pressure is held as long as you are in the bank. Now you can turn indefinitely.

To roll out of the left turn:

1. Right aileron and right rudder.
2. As the bank decreases, ease off the back pressure.
3. When the plane is level, the ailerons and rudder are neutralized and there should be no more back pressure.

If the rudder and aileron are not coordinated properly, the plane will skid or slip. The skid occurs when *too much* rudder is used. You'll try to

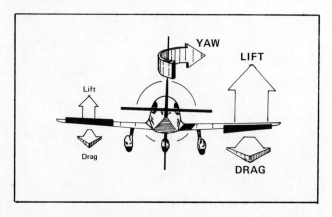

Fig. 9-1. Adverse aileron yaw.

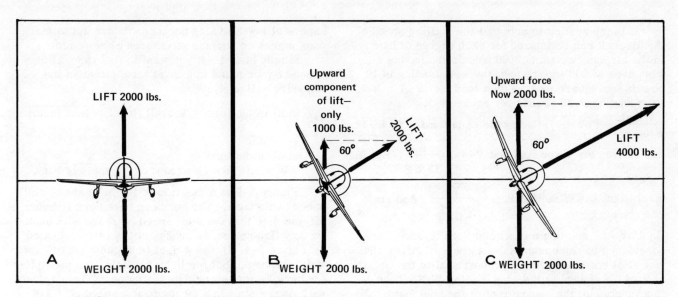

Fig. 9-2. The vertical component of lift must be equal to weight in a constant-altitude turn.

slide toward the outside of the turn as you do when a car turns a corner. The slip is a result of *too little* rudder, and you'll feel that you are sliding toward the inside of the turn. These errors can be felt and give you an idea of the expression "seat of the pants flying." Students have been known to wear out the seats of perfectly good pants, sliding around during the presolo phase.

If, in our example of the 60° bank, you roll out level but don't get rid of the extra 2000 pounds of lift you have, obviously the airplane will accelerate upward (the "up" and "down" forces will no longer be in balance). Maybe your idea of coordination is Miss Fifi LaTour's bubble dance routine, but it's necessary in flying too. Think of control pressures rather than movement. The smoother your pressures the better your control of the airplane.

If you aren't particularly interested in the trigonometric approach to back pressure, Figure 9-3 gives another approach.

LOAD FACTORS IN THE TURN

The turn introduces a new idea. It is possible to bank so steeply that the wings cannot support the airplane. The lift must be increased so drastically that the critical angle of attack is exceeded, and the plane stalls. In the previous example at 60° of bank it was found that our effective wing area was halved; therefore, each square foot of wing area had to support twice its normal load. This is called a *load factor of 2*. A plane in normal, straight and level flight has a load factor of 1, or 1 "g." You have this same 1 "g" load on your body at all times. Mathematically speaking, the load factor in the turn is a function of the secant of the angle of bank. The secant varies from 1 at 0° to infinity at 90°; so to maintain altitude in a constant 90° bank, an infinite amount of lift is required — and this is not available.

For those interested in the mathematics of the problem, the following is presented.

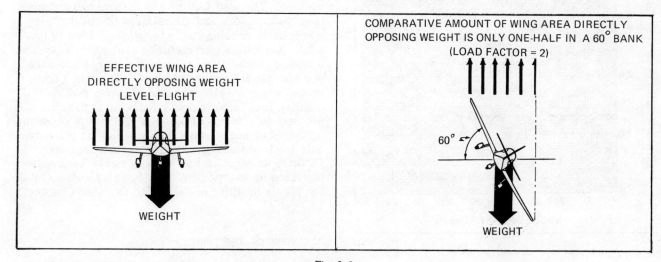

Fig. 9-3.

49

It is interesting to note that the stalling speed of the aircraft can be figured for each degree of bank. In the airplane weighing 2000 pounds and having a wing area of 200 square feet, the wing loading is 10 pounds per square foot. With a load factor of 2, the wing loading is 20 pounds per square foot = $\frac{\text{Weight}}{\text{Wing Area}}$ (or $\frac{W}{S}$). Using the equation $L = C_L S \frac{\rho}{2} V^2$ and solving for V you find that $V = \sqrt{\dfrac{L}{C_L S \frac{\rho}{2}}}$. But in level flight $L = W$ so that $V = \sqrt{\dfrac{W}{C_L S \frac{\rho}{2}}}$. And since C_L *Max* (the maximum coefficient of lift) and ρ are considered to be constants for a given situation, the new stall speed is directly proportional to the square root of the change in the wing loading W/S. Then V is a function of the square root of the load factor. So the stall speed in a 60° bank is $\sqrt{2}$ times that of the stall speed in level flight. If the plane stalls at 50 K in level flight, then its stall speed in a 60° bank is $50 \times \sqrt{2} = (50) \times (1.414) = 70.7$ K. *All of this is assuming that you hold enough back pressure to maintain level flight* (Fig. 9-4). If no back pressure is held, the airplane will be in a diving turn, there is still a load factor of 1, and the stall speed is not increased. If you make this kind of turn, it is wise to have a lot of altitude. Needless to say, the Federal Aviation Administration frowns on such capers at low altitudes because you are apt to leave pock marks on surface structures when you hit.

Simply stated — if you want to find the stalling speed of your plane in a level turn, either of the following will apply.

V stall in the turn = V stall (level) $\sqrt{\text{load factor}}$

or

V stall in the turn =
V stall (level) $\sqrt{\text{secant of the angle of bank}}$.

Figure 9-5 is a diagram of the increase of stall speeds with bank. The numbers have been rounded off, but note that the stall speed increase with bank for any flap setting increases at the ratio indicated by Figure 9-4. Gross weight (maximum certificated weight) is used, but for lighter weights the multiplier for bank increase would be the same. (The airplane will always stall in a 60° bank at a speed of 1.414 times the wings-level stall speed whether it's given in mph or knots.)

=Power Off= STALLING SPEEDS MPH = CAS				
⌐Gross Weight⌐ — 1600 lbs. —	ANGLE OF BANK			
CONDITION	0°	20°	40°	60°
Flaps UP	55	57	63	78
Flaps 20°	49	51	56	70
Flaps 40°	48	49	54	67

Fig. 9-5. Stall speed increase with bank. (*Cessna Aircraft Co.*)

Now back to the important, practical side of flying. Putting it simply: The stall speed goes up in the turn, and the steeper the bank the faster the stall speed jumps up, as can be seen in Figures 9-4 and 9-5. The load factors just discussed are "positive" load factors and are attained by pulling the wheel back, causing you to be pressed down in the seat. A negative load factor is applied if the control wheel is pushed forward abruptly, and in this case you feel "light" and tend to leave the seat. Light-planes are generally stressed to take a maximum positive load factor varying from 3.8 to 6, and a negative load factor of between 1.52 and 3, depending on the make and model. Both you and the plane are able to stand more positive "g's" than negative. Positive or negative load factors can be imposed on the plane by sharp up or down gusts as well as by the pilot's handling of the elevators. (See Chapter 23.)

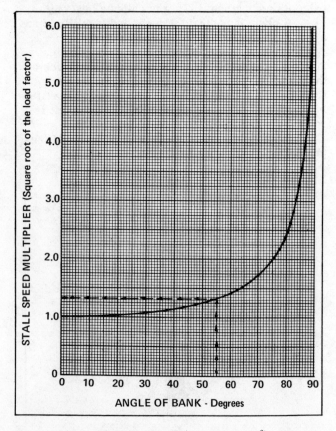

Fig. 9-4. Choose an angle of bank (in this case, 55°). Multiply the corresponding number (1.32) times the wings-level (normal) stall speed to get the stall speed at this angle of bank.

A REVIEW OF THE TURN

1. Aileron and rudder in the direction of turn.
2. Begin back pressure.

3. When desired steepness of bank is reached, neutralize the ailerons and rudder but hold enough back pressure to keep the nose at the correct place on the horizon — turn until you get ready to roll out. Check the nose, wings, and altimeter for smooth level turn.

THE ROLLOUT

1. Opposite ailerons and rudder. Gradually ease off the back pressure as the wings become level.

2. As the wings become level, neutralize the ailerons and rudder (the back pressure will be completely off at this point).

The idea is to be smooth. You have better control over the plane by using control pressures rather than movements.

Ride with the turn. You'll have a tendency at first to lean against the turn. Remember that in a proper turn the centrifugal force will hold you upright in the seat.

If you are in a side-by-side airplane, the position of the nose seems different in left and right turns. You will be sitting to the left of the centerline of the fuselage so that when the plane is turning left the nose will seem high; in a right turn the nose will appear low. Your instructor will demonstrate the proper nose position for climbs, glides, turns, and straight and level.

Figure 9-6 shows the views from the left seat during left and right level turns.

COORDINATION EXERCISES

After you are familiar with the idea of the turn, the instructor may have you do what is known as a coordination exercise. This consists of heading the plane at a point on the horizon and rolling from left to right bank, and so forth, without letting the nose wander from the point. It is a very good way to discover how much control pressure is needed to get the desired effect with the plane.

The beginning of the maneuver is like that of the beginning of the turn. Ailerons and rudder are used together. Then, before the nose has a chance to move, hold it on the point with opposite rudder. Apply opposite aileron and rudder and roll it to the other side and repeat the process. You will find it difficult at first but will soon get the knack and be able to roll smoothly from one side to the other without the nose moving from the point.

Although in parts of the maneuver the controls are crossed and not coordinated as they are in the turn, you will find that your turns will profit by a short period of this maneuver.

NORMAL CLIMB

Another of the Four Fundamentals is the normal climb, and at first you will practice starting it from normal cruising flight. To climb, the nose is eased up to the proper position relative to the horizon, the throttle is opened smoothly to the recommended climb power, and, as the airspeed starts to decrease, right rudder is applied to correct for torque. The recommended airspeed for best rate of climb is maintained.

You had a brief introduction to the climb in Chapter 8 when the elevators were discussed. There you noted that the elevators do not make the airplane climb; they are used to attain and maintain the *airspeed* at which the best rate of climb is found. That airspeed, engineers have found, is the one at which the greatest amount of excess horsepower is available for your airplane. (The rate of a steady climb depends on the amount of excess horsepower available.) An equation for determining rate of climb is:

$$\text{Rate of climb (fpm)} = \frac{33,000 \times \text{excess horsepower}}{\text{weight of plane}}$$

The horsepower in that equation is *thrust* horsepower, or the power being effectively developed

Fig. 9-6. Perspectives in left and right level turns. Note that your reference (which is a point on the cowling *directly in front of you*, and not the center of the nose) is at the same position in relation to the horizon. Don't use the center of the cowling as a reference.

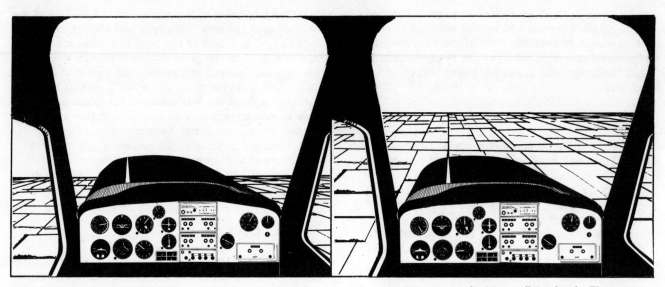

Fig. 9-7. The climb and level flight attitudes. This doesn't necessarily mean that you are climbing or flying level. These are attitudes only.

through the propeller, as was mentioned in Chapter 2. You also remember from that chapter that *power* is *force* times *distance per unit of time*, and 1 horsepower is equal to 550 foot-pounds per second, or 33,000 foot-pounds per minute. That's where the 33,000 in the equation comes in; it's set up for a rate of climb in feet per minute. By illustration, suppose your plane weighs 1500 pounds, has an engine capable of developing 100 *brake* (or shaft) horsepower at the recommended climb power setting at a particular altitude, and the propeller is 85 percent efficient at the climb speed. This means there will be 85 *thrust* horsepower available at the climb speed. Suppose, also, that at that speed 55 *thrust* horsepower is necessary to maintain a constant altitude. This means that 30 thrust horsepower is available for use in climbing. From the above equation we find the rate of climb to be 660 feet per minute:

$$R/C \text{ (fpm)} = \frac{33,000 \times 30}{1500} = 660 \text{ fpm}$$

So the excess horsepower is working to raise a weight (the airplane) a certain vertical distance in a certain period of time (rate of climb). If no excess horsepower were available at the climb speed the rate of climb would be zero. If you throttled back until the power being developed was *less* than that needed just to keep the airplane flying at a particular airspeed, a "negative" rate of climb would result; the airplane would descend at a rate proportional to your "deficit" power.

As a pilot you won't worry about excess horsepower, but you will use the recommended climb airspeed and power setting and let the rate of climb take care of itself.

The revolutions per minute of a fixed-pitch prop such as on a light trainer are affected by the airspeed. Assume you set the throttle for cruising at 2400 rpm. If the airplane is dived, the added airspeed will give the propeller a windmilling effect

and the rpm will speed up to, say, 2500 or 2600 rpm. If you pull the nose up for a climb, the airspeed decreases and the rpm drops below the cruising setting. Therefore, it is necessary to apply more throttle to obtain climb power. Normal climb speed is about 1.4 to 1.5 times the stall speed and is the speed that results in the best *rate of climb*. Your instructor will show you the correct climb attitude and airspeed for your particular plane (Fig. 9-7).

TO CLIMB

1. Ease the nose up to normal climb position and maintain back pressure to keep it there.
2. Increase the power to the climb value.
3. As speed drops, apply right rudder to correct for torque.
4. Don't let the nose wander during the climb or transition to the climb.

TO LEVEL OFF FROM THE CLIMB

1. Ease the nose down to level flight position.
2. As speed picks up, ease off right rudder.
3. Throttle back to maintain cruise rpm.
4. Don't let the nose wander during the transition.

PROBABLE ERRORS

1. Climbing too steeply — overheating the engine and actually decreasing the rate of climb.
2. Too shallow a climb — easy on the engine but not a good way to gain altitude.
3. Over- or undercorrecting for torque during the climb transition.
4. Rough transition to the climb or straight and level flight.
5. Not keeping the nose lined up on a reference point — letting it wander.

THE CLIMBING TURN

This is a combination of the two Fundamentals covered so far. It is, as the name implies, a turn while climbing.

For practice, at first, the climbing turn will be executed from a straight climb. That is, establish a normal climb and then start your turn.

Make all your climbing turns very shallow (Fig. 9-8). Steep banks require added back pressure (angle of attack) to keep the nose up, which sharply reduces the rate of climb because of greater drag (induced drag — see Chapter 2). *A 15° bank is plenty.*

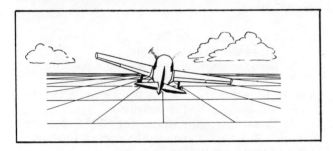

Fig. 9-8. Keep the bank shallow in the climbing turn or else the climb will suffer.

Torque must be considered in making a climbing turn. *Any time the plane is climbing, right rudder pressure or right rudder trim must be used.*

Suppose you are climbing and want to turn to the right. You are already holding right rudder, but as right aileron is applied more right rudder is needed to take care of aileron yaw, so the turn is something like this:

Climb
1. Back pressure.
2. Right rudder.

Climbing Right Turn
1. Right aileron and more right rudder -- make the turn shallow.

2. More back pressure.
3. Neutralize the ailerons and return to enough right rudder to correct for torque.

Rolling Out to Resume the Straight Climb
1. Left aileron and very little left rudder (in some planes, easing off the correction for torque may be all that is needed).
2. As the wings become level, neutralize the ailerons and get back on that right rudder.

Again, any time you make a turn it requires added back pressure.

The torque effect is as if slight left rudder were being held. In a left-climbing turn, torque will tend to skid you into a steeper bank. In a right-climbing turn, it will tend to skid you out of the turn.

When you have the climb and climbing turn idea well in mind and are able to control the aircraft in a reasonable manner, you should start the habit in your climbing turns of maintaining a constant bank and making definite 90° turns as you climb. (This will be your introduction to precision flying.)

NORMAL GLIDE

The normal glide is a third Fundamental and the least understood by the beginning student. The nose is not pushed *down* to glide as is commonly believed but, on the contrary, back pressure is needed to keep the glide from getting too steep.

In Figure 9-9A the airplane is trimmed for straight and level flight. The force caused by the slipstream and relative wind acting on the stabilizer just balances the force of the weight trying to pull the nose down. The plane is in balance. Pulling the throttle back to idle causes a lessening of the tail force by two factors: (1) The slipstream effect has dropped to nil, because the propeller of an idling engine produces a very weak slipstream; and (2) the plane starts slowing immediately now that the drag

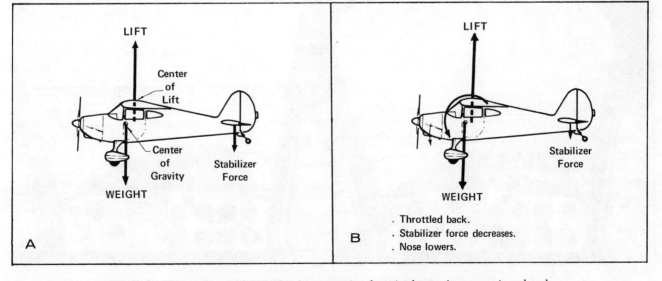

Fig. 9-9. The airplane is designed to have a nosing down tendency when power is reduced.

53

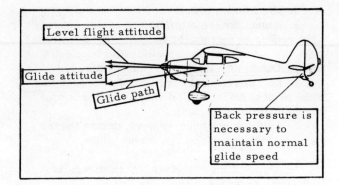

Fig. 9-10.

is greater than the thrust — hence the relative wind speed decreases. (The decreased slipstream is by far the biggest factor in this nosing down process, however. Item 2 mentioned above can be neglected for all practical purposes.)

The result is shown in Figure 9-9B. The plane noses down until the forces are balanced again. Your speed now may be higher than desired for the glide. If you want to glide at 70 K, you must slow the plane to that speed by holding back pressure so that the plane's glide attitude is something like that in Figure 9-10. Normal glide attitude in most light-planes is only slightly more nose down than the straight and level position (Fig. 9-11).

Tailwheel type airplanes are shown in Figures 9-9 and 9-10 but the tricycle-gear trainer reacts the same way.

The recommended normal glide speed is the speed that gives you the most feet forward for altitude lost. For a fixed-gear trainer the normal glide ratio is about 9 to 1, that is, 9 feet forward for each foot of altitude lost.

If you glide too steeply, the 9 to 1 ratio drops off to maybe only 5 to 1. You can tell the steep glide by sight (nose position, airspeed increase), sound (increase in pitch of sound of wind), and feel (the controls become firmer).

Trying to "stretch the glide" by pulling the nose up also causes the glide ratio to suffer. You've increased the angle of attack to such a point that drag holds the plane back, but gravity is still pulling the plane down with the same force, resulting in a lower glide ratio. *So stick to that recommended glide speed.*

Pull the carburetor heat "ON" before closing the throttle in flight unless the Pilot's Operating Handbook *recommends otherwise.* Its use will be mentioned here each time the glide is covered, but your trainer and conditions may not always require it.

Assume that you are flying straight and level and want to glide:

1. Carburetor heat "ON."
2. Close the throttle (to idle).
3. Hold the nose in the level flight position.
4. As the airspeed drops to normal glide speed ease the nose down slightly to the normal glide position as shown you by the instructor.
5. Clear the engine about every 200 feet of the descent. This means running the rpm up to about 1500 and then back to idle.

You'll notice that quite a bit of back pressure is necessary to hold the nose up. The instructor may let you trim the plane for the glide. In that case, roll or move the trim until you feel no force against the wheel. Most instructors want you to get the feel of the plane and will probably only demonstrate trim in the glide at first.

To return to straight and level flight:

1. Apply power smoothly to cruise rpm as you simultaneously ease off the back pressure.
2. Push carburetor heat "OFF" after cruising flight is established.

With more experience you'll open the throttle up to about 100 rpm less than the cruise setting so that when the carburetor heat is pushed "OFF" the rpm will be at the cruise setting.

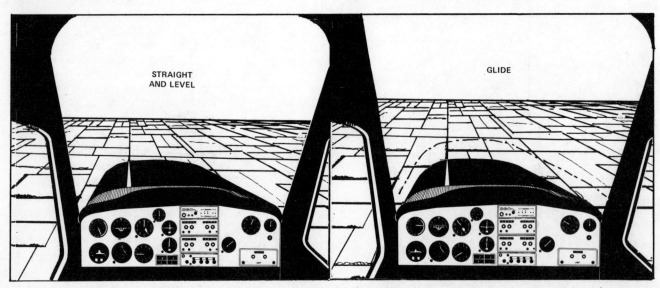

Fig. 9-11. Notice that the glide attitude is only slightly more nose down than that for straight and level flight.

The altimeter appears to "lag" in the climb or glide, particularly in the glide. If you want to level off at a specific altitude, say 1500 feet, it is wise to start the above procedure about 50 feet above that, or 1550 feet. The plane has momentum downward that requires altitude to change, and maybe your reactions aren't perfect yet — so give yourself about 50 feet for recovery from the glide. Of course, the bigger the airplane and the faster you are descending, the more margin you'll use.

If the back pressure is not eased off as you open the throttle, the nose will rise sharply as the slipstream strikes the up-elevators. The elevators are comparatively ineffective in the glide so you use a lot of up-elevator, and when the prop blast hits all that surface something's bound to happen.

COMMON ERRORS

In Starting the Glide:

1. Not giving the carburetor heat enough time to work before closing the throttle.
2. Abrupt throttle movement — jerking it back to idle.
3. Holding the nose up too long, resulting in too slow a glide speed.
4. Letting the nose wander as the glide is entered.
5. Forgetting to clear the engine in the glide.

In the Recovery from the Glide:

1. Opening the throttle abruptly.
2. Letting the nose wander.
3. Not releasing back pressure in time — nose goes up and plane climbs.

The carburetor heat is the first thing before, and the last thing after, the glide.

If icing conditions are bad, the carburetor may ice enough to cause engine stoppage between the time you push the heat off and get around to opening the throttle, particularly if you are the fumbling-fingers type. Granted that this would be an unusual occurrence, but why take the chance? Do it correctly now until it becomes a habit.

Clear that engine! In the winter, the engine may cool so much after an extended glide without clearing that it won't take throttle. In the summer the engine may "load up" and quit.

If you want to see what an actual emergency landing is like, don't clear the engine.

GLIDING TURN

Like the climbing turn, the gliding turn is a combination of two of the Four Fundamentals. Combine the glide and the turn and you get a gliding turn. An extended steep gliding turn is called a spiral. A greatly extended steep gliding turn is called a crash.

Probably the first thing you'll notice about the gliding turn is that the rudder seems to have lost much of its effect. Although the ailerons are ineffec-

tive in comparison with level flight, they still feel the same as they did in the climbing turn because the airspeed is approximately the same for climb and glide. The rudder, however, is suffering from lack of slipstream (Fig. 9-12). Concentrate on coordination again. Use the controls so that the airplane reacts correctly.

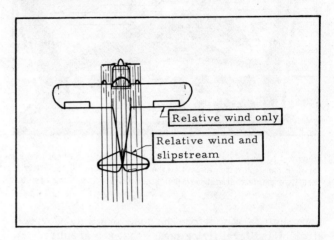
Relative wind only

Relative wind and slipstream

Fig. 9-12. Rudder and elevator get slipstream during cruise and climb.

Any time a turn is made, back pressure is required. If you have back pressure in the glide and make a turn, it will require more pressure. The principle is the same for climbing, gliding, or level turns. When the plane banks, the lift vector must be increased.

If you use insufficient back pressure:
In the climbing turn — no climb, only turn.
In the level turn — turn plus a shallow dive.
In the gliding turn — turn plus a steeper dive.
In rolling into or out of a gliding turn, the rudder is not as effective as you've been used to because of the weaker slipstream.

Common Errors
1. Not enough back pressure in turn — plane dives.
2. Not enough rudder on roll in and roll out.
3. Not easing off back pressure when rolling out — the nose comes up and the plane slows up.

Your instructor will have you make 90° gliding turns in each direction after you have a good idea of the procedure.

STRAIGHT AND LEVEL FLYING

One of the most important of the Four Fundamentals is straight and level flying. Some pilots have trouble with straight and level flying even after years of experience. Nearly every student has difficulty keeping the wings level. The average student tends to stare out over the nose with the glazed gaze of a poleaxed steer. Don't try to keep the wings level by watching for the cant of the nose, because the nose line is so short that one of the wings can be

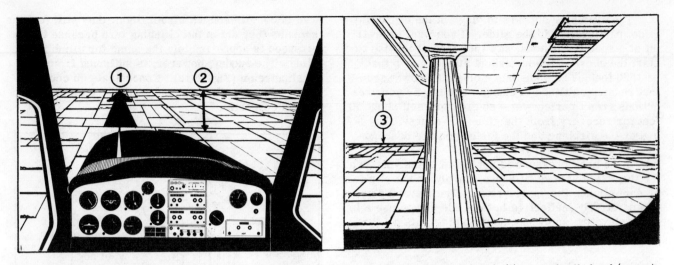

Fig. 9-13. In straight and level flight the airplane should be kept (1) directionally straight (no yaw), (2) longitudinally level (nose at proper position with respect to the horizon), and (3) laterally level (the wings the same distance above the horizon for the high-wing craft, or same distance *below* horizon for the low-wing airplane).

down quite a way before the nose shows it. Correct straight and level flying means that you are directionally straight and longitudinally and laterally level (Fig. 9-13).

The plane, if trimmed properly and left alone, will do a better job of flying than you are able to do. Many a student flies a "Chinese Cross-Country" (WUN WING LO) and wonders why he has that slightly uncomfortable feeling.

This is what's happening. He is unconsciously holding aileron one way or the other. A plane with a stick is flown with the right hand and sometimes the student allows the weight of his arm to pull the stick in that direction, resulting in a right slip. As the wheel is flown with the left hand, sometimes left aileron is slipped in.

The plane is banked and wants to turn, so the student helpfully holds opposite rudder to keep the nose from moving and is now in a slip. In Figure 9-14, the resultant is downward and the plane starts losing altitude gradually. To stop this, the student uses back pressure to maintain altitude, and the controls are in the position as shown in Figure 9-14.

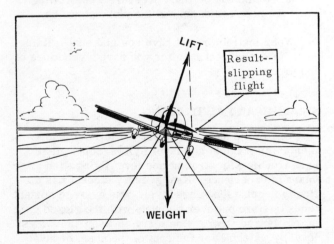

Fig. 9-14. Exaggerated view of wing-low flying.

He's holding right aileron, left rudder, and up-elevator when he should be able to fly "hands off."

The instructor will show you how to trim the airplane for straight and level flight. Generally this is done as soon as you reach the assigned practice altitude and consists of placing the nose at the correct attitude and trimming until the stick or wheel force against your hand is zero, the same technique as described in the normal glide.

Larger planes not only have controllable tabs for the elevators but have tabs for the rudder and ailerons as well. The pilot can trim the plane for any attitude or speed he desires.

Most lightplanes have a bendable aileron tab similar to the one on the rudder. If the plane has a tendency to fly wing-low at cruise, the pilot is able to bend the aileron tab so that this is corrected. The procedure is the same as used for that of the rudder tab. Bend the tab and fly. If further correction is needed, land, make the correction, and fly it again.

Once you have established good straight and level flight, there's nothing to do but watch the plane to see that it keeps this attitude. Some students feel that they should do *something* and consequently the plane receives quite a workout.

Try not to be tense, but if you are, don't worry about it. Flying is a strange experience at this point, and if you are completely relaxed you're one student in a million. However, if you are *too* tense the learning process slows down.

If a wing goes down momentarily, as may happen on a hot, bumpy day, bring it up with aileron and rudder together and as soon as the wings are level, neutralize the controls. If you try to use aileron alone, the plane will yaw from its heading.

Usually another "bump" will raise that wing but this return to wings-level flight is not always immediate, so you can help the process. But don't overdo it, because on bumpy days you'll be worn out in 30 minutes.

All through this book so far it has been stated that power controls altitude and that elevators are to be used to establish the proper airspeed for the maneuver involved. You will find, however, that in straight and level cruising flight, for minor altitude adjustments it's a lot simpler to use the elevators. For instance, if you are 50 feet low you will exert back pressure on the wheel and regain the altitude rather than adding power, which from previous discussions would be the "proper" thing to do. (Use "Energy Effect.") However, you might also take a look at the tachometer to make sure that the altitude loss (or gain) wasn't caused by an improper setting.

COMMON ERRORS

1. Flying with one wing low.
2. Holding back pressure unconsciously, causing the plane to climb.
3. Fighting the bumps.

These are the Four Fundamentals. These and stalls will be the backbone of your presolo flying.

THE FOUR FUNDAMENTALS AND INSTRUMENT INDICATIONS

The FAA requires on the flight test that you demonstrate the ability to recover from an emergency situation such as accidentally flying into clouds or fog. This means that you must be able to get out of such a situation through use of the flight instruments.

Tests have shown that students got better grades on the flight test when this training started early, that is, when flight with reference to instruments was integrated with the pre- and post-solo maneuvers. The FAA recommends that this integrated method be used in training all student pilots.

As in all of your flight training, the steps must be taken logically, when you are able to do the Four Fundamentals and feel at ease in the airplane, the instructor will have you go through these same maneuvers, directing attention to the instrument indications during the process of each. Later, you will use an extended visor cap, or "hood," that will restrict your vision to the instrument panel. At this point, however, it will be better to see the plane's attitude as

Fig. 9-15. A balanced constant altitude turn (standard rate). Airspeed slightly less than cruise because of bank (and back pressure). Heading indicator shows left turn, and turn coordinator shows balanced standard-rate turn. Altitude constant.

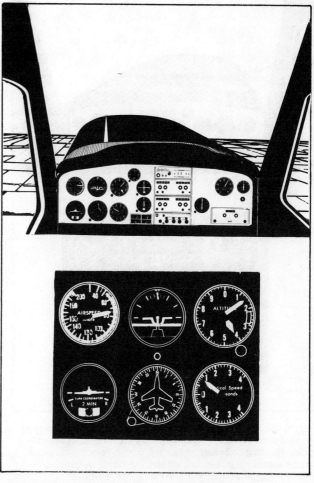

Fig. 9-16. Normal straight climb. Airspeed steady at climb speed. Attitude indicator shows attitude is nose up, wings level. Heading indicator shows constant heading, turn coordinator indicates balanced straight flight. Altitude increasing as shown by altimeter and vertical speed indicator.

well as the instruments so that you will be able to tie in the plane's actions with the instrument indications (and vice versa). In order to fly without outside visual references you must be able to "see" what the plane is doing through the instruments.

Figures 9-15 through 9-20 show the Four Fundamentals (plus climbing and descending turns) as seen from the cockpit and by the instrument indications.

It will likely be at this stage that you will first note the idiosyncrasies of the magnetic compass. You will see for yourself that in actual flight the compass is affected by steep banks, attitude changes, and acceleration or deceleration of the airplane. In many cases the compass may initially show a change of direction of up to 30° as soon as the plane is banked for a turn and in some may show a turn in opposite direction at first. In any event, the various actions of the compass for each maneuver cannot be

shown here; in Chapter 15 more information will be given about it. The heading indicator gives a true indication of the amount of turn, but the compass is accurate only when the plane is flying straight and level in balanced, unaccelerated flight.

During these maneuvers your attention will be on the instrument panel a large part of the time and the instructor will maintain a close watch for other airplanes.

There is no specific amount of dual required on the emergency maneuvers for the private certificate; it will rest on the instructor's judgment of your ability in this area.

However, the instructor will require that you be able to safely control the airplane by use of the instruments *before* you go on a solo cross-country. He won't want precision instrument flight but will expect you to stay ahead of the airplane in this area.

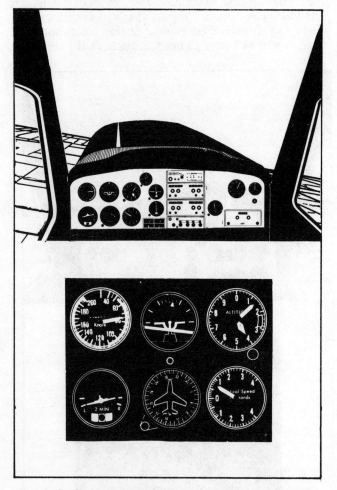

Fig. 9-17. Climbing turn, standard rate. Airspeed steady at climb speed. Attitude indicator shows 11° bank, climb attitude. Heading indicator shows left turn. Turn coordinator shows standard-rate balanced turn. Altitude increasing as indicated by altimeter and vertical speed indicator.

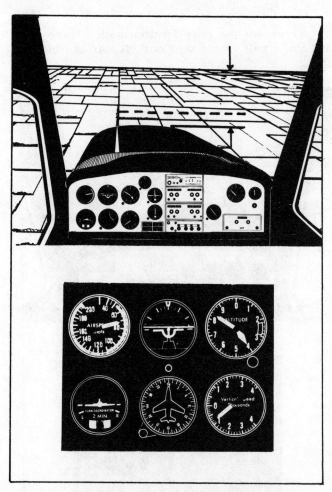

Fig. 9-18. Normal power-off glide (straight descent). Airspeed steady at proper glide speed. Attitude indicator shows slight nose-low, wings-level attitude. Heading indicator shows constant heading; the turn coordinator indicates straight balanced flight. Altitude decreasing as indicated by altimeter and vertical speed indicator.

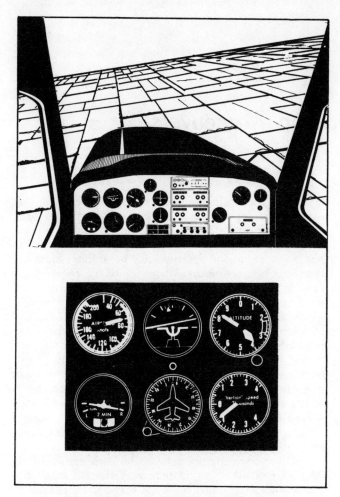

Fig. 9-19. Balanced, standard-rate, gliding turn. Airspeed steady at glide speed. Attitude indicator shows slight nose-low, 10° bank. Heading indicator shows right turn. Turn coordinator indicates balanced, standard-rate right turn. Altitude decreasing as shown by altimeter and vertical speed indicator.

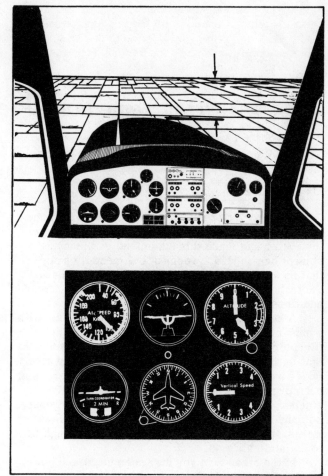

Fig. 9-20. Straight and level flight. Airspeed steady at expected cruise value. Attitude indicator shows nose- and wings-level flight. Heading indicator shows a constant heading. Turn coordinator, straight and balanced flight. Altitude constant as shown by altimeter and vertical speed indicator.

T-TAIL AIRPLANES

The current trend is toward building airplanes with "T-Tails" (the horizontal tail surfaces are on top of the fin and rudder). The horizontal tail is out of the slipstream and changes in power don't cause the pitch changes discussed earlier in the chapter (Figures 9-9 and 9-10) or at least such changes are smaller. You might watch for the differences if you go from one type to the other (T-Tail or standard) during your flying career.

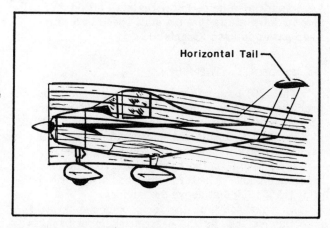

Fig. 9-21. The T-Tail is usually out of the slipstream so that pitch change with power is decreased.

10. Elementary Precision Maneuvers

STEEP TURNS

The only difference between the steep turn and the normal turn is the steepness of bank. Many an instructor has made this statement, and many a student has nodded agreement but mentally noted that he didn't believe a word of it. The fact is that the techniques are the same, with one or two minor additions.

A steep turn, as defined by the FAA, is one with a bank of over 30°. In EFFECTS OF CONTROLS (Chapter 8) and "The Turn," (in Chapter 9), you noted that in medium turns (15°-30° bank) you were able to take care of the need for increased lift by increasing back pressure. As the turn gets progressively steeper, you will find that the lift must be increased so much that you run out of angle of attack. In other words, the airplane stalls before you get enough lift to maintain altitude.

In the steep turn you may need increased power to maintain altitude because two things are happening: (1) The required added back pressure means a higher angle of attack and greater induced drag (see Chapter 2) and (2) the added load factor in the turn causes an increase in the stall speed. The added power serves to compensate for the added drag (which might otherwise finally result in an altitude loss) and it also helps lower the stall speed. You'll note in doing stalls that the stall speed is lower when power is used (Chapter 12).

THE 720-DEGREE POWER TURN

The 720° power turn is a confidence-building precision maneuver and consists of 720° of turn with a coordinated roll-in and roll-out and a bank of 45°-60°. You will use added power and will vary your bank as needed to maintain altitude.

Pick a point on the horizon or a road below as a reference point. The turns are done at an altitude of at least 1500 feet above the surface.

As your roll into the turn, open the throttle smoothly so that as the desired angle of bank is reached the power setting is approximately that of climbing power. Because of the great amount of back pressure needed after the turn is established, the angle of attack will be such that the airspeed will drop appreciably. You have a high power setting and low airspeed, so you will have to correct for torque effect.

Once the desired amount of bank is reached, the ailerons are neutralized, sufficient right rudder to correct for torque is held, and back pressure is held as needed to keep the nose at its proper place on the horizon. This nose position may be slightly higher than that in medium turns because of the required increase in angle of attack (added back pressure). A good rule of thumb is to have your bank and power established before you have made over 45° of turn.

You will find that the back pressure required is somewhat greater than you had anticipated.

If you see that the plane is losing altitude, the best method of bringing it back is to shallow the bank slightly. This will increase the vertical component of lift and the nose will return to the correct position — then resume your steeper bank. Or, if the plane is climbing, steepen up slightly and/or relax back pressure slightly.

The reason for not making the back pressure take care of all of the altitude variations is this: If you are in a 60° bank, the stall speed is increased 1.414 times that in level flight. If you have to climb or increase the lift at this bank, obviously you will run out of angle of attack. At 60° it takes 2 pounds of lift to get 1 pound of the vertical component. This is a losing proposition and with steeper banks these odds jump sharply (see Figs. 9-4 and 9-5).

Check your wings, nose, and altimeter as you turn. Watch for the checkpoint. Some students make three or four complete turns instead of two because they aren't watching for the point. After all, this is a precision maneuver.

After you've completed the first 360° of turn — if you held altitude — the plane may wallow or bump slightly as it flies through its wake turbulence. The more slipstream you hit on the second 360° the better your turn. It's possible, however, to hit a bump even if the altitude ran wild.

The idea is not to start out, say at 3000 feet, lollygag around from 2800 to 3200, and then feel proud because you happen to be back at 3000 feet when you roll out.

While your instructor won't be too critical about your performance at this stage of the game, it's a good idea to learn the technique now. Then you won't have to sweat 720s later when you should be practicing advanced stalls or other maneuvers.

The second 360° is a continuation of the first — make corrections as needed. Watch for the checkpoint and start rolling out and throttling back about

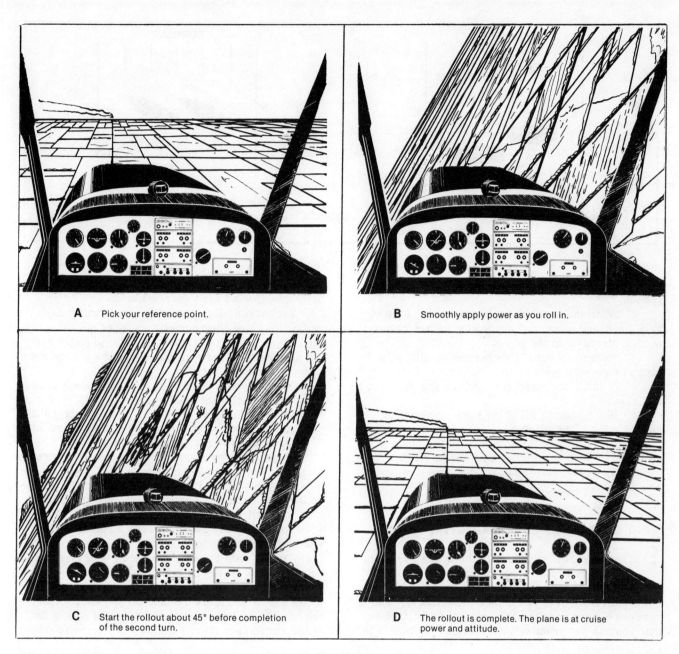

A Pick your reference point.	**B** Smoothly apply power as you roll in.
C Start the rollout about 45° before completion of the second turn.	**D** The rollout is complete. The plane is at cruise power and attitude.

Fig. 10-1.

45° before you are lined up with the checkpoint. The rollout should be smooth and timed so that the plane is in a straight and level attitude and at cruising power when the checkpoint is reached.

The hardest part about the rollout is keeping the nose from coming up. It takes a lot of back pressure to hold it up in the turn and it will take concentration in easing off that back pressure. During the first few times, it will seem you don't relax back pressure — you press forward to get the nose down where it belongs. To review the 720° turn:

The 720° power turn uses the same fundamentals as the shallow or medium turn. A steep turn requires only a longer period of deflection of the ailerons and rudder in order to obtain the steeper bank.

The reason slight right rudder may be needed is because of the torque effects caused by added power

and slower airspeed, not the steepness of bank.

Power is used because (1) the angle of bank is such that the stall speed is increased, plus (2) the required added angle of attack is increasing drag to the point where altitude may no longer be efficiently maintained by back pressure alone.

Some students get the idea that the nose can be held up by top rudder. The infinitesimal amount of the upward thrust angle doesn't compare with the great loss of efficiency suffered by slipping the airplane and slowing it down. It just won't work.

PROBABLE ERRORS

1. Back pressure added too soon at beginning of the turn — nose rises and plane climbs.

2. Applying full power or opening throttle too

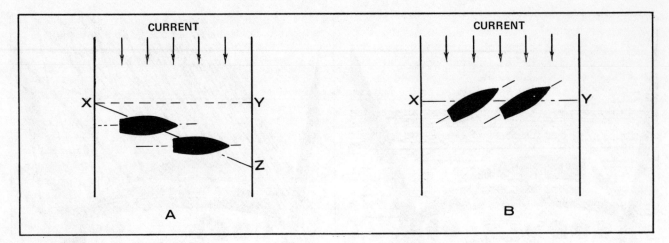

Fig. 10-2.

soon — airspeed has not dropped yet and engine over-speeds.

3. When the nose drops, trying to pull it up by back pressure alone, not shallowing bank — results in high stresses on the plane.

4. Failure to watch for checkpoint. (Make a mental note as it goes by the first time. That way you won't make the instructor sick as you go around and around.)

5. Not releasing all of the back pressure on rollout — the plane climbs.

6. Forgetting to throttle back as the plane is rolled out — also causes the airplane to climb.

7. The usual coordination problems of slipping and skidding.

WIND DRIFT CORRECTION MANEUVERS

The instructor will usually introduce you to the idea of wind drift correction by choosing a road or railroad that has a crosswind component and having you fly directly over it and then alongside it. You'll reverse course and fly in the opposite direction so that you can get practice in correcting for both a left and right crosswind. But first, take a look at the principle of wind drift correction:

You've seen lightplanes flying on windy days and noticed that they sometimes appeared to be flying sideways. In relation to the ground they were, but as far as the air was concerned the planes were flying straight as a string.

Suppose you wanted to cross a stream in a boat, paddling or motoring briskly from X to Y. The current is swift so if you start out, as in Figure 10-2A, you can see what happens — there's much sweat but little progress toward your destination.

By pointing the nose directly across the stream at Y, you wind up at Z. In Figure 10-2B, you play it smart. You point the boat upstream, how far up depends on the current speed, and you keep experimenting until you get the correct angle.

The same idea applies to the airplane. The wind is the current in this case. If you want to fly from X to Y with the wind as shown, you must angle into the wind, or set up a "crab."

If you start out pointing the nose at Y, you end up as shown in Figure 10-3A. So you correct for the wind by making a balanced turn and rolling out at the correction angle as shown in Figure 10-3B.

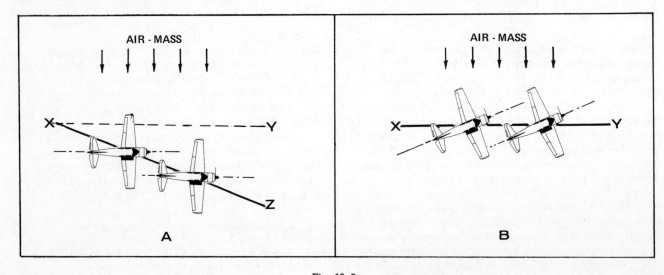

Fig. 10-3.

The purpose of the rectangular course is to give you a chance to fly the airplane while your attention is directed outside. As you learned the Four Fundamentals, you concentrated on the airplane and only noted its reference to the ground as a whole. Now you'll begin to use the plane and make it follow a definite path over the ground. During the first few minutes you'll feel as frustrated as a one-legged man in a kicking contest.

This maneuver consists of flying a rectangular pattern around a large field or fields and is done for three reasons:

1. To get into the habit of flying the plane while dividing your attention from the cockpit to objects outside.

2. To learn to correct for wind drift in flying a straight course in preparation for cross-country flying.

3. To get practice in low precision flying in preparation for traffic pattern flying.

The rectangular course is done at 600 feet because mistakes are easily seen at that altitude and because it builds confidence to fly at a lower altitude.

The instructor will try to pick a field lying so that the wind is blowing diagonally across it. This will give you practice in wind correction on all four legs (Fig. 10-4).

Procedure

Enter the pattern at a 45° angle, flying downwind (1). It is easier to set up your first correction downwind because drift can generally be seen more easily. This is just a human foible, but it works out that way. The turns around the field can be made either left or right. Assume in this case that the turns are to the left (Fig. 10-4).

Roll out of the turn at what you think is the proper correction angle. The plane's distance from the field should be far enough away that the boundary is easily seen and yet not so far away that your mistakes can't be seen. About 600-800 feet from the boundary would be a good distance for the average lightplane. Some students roll out parallel to the boundary and then make the correction, but it's advisable for you to get into the habit of making a correction as soon as possible.

Assume that in (2) you undercorrected and the plane is drifting into the field. Make a balanced turn of a few degrees into the wind and see how things fare. If you are now holding your own and are not too close to the field to see the boundary without straining, fly the plane to the end of the field.

At (3) you'll have to make a left turn. Since there is a quartering tail wind, it will tend to push you away from the field, particularly if a shallow turn is made (4). The best thing, then, is to make a fairly steep turn at this point. The steepness of bank will be dependent on the wind velocity—the greater the wind velocity, the steeper the bank. Roll out of

the turn with whatever correction you think necessary (5). Don't count on having the same angle of correction as you had on the other leg. The wind probably won't be crossing this leg at the same angle. As shown in the diagram, the wind is more from the side here, so more correction is needed. The vector of the wind pushing you into the field on the first leg was not as great as the vector you're fighting on this second leg.

In the second leg the wind is still somewhat behind the plane, so when you get to point (6) you can figure on another fairly steep turn. This turn will not be as steep as the one at (3) because the wind component on your tail is not as great as it was at (3).

Your angle of bank (the steepness of the turn) is directly proportional to your speed over the ground.

Continue the rectangular course. At point (7) the bank must be shallow, as you are flying into the wind (your ground speed is low). At point (8) the first part of the turn is shallow and then it is steepened to keep the plane at the correct distance from the field.

Probable Errors

1. Poor wind drift correction—not setting up correction soon enough.

2. Not recognizing drift or not making a firm correction after recognizing it.

3. Not maintaining altitude. Most students tend to climb in a rectangular course—there are a few rugged individualists who lose altitude.

4. Coordination problems—some students who make perfect turns at higher altitudes get so engrossed in watching the field that their turns are awesome spectacles indeed.

When the airspeed indicator was being discussed in Chapter 3, it was mentioned that the airplane was part of the air when it was flying. Let's go into it a little deeper:

Suppose that you are flying from point A toward point B, as shown in Figure 10-5. The wind is 20 K. You are to point the nose at B and make no correction for the wind. At the same time you leave A, a balloon is released there. At the end of an hour both you and the balloon are 20 nautical miles south of the A-B line. You covered a lot of ground but still ended up as far south of the line as the balloon. You were both carried by the air mass itself.

A jet or rocket plane, flying the same heading, would be 20 NM south of the A-B line at the end of an hour, even if it cruised at 1500 K.

Old-time pilots used to say, "I was flying along and all of a sudden the wind got under the wing and almost flipped the plane over." They hit turbulence, or disturbances within the air mass. The air mass itself didn't suddenly "blow" against just a part of the plane.

Another idea that died a hard death in that holding rudder corrects for wind drift. Stories are still told of pilots flying the mail in the 1930s landing with one leg numb from holding rudder for "that blank crosswind." If you hold rudder you defeat

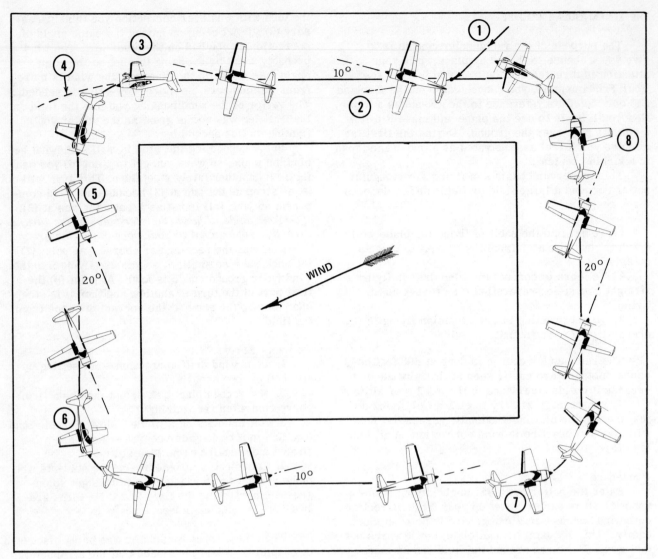

Fig. 10-4. The rectangular course.

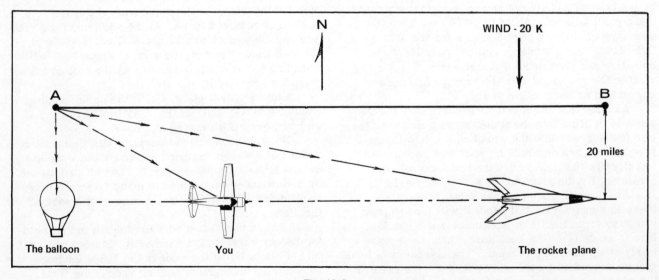

Fig. 10-5.

your purpose. When you skid a plane, it tends to continue in a straight line, and because of the added drag its airspeed will drop off. You'll end up in cross-controlled flight.

Skidding the plane defeats your purpose. The most comfortable and efficient means of compensating for drift is to maintain balanced flight (no slip or skid). You will be shown later that there is one time, and one time only, when this does not apply (Chapter 13 – THE CROSSWIND LANDING).

S-TURNS ACROSS THE ROAD

S-turns across a road, like the rectangular course, are good maneuvers for getting you used to dividing your attention between the airplane and the ground. The primary purpose, however, is to show you how to correct for wind in a turn. There was a brief introduction to this idea in the rectangular course, but S-turns give you a chance to acquire finesse.

S-turns are a series of 180° turns of about a quarter-mile radius using a road as nearly perpendicular to the wind as possible. (This is for planes of 90-95 K cruise. Faster planes will use a greater radius.)

The reasons for S-turns are:

1. To fly the airplane while dividing your attention between cockpit and ground.
2. To learn to correct for wind drift by varying the bank. This will come in handy later in circling and remaining near the same spot in a strong wind.
3. To get practice in precision flying in preparation for advanced maneuvers later.

S-turns are also done at 600 feet for the same reasons as were given for the rectangular course.

The object is to fly a series of semicircles of the same size, making smooth balanced turns and correcting for wind drift by varying the steepness of the bank. The plane should cross the road in a level attitude and with the wings parallel to the road.

Procedure

A road that runs as nearly 90° to the wind as possible is picked. It is best to enter the S-turns downwind, because drift is more easily detected and corrected by the student if correction requires a steepening of the bank rather than shallowing it out. The first turn can be made in either direction.

As shown in Figure 10-6, the initial bank must be steep; otherwise, the wind would push the plane too far from the road before the turn is completed (1).

Assuming that you have the correct steepness of bank set in, when point (2) is reached the bank must be shallowed or the plane would be turning at the same rate of turn in degrees per minute but, as it began to head into the wind, the ground speed would drop. It would appear to "pivot" and would not follow the smooth curve of the semicircle but would end up at (3).

The shallowing of the turn should be such that the wings are level as the plane crosses the road, still at 600 feet (4).

After crossing the road the bank should be a shallow one in the opposite direction. If a steep bank is used, a path such as at (5) would result.

When point (6) is reached the bank must be steepened in order to have the turn completed as the plane crosses the road again. If the bank were not steepened at point (6) a path like that of (7) would occur, and the plane would not cross the road at the correct place — nor would the wings be level or parallel to the road.

Continue the series until you get tired or run

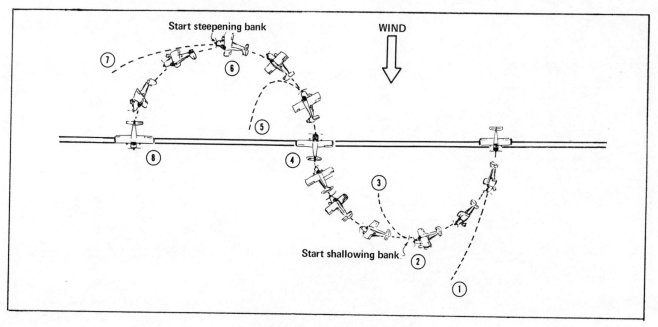

Fig. 10-6. S-turns across the road.

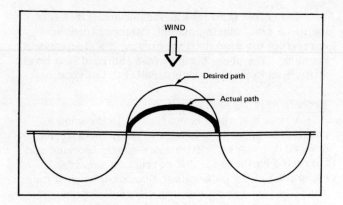

WIND

Desired path

Actual path

Fig. 10-7.

out of road. Remember: *The angle of bank is directly proportional to the ground speed.* (The greater the ground speed, the greater the angle of bank.

The angle of bank in S-turns must be constantly changing. The hardest part of trying to keep the maneuver smooth is at point (8), where you have to roll from a steep bank one way to a steep bank in the opposite direction.

If the wind is strong many students do not have a shallow enough bank on the upwind side of the road. Strangely enough they are able to correct on the downwind side without much trouble. Many times in this situation the plane's path over the ground looks like Figure 10-7.

Probable Errors
1. Failure to properly correct for drift.
2. Rolling out of the turn too soon or too late, resulting in crossing the road with wings not parallel to it.
3. Gaining or losing altitude.
4. Coordination problems in the turns (jerky or slipping and skidding).

In the S-turn you are interested in a definite path over the ground and therefore must correct for the movement of the air mass of which you are a part.

11. Elementary Forced Landings

At some time during the period of rectangular courses or S-turns, your instructor will demonstrate an elementary forced landing or "simulated emergency," as you may hear it called.

Engines nowadays are very reliable. Cases of engine failure are rare, but you will still be given forced-landing practice because pilots still run out of gas and leave oil caps off. It is still possible, too, that the engine could fail structurally, so it's better to be prepared.

The elementary emergency is given below 1000 feet and requires a 90° gliding turn at most. The instructor will pull the carburetor heat and close the throttle at some point during the maneuvers and demonstrate the procedure.

If it is at all possible, you want to land into the wind. If the plane stalls at 50 K and you have a 15 K head wind, your ground speed, or relative velocity to the ground, at touchdown will be 35 K. The advantages of this are obvious. However, sometimes a field may not be available for an upwind landing. Or if the field is steeply sloped, it's better to land uphill even if it's downwind. Obstacles may require that you land downwind.

Sometimes students who've been doing the rectangular course or S-turns for several minutes and have been correcting for a stiff wind forget the wind direction as soon as the throttle is closed for the simulated emergency.

Picking the right kind of field (at low altitude you don't have much time to shop around) comes with experience. If you've lived on a farm you can spot a good field without much trouble.

Here is a list and description of various types of fields with comments about each type:

Obviously there will be times when some of the landing spots labeled "poor" and "very poor" will be the only ones available. It then becomes the case of making the best of a bad situation. As one instructor put it, "Hit the softest, cheapest thing in the area as slowly as possible" — which pretty well covers it.

In the case of an actual forced landing below 1000 feet:

1. Establish a normal glide.
2. Pull on the carburetor heat. The carburetor may have iced up and will clear out when heat is applied. Normally you will have some warning beforehand, such as rpm dropping, but you may not have noticed.
3. Pick your field and start the approach.
4. Switch to another fuel tank (if your airplane has more than one).
5. Electric boost pump "ON" (low-wing trainer).
6. Mixture "RICH."

Do not waste time trying other methods of starting. Do 4-6 after you have the field selected and the approach set up. Then get back to your approach. Don't try to use the starter.

The propeller usually windmills after an engine failure and, if the fault is remedied, will start again. If it does, climb to an altitude of 2000 or 3000 feet while circling the field. If you are *sure* of the reason for the failure (tank run dry, carburetor icing, etc.) and have remedied it, continue your flight. Otherwise keep your high altitude and pick a route of good terrain back to the airport.

Once you have selected a field you don't have time to change your mind. Pilots have been killed trying to change fields in an emergency because they made turns too steep and stalled at low altitudes.

Type of Field	Description	Comments
Good -- Pasture.	Brown-green. May have livestock or cow paths across it.	You can land in a pasture, but land in the part well away from the stock. Cows like to eat airplane fabric so don't be gone too long to telephone (unless you have a metal plane).
Good — Freshly cut wheat, barley, oat fields, etc.	Brown grass but mower marks can usually be seen.	Very good for forced landing, if any place could be considered good for a forced landing.
Fair — Field of high grass, wheat, etc.	Rich green or golden.	Not much landing roll, but field may be soft under camouflage of grass. Possible nose over.
Poor — High corn.	Green, or later brown.	Field itself usually rough. Plane will probably be damaged.

Type of Field	Description	Comments
<u>Poor</u> — Freshly plowed field	Dark brown.	If the field is soft the plane will nose over. If you must land in a plowed field, land parallel to the rows.
<u>Poor</u> — Terraced field.	Contour lines.	Contour lines show that it is sloping. Never land across the contours.
<u>Very Poor</u> — swamps, woods, etc.		Land as slowly as possible but don't stall it in.

A normal glide is a must for an emergency landing. If you are high and dive at the field the airspeed goes to high that the plane "floats" and you still overshoot, or go past the field.

If you try to "stretch a glide," the rate of descent actually increases as the angle of attack gets in the critical range. It's better to hit something when you have control than to stall and drop in (Fig. 11-1).

If you are going to land in trees, don't stall the plane above and drop in. Get it as slow as possible, still having control, and fly it into the trees.

It's impossible to list exact procedures for every situation, but you'll try to keep the airplane under control without stalling and will try to pick a landing point that will allow the lowest deceleration (something soft like shrubs or weeds, rather than a stone wall or solid tree trunk). As for when to turn off all switches before impact, your *Pilot's Operating Handbook* will have such information. Keep the cockpit intact.

Sometime after you have had the simulated emergency demonstrated, the instructor will close the throttle and say "Forced Landing." You will then go through the procedure. The instructor will let you glide to a reasonably low altitude or an altitude where you could see whether the field could be made. He will say, "I got it," open the throttle, take the plane up, and point out any mistakes you may have made.

PROBABLE ERRORS

1. Failure to establish a normal glide promptly.
2. Indecisiveness in selecting a field.
3. Trying to stretch the glide if low and diving if high.
4. Making steep turns close to the ground.

THIS   NOT THIS

Fig. 11-1.

12. Stalls and Slow Flight

A stall is a condition in which the angle of attack becomes so great that the flow over the airfoil breaks down so that the wings can no longer support the airplane. An airplane can be stalled at any speed, attitude, or power setting — as many a dive bomber pilot found out when he tried to pull out of a dive too quickly. He may have been doing 400 K but the plane was stalled as completely as if he had climbed too steeply. What happens is shown in Figure 12-1.

With the knowledge that a stall is caused by too great an angle of attack, the proper recovery is always to decrease that angle of attack and get the air flowing smoothly again whether you are doing 40, 400, or 4000 K.

You won't be doing accelerated stalls until later, but if you know what a stall is, the accelerated stall will be no different from the first elementary ones. The stalls in this phase will be done by gradually pulling the nose up and slowing the plane to the stalled condition.

In the earlier days of aviation, keeping the wings level during stalls was a problem. In the older planes, control effectiveness in the stall was lost in alphabetical order — AER. The ailerons were the first to go, followed by rapidly decreasing elevator effectiveness, and last of all by the rudder. Generally, if power was used during the stall the rudder was effective throughout.

In many cases, use of ailerons alone to raise a wing during a stall resulted in an opposite effect to that which was desired. When the aileron was applied, the down aileron on the low wing caused adverse yaw effects, resulting in a further slowing of that wing and causing it to stall first. This was disconcerting, to say the least, and led to some interesting wing-leveling techniques. Pilots found that it was possible, for instance, to raise the low wing during the stall by applying opposite rudder — which yawed the plane in that direction, speeded up the low wing, gave it added lift, and caused it to rise. Sometimes this opposite rudder was applied so enthusiastically that the high wing was slowed to the point that it abruptly exceeded the critical angle of attack and stalled first, thereby causing a great deal of adrenalin to flow in occupants of the plane.

Planes type-certificated under the Federal Aviation Regulations (as all general aviation planes are now) must maintain aileron control throughout the stall. The Federal Aviation Administration, therefore, now encourages the use of coordinated controls to keep the wings level during the stall. While keeping the wings level is not critical at the altitudes where stalls will be practiced, it will be very important when you start landings, as will be shown later.

Several methods of design are used to aid lateral control throughout the stall. The idea in each case is to have the wing tips stall last. If a wing tip stalled first (and it is extremely unlikely that both will stall at the same time) a dangerous rolling tendency may occur as the stall breaks.

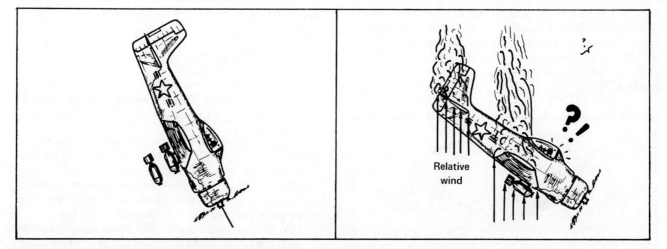

Fig. 12-1. Pilot releases bomb, discovers that he is very low. He pulls back stick abruptly. Plane changes attitude but momentum carries it down. Result—a high-speed stall. Lacking altitude for a smooth pullout, plane strikes the ground.

The tips may be made to stall last by "wash out." The manufacturer builds a twist into the wing so that the tips always have a lower angle of incidence (and a resulting lower angle of attack) and will still be flying when the root area has stalled (Fig. 12-2).

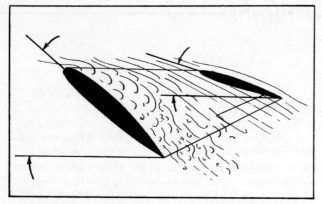

Fig. 12-2. Exaggerated view of wing tip washout. Ailerons still effective even though wing root is in the stalled condition.

Another method of having the root stall first is the use of slots near the tip. The opening (Fig. 12-3) near the leading edge allows the air to maintain a smooth flow at angles of attack that would result in a stall for the unslotted portion of the wing.

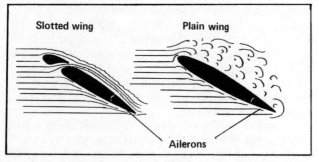

Fig. 12-3. Plain and slotted wings at equal angles of attack.

Still another method is that of stall strips (Fig. 12-4) or spoiler strips being placed on the leading edge of the root area of the wing, breaking the air-flow and resulting in an earlier stall for this portion. Some airplane wings have higher lift-type airfoils at the tip, causing the wing tip to stall last. In some cases several of these design techniques may be combined.

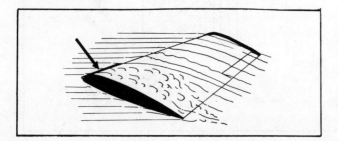

Fig. 12-4. The stall strip as a means of insuring that the root section stalls first.

STALLS AS AN AID TO LANDINGS

As you'll see, a normal landing is nothing more than a stall. The landing is begun at an altitude of about 15 or 20 feet from a normal glide. At this point you begin the landing transition, or start "breaking the glide." From this point, it becomes a matter of your judgment in trying to have the airplane completely stalled just as it touches. This means that you have the wheel full back and the plane stops flying at the instant it contacts the ground.

The instructor will show you a series of straight-ahead stalls that will be good preparation for landing practice later.

In practicing stalls, it's important not to stare blindly over the nose. Get an idea of what the plane is doing by looking out of the corners of your eyes. The instructor will probably have you practice landings from a normal glide at 2000 or 3000 feet above the ground. It's impossible to see the ground by looking over the nose of the average trainer when it's in the landing attitude, so as soon as you start the transition, switch your scan to the left side of the nose, noting the plane's attitude out of the corner of your eye and keeping the wings level through co-ordinated use of the controls.

Once the nose is at the landing attitude (the instructor will show you the proper nose position), it becomes a matter of pinning it at that position by continued back pressure.

IMMINENT STALLS—POWER ON OR POWER OFF

You'll practice these stalls in take-off or climb configuration (power on) or approach configuration (power off), straight ahead or in 20° banked turns. For the straight ahead stalls be sure to "clear the area" by making two 90° turns in opposite direction because the nose will be in one place and form a blind area. Recover at least 1500 feet above the ground.

The imminent stalls are so named because the airplane is not allowed to stall but recovery is effected as soon as indications of a stall occur (buffeting or decay of control effectiveness).

PARTIAL OR IMMINENT STALL—POWER OFF

Procedure (straight ahead)
1. Clear the area.
2. Carburetor heat "ON" — throttle back to idle.
3. Apply gentle back pressure to raise the nose to about the landing touchdown attitude — don't let the nose wander.
4. Hold the nose at this point by continued back pressure — keep the nose directionally straight. The use of the elevators in approaching the stall can be likened to a vicious cycle. As the plane is slowed up by the elevators, the nose tends to drop — requiring more up-elevator, which slows the plane further, requiring more elevator, etc. The point where the wheel is all the way back and the nose drops is the stall "break." In the imminent stall the process does not go as far as the break (Fig. 12-5).

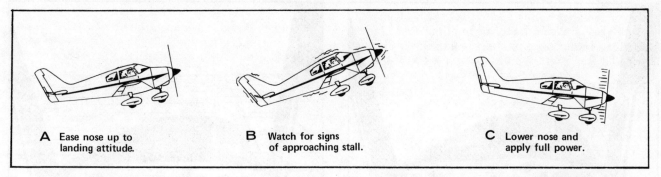

A Ease nose up to
   landing attitude.

B Watch for signs
   of approaching stall.

C Lower nose and
   apply full power.

Fig. 12-5.

5. When indications of the approaching stall are sensed by:
   a. Sight — the attitude and airspeed indicator.
   b. Feel — the controls are ineffective and mushy. The airplane may shudder or vibrate as the stall approaches.
   c. Sound — the wind and engine noise level drops as the plane slows.
lower the nose to level flight and apply full power simultaneously. (Easy with that throttle — don't ram it open.)
   6. Carburetor heat "OFF."

The idea of this maneuver is for you to learn to recognize the approaching stall. You could recover easily leaving the throttle back at idle — it just takes a little longer, that's all. Don't start thinking that power is the big thing in the recovery. The change in the plane's attitude is the most important part. Your instructor will also have you practice these stalls in 20° banked turns in each direction.

PARTIAL OR IMMINENT STALL—POWER ON

Use cruising power on this one (Fig. 12-6). The technique is fundamentally the same except you'll have to raise the nose higher in order to speed up the approach to the stall. The plane wants to "hang on" longer when power is used. A thing to remember — at higher rpm you have torque effects as the plane slows and also the plane is less laterally stable because of gyroscopic effects. That is, you may have more trouble keeping the wings level.

Procedure
   1. Clear the area.
   2. Slow the airplane to approximately the climb speed or slightly below by throttling back and maintaining a constant altitude, then set the rpm to cruise.
   3. Ease the nose slightly higher than for the power-off version, maybe 5° higher. (Your instructor will demonstrate the nose position.) Keep the wings level.
   4. Keep the nose in line with a point on the horizon. Remember that torque will be acting on the plane.
   5. As the approaching stall is noted (sight, sound, feel), lower the nose and open the throttle fully (Fig. 12-7).

Granted, you'll be practicing imminent stalls at an altitude where the recovery will be no problem. Still you might as well get in the habit of using full power and recovering as soon as possible, because someday you may be low and won't have time to reason, "Well, I'm pretty low so maybe I'd better use full power; on the other hand, possibly I should . . ." (CRUNCH).

You'll also get practice in power-on imminent stalls in banks of about 20°.

Open that throttle each time unless you are called upon by your instructor or the FAA check pilot to demonstrate a power-off recovery.

SOME STRAIGHT-AHEAD STALLS

NORMAL STALL—POWER OFF

Another step in the stall sequence is the wings level normal stall. This is the one you'll use for landing practice at altitude. The first part of the stall is quite similar to the imminent stall. In this case, however, you continue increasing back pressure until the stall breaks and the nose starts to drop. Recovery is effected by releasing back pressure and applying full power (easy with that throttle). Try to recover with a minimum altitude loss. Many students get eager to recover from the stall, release the back pressure, and immediately come back again with the wheel to minimize the altitude loss (they think). The plane stalls again (called a secondary or progressive stall) and the process of recovery must be redone. It is possible to do a series of secondary stalls (even the fifth stall is called a secondary stall) and, if the ground is close, you'll feel as uncomfortable as a dockworker in a lingerie shop until the plane is flying normally again.

Recover firmly but don't get rough with the airplane. Minimize your altitude loss but don't get a secondary stall.

During your first series of stalls, the plane seems to have a mind of its own. The wings don't want to stay level and maybe you push forward on the wheel a little harder than you mean to and your stomach comes up in your throat. Don't worry about it; there were several hundred thousand other people who felt the same way before you came along.

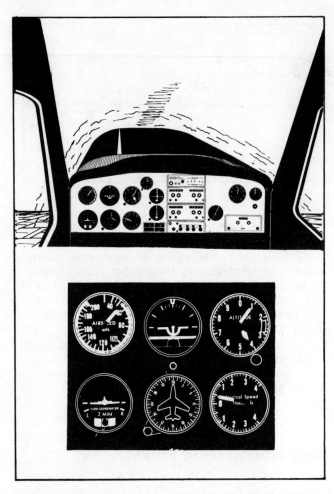

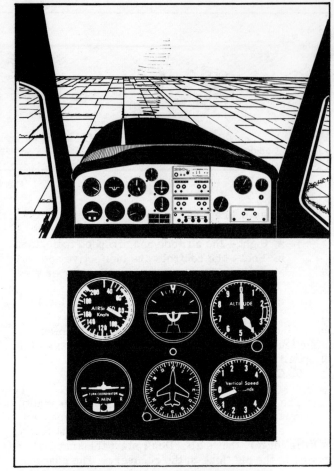

Fig. 12-6. Power-on partial (imminent) stall. Airspeed near stall. H/I, no turn. A/I, nose high, wings level. Turn coordinator, straight balanced flight. Altitude, steady or increasing slightly.

Fig. 12-7. Lower nose to level flight and open throttle at the same time. Airspeed increasing. H/I, no turn. A/I, level flight. Turn coordinator, straight balanced flight. Altitude, constant or slightly decreasing.

After several stalls you'll get the idea and they'll begin to make sense.

Procedure
    1. Clear the area.
    2. Carburetor heat "ON" — close the throttle to idle.
    3. Bring the nose up to the three-point position.
    4. Pin it at that position with continued application of back pressure. If you are preparing for landings, practice looking out the left side, keeping the wings level and the plane at the correct nose-up attitude by checking it from the corners of your eyes.
    5. When the stall breaks, recover by lowering the nose, applying full power as you do so, minimizing altitude loss.
    6. Carburetor heat "OFF."

More about this idea of keeping the wings level: If a wing drops, the plane is banked and will turn. This doesn't matter at high altitudes, but runways are only a couple of hundred feet wide at best (some of them will be 50 feet) and the plane will be off into the boondocks before you know it. Here's a good place to get the wings-level idea down pat. Then

you won't have any trouble when landing practice starts.

If the wing drops slightly, use coordinated controls. Exact stall recovery techniques will vary from airplane to airplane, but the general principle is the same for all airplanes and airspeeds. *Get the air flowing smoothly over the wings with the minimum loss in altitude.*

If you are flying an older airplane the ailerons may not be effective throughout the stall and use of rudder may be needed to stop rolling tendencies. Your instructor will demonstrate the best technique for maintaining lateral control during the stall for your particular airplane. However, the chances are that coordinated aileron and rudder usage will be the most effective means.

NORMAL STALL—POWER ON

Fundamentally, this is the same as the stall just discussed. The nose position will be higher because of the power. As seen in Figure 12-8, when the plane uses power, its path is changed and the attitude will be more nose high, but the angle of attack at the stall will be roughly the same.

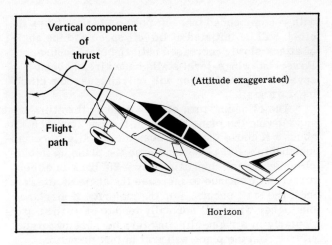

Fig. 12-8. Attitude more nose high than for power-off version.

A plane will stall at a slightly slower airspeed with power on than it does with power off. The effect of the slipstream over the center section of the wing makes a slight difference. The more nose-high attitude also gives a vertical component to the thrust, which in effect lowers the wing loading.

Procedure

1. Clear the area. (You're probably getting tired of hearing this by now, but do it anyway.)
2. Ease the nose up to a slightly higher position than was used for the power-off normal stall — your instructor will demonstrate.
3. Keep the wings level.
4. When the stall break occurs, lower the nose and open the throttle the rest of the way. Level the wings with coordinated aileron and rudder if you fell asleep in 3 above (Fig. 12-9).

COMPLETE OR FULL STALL—POWER ON AND POWER OFF

The stall has little application other than as an exercise in keeping the wings level during the stall, but if you're having that problem, a few of these will help you see the light.

Procedure—Power Off

1. Clear the area.
2. Carburetor heat "ON" — throttle at idle.
3. Ease the nose up to an attitude of 30° above the horizon. Keep the wheel back until the nose falls

to the horizon. Keep the wings level during the recovery.

4. As the nose crosses the horizon, effect a normal recovery. Release the back pressure and apply power. You will notice that the nose will be somewhat lower during the recovery from the complete stall as compared to the normal stalls.
5. Carburetor heat "OFF."

The power-on complete stall is fundamentally the same except for higher nose attitude and the increased difficulty in keeping the nose straight and the wings level because of torque and gyroscopic effects.

CHARACTERISTIC STALL

This stall is a good demonstration of the built-in stability of the airplane. It disproves the non-flyer's idea that the airplane is just waiting for a chance to "fall."

This stall can be done either power on or off, as your instructor may want to demonstrate for you. For discussion purposes assume that you are going to make it power off. The idea is to start a normal power-off stall (trimmed for cruising flight), getting the break, but, instead of recovering as usual, take your hands and feet off the controls. The nose will drop and the plane will make its own recovery. In most lightplanes you will have to ease the plane out of the dive in the power-off characteristic stall. It would come out of the dive by itself but the airspeed might be in the region of the red line, or "never exceed" speed, at the bottom of the first oscillation.

If the plane had cruising power throughout the maneuver the initial dive would not be nearly as steep as the power-off one and the recovery would be back to level cruising flight. Generally, it is not necessary to pull it out of the dive when you are using cruising power. These oscillations that result are called phugoid oscillations, which sounds very technical. Sometime during the course of an ordinary conversation, work the talk around so you can mention "phugoid oscillations" — it's quite impressive.

Put bluntly, the idea of this maneuver is to show that most of the trouble that happens during stalls is caused by some heavy-footed, ham-handed pilot groping around in the cockpit. The characteristic

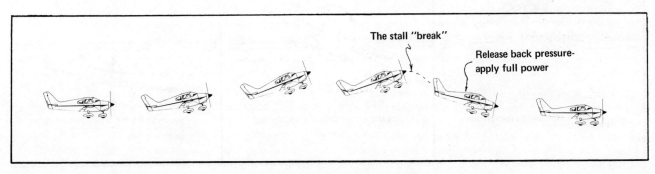

Fig. 12-9. Power-on normal stall.

stall is not required on the private flight test but is a good maneuver for building up your confidence in the airplane.

Procedure
1. Clear the area.
2. Start a normal power-on or power-off stall.
3. When the stall breaks, take your hands and feet off the controls.
4. Ease the plane out of the dive and return to level flight.

Common Errors
1. Not getting the break before releasing the controls.
2. Letting the plane pick up excessive speed in the dive.

ELEMENTARY TURNING STALLS

TAKE-OFF AND DEPARTURE STALLS—CLIMBING TURNS

Many a pilot has taken off in front of his friends on a bright Sunday afternoon and decided to give them a little extra show — a take-off, followed by a steep climbing turn. The result — a little more show than he bargained for when he stalls at the top of one of these colorful maneuvers.

Or, suppose you are landing at a very short airport with trees at the far end. You are just about to touch down when you realize that you're almost out of runway. The trees are close. You open the throttle and try to climb and turn out of the way. What happens then? If you've practiced a few departure stalls it will be evident just what can happen, and you will have learned a method of recovery. Better to have used headwork in the first place and not gotten into such a predicament.

The take-off and departure stall is designed to give you practice in recognizing and coping with such a situation. You will do these stalls both from straight flight and moderately banked (20°) turns

with recommended take-off power. In both types the climb will be initiated at lift-off speed and the angle of attack slowly increased until the stall occurs. Power-on, wings-level stalls have already been covered, so this section will only discuss the climbing-turn stall.

The climbing-turn stall is done by throttling back and slowing the plane as if on a landing approach. At about 5 K above the stall, open the throttle to recommended take-off power and ease the plane up into a climbing turn of approximately a 20° bank in either direction. Continue to increase the angle of attack until the stall occurs. For the majority of airplanes the higher wing will normally tend to stall first, particularly in a right-climbing turn because of torque effects, and the plane will roll in that direction. Here's why the top wing tends to stall first: As you pull up into the stalled condition, the wings start losing lift and the plane mushes and starts to slip. In the right-climbing turn, torque is working to yaw the nose against the turn and aggravates the slipping condition.

As shown by Figure 12-10, the higher wing receives turbulence when a slip occurs, while the lower wing is comparatively free; consequently the high wing will stall first. When the break occurs the plane rolls in the direction of the high wing. In such a case the ball of the turn and slip (needle and ball) will indicate a slip just as the break occurs. The rigging of the wings of your particular airplane can affect its reaction; also, if the plane is skidding at the stall break, the low or inside wing will be the first to go. If your plane has a needle and ball you can note that the roll at the stall break is "away from the ball." (If the ball is to the right, the roll will be to the left — if the ball can be kept centered, any tendency to roll is minimized, but it still might roll in either direction, so be ready for it. The only problem is that with most airplanes the rapid decay of rudder effectiveness as the stall is approached may not allow the pilot to keep the ball centered.)

When you are practicing these turning stalls, dual or solo, you might notice that the nose will

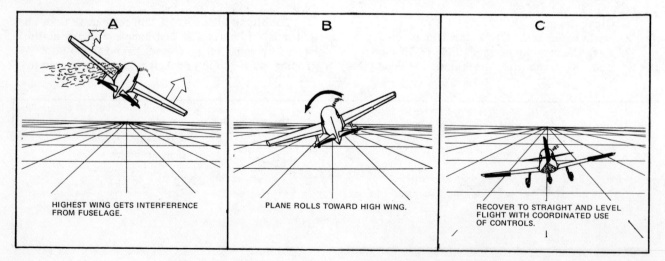

HIGHEST WING GETS INTERFERENCE FROM FUSELAGE.

PLANE ROLLS TOWARD HIGH WING.

RECOVER TO STRAIGHT AND LEVEL FLIGHT WITH COORDINATED USE OF CONTROLS.

Fig. 12-10. A rolling moment may be set up as the plane stalls.

usually drop at the stall break, an instant before the roll occurs. This follows the analysis as shown by Figure 12-10.

Relax back pressure to recover. You already have a fair amount of power on throughout the maneuver, but you should increase it to maximum. But relaxing the back pressure is the main stall-recovery aid here, as always. In a few airplanes with good rudder effectiveness, in keeping the ball centered, the *right*-climbing turn can result in the low wing dropping! This is, of course, the reason you practice these stalls — to see what *your* airplane will do.

With more practice you'll be able to recognize the start of the roll and the break and recover in level flight by catching the stall at the right point.

The angle of bank must be moderate in order to get a good break. If you bank the plane too steeply the nose may drop, tending to make the stall harder to attain because of the increase in airspeed. In many cases the nose will be low enough that the plane will merely mush and you'll be turning in a tight circle, losing altitude with the plane shuddering but not getting a definite stall break. This too-steep bank will give you more trouble during solo practice of these stalls. It's a matter of stall speed being a function of wing loading. Without the instructor's weight, the wing loading is lower and the plane is harder to stall.

In doing these stalls note the altitude at the point of assumed take-off and compare it with the altitude on recovery.

Procedure
1. Since you will be turning, it is not necessary to make special clearing turns. Keep looking around during the approach to the stall.
2. Pull the carburetor heat (if required for your airplane) and slow down to lift-off speed.
3. When the airspeed drops to 5-10 K above the stall, apply recommended climb power and attempt a comparatively steep climbing turn (the climb is comparatively steep, the bank is shallow) in either direction.
4. When the top wing starts to drop and the break is definite, relax back pressure and apply *full* power.
5. Level the wings with coordinated controls after the recovery is started. (Don't just go by the airspeed; you should feel and hear this pickup in speed as well.)

Common Errors
1. Too steep a bank — the plane doesn't stall but mushes instead.
2. Too early a recovery — the plane does not get a chance to break before the recovery is started.
3. Too late a recovery — the plane may rotate too far before you get a recovery started.
4. Nose too low — climb not steep enough, plane mushes.

APPROACH TO LANDING STALLS—GLIDING TURN

This is the power-off version of the take-off and departure stalls, and like them will be done from both straight glides and moderately banked (approximately 30°) gliding turns in landing configuration (full flaps and trim set). Power-off, wings-level stalls were covered earlier, so only the gliding-turn stall will be covered here (Fig. 12-11).

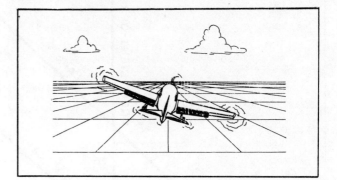

Fig. 12-11. The approach-to-landing stall (gliding turn).

You will notice that the rolling tendency is not nearly so great with the power off. The plane tends to mush and shudder and it is harder to get a sharp stall break, particularly if you are solo. It may require a faster rate of applying back pressure to get the break as compared with the departure stall. When you fly heavier planes you will find that in most cases you don't have to work to make them stall. The faster planes will stall and generally give comparatively little warning. You are more interested in the technique of recovery than in the effort required to get into the stall. So don't get complacent about stalls.

Procedure
1. Carburetor heat "ON." Set the plane up in the landing configuration. Establish a normal gliding turn in either direction.
2. Continuously add back pressure, raise the nose to about the climb position.
3. When the break occurs (or you have full up-elevator), stop any rotation and recover by releasing back pressure and applying full power.
4. Carburetor heat "OFF."
5. Clean up the airplane (gear and flaps, as applicable) and climb to an altitude at least 300 feet above the altitude at which full control effectiveness was regained.

Probable Errors
1. Too steeply banked — plane mushes in a turn rather than stalling.
2. Nose not high enough — again the plane mushes with no definite stall break.
3. Improper throttle handling — too fast or too timid application of power.

FLAPS AND STALLS

Figure 12-12 shows the coefficient of lift versus angle of attack (also see Fig. 2-8) for a wing — clean

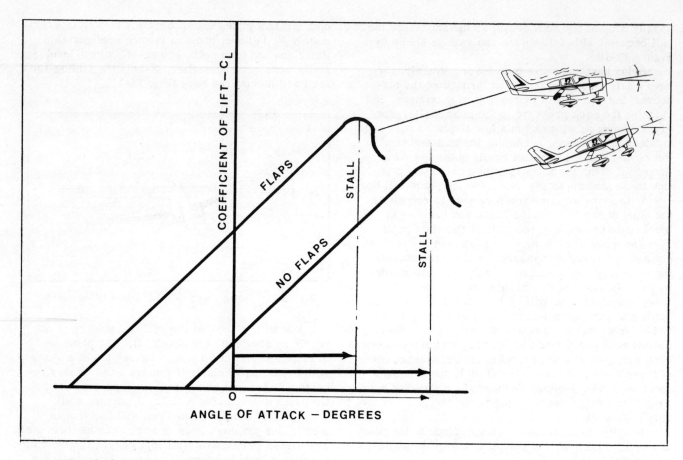

Fig. 12-12. Coefficient of lift and stall break attitudes for a fictitious airplane — clean and with landing flaps down.

and with landing flaps extended (20° in this case). Note that the maximum coefficient of lift is noticeably higher with flaps extended. Using, for example, the 0° angle of attack as a common starting point, you'd see that by slowly increasing the angle of attack, the flapped condition would reach its critical angle of attack (stall) well before the clean wing would have problems.

The point is this: Pilots tend to think that stalls can only occur with the nose well above the horizon. You can see that some airplanes with full flaps, approaching landing in a turn, might stall with the nose well below the horizon. This is because the airplane's "normal" approach attitude is much lower and the stall attitude will also be equivalently lower as compared to the nonflapped condition (same power setting).

The principle just covered stands whether your airspeed indicator is in miles per hour or knots. Your instructor may cover the airspeed indicator during the slow-flight practice so that you can fly the airplane by pitch attitude and power.

FLIGHT AT MINIMUM CONTROLLABLE AIRSPEED (SLOW FLIGHT)

This is designed to show you how to recognize the stall and to help you get to know your airplane. Someday you may have to fly the plane close to the stall, and knowing how the plane flies in that region may save your neck.

Such flight (sometimes called "slow flight") is usually considered to be level, sustained flight at a speed close enough to the stall (about 5 K above) so that if power were chopped, you would get immediate indications of a stall. You will be expected to demonstrate minimum-speed flying to the FAA inspector during the private flight test. He will ask you to make minimum-speed climbing, gliding, and level turns with banks from 20° to 30°. The flight test tolerances in straight and level slow flight will be to maintain within 10° of heading and 100 feet of altitude. Unless a stall warning indicator is required equipment on your airplane, you won't be allowed to use it on the flight test.

Don't get the idea that the speed for slow flight (or minimum maneuvering speed) is always the same for your airplane. The *angle of attack* at the stall *is* always the same (for a given flap setting), but the airspeed at the stall varies with the *weight* of the airplane. The less a particular airplane weighs, the less its airspeed when that fixed maximum angle of attack is reached. The stall airspeed is also lowered by the lowering of *flaps*. Take a look back at Figure 9.5. The stall speeds given there are at the maximum certificated weight of 1600 pounds and are power-off. Note that the stall speeds decrease with an increase in flaps for any condition of bank. For instance, looking at the effects of flaps at 0° bank (wings level), the stall speed decreases from 55 mph to 49 mph at 20° of flaps, and then down to 48 mph at the 40° flap setting. Note that the second 20° only lowered the speed by another 1 mph. Added drag is a greater factor than added coefficient of lift in this area (20°-40°) of flap setting.

Okay, take an airplane that stalls at 55 mph (no-flaps) at 1600 pounds with the *power at idle*. If you wanted to fly slow flight in this condition (idle) you would probably set up a speed about 5 mph faster, *or 60 mph calibrated* airspeed.

Now use 20° of flaps. At this same airplane weight you would add 5 mph to the stall speed (49 mph) and set up a descent at about 54 mph. For 40°, 53 mph (C.A.S.) would be a good number.

At a *lighter weight* of 1300 pounds you might use *55, 49,* or *48* mph respectively in slow flight, to have a 5 mph margin.

A little earlier in the chapter, it was noted that the use of power decreased the stall speed (Fig. 12-8), so that the airspeed, as an example, could be lowered another 3 mph for each condition. Now the new speeds would be *52, 46,* and *45* mph C.A.S. respectively for slow flight in the three flap settings, at a lighter weight, *and using power*.

While numbers have been cited here to make the point that *flaps, lower airplane weights,* and *more power* all will *lower* the airspeed given for stall (and hence the required slow-flight speed if the same margin is kept), the idea is to *fly* the airplane here by your feel and senses. Figure 9-5 and the discussion about it in this chapter use miles per hour as examples. The principle remains the same whether expressed in mph or knots.

PROCEDURE

1. Throttle back to a power setting much less than is required to maintain level slow flight. After the first time you'll have an approximate idea of what's needed. Maintain altitude as the plane slows. This means that the nose must be slowly raised. As the required speed is approached, start adding power as necessary to keep the altitude constant. You can see in Figure 12-12 that the power required to fly the airplane *increases* again after the airspeed is decreased from cruise down past a certain point.

2. Maintain your heading. You have power on and a low airspeed, and torque must be taken care of.

3. Notice that elevators and throttle are coordinated in maintaining airspeed and altitude. If you are losing altitude, add power and adjust the nose position to maintain the proper airspeed. If you are too slow but are maintaining altitude, ease the nose slightly lower and adjust your power to assure staying on that altitude. Keep checking the altimeter and airspeed. *You'll also be watching for other planes.*

4. Make a shallow turn in each direction. Maintain altitude in the turn. This will mean increased power and a slight raising of the nose.

5. Level the wings and gradually throttle back to idle as you lower the nose to maintain a glide at the minimum control speed of 5 K above the stall. Make 20°-30° banked turns in each direction.

6. Return to level, slow flight by applying power and easing the nose up. Try to keep the airspeed from varying during this transition. You'll note in slow flight, as in other phases of your flying, that an increase in power tends to make the nose rise, which will make it seem as if all you have to do as power is applied is to *think* about the nose easing up.

7. Increase the power and ease the nose up to a climb at minimum speed. Make shallow turns in each direction. (Don't climb too long, as the engine will overheat at the low airspeed.)

Making the transition from level flight to glide to climb, etc., without varying the airspeed more than 5 knots, takes some heavy concentration, but when you can do it you'll have an excellent feel of the aircraft.

The instructor will probably not do any more before solo than have you fly the plane at the minimum speed to get the feel of slow flight. He will not require as close tolerances of altitude as he will later in your training. However, if you seem to get the hang of slow flight you may go on with the transition to climbs and glides. You will probably review slow flight before going on the cross-country solo.

Remember that you should also be able to do slow flight by reference to the instruments. In this condition, you don't rely on your senses, but on the instruments. The instructor will give you a chance to practice this both hooded and with visual references during periods of dual.

You should get slow-flight practice in as many combinations of flaps and power as possible. If your trainer has retractable gear (it's doubtful), you should fly at minimum controllable speeds in cruise and landing configurations. You might repeat steps 1 through 7 in various flap configurations. (Don't try to climb very long at the low speed with the flaps extended.)

COMMON ERRORS

1. Losing or gaining altitude in the transition from cruise to slow flight.
2. Poor speed control in the transitions.
3. Stalling the airplane.
4. Poor altitude control during the level portions of slow flight.

POWER VERSUS AIRSPEED

You might be interested to know that in slow flight you will be operating in a condition that pilots call the "back side of the power curve." Figure 12-13 shows the attitudes and power required to maintain a *constant altitude* at various airspeeds for a typical light trainer at one particular weight at sea level. Other weights and/or altitudes would have separate curves. To simplify matters, Figure 12-13 is set for brake horsepower and indicated airspeed, because these will be the two factors you'll be working with as a pilot. The engine of this plane is able to develop 100 brake horsepower at the altitude used here (sea level).

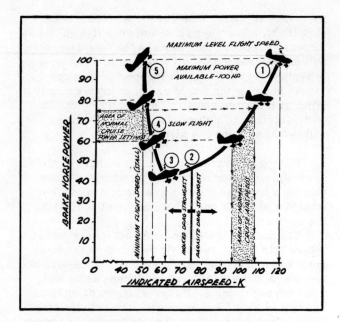

Fig. 12-13. The power required to maintain a constant altitude (sea level) for a fictitious light trainer at a particular weight.

All the vehicles you've been operating before (bicycles, motorcycles, automobiles) always require *more power to go faster* at any particular road condition or grade; in your flying of the airplane in straight and level cruising flight this has seemed also to be the case. The kicker is that the added power in the normal cruise area doesn't directly make the airplane go faster, but *allows it to go faster without losing altitude*. This is important to remember. The airplane in the example *can* go faster than the maximum speed shown, but only at a cost of altitude. Road vehicles are supported by the ground and don't have to rely on producing lift; hence their horsepower is used basically only to overcome parasite drag.

The power curve gets its characteristic "U" shape because the airplane is subjected to *two* types of drag. Looking back to Chapter 2 you remember that *total drag* is composed of *parasite drag,* which increases with airspeed, and *induced drag,* which becomes much stronger as the airplane slows up. You've been doing all of your straight and level flying in that area of the power curve (normal cruise) where parasite drag is the big factor. Because you're more used to talking in terms of horsepower, Figure 12-13 shows the horsepower required to overcome a combination of the two types of drag throughout the speed range of the airplane.

Note in Figure 12-13 that the area of normal cruise power settings for the airplane in the example runs from 60 horsepower (60 percent power) to 75 horsepower (75 percent power). This is the normal range of cruise power settings for most airplanes, from *60 to 75 percent* of the normal rated power, the power the engine can use continuously at sea level. To make things easier, assume that the airplane in the example can use full power (100 hp) continuously (this is not the case for all airplanes).

Point (1) shows the maximum level-flight speed of the airplane. It requires 100 horsepower to fly this airplane at a constant altitude (sea level) at this speed, and that's all that this particular engine has available. From that point, as the airplane flies at slower airspeeds, less horsepower is required; and moving down the curve, Point (2) is reached. This is the point where parasite drag and induced drag are equal. Incidentally, this is the point of maximum cruise efficiency, or maximum range, of the airplane. You'll get more miles to the gallon while maintaining altitude at that speed, which is about 150 percent of, or 1.5 times, the stall speed (for trainers). This would be the airspeed at which to fly if you got in a bind for fuel and had to stretch it to make an airport some distance away.

As you move back down the curve, Point (3) is the airspeed at which the minimum power is required to maintain altitude. This would be the airspeed you'd use if you were looking for maximum endurance, or longest time airborne, and is roughly about 120 percent of the stall speed (or 1.2 times the stall speed, however you like to think of it).

Decreasing the airspeed below Point (3) results in the power required to fly the airplane (at a constant altitude) starting to increase sharply; induced drag is beginning to make itself known. The part of the curve from Point (3) back to the stall is called the "backside of the power curve," which implies that something unnatural is occurring. It's only unnatural if you don't have the full picture of what happens to drag at various airspeeds, and the term is a rather poor one (like "elevators"). Note that for this airplane it requires as much power (60 horsepower) for slow flight, 5 K above the stall, Point (4), as it does to cruise at an I.A.S. of 96.

Finally, as the stall is approached at Point (5), all of the power is needed to maintain altitude; if the angle of attack is increased further the stall occurs, even though full power is being used. (The attitudes of the airplane at the extreme ends of its speed range are exaggerated in Figure 12-13.)

Practice-flying at minimum controllable airspeeds is extremely important; it shows you what to expect when you are flying at speeds fairly close to the stall (as might be done on a power approach to a short field). If you find yourself too low and slow and close to the stall on the power approach, you would *not* pull the nose up. This would demand more horsepower and make you sink faster. You would, instead, ease the nose lower and add power. In less critical situations you wouldn't even have to add power but would just ease the nose down to pick up a slightly higher airspeed (where less power is required).

Notice also how steeply the curve goes up at the maximum level-flight speed, Point (1). If this same airplane had another 30 horsepower it wouldn't have a much greater top speed. In fact, an added 30 horsepower (an added 30 percent) would only mean an increase in top speed of about 10 percent. As a rule of thumb for high cruising speeds or top speeds, the increase in airspeed (percentage) is about one-third of the increase in power (percentage) for a particular airplane. Speed can be expensive.

Chapter 23 will go into more detail as to how to set up specific *cruise* power conditions for your airplane.

SPINS

While stalls are fresh in your mind, it's a good idea to discuss spins. The Federal Aviation Administration does not require the demonstration of spins for any certificate or rating other than the flight instructor's certificate. But sometime you may want to have a spin demonstration by an instructor, and it's a good idea for anybody to know what they are and how to cope with them. You are no longer required to wear a parachute during such demonstrations.

Spins are naturally to be practiced in a properly certificated airplane. Before getting a demonstration, you should have a good idea of what to expect. The spin is an aggravated stall resulting in autorotation. In short, it is a condition where one wing stalls first and the plane "falls off" in that direction. One wing has more lift left and it is chasing the other stalled wing like a dog after its tail.

You've had experience with this in the departure and approach stalls. One wing stalls and the plane starts to rotate in that direction. If you had kept the wheel back, not recovering from the stall, and held rudder in the direction of rotation, a spin would have resulted. *But a lightplane has to be held into a spin. If you relaxed the back pressure, the spin would have turned into a tight diving turn and you would know how to get out of that.*

Okay, so a spin occurs when you stall one wing before the other and continue to hold back pressure, not allowing the plane to recover from the stalled condition.

The normal spin procedure is to start a normal power-off stall (after clearing the area) and just before the stall occurs, apply *full rudder* in the direction you want to spin. It's a good idea to begin no lower than 4000 feet above the ground. A one-turn spin in the average lightplane takes about 1000 feet of altitude from start to finish. Have enough altitude that you will recover at least 3000 feet above the ground. *Never deliberately spin with flaps down.* For instance, a spin to the left:

PROCEDURE

1. Clear the area and start a normal power-off stall. Carburetor heat "ON."

2. Just before the break occurs, apply full left rudder. The left wing stalls (Fig. 12-14).

3. Hold the wheel fully back and keep that left rudder in. Sometimes it may be necessary to apply a burst of power to start the spin. The prop blast gives the rudder added effectiveness to yaw the plane. Because of the yaw created by your use of the rudder, the left wing "moves back" and has less relative lift. The right wing, being moved forward, has

Fig. 12-14. As plane stalls, apply rudder in desired direction of spin.

relatively higher lift. The result is a roll to the left, causing the left wing to increase its angle of attack (which was right at the stall, anyway), and so the left wing has stalled and is now developing much less lift — and more drag — than the right wing. A spin can only occur if the airplane (or at least one wing) has passed the stall angle of attack and stays there. So the spin is created by a too-high angle of attack with yawing or rolling (the rolling can be induced by the yaw *or* other factors). For instance, look back to Figure 12-10. You're out practicing take-off and departure stalls solo one day and are making a right-climbing turn entry as shown. The airplane rolls to the left briskly and you use full right aileron to stop the roll — before you release the back pressure. Also, maybe your feet were lazy and you didn't use rudder like you should have. The down-aileron acts as a flap and the left wing is suddenly shifted to the left-hand "flap" curve in Figure 12-12; in addition, the angle of attack on that down-moving wing is increasing. Things meet in the middle (at the stall) pretty fast, and the wing starts the autorotation part. You'll have to break it by closing the throttle, neutralizing the ailerons, using opposite rudder and moving the wheel forward briskly. But getting back to talking about a deliberate spin:

4. The nose drops, but the full up-elevator does not allow the plane to recover from the stall. The unequal lift of wings gives the plane its rotational motion (Figs. 12-15 and 12-16).

The nose is not pointed straight down, though it will certainly appear this way to you during the first spin (Fig. 12-17).

Figure 12-18 shows the developed spin as seen from the cockpit.

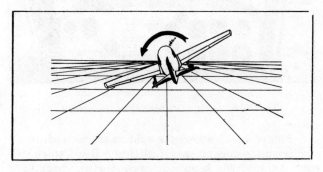

Fig. 12-15.

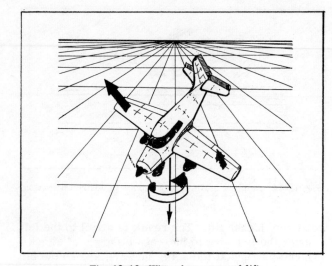

Fig. 12-16. Wings have unequal lift.

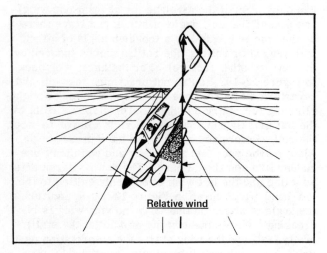

Relative wind

Fig. 12-17.

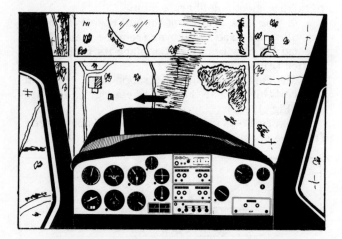

Fig. 12-18. The spin as seen from the cockpit.

Figure 12-19 shows the spin as it may look to *you* from the cockpit that first time. Don't stare over the nose, but keep your eyes moving, checking different objects on the ground.

Fig. 12-19. The spin as it will probably be seen from the cockpit your first time. The ball in the turn coordinator is to the left side of the instrument, you will notice, not to the right as might be assumed by theory. (You are holding full *left* rudder, which under normal flying conditions would put the ball to the right — but not in a developed spin with the instrument in the position shown.)

The plane's rotational motion tends to keep the imbalance of lift as seen in Figure 12-20.

As you can see, the relative wind caused by the plane's path toward the ground is the same speed and direction for both wings and the relative wind caused by rotation is the same velocity but from an opposite direction for each wing — giving a great difference in the angles of attack of the wings. You can get a "roll stall" if a wing is lowered too fast and causes the angle of attack to become too great for that wing.

Once the spin is established, you can maintain it as long as you like with full up-elevator and full left rudder.

Relaxing the back pressure will result in the plane's going from the spin into a spiral.

A properly executed spin is not any harder on an airplane than a stall. The airspeed remains low. (If you get a chance during the demonstration, look at the airspeed indicator. It will be showing a speed in the vicinity of the normal stalling speed.)

A sloppy recovery puts far more stress on the airplane than does the spin itself.

RECOVERY

1. Apply opposite rudder as needed to stop rotation. Opposite rudder would stop rotation on older, lighter trainers. Newer planes may require full opposite rudder and then brisk forward pressure before rotation will stop.

2. Relax the back pressure. Again, older light-planes need only for you to relax the back pressure. A newer model may require the stick to be moved forward briskly and held there. But more about this shortly.

3. Ease the plane from the dive. You converted the plane's actions from a rotating stall to a straight

80

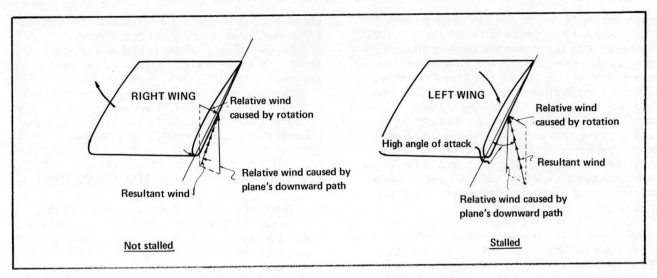

Fig. 12-20. Differences in angles of attack in a spin.

dive. Don't wait too long to pull the plane out of the dive because the airspeed will be building up. On the other hand, don't jerk it out because you don't want to put undue stress on the airplane.

COMMON ERRORS

1. Failure to get a clean spin entry — getting a spiral instead. (More about this shortly.)

2. Overenthusiasm on the releasing of back pressure, that is, pushing forward abruptly on the wheel and causing a negative load factor to be put on the plane.

3. *Not* releasing the back pressure enough. Some students get so eager to get out of the left spin, for instance, that they stop the rotation by full right rudder, quickly releasing back pressure, then pulling right back with the wheel to pull out of the dive. They are astounded to notice that they restalled the airplane and that the still held right rudder caused them to enter a spin to the right. This is called a progressive spin but is really the same as any other spin. In this case it requires that you start a new recovery procedure for a spin to the right. This is embarrassing unless you can convince the instructor that it was a deliberate demonstration of your skill. Flight instructors are pretty skeptical people.

In discussing spin recovery it was noted that most older lightplanes need only a little relaxation of rudder or back pressure to ease them out of a spin. However, improper loadings may cause even a "docile" airplane (or maybe it's a type of light airplane that doesn't know it's supposed to get out so ridiculously easy) to surprise you. One recommended type of recovery would be to apply full opposite rudder, followed immediately by a brisk forward motion of the control wheel or stick, and held until the rotation stops. If you've tried the "relaxation of control" type of recovery and the spin is continuing, go back to pro-spin controls and institute the type of recovery just cited. You could get into an accidental spin at altitude during a stall and you should also know that *closing the throttle helps the recovery.*

If you do accidentally get into a spin situation someday when you are at altitude practicing stalls, your initial instinct will be (as the airplane rolls and the nose drops to a very low pitch attitude) to hold the wheel or stick all the way back to pull the nose up. *Don't.* You'll need to get the wheel or stick forward to break the stall, and this is hard to make yourself do, sometimes.

One instructor experienced in spins, when asked what he recommended as a "spin warner" — that is, when the airplane is being stalled and yaw or roll is being induced — answered that a boxing glove should come out of the instrument panel hitting the pilot and making him release the wheel.

If you think that during a practice stall things are going too far, as a general approach you should take the following steps:

1. Close the throttle. This makes initial recovery much easier for most airplanes.

2. Neutralize the ailerons.

3. Apply full rudder opposite to the roll or yaw, then:

4. When the rudder hits the stop, briskly move the stick or wheel forward to break the stall *and* help stop the rotation. Again, you'll automatically tend to hold back the wheel in an attempt to pull the nose up. (*Don't.*)

5. When rotation stops, neutralize the rudder and ease the airplane out of the dive.

SPINS AND SPIRALS

Some people have problems knowing the difference between spins and spirals. Figure 12-21A shows the airspeed, turn coordinator, and turn and slip indications in a spiral.

Spiral — This is nothing more than a steep diving turn. The airspeed is rising rapidly and the turn and slip (or turn coordinator) shows a moderate to high rate of turn in the well-developed spiral. The ball will probably be to the left in most airplanes because it takes left rudder in a dive to keep it centered, and you've gotten into this situation unconsciously so you

81

aren't correcting for it. (Right rudder is needed at low speeds and high power settings to keep the ball centered.) The spiral is a low angle of attack/high speed situation and the recovery procedure is to use *normal control pressures*. You'd level the wings with coordinated aileron and rudder and then ease the nose back to level. You'd also throttle back as soon as you realized the airspeed was picking up so as to keep the rpm under the red line (fixed-pitch prop). But the point is that the spiral is nothing more than an exaggerated combination of two of the four fundamentals — a turn and a descent — and the average 2-hour student should be able to recover from it.

Spin — This is a high angle of attack/low air-speed situation; the airspeed will be hovering some-where down in the stall area (Fig. 12-21B). The recovery requires an apparently unnatural use of the controls. You don't use aileron and rudder together to "level" the wings. You neutralize the ailerons just to keep from complicating matters and use rudder alone against the rotation. Instead of "naturally" getting the nose up by added back pressure, you'll have to try to push it even farther down to decrease the angle of attack and get out of the stalled condition — then bring it up by back pressure after the airplane is in the dive.

Note that the ball is well to the left side of the two turn instruments. It's assumed that this is a side-by-side trainer and those instruments are on the left side of the panel; this could well be the indications of the ball in a *left* spin. The slip indicator (ball) tends to go to the left side of the instrument in spins in either direction. Usually the rate of yaw and/or roll is much greater than in the spiral, with the indicator(s) pegged in the direction of spin. You, however, will have no comparison as shown by (A) and (B) in Figure 12-21 and the low airspeed (con-stant or oscillating in a low speed range) will be the

big clue for detecting a spin situation. The ball is to be ignored as an indication of spin direction.

So, the spiral problem is that of a too-high air-speed. "Normal" control *pressures* are used to recover.

The spin problem is that of a too-low airspeed (too-high angle of attack). Mechanical control *move-ments* are used to initiate the recovery. The air-plane is then flown normally out of the dive.

SUMMARY OF ELEMENTARY STALLS AND SPINS

The elementary stall recovery requires that you get the air flowing smoothly over the wing again. Control pressure or abruptness of control move-ments will vary between lightplanes and heavy planes and will even vary between different types of light-planes. Whatever the type of plane — the required result is the same.

An airplane can be stalled at any speed and attitude.

The fact that spins were covered right after the elementary stalls does not necessarily mean that this is the phase in which you will practice spins. Your instructor will likely want to wait until after you solo, or he may not demonstrate them at all. It is a good idea to be able to recognize and recover from the spin and, after you have done this, to move on to other maneuvers.

All "Normal" category airplanes that are capa-ble of spinning are placarded against spins, and if your trainer is so certificated you won't be doing them.

The airplane's attitude and heading will be changing rapidly during these maneuvers, and you'd better keep those eyeballs moving. The practice area is no place to "run into an old friend" (or any-body else, for that matter) (Fig. 12-22).

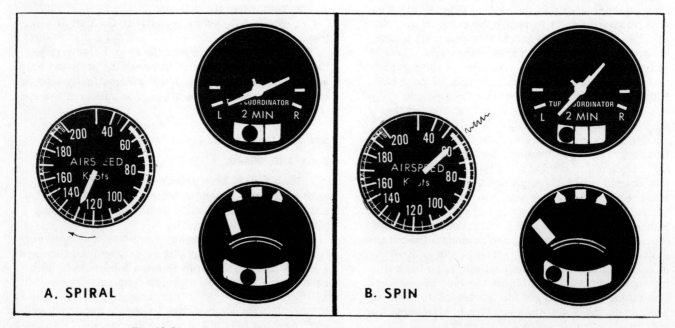

A. SPIRAL   B. SPIN

Fig. 12-21. Instrument indications in a spiral and a spin (to the left, in both cases).

Fig. 12-22. Other airplanes may be using "your" practice area.

As you progress to faster, heavier airplanes you will rely less on feel and sound and more on the airspeed indicator and stall warning indicators. The supersonic airplane has power-boosted controls, and a spring or bungee arrangement furnishes stick "feel." With this arrangement there's no hope of feeling the control pressures as the plane approaches the stall. While "seat-of-the-pants" flying may still apply to older lightplanes, the stall warning indicator is being added as an aid to pilots of newer, heavier craft.

The stall warning indicator may be electrical or reed type (sound). The electrical type is attached to a cockpit warning device such as a light or horn, depending on the make or model. A general idea is shown in Figure 12-23.

The tab is set at the correct angle for the particular airfoil being used. The indicator "warns" of any approaching stall. Generally it is set slightly ahead of the stall so that under normal conditions, such as a landing, the pilot is warned 5 to 8 knots before the stall. The warning may be given anytime the angle of attack becomes too great — regardless of the airspeed.

The pneumatic-type stall warning system used on some current trainers has an inlet on the leading edge of the left wing, connected by tubing to an air-operated horn within the pilot's hearing. The air pressure variations at changing, higher angles of attack draws air through the horn, giving warning of the impending stall at several knots before the stall break occurs. The tone usually gets higher in pitch as the stall approaches.

The military uses angle of attack indicators for performance information, particularly for approaches. The advantage of this is that the airplane always stalls at the same angle of attack (for a given flap setting) regardless of weight or g forces acting on the airplane. The angle of attack indicator hasn't gotten general acceptance for light general aviation airplanes, but may be used in the future.

And a couple of last notes on spins: The *Pilot's Operating Handbook* and an instructor current in spins in that model are the final authorities on spins for a particular airplane. *In an accidental spin with flaps, get them up as soon as possible, for easier recovery and to avoid exceeding the flaps down airspeed in the recovery dive.*

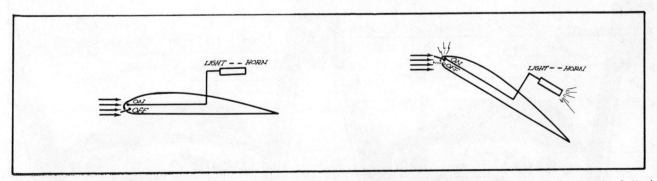

Fig. 12-23. At normal angles of attack, relative wind keeps switch in "OFF" position. As airfoil approaches critical angle of attack, relative wind pushes tab to "ON" position. Horn or light operate as long as critical angle of attack continues.

13. Take-offs and Landings

NORMAL TAKE-OFF

After you have about five or six hours and are proficient in the Four Fundamentals, stalls, the wind correction maneuvers, and elementary emergencies, the periods of shooting take-offs and landings will begin.

Maybe you feel that take-offs and landings are the most important parts of flying, but as far as your training is concerned they are just another maneuver. The average student even places more weight on landings than take-offs.

Take-offs are not important, he thinks, but LANDINGS are. So with this attitude, he finds himself having plenty of trouble when it comes to getting the bird smoothly into the air.

The instructor will have you follow him through on the take-offs during the first flight or two, and probably by the third or fourth flight you will be making the take-offs yourself.

Most of the trainers being used today are the tricycle-gear types. As was the case for taxiing, the lower nose position gives better visibility during the ground roll parts of the take-off and landing.

Because the airplane is in level flight position, the take-off becomes a matter of opening the throttle smoothly, keeping the airplane straight, and, as the controls become firm, applying back pressure to ease the nosewheel up to attain the take-off attitude

and letting the airplane fly itself off. As you found in taxiing, most tricycle-gear airplanes have nosewheel steering and during the initial part of the ground roll, right rudder pedal pressure will be needed to take care of the left-turning tendency always existing in a low-speed, high-power situation. While the nosewheel is on the ground the steering is divided between the nosewheel and the aerodynamics of the deflected right rudder; as the nosewheel is lifted, be ready to use more right rudder to compensate for the loss of nosewheel steering.

TRICYCLE-GEAR AIRPLANE TAKE-OFF PROCEDURE

1. See that no airplanes are landing. Taxi to the centerline of the runway.

2. Line up with the centerline or, if there isn't one (say, as on a grass strip), use a reference at the far end of the runway.

3. Apply power smoothly to get rolling, then move on to full throttle. Keep your hand on the throttle and check the engine instruments.

4. As the controls become firm (particularly the elevators), use back pressure to obtain the proper angle of attack for take-off. Be ready to add right rudder as the nosewheel lifts clear.

5. After the lift-off, relax back pressure slightly to assure that the nose maintains the proper climb

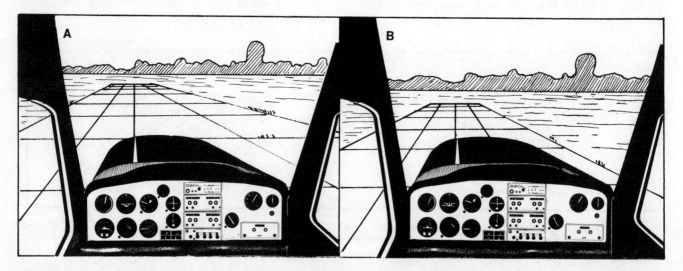

Fig. 13-1. (A) Line up with the centerline and apply power to start rolling, then smoothly go to full power for take-off, keeping the airplane straight by smooth application of right rudder. (B) As the controls become firm, start applying more back pressure to ease the nose up to the take-off attitude.

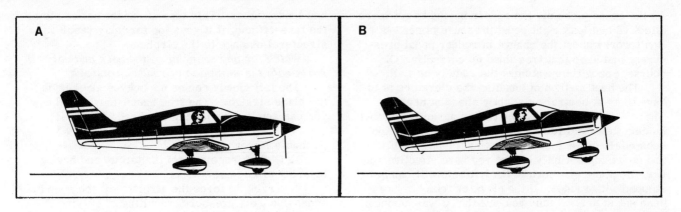

Fig. 13-2. A side view of the initial roll (A) and lift-off (B) attitudes for a tricycle-gear airplane.

attitude. Maintain that attitude and climb straight ahead, correcting for torque and keeping your hand on the throttle to make sure that it's at climb power. Ease the flaps up (if used) at a safe altitude.

Common Errors

1. During the initial part of the roll, allowing (or "helping") the control wheel to move forward so that the elevators are slightly or well down. This could put too much weight on the nosewheel and could cause a delay in the take-off or steering problems — called "wheelbarrowing" (to be covered later in the chapter).

2. The average student at first is usually timid in applying back pressure at the right time to ease the nose up to the take-off attitude. This results in the airplane staying on the ground to too high an air-speed, wasting runway and possibly getting some nosewheel "chatter." Some King Kong types give a mighty heave too early and pull the airplane abruptly into the air before it's quite ready to go. You'll find that after a couple of take-offs you'll be able to apply the right amount of back pressure at the right time.

3. Not relaxing back pressure after the lift-off (or continuing to hold the back pressure used to bring the airplane off) so that the airplane's nose rises sharply and doesn't maintain the best rate of climb speed (V_Y).

Figure 13-2 shows the side view of a take-off for a tricycle-gear airplane.

TAKE-OFF FOR AIRPLANES WITH TAILWHEELS

You are trying to leave the ground as smoothly and efficiently as possible. Taxi onto the runway, first making sure no other planes are on final approach, and line up with some object such as a tree at the far end (Fig. 13-3). In most planes with tailwheel type landing gear it is difficult to see over the nose in the three-point attitude, so you must look at your object alongside the nose for the first part of the take-off run. You may ask, "What if there's no tree?" Lacking a reference point at the end, watch the left side of the runway. The take-off consists of three phases: (1) the initial or three-point position part of the run, (2) the roll on the front two wheels in which the plane is streamlined to pick up speed quickly, and (3) the lifting off, or transition to flight.

Phase 1

Open the throttle slowly to get the plane rolling, then continue to apply full power smoothly.

The torque situation is this: You are now using full power but the plane is barely moving. The rudder itself is comparatively ineffective and the greater part of the steering must be done with the tailwheel.

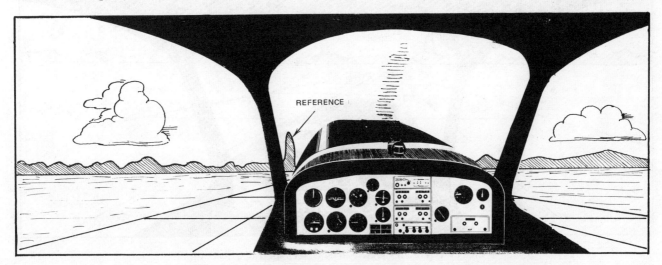

REFERENCE

Fig. 13-3. Pick an easy-to-recognize object to line up on.

As the speed picks up, the rudder begins to get more effective and less right pedal pressure is needed. Don't worry about the change in rudder pedal pressures, just keep that tree lined up correctly. Of course, you will be watching the runway as well.

The best method of handling the elevators is to have them at neutral or slightly ahead of neutral. There's no need to force the tail up abruptly. In fact, holding the wheel full forward to get the tail up too soon might cause loss of directional control. If the tail comes up abruptly before you have effective rudder, the plane may turn to the left before it can be stopped with rudder. If the elevator trim tab has been set at neutral (and you saw that it was during the pretake-off check) the tail will come up by itself when the time gets ripe. You can, however, help the process by exerting slight forward pressure on the elevators as the plane picks up speed.

Don't "walk" the rudder, hoping to average out the swing of the nose — you'll never get the feel of the take-off that way.

Probable Errors in Phase 1

1. Abrupt throttle usage resulting in poor directional control at the beginning of the run.

2. Not keeping the plane lined up with the object at the end of the runway.

3. "Walking" the rudders.

Phase 2 — The Tail-up Part of the Roll

Many students have trouble in the transition from Phase 1 to Phase 2. While the plane is rolling in the three-point position you have both tailwheel steering and, in the latter part of Phase 1, a fairly effective relative air moving past the rudder. When the tail comes up, the tailwheel no longer helps and a further deflection of the rudder is required for torque correction. Students sometimes have trouble correcting for torque and keeping the nose lined up. Their take-offs are smooth rolls interrupted by a period of mad maneuvering because they use the rudder too enthusiastically. The plane weaves down the runway, putting great side stresses on the tires

and landing gear. This type of rudder action slows the take-off and, if it goes too far, may result in structural damage to the airplane.

Watch for any swinging of the nose and catch it early with the minimum of rudder pressure.

The tail slowly comes up and you are keeping the plane straight. The tree hasn't moved and now you can see the whole runway ahead (Fig. 13-4).

Probable Errors in Phase 2

1. Getting eager to get the tail up and having steering problems.

2. Trying to force the airplane off too soon by excessive back pressure, resulting in slowing the airplane and delaying the take-off.

A good demonstration of the effects of gyroscopic precession can be given by forcing the tail up suddenly on take-off. The rotating propeller acts as a gyro wheel. When the tail is raised the rotational plane of the propeller is changed. As the tail comes up the effect is that of a force being exerted against the top of the propeller arc from behind. You know that a gyro reacts as if the force had been exerted at a point 90° around the wheel (measured in the direction of rotation). The airplane reacts as if the force had been exerted at the right side of the arc, and this tends to turn the plane to the left. The faster the tail is raised the more abrupt this left-turning action. This only acts as long as the plane's attitude is being changed. Once the take-off attitude is reached and maintained, precession is not an important factor. You will not be worried so much about what causes certain effects on take-off as about correcting them. If the nose veers to the left, no matter what the cause, you'll have to straighten it out. This is the most important thing to remember.

Phase 3 — Lift-off

As the plane picks up speed the controls become firmer. The attitude is that of a shallow climb. This makes it possible for the plane to lift itself off as flying speed is reached.

Fig. 13-4. Now all you have to do is keep it straight and wait.

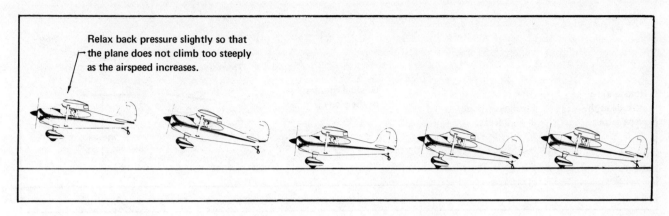

Relax back pressure slightly so that the plane does not climb too steeply as the airspeed increases.

Fig. 13-5. The normal take-off (tailwheel type).

As the airspeed approaches the take-off value the plane will become "light" and may start skipping or bouncing. If this happens, use more back pressure and bring the plane off. The skipping or bouncing is an indication that the plane is ready to fly but there is not quite enough angle of attack to lift it off. Once the plane breaks free, keep it in the air. It doesn't help matters to hit again. If there is a crosswind, you may be drifting across the runway the next time you hit, thus putting a heavy side load on the landing gear.

After you are off the ground with no danger of hitting again, relax back pressure slightly so that the nose does not rise too steeply as the plane accelerates and the elevators become more effective (Fig. 13-5). After this point it's no longer a take-off but a normal climb — and you've been able to cope with that for some time.

As soon as the wheels leave the ground, the rudder no longer steers the airplane. Use coordinated aileron and rudder to turn until you get back on the ground again.

Procedure

1. See that no planes are landing. Taxi to the centerline of the runway. Use all the runway available; that portion behind doesn't help you.

2. Line up with some object at the far end of the runway.

3. Apply power smoothly to get it rolling, then apply full throttle smoothly.

4. Keep the plane lined up with the object at the end of the runway.

5. As the tail comes up be prepared for the need of added right rudder.

6. As controls become firm, bring in back pressure to lift the plane off, and when it is off, keep it off.

7. After take-off, level off to pick up climb speed. Remember the take-off speed is slightly above stall speed and well below proper climb speed.

If the runway is smooth and you use proper techniques it should be hard to tell when the plane leaves the ground.

NORMAL LANDING

The normal landing is nothing more than a normal power-off stall, with the stall occurring just as, or very shortly after, the plane touches the ground. Why stall the airplane? You can put a lightplane on the ground at 100 K but this is hard on the plane, and on you, and also uses up more runway than is practical. The best idea is to land at the slowest speed possible and still have control of the airplane.

The first thing you want to learn is that the importance of landings is vastly overrated by the public (and probably by you, too, at this stage). If you make a smooth landing, you're the greatest pilot alive to your passengers. There are several reasons for this: (1) landings are always made at the airport (you hope) where everybody can see them and know what they are, (2) this flying is still somewhat mysterious to the layman and he figures it must take a high degree of skill to be able to come back down after defying gravity and the elements, and (3) the landing is a maneuver done close to the ground where the smallest mistakes may look like near crashes. At 3000 feet you may skid a half mile, but since there are no references up there it doesn't show up.

This disease of sweating landings even strikes old pilots who should know better. It is interesting to note that the perfect landing is always made on a day when the airport is deserted. But bounce your way in on a sunny Sunday afternoon, with somebody special along for that first ride, and there'll be a fence full of jeerers as you try to park as inconspicuously as possible.

But speaking on a pilot's level, the idea of a landing is to get the plane on the ground without fanfare. *That's all that it is.*

PROCEDURE

The landing is started from a normal glide at a height of about 20 feet (or about hangar height) above the ground. This starting height depends on the size of the airplane and is also affected by the rate of descent. Large planes may start the transition at 75 feet, but hangar height is about right for the

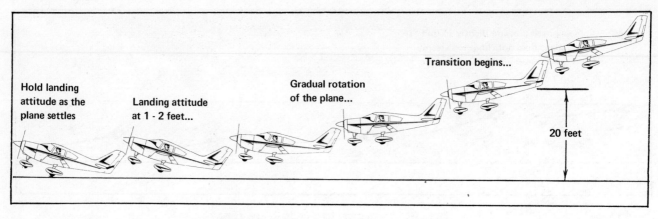

Fig. 13-6. Landing the tricycle-gear airplane.

lightplane. Start the landing transition or "break the glide" at hangar height by gradually easing the wheel back to stall the airplane. About 19 of that 20 feet is used to change the airplane's attitude from that of the normal glide to the landing attitude.

Transition must be gradual. If you pull the wheel back abruptly the plane will go up. This is called ballooning. Ease the nose up to the landing attitude, disturbing the plane's flight path as little as possible. *This takes a certain amount of skill, you will discover.* The plane is slowing up all this time as the angle of attack is being increased. By the time you are down to about a foot off the ground, the transition to landing attitude is complete and your job is to keep that attitude by using more and more back pressure. *The best way to make a landing is to try to hold the plane off as long as possible.* The faster the plane settles, the faster the rate of application of back pressure must be. The plane continues to settle and slow up. Remembering stalls, you know that the slower the plane gets, the more elevator is needed to hold its attitude, which slows it, etc. You should run out of elevator just as the plane touches the ground.

Thermals, gusts, or downdrafts affect the transition. Only in theory, or on a perfectly calm day, will the wheel be moved smoothly back at a near constant rate.

In other words, there may be times during the transition when you have to relax back pressure.

Never *push* forward. Remember you are at a low speed and a high angle of attack. If you decrease the angle of attack suddenly, there will be a lag before the speed picks up. During this time, lift will be practically nothing and you might find that you've made a serious mistake. There may be times when the back pressure must be stopped where it is and other times when it seems that you must pull back rapidly on the wheel. Well, that's the way it is. But one thing of importance — start the landing from a normal glide. Generally a poor approach means a poor landing.

Land the tricycle-gear plane so that the initial contact is made on the main wheels. Try to hold the nosewheel off so that the airplane's attitude causes aerodynamic drag and helps slow it down on the landing roll (Fig. 13-6).

Later you'll find that there is an optimum time to ease the nosewheel down to get the maximum drag on the landing roll for each plane.

The tailwheel airplane should be landed so that the tailwheel and main gear touch simultaneously, though for some airplanes, some pilots argue, the tailwheel should touch an instant early.

WHERE TO LOOK

In order to know when and how much back pressure is to be applied, you must know where the plane is in relation to the ground. The nose will be coming

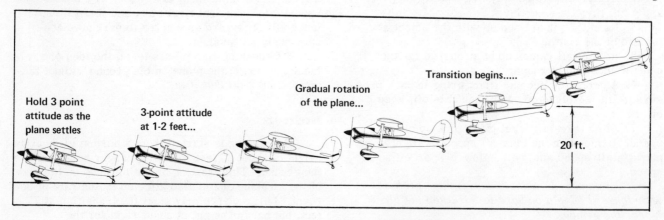

Fig. 13-7. The three-point landing (tailwheel type).

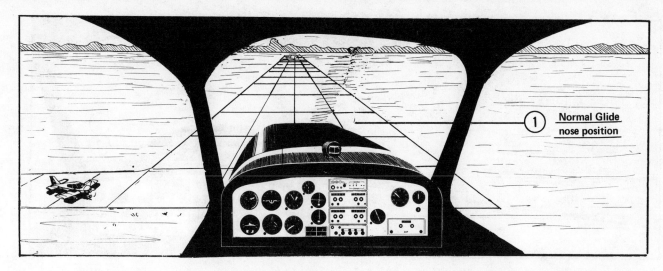

Fig. 13-8. Maintain a constant attitude/airspeed during the latter (power-off) part of the approach.

up higher and higher as you approach the landing attitude. It will be impossible to see the ground over the nose in the last stage of the transition, as you will see during the landing demonstrations in the early part of your training.

You will be sitting on the left in a side-by-side airplane, and the stick and throttle arrangement in a tandem plane makes it easier for the pilot to turn his head to the left. So you will look out this side after the transition begins.

The best place to look is about 20° to the left of the nose and far enough ahead so that the ground is not blurred. Don't stare at one spot. Scan the ground; your depth perception depends on a lot of eye movement. If you look only straight down, the relative movement of the ground is great and you may have a tendency to stall the airplane while it's still a fair distance off the ground. The plane will "drop in" and could be damaged. If you look too far ahead, the error in your depth perception may cause you to fly the plane into the ground.

As you reach about 20 feet, or hangar height, begin the transition (Figs. 13-9, 13-10, 13-11).

Don't try to look over the nose. If you can see over the nose during the landing you don't have the correct landing attitude and you will fly into the ground. If you get the nose at the right position and stare blindly up at it, you won't have the faintest idea where the ground is. You'll find out exactly where when you hear the sickening thud.

Keep the plane lined up with the runway and have the wings level when you touch down. The stall warner should be making its presence known, under normal conditions.

GROUND LOOPS

In Figure 13-12 you see that the momentum of the plane will act through the center of gravity, and the center of friction with the runway may be considered to act at a point midway between the wheels.

If the plane isn't pointed the way it's flying when it hits, a ground loop might result. A ground loop is an abrupt turning of the airplane on the ground. If the ground loop is violent enough, the plane may rock over and drag a wing. The best way to avoid a

Fig. 13-9. After starting the transition at about 20 feet, continue to ease smoothly back on the wheel (altitude shown here about 15 feet).

Fig. 13-10. Landing attitude is reached at a height of about 1 foot — continue back pressure to maintain this attitude.

The plane touches just as you run out of elevator.

Fig. 13-11. The plane continues to settle as you keep easing back on the wheel and it touches in the correct landing attitude. Keep wheel full back and maintain directional control with the rudder.

ground loop is to make sure the plane is lined up with the runway when the touchdown is made.

If the ground loop has started and a wing has dropped, don't get any ideas of bringing it up with rudder. This works in the air, but makes matters worse on the ground. The plane rocks over because of the sharpness of the turn. Applying rudder to

"speed up" that down wing in hopes of bringing it up only results in a sharper turn. Use all controls including the throttle to stop or slow down the ground loop. A burst of power coupled with prompt rudder and/or brake action against the turn is usually effective as a means of recovery.

If a wing is down during the landing transition, the plane will turn. You'll have to concentrate on keeping those wings level, the plane straight, and making the transition all at the same time. Later

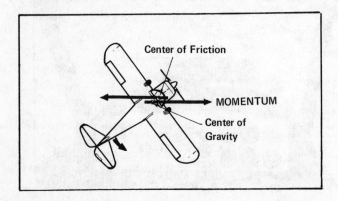

Fig. 13-12. Center of gravity, momentum, center of friction (tailwheel plane).

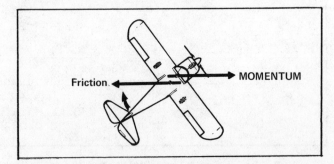

Fig. 13-13. The tricycle-gear plane tends to straighten out.

you'll be shown how holding a wing down and applying opposite rudder will help in a crosswind landing.

In moving the wheel back during the landing process, students sometimes pull *up* on the left side of the control wheel as well as moving it back (the wheel is generally held on the left side by the left hand). This means that aileron is being applied, the wing is lowered, and the airplane "drifts" toward the right edge of the runway. The stick control, being used by the right hand, is often pulled to the right with the same results.

When you're flying cross-country, a slightly lowered wing for a short time may mean that the plane's path will vary several hundred feet to that side. It's not noticeable up there, but because many runways aren't even a hundred feet wide, you may end up out in the gravel pits and tall grass alongside the runway.

One common error students make during the landing roll is to relax back pressure and allow the control wheel to move forward. In the tailwheel type, this doesn't keep that tailwheel down firm on the ground for good steering; in the tricycle-gear airplane it will allow too much weight on the nosewheel, causing "wheelbarrowing." Wheelbarrowing occurs when the added weight on the nosewheel causes it to become extra sensitive to rudder pressures during the ground roll. Your correction for a slight nose movement on the roll-out may be exaggerated and the airplane overreacts, abruptly turning toward the direction of that corrective rudder.

The first hour of landings will keep both you and the instructor busy. You'll be worn out at the end of the hour but will discover that landings are quite interesting.

SHOOTING TAKE-OFFS AND LANDINGS

Most students have three to four hours of take-offs and landings before solo. Some may have two and others six hours. This will be the most enjoyable part of your presolo work. You won't have to take the instructor's word for it if you foul up. You can see and feel it for yourself.

THE TRAFFIC PATTERN

Now that you know the theory of take-offs and landings, it's good to have an idea of how to go about practicing them.

The airport traffic pattern is established so that planes flying from that field will have some standard of operation for safety's sake.

A typical traffic pattern for a small airport is shown in Figure 13-14. Some airports have a right-hand pattern for some runways, as will be shown by their segmented circles, but the principle is the same.

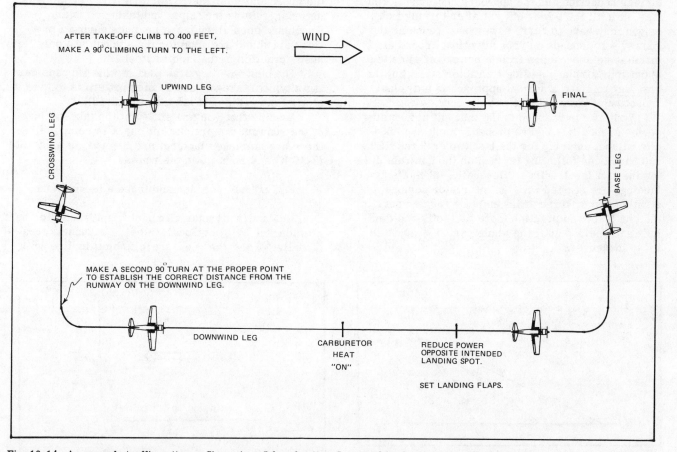

Fig. 13-14. An example traffic pattern. Shown is a "closed pattern" as used in shooting take-offs and landings. Your instructor will demonstrate, and you will practice, departing and entering the pattern. (Substitute your own numbers.)

91

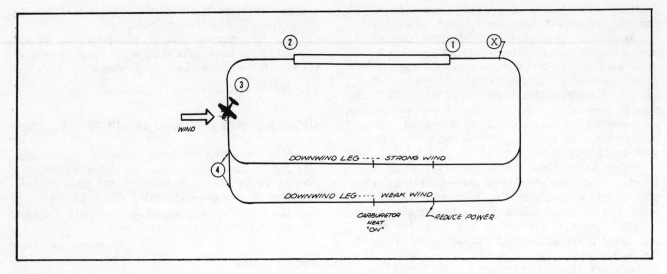

Fig. 13-15.

Back in the olden days of flying, most lightplane approaches were made from a normal power-off glide so that should the engine quit during any part of the approach the airplane could still make it to the runway. Nowadays, the aircraft engine is so reliable that this is an extremely minor factor; the recommended method of making the approach is to reduce power (as recommended by your instructor) opposite to the point of intended landing and make further reductions as the approach continues. You may have all the power off just after turning final, or you may have to carry power until reaching the runway — it depends on your situation. You'll also make some approaches from a power-off glide to learn your airplane's glide characteristics, but the best way to make a normal approach is a gradual reduction of power all the way around.

You'll be introduced to the take-off and landing series gradually. You've probably made the take-offs without any help for the last two or three flights and have been following through on the controls during the last few landings. Generally, take-offs and landings are started with the instructor demonstrating two or three at the end of a regular period; then he'll let you practice more take-offs and landings each period until the whole period is spent on these maneuvers.

The first couple of hours of landing practice will probably be full-stop landings. That is, you will let the plane slow down; then you'll turn off the runway and taxi back to make another take-off. This is a good practice in learning to control the airplane as it slows up on the landing roll, as well as smoothing out any taxiing problems. Later you'll probably shoot "touch and goes" — opening the throttle, pushing the carburetor heat off (if it was used throughout the approach; your instructor will have recommendations), raising the flaps, and taking off again. Touch and goes allow more landings during a practice period and are good for the student who only needs practice in the landing itself.

The best way to get an idea of what happens during a typical take-off and landing pattern is to take it step by step (Figs. 13-15 through 13-18).

Assume that you are sitting at the take-off end of the runway, the pretake-off check is complete, there are no planes landing, and the wind is moderate (8-10 K) and right down the runway.

1. Taxi into position and make a normal take-off.

2. Make a normal climb straight ahead to the altitude set by your local rules. Look back occasionally to see that you are climbing in line with

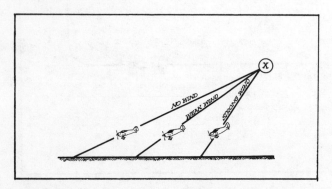

Fig. 13-16. Variation of approach angle with wind. Constant glide attitude and airspeed (angles exaggerated).

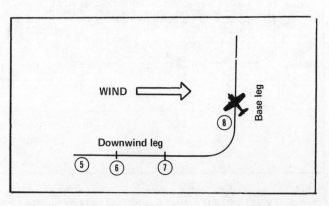

Fig. 13-17.

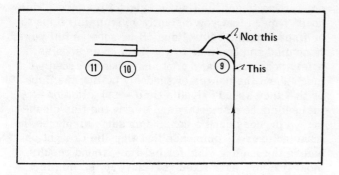

Fig. 13-18.

the runway and not headed out cross-country.

3. When the turn altitude is reached, look behind again to make sure you aren't going to turn into a faster plane coming up from behind. Make a 90° climbing turn to the left. Actually the turn should not be quite 90° since you will have to compensate for the wind. Incidentally, don't make any turns inside the airport boundary. It's better to be at least 1000 feet past the end of the runway before turning.

4. Make the second 90°, left-climbing turn whenever it is necessary in order to establish the correct distance from the runway on the downwind leg. The principle of establishing a distance from the runway is this: If the wind is strong, the approach angle is steep on the final approach for a particular power setting; therefore, more altitude is needed at point X (Figs. 13-15 and 13-16). Maybe you say, "Why not stay the same distance from the runway for every wind velocity and just make that first turn sooner?" It can be demonstrated that you will be critically low at the point of the final turn if the wind is strong and also you'll have no "straight-away" or final to establish yourself for the landing.

5. Climb to 1000 feet. Keep the plane flying parallel to the runway (Fig. 13-17).

6. Pull the carburetor heat a few seconds before you reach the position directly opposite the intended landing spot. Give it a chance to clear out any ice before you start reducing power. The use of carburetor heat will depend on the airplane and conditions: (a) you may not use carburetor heat for certain airplanes if conditions preclude icing, or (b) you may be told to apply carburetor heat on the downwind leg to check for icing, and then push it off if no evidence of icing is found, or (c) use full carburetor heat throughout the approach.

7. Reduce power and set up the approach speed.

8. Make a slightly more than 90° turn to the left. Continue to reduce the power as necessary to control the approach path. One problem students have is making this turn too shallow, so the airplane is nearly over to the final leg before the first 90° of turn is completed. This would then require a steep 90° turn onto final, at a low altitude, to line up with the runway centerline — a disconcerting and possibly dangerous practice. This is more apt to happen in a high-wing trainer because the down-wing may keep the runway hidden throughout the turn onto the base leg. You may not realize that you are moving so

close to the final leg. This is particularly a problem if the airplane on the base leg has a tail-wind component as is shown in Figure 13-31. It's best to have a symmetrical pattern, but most instructors prefer that the turn at point (8) (Fig. 13-17) be slightly steeper than the one at point (9) (Fig. 13-18), because (a) the steeper turn is done at the higher altitude and (b) the turn will be completed soon enough so that the wings can be leveled for a straight base leg (and a good look at the runway).

9. Make the final turn as needed to line up with the centerline of the runway. A common fault of students is overshooting the runway on the final turn. This happens when the final turn is not started soon enough and the plane must be turned back into the runway. Another error is making the final turn too soon, angling toward the runway. Shoot for at least a 1/4-mile final.

10. When your height above the ground is approximately 20 feet, begin the transition to the landing attitude. Keep the plane straight and the wings level. At about 1 to 2 feet, the landing attitude should be reached. Continue the back pressure, maintaining this attitude as the plane settles. The wheel should reach its full back travel just as the wheels touch.

11. Keep the plane rolling straight down the runway. As it slows to taxi speed turn off the runway and taxi back for another go.

Don't try to turn off the runway at too high a speed — you may ground loop.

Don't try to slow the airplane quickly by using brakes. It's not good for a tricycle gear-equipped plane, and you may nose over in a tailwheel type plane. It takes experience to be able to apply brakes on the landing roll without nosing over. It's hard on tires, too.

FLAPS

You've seen the flaps during the preflight checks and the instructor has shown you how to use them in the approach to landing stalls as well as during his approach demonstrations. But now another closer look at how *you* are to use them during these take-off and landing sessions, and in future pattern work, also (Fig. 13-19).

By extending the flaps you increase the camber (curvature) of the wing which results in more lift *and*

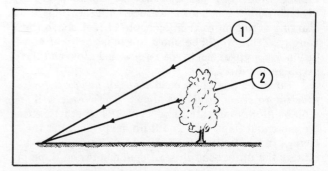

Fig. 13-19. (1) Approach path at normal glide speed with flaps. (2) Approach path at normal glide speed — no flaps.

more drag for a certain nose position. This means you can have a steeper angle of descent to clear obstacles because of the drag, and you will land at a lower airspeed because of a higher coefficient of lift. There may be a pitch change with flap extension.

As the flaps are extended (lowered) in the approach, the nose must be lowered to maintain the normal glide speed. After the landing, the drag of the flaps helps shorten the landing roll.

For take-off the flaps are set at the position recommended by the manufacturer. This may vary from no deflection for normal take-off to 10 degrees or more for special procedures such as for soft or short field take-offs. If your airplane has flaps you'll be shown their use from the beginning.

The flap operation range is marked by that white arc on the airspeed indicator. The bottom of the white arc is the flaps-down, power-off stalling speed at the maximum certificated weight of the airplane. The high value (top of the white arc) is the maximum speed at which full flaps may be used at any weight. (For safety, think of this speed as the maximum at which *any* flaps may be used.) If the flaps are lowered at an *indicated* (calibrated) airspeed higher than noted at the top of the white arc, possible structural and trim problems could occur. Because the flaps add both drag and lift for any given airspeed you will find that your angle of descent will be steepened by their use; you will also find that the landing speed is measurably lowered. Generally it's best *not* to combine slips and flaps; some airplanes don't like it. You might check this for your airplane at a safe altitude with an instructor.

On the private flight test you may have to make at least one landing *without* flaps in an airplane equipped with flaps, unless the operations limitations prohibit no-flap landings. If you've been using flaps a lot lately, that first practice no-flap landing will give the impression that you're going to float all the way down the runway; you'll tend to let the airspeed get too great on final approach. For most airplanes the actual landing technique is easier without flaps; the nose can be eased up with less effort or trim. You should be familiar with how the airplane handles on landing both with and without flaps.

While flaps are a great aid to the pilot on final approach and landing, they are nothing but a problem when a sudden go-around is required. Flap drag eats up horsepower that could be used for needed climb. Some day you may have to make a go-around from a touchdown attitude with full flaps, starting at not more than a couple of feet above the runway. This would be about the most critical condition for a go-around; you're low and slow and the airplane is "dirty."

First, on any go-around *add full power before starting to clean up the airplane.* The power will stop or slow your rate of descent. Then start getting the gear and flaps up. You'll be surprised, but the change in stall speed from idle to full power almost offsets the difference in stall speed between flaps up and flaps down (it depends on the particular airplane). In other words, apply full power and figure

on starting to get the flaps up right afterward. This doesn't mean that you instantly go from full flaps to no flaps, but get *some* flaps off as soon as full power is applied and continue to get them up as soon as safely possible. Many pilots have been warned so much about the danger of suddenly pulling the flaps up that they spend valuable time — and attention — just seeing how smoothly and slowly the flap cleaning-up process can be done. For some airplanes the manufacturer recommends that flaps be brought up before the landing gear for best go-around results. Most trainers have fixed gear anyway, so this is a decision you probably won't have to make — now.

SLIP

The slip is a very important maneuver for airplanes not equipped with flaps and is used to increase the angle of descent without increasing the airspeed. If you are high on the final approach and dive the plane (Fig. 13-20A), you will get down to the runway but will also have excess speed that will cause the plane to float down the runway. In the slip the pilot turns the plane so that an unstreamlined shape is presented to the relative wind (Fig. 13-20B). Airspeed will stay low even in a steep descent because of this drag.

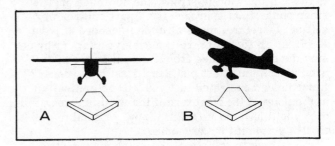

Fig. 13-20. (A) Silhouette of the drag area of a plane in a dive. (B) Silhouette of the drag area of a plane in a slip.

There are two kinds of slips, the side slip and the forward slip. The difference is a matter of the path over the ground. The idea is the same for both.

Take a slip in general. The technique is to use aileron in the direction of slip. When aileron alone is used, adverse yaw occurs, as you know from experience by now. If you give it left aileron, the plane banks to the left and the nose yaws to the right. Stop the nose at the peak of its yaw with right rudder. Continue to hold left aileron and right rudder and whatever back pressure is needed to maintain glide speed. The more aileron and opposite rudder used, the steeper the slip, which means a steeper angle of descent (Fig. 13-21).

The steeper the slip, the more the airplane's path varies from the way the nose is pointing. Bank an airplane 15° and notice the difference between the forward slip and the side slip. *Remember, for a 15° bank the flight path of the airplane will vary from the way the nose is pointing by a certain number of degrees.* Assume, for instance, that in the case of a 15° bank the variation is 10° (Fig. 13-22).

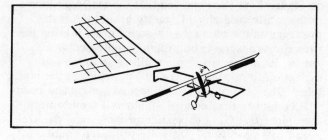

Fig. 13-21.

The forward slip is used to lose altitude while following your original flight path and is considered as a means of losing altitude faster without picking up excess speed, as would be done in a dive.

The side slip is normally used to correct for wind drift (as you will see later in crosswind landings) *or to change the flight path of the airplane as you increase the angle of descent.*

Right now let's discuss the forward slip. It's a handy maneuver in a forced landing. After you are able to do slips, the forced landing becomes a matter of picking a field, making a slightly high approach, and slipping into the field. If you try to hit the field right on the nose, make an error in judgment and undershoot, you can never get that altitude back and will hit short of the field. You can always lose altitude, so make the approach slightly high and slip off the excess altitude as you need to.

If there is a slight crosswind on the runway that you are slipping into, always slip into the wind. This

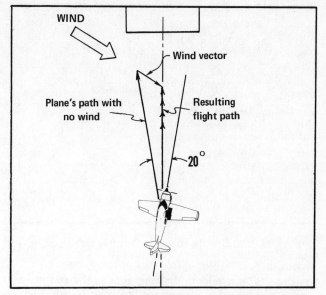

Fig. 13-23.

way you can make a slight side slip so that your path is straight down the runway. Say, for instance, that for a 30° banked slip the flight path is 20° from the nose. Just don't turn the nose so far from the wind (Fig. 13-23).

Also, it's easier to convert the forward slip to a side slip for wind drift correction on the landing (Fig. 13-24).

If you slipped to the right with a left crosswind, it would mean that it would be necessary in recovering to roll from a right bank to a left wing-down

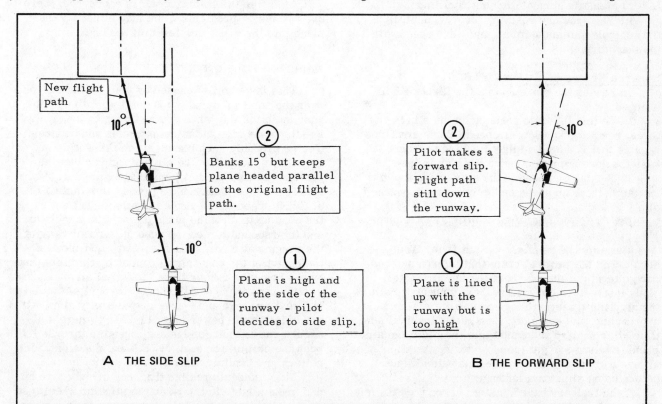

A THE SIDE SLIP   B THE FORWARD SLIP

Fig. 13-22.

95

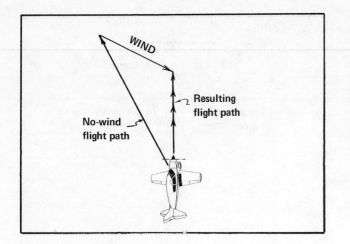

Fig. 13-24. The side slip as used to correct for wind drift on landing.

position. You would be drifting across the runway at a good clip by the time you got the wing lowered and drift correction set up.

A left slip means using left aileron. A right slip means the use of right aileron. The aileron is considered to be the main control in the slip, with the rudder used as an auxiliary.

Procedure
A Forward Slip to the Right from a Normal Glide
1. Right aileron is applied. As the nose yaws left, stop it at that position with left rudder. If added steepness of bank is needed, add more right aileron and left rudder.
2. Maintain normal glide pitch attitude.
3. When you are ready to recover, neutralize the controls and maintain normal glide speed with the elevators.

Common Errors in the Forward Slip
1. Yawing the plane so that the flight path is changed.
2. Letting the nose come up as the slip is entered, resulting in a low airspeed. Some airplanes require that you hold a slight forward pressure to keep the nose from coming up too high in the slip.
3. Picking up speed in the slip — nose too low.
4. Picking up speed on the recovery from the slip.
Don't slip too low, it takes altitude to recover.

The slip will be fairly hard at first. You've been taught for several hours that aileron and rudder go together and now have to "uncoordinate." Many instructors don't allow their students to slip the airplane if they are high on one of the first solo approaches, and some don't instruct slips until sometime after solo. You can get into trouble if the airplane is allowed to get too slow during the slip. It's always a good idea to practice at a safe altitude before using slips on a landing.

Some trainers have a static port only on the left side, as shown back in Figure 3-4. This can cause some errors of airspeed in slips. Take a good look

at Figure 3-4: You can see that the static pressure in the static tube should exactly cancel the static pressure in the pitot tube (it says here), leaving the dynamic pressure to be properly indicated as airspeed. In a forward slip, or side slip to the *left*, dynamic (or ram) pressure will be entering the static tube. The pressure in the airspeed instrument case will be higher than normal. This will tend to keep the diaphragm from expanding properly and the airspeed will read *low*. (Dynamic pressure coming in the wrong way tends to cancel out the "proper" dynamic pressure coming in the pitot tube.) In a slip to the right, a low pressure area tends to be formed on the left side of the airplane, *lowering that static pressure*, so that it doesn't "cancel" the static pressure in the pitot tube (and diaphragm). The airspeed indicator "thinks" that the airplane is going faster than it really is, and so reads *high*. The point is, if you rely on the airspeed indicator rather than the airplane's attitude, you may be too fast in the slip — and lose the benefit of the maneuver — or too slow — and have an abnormally high sink rate. Some airplanes have static ports on both sides, which system tends to cancel out static pressure problems.

RECOVERIES FROM BAD SITUATIONS DURING THE LANDING

As everyone knows, you will not always make perfect landings, so you will be shown the corrective procedure if you happen to foul up a little on an approach or landing.

As far as the landing itself is concerned, there are two major problems: You may either fly the plane into the ground or level off too high.

FLYING INTO THE GROUND

This is generally caused by your trying to look over the nose. Naturally you don't want to pull the nose up in the way when you're trying to look over it — the plane hits on the main wheels and bounces. You've probably seen planes hit on the wheels and go up 10 or 15 feet in the air and figured that the plane hit mighty hard to jump that high. Here's what happened. The plane hit the ground with quite a bit of flying speed left because the pilot hadn't gotten the nose up to slow the plane down. The wheels hit and the rebound forced the nose up suddenly, giving the wings added lift. The result was that most of the height of the bounce was caused by this lift — not by the bouncing rubber tires (tailwheel airplanes).

To recover, *ease* the nose over and, if the height is 5 feet or more and you've gotten pretty slow, it's a good idea to add power (Fig. 13-25). If there's not enough runway left for landing, open the throttle full, push the carburetor heat "OFF," and make another pattern and landing, and *this time don't bounce*.

Many students realize that they are about to hit and make a last ditch jerk on the stick or wheel just as the plane touches. This aggravates the situation considerably. It's also poor form to sit there doing

Fig. 13-25. The bounce recovery.

nothing after the bounce, with the plane pointed up and the airspeed dropping.

Most bounces are minor — maybe only a foot or so. If this is the case it's generally not necessary to add power; reland, making sure the plane has the correct landing attitude when it touches again.

Pilots have the problem of getting out of phase with the bounces, thus making matters worse. Even the tricycle-gear plane can produce a series of impressive actions when the pilot touches down on the nosewheel, yanks back on the wheel, and manages to be 180° out of phase with the airplane. . . . *Land again, making sure the airplane has the correct landing attitude when it touches.*

DROPPING THE PLANE IN

When the plane is stalled too high above the ground, the resulting back-bending maneuver is called "dropping it in."

A student flying his plane into the ground, to the accompanying anguished screams of the instructor, may go to such efforts to keep from repeating this mistake on his next landing that he "drops it in." This usually results in even louder cries from the instructor.

Dropping in is caused by the student's not knowing where the ground is. He is looking too close to the airplane and the ground is blurred. His depth perception is poor and he is perfectly happy landing 5 feet off the ground. Many an airport operator has wished for a runway jack as he sees his shiny new airplane being stalled several feet above the ground (Fig. 13-26).

More airplanes have been damaged by dropping in than by touching on the wheels and bouncing.

As soon as you realize that you and the runway have not made connections and the plane is stalling, *apply power!* You won't have room to completely recover, but the power may slow the descent enough to soften the impact and keep the plane from being damaged.

Another cause of dropping in is ballooning (coming back on the wheel too abruptly) during the transition and then not relaxing back pressure, thus letting the speed get too slow. Being too low on the approach while trying to stretch the glide is another cause. The student unconsciously pulls the nose up as he sees that it's going to be a pinch making the runway and, by the time he starts breaking the glide, the airspeed is very low (the angle of attack is very high) and he runs out of airspeed and inspiration before the airplane reaches the ground.

Fig. 13-26. Sometimes a runway jack is needed for the guy who keeps landing up in the air.

TOO LOW IN THE APPROACH

There'll be quite a few times during the pre-solo part of your flying when you'll misjudge the approach and realize the plane is going to hit short of the runway. Maybe it was caused by the downwind leg being too far out from the runway or because that first approach turn wasn't started soon enough or you chopped off all the power too soon. At any rate you're going to run out of altitude before reaching the runway. *Don't try to stretch the glide; power is needed.*

As soon as you realize that you are low, apply power. Don't wait until the plane is skimming over that cornfield a fourth of a mile from the runway before doing something about it.

Apply enough power to get to the runway and still maintain the normal approach speed. In applying the power you'll raise the nose slightly. A mistake some students make is forgetting to lower the nose again when they have the runway made and close the throttle. With the nose up and power off, the plane loses airspeed quickly and the end result is that the student drops the plane in.

Another mistake made by some students is to apply full power and fly the plane to the runway at about cruising speed and then wonder, when the power is chopped off, why the plane won't land but floats to the far end of the runway. The sad thing is that it happens all the time.

The sooner you recognize the fact that you are low and do something about it, the more credit you'll be given for judgment.

TOO HIGH IN THE APPROACH

On a hot summer day a light airplane will be affected by updrafts and may end up too high to land — or you may have flown the downwind leg too close to the runway. With your inexperience, the only thing to do is open the throttle and take it around. Again, the sooner you recognize this condition (called a *balked landing*) and do something about it, the more credit you'll be given for headwork.

Later, as you become proficient in slipping the plane (or using more flaps), you'll be able to land under conditions that now require a go-around.

Once you've decided to go around — do it! Use full power. Sometimes a student forgets this simple rule and staggers out at partial power, nearly causing heart failure for himself, the instructor, and any spectators present. Open the throttle all the way, get the carburetor heat "OFF" (if used), and get the flaps up, using the procedure recommended by your instructor. The instructor will be watching your reactions during the latter stages of pre-solo landing practice. He'll ask himself, "Can I trust this student to do the right thing if he bounces or comes in too high or too low on his first solo?" How you take action when action is needed will help him decide when you are ready to solo.

EMERGENCIES ON TAKE-OFF AND IN THE PATTERN

During take-off is the worst time to have an engine failure and the most likely time for it to happen. You are climbing out after an extra good take-off. Suddenly the engine starts kicking up and then quits cold. What now?

The worst possible move on your part would be to try to turn back to the runway. Sure, there's some pretty rough country right off the end of the runway. But you'll have a better chance for survival there than by trying to turn back to the field. Analyze what happens: The engine quits. The plane is in the climb attitude with no power. If you had time to think about it now, the situation would look like the first part of the normal power-off stall — and that's what it is. While you sit there, the airspeed is dropping fast. You realize what's happening and quickly whip the plane around to get back to the runway. A few seconds later you're sitting in a pile of junk wondering what happened. You gambled and lost. The plane was very slow, and when you turned it the speed was less than the stalling speed for that bank.

Experience has shown that an attempt to make a 180° turn to get back to the runway after engine failure on the climb-out is fraught with peril. It depends on the altitude at which the failure occurs, but statistics argue against trying to turn back. This doesn't mean that you have to just sit there when a shallow turn would let you miss that crockery factory. A rule of thumb for lightplanes is: Don't make 90° of turn at less than 200 feet and 45° of turn at less than 100 feet. You say, "I've been making 180° side approaches from 1000 feet in the traffic pattern, so what's this lower requirement idea?" When you made that 180° or those two 90° turns you were set in a normal glide with the nose down and plenty of airspeed. In the take-off emergency, you start with the nose up and sit there for a while before you realize what's happened. The 200 and 100 feet take this (and your probable nervousness and roughness in an actual emergency) into consideration.

Get the nose down as soon as possible after the engine failure and make as good a landing as possible under the conditions.

In case of a partial power failure on take-off, fly straight ahead and try to gain altitude without slowing the plane critically. Make all turns shallow. Don't try to turn back to the airport too soon. You're headed into the wind and, if the engine quits completely, will land at a much slower ground speed this way.

In any actual forced landing, once you are definitely committed, cut the ignition and master switches and fuel off before you land. This will lessen chances of fire after impact if things don't work out as you plan.

One problem found with students is that once they have opened the throttle for take-off they feel the take-off *must* be made. If you are rolling down the runway and things don't feel right to you (perhaps the engine doesn't sound like it should or the trim doesn't feel right), throttle back immediately and keep the airplane straight, hold the wheel back, use careful braking as necessary, and taxi back to find out what the problem is. Don't be afraid to abort a take-off.

Your instructor may cover the airspeed indicator during the pre-solo landing sessions to let you see that you can make safe approaches by checking the airplane's attitude and power combinations as you complete the pattern. It could be that sometime you may neglect to check the pitot tube during the preflight and discover after you've lifted off that it's not working — mud daubers built a home in there. Or maybe water had gotten in and froze when the airplane was pulled out of a warm hangar to subfreezing conditions. You'll find after demonstration and practice that making an approach and landing without an airspeed indicator isn't as bad as you imagined. Remember also, once you get to the point of transition to landing you won't be looking at the airspeed indicator, anyway.

The instructor also may include a pattern or two with the altimeter covered to allow you to estimate the various pattern altitudes.

CROSSWIND TAKE-OFFS AND LANDINGS

The wind may be directly down the runway on all of your pre-solo flying days. But the chances are slim that this will happen, so you'll doubtless get some instruction in crosswind landings during one of the pre-solo landing periods. At any rate, there'll be many times during your flying career when crosswind take-offs and landings must be made.

You already know how to correct for wind drift in the air and have had a chance to get some crosswind taxiing earlier, so you know how the wind affects the airplane both in the air and on the ground.

CROSSWIND TAKE-OFF

As a review, look at the diagram of a tailwheel airplane sitting crosswind on the ground (Fig. 13-27). Because all the weight is centered near the wheels and because the fin and rudder present a large area and the tail is light, the plane wants to weathercock, or turn into the wind. Since the points of friction (the wheels) are low, the plane also tends to "lean over." These two actions must be taken care of any time the plane is on the ground in a crosswind — the amount of compensation depends on the strength of the wind.

Procedure

The tricycle-gear airplane is lined up with the centerline of the runway as with a normal take-off. Assume in this case a moderate (8 K) crosswind is from the left. As you smoothly apply power, hold full left aileron and be prepared to use enough rudder to correct both for torque and the weathercocking tendency. The controls for both types will look like Figure 13-28.

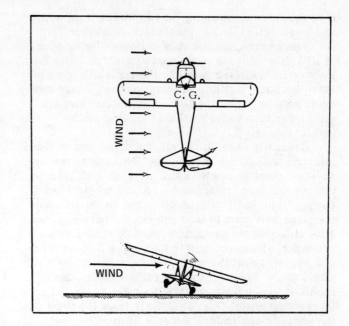

Fig. 13-27. The airplane tends not only to lean away from the wind but also to turn into it (weathercock).

If the wind is directly across the runway, the ailerons will be ineffective until the plane picks up speed. At low speeds, any effect you get from the aileron will be due to impact pressure and will be comparatively small.

As the plane picks up speed, the ailerons and rudder will become more and more effective and less control deflection will be needed.

If you ease the nosewheel off early, the tendency to turn to the left will be much greater than usual because not only have you lost the nosewheel steering and now must depend on the rudder alone, but also the nosewheel friction no longer fights the weathercocking tendency.

The tailwheel airplane should have the tail lifted slightly higher than normal and you should also be prepared to add even more right rudder than in a no-wind or no-crosswind condition. The tailwheel is free and its friction no longer opposes the wind's sidewise force. The tricycle-gear type, all other factors equal, has less tendency to weathercock during the early part of the run because of the greater weight on the (large) nosewheel. In a

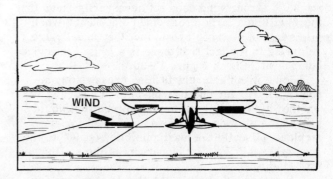

Fig. 13-28. Starting the crosswind take-off roll.

crosswind from the right, the two forces (torque and weathercocking) tend to counteract each other.

You want to make sure of sufficient flying speed at lift-off so that the plane doesn't start skipping. As soon as the plane gets into the air it will want to start drifting. If it hits the ground again, heavy side loads may be put on the landing gear. So raise the tail higher than usual and hold the plane on the ground longer.

Gradually ease off the aileron deflection as the ailerons become more effective. As soon as you are sure the plane is ready to fly, lift it off with definite, but not abrupt, back pressure. At the take-off point, there will be some aileron deflection to the left and the plane will start to bank slightly in that direction after it leaves the ground. Apply left rudder as well and make a balanced turn to the proper drift correction angle: Level the wings, then continue a normal climb (V_Y). Look back at the runway during the climbout to see that you have the right amount of crab (correction angle) (Fig. 13-29). Retract the flaps (and the gear, as applicable) at a safe altitude.

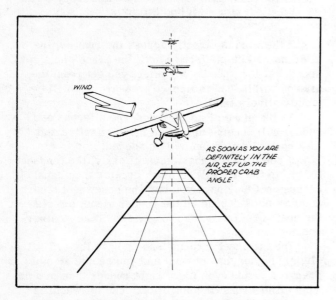

Fig. 13-29. The crosswind take-off.

You'll hear talk of "the crosswind component" from time to time. This is the component of the wind vector that is actually trying to push you sideways. A strong wind does not necessarily mean that there will be a large crosswind component. When pilots talk of a strong crosswind, they usually are referring to the fact that there is a large crosswind component. Check Figure 13-30.

Some manufacturers furnish crosswind component charts for their airplanes and you can find whether a particular runway wind condition would exceed the allowed crosswind component for your airplane. Usually the maximum cited (at 90° to the runway) is 0.2 V_{SO}, or 20 percent of the stall speed with landing flaps.

A crosswind slightly complicates matters for all legs of the traffic pattern. This is where the

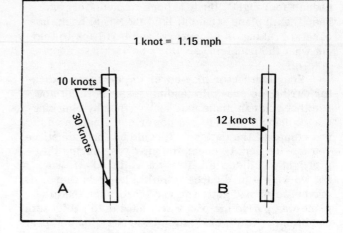

Fig. 13-30. (A) Although the wind has a velocity of 30 K, it has a crosswind component of only 10 K. (B) The wind velocity is 12 K, all of which is crosswind component.

rectangular course pays off (Fig. 13-31).

<u>Probable Errors</u>

1. Not enough aileron into the wind at the beginning.

2. Pulling the airplane off before it's ready to fly — letting the airplane skip and drift.

3. Holding too much aileron at the latter stages of the take-off so that the plane banks steeply into the wind as soon as the wheels leave the ground.

4. Not making a turn to set up a crab — holding the wing down and slipping after take-off.

5. Not looking back at the runway occasionally on climb-out — resulting in not flying in line with the runway.

CROSSWIND LANDING

You know that the plane must be headed straight down the runway when it lands, and in normal landings it was just a matter of keeping the nose straight and the wings level. It's a different proposition if there is a crosswind. If the nose is kept straight and wings level on final, the plane may drift completely away from the runway before you have a chance to land. Or, at best, it will land drifting across the runway and put heavy stresses on the landing gear.

The plane will tend to ground loop because not only are the forces of the impact at work, but the plane wants to weathercock as well (Fig. 13-32).

<u>Crab Method of Correction</u>

One way to correct for drift is to set up a crab on the final approach and then, just before the plane touches, skid it straight with the runway using the rudder. True, the crab will compensate for drift, but it requires no small amount of judgment to know when to straighten the plane. You've had the experience during normal landings of thinking you're about to touch down and then a thermal or ground effect holds the plane up for a good distance down the runway. The same thing can happen in a crab

100

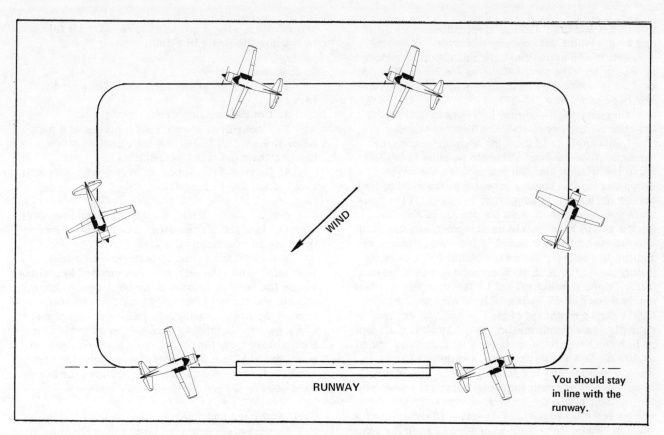

Fig. 13-31. The rectangular course as applied to the airport traffic pattern.

approach. You may straighten the plane out. It starts drifting again and there you sit — too little time to set another crab — so the plane lands drifting. For the next few seconds you're as busy as a one-eyed cat watching two mouse holes.

Another common error is not straightening the plane soon enough and landing while still in a crab. This doesn't do the landing gear any good, either. It's best, then, that the crab method be avoided at this point of experience.

Wing-Down Method

The simplest way for the student to make a crosswind landing is by the wing-down or slip correction method. This is accomplished by lowering the upwind wing and holding opposite or downwind rudder. When the plane is banked it wants to turn. The opposite rudder stops any turn and causes the plane to slip.

The procedure is this: As you roll out on final approach, lower the upwind wing the amount needed

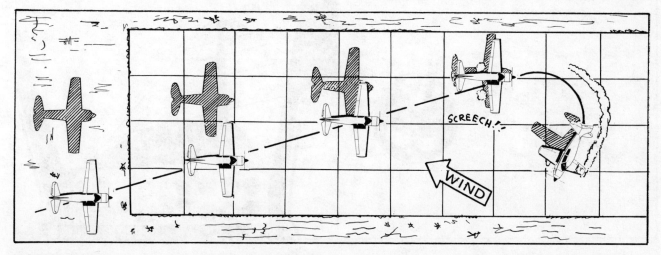

Fig. 13-32. *Hoping* that you'll touch down before the wind drifts you off the runway is no way to take care of a crosswind. A ground loop could result.

101

to correct for drift and apply opposite rudder to stop any turn. Watch for any signs of over- or under-correcting and adjust the bank and opposite rudder accordingly. *The lower the wing the more drift correction is being applied and the more opposite rudder is needed* (Fig. 13-33).

On gusty days you may be continually varying the bank as the crosswind's velocity changes.

Continue to hold the wing down as necessary throughout the landing. There's no need to try to raise the wing at the last second. As the plane slows during the landing process, more aileron and rudder deflection is necessary because (1) the controls are less effective as the speed lowers, and (2) the actual bank should be steeper since the ratio of wind speed to your speed is increasing (more correction is needed). As an example, if you were approaching at 100 K, a 10 K crosswind would mean a fairly minor correction, but by the time the airplane touches down at 50 K, the 10 K of wind would represent a high percentage of your speed. Of course, if your plane's normal stalling speed is 50 K you have no business approaching at such an excessive speed as 100 K. But it makes a good example. Land on the one main wheel and the tailwheel. The other main wheel will touch immediately after. After you are on the ground the controls are used in the same way as for the crosswind take-off — ailerons into the wind and opposite rudder as needed to keep the plane straight. Land the tricycle-gear plane on the one main wheel also. Ease the nosewheel down immediately after touchdown for effective ground steering in the crosswind. This method is so simple and effective that it is the most popular way of correcting for drift during the approach and landing.

As you are slipping, a slightly steeper glide results, but this is of no great significance.

The only time that slipping is used to correct for a crosswind is on the final approach and landing. After shooting crosswind landings some students

climb with a wing down after take-off. All this does is cut down the rate of climb.

Probable Errors

1. Letting the plane turn when the wing is lowered.
2. Not recognizing drift.
3. Mechanical corrections — putting the wing down at a certain angle and not changing it, even through the crosswind varies.
4. Getting so wrapped up in the drift correction that the landing is forgotten.

If you bounce during a crosswind landing, remember that the plane will start drifting. Lower the wing as you reland the plane.

The crosswind landing technique is a form of side slip. The side slip, you remember, is a slip where the nose is pointed at an object (say, for instance, the runway) and the plane slips to one side — toward the lowered wing. In this case, the plane's movement to the side is counteracted by the wind. If you overcorrected for drift or if there were no wind, the side slip idea would be evident. In strong winds the two methods may be combined (crab and wing down).

Crab Approach and Wing-Down Landing

You may like this idea better than the long slipping approach, which can be uncomfortable to both pilot and passengers.

As is shown in Figure 13-34, this technique is to set up the proper crab angle (it will have to change as the wind changes on the approach), and maintain a straight path over the ground by this method until the point of round-out is reached. The airplane is then lined up with the runway and the wing is lowered into the wind (and opposite rudder is used), as necessary, to correct for drift as the landing is completed. It takes time getting used to making the transition, but

Fig. 13-33. A crosswind approach as seen from behind the airplane and from the cockpit. The slipping resultant (R) compensates for the crosswind component. If you had time to check it, the needle in the turn and slip indicator would show no turn, but the ball would show a slip.

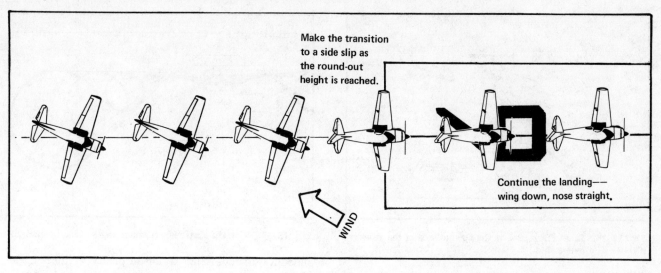

Make the transition to a side slip as the round-out height is reached.

Continue the landing—wing down, nose straight.

WIND

Fig. 13-34.

with practice you'll probably find this method more to your liking than the long wing-down final.

GUSTY AIR AND WIND GRADIENTS

If the velocity of the wind changes suddenly it can affect your airplane. Take a particular situation:

You know that it is possible to have different wind directions and velocities at different altitudes, so take a theoretical situation as is shown in Figure 13-35.

You are gliding at 70 K and the plane stalls at 50. Your speed in relation to the air is, of course, 70 K. But your speed in relation to the ground and to the calm wind is 70 minus 30, or 40 K. What happens as you suddenly fly into the area of calm air? The airspeed or speed relative to the calm air mass is only 40 K. The balance between lift and weight is broken (lift decreases suddenly) and the airplane accelerates downward, increasing the angle of attack to the point that the airplane stalls — which aggravates the situation.

The above illustration is exaggerated, but the principle applies on any gusty day. Many a pilot has been set for a landing on a gusty day and had the bottom drop out on him. He clambers from the wreckage

and wonders why the airplane "fell." It's not unusual to have fluctuations of plus or minus 10 K on the airspeed indicator during an approach.

If there are gusty winds, fly your approach 5-10 K faster than normal. That way you won't be in such a bind when the wind speeds kick back and forth.

If you hit sudden turbulence on an approach, apply power first and then ask, "Was that a shear area? Was the wind dropping or picking up?" The chances are that the plane won't stall, but you may find the airspeed low with the ground coming up fast.

WAKE TURBULENCE

Always be leery of taking off or landing close behind another plane. The bigger the plane, the more cautious you should be. Lightplanes always come out second best in a contest with an airliner's prop or jet-wash or wing tip vortices. If the wind is calm, wake turbulence may hang over the runway for several minutes — even after the plane has gone out of sight. If you *have* to take off or land behind another plane, get on the upwind side of him if there is a crosswind (Fig. 13-36). In light crosswinds one vortex may stay over the runway.

Better yet — don't take off for a while. Always be prepared for wake turbulence if the wind is calm and big planes have taken off in the last few minutes. Lightplane wake turbulence is bad enough, but airliners and heavy aircraft can set up a fatal crash for you.

The wing tip vortices are as shown in Figures 13-37 and 2-16, but not so well shown is the fact that the vortices descend after being formed, moving downward at 400-500 feet per minute, and tend to level off about 900 feet below the aircraft. Flying behind and below a large jet when it's clean and slow could cause big problems for you.

Read Appendix A, which covers information you should know about wake turbulence. Look it over carefully for some facts that could save your neck someday.

Don't fly directly behind a large aircraft or cross its flight path if you can avoid it. The

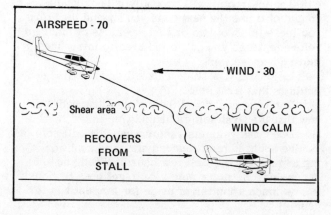

AIRSPEED - 70

WIND - 30

Shear area

WIND CALM

RECOVERS FROM STALL

Fig. 13-35.

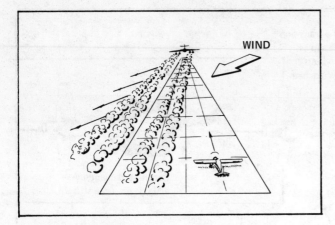

Fig. 13-36. Take off or land on the upwind side of the runway if there is a crosswind.

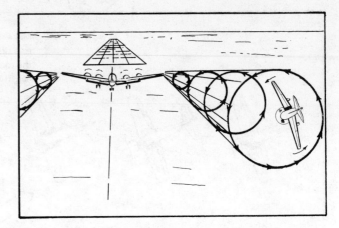

Fig. 13-37. Wing tip vortices are much worse than propwash.

turbulence may cause load factors so great as to cause structural failure of your plane.

Again, don't be proud — take it around if you think there'll be wake turbulence on landing. Wait a while longer before taking off if you're in doubt. (Don't sit on the runway — taxi out of the way.)

SOLO

When you are able to make good take-offs and landings and use good judgment in your flying — then you will solo. By this time you should have your medical certificate and student pilot certificate and have passed a brief quiz on Federal Aviation Regulations, Parts 61 and 91, and your airplane and the local traffic rules.

Students, particularly in group training programs, get anxious to solo. (Joe Doe soloes in 10 hours, how come I have 12 hours and still haven't?) Don't worry, maybe Joe's 6-hour slump wasn't as pronounced as yours or maybe he didn't have one. Very few students solo without hitting a slump somewhere along the line. It hits a large number of students at about the 6-hour point — and oddly enough it's called a 6-hour slump.

Usually it strikes after you've had an hour or two in the pattern and had a good first period of shooting landings. You feel pretty good and are all set to get these landings down pat and solo earlier than that Horace Numbskull who thinks he's such a hot pilot. Things don't go too well, and suddenly you can't find the ground with both hands. You're right in the middle of the 6-hour slump and you feel lower than a whale's stomach.

You go on shooting landings and it seems for a couple of hours that absolutely no progress is being made. Then suddenly one day you start landing like a pro — the instructor gets out — and you solo.

The instructor will tell you that the plane will get off quicker, climb better, and want to stay up longer without him — and so it will. You'll be so busy flying the plane that you won't notice that the other seat is empty. The first solo is the point where you

suddenly discover that flying is pretty wonderful; when you get down and receive the congratulations of the people in the airport office, you're standing about a mile high.

The procedure for solo will generally be this: The instructor will get out and you'll shoot one landing and taxi back to where he's standing. He may wave you on or stop you to discuss points of the solo take-off and landing. In most cases you'll shoot three landings — for this reason: If you shoot one and then lay off for a few days you'll probably start thinking, "That one good landing could have been luck. . . ." If you shoot three you'll know it wasn't luck and won't talk yourself into a state of nervousness before the next solo flight.

Students sometimes worry about what the instructor will think if they have to take it around on that first solo approach. Traffic may require that you have to make a go-around during one or more of the first-solo approaches. So what? More than one first-solo student has had to circle while somebody else makes an approach and landing. So don't worry about it. The instructor demonstrated, and you've practiced this enough, so that you'll know what to do. The main thing is to not talk yourself into a dither if you have to go around. The instructor will think it good judgment on your part, even if you lean to the cautious side. There will be plenty of times during your flying career when you'll have to take an airplane around, so do it now, as necessary.

The instructor will probably ride around a couple of times the next time you fly and then turn you loose to shoot two or three periods of landings before he takes you out to the area to introduce more advanced work.

Incidentally, a student usually makes his best landings that first solo.

Don't get cocky and think you've learned it all now that the first solo is behind you.

Don't ask your instructor when you will solo. You've bounced him, jounced him, and kept him chewing aspirin for the past few hours. When you are ready, he'll be *more than glad* to get out. Seriously, it's as much a matter of pride for him as it is for you.

14. Advanced Stalls

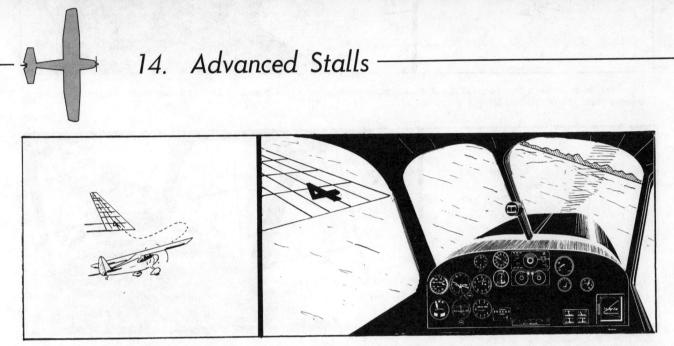

Fig. 14-1. Pilot sees that he will fly past runway if rate of turn is not increased.

CROSS-CONTROL STALL

This stall is a perfect illustration of the dangers of abusing the controls. A typical case of a cross-control stall accident is this: A pilot sees in the turn onto final that it will require a sharper turn to line up with the runway. He's always been told the dangers of banking too steeply at low altitude, so to avoid this and still make the turn, he does something much worse.

A small voice inside says, "Go on, use rudder, skid it around and you won't have to bank it."

So the pilot skids it. As you know full well, when a plane is skidded, the outside wing speeds up, gets more lift than the inside one, and the plane starts to increase its bank. The pilot realizes this and unconsciously holds aileron against the turn. The down aileron on the inside of the turn helps drag that wing back more, slowing it up and decreasing the lift, which requires more aileron to hold it up—

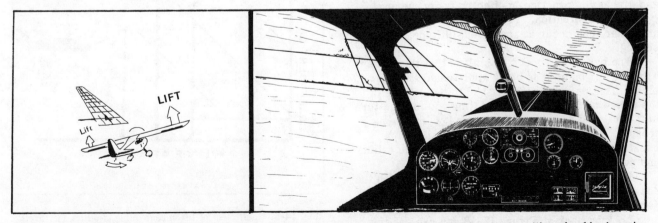

Fig. 14-2. He doesn't want to make a steep bank at low altitude. He knows that stalling speed increases with angle of bank, so he uses rudder to cheat a little. Lift is greater on the outside wing because of its increased speed. The bank starts to increase because of difference in lift. Pilot doesn't want bank any steeper so opposite aileron is applied.

Fig. 14-3. Nose tends to drop because of rudder and aileron, so up-elevator is added. Down aileron drags wing back causing a steeper bank. More opposite aileron is applied, etc.

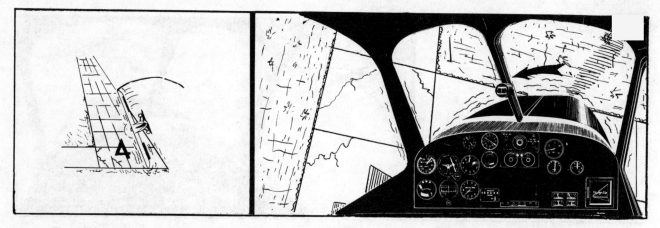

Fig. 14-4. Inside wing stalls and plane rotates abruptly toward low wing. The altitude is insufficient for recovery.

and so the cycle goes. As the plane is banked, use of bottom rudder and opposite aileron will tend to cause the nose to drop. The pilot helpfully holds more back pressure to keep the nose up. This, then, is the perfect setup for one wing to stall before the other. Figures 14-1 through 14-4 show the maneuver as seen from outside the airplane and from the cockpit.

The practice cross-control stall is aimed at teaching you to recognize how such a stall occurs and giving you practice in effectively recovering from such a situation. The cross-control stall, like any other, can occur at any speed, altitude, or power setting.

The bad thing about this stall is that the forces working on you as it is being approached are "normal." That is, you'll feel pushed to the outside of the turn — as is the case every time you make a turn in a car — and so may not be warned of impending trouble. The slipping type stalls (over the top) usually have people scrambling around in the cabin and putting things to rights.

Figure 14-5 shows why the inside wing (with the down aileron) tends to stall first, when by "common sense" the down aileron should hold that wing up.

Looking back at Figure 12-12 you can see the effect on the coefficient of lift curve of extended flaps. Down ailerons will give the same general

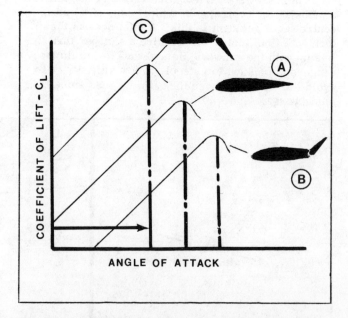

Fig. 14-5. Coefficient of lift versus angle of attack for three conditions: (A) Airfoil with no aileron or flap deflection, (B) the right wing (aileron up), and (C) the left wing (aileron down).

effect (although they're farther out on the wing). The up aileron (B) in Figure 14-5 gives the effect of the wing being twisted to a lower angle of incidence.

As you increase the angle of attack, as indicated by the arrow, the inside wing with the down aileron (C) will reach its "break" first and will stall. The question comes up: Shouldn't there be more lift on that wing and therefore no stall? By his bizarre arrangement of the controls to stop the airplane from rolling into a steeper bank, the pilot is assuring that the actual lift of each wing (in pounds) is equal to the other. And, since angle of attack is the only criterion of the stall, that inside wing goes first.

PROCEDURE—POWER OFF

1. This is a turning stall, so the clearing turns are not necessary. Keep looking around during the stall.

2. Pull the carburetor heat "ON" and make a shallow gliding turn. (The direction of turn will be left up to you — practice them in both directions.)

3. Gradually apply more and more inside rudder to "cheat" on the turn.

4. Use opposite aileron as necessary to keep the bank from increasing.

5. Keep the nose up by increasing back pressure.

6. When the break occurs, neutralize the ailerons. Stop any further rotation with opposite rudder. Relax back pressure.

7. Roll out of the bank with coordinated controls.

The rotation is so fast that it is quite possible that the bank will be vertical or past vertical before it is stopped. Because of the great difference in the lift of the wings at the point of stall, a rolling moment is produced.

In many ways, the recovery from this stall is close to the recovery from a spin. The wings' lift must be made equal. This is done by neutralizing the ailerons and stopping further rotation with rudder *at the same time* as the back pressure is released. The neutralizing of the ailerons speeds the equalizing of lift.

Because of the low position of the nose when the rotation is stopped, the speed will build up quickly. Recover to straight, level flight with coordinated controls as soon as possible, without overstressing the plane or getting a secondary stall.

COMMON ERRORS

1. Not neutralizing the ailerons at start of the recovery.

2. Using too much opposite (top) rudder to stop rotation, causing the plane to slip badly during the recovery.

3. Waiting too long to roll out with coordinated controls; too great an altitude loss.

Cross-control stalls, as such, are not required on the private flight test but were included here to show the hazards of trying to "cut corners" and the effects of neglecting coordination at critical times.

ACCELERATED STALLS

The accelerated stall is a maneuver for proving that the stall is a matter of angle of attack, not speed. The accelerated stall is to be started no higher than 1.25 times the normal stalling speed because of extra stresses that may be put on the plane by stalling at higher speeds. The term "accelerated" means that the airplane is under forces of acceleration or "g" forces when the stall occurs.

Chapter 9 (THE TURN) introduced the expression "load factor." In the 60° banked turn (constant altitude) the load factor was 2, or the airplane was subjected to 2 "g's." As far as the wings were concerned the airplane weighed twice as much, and by working out the math it was shown that the stall speed was increased by the square root of the load factor, which turned out to be a figure of 1.414. In the 60° banked turn the airplane stalled at a speed over 41 percent higher than normal stall speed. The same increase in stall speed effect would have occurred if instead you had loaded the plane to *twice* its normal weight and done an old-fashioned straight-ahead stall. (Don't load it that way!)

The pilot in Figure 14-6 can't understand why he's getting evidences of a stall when the airspeed is so high. (In a 60° banked level turn the stall speed is increased by a factor of 1.414, from 62 to 88 K. He's feeling a load factor of 2 g's.)

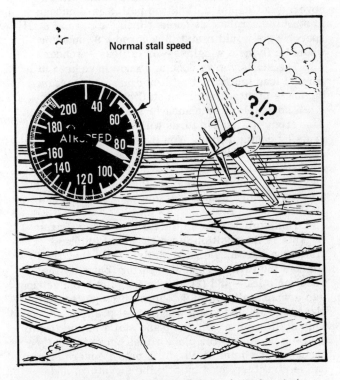

Fig. 14-6. The stall is a function of angle of attack, not airspeed. This pilot is learning that the load factor is 2 g's and the stall speed in a 60° banked level turn is 1.414 times that of normal 1 g flight.

You can also encounter positive acceleration forces when pulling up from dives or brisk pull-ups from straight and level — acceleration doesn't just happen in a turn, although in everyday flight this is the most likely place to meet it. Of course, you could run into strong negative acceleration forces (or negative g's) if you were to shove the wheel forward abruptly at high speeds. (Don't do *that* either!) You've been used to thinking of acceleration in terms of increasing speed — this is not the type of acceleration of interest here.

Your elevators are not only the airspeed control but are also your "g" control. By rapidly pulling back on the wheel or stick, positive g forces are created. (They may be too positive at speeds well above the stall and problems could result.) Pulling back abruptly means that excess lift is temporarily in existence. The airplane will start slowing immediately to reestablish the old lift value (*the airplane always tends to remain in equilibrium as far as lift and weight are concerned*). You may, however, exceed the airplane's limit load factor (maximum allowed g's) before the airplane has a chance to slow and equilibrium can be established. Normal category airplanes are required to have a maximum limit load factor of 3.8 positive and 1.52 negative g's. Utility category planes have limit load factors of 4.4 positive and 1.76 negative g's. Your trainer will fall into one of these two categories. If you pulled hard enough to stall the airplane at twice normal stall speed, you'd pull 4 g's (2 squared is $2 \times 2 = 4$ g's). And this would be over the limit for a normal category airplane. (A more complete explanation of the various category requirements will be covered in Chapter 23.) If you pulled hard enough to stall the airplane at *three* times the normal stall speed, 9 g's would result (3 squared = 9), and you would be flying a wingless — or tailless — wonder.

The stalls you've done up to now have been at a normal load factor of 1 g. You *gradually* increased the angle of attack until the stall occurred.

The accelerated maneuver stalls will best be done from 45° banked turns with reduced power in cruising configuration. You'll increase the angle of attack smoothly in a level or slightly climbing turn until the stall occurs just above the normal stalling speed. Don't start increasing the angle of attack at a speed of more than 25 percent above the normal stall speed.

This stall is done in the turn for two reasons: (1) This is the position in which most lightplane pilots run into accelerated stalls — when they try to "tighten the turn" by rapidly pulling back on the wheel or stick — and (2) to keep the pilot from getting into a whip stall, as might happen if he pulled the plane sharply up from a wings-level position. A whip stall occurs when the plane stalls in a vertical nose-up position — the plane slides backward before recovery can be effected. This puts a severe strain on the structure, particularly the elevators, and could cause structural failure. If the plane is banked, the position of the center of gravity and the effects of the fin and rudder wouldn't allow the plane to get into

such a predicament; the nose will fall to one side.

The stall break and recovery is fundamentally the same as the turning departure and approach stalls. The high wing will generally stall first unless you are skidding. Release back pressure and, after the recovery is started, return the plane to level flight with coordinated controls. The check pilot may want you to recover (1) as soon as you recognize the stall and (2) after the stall develops and the nose falls down through the horizon.

In (1) the recovery can be simple and quick. Relaxing the back pressure at the right time will cause the plane to recover in straight and level flight if the high wing stalled first and you can effect a recovery just as the wings roll level.

In (2) the plane may have rolled over into a bank in the opposite direction and the nose will be low. Recover from the stall, *then* bring the plane to wings-level flight. Too many students try to do everything at once, in this case, and end up stalled again. The check pilot is very unhappy — and so is the student, when the flight is over.

Bring the wheel back smoothly. Don't jerk the wheel back and put a lot of unnecessary stress on the plane. You will be expected to be able to recover from the accelerated stall both with and without application of power. Use power to recover unless specifically asked not to.

PROCEDURE

1. At reduced power in cruise configuration make a turn with about 45° of bank. Slow the airplane to 25 percent above normal power-off stall speed by slowly increasing the back pressure.
2. When a speed of less than 25 percent above normal stall is reached, increase the back pressure rapidly but smoothly until the stall occurs.
3. Release back pressure, open the throttle, and recover to straight and level flight using coordinated controls. Also practice recoveries without use of power.

On the flight test you may be asked to set up the 45° bank and *gradually* slow the airplane up at a constant altitude or a moderate rate of climb until the stall occurs.

COMMON ERRORS

1. Jerking the wheel back — putting too much stress on the plane.
2. The other extreme — too slow in applying back pressure so that the stall isn't an accelerated one.
3. Too brisk a forward pressure on recovery so that negative load factors are applied.

STABILATOR OR ELEVATOR TRIM TAB STALL

When the elevator trim tab was discussed in Chapter 8 it was noted that the elevator trim tab or the stabilator trim could get you into trouble under certain conditions.

The combination of high power setting and full nose-up elevator — or stabilator — trim can result in a tendency for the airplane to assume some pretty impressive nose-up attitudes. (These spectacular reactions are most likely to occur accidentally close to the ground.)

You saw the effects of power when you were first practicing recoveries to level flight from a glide. The nose wanted to rise as cruise power was applied and it took a definite concentration on your part to keep it down where it belonged. You had the plane trimmed for level flight those times; picture the situation if you had been using *full power* as would be done on a take-off or a go-around with the trim in the *full nose-up* condition. Add to these problems outside distractions — plus the fact that you are at a low altitude — and you have a bad combination.

The instructor will demonstrate this stall at a safe altitude, as is done for all the other stalls. The conditions will be set up and he will apply full power and probably keep his hands off the wheel to show you what the plane will do. (You guessed it; the nose will claw upward and the stall break, when it comes, will most likely be to the left because of torque effects.)

You'll then get a chance to practice recovering before things get out of hand. The main idea is to keep that nose down. For most light trainers the nose can be held down without too much trouble. The hazard is in the surprise associated with an actual situation. Practicing these stalls will give you quick recognition of the problem and the best means of recovery for your particular airplane and the following will generally apply:

1. *Recognize the problem immediately* (improper trim).

2. *Get the nose down to no higher than the normal climb position with whatever forward pressure is needed*. Then get the trim back to neutral as soon as it is practicable. If the forward pressure required is so strong as to require both hands on the wheel, keep them there and climb to a safe altitude before trying to get on the trim. Then you can use one hand intermittently to get the trim squared away.

3. *Do not chop the power after the nose has risen*. You'll be too low to clear the problem and add power again. If the situation has progressed, the chopping of power could cause an immediate stall.

EXCESSIVE TOP-RUDDER STALL

Rough usage of the controls during a slip is a good way to discover the excessive top-rudder stall. By using excessive top rudder in a slip or turn, the high wing is stalled and the stall is quite similar to the departure and approach stalls. As you remember, in these stalls the high wing stalled first because the plane started slipping and part of that wing's airflow was disturbed or blanked out. In the excessive top-rudder stall you speed up the process by holding top rudder and causing the plane to slip. The high wing drops a little faster because of this "help," but the recovery is the same as for the departure or approach stall, or any stall, for that matter. Relax back pressure as you apply coordinated control pressure to return to straight and level flight.

EXCESSIVE BOTTOM-RUDDER STALL

This one is close to the cross-control stall except that in the turn rudder alone is used to stall the low wing. You skid the plane as back pressure is increased and the high wing has more lift, so that when the plane stalls the low wing is the first to go. Recovery is standard. Relax the back pressure as you stop further rotation with the rudder and return to level flight by coordinated control usage.

GENERAL TALK ABOUT STALLS

By now you should realize that the plane can be stalled flying straight down or straight up. You can make the high wing or low wing stall in a turn. You see that one thing has remained true in all stall recoveries — *get the air flowing smoothly over the wing*. This may mean relaxing the back pressure in a lightplane or a brisk forward movement of the stick or wheel in a heavy plane.

The problem with any stall is that at the break the nose pitches down and your instinct is to hold back on the stick or wheel to bring it back up. At low altitudes in an inadvertent stall this is even more the case. It may take some doing to move the control wheel or stick forward to recover from the stall. (You'll have to move the wheel back again to stop loss of altitude; but don't get a secondary stall.)

By the time you finish these advanced stalls you'll know a great deal more about the airplane and will be confident in your ability to fly it.

15. Emergency Flying by Reference to Instruments

BACKGROUND

The idea of giving student pilots emergency instrument instruction was debated in aviation circles for several years before the ruling was made. Some argued that "a *little* knowledge is a dangerous thing," and felt that the student or private pilot might get just enough confidence in his instrument flying ability to attempt to fly in marginal weather. Others said that it was up to the individual. Some might try it, but many more lives would be saved by this training than would be lost by student overconfidence.

These maneuvers are emergency maneuvers like the low- and high-altitude emergencies and simulated engine failure on take-off. You would not deliberately cut the ignition to practice these emergencies nor would you deliberately fly into conditions where flying by reference to instruments is necessary.

In requiring this training the FAA still does not authorize instrument flying by anyone other than a properly rated instrument pilot. If you accidentally fly into a control area or control zone when the weather is below visual flight minimums, the FAA will be interested in talking to you, since you would be a collision hazard for airplanes on authorized instrument flight.

Flying under actual instrument conditions is quite different from simulated instrument flying. If you foul up during the practice sessions you can always pull the hood up and recover by looking out (if the instructor hasn't already recovered for you). "Practicing" actual instrument flying is like "practicing" actual parachuting. There's no practice about it — it must be done correctly each time. As the Navy would say, "This is no drill!"

To insure that you have a good grasp of emergency instrument flying you will get instruction on the following items:

1. Recovery from the start of a power-on spiral.
2. Recovery from the approach to a climbing stall.
3. Normal turns of 180° duration left and right to within 20° of a proper 180° heading.
4. Shallow climbing turns to a predetermined altitude.
5. Shallow descending turns at reduced power to a predetermined altitude.

6. Straight and level flight.

These will probably be introduced and practiced as definite exercises during the dual flights of the second or post-solo phase of the syllabus. A portion of each dual period will be spent on the above requirements as well as the strictly visual flight maneuvers as covered in Chapters 14, 16, 17, and 18.

One thing will be stressed at all times. *Fly the airplane in exactly the same manner as in normal flight. There are no gimmicks, short cuts, or special techniques. The instruments "see" the plane's attitude and give you the information.* Instrument practice is to teach you to interpret the information given by the instruments and to make the plane respond in the desired manner by use of the indications.

The six maneuvers are based on the premise that you have just flown into worsening weather conditions and suddenly the ground has disappeared and there's nothing left but a gray mist. Which way is up? Or down? Even though for the first few seconds the plane may continue flying straight and level, your body may want to lie to you. The balance center in the middle ear may get a bum signal. (It's surprising how much that balance depends on sight.) You are *convinced* that the plane is in a left-climbing turn or right-diving turn or any other maneuver that may strike your fancy at the moment. The number of flying hours has no bearing on a pilot's ability to fly the plane by "feel" alone. *No pilot can do it.*

Nearly all trainers used today have a full panel of flight instruments as shown in Figure 15-1, but for training purposes, some of the explanations will also assume that a heading indicator and attitude indicator are not available. *Coordinated use of the ailerons and rudder is needed, as always, and the turn indicator and ball should be thought of as working together.* The wheel and throttle will also be coordinated throughout these maneuvers. Again, if the plane you are using for training has an A/I and a H/I, you would use them in all of the following maneuvers.

RECOVERY FROM A POWER-ON SPIRAL

The power-on spiral is probably the most common result of trying to fly the plane under instrument conditions without proper training and/or instrumentation.

Many fatalities have been caused by pilots entering this flight condition when visual references are lost. The plane picks up speed rapidly in the diving turn; the pilot sees the airspeed increasing and tries to stop the descent by increasing back pressure — which actually tightens the turn and makes the situation worse. Two things usually happen with this type of recovery attempt: (1) The plane strikes the ground while still in the spiral or (2) it comes apart in the air due to the high stresses imposed by the excessive back pressure (which, as you know, causes a high load factor). The maneuver is aptly named the "Graveyard Spiral."

You learned in the "720° Power Turn" that if the nose started dropping in the steep turn there was little use in trying to bring it up by back pressure. The situation was generally made worse instead of better. The bank had to be shallowed to stop the loss of altitude.

The bank in the power-on spiral under actual conditions may be approaching vertical. The "basic" instruments would indicate as follows in the power-on spiral (Fig. 15-1):

1. Turn and slip (T/S) or turn coordinator (T/C) indicator — shows a great rate of turn, ball may or may not be centered. It is shown as not centered in the diagram; and knowing the effects of the offset fin at higher speeds, it is more likely to be to the left because of right yaw effects. See "Torque," Chapter 2.

2. Airspeed — high and increasing.

3. Altimeter — showing a rapid loss of altitude.

RECOVERY (BASIC INSTRUMENTS)

To recover from the condition as effectively as possible, do the following:

1. Center the turn indicator and ball through coordinated use of ailerons and rudder. If the needle or small airplane is to the right, apply left rudder and aileron until the indicator is centered.

This coordination is necessary because through harsh application of top rudder the turn might be stopped (the needle centered) and the plane may stay in the bank, with the result that back pressure would still put stresses on the plane with little action toward recovery. A glance at the ball, however, would immediately show the imbalance.

2. Check the airspeed. As you roll out of the bank apply back pressure (easy!) to stop the increasing airspeed. A rough approximation is that in a spiral or dive recovery, at the instant the airspeed

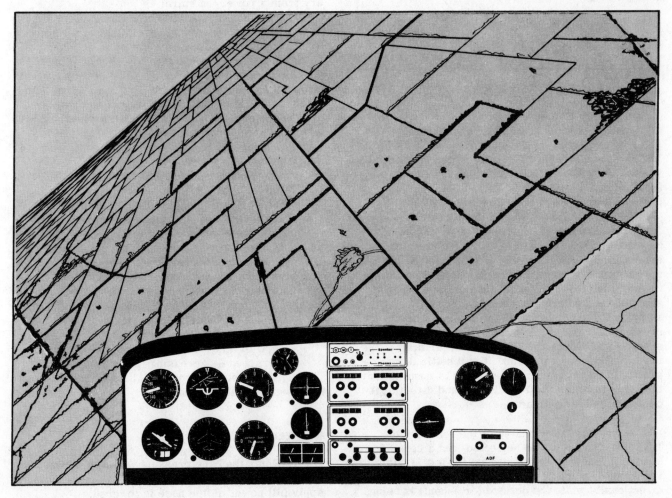

Fig. 15-1. A diving spiral to the right.

111

starts to decrease, the plane's nose is in the level flight attitude. When this is indicated, ease on forward pressure so that the nose is not pulled up into a steep climb or stall attitude. As the plane returns to steady, straight and level flight, the airspeed will continue to decrease until the cruise speed is attained (assuming the power is at cruise setting).

The reason for applying back pressure only until the airspeed shows the change is that in trying to go any further toward recovery by watching the airspeed you may get the result shown in Figure 15-2. The nose will want to continue up past the level flight position because of the excess speed of the dive; forward pressure is needed to stop this.

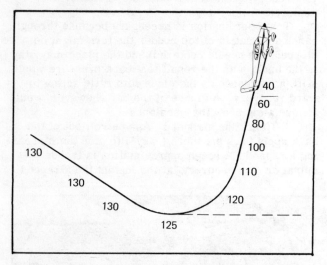

Fig. 15-2. Don't chase the airspeed.

In the 130 K dive of the illustration the plane has a lot of energy to dissipate. If you pull the nose up (remembering that there's no outside visibility) or let the nose come up until cruise speed is reached, you will find that the attitude is quite nose high and the airspeed drops rapidly to the stall, requiring forward pressure, or a stall recovery.

3. The third main step in the recovery is to "stop the altimeter." This is the finer adjustment to be made immediately after getting the plane to the approximate level flight attitude through use of the airspeed indicator. Little attention will be paid to the altitude of leveling other than recovering as smoothly and quickly as possible. You will find that stopping the altimeter, with the power setting at cruise, will result in a stable cruise airspeed in a short while. Check the airspeed in your scan of the instruments, but realize that it will settle down shortly of its own accord. Don't try to rush it. After the plane is under control, altitude and directional adjustments may be made.

During the latter phases of the recovery the T/C or T/S must not be neglected, and a constant scan of all instruments is needed for a safe, firm recovery. The plane must be kept under control directionally while the descent (or ascent) is being controlled or stopped.

You will note that nothing was mentioned about heading in this case. It doesn't matter. Recover from the spiral, let the compass settle down, and make a timed turn back toward the good weather area. Timed turns will be discussed later in this chapter.

One important thing should be mentioned. As you know, the fixed-pitch prop will windmill in a dive and the engine will overspeed. It is better if you throttle back at the start of the spiral recovery to avoid this abuse of the engine.

SUMMARY OF THE POWER-ON SPIRAL RECOVERY

1. Power retarded.
2. Center the T/C or T/S.
3. Start back pressure smoothly. Check airspeed for first indication of a change. Stop the back pressure.
4. Stop the altimeter.
5. Maintain the instrument scan throughout the recovery.
6. When the plane is under control make adjustments in power, altitude, and direction as needed.

Figure 15-3 shows the steps used in the recovery from a power-on spiral.

You should know how to effect a recovery by use of the basic instruments shown in Figure 15-3, but will, in most cases, have the use of an attitude indicator. (Of course, you could have tumbled it with your outrageous maneuverings while getting into this situation.) Figure 15-4 shows that the attitude indicator can be used to level the wings and bring the nose up to level flight. You would readjust the power as the airspeed approaches the cruise value.

RECOVERY FROM THE APPROACH TO A CLIMBING STALL

The climbing stall sometimes occurs when visual references are lost, or it may be a result of letting the nose rise too high in the spiral recovery. In either case the recovery technique is the same. You have had a chance to practice stalls visually, as well as noting the instruments during the maneuver.

As a review, check the indications as the stall is approached (at cruising power).

1. T/C or T/S — may or may not be centered.
2. Airspeed — decreasing (probably rapidly).
3. Altimeter — increasing altitude, or steady in last stage of stall approach.

RECOVERY

1. Relax the back pressure (or push forward if necessary) until the airspeed starts to increase. Apply full power as the nose is lowered.
2. Center the T/C or T/S.

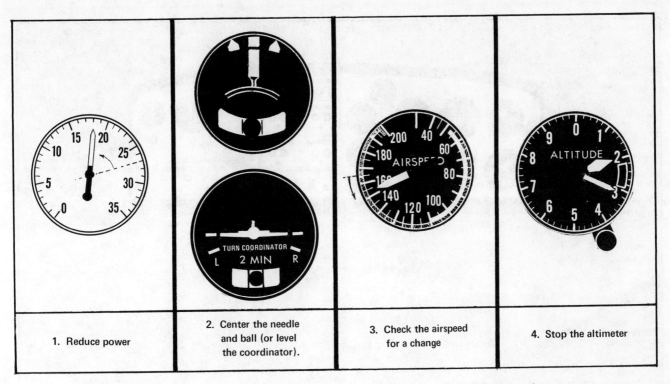

| 1. Reduce power | 2. Center the needle and ball (or level the coordinator). | 3. Check the airspeed for a change | 4. Stop the altimeter |

Fig. 15-3. The steps in recovery from a power-on spiral, using the basic instruments.

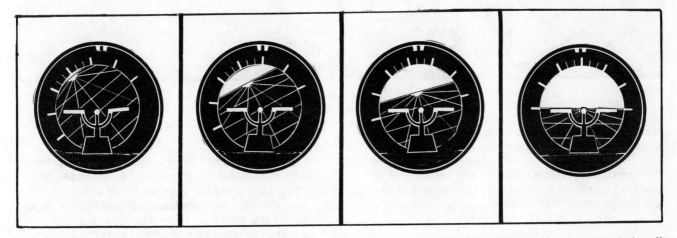

Fig. 15-4. The attitude indicator gives a better picture of the spiral situation. You would retard the power, then simultaneously roll out as you bring the nose up to the level flight attitude.

3. Use the altimeter to level off. Lose a minimum of altitude but don't get a secondary stall.

4. Maintain the instrument scan throughout the recovery. Keep the T/C or T/S centered.

5. After recovery to cruising flight is made, make power, altitude, and directional adjustments as needed.

Use of the airspeed for recovery from an approach to a stall follows the same general idea as that in the spiral. In this case, however, the airspeed starts *increasing* when the attitude of the plane is approximately level. To be on the safe side, this point should be passed so that the plane will be in a slightly nose-down attitude to insure a definite recovery. This is more important when the stall breaks than in an approach where the plane still has some flying speed.

You will notice that in the case of the stall recovery the primary need is to get the airspeed back into a safe range, and any deviation in direction can be corrected after the recovery is made.

Again, the use of the attitude indicator makes things much easier; you can simultaneously lower the nose as the wings are leveled. If you are sure the attitude indicator is working properly, the following would apply:

1. Relax back pressure as full power is applied.

2. Ease the nose down (leveling the wings) to a pitch attitude below level flight.

3. As the airspeed approaches cruise value,

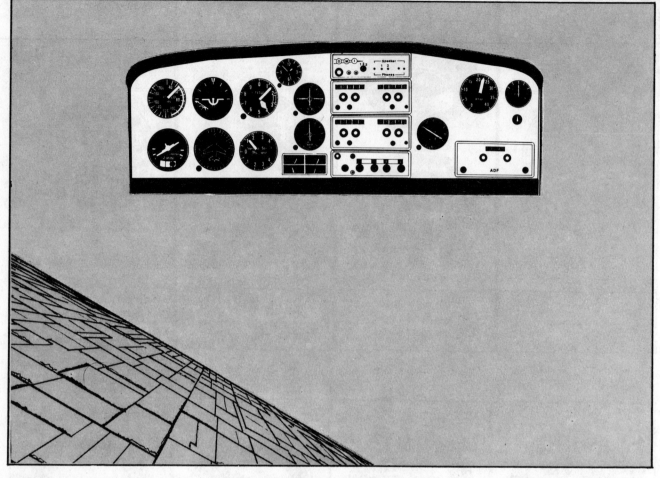

Fig. 15-5. Approach to a climbing stall.

ease the nose up to level, readjust power, and make altitude and heading corrections as necessary.

The reason for the lowering of the nose below the normal level flight attitude is to assure that no new stall is encountered by trying to stop it at the level flight attitude (Fig. 15-6).

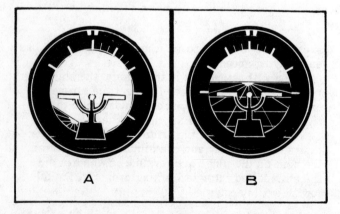

Fig. 15-6. (A) The attitude indicator shows that the airplane is in a nose-high left turn. (B) Level the wings and ease the nose below the normal level flight attitude until the airspeed approaches the normal cruise. Then bring the nose to the level position and adjust power.

180° TURN

You had a chance to practice turns with reference to instruments during the pre-solo phase and will now have a chance to make turns using the T/C or turn and slip, airspeed, and altimeter as well as using the full panel for these maneuvers.

A heading indicator makes 180° turns (or any turn) simple (Fig. 15-7); just turn and roll out when the H/I reads correctly. (Your problem with the older type of instrument may be figuring out just *what* heading is 180° from the present one.)

TIMED TURN—RECOMMENDED METHOD

The recommended method of making a 180° turn, if you don't have a good heading indicator, is by timing the entire turn using the T/C or T/S (and, of course, your airspeed and altimeter). One advantage here is that the turns may be made in either direction without the necessity of making separate calculations for each direction. Another advantage is that you can merely set up a standard-rate turn and hold it for 60 seconds. A timepiece is needed.

Test programs showed that students had trouble with the timed turn in that they would forget the time the turn started. One other thing that may bother

Fig. 15-7. With the newer type heading indicators, finding your reciprocal heading and turning to it is easy. Other methods of turning will be discussed, anyway.

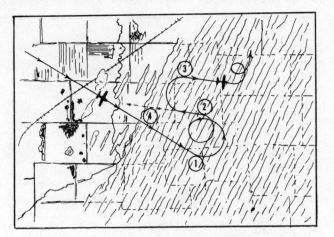

Fig. 15-8. (1) A power-on spiral is accidentally entered. (2) Recovery is effected on a heading of 280°. (3) Without thinking, the pilot mechanically makes a 180° turn. (4) Pilot would have been out of the weather in a short time.

you — a minute can be a long time. Students sometimes lose track of the time and think that they have been turning a minute and 30 seconds instead of an actual 30 seconds. Or you may check the clock and continue the turn for 2 minutes, instead of the 1 minute required.

In bumpy weather the needle or turn coordinator will oscillate and you will have to fly the average position rather than try to keep the indicator exactly at the standard-rate turn position.

Remember that the T/C (or T/S) is not the only instrument to be watched during this maneuver. Keep up your scan. If the airspeed and altitude start getting away, stop the turn, recover to straight and level flight, and, after the plane is under control, continue the turn.

When you are flying cross-country always have the reciprocal of your course in mind. *This is the heading you will want to turn to.* If the plane stays under control after entry into the weather, then a 180° turn is desired. On the other hand, if you have inadvertently turned while in the clouds or fog, a 180° turn could put you deeper into the weather. As an illustration:

You are on a heading of 120° and suddenly fly into a condition where outside visibility is lost. The plane enters a spiral and you recover to straight and level. After recovery the plane's heading is 280°. You don't particularly notice the heading but mechanically set up a 180° turn, which will actually carry you farther into the weather, when a turn of 20° to the right would put you on the desired reciprocal heading. Even holding the 280° heading would be accurate enough to leave the weather area (Fig. 15-8).

USING THE FOUR MAIN DIRECTIONS

In a *shallow*-banked turn the magnetic compass is fairly accurate on the headings of East or West and lags by about 30° as the plane passes the heading of North and leads by about 30° as the plane passes the heading of South. (The exact lag or lead will have to be checked for your situation, which will include latitude and other variables. For illustration purposes here it is assumed to be 30°). This is called

'northerly turning error" and affects the compass while the plane is turning.

Assume that you are flying on a heading of 120° and want to make a 180° turn. The desired new heading will be 300°. By turning to the right you will have a cardinal heading (West) reasonably close to the new heading. A standard-rate turn is made to the right but no timing is attempted. You will be watching for West on the compass, and as the plane reaches that heading you will start timing. The desired heading is 30° (300° minus 270°) past this and will require 10 seconds at the standard rate. The timing can be done by counting "one thousand and one, one thousand and two" and so forth, up to ten, at which time the needle and ball are centered (Fig. 15-9).

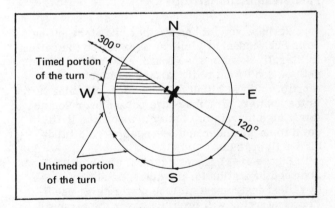

Fig. 15-9. The 180° turn to the right.

A turn to the left could have been made realizing that the nearest major compass heading (North) will be 60° or 20 seconds short of the desired heading of 300°. In that case you will set up a standard-rate turn to the left and will not start timing until the compass indicates 030 degrees. Remember that the compass will lag on a turn through North and will be behind the actual heading by about 30° (Fig. 15-10).

When the 030° indication is given, the 20-second timing begins, either by the sweep second hand of the aircraft clock or your watch, or by counting.

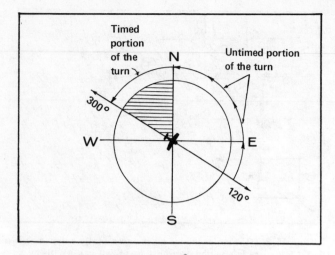

Fig. 15-10. The 180° turn to the left.

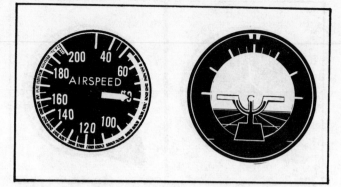

Fig. 15-11. At climb power, a certain pitch attitude will give the correct climb airspeed. You should use this fact in initially setting up the climb. You may hear the expression, "Power plus attitude equals performance," among the instrument-rated pilots at the airport.

There are several disadvantages to this system, the major one being that it requires a visual picture of the airplane's present and proposed heading — and mental calculations. You may not have time or be too excited for a mental exercise at this point. Also, in bumpy weather the compass may not give accurate readings on the four main headings.

The main advantage is that reasonably accurate turns may be made without a timepiece, as the new heading will never be more than 45°, or 15 seconds, away from a major heading. This method then is presented as something to be filed away and used if necessary.

SHALLOW-CLIMBING TURNS TO A PREDETERMINED ALTITUDE

Perhaps you hit bad weather and start letting down but suddenly fly into an area where the ceiling is literally down on the ground. Altitude is needed, yet you don't want to fly farther into the unknown territory as you climb. The shallow-climbing turn is the answer. You may have passed over some fairly high terrain or obstructions before letting down to sneak under and now need more altitude before flying back.

Figure 15-11 shows a typical climb attitude and airspeed indication for a trainer, as shown by the two flight instruments (climb power being used). Your instructor will probably cover the airspeed and attitude indicator at separate times to show how a proper climb can be set up by either instrument.

If you are using the full panel of flight instruments, the instructor may set up a spiral and require that after recovery you climb back up to a specific altitude and heading, as would be the case in a real situation. (You need to recover lost altitude; you also need to turn out of the bad weather.)

Suppose that at the end of a spiral recovery you are at 2800 feet and your heading is 035°. You need 3500 feet altitude and a heading of 125° to safely get back to good weather. The airplane climbs at 700 fpm and you'll be back up to the safe altitude in 1

minute. A 90° turn to the right is required, so, using a standard-rate turn, you'll get there in 30 seconds. Fine. Set up your climb and turn. You'll be at your heading of 125° when you still have 350 feet of altitude to go. Roll out and make a straight climb until the required altitude is reached. *Keep an eye on that heading indicator during the straight climb.* Students sometimes get so interested in the altimeter that they let the airplane turn right on around — back into the imaginary, or actual, bad weather. ("Torque" sometimes is a culprit, too.) So, if you get to the heading first, maintain it as you climb, and vice versa. The problem is not completed until you are at both the required altitude and heading (Fig. 15-12).

The following explanation will assume that your heading and attitude indicators are out of action. One point: While the A/I may be tumbled and out of action for several minutes (if you don't have an instrument with a caging knob), you can reset the *heading indicator* immediately and use it as an aid to keep your wings level. (If you are getting indications of a turn to the right, that wing is down, etc.) You'll be surprised at how much aid the H/I can give you. Your first resetting of it with the magnetic compass will be a rough one, but you can reset it later, after the compass has settled down.

PROCEDURE (BASIC INSTRUMENTS)

Right rudder will be needed to keep the ball centered, as always in a climbing turn.

If climbing power is set, the turn kept shallow, and the airspeed is held at that of climb, the rate of climb will take care of itself. The rate of climb indicator is a very useful reference here. But "chasing" the vertical speed indicator will only result in a varying flight path. *Corrections must be smooth, and deliberate.*

As in the case of the shallow-climbing turn with visual references, you will ease the nose up to the required position and apply climbing power. When you could see outside, the nose position, power setting, airspeed, and altimeter showed that the plane was in a normal climb. You found that by combining the proper nose position and power setting the altimeter and airspeed took care of themselves. Here you will use the airspeed and power setting to assure that the proper climb is maintained (take care of the airspeed and power and the nose attitude will take care of itself as long as the other instruments are not neglected). It would be advisable to establish the climb first before the turn is started.

The idea of starting the level-off about 20 feet below the desired altitude still stands (for most lightplanes). This allowance depends on the rate of climb — a fast-climbing jet may need several hundred feet to level off.

In visual flying the leveling-off was accomplished by easing the nose over to the straight and level position, checking the altimeter, and throttling back to cruise rpm. You paid little attention to the airspeed during the leveling process. The same applies here. If the altitude is kept constant and the power setting is at cruise, the airspeed will take care of itself and will soon settle down at the cruise value. It will still, however, be covered in the scan.

1. With the T/C or T/S centered, apply back pressure slowly to decrease the airspeed to the climb value. It will take a little time for the airspeed to drop to that of the climb. The best technique is to apply a certain amount of back pressure, let the airspeed stabilize, and apply more or less back pressure

as needed. After you have practiced a few climb entries this back pressure can be estimated. The trim tab can help maintain the climb, and you are encouraged to use it.

2. Apply climb power as the airspeed drops to the climb value.

3. After the climb is established with the airspeed and power setting (you've been keeping the wings level with the T/C or T/S), set up a standard-rate turn in the desired direction. At your plane's probable climb speed the bank required for a standard-rate turn will be in the vicinity of 10° - 15°, so that the standard-rate turn is easy to maintain as well as giving the proper shallow bank required for a climbing turn.

Make all turns standard-rate. Later you may start the turn and climb at the same time. It may be desired to climb to a specific altitude and turn to a definite heading, so stop the turn but continue the climb — or vice versa — to get what you want.

LEVELING-OFF PROCEDURE

1. At the proper distance below the chosen altitude start the leveling procedure. Relax back pressure to stop the climb.

2. Fly the altimeter; maintain the chosen altitude.

3. Center the T/C or T/S as you "stop the altimeter."

Fig. 15-12. (A) Control of the airplane is recovered on the heading (035°) and altitude (2800 MSL) shown. The desired heading is 125° and the required altitude is 3500 feet. A standard-rate turn and climb is started. (B) The heading is reached and the turn is stopped. A straight climb is continued to the required altitude. (C) The requirements are complete when the airplane is on both the required heading and altitude.

4. As the airspeed increases, throttle back to cruise power. Trim the airplane.

SHALLOW-DESCENDING TURNS AT REDUCED POWER TO A PREDETERMINED ALTITUDE

A descent (or ascent) at a given airspeed can be controlled by the amount of throttle used. The simplest form of descent is one that you have used in losing altitude by maintaining the cruise airspeed and throttling back until the desired rate of descent was obtained. You probably didn't measure the exact rate in feet per minute but used the controls to get what "looked good."

As in the other turns on instruments, you are advised to make these descending turns standard rate. A steeper banked turn may get out of hand and what started as a shallow-descending turn may wind up as a graveyard spiral.

The descent could be made at any airspeed, but you wouldn't want to be slower than the normal glide or much faster than cruise because of the possibility of loss of control at the extremes of the airspeed range. The plane may be overstressed if turbulence is encountered at high speeds or a stall might be gotten into at the lower end of the airspeed range. The leveling-off process will be dependent on the rate of descent. For lightplanes, starting the level-off approximately 50 feet above the altitude will work for an average controlled descent of 500-800 feet per minute. You will be flying the T/C or T/S, airspeed, and altimeter (plus A/I and H/I, if available) for attitude, rate of turn, and descent.

After leveling off, the power will have to be increased to that of cruise in order to maintain altitude. Your instructor will have a recommended speed and power setting for descent available for your airplane. A 500 fpm descent is a good one to shoot for. It won't be so great as to risk loss of control (this is a "standard" rate of descent for instrument flying). For one high-wing trainer, a speed of 80 K is in the center of the green arc on the airspeed indicator (a good place to be) and a power setting of 1900 rpm gives a 500 fpm descent. (You'll find that the rate of descent at your given airspeed and rpm will vary slightly with altitude and/or airplane weight, but the difference will not be enough to cause any problems.)

A normal glide can be used also. The vertical speed indicator will be useful in this maneuver.

STRAIGHT DESCENTS USING THE MAGNETIC COMPASS

Suppose you've lost all three gyro instruments and need to let down through a cloud layer. As a last resort and if there is a good ceiling below, the magnetic compass may be used as a combination attitude indicator and heading indicator. The letdown should be made on a heading of South because the compass will react "normally" if a wing drops and a turn is started. In other words, on that heading the compass

will show an increase in heading numbers if a right turn is starting or a decrease for a left turn. On a North heading you recall that the compass will start moving the "wrong" way at the initiation of a turn — which could be fatally confusing. The South heading gives a quick and proper reference to keep the wings level. You might ask your instructor to demonstrate this on the way back from the practice area sometime.

STRAIGHT AND LEVEL

Although you have been practicing straight and level flying by reference to instruments for some time, it might be well to mention a few other points:

Talking about the full flight panel, it would seem that flying straight and level using attitude and heading indicators should be duck soup. But the problem is that the student sees the means to keep a precise heading (the H/I) and so works too hard and overcompensates. You might have this problem: You see that the airplane has turned a few degrees off heading. You want to get back on the heading right away so you roll into a bank to accomplish this. You find that you've overshot and now have to reverse the procedure. This game can go on as long as the instructor allows it — which is not too long. This is known as "S-turns across the route." The thing to keep in mind is that you will make *minor* corrections (more about that shortly) — and this will also apply later as you work on that instrument rating — *ease* up (or down) to an airspeed, altitude, or heading if you've slipped off a little.

You may have to fly several minutes to get out of the weather. The ability to fly a straight and level path and not wander means a quicker return to a place where visual references are available. The needle and ball is the primary indicator for keeping a fixed direction of flight if the other gyro instruments aren't available. Fly the T/C or T/S and use the compass for a cross-check. If the compass has settled down and shows that you are off heading, correct with a balanced turn in the proper direction. For minor variations from heading (up to 15°), a half standard rate correction is preferred. If you are 10° off, make a one-half standard-rate turn (1-1/2° per second) for 7 seconds. In straight and level flying the student sometimes has a tendency to stare at the T/C or T/S, neglecting the rest of his scan. It's important that the instruments be continually cross-checked with each other.

You may get practice in flying straight and level using one or two of the instruments to show how a reasonable heading and altitude can be maintained. The procedure might be like this: You'll have on the hood and the instructor will set up the airplane on a heading of, say, 090° and altitude of 3500 feet. When everything has "settled down" he will, for instance, cover all of the flight instruments except the attitude indicator and have you fly the airplane, keeping the proper pitch and wings level position by this instrument only. After 2 minutes he will uncover the altimeter and heading indicator and you can see how close you are to the original requirements.

He may use combinations of instruments to make the point that you *can* keep the airplane under control when ground references are lost. It's a good confidence-building exercise.

SIMULATED RADAR ADVISORIES

If your airport traffic permits, your instructor on dual flights may bring you back from the practice area "on radar" several times. You'll go under the hood and he will be "approach control radar" and direct you back into the traffic pattern and, perhaps, down to a few hundred feet on final. He can give you problems that use the instrument training you've had. It will be good practice if you should later accidentally get into actual instrument weather and need radar service.

ASR — Airport Surveillance Radar is a non-precision radar that allows the controller to vector you into the pattern and tell you what altitude you should be at various distances on final. (The controllers have no altitude information, just direction and distance.) Usually the weather minimums for ASR approaches are a 500-foot ceiling and 1 mile. Its primary purpose, however, is to expedite traffic flow in the terminal area.

PAR — Precision Approach Radar is used as a *landing* aid. The operator can check your approach path and advise whether the airplane is on course and/or on the glide path. This is the system that is used on the Late Late Show where the crippled jet has 5 minutes of fuel and the weather has just gone to zero-zero at the only airport available within several hundred miles. After much suspense (did he make it?) the jet taxies out of the fog. The mini-mums for the PAR approach are naturally lower than the ASR, but never as low as shown on the Late Late Show.

Later you will also get practice in tracking to or from a VOR station (see Chapter 21) while flying the airplane by reference to the instruments.

SUMMARY

The instruments give information on the plane's actions and attitudes and take the place of the horizon in visual flight. A certain amount of practice is needed to be able to see the plane's actions through the instruments. A plane's responses to the controls are the same under instrument conditions as under visual conditions; hence, no special control technique is used, but throttles and elevators, ailerons and rudder are coordinated as always.

If you can do the maneuvers cited in this chapter you should have no trouble passing this area of the private flight test.

You may use the techniques discussed in this chapter to save your neck someday. If you should inadvertently find yourself in a situation of being on actual instruments, your worst enemy will be panic. You'll have practiced under the hood (dual) and will be able to keep control of the airplane *before* you go on that first solo cross-country. Take a couple of slow, deep breaths to slow yourself down, and remember the numbers (airspeeds, etc.) you've been taught. As will be covered later in this book, and by your instructor, there are FAA people on the ground who can help, but *you* will have to fly the airplane and make the decisions (often the man on the ground is not a pilot).

Make a 180° turn *before* getting into the bad weather and save yourself some sweat.

16. Post-Solo Precision Maneuvers

TURNS AROUND A POINT

This maneuver is very close to the S-turn across a road because you're correcting for wind while in a turn. It is suggested that the steepest bank be approximately 45° and the altitude not be lower than 500 feet above the highest obstruction in the maneuver pattern. The idea of the turns about a point is to show the check pilot how well you can fly the plane when your attention is directed outside. He'll also want to find out if you understand wind drift correction principles (Fig. 16-1).

PROCEDURE

1. Pick a tree or some other small but easily seen object and set up the radius small enough so that the steepest bank is **approximately 45°**.

2. Enter the pattern downwind. Practice both left and right turns around the point. Many students only practice left turns and get a rude awakening when they are asked to make a turn around a point to the right on the check flight. The best altitude for keeping the point in sight is about 700 feet above the surface.

3. Vary the turn as needed to maintain a constant distance from the point—the greater the ground speed, the steeper the bank.

4. Maintain a constant altitude.

5. Keep your eyes open. This is a perfect place to have a **low-altitude emergency** thrown at you.

6. The check pilot may give you a free turn to get set up, but keep up with the number of turns after the maneuver is started.

COMMON ERRORS

1. Starting the maneuver with the plane too far from the point so that the steepest bank does not reach 45°.

2. Poor altitude control.

3. Pointing the wing at the tree—trying to keep the plane's attitude the same in relation to the point rather than having the plane's path constant, as it should be.

4. Failure to recognize wind drift or, if recognized, not doing anything about it.

5. Coordination problems.

Students sometimes have trouble with this

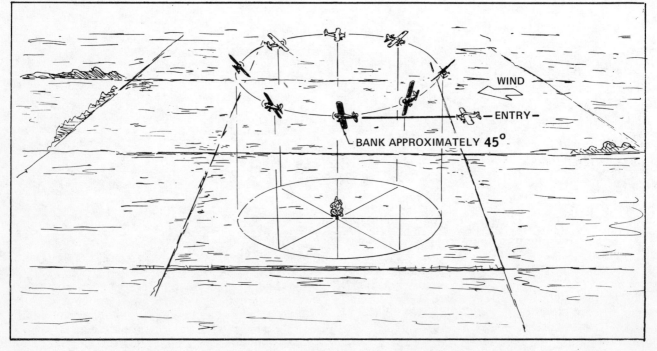

Fig. 16-1. Turns around a point. The steepest bank is required when the plane is flying directly downwind.

maneuver because they can't seem to convince themselves that the steepest bank is required when the airplane is headed *directly* downwind, as indicated in Figure 16-1.

Suppose an airplane is flying tangent (wings level) to the circle at the positions shown by A, B, C, and D in Figure 16-2. At A, the airplane is moving at its true airspeed *plus* the wind speed. This results in the highest relative speed to the reference point of any position around the circle. At C, its relative speed is the lowest, because it is moving into a headwind. The arrow (vector) behind each airplane gives a picture of the relative speed at the four positions. The dashed lines show the comparative distances the airplane would be "away" from the circle for any given interval of time, if no turn were made.

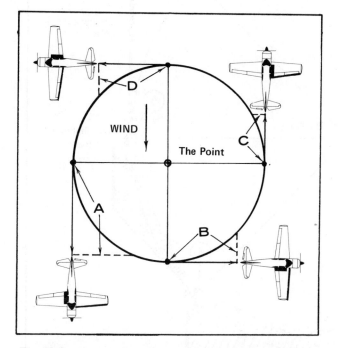

Fig. 16-2. A comparison of rates of "leaving the circle" for an airplane flying at the same true airspeed at four positions on the circle.

The rate of turn, then, must be greatest at A if it is to "follow the circle." Since this is a coordinated maneuver, the bank must be greatest at that position (and the bank is most shallow at C). The banks at B and D will be comparable.

VECTOR APPROACH TO THE MANEUVER

If you are interested in the mathematics of turns around the point, Figure 16-3 shows wind triangles for the airplane at 8 points around the circle. As noted, the airplane's true airspeed is 100 K and the wind is from the top of the illustration (North) at 40 K. The solid thin arrow represents *groundspeed, or the airplane's path and speed with respect to the ground.* This groundspeed vector varies in size (speed) because of the wind, but at each of the 8 points shown (or at *any* point on the circle) it must

be tangent to the circle — or else the plane would not be following the prescribed path; so this is the first consideration.

The true airspeed is indicated by the dashed arrows and is always 100 K for this problem. (Disregard slowing the airplane in the steeper banks.) The 100 K true airspeed vector, however, must be "pointed" in such a manner that the result of the plane's heading, plus the wind, makes the airplane's path tangent to the circle at any position. The wind is a constant velocity and direction.

Maybe you haven't done any work with the navigation computer yet, but you will, and you can come back to this later.

The circle can be thought of as an "infinite number of short, straight lines" and the airplane is flying "one leg" of a rectangular course for each one. In order to do this, the plane must be crabbed to fly the line tangent to the circle. The reason for the bank is to get the proper heading for the next "leg." The bank at Point (1) must be steepest because the airplane is approaching the next "leg" at the greatest rate. At Point (5) the opposite is true.

Of course, practically speaking, you fly the airplane and maintain the proper distance from the point by looking at it. But given the true airspeed and wind, you could work out on a navigation computer the required headings for each of the 8 points given here. For instance, the course at Point (1) is 180°. At Point (2) the course would be 135°. At Point (3) it would be 090°, etc., and you could find the wind correction angle. The required banks at each point could be obtained mathematically for the radius of the circle to be flown, using a turn equation similar to that given in Chapter 3. The maneuver could be theoretically flown "under the hood" once the airplane is established in the maneuver. You would just match the proper banks to the various required headings you found for the 8 (or more) points around the circle.

Maybe this approach to the maneuver doesn't interest you, and you can certainly do it well if you don't know a vector from a victor. But the main point here is that the rectangular course, S-turns across a road, this maneuver, and others are designed to teach you to fly the airplane on a certain path or track, correcting for wind.

EIGHTS AROUND PYLONS (AROUND-PYLON EIGHTS)

SHALLOW EIGHTS

This maneuver is closely akin to the turns around a point but, as the name implies, a figure eight is flown around *two* points, or pylons. The pylons are picked so that an imaginary line between them is perpendicular to the wind (Fig. 16-4).

Shown in Figure 16-4 is a shallow around-pylon eight maneuver. The steepest bank should be approximately 30°. Your instructor will note that you may use the same pylons for steep or shallow pylon

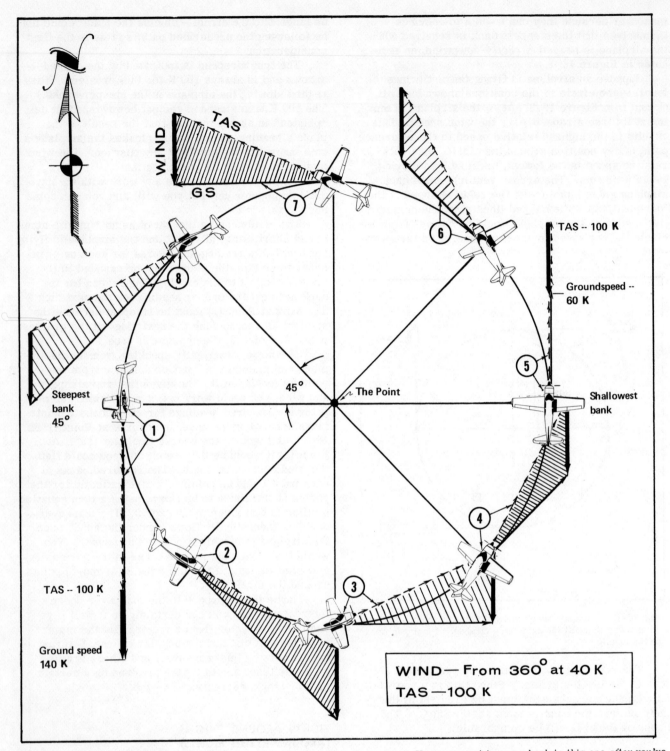

Fig. 16-3. The turns around a point maneuver as seen as a problem in vectors. You may want to come back to this one *after* you've done some work with the computer.

eights, using a straightaway portion between the pylons as shown. While at first you will enter downwind between the pylons, you will later enter from any point of the maneuver — but will fly it so that the outer parts of the turns are made into the wind.

Looking at Figure 16-4, the entry is set up (1) and will be slightly wider from the pylon(s) than turns around a point (which required 45° maximum banks). You should be flying directly downwind

and tracking to a position exactly between the pylons. When (2) is reached, a turn is started in either direction (to the right, here). At this stage it's like the maneuver in Figure 16-3. (The bank will be steepest at Point 2.) Note that at Points (3), (4), and (5) the airplane is crabbed in the turn. Point (6) has the shallowest bank and (7), (8), and (9) require crabbing. When (10) is reached (or 2, again), the airplane is rolled into a turn in the opposite direction and the second pylon used (Points 11, 12, etc.). *Not only should each circle be of constant radius, but both should be the same size.* One of the common errors students make is to have a too-wide turn on one pylon and a too-narrow turn on the other. Because of this tendency, careful planning and orientation are needed to get back to the spot exactly between the two pylons. You may repeat the pattern any number of times, but usually four or five are the maximum done without a break.

The blacked-out ellipse in the center of the illustration might be called the "zone of confusion" because, even though the circles are supposed to be tangent, it's impossible for an airplane to be rolled from one turn to the other instantly. So, in actual practice, they can't be tangent, but you should make them as near tangent as is *safely* possible.

Common Errors
1. Poor pylon picking (which will be covered shortly).
2. Coordination problems (slipping or skidding).
3. Altitude problems. The altitude should be the same as used for turns around a point and kept *constant.* The usual problem is a tendency to climb as the airplane is rolled from one bank to another, and then lose altitude as the new turn (steep bank) is established.
4. Orientation loss, or "losing" a pylon. You may continue well on past the point to roll in for the opposite turn. If you do this, you could make another 360° turn around the pylon, attempting to divert the

attention of the instructor (or check pilot) by pointing out objects of local interest as you go around. (He'll notice your problem, anyway.)
5. Nonsymmetrical circles — the turn around one pylon steep, the other shallow. This, too, can usually be attributed to losing the other pylon, as well as losing the center point of the pattern (Point 2 or 10 in Fig. 16-4).
6. Having too large an eight; the airplane is too far from the pylons and very shallow banks are required.

STEEP EIGHTS

Figure 16-5 shows the steep around-pylon eight. The turn pattern is closer to each pylon and a straight leg is used to get set up for the other pylon. This maneuver uses wind drift corrections in straight flight and a turn. You'll have to plan the roll-out from one pylon so as to have the proper drift correction set up for the leg to the other pylon.
Note the steps at the following points:

(1) The airplane is in a position to enter the maneuver.
(2) Drift correction is set up in the straight leg.
(3) When the proper radius is reached, a turn is set up. Points (3) and (9) will require the steepest banks in this maneuver since the ground speeds will be greatest at these positions.
(4) — (9) The bank is varied to maintain a constant radius. As (9) is approached the airplane is

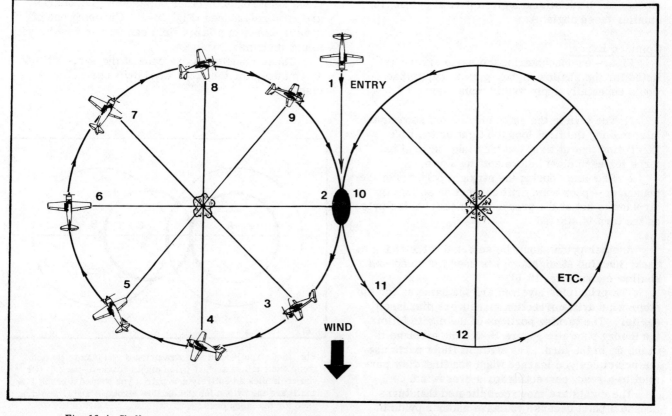

Fig. 16-4. Shallow around-pylon eights. This maneuver is a more complicated version of turns about a point.

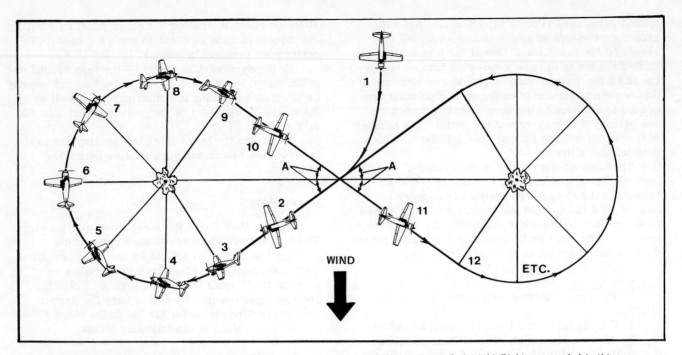

Fig. 16-5. Steep around-pylon eights. Wing drift corrections in both turning and straight flight are needed in this one.

rolled out to set up the proper crab angle, (10) and (11), to be at the required radius at Point (12). This loop of the eight uses the same principle as the first.

The four angles indicated by the two "A's" may be that as desired by the instructor. Later, you will pick the pylons and set the maneuver up so that each of these angles will be 45°. (You can figure that the steeper the bank around a given pair of pylons, the smaller these angles.)

Common Errors

Figure on encountering the same errors as listed for the shallow eights, plus a couple that would especially apply to this maneuver:

1. The turn in the entry may be too soon or too late, making the first loop too tight or too wide. You'll find that at first you may take several patterns for each eight before settling down.
2. Problems during the straight portions of the maneuver — poor wind drift correction so that the airplane is not at the proper distance from the pylon as the turn is started.

Another pylon should be selected if the "back to back" idea (no straightaway) is used for steep *and* shallow eights (Fig. 16-6).

The principles involved are the same as for the other wind drift correction maneuvers discussed earlier. The turning portions of the eights follow the theory shown in Figure 16-3 — the airplane is crabbing in the turn. The straight flight parts use the principles you learned when you first flew parallel to a road, correcting for a crosswind.

The eights are more complicated than turns around a point because you have another pylon to

consider and must be planning your transition from one to the other, even while maintaining a constant radius around one pylon. It's easy to lose that other pylon by getting too involved in the one you are working with. It makes for a sinking feeling on a check flight when you roll out and don't see anything that looks like the other pylon you selected earlier. Picking your pylons is very important; isolated trees near roads or other outstanding landmarks are good references (Fig. 16-7). Choosing one of several trees in a large field can lead to results you might imagine.

These maneuvers are done at the same altitude as you used for the other wind drift correction exercises.

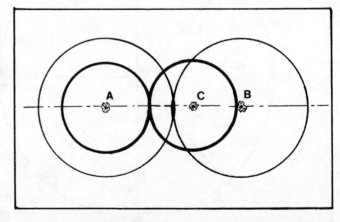

Fig. 16-6. You'll need an extra pylon if you plan to fly both steep and shallow around-pylon eights "back-to-back." (Or you could pick an entirely new pair if you wanted a break.) A and B are the pylons for the shallow eights; A and C would be used for the steep ones.

124

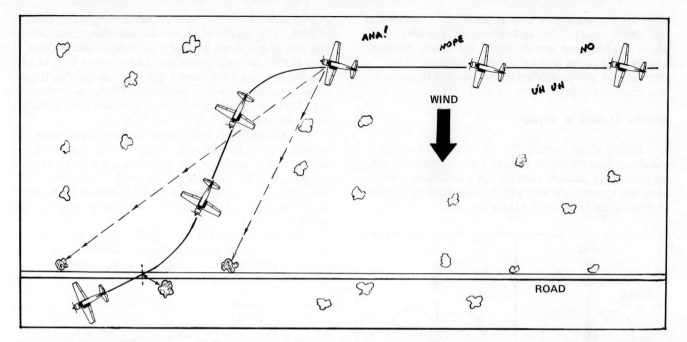

Fig. 16-7. Picking pylons. Points beside a road are best for keeping your orientation. If there is no good reference exactly between the pylons, you should find the center with relation to some object, such as the tree shown here.

THE PERPLEXING PROBLEM OF PROPER PYLON PICKING

Probably one of your biggest problems is finding pylons the proper distance apart, and oriented perpendicular to the wind. Students have gone on pretty good cross-country flights looking for pylons that were "just right," while the instructor or check pilot grew restless in that right seat. A good method of picking pylons is to fly crosswind, looking to the downwind side. As soon as a proper pair of pylons are spotted, the airplane can be turned downwind to enter. Picking pylons beside a road helps a great deal in orientation. (Pylons don't have to be trees, they can be other *immobile* objects; one student picked a cow for one and, needless to say, his pattern was affected as the animal walked across the pasture. An automobile

that drives off is also considered a poor choice in most quarters.)

EIGHTS ACROSS A ROAD

Another good maneuver for practicing wind drift correction is eights across a road as shown in Figure 16-8. This is often used as an introduction to the idea of correcting for wind drift while flying a pattern eight. If you develop problems with the eights around pylons you may come back to this maneuver to work them out.

The road should be perpendicular to the wind, and an intersection — or some other well-defined object — should be used as a center reference.

Steep, medium, and shallow-banked turns may be

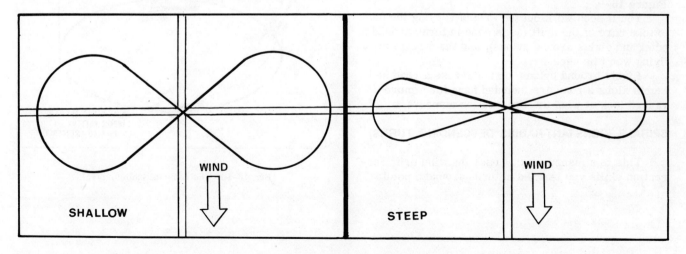

Fig. 16-8. Eights across a road.

125

used for variation (but they shouldn't be combined in the *same* eight). The instructor, by choosing the angle at which you are to cross the road, decides whether the turns will be steep or shallow. The corrections and problems of the other drift correction maneuvers apply here as well.

EIGHTS ALONG A ROAD

Eights along a road (Fig. 16-9) look like they should be named eights across a road since the centerline of the pattern crosses the road. One way to keep the maneuvers straight in your mind is to note that the wind is blowing "along the road."

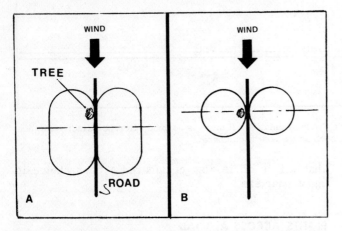

Fig. 16-9. Eights along a road. (A) A turn of a constant bank requires some straightaway flying to get back to the reference (tree). (B) The bank is varied as necessary to maintain constant radii.

This maneuver is started by picking a road parallel to the wind and flying downwind. A 360° turn is made either way (after checking a geographic reference by the road), using a constant medium bank. You'll find that a constant bank allows the airplane to move to a position downwind of the original point. So some straight flight into the wind is necessary to get back to the reference (tree) as shown by Figure 16-9.

You'll soon work out the idea of varying the bank to take care of the drift (as is done in turns around a point and eights around pylons), and the straightaway flying won't be necessary.

Eights around pylons, eights across a road and eights along a road are included here for a more advanced look at wind drift correction maneuvers.

SPIRALS (CONSTANT-RADIUS DESCENDING TURNS)

This is a maneuver that uses the wind drift correction skills you learned in turns around a point;

in this case, however, you're descending with power at idle. The practical aspect is that with practice you can spiral down around a particular point to set up a traffic pattern in the event of a power loss at altitude. (Figure 18-3 shows the idea also.) You'll get some practice with this before the flight test, when the flight instructor gives you simulated high altitude emergencies.

The spiral is a little more difficult than turns around a point because the airplane will be getting closer to the reference as you descend and the perspective will be changing. (The bank is steepest when flying directly downwind and shallowest when headed upwind, as was discussed in turns around a point.)

The main problem in a spiral is that the airspeed may tend to get away from you — the usual error is to be too fast. Hold the airspeed to within ±15 knots of that desired.

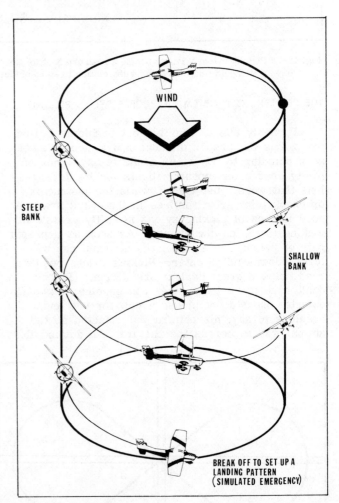

Fig. 16-10. The constant radius spiral.

126

17. Special Take-off and Landing Procedures

SHORT-FIELD TAKE-OFF

Now you've done it! You're a victim of that old tried and true aviation saying, "You can land a plane in places where you can't get it out." The field seemed short when you landed, and now the wind has died and things look pretty grim. There are some 50-foot trees at the other end of the runway that you'll have to get over. A special type of take-off is needed here. (*Or maybe you shouldn't take off.*)

The short-field take-off is a maneuver aimed at just such a situation. You must take off efficiently and make the steepest angle climb that is safely possible after take-off. As a rule of thumb, a plane's maximum angle of climb is at a speed of approximately 1.3 times the power-off stall speed, but check the *Pilot's Operating Handbook* for the exact figure. In the normal climb you are interested in the maximum altitude gain over a given length of time (and still not ruin the engine). The maximum *angle* of climb gives you more altitude for the distance traveled forward (Fig. 17-1). *The situation obviously calls for a maximum angle climb.*

PROCEDURE

1. Start the take-off at the extreme end of the runway. Hold the wheel back and smoothly open the throttle.

2. As soon as you are certain the engine is developing full power, and the plane is accelerating properly, proceed with a tail-low take-off. This is to let the plane get into the air as soon as possible. The plane will accelerate faster when airborne because of the lesser drag of the air. Don't try to rush the process, because this will slow the take-off as

explained in "Normal Take-off" (Chapter 13). The attitude of the plane during the take-off will naturally vary between airplanes.

3. The plane will lift off when the minimum flying speed is reached.

Some pilots suggest that the airplane should be held on the ground until V_X (the max angle of climb speed), but this can cause two possible minor problems: (a) If the field is rough, this can be hard on the landing gear; if the surface is soft or consists of taller grass, you'll take a lot of room to get V_X. (b) For some nosewheel airplanes a shimmy could develop at high speeds on the ground, even on smooth, firm runways. The instructor will have suggestions for your particular airplane.

4. Attain and maintain the recommended maximum angle climb speed. Keep the throttle wide open. If conditions require this sort of take-off they also require all the power you can get from the engine.

5. At about 100 feet above the ground, assume a normal climb (V_Y) and use normal climb power.

For check-ride purposes the obstacle to be cleared is considered to be 50 feet high and the field is considered to be firm. If the plane has flaps use the take-off flap setting as recommended by the Airplane Flight Manual or *Pilot's Operating Handbook*.

Some pilots argue for making a 90° rolling take-off as against the straight roll technique. The fixed-pitch propeller of the lightplane is inefficient at low speeds. This means comparatively slow acceleration as the plane starts rolling. But the added efficiency gained by the 90° rolling take-off does not offset the chances of an inexperienced pilot losing directional control. Also, there have been instances

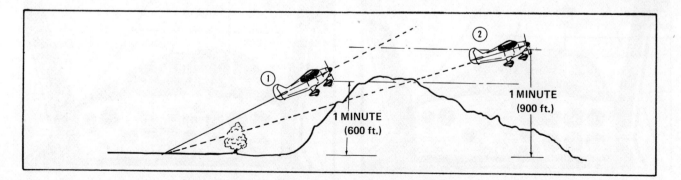

Fig. 17-1. Exaggerated view of maximum angle climb (1) versus maximum rate of climb (2).

where the sharp turn moved fuel away from a wing tank outlet (called "unporting") so that the engine suffered fuel starvation during the take-off or initial climb.

Your instructor may demonstrate various techniques used.

COMMON ERRORS

1. Poor directional control when the brakes are released.

2. Trying to hurry the plane off the ground — resulting in high drag and slowing the take-off.

3. Letting the airspeed pick up past the best angle of climb speed after take-off and not getting a maximum angle climb.

SHORT-FIELD LANDING

MORE ABOUT POWER APPROACHES

The approach you've been making by gradually reducing the power to make the runway is a crude version of the power approach. (Sometimes you had to add power again to make the runway after you were too hasty in reducing it.) Power is a means of controlling the airplane's path on an approach and makes it possible to land on a particular spot. In the pre-solo work little effort was made to make a "spot landing" or landing at a chosen point on the runway, but now you'll start making precision landings.

The power approach is a general term. It doesn't say at what speed the approach is made, but only that power is used to control the glide path. There are two power approach speeds in which you will be particularly interested, however. These are the power approach at normal glide speed and the short-field approach with a speed of approximately 1.3 times that of the stall speed.

Before, you were able to tell fairly soon whether you were too high or too low to make the runway, but now you want to predict your landing place within a few feet — and land there. By controlling the airspeed you will be able to estimate the point of landing. By controlling the airspeed *and* the rate of descent you will be able to pick the point of landing.

On a day of steady wind in a normal power-off approach, your point of landing has already been determined. But you don't know what this point is. How do you tell? Assume that you are trying to land at a particular spot on the runway — maybe it's a big clump of grass or oil spot that is easily seen. You want to land there, so watch it. If the spot apparently moves toward the nose you will glide over it. If it moves out away from the nose the plane will be short of the point. So you say, "By controlling the airspeed I can set up means of telling whether I'm overshooting or undershooting; now what?" You can slip, add flaps, or add power as needed to hit the spot (Fig. 17-2).

You keep a perfect glide speed and the approach is such that the oil spot or clump of grass doesn't move. As soon as you start breaking the glide the nose will start moving up and the spot will move under the nose. Let it; you've done everything possible, so forget the spot and make the landing.

Allowing for round-off, your path will look something like Figure 17-3.

The landing will be slightly past the spot.

You could hit the spot exactly if the plane followed its original path all the way to the clump of grass, but who wants to glide right into the ground? It's hard on airplanes for one thing. When maneuvered properly, *the airplane will always land slightly past the spot because of the rounding-off of the landing. There's always a certain amount of float to a landing, even one made from a normal glide.*

Your best bet is an approach speed that has a minimum amount of float plus a definite margin of safety. There is such a speed, and a rule of thumb gives it as about 1.3 times the power-off stalling

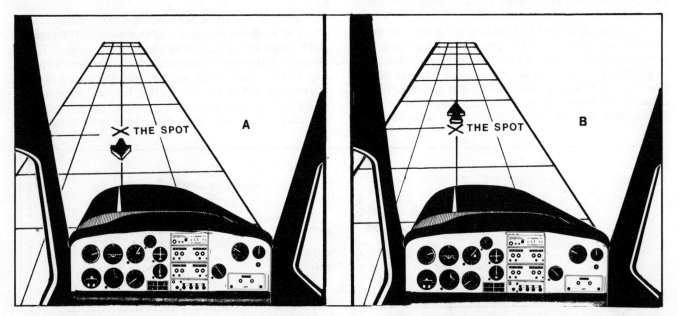

Fig. 17-2. (A) If the spot appears to be moving toward the airplane, you will be too high to land at the spot. (B) If the spot is "gaining" on the airplane, you will land short of the spot.

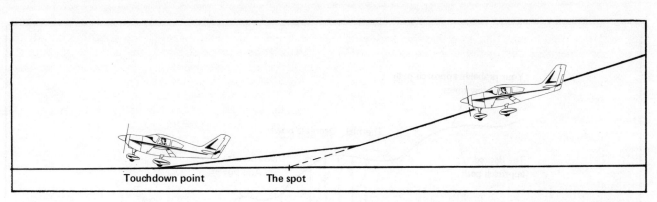

Fig. 17-3.

speed. It's suggested that the airspeed on a short-field approach be *no greater* than this figure. For safety's sake don't get too close to the stall speed — remember the gradient wind and gust effects. *There is no way of predicting the point of landing from a power-off approach on a gusty day.* Reviewing the wind effects — the plane's glide angle will be different for different wind strengths. The glide angle in relation to the ground may change from approach to approach or it may change several times during one approach (Fig. 17-4). By making a power approach the pilot can compensate for wind variation and errors in judgment.

SHORT-FIELD APPROACH AND LANDING

The short-field approach is the most useful type of power approach. It allows the pilot to control the glide path and make a landing with a minimum of float; therefore, as the name implies, it is a good approach to make to short fields. The approach is made at a maximum speed of 1.3 times the power-off stall speed. (If your plane stalls at 50 K, the maximum approach speed is 1.3 times 50, or 65 K.) At this speed the plane's glide path is particularly sensitive to power adjustments, because there is little excess airspeed to cause floating when power is removed.

The traffic pattern will be slightly wider and longer than normal. In essence you'll fly the pattern

so that using a normal glide would cause undershoot-ing of the runway — otherwise, if power is used in a normal pattern you'll overshoot.

Procedure

1. From a slightly wider downwind leg start a power-off approach. Keep the airspeed at normal glide or slightly below.

2. After the first 90° turn, slow the plane to 1.3 times the stall speed and control the angle of descent with the throttle. Set final flaps.

3. Use power as needed to make the landing. It may be necessary to keep power on all the way to the ground if you get low and slow.

After the landing, hold the control wheel (or stick) full back as you apply braking. This helps put most of the weight on the main wheels of the tricycle-gear plane and makes for more braking efficiency. If it's not too much of a distraction, upping the flaps will kill some of the residual lift and put more weight on the braking wheels.

Common Errors

1. Gliding too fast in the normal part of the approach, so that when the nose is raised to slow to the final approach speed, the airplane balloons and is too high to make a power approach.

2. Not keeping a constant airspeed during the power approach. Letting the speed pick up and

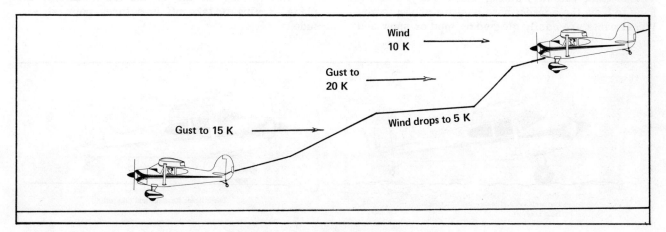

Fig. 17-4. Approach path on a gusty day.

129

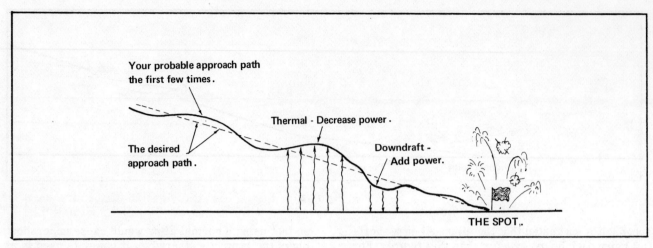

Fig. 17-5.

drop as the power is increased or decreased.

3. Not establishing a constant angle of descent — either using full power or idle. You are free to use as much or as little power as needed, but it looks pretty bad on a check ride if you're a throttle jockey.

4. Closing the throttle while the plane is near stalled and still off the ground — letting the plane drop in.

With more experience you'll be able to leave the throttle at a constant setting once the path is established. This is under constant wind and thermal conditions, of course (Fig. 17-5).

SOFT-FIELD TAKE-OFF

In mud, snow, or tall grass the drag on the wheels of the airplane tends to make acceleration suffer badly, and a special technique is required for taking off from a soft field.

The soft-field take-off requires that the tail of the plane be held as low as possible for two reasons: (1) To lessen the chances of nosing over (tailwheel type) or the nosewheel digging in (tricycle-gear type) and (2) to have the angle of attack such that the weight is taken from the main wheels as soon as possible. This attitude will vary among planes and you will have to have the correct nose position shown to you. Wheel pants are easily clogged by mud or snow and

are usually removed from planes operating under these conditions.

PROCEDURE

Use flaps as recommended by the *Pilot's Operating Handbook.*

1. Taxi onto the runway and keep the plane rolling — make a "rolling take-off." In a soft field the plane will require a great deal of power to start it rolling again, and at high rpm on the ground the prop will pick up mud and gravel and be damaged.

2. Hold the wheel back to stop any tendency to nose over as you apply full power.

3. Put the nose in the proper attitude.

4. Lift the plane off as soon as possible without stalling.

5. As soon as the plane is flying, lower the nose and assume a normal climb. If obstacles are to be cleared, use V_X.

The tailwheel airplane should be set up in a tail-low attitude as the take-off run progresses (Fig. 17-6).

COMMON ERROR

Not raising the tail on the tailwheel type airplane — trying to take off in a three-point attitude.

The airplane's attitude — soft or rough field take-off.

The attitude for a normal take-off.

Fig. 17-6. Soft or rough field and normal take-off attitudes (tailwheel airplane).

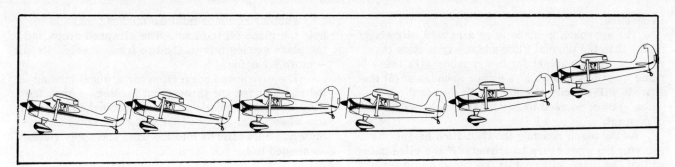

Fig. 17-7. The wheel landing.

SOFT-FIELD LANDING

The tendency to nose up on the soft-field landing is a problem, as on the take-off from a soft field. On the take-off the force trying to nose the plane over is normally not a sudden thing but may build up as the plane accelerates. As the plane lands, this force may be applied suddenly as the wheels take the weight of the plane. Although this effect will always be there, you can make it as small as possible.

Land the plane as slowly as possible. Use power to decrease the landing speed and to have as much nose-up attitude as is safely possible at touchdown.

Keep the tail down. Hold full back pressure.

The same principle applies on the soft-field landing for the tricycle-gear equipped plane. Land as slowly as possible and try to keep the nosewheel off. The drag of the main wheels will force it down, but you can keep as much weight off the nosewheel as possible by back pressure.

GUSTY WIND LANDINGS

TRICYCLE-GEAR PROCEDURES

The glide speed should be slightly higher to take care of the variance in wind velocity and, for some airplanes, the use of full flaps should be avoided for gusty conditions.

The airplane should be landed at a lower nose attitude than for smooth air, though you shouldn't land it on all three wheels at once (or the nosewheel first). The airplane will tend to rotate forward on the nosewheel at the landing impact; this decrease in angle of attack generally results in the airplane staying firmly on the ground—a decided advantage in gusty winds.

WHEEL LANDING—TAILWHEEL TYPE AIRPLANE

The wheel landing (Fig. 17-7) is used when the wind is strong and/or gusty and gives you a means of having good control all the way down to the landing. The airplane is literally flown onto the ground, landing on the main wheels to keep a low angle of attack and stop any tendency for a sudden gust to pick the airplane off the ground, as might happen in a normal landing under such conditions.

The technique at one time was to use power all through the landing, but this resulted in the pilot "juggling" the throttle, using up runway and fouling up the landing as he tried to control the landing time with power (Fig. 17-8).

Use only enough power to control your rate of descent and get to the position to make your power-off landing. Some pilots advocate using 1300 to 1600 rpm for a wheel landing, but you have found out that the average lightplane will maintain altitude at a power setting only slightly higher.

Use power only as is needed to make the landing. The less used at touchdown the better. Without power the plane will land—not float halfway down the runway. *Elevators and throttle go together. Don't be mechanical with either one.*

True, the wind will be strong and the ground-speed will be low. This will keep the plane from using as much runway as it would under lesser wind conditions, but you can still eat up a lot of runway using poor techniques.

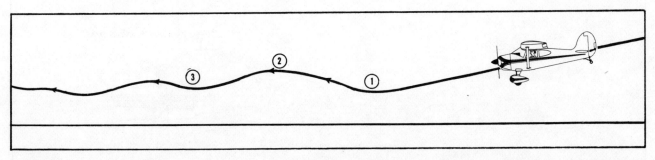

Fig. 17-8. (1) Pilot sees that he is settling fast, adds more power (oops, too much). (2) Now he throttles back. (3) Plane now settling fast—adds more power again, etc.

Procedure

The approach is made at an airspeed slightly faster than the normal glide and the transition is made at a lower height for two reasons: (1) The plane must touch down at a higher speed, and (2) the attitude will be only slightly tail-low — not three point. Power is used to control the angle and/or rate of descent.

As the plane reaches the transition height, start applying back pressure to "round off" the glide path so that the plane will contact the runway with the main wheels, in a slightly tail-low attitude. After the plane has touched, apply slight forward pressure to keep the tail up. This is to keep gusts from causing the plane to leave the ground again.

As the plane slows up, more and more forward pressure will be required to keep the tail up. When the wheel is all the way forward and the tail drops, move and hold the wheel completely back so the up elevator will now hold the tail down. The reason for holding the tail up is to keep a low angle of attack as long as possible. When the elevators become ineffective the plane's speed is slow enough that the wings have lost all lift. If you try to put the tail on the ground too soon after landing, you may find yourself several feet in the air, with very little airspeed. One disadvantage in keeping the tail up as long as possible is that directional control may be lost before the steerable tailwheel contacts the surface. However, generally the plane with this characteristic has a higher wing loading and is not as apt to be lifted by gusts during the landing roll. A suggested technique in this case is to maintain the forward pressure applied at touchdown, allowing the tail to lower gradually as the speed diminishes. The tailwheel will contact the runway before loss of rudder control occurs and at a speed allowing a smooth steady movement of the wheel to the full rear position without danger of becoming airborne again.

Too many students get impatient as the plane is skimming just above the ground and apply forward pressure to "put it on." This sets off a series of bounces that would make a kangaroo turn white. The trouble is that once you start bouncing, it usually gets worse until you take it around again or something (usually the landing gear) gives (Fig. 17-9).

Another common mistake students make is to hold the plane off too long. The airspeed drops and the plane settles fast on the two front wheels. Result — more bouncing.

The crosswind correction for a wheel landing is the same as for the three-point landing. Lower the wing and hold opposite rudder as needed and land on one wheel. The other wheel will come down immediately. Hold aileron into the wind and apply rudder as needed to keep it straight.

Common Errors

1. Too fast an approach — the plane floats.
2. Too slow an approach — the plane settles fast and bounces.
3. Getting impatient — shoving forward on the wheel "to make it stay on" (Fig. 17-9).

If the plane starts bouncing, open the throttle and take it around and make a new landing.

Although wheel landings are best for gusty air, a good three-point landing can be made under these conditions if care is taken.

DRAGGING THE AREA

Before you go on a solo cross-country the instructor will demonstrate how to drag the area, a procedure used in checking a strange field for landing. The idea is to pick a field and land before you run out of gas and have no choice.

Suppose that you become lost on a cross-country. You have about fifteen minutes of gas left and there are no airports or recognizable towns in sight. Or maybe you locate yourself but realize there's no airport close enough to make with the fuel remaining. Should you fly on to get as close to an airport as possible before the engine quits? Or should you pick a good field, look it over, and land there? Obviously this is a loaded question. You should pick a field.

PROCEDURE

1. Pick a likely looking field and circle it at about traffic pattern altitude. Know the wind

"I'LL *PUT* THIS ☆-##☺-! THING ON!"

Fig. 17-9.

direction. Pick a field near a road or farmhouse if possible.

2. Set yourself up on the downwind leg and start a normal approach to the portion of the field you want to land on.

3. Fly at a height of about 50 to 75 feet, just to the right of the intended landing path.

4. Look for obstructions or hazards that could not be seen from traffic pattern altitude.

5. If the field is suitable, make another traffic pattern with a short-field approach.

6. After the landing, go to the farmhouse and ask the farmer's daughter if you may use the phone.

Dragging the area is done any time you feel that for safety's sake the plane should be on the ground and you aren't close to an airport. If the engine is in imminent danger of quitting, you may not have time to drag the area but must land immediately in the first likely looking field. This will be covered more thoroughly in "Problems and Emergencies," Chapter 25 (FLYING THE CROSS-COUNTRY).

ACCURACY LANDINGS

180° ACCURACY LANDING—POWER OFF

The technique is different from that you used for the pre-solo take-offs and landings. In this case you're trying to land at a definite point *without* using throttle.

Fly downwind at the normal altitude and distance abeam of the runway. Pull the carburetor heat and close the throttle opposite the selected point of landing.

You'll play the turns and glide to land on or just over the spot. You may slip or use flaps, but the use of throttle should be avoided. Some students see they are low and "clear the engine" to make the field. You should clear the engine but no more often or for longer duration than usual.

If you are too low or too high, move the downwind leg in or out as needed to hit the spot on the next approach.

Remember: If you know the basic points of flying you can combine them in any way desired.

TAKE-OFF AND LANDING PERFORMANCE

It's very important to know the required take-off and landing roll distances of your airplane, plus the *total* distances required to clear a 50-foot obstacle. Figure 17-10 shows typical take-off and landing performance charts. Look at the *Pilot's Operating Handbook* for your airplane and be able to use these and other performance charts (climb, cruise, etc.)

The airplane (and engine) is only aware of the *density*, or standard, altitude and this results from a combination of pressure altitude and temperature. (Pressure altitude is that altitude shown on the altimeter when it is set to 29.92 inches of mercury —

review Chapter 3.) The sea level standard temperature is 59°F (15°C) and the normal lapse rate, or normal temperature drop, is 3 1/2°F (2°C) per thousand feet; a higher temperature than normal would mean that the air density is less for that particular altitude. The air could be as "thin" as that found several thousand feet higher under standard conditions. The altimeter is only capable of measuring air pressure, not air density, so you must take variations from standard temperature into account.

In using the take-off and landing charts (Fig. 17-10) you may have to interpolate between values given. For instance, assume that you will be taking off from a field with a pressure altitude of 3000 feet with a 14 K headwind at a temperature of 15°C: First, you'd interpolate between 10° and 20°C at that pressure altitude for the ground run and total distances to clear a 50-foot obstacle. At 10°C the values are 935 and 1780 respectively. At 20°C the distances are 1010 and 1915 feet, so you could expect them at 15°C to be 975 and 1850 feet (rounded off). As the NOTES indicate, you should subtract 10 percent for each 9 K of headwind, so at 14 K (about 1.5 times 9 K) the reduction should be 15 percent for final figures of 830 and 1575 feet (rounded off). The same idea would be used for the landing distance. *These distances given are for a hard-surface runway; the take-off run could be doubled by*

TAKEOFF DISTANCE
SHORT FIELD

CONDITIONS:
Flaps Up
Full Throttle Prior to Brake Release
Paved, Level, Dry Runway
Zero Wind

NOTES:
1. Short field technique as specified in Section 4.
2. Prior to takeoff from fields above 5000 feet elevation, the mixture should be leaned to give maximum RPM in a full throttle, static runup.
3. Decrease distances 10% for each 9 knots headwind. For operation with tailwinds up to 10 knots, increase distances by 10% for each 2 knots.
4. Where distance value has been deleted, climb performance after lift-off is less than 150 fpm at takeoff speed.
5. For operation on a dry, grass runway, increase distances by 15% of the "ground roll" figure.

WEIGHT LBS	TAKEOFF SPEED KIAS		PRESS ALT FT	0°C		10°C		20°C		30°C		40°C	
	LIFT OFF	50 FT		GRND ROLL	TOTAL TO CLEAR 50 FT OBS	GRND ROLL	TOTAL TO CLEAR 50 FT OBS	GRND ROLL	TOTAL TO CLEAR 50 FT OBS	GRND ROLL	TOTAL TO CLEAR 50 FT OBS	GRND ROLL	TOTAL TO CLEAR 50 FT OBS
1600	53	60	S.L.	655	1245	710	1335	765	1435	820	1540	880	1650
			1000	720	1365	775	1465	835	1575	900	1690	970	1815
			2000	790	1500	855	1615	920	1735	990	1865	1065	2005
			3000	870	1650	935	1780	1010	1915	1090	2065	1170	2225
			4000	955	1820	1030	1965	1115	2125	1200	2290	1290	2475
			5000	1050	2015	1140	2185	1230	2360	1325	2555	1430	2770
			6000	1160	2245	1255	2435	1360	2640	1465	2870	1580	3120
			7000	1285	2510	1390	2730	1505	2970	1625	3240	---	---
			8000	1420	2820	1540	3080	1670	3370	---	---	---	---

LANDING DISTANCE
SHORT FIELD

CONDITIONS:
Flaps 40°
Power Off
Maximum Braking
Paved, Level, Dry Runway
Zero Wind

NOTES:
1. Short field technique as specified in Section 4.
2. Decrease distances 10% for each 9 knots headwind. For operation with tailwinds up to 10 knots, increase distances by 10% for each 2 knots.
3. For operation on a dry, grass runway, increase distances by 45% of the "ground roll" figure.

WEIGHT LBS	SPEED AT 50 FT KIAS	PRESS ALT FT	0°C		10°C		20°C		30°C		40°C	
			GRND ROLL	TOTAL TO CLEAR 50 FT OBS	GRND ROLL	TOTAL TO CLEAR 50 FT OBS	GRND ROLL	TOTAL TO CLEAR 50 FT OBS	GRND ROLL	TOTAL TO CLEAR 50 FT OBS	GRND ROLL	TOTAL TO CLEAR 50 FT OBS
1600	52	S.L.	425	1045	440	1065	455	1090	470	1110	485	1135
		1000	440	1065	455	1090	470	1110	485	1135	505	1165
		2000	455	1090	470	1115	490	1140	505	1165	520	1185
		3000	470	1115	490	1140	505	1165	525	1195	540	1215
		4000	490	1140	505	1165	525	1195	545	1225	560	1245
		5000	510	1170	525	1195	545	1225	565	1255	585	1285
		6000	530	1200	545	1225	565	1255	585	1285	605	1315
		7000	550	1230	570	1260	590	1290	610	1320	630	1350
		8000	570	1260	590	1290	610	1320	630	1350	655	1385

Fig. 17-10. Take-off and landing distance charts. (*Cessna Aircraft Co.*)

RATE OF CLIMB
MAXIMUM

CONDITIONS:
Flaps Up
Full Throttle

WEIGHT LBS	PRESS ALT FT	CLIMB SPEED KIAS	RATE OF CLIMB - FPM			
			-20°C	0°C	20°C	40°C
1600	S.L.	68	770	710	655	595
	2000	67	675	615	560	500
	4000	65	580	520	465	405
	6000	64	485	430	375	310
	8000	63	390	335	280	215
	10,000	62	295	240	185	---
	12,000	61	200	150	---	---

Fig. 17-11. Maximum rates of climb chart. (*Cessna Aircraft Co.*)

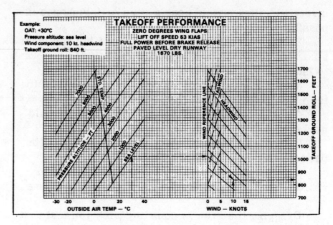

Fig. 17-12. A graphical presentation of take-off performance.

mud, snow, or high grass. Also, these are "average" values — you can use a lot more runway with poor pilot technique.

Figure 17-11 is a climb chart for the airplane just discussed.

Figure 17-12 shows a graphical method of computing the ground roll required under different conditions. This airplane also has a chart for total distance over a 50-foot obstacle under varying conditions (not included here).

Figure 17-13 shows the take-off distances (ground roll and to clear a 50-foot obstacle) for a current trainer. Two propeller options are available for this airplane: (1) A climb propeller of lower (flatter) pitch, which is more efficient at lower airspeeds, and (2) a cruise propeller with a higher

average pitch, which is not as efficient in lower speed regimes but comes into its own at cruise speeds. Note that at a pressure altitude of 2000 feet and a temperature of $20°C$ (at a weight of 1600 pounds) the climb prop-equipped airplane uses less distance to lift off or to clear the 50-foot obstacle (arrows).

While the subjects of special take-off and landing procedures and performance charts are being covered, it might be well to take a look at Figure 17-14.

The example shown gives an answer to 35-knot headwind and 20-knot crosswind components respectively. Looking at another problem, suppose an airplane is limited to a crosswind component of $0.2 V_{so}$ (see Fig. 3-27) and its V_{so} is 60 knots. Can it legally land in a 30-knot wind at a 25° angle to the

TAKEOFF DISTANCE. CLIMB PROPELLER

ASSOCIATED CONDITIONS:
Power — Maximum
Flaps — Up
Runway — Hard surface (level & dry)
Fuel Mixture — Full throttle climb, mixture leaned above 5000 feet to smooth engine operation

NOTES:
1. Decrease distance 5% for each 5 knots headwind. For operation with tailwinds up to 10 knots increase distance by 10% for each 2.5 knots.
2. Where distance value is shaded, climb performance after lift-off, based on the engine operating at takeoff power at takeoff speed, is less than 150 feet per minute.
3. If takeoff power is set without brakes applied, then distances apply from point where full power is attained.

WEIGHT LBS	TAKEOFF SPEED KIAS (MPH) LIFT OFF	CLEAR 50 FT.	PRESS. ALT. FT.	0°C (32°F) GROUND ROLL	0°C CLEAR 50 FT.	10°C (50°F) GROUND ROLL	10°C CLEAR 50 FT.	20°C (68°F) GROUND ROLL	20°C CLEAR 50 FT.	30°C (86°F) GROUND ROLL	30°C CLEAR 50 FT.	40°C (104°F) GROUND ROLL	40°C CLEAR 50 FT.
1600	57 (66)	66 (76)	S.L.	719	1313	798	1455	883	1607	973	1769	1069	1940
			2000	857	1554	951	1722	1051	1901	1159	2092	1273	2295
			4000	1022	1842	1135	2042	1255	2254	1383	2481	1520	2772
			6000	1224	2190	1358	2427	1502	2680	1655	2949	1819	3236
			8000	1468	2610	1629	2892	1802	3194	1986	3515	2182	3856
1500	56 (64)	64 (74)	S.L.	616	1132	684	1254	756	1385	834	1524	916	1672
			2000	734	1339	814	1483	901	1638	993	1802	1090	1977
			4000	876	1587	972	1759	1075	1942	1185	2137	1302	2345
			6000	1048	1887	1163	2091	1286	2308	1418	2541	1558	2787
			8000	1257	2248	1395	2491	1543	2751	1701	3028	1869	3322
1400	55 (63)	62 (71)	S.L.	522	965	580	1069	641	1181	706	1299	776	1425
			2000	622	1141	690	1265	763	1397	841	1537	924	1686
			4000	742	1353	824	1500	911	1656	1004	1822	1103	1999
			6000	888	1609	986	1783	1090	1968	1201	2166	1320	2376
			8000	1065	1917	1183	2124	1308	2345	1441	2581	1584	2832

TAKEOFF DISTANCE, CRUISE PROPELLER

ASSOCIATED CONDITIONS:
Power — Maximum
Flaps — Up
Runway — Hard surface (level & dry)
Fuel Mixture — Full throttle climb, mixture leaned above 5000 feet to smooth engine operation

NOTES:
1. Decrease distance 5% for each 5 knots headwind. For operation with tailwinds up to 10 knots increase distance by 10% for each 2.5 knots.
2. Where distance value is shaded, climb performance after lift-off, based on the engine operating at takeoff power at takeoff speed, is less than 150 feet per minute.
3. If takeoff power is set without brakes applied, then distances apply from point where full power is attained.

WEIGHT LBS	TAKEOFF SPEED KIAS (MPH) LIFT OFF	CLEAR 50 FT.	PRESS. ALT. FT.	0°C (32°F) GROUND ROLL	0°C CLEAR 50 FT.	10°C (50°F) GROUND ROLL	10°C CLEAR 50 FT.	20°C (68°F) GROUND ROLL	20°C CLEAR 50 FT.	30°C (86°F) GROUND ROLL	30°C CLEAR 50 FT.	40°C (104°F) GROUND ROLL	40°C CLEAR 50 FT.
1600	58 (67)	66 (76)	S.L.	762	1365	846	1513	963	1670	1031	1838	1133	2017
			2000	908	1615	1007	1789	1114	1976	1228	2175	1349	2386
			4000	1083	1915	1202	2122	1330	2344	1466	2579	1610	2830
			6000	1296	2277	1439	2523	1591	2786	1754	3067	1927	3365
			8000	1555	2714	1726	3008	1909	3321	2104	3655	2312	4011
1500	57 (66)	64 (74)	S.L.	653	1176	725	1303	801	1439	883	1583	970	1737
			2000	777	1391	863	1541	954	1702	1052	1873	1155	2055
			4000	928	1650	1030	1828	1139	2019	1255	2221	1379	2437
			6000	1110	1961	1232	2173	1363	2400	1502	2641	1650	2898
			8000	1332	2338	1479	2590	1635	2860	1802	3148	1980	3454
1400	56 (64)	62 (71)	S.L.	553	1003	614	1111	679	1227	748	1350	822	1481
			2000	659	1186	731	1314	809	1451	891	1597	979	1752
			4000	786	1406	873	1558	965	1721	1064	1894	1169	2078
			6000	841	1672	1044	1853	1155	2046	1273	2252	1398	2470
			8000	1129	1993	1253	2208	1386	2438	1527	2684	1678	2944

Fig. 17-13. Take-off distances for a current two-place trainer for climb and cruise propellers. (*Grumman American Aviation Corp.*)

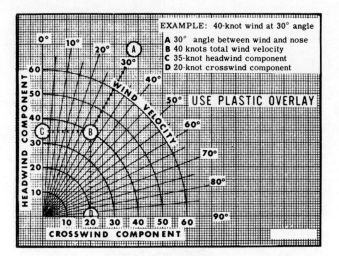

EXAMPLE: 40-knot wind at 30° angle
A 30° angle between wind and nose
B 40 knots total wind velocity
C 35-knot headwind component
D 20-knot crosswind component

USE PLASTIC OVERLAY

WIND VELOCITY

HEADWIND COMPONENT

CROSSWIND COMPONENT

Fig. 17-14. A crosswind-headwind component chart. (FAA).

runway? The actual value of the maximum allowable crosswind is 0.2 × 60 = 12 knots. Using Figure 17-14, you'll find that the crosswind component is 12.5 to 13 knots, which is over the limit. (The headwind component is about 27 knots.) The problems you'll be given on the written test will require that you find the angle ("you are landing on Runway 27 with a wind from 310° at 20 knots") and then use the chart. The problems apparently assume that the runway is lined up exactly with 270°, and the wind and runway are both given in the same terms (magnetic or true directions – see Fig. 6-3).

SIMULATED HIGH-ALTITUDE TAKE-OFFS

Before you get to the private flight test you should make a simulated high-altitude take-off. The instructor will limit your power for take-off, and you can see how the airplane would do (or not do) at some high altitude. The biggest problem you'll have is the very strong tendency to rush the airplane off. (This is also the tendency the first time you fly the airplane at maximum certificated weight from a comparatively short field.) The airplane seems to be dragging its feet, and you'll want to pull it off before it's ready. After you become airborne, don't pull the nose up "to get extra climb." You might put yourself in Position (4) or (5) back in Figure 12-13, and performance will suffer even more.

Talking a little more about the density altitude idea, every 15° F (8 1/2° C) above the standard temperature for your pressure altitude bumps the density altitude up another 1000 feet. Suppose you are going to take off at an airport at an elevation of 2200 feet. The altimeter setting is 30.12 inches of mercury, which makes your pressure altitude right about 2000 feet (1 inch of mercury equals approximately 1000 feet of altitude). The pressure corrected to sea level is 0.20 inches of mercury higher than standard, so the pressure altitude is (0.20 × 1000) = 200 feet lower than the elevation. The pressure altitude is 2000 feet (which could have also been found by rolling 29.92 into the setting window).

The temperature is 82° F, which certainly is not unusual in the summer. The standard temperature for this pressure altitude is 52° F (59° F - [2 × 3 1/2° F] = 52° F), since the normal lapse rate is 3 1/2° F per thousand feet. The temperature (82° F) is 30° F above the standard. Since each added 15° F makes an additional 1000 feet of density altitude, your real density altitude is the pressure altitude (2000 feet) *plus* 2000 feet, or *4000 feet. You* think you're sitting at 2000 feet, but the airplane knows that it is at 4000 feet – and acts accordingly. If the temperature had been 97° F at that airport (entirely possible), another thousand feet would have been tacked on and the density altitude would have been *5000 feet.*

At an airport in the summer it's not at all unusual for the temperature to be 15° F (or much more) above its "standard." The temperature, rather than atmospheric pressure changes, is the big factor. The not-unusual temperature of 82°F in the example added 2000 feet of density altitude. To get that effect by pressure decrease (assuming a standard temperature) would mean that the pressure would have to be *2 inches* of mercury below normal, or the sea level pressure would be 27.92 instead of 29.92 inches of mercury (in/Hg). This *is* unusual, and such pressure conditions could only be found in the eye of a very strong typhoon.

Talking in terms of Celsius for the earlier example problem, the standard sea level temperature is 15°C and the normal lapse rate is 2°C per thousand feet, so the following would apply:

Standard temperature for the 2000 feet is 11°C; the actual temperature is 28°C, or 17°C above standard. Since each 8 1/2°C adds another 1000 feet of density altitude, the answer is again 4000 feet.

One thing that you may not have considered is that the *moist air is less dense than dry air* (all other factors equal) and so the airplane will not perform as well in take-offs and climbs when the air is moist. (You might figure on up to about 10 percent less performance under wet conditions.)

One last thing about density altitude: You may not know what it is at a particular time, but the airplane *always* does.

Fig. 18-1. The instructor will discuss your errors on the forced landing.

The high-altitude emergency gives you more time and a greater choice of fields. In earlier stages, however, this is a handicap, so practice is usually reserved for the post-solo period. The average student, when given his first high-altitude emergency, is as busy looking around as a one-eyed man watching a beauty contest. There are *too many* places to land. He may get confused and change his mind on the choice of a field several times and finally end up too low to do anything but land in the worst field within a 15-mile radius (Fig. 18-1).

The high-altitude emergency requires that you do the following: (1) Know the wind directions; (2) pick a field; (3) glide to a position over it; (4) and try to find out what caused the failure (carburetor ice, tank ran dry, etc.) and remedy it if possible. Set up a glide pattern so that you will hit a "Key Position" at about the same point and at a slightly higher altitude above the ground as the point at which you closed the throttle to make a 180° power-off approach (the windmilling prop will hurt the glide).

This Key Position is chosen because by this time you've shot many power-off approaches from this position. It's literally impossible to glide for a distant field from 2000 or 3000 feet above the ground and consistently hit it. It's been found to be easier to judge the glide angle if the approach involves a turn. Let's take the emergency point by point.

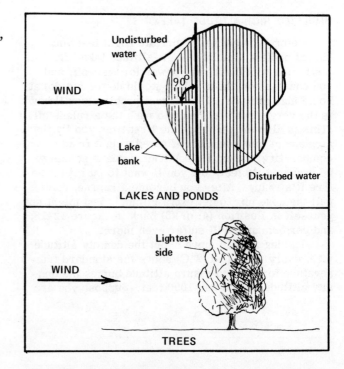

Fig. 18-2. Lakes or ponds help you tell the wind direction, even if you are too high to see the actual wave movement; the bank on the windward side keeps the water undisturbed. The wind turns tree leaves over, showing their lighter side in the direction from which it is blowing.

TELLING WIND DIRECTION

There are many ways of telling the wind direction when you are away from the airport: smoke, waves moving across a field of grain or waves on lakes, dust blowing, trees, etc. (Fig. 18-2).

Know the wind direction and approximate velocity at all times. Don't be like the student who didn't know the wind direction and stuck his hand out the plane window to find out. (He figured that the wind was right on the nose at about 100 K.)

It's better not to waste time trying to find out the wind direction *after* the emergency has occurred.

PICKING YOUR FIELD

Know the types of fields in your part of the country. Has it been raining a lot lately? If so, that field of young wheat may be too soft to land on.

Look for electric or telephone poles across the field because you won't see the wires themselves, from altitude.

Look for fences across the middle of pastures. These are sometimes hard to see because the field on both sides looks alike.

If two fields are equally near and good for landing, pick the one closest to the highway or houses, for several reasons. If the landing is a success (and with good planning it's bound to be) you will want to call the airport. If the plane is damaged or the engine is in bad shape (maybe there was an oil leak and the engine seized) the airport personnel may want to dismantle the plane and haul it back. If the landing was not a success and you are injured, people will see the crash and come to your aid.

If your airplane has flaps, they'll be a great help in hitting the field. The idea is to add flaps in increments as necessary to hit the field. The usual student error in practice emergencies is to add flaps too soon (and *full* flaps at that) and sit there helplessly while the airplane starts to sink into the woods a quarter of a mile short of the chosen field. *If you have added flaps and start losing ground (it looks as if the field is gaining on you), get the flaps*

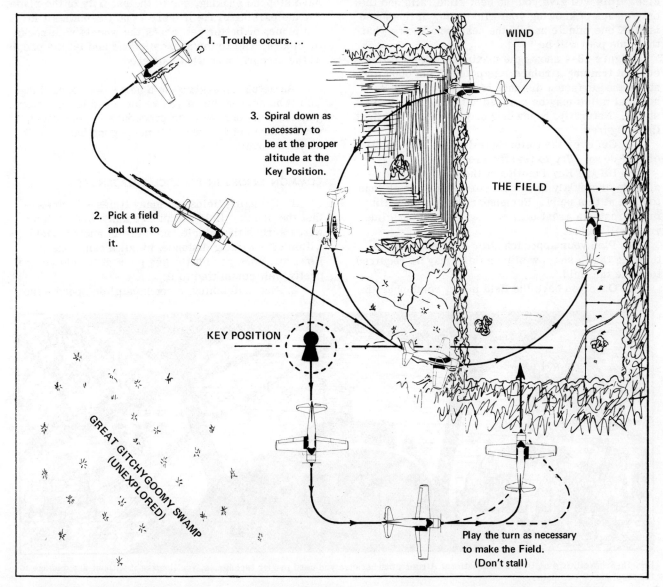

Fig. 18-3. The Key Position helps to turn an unusual situation into one more familiar. Keep that glide speed constant.

up and watch things start improving. Then when you get to the proper position, put 'em back down again.

The big misconception about flaps concerns the idea that once the flaps are down, they should never be retracted because the airplane will "fall" because of a loss of "lift." If you are close to the flaps-down stall speed and suddenly raise the flaps, you might find that the airspeed is *below* the flaps-*up* stall speed, and a stall could result. *But,* if you are at the normal glide speed and at a reasonable altitude (say, a couple of hundred feet or more) you'll be a lot better off in getting distance, even if that initial, slight sink bothers you. Putting the flaps down in increments is the best way to do it to avoid flap juggling (up and down).

PROCEDURE

1. When the engine stops, establish a normal glide. Pick the best field and turn to it (Fig. 18-3). Maintain the normal glide speed throughout the exercise. This will give you the best glide ratio and the only means of knowing your glide path. If the speed is 70 K one minute and 50 the next, who knows what the glide path will be?

Figure 18-4 shows the maximum glide ratio of a current training airplane. As noted, from 6000 feet above the surface a distance of approximately 8 nautical miles may be covered with the conditions stated. Naturally, headwinds or tailwinds will affect these figures.

2. Get over the field. Spiral to the Key Position or "S" down. Try to find the problem.

3. Hit the Key Position at the traffic pattern altitude or slightly higher — better slightly high than too low at this point. Remember that a windmilling prop creates a great deal of drag, hence your glide ratio will suffer.

4. Plan your approach after the Key Position thinking that a shallow slip or flaps may be required to make the field.

5. Once you have the field made, remember the

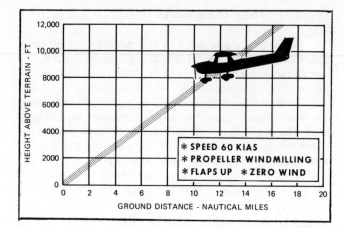

Fig. 18-4. Maximum glide performance. (*Cessna 150*)

landing is just like the one back at the airport (Fig. 18-5). A normal landing will minimize the damage if the field is rougher than it looked from 3000 feet.

6. After the plane is stopped and your knees have stopped shaking, see to the security of the plane. Set the parking brake if there is no tie-down kit in the plane, or better yet, chock the wheels with rocks or blocks. Get to the nearest phone and let the people at the airport know what happened.

An actual emergency is a nerve-wracking thing. You'll be scared, but if you've had practice in emergencies and gone over the procedure in your mind, you'll make out fine and it'll make good hangar talk after it's over.

COMMON ERRORS IN PRACTICE EMERGENCIES

1. Changing fields too many times — if you see that the original field you picked has a big ditch or wires across the middle and there is another field within easy gliding distance, by all means take it. However, once you hit the key point at a field you're pretty well committed to it.

2. Not maintaining a constant glide speed — the

Fig. 18-5. Well, it's no Dulles International Airport, but because you used proper techniques, you'll make it without any damage to the airplane or occupants.

result is usually that the field is missed and an airplane is "pranged."

3. Poor wind correction after the key point, that is, being too high or too low to make the field.

DISCUSSION

After the field is "made" the instructor will take over and discuss the emergency with you.

Keep the engine cleared on the descent. The high altitude emergency means an extended glide and cooling of the engine, particularly in cold weather.

Use carburetor heat as recommended by the manufacturer.

You will not practice emergencies solo. But while we're on the subject of extended glides, if sometime in cold weather you've glided from 3000 feet down to 600 feet above the ground the engine may cool and not want to take throttle at first. Don't ram the throttle open — open it slowly. Give the engine a shot of primer if it's particularly hard to get going again. One quick shot will usually do the trick. In hot weather the engine tends to load up during an extended glide and will require careful clearing.

19. *The Navigation Idea*

A flight is a success or failure before you leave the ground. Preflight planning is important at all times but particularly so before a cross-country flight. Too many pilots jump into a plane and head for distant airports with little thought of weather, the condition of the destination airport, or what kind of fueling or repair service can be obtained there.

BACKGROUND

There are several types of navigation used by pilots: (1) *pilotage*, or flying by reference to landmarks; (2) *dead* (deduced) *reckoning*, which is drawing vectors of the wind and your true airspeed and computing the heading, ground speed, and estimated time of arrival at the destination; (3) *celestial navigation*, using a sextant to measure angles to heavenly bodies; and (4) *radio navigation*, or navigation through the use of radio aids.

Pilotage is the major means of navigation for the student pilot, but radio navigation is coming into more use as trainers become better equipped.

Unfortunately, too many pilots rely on radio navigation and find themselves rusty in pilotage or use of the sectional chart if the radios go out.

MERIDIANS AND PARALLELS

The earth is laid off in imaginary lines called meridians and parallels. The meridians run north

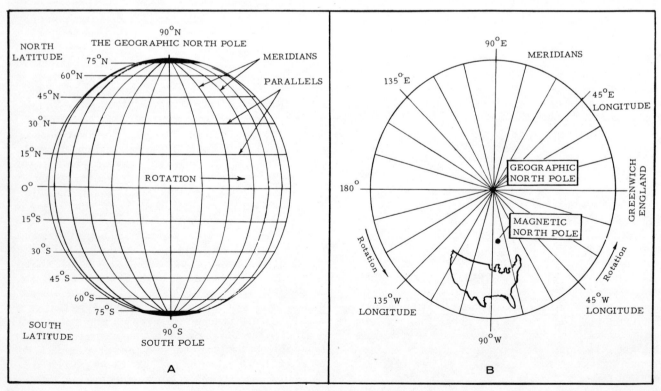

Fig. 19-1. Navigation basics.

and south and divide the earth like the sections of an orange (Fig. 19-1). The prime meridian goes through Greenwich, England. All longitude (east or west measurements of position) is measured east or west from this line to the 180° meridian on the opposite side of the earth. Since the earth turns 360°, or a complete revolution, in 24 hours, each 15° of longitude means a difference of 1 hour as far as the sun is concerned. You can see this roughly in the time zones in the United States.

If someone said that a ship is at 15° west longitude, it would be almost impossible to locate. It could be anywhere on that meridian between the north and south poles. It would be much like telling a friend to meet you on 54th Street in New York City on a busy day. If you said instead, "Meet me at 54th and Blank Street," it would help matters considerably. The United States extends from about 67° west longitude to about 125° west longitude.

For navigational purposes, time is standardized to that at Greenwich. This Greenwich Mean Time or Universal Time is based on the 24-hour clock. Looking at Figure 19-1, you see that the earth rotates toward the "east." The day starts at 0000GMT, and since parts of the United States are from 67° to 125° "behind" Greenwich, as the earth rotates, our time will also be behind accordingly. If you are at 90° west longitude, your time will be 6 hours behind that of Greenwich (each 15° longitude = 1 hour of time). If the time is 0600 (6:00 a.m.) at your position, add 6 hours to obtain the Universal Time (1200 or 12:00 noon). If you are in the Eastern Standard Zone add 5 hours to get GMT (or "Zulu") time, add 6 in the Central Standard Time Zone, and so on.

The earth is further divided north and south by parallels — so called because, instead of converging at two points as the meridians do, they are parallel to each other (Fig. 19-1). The equator is the prime parallel, and latitude is measured north and south from it. The equator is 0° latitude and the United States runs from about 25° north latitude at the Florida tip to about 49° north latitude on the Canadian border. The North Pole is at 90° north latitude and the South Pole at 90° south latitude.

Each degree of latitude and longitude is broken down into 60 minutes, and each minute of *latitude* equals a nautical mile, or 6080 feet. You can measure a distance on the map by laying the length to be measured north and south on the map and reading the minutes of latitude that it extends. This gives the distance in nautical miles; to convert these to statute or land miles, multiply the result by 1.15. In other words, a nautical mile equals 1.15 or about 1 1/7 statute (land) miles.

Don't measure distances between meridians this way, because the equator would be the only place where 1 minute of longitude equals a nautical mile. The meridians converge as they get farther north or south, so while the distance between them in degrees is always the same, the distance in miles is not. All aeronautical charts have a scale in statute and nautical miles.

The meridians converge on the "true" North Pole so that any angle measured from a meridian is the angle from true North. If you were at a point on a map and wanted to know the direction to another point, you would measure it as an angle clockwise from true North, using a meridian midway between the two points. The reason for choosing a middle meridian is because of the type of map you'll be using, as will be discussed later in "Plotter."

Then, directions are measured clockwise from true North using 360° (a full circle). East is 90°, South is 180°, West is 270°, and North is 0° (or 360°). Northeast is 45°, Southeast 135°, etc. This means that the pilot can plan his course to the nearest degree.

The idea is to always use three numbers in speaking or writing of directions; 90° should be 090°.

MORE ABOUT THE COMPASS

Certain errors of the compass were discussed earlier in the introduction to the instrument and emergency flying by instruments. You know of the properties such as northerly turning error, which affects the compass in a turn, or the acceleration errors that affect it with speed changes. Other factors important in aircraft navigation should be considered in using the compass in straight, unaccelerated flight.

VARIATION

The fact that the Magnetic North Pole and the True North Pole are not the same means a little more work for you in navigating. The Magnetic North Pole is in Canada, and your compass points to this magnetic pole rather than the true one.

The angle between your direction to the True North Pole and the Magnetic North Pole is called variation. If at your position the Magnetic Pole is 6° farther "east" than the True North Pole, you say that a 6° east variation exists. The variation in the United States runs from about 22° West in Maine to about 20° East in Oregon. Isogonic lines, or lines of equal variation, are on the aeronautical charts and are given in 1° increments. If you should be flying in an area where the two poles are in line, no correction for variation is needed. The isogonic line will show as 0° variation, or more properly, the 0° line is called the agonic line (Fig. 19-2).

In plotting a course, you will measure the true course at a middle meridian. Because you will be referring to the compass, the course must be plotted in relation to the Magnetic North Pole. You will add or subtract variation to accomplish this. *Remember: East is least and West is best.* This means that you will look at the isogonic or variation line that is nearest to the halfway point of your course and subtract 5° from the true course if the variation is 5° E or add 5° if the variation is 5° W. *Going from true to magnetic, subtract easterly variation and add west-*

erly variation. How much to subtract or add will depend on the value of the midpoint isogonic line.

The British have a saying "Variation East, Magnetic Least; Variation West, Magnetic Best," which could also help you to remember.

If you measured the true course with a protractor and found it to be 120°, and the midpoint isogonic line showed 5° E, your magnetic course would be 115° (Fig. 19-3).

The terms "east" and "west" used for variation may be misleading to the newcomer. 'East" and "west" might appear to have something to do with the direction the airplane is flying. *This is not the case at all.* Since the magnetic compass starts *its* measurements at the Magnetic North Pole, in Figure 19-3 it starts "counting" 5° later than your map reference (true North). This is the case whether you are flying on a course of 320°, 120°, or what have you. It might be better to speak in terms of "plus 5° variation" or "minus 5° variation," but the current method seems to be permanent. *Variation at a particular geographic position is the same for all types of airplanes, whether J-3 Cubs or B-52s.*

DEVIATION

The compass will have instrument error called deviation, due in part to attraction by the ferrous metal parts of the plane. This error will vary between headings, and is usually noted for every 30° on a compass correction card, which is located on the instrument panel near the compass (Fig. 19-4).

The compass is swung or corrected on a compass rose, a large calibrated circle painted on the concrete ramp or taxiway away from metal interference such as hangars. The plane is taxied onto the rose and corrections are made with a nonmagnetic screwdriver. Attempts are made to balance out the errors as much as possible. The engine should be running and radio and electrical equipment should be on to give a true picture of the deviation as would be experienced in flight. To be completely accurate the plane should be in level flight attitude (no problem with a tricycle gear) with the tail supported by a sawhorse or short ladder (tailwheel type).

Suppose, for example, your magnetic course is 115°. This is not shown on the correction card, so some averaging will be necessary. Practically speaking, pick the reading on the card that is 120°. You see that for 120° you must fly 118° or subtract 2°. Subtract 2° from 115° and the compass course is 113°.

Unlike variation, which is a function of your geographic position, deviation varies between individual airplanes (and may vary in a particular airplane, depending on what electrical or radio equipment is currently in operation).

For the steps used to go from a true course (or true heading) to the course (or heading) with respect to the *compass,* remember that "*True Virgins Make Dull Company*":

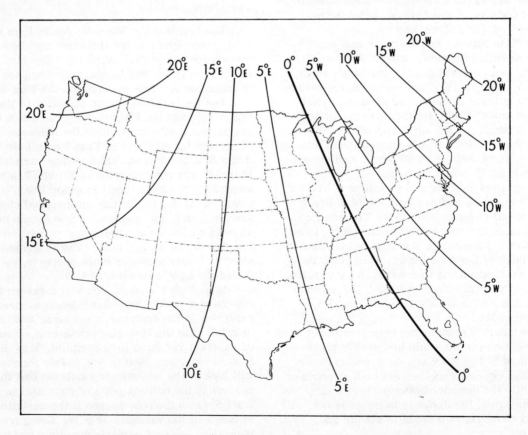

Fig. 19-2. Approximate location of isogonic lines in the United States.

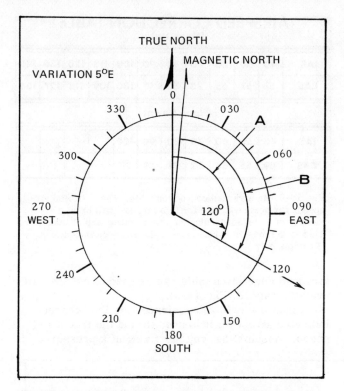

Fig. 19-3. True and magnetic courses and variation. You measure the course from the map reference (True North Pole) and find that the angle is 120° (A). The Magnetic North Pole, in this example, is 5° "east" of the True North Pole and your compass measures its angle from this and starts 5° "later" (B). The angle with reference to the Magnetic North Pole to the course line is 5° less than the true course. This is the condition for *any* course in the geographic area of 5° E variation. If the problem had been for a place where the variation is 5° W, the MNP would have been 5° "west" of the TNP and the 120° *true* course would mean a *magnetic* course of 125°.

1. *True* course (or heading)
2. Plus or minus *Variation* gives
3. *Magnetic* course (or heading)
4. Plus or minus *Deviation* gives
5. *Compass* course (or heading).

Remember that the 'east is least . . .' idea is true only when going from a true course (or heading) to a magnetic course or heading. Working from magnetic to true, you would *add* easterly variation and *subtract* westerly variation. The normal procedure is to go from true to magnetic courses or headings, but written tests have asked questions on the reverse procedure.

FOR (MAGNETIC)	N	30	60	E	120	150
STEER (COMPASS)	O	26	58	87	118	150
FOR (MAGNETIC)	S	210	240	W	300	330
STEER (COMPASS)	183	214	243	275	303	332

Fig. 19-4. A typical compass correction card.

PLOTTER

The plotter is a small transparent plastic circle or semicircle marked from 0° to 359° (the semicircular plotter has a double row of figures at each

point) to measure course angles on the map. Plotters have an attached plastic rule in scale miles for both the sectional (1 inch equals about 7 NM) and the World Aeronautical Chart (1 inch equals about 14 NM).

When you plan a cross-country you'll draw a line between your departure airport and the destination airport and measure the true course with the plotter.

Measure the course at a midway meridian, because the sectional chart is a Lambert conformal conic projection; that is, the meridians are closer together at the top of the map. By measuring from the middle meridian a more accurate course will be obtained. However, the error is so small that little trouble will be caused by not doing this — but again you might as well get another good habit now.

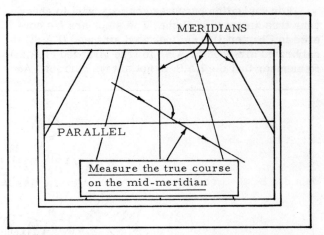

Fig. 19-5. Exaggerated drawing of meridian convergence on a sectional chart.

It's possible to get confused when laying off a course by using a plotter, and students sometimes arrive at an answer that is 180° off. *Draw the course line and figure about what the direction is* (Jonesville is east-southeast of Smithtown, so you would figure somewhere between 90° and 135° true course). *Don't mechanically measure a course but think about what you're doing.* You'll soon be able to look at a course line on a map and guess within 5° of it. You should *very carefully read the plotter when checking the course.*

You will notice azimuth circles around each VOR station on the sectional chart. These are calibrated from 0° to 360° in 5° increments and are oriented on magnetic north. These are an aid to the pilot who is combining pilotage and radio navigation, as will be covered later. If you can't find your plotter and one of these omni roses is near your course line on the map, you may measure the magnetic course by laying a straight edge parallel to the course line and through the center of the circle (or use a parallel rule if you have one). The *magnetic* course is then read because of the orientation with magnetic north rather than a meridian, and you've saved the step of adding or subtracting variation.

COMPUTER

A computer is a useful addition to any student pilot's equipment. It's a circular slide rule with the inside circle calibrated in time (hours and minutes) and the outside circle in velocity (miles per hour or knots) or gallons. With it you can check fuel consumption or speed. You learned in Chapter 3 that the 2 percent per thousand feet airspeed correction is only good for a standard day (59°F or 15°C at sea level) and for a normal temperature lapse rate, or drop, of 3 1/2°F or 2°C per thousand feet. If you know the outside air temperature at your pressure altitude, the true airspeed can be readily found on the computer.

FINDING TRUE AIRSPEED

For navigation purposes you may want to check your true airspeed in flight. The steps are (as covered in Chapter 3) from indicated airspeed (I.A.S.) to calibrated airspeed (C.A.S.) to true airspeed (T.A.S.). Remember that the I.A.S. is not always correct. An

AIRSPEED CORRECTION TABLE											
(Flaps Up)											
IAS	40	50	60	70	80	90	100	110	120	130	140
CAS	51	57	65	73	82	91	100	109	118	127	136
(Flaps Down)											
IAS	40	50	60	70	80	90	100				
CAS	49	55	63	72	81	89	98				

Fig. 19-6. An airspeed correction table. The indicated airspeeds for normal cruise for this airplane will be in the vicinity of 100 K (depending on power setting and altitude). This is the most accurate area of the airspeed indications. (Example only.)

airspeed correction table can be used to get the calibrated airspeed (Fig. 19-6).

Since the *calibrated* airspeed is the "correct" indicated airspeed, it is used to find the true airspeed. Assume that you are flying at a pressure

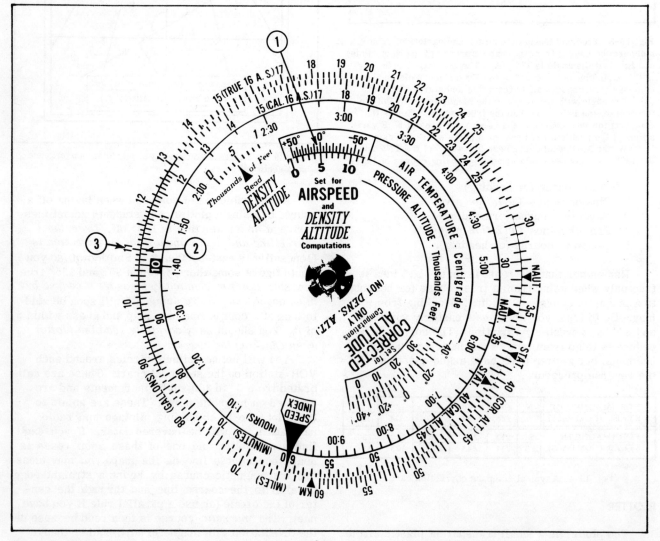

Fig. 19-7. Finding the true airspeed. (1) The temperature (+5° C) and pressure altitude (4500 feet) are set together, and opposite the calibrated airspeed (2) of 103 K, the true airspeed (3) of 110 K is found.

altitude of 4500 feet (indicating 103 K), the outside air temperature is +5°C, and you want to find the T.A.S. Looking at Figure 19-6 you see that the I.A.S. and C.A.S. can be considered the same at 103 K. That takes care of the first step.

Figure 19-7 shows the method of getting the true airspeed.

Practically speaking, you'll seldom get your T.A.S. in flight. You will be more interested in finding out your ground speed. The cruise information in the airplane's *Pilot's Operating Handbook* is given as true airspeed for various power settings and altitudes (see Chapter 23). However, you can check your T.A.S. to see if you're getting the proper performance for your power setting and altitude.

Some pilots use their indicated altitude instead of setting the altimeter to 29.92 for the pressure altitude to get the T.A.S. There is an error of about 2 percent for each thousand-foot difference between the indicated and pressure altitudes. Since this difference is generally much less than 1000 feet, this method is considered accurate enough for practical use.

GETTING THE GROUND SPEED

You'll find that the computer is used most often in practical situations to find ground speeds and estimated times of arrival.

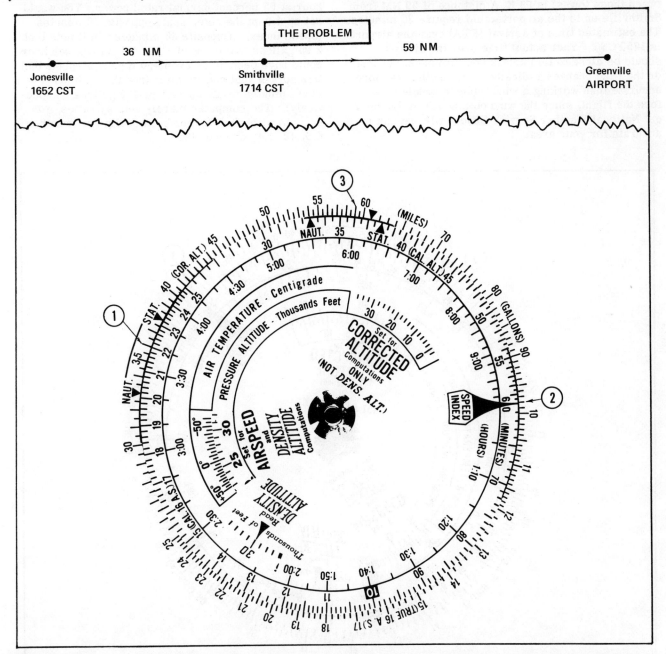

Fig. 19-8. Find the ground speed. (1) Set up the time (22 minutes) opposite the distance traveled (36 NM) to get the ground speed (98 K here) at (2). Once the relationship is established, the time required to fly other distances (59 NM in this case) can be found (36 minutes) as shown at (3). It is not necessary to actually know that the ground speed is 98 K — but you can go directly to (3). The estimated time of arrival over Greenville would be 1714 + 36 minutes, or 1750 CST.

The written examination for the private pilot's certificate contains questions that would concern a practical cross-country flight with multiple choice answers. A question might be: "You are over the center of the town of Jonesville at 1652 (4.52 p.m.) CST and over the center of Smithville at 1714 (5:14 p.m.) CST. What is your estimate of time and distance to the destination airport at Greenville?" Using the sectional chart issued to you for the examination, measure the distance between Jonesville and Smithville — it is 36 NM. So knowing that the distance from Jonesville to Smithville is 36 NM, and flying time is 22 minutes, set up the problem as shown in Figure 19-8. Your ground speed (or the speed over the ground between those towns) is 98 K. A distance of 59 NM from Smithville on to the airport would require 36 minutes. The estimated time of arrival (ETA) over the airport is 1750 CST. Your actual time over the airport should be close to this unless you turn back, get lost, or the wind changes radically. This method is more accurate than working a wind triangle problem before the flight, since the wind obtained from the nearest National Weather Service Office still may not be accurate for your area.

Notice also: In the area of point (3) in Figure 19-8 is the nautical miles (or knots) converter to statute miles or miles per hour. Note that 54 NM is equal to 62.5 statute miles. You could set the computer to whatever values you wanted to convert.

FINDING FUEL CONSUMPTION

Figure 19-9 shows how to find how much fuel you'll use flying from Smithville to Greenville. As Figure 19-8 showed, after checking the ground speed as 98 K, you'd expect to take 36 minutes to fly the 59 NM. A typical light trainer uses 4.9 gallons an hour at 65 percent normal rated power. You would set up 4.9 on the outer scale opposite 60 minutes (speed index). Opposite 36 minutes you'll note that 2.95 gallons will be used. The 4.9 gallons per hour could have been 49 or even 490 if your airplane had this sort of fuel consumption (and the fuel consumed in 36 minutes would be 29.5 or 295 gallons, respectively). The computer merely sets up ratios; *you* keep up with what the numbers really are (whether 4.9, 49, 490, or even 4900).

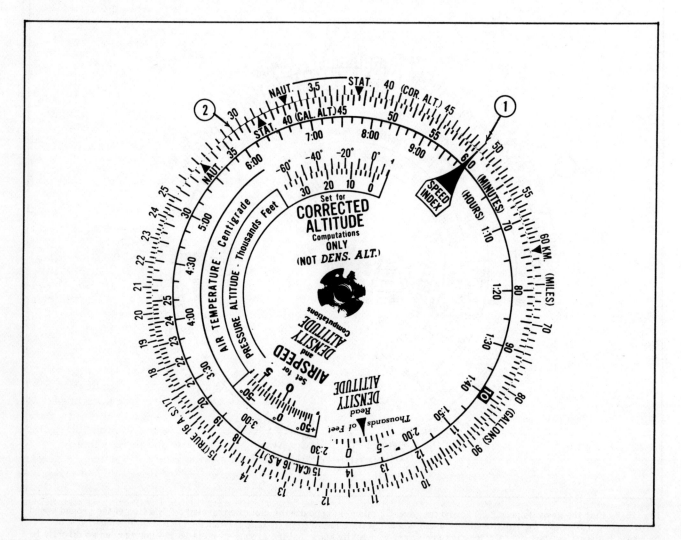

Fig. 19-9. Find fuel consumption.

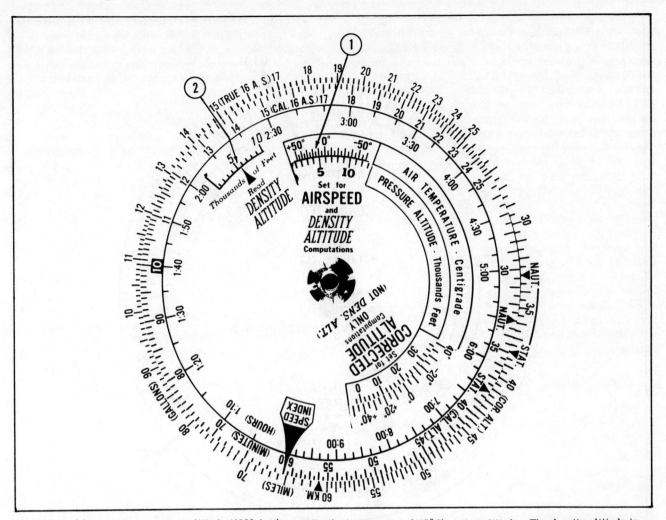

Fig. 19-10. (1) Set up the pressure altitude (4500 feet) opposite the temperature (+15°C) at that altitude. The density altitude is approximately 5500 feet as shown at (2). The standard temperature at 4500 feet is +6°C so that the actual temperature for this problem (+15°C) is high. The warm air is "thinner" and the airplane is flying at a lower air density than would be shown by the altimeter alone and would be performing as if at an actual standard altitude of 5500 feet, since performance depends on air density (among other things).

DENSITY ALTITUDE

Density altitude, which is used for calculating aircraft performance, may be found on the computer. As an example, suppose you are flying at a pressure altitude of 4500 feet and the outside air temperature gage indicates +15°C. Figure 19-10 shows how to set up a problem.

CORRECTING INDICATED OR PRESSURE ALTITUDE

Also shown on the computer is a *corrected altitude* function. The altimeter may read incorrectly because of a nonstandard temperature (which would affect the pressure working on it). Figure 19-11 shows how the altimeter can be corrected for this error.

In this case, the altimeter goes through the same steps as the airspeed indicator (from indicated altitude — which is what the instrument actually reads — to *calibrated* — which would be the indicated altitude corrected for instrument and system error to "true" altitude after the effects of nonstandard

temperature are taken into consideration). The standard temperature for 10,000 feet is -5°C, so the actual temperature is 10°C lower than standard (1). The computer shows that the actual pressure altitude is approximately 9650 feet — not the 10,000 shown by the altimeter (2). This would be of interest in clearing obstacles such as mountain ranges.

WIND TRIANGLE

Flying cross-country requires application of the principles learned in the rectangular course. Instead of having a well-defined line such as a field boundary to follow, you must use the imaginary line between your home airport and the destination.

The wind triangle is a vector system. A vector is an arrow representing the direction and magnitude of a force, as was seen in Chapters 8, 9, and 16. In the case of airplane navigation, these vectors are set up for a 1-hour period. On the earlier sample trip we found that the true course was 120°. Winds aloft are always given in true directions and in knots, and the

147

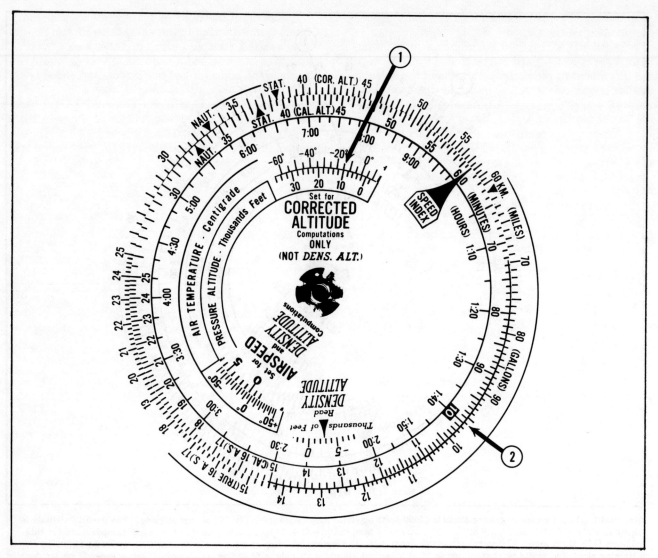

Fig. 19-11. Correcting indicated or pressure altitude for nonstandard temperature conditions.

altitudes given are above sea level. Rather than go through the steps to convert the true course to compass course, work the wind triangle with respect to true North and then convert the answer — your *true heading* — to compass heading, using corrections for variation and deviation.

Given: (1) The measured true course from Dover to Erin is 120°. (2) The Federal Aviation Regulations require that planes flying at 3000 feet or more above the surface fly at odd thousands plus 500 if the magnetic course to be flown is from 0° to 179°, and even thousands plus 500 from 180° to 359° (Visual Flight Rules — cruising altitudes). You see that the variation is 5°E, so the magnetic course is 115° (which is well within the eastern semicircle). Above 3000 you must fly odd plus 500 feet. You checked the winds aloft at the National Weather Service Office or FAA Flight Service Station and found that the wind at 5000 feet is from 220° true at 30 K. Because this gives you the best tailwind, you decide to fly at 5500 MSL, which is the closest odd plus 500 altitude. (3) You've checked the *Pilot's Operating Handbook*

and found that the true airspeed for this altitude will be 95 K.

On a blank piece of paper draw a line representing a true North line or meridian. Measure the true course with a plotter through some point on the true North line (Fig. 19-12A).

This line is of indefinite length (1). Pick a scale and draw a wind vector in the correct direction and at the proper length from some point on the course line. The wind given for this altitude is in knots, so that length is drawn to scale and in the proper direction (2). We are assuming in this case that the wind is the same at 5500 feet as that at 5000. However, many times you can interpolate between altitudes if there is a large variation between the wind's direction and/or velocity. For instance, if the wind is 270° and 20 K at 5000, and 310° and 30 K at 6000, a reasonable assumption would be that the wind at 5500 is halfway between these values, or 290° at 25 K.

From the wind arrow point swing a line the length of your T.A.S. (95 K) until it hits the course

148

line (3) (Fig. 19-12B). This gives you the vector picture (Fig. 19-12C).

The line EW (earth-wind) represents the wind with respect to the earth. The line WP represents the movement of the plane with respect to the wind, and its length (the T.A.S.) and angle (the true heading) tell you of the plane's movement and heading within the air mass.

The line EP (earth-plane) represents the plane's movement and speed with respect to the earth, and its direction is the true course you originally measured. The length of the line gives your ground speed from Dover to Erin at 96 K. You could figure the return trip ground speed and heading by extending the reciprocal course line through the point E and swinging another 95 K line from W to strike the course line, then reading the information as before.

A point of interest: A plane does not make a round trip with wind in the same time as can be done with no wind. It would seem that the plane having a headwind one way and a tailwind the other would average the same as a plane making the round trip under no wind conditions — but it won't.

Assume a round trip of 100 NM each way. Both planes cruise at 100 K true airspeed. Plane A has a 20 K tailwind on the outbound leg and a 20 K headwind on the return trip. Plane B flies the same trip under no-wind conditions.

PLANE A—WIND 20 K

Trip out - 100 miles at 120 K =		50 min.
Trip back - 100 miles at 80 K =		1 hr. 15 min.
		2 hr. 5 min.

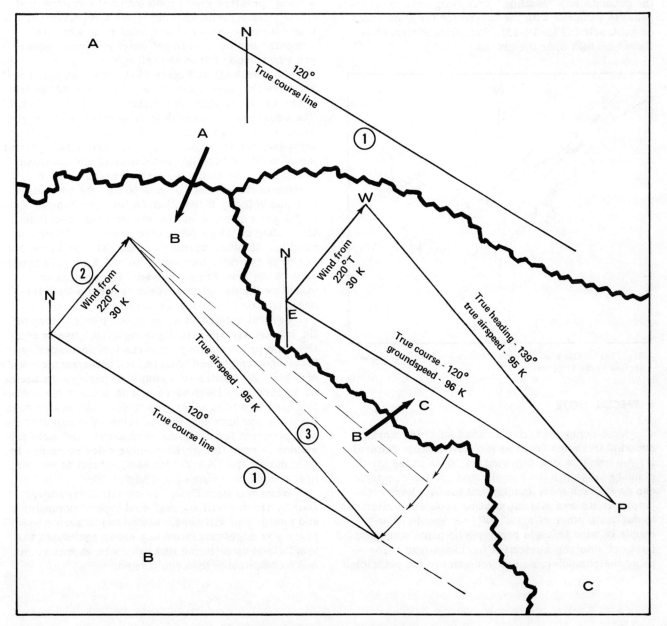

Fig. 19-12. Working a wind triangle.

Plane B—Wind Calm

Trip out   - 100 miles at 100 K = 1 hr.   0 min.
Trip back - 100 miles at 100 K = 1 hr.   0 min.
                                    2 hr.   0 min.

The stronger the wind as compared to the plane's cruise, the greater the divergence in time between the two conditions. The answer is that the plane with the wind flies longer in the headwind condition than the tailwind condition and loses the chance at equalization. Don't cut your fuel figuring too close under these conditions — *it won't average out.*

Back to the wind triangle. You now convert the true heading to compass heading by correcting for variation and deviation.

Remember any "course" (true, magnetic, or compass) deals with the plane's proposed path over the ground. Any "heading" (true, magnetic, or compass) is a course with the correction for wind added or subtracted (Fig. 19-13). The plane's "track" is its actual path over the ground.

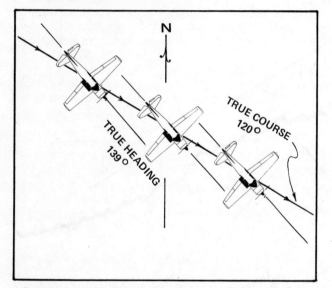

Fig. 19-13. The wind triangle solution for Figure 19-12 as applied to the airplane.

A SPECIAL NOTE

Most computers have a "wind side" for working out wind triangles (such as just discussed). Naturally, you won't be drawing wind triangles in the airplane because it's too complicated and the computer can do it much more quickly and easily. Each computer has its own manual and this book won't attempt to duplicate other efforts. *But,* you should draw a couple of wind triangle problems on paper when you first get into the navigation business, and before using the computer, so that you can see the principles

involved. Later, when you are using the computer to solve wind triangle problems, don't just insert a bunch of numbers and get an answer — *it may be wrong.* Have an idea of how the problem looks before setting it up on the wind side of the computer.

For instance, you have a problem as follows: True course — 090°, wind from 135° true. The true airspeed and wind velocity need not be available in order to know that (1) the wind is from the right and the true heading will be greater than 090° if a track of 090° is to result. (You will have a correction to the right.) You will have to correct right and 'add" numbers to the true course if you are to track 090°. (2) The *ground speed* will be *less* than the *true airspeed* because there is a head wind component also. Too many students mechanically use the computer and come up with wrong answers because they couldn't "see" the problem. If necessary, when working practice wind problems on the computer at first, make a crude drawing of the wind direction and true course to get an idea of what to expect. The computer can be used to get exact answers. Later you won't need to draw the triangle.

Looking back at Figure 19-12, you can see that if you have the information on any two sides of the triangle the information on the third side may be found. The usual practical problem is as given in the earlier example of known wind (direction and velocity), true airspeed, and true course, and you are to find ground speed and true heading (and magnetic and compass headings). The computer manual will also have sample problems such as how to find the wind direction and velocity if the other factors are known. You might get a question on the written exam requiring the finding of things other than ground speed or true heading. In other words, you may get a problem that requires "working backward" to check on your knowledge of the principles involved. The point is to visualize the situation whether drawing a wind triangle on paper or using a computer.

Several electronic computers or calculators on the market are specifically designed for use in aviation, and problems may be worked on navigation, performance, weight and balance, and other requirements of flight. As mentioned a couple of paragraphs back, computers have their own manuals and sample problems, so this book won't go into detail on how to work them. If you have that type of talent, you can also set up a program for using the "ordinary" hand-held calculator in your flying. Electronic calculators can be used during the FAA written test, subject to certain precautions as indicated in Chapter 27.

When you start flying, or shortly thereafter, your instructor will suggest what type of computer and plotter you will need. Listen to his advice because you might otherwise buy cheap equipment that won't stand up or items that are more expensive or more complicated than you'll need.

20. The Chart and Other Printed Aids

SECTIONAL CHART

The sectional chart, printed every six months, is the backbone of cross-country flying for the student and private pilot. It is printed by the National Oceanic and Atmospheric Administration and is extremely accurate. The scale is 1:500,000; that is, 1 inch on the chart equals 500,000 inches on the ground, or, as noted in the last chapter, the scale is about 7 NM to the inch. The chart contains such items as:

1. Aeronautical symbols used on the chart.
2. A map of the United States showing each sectional chart's coverage (named for a principal city on the chart such as Atlanta, Charlotte, etc.).
3. Topographical symbols — an explanation of the topographical or terrain symbols used on the chart.
4. Radio aids to navigation and airspace information, plus data on obstruction symbols.
5. A list of the frequencies used by control towers in the area of the chart.
6. A list of Prohibited, Restricted, Warning, and Alert areas on the chart.

Terminal areas of heavy air traffic concentration and complicated approach requirements (such as Chicago, Washington, Atlanta, etc.), publish VFR local area charts, using the same typography and symbols as the sectional, but in more detail. These charts use a scale of 1:250,000. If you plan to go into such a congested area you should have one of these up-to-date charts along.

Part of a sectional chart with a sample cross-country flight is reproduced in the back of this book.

AIRMAN'S INFORMATION MANUAL (AIM)
BASIC FLIGHT INFORMATION AND ATC PROCEDURES

This publication, issued twice a year, contains instructional, educational and training material — things that are basic and not often changed, such as:

Pilot Controller Glossary — Definition of control zones and areas and other terms used in air traffic control.

Air Navigation Radio Aids — Theory and operations of such aids as LF/MF ranges, VORs, radio beacons, Distance Measuring Equipment, Instrument Landing Systems (ILS), and marker beacons. VHF/DF (VHF Direction Finding) is included.

Airport, Air Navigation Lighting and Marking Aids — Information on airport beacons and runway lighting and marking. Information about enroute beacons and landmark lighting, including obstructions hazardous to flight, is in this part also.

Radar — General information on FAA and military radar plus specifics on precision and surveillance radar approaches.

The Airspace — A discussion of the various types of airspace and their visibility, cloud clearance, and airplane equipment requirements.

Air Traffic Control — Services available to pilots from Flight Service Stations, Towers, Air Route Traffic Control Centers (radar, transponder operations and advisory services available).

Airport Operations — Operations at tower-controlled airports and non-tower airports, use of runways, traffic pattern indicators, tower light signals and hand signals for taxi directors.

Radiotelephone Phraseology and Techniques — Background on microphone technique and procedure words and phrases. Includes the phonetic alphabet and Morse code.

Altimetry — Background and use of the altimeter in the airways system.

Weather — The weather reporting aids available, in-flight weather safety advisories, weather radar, pilot reports (PIREPS). Information on thunderstorms, such as at which altitudes the most turbulent conditions exist, etc.

Wake Turbulence — Information on Airplane Wake Turbulence (how it's developed, the places where it's most likely to be found, and suggested pilot action if it is encountered).

Medical Facts for Pilots — Discussions of the effects of hypoxia (lack of oxygen), use of alcohol and tips on how long to wait before flying after its use, plus sections on use of drugs, effects of vertigo and carbon monoxide on the pilot, and the danger of flying shortly after scuba diving.

Preflight — Preflight preparation and how to file and cancel a flight plan.

Departure IFR (Instrument Flight Rules) — Communications information (ground control and tower). Light signals. Clearances for taxi and take-off.

Departure control procedures.

Enroute IFR — The VOR and LF/MF airways systems and special control areas. (See Chapter 21.) Communications and operating procedures enroute (Instrument Flight Plan). Diagrams of cruising altitude requirements (VFR and IFR).

Arrival IFR — The use of approach control, approach procedures, radar controlled approaches, and IFR weather minimums.

General — Airports of entry and departure, and procedures. ADIZ (Air Defense Identification Zone) procedures.

Emergency Procedures — What to do under various emergency situations. Search and rescue procedures and visual emergency signals and codes. Radio communications failure procedures.

(This is only a part of the material in the AIM; the airport office should have a copy for you to study.)

Figure 20-1 is from the *Basic Flight Information and ATC Procedures* and shows recommended traffic patterns at non-tower airports.

AIRPORT/FACILITY DIRECTORY

This publication is available in seven subscriptions, each for a certain part of the United States (Fig. 20-2). The smaller (5 3/8 × 8 1/4 inches) size and compactness makes it handier to carry in the airplane.

The A/F Directory also includes VOR Receiver Check Points for the states covered in that particular section of the country and major changes in aeronautical (sectional) charts. There are Special Notices including Flight Service Stations and National Weather Offices telephone numbers.

Appendix B of this book is the legend and information on the Sewanee (Tennessee), Columbia-Mount Pleasant (Tennessee), and Huntsville (Alabama) airports. The airports will be used in the sample cross-country discussed in Chapters 24 and 25.

NOTICES TO AIRMEN

Issued *every 14 days*, this publication lists NOTAM (Notice to Airmen) information, Airman Advisories, hazardous airspace activities, and other items considered essential to flight safety. Listed alphabetically by state. You'll see notices of VOR (VHF Omnirange) errors in the individual listings in the *Airport/Facility Directory*.

During your preflight planning for a cross-country you'd check this part carefully (as well as checking later NOTAMs with the nearest FAA Flight Service Station — see the next chapter).

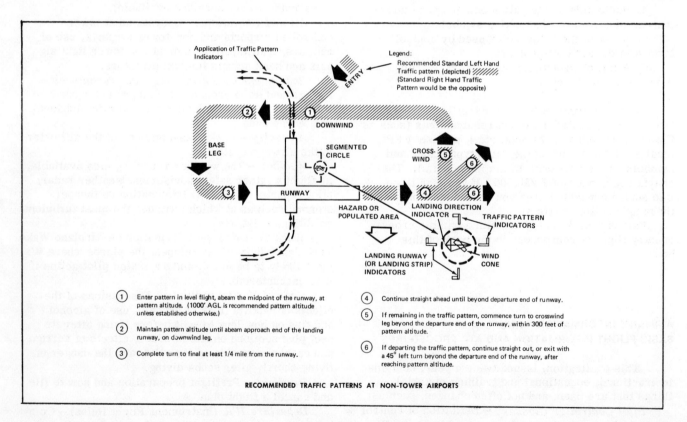

RECOMMENDED TRAFFIC PATTERNS AT NON-TOWER AIRPORTS

Fig. 20-1.

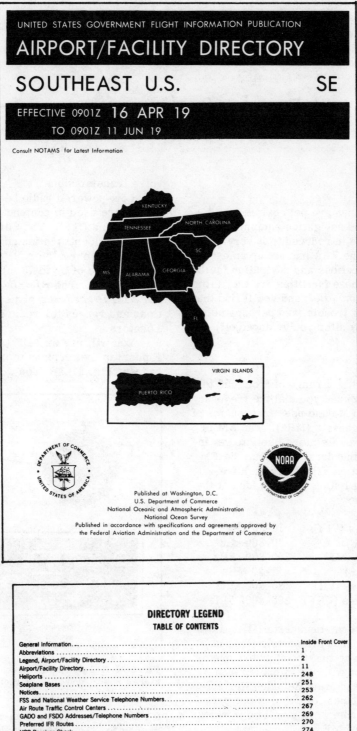

UNITED STATES GOVERNMENT FLIGHT INFORMATION PUBLICATION

AIRPORT/FACILITY DIRECTORY

SOUTHEAST U.S.   SE

EFFECTIVE 0901Z **16 APR 19**
TO 0901Z 11 JUN 19

Consult NOTAMS for Latest Information

Published at Washington, D.C.
U.S. Department of Commerce
National Oceanic and Atmospheric Administration
National Ocean Survey
Published in accordance with specifications and agreements approved by
the Federal Aviation Administration and the Department of Commerce

DIRECTORY LEGEND
TABLE OF CONTENTS

Fig. 20-2.

153

BACKGROUND

Nowadays few airplanes are not equipped with radio communications and navigation equipment — chances are that you'll be introduced to it very soon after you start flying. The FAA has set up an extensive system of communications and navigation facilities. The personnel at those facilities are there for only one reason, to *help the pilot*, and you'll find that they can save you a lot of trouble (and perhaps help you out of a bind someday after you've doped off).

FREQUENCIES

Your AM radio dial has a range of from 550 to about 1600 kilohertz (kHz) and you dial the frequency (station) you want. The FM band uses frequencies of from 88 to about 107 megahertz (MHz). The AM is MF (medium frequency) and is more likely to get interference from nearby thunderstorms than the FM stations, which broadcast on VHF (very high frequencies). The following listing gives an idea of the frequency bands in use now:

Very low frequencies (VLF)	10–30 kHz
Low frequencies (LF)	30–300 kHz
Medium frequencies (MF)	300–3000 kHz
High frequencies (HF)	3–30 MHz
Very high frequencies (VHF)	30–300 MHz
Ultra high frequencies (UHF)	300–3000 MHz

At the HF band the term megahertz (MHz) is introduced (1 megahertz = 1000 kilohertz). This is done to keep things from getting too cumbersome as would be done by going on with the kilohertz idea. The term "hertz" is named after Heinrich Hertz, German physicist, and stands for "cycles per second." In your aviation radio work you'll be working mostly with VHF, LF, and MF.

RADIO NAVIGATION AIDS

RADIO BEACON

Radio beacons or nondirectional radio beacons (NDB) are assigned broadcast frequencies between 190 and 535 kHz, which makes them LF/MF facilities.

Each station continually transmits its particular assigned three-letter identifier in code except during voice transmissions.

Low-powered radio beacons called Compass Locators are used in conjunction with Instrument Landing Systems (ILS). The Compass Locators have a two-letter identification and a range of at least 15 miles. The enroute or "H" (homing) facilities may have a range of up to 75 miles for the more powerful installations. The *AIM-Basic Flight Information and ATC Procedures* gives more details on designations and ranges for radio beacons and Compass Locators.

You will use an ADF (Automatic Direction Finder) in the airplane to navigate with the radio beacon (Fig. 21-1). You would select REC (Receive)

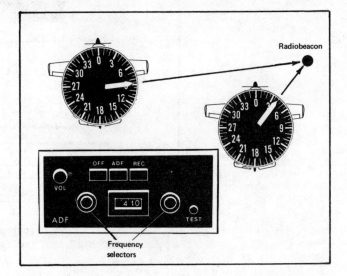

Fig. 21-1. The Automatic Direction Finder (ADF) needle points to the radio beacon or commercial broadcast station (if properly tuned).

for better audio reception and set in the proper frequency for the desired radio beacon or broadcast station. Some sets have a selection of ANT (Antenna) for this purpose. After the station is coming in loud and clear, you'd switch to the ADF setting.

The needle of the ADF points to the station you have selected and gives a relative bearing to that station. Always make sure that the station has been properly identified — it would be embarrassing on the flight test if you homed in on the wrong station. It can happen!

Figure 21-2 shows some magnetic headings and relative bearings to fictitious radio beacons. (Assume no deviation for these illustrations.) (A) Shows

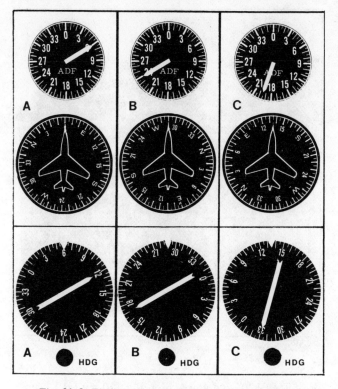

Fig. 21-2. Finding magnetic bearings to the station.

that the magnetic heading is 060° and the relative bearing is 060°, for a magnetic bearing to the station of 120° (60° + 60°). (B) Indicates a magnetic heading of 290° with a relative bearing of 240°. You can find the magnetic bearing to the station in two ways: You can add the two values and subtract 360 from the answer (290° + 240° = 530°; 530° - 360° = 170° to the station); or, you note that the needle is pointing 120° to the left of the nose, so you can subtract this amount from the heading (290° - 120° = 170°). If the addition results in a number greater than 360°, subtract 360° from the result. (C) The heading is 135° with a relative bearing of 195°. You can add the two numbers (135° + 195° = 330°) to the station. If you wanted to "visualize" the situation you could say that the reciprocal of your heading is 315° and the station is 15° "farther around," so this would also give a result of 330°.

Looking at the lower part of Figure 21-2, you'll see a different presentation as found in newer ADF sets. The knob marked HDG (Heading) is used to mechanically turn the card to set the airplane's heading under the indicator or lubber line. The needle then indicates the actual bearing to the station. In (A) the airplane is heading 060°; this is set up on the card and the needle shows that the bearing to the station is 120°. This answer was found in the last paragraph by addition. (B) Indicates that the bearing to the station is 170°. (C) The bearing to the station is 330° as found before. This presentation is an improvement over the addition and subtraction method required by the first type, but you have to be sure that the number you set in on the card is the same as the heading indicator shows. Anytime you change the airplane's heading, the ADF card has to be mechanically reset

to that new figure if you want to have an accurate relative bearing to the station.

It would be good if this could be done automatically for you, so the RMI (Radio Magnetic Indicator) was designed. It's a combination of heading indicator and ADF and VOR pointers. The H/I can be slaved to a remote magnetic compass so that precession is continually being corrected. You'll probably use an RMI when you start working on that instrument rating.

You "home" into a station by turning the airplane until the ADF needle points to a relative bearing of 000° (the station is straight ahead) and by keeping the needle in this position. A crosswind will result in a curved path (Fig. 21-3). This is the most simple, but not the most efficient, way of getting to the station.

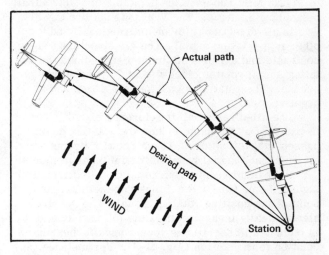

Fig. 21-3. A curved path results if there is a crosswind during "homing" (the nose is kept pointed to the station). The effect shown is exaggerated for purposes of illustration.

As you pass the station the needle will swing and point to the rear (180° position on the dial). Later you will learn how to *track* into the station, setting up the proper wind drift correction that would result in a straight flight path (the same principle covered in "Wind Triangle" in Chapter 19).

Your ADF set is able to pick up stations in the frequency range of 190-1750 kHz, which means that you can also home into commercial broadcasting stations. While those stations are normally more powerful than the radio beacons or "H" facilities, they have the disadvantage of not having continuous identification. You may have to suffer through several minutes of rock music before learning that you've been tuned to the right (or wrong) station.

Because the ADF operates in the LF/MF bands, it is subject to the troubles of the regular home radio when thunderstorms are in the vicinity. Precipitation static and thunderstorms may make reception difficult or impossible. Precipitation static is the result of static electricity generated when the airplane flies through rain, snow, etc.

The radio beacon has one advantage over VHF navigational equipment; it is *not* "line of sight." You can pick up the signals even when you are low and the station is over the horizon (just like the home radio).

If your trainer does not have an ADF you might ask your instructor for a ground checkout on the operation of that equipment in one of the other planes on the field.

When you work on the instrument rating you may get an introduction to MDF (Manual Direction Finder), wherein the loop is manually rotated to obtain bearings.

VOR

The most useful of the enroute radio navigation aids is the VHF Omnirange, or VOR as it is sometimes called. The VOR frequency band is from 108.00 to 117.95 MHz and uses the principle of electronically measuring an angle. The VOR puts out two signals. One is all-directional (or omnidirectional) and the other is a rotating signal. The all-directional signal contracts and expands 30 times a second and the rotating signal rotates clockwise at 30 revolutions per second. The rotating signal has a positive and a negative side.

The all-directional or reference signal is timed to transmit at the same instant the rotating beam passes *magnetic north*. These rotating beams and the reference signal result in radial measurements.

Your omni receiver picks up the all-directional signal. Some time later it picks up the maximum point of the positive rotating signal. The receiver electronically measures the time difference, and it is indicated in degrees as your *magnetic* bearing in relation to the station (Fig. 21-4). For instance, assume it took a minute instead of 1/30 of a second for the rotating signal to make one revolution. You receive the all-directional signal and 20 seconds later you receive the rotating signal. This means that your position is 20/60 or 1/3 of the way around. (One third

Fig. 21-5. A VOR receiver. (*Narco Avionics*)

of 360° is 120° and you are on the 120 radial.) The omni set does this in a quicker, more accurate way.

The aircraft VOR receiver presentation is composed of four main parts: (1) a dial to select the frequency of the station you want to use, (2) an azimuth or Omni Bearing Selector (OBS) calibrated from 0 to 360, (3) a Course Deviation Indicator (CDI), a vertical needle that moves left or right, and (4) a TO-FROM indicator.

Figure 21-5 shows a compact VOR receiver. Note that the frequency selector and all parts are together. The OBS is the left knob and the window ("NAV") would indicate TO, FROM (or a flag) as applicable.

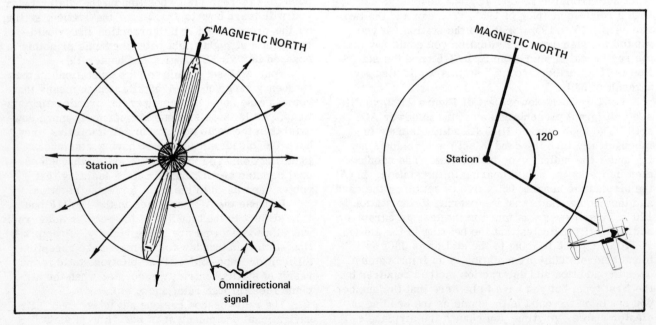

Fig. 21-4. Principle of the VOR.

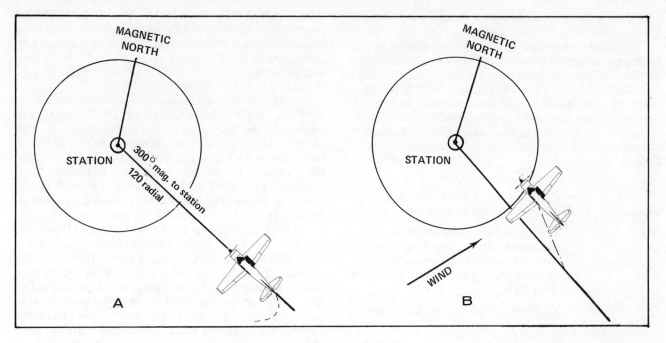

Fig. 21-6.

Suppose you want to fly to a certain VOR 30 miles away. First you would tune the frequency and identify the station. You should have some idea where you are in relation to the station but if not, turn the azimuth or direction selector until the deviation indicator or needle is centered and the TO-FROM indicator says "TO." Read the Omni Bearing Selector. This is your course TO the VOR. If you turn on that magnetic course and keep the needle centered you'll fly right over the VOR. If the TO-FROM says "TO" and you are going to the station, fly the needle. If the needle moves to the left, the selected bearing is to the left and you will turn the plane in that direction and fly until the needle is centered again. You will have to correct for wind to stay on the selected bearing (Fig. 21-6).

In this case your position from the VOR looks something like that shown in Figure 21-6A.

While your bearing to the station is 300°, *you are on the 120 (one-two-zero)* radial. (The radials are like spokes from the VOR.) (Fig. 21-6A) The radials are numbered from 0 through 359, so if the station asked where you were you'd say, "I'm inbound to the station on the 120 (one-two-zero) radial." For example, if there's a west wind, the plane may drift from the selected bearing as shown in Figure 21-6B, and the LEFT-RIGHT needle would look like Figure 21-7.

The angle of correction or the "cut" you'll take will depend on the amount that you've drifted from course. Usually 30° would be the maximum even at some distance from the station. It may take some time for the needle to center again if you're far out. After the needle returns to center, turn back toward the original heading, but this time include an estimated wind correction on your compass, or heading indicator. Watch the needle and make further corrections as needed.

When you cross over the station the TO-FROM indicator will oscillate, then fall to FROM. The receiver now says that you are on a bearing of 300° FROM the station. Always make sure your Omni Bearing Selector is set close to your compass heading. This way the needle always points toward the selected radial. If you turned around and headed back to the station after passing it on a course of 300° and did not reset the bearing selector to coincide with your heading, the needle would work in reverse. *Always set your Omni Bearing Selector to the course to be followed — then the needle senses correctly.*

The sensing is incorrect if you correct toward the needle and the needle moves farther away from the center as you fly.

But, back to the station passage: The TO-FROM says FROM and your plane is on a course of 300° FROM the VOR, so the needle is correct. Continue to fly the needle as you did before the VOR was reached.

Most omni needles are set up so that a full deflection from center is 10° or more. If the needle is

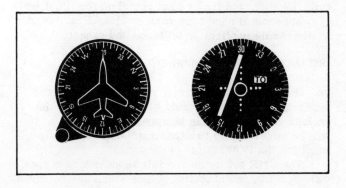

Fig. 21-7. The selected radial is to the left.

157

deflected halfway, you can figure that you are about 5° from your selected bearing.

VORs are identified by Morse code and/or by the automatic recorded voice identification ("Airville VOR").

The accuracy of the VOR ground facility is generally plus or minus 1°, but some stations in mountainous terrain may have errors greater than this for some radials or may be unusable below certain altitudes; this is duly noted in the *Airport/Facility Directory*.

Summary

Frequency Band: 108.0 to 117.95 megahertz

Use:	Navigation and instrument approaches. (A few don't have voice facilities. See the *Airman's Information Manual* and *Airport/Facility Directory*.)
Identification:	Continual code or code and voice.
Advantages:	1. Very high frequency — not as affected by weather as LF/MF facilities.
	2. Omni or all-directional signals — pilot is not limited to 4 legs, as was the case for the old LF/MF range.
Disadvantages:	Line of sight — cannot be picked up if plane is low (Fig. 21-8).

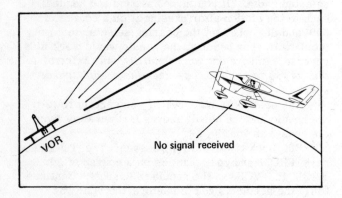

Fig. 21-8. Omni is line of sight.

The check pilot will require that you be able to tune, identify, and fly an omni radial on the flight test.

Appendix B shows the various classifications of VORs and their effective altitudes and ranges.

DISTANCE MEASURING EQUIPMENT (DME)

DME is a comparatively recent addition to the family of air navigation aids. It's doubtful that the trainer you are flying is equipped with a DME, so it will be covered only briefly. Special ground equipment for the VOR station is needed.

The DME set in the aircraft sends out, at a specific spacing, interrogating pulses which are received by the ground station. The ground station then trans-

mits a paired pulse back to the aircraft at a different pulse spacing and on a different frequency. The time required for the round trip of this signal exchange is measured by the DME unit in the aircraft and is indicated on a counter or dial as nautical miles from the aircraft to the station.

DME operates on frequencies between 962 and 1213 MHz (UHF), but because each DME frequency is always paired with an associated omni frequency the selector of the set may be marked in terms of the omni frequency band. All you have to do is to know the frequency of the associated omni and set up the selector of the DME on this number, rather than having to remember the various DME frequencies or "channels."

VORTAC stations are combinations of two components: the VOR, giving azimuth information, and the TACAN equipment, giving distance (DME) information. TACAN is the term for Tactical Air Navigation, a military innovation being used in FAA facilities. Note in the sectional chart in the back of this book that Huntsville has a VORTAC (named *Rocket*), and you would set up 112.2 MHz on the VOR set and the same on the DME equipment and get directions, ground speeds, and distances from that station. The "Channel 59" is for TACAN equipment, and all VORs in the United States having the frequency 112.2 MHz would have a channel 59 assigned. (See Appendix B.) Note also on the chart that Shelbyville has a VOR/DME which is used in the same way as indicated for the VORTAC but the ground equipment is different.

Like the VOR, the DME depends on line-of-sight reception. Because it is a transmitter (it sends signals rather than words, however), airplanes so equipped must have an Aircraft Radio Station License for the DME. (See Chapters 3 and 23.)

COMMUNICATIONS

FLIGHT SERVICE STATION (FSS)

The Flight Service Station has several functions in its job of assisting the pilot (*you*).

Flight Plan Service — You file all flight plans with an FSS in person, by telephone, or by radio. (If possible, avoid filing by radio; it ties up the frequencies too much.) A discussion of flight plans and how to file them will be covered in more detail in Chapter 24, which covers navigation planning.

Pilot Briefing Service — You may obtain preflight briefing on weather (existing and forecast) along your route and information on the operating status of navigation aids and airport conditions either in person or by phone. Incidentally, when getting flight weather information by phone from either Flight Service Stations or Weather Service Offices, always tell them that you are a pilot, give the aircraft identification, and also note the approximate departure time, route, and expected time enroute to your destination. Your briefing will normally cover the following information: (1) adverse weather, (2) current weather at the departure point, destination and enroute, (3) forecasts for the points just mentioned, (4) advisories, Pilot Reports (see Chapter 22) and NOTAMS (Notices to Airmen) plus Military Training Routes within 100 NM of the FSS. About NOTAMS: ask for them every time. Ask for a *weather briefing* when you talk to the facilities, rather than taking it upon yourself to just request information on individual stations along your route. The latest telephone numbers for Weather Service and Flight Service Stations can be found in the *Airport/Facility Directory*.

For in-flight briefing call the FSS on the proper frequency and let them know on which frequency you'll be listening. It is suggested that you call Flight Service Stations on 122.1 MHz (which is a one-way frequency *from* aircraft to them) and listen to one of the VOR frequencies they can transmit on. This practice cuts down interference from other stations. Don't be impatient, because the people in the FSS could be tied up on another frequency. Also let them know that you are a student pilot; they'll appreciate the information and will give you extra consideration. (This goes for contacting approach controls and towers also.)

Assume you are on a cross-country and the weather ahead doesn't look too good. You can give a call to the nearest FSS and get the latest weather and the forecast for your destination.

You: "BLANKTOWN RADIO, THIS IS CHERO-KEE 6789 WHISKEY, STUDENT PILOT, LISTEN-ING JONES VOR, OVER." (This is not official, but you might repeat the station name twice on the initial call; such as, "BLANKTOWN, BLANKTOWN RADIO . . ." The reason for this is that the station name would sometimes be missed by the FSS personnel and they might only hear ". . . RADIO." This would mean that the personnel in every FSS within reception distance of your transmitter think that you're calling them and time is wasted until the matter is straightened out.)

Blanktown Radio: CHEROKEE 6789 WHISKEY, THIS IS BLANKTOWN RADIO, OVER." (Notice that you'll make an initial contact, letting them know *who* you are and on *what* frequency you'll be listening for their reply. The FSS has identified itself to you and by saying "over" has handed the ball back. You should *always* let the FSS know on which frequency you expect a reply because the stations can transmit on several frequencies and may have to transmit simultaneously on all of them to make sure they get you. This causes interference with other stations and other aircraft. Keep in mind that some Flight Service Stations have jurisdiction over several VOR stations, so if you are listening on an omni frequency, tell them which one.)

You: "THIS IS EIGHT NINER WHISKEY, I'M ABOUT FIVE MILES EAST OF BLANKTOWN AT FOUR THOUSAND FIVE HUNDRED (4500 feet), ENROUTE TO JONESVILLE. I'D LIKE THE LATEST JONESVILLE WEATHER AND THE FORECAST FOR THE NEXT TWO HOURS, OVER."

(Once you have established contact it is not necessary to use your full number each time.)

Blanktown: "EIGHT NINER WHISKEY, WAIT,

OUT." (The "out" is to let you know that he doesn't expect a reply to this transmission.)

Blanktown: "THE LATEST JONESVILLE WEATHER IS . . ." (Gives the Jonesville weather and the Blanktown altimeter setting.)

You: "EIGHT NINER WHISKEY, THANK YOU. OUT."

You acknowledge receipt of transmissions or instructions by the last three digits (and/or letters) of your registration number.

Although it's not required, you should give your position and altitude when contacting an FSS, even if you're not on a flight plan, because later, if you do not show up at the destination, your friends may start checking. The FSS will have on file a record of having talked to you at such-and-such a time, at such-and-such a position and altitude, and the search can start from there. You might as well get in the habit of giving your position and altitude in each contact.

Enroute Services — You can report your position at any time to an FSS whether on a flight plan or not. If you are on a VFR (Visual Flight Rules) flight plan the Flight Service Stations are the facilities to which you would normally make your position reports. In a bind you could report to a tower and they would relay the message. Position reports for IFR (Instrument Flight Rules) flight plans can be made either directly to Air Traffic Control Centers or to Flight Service Stations (for forwarding to the Centers), but IFR position reports won't be something for you to worry about yet.

Another Enroute Service available from Flight Service Stations is that of giving aid in emergencies arising in flight. The personnel are trained to help in situations such as orientating the lost pilot (using radar, Direction Finding, omni receiver manipulation, or their knowledge of prominent landmarks reported by the pilot). If you have a problem call the FSS and let *them* worry. (Of course, you are allowed to worry also, if you like.) Emergency frequencies are discussed in the *AIM — Basic Flight Information and ATC Procedures.*

Airport Advisory Service — This is provided by Flight Service Stations at airports not served by a control tower.

For Airport Advisory Service you would normally make initial contact with the FSS about 15 miles out and transmit and receive on 123.6 MHz.

Remember that it's only an advisory service. No airport control can be as complete as a control tower. Such information as wind, favored runway, field conditions, and *known* traffic will be given to you. If you have two-way radio it's a good idea to maintain communications with the FSS within 5 statute miles of such airports. If you only have a receiver you can maintain listening watch on the appropriate frequency when within 5 statute miles of the airport. You could also call them when taxiing out for departure. (AAS is *not* mandatory.)

Broadcast Service — Continuous weather broadcasts are made over selected LF/MF navigation aids. (Chapter 22 — WEATHER INFORMATION — goes into more detail.)

Pilot Weather Reporting Service — The FSS acts as a clearinghouse between pilots for exchanging information concerning turbulence, significant weather encountered, or other pertinent information. These pilot reports, or PIREPS, will be passed on by the FSS to other pilots in the area by direct communication or through the teletype and scheduled weather broadcasts.

Check the latest *Airport/Facility Directory* for frequencies, because the sectional chart data may be out of date. Note that not all Flight Service Stations have all of the same frequencies (Fig. 21-9).

Civil communications frequencies used in the FSS air/ground system are now operated simplex on 122.0, 122.2, 122.3, 122.4, 122.6, 123.6; emergency 121.5; plus receive-only on 122.05, 122.1, 122.15 and 123.6.

    a. 122.0 is assigned as the En Route Flight Advisory Service channel at selected FSS's.

    b. 122.2 is assigned to all FSSs as a common en route simplex service.

    c. 123.6 is assigned as the airport advisory channel at non-tower FSS locations, however, it is still in commission at some FSSs collocated with towers to provide part-time Airport Advisory Service.

    d. 122.1 is the primary receive-only frequency at VORs. 122.05, 122.15 and 123.6 are assigned at selected VORs meeting certain criteria.

    e. Some FSSs are assigned 50KHz channels for simplex operation in the 122–123 MHz band (e.g. 122.35).

Pilots using the FSS A/G system should refer to this directory or appropriate charts to determine frequencies available at the FSS or remote facility through which they wish to communicate.

Fig. 21-9. Flight Service Station frequencies. (*Airport/Facility Directory*)

The FAA is planning in the near future to have automated Flight Service Stations at various locations around the United States. This changeover may take some time; your instructor can keep you posted on what's happening in your area.

CONTROL TOWER

If you've never been into a controlled field you'll face the prospect with some misgiving. It's best if you have a brief idea as to the various functions of the tower so that things won't be so confusing that first time.

You can think of the operations of the tower as being broken down into three main divisions or "positions."

1. *Local Control* — This is the function that pilots think of as "The Tower." Local control has jurisdiction over air traffic within the airport traffic area. (*Airport traffic areas* are 5 statute miles in radius from the center of a *controlled* airport and extend from the surface up to, but not including, 3000 feet above the surface. The ATA exists only during the hours when the control tower is in operation.)

A *control zone* also extends in a 5-mile radius from the center of the airport but may have legs or extensions for IFR approaches or departures as shown in Figure 21-10. Control zones extend upward from the surface to the continental control area —

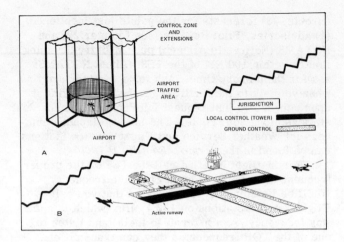

Fig. 21-10. (A) Control zone and airport traffic area. The airport traffic area extends from the surface up to, but not including, 3000 feet above the surface. (B) The areas of jurisdiction of local control (tower) and ground control.

14,500 feet MSL (Mean Sea Level), or ASL (Above Sea Level) except in Hawaii and upper Alaska (they go up to infinity there) — and are thought of more in terms of IFR operations.

The tower is considered to control the traffic pattern entry and the pattern itself, including take-offs and landings. The local controllers are in the glassed-in part of the tower because their control is dependent on visual identification of aircraft for take-offs and landings. The local control (tower) frequencies are in the *Airport/Facility Directory*, as was mentioned in the last chapter.

2. *Ground Control* regulates traffic moving on the taxiways and those runways not being used for take-offs and landings. (Ground control will coordinate with the tower if you have to cross a "hot," or active, runway.) Ground control is on a different frequency than that of the tower because you could imagine what radio clutter would result if some pilots were asking for taxi directions to Joe's Flying Service while other pilots were calling in for landing instructions.

Take a typical flight into a controlled airport: You'll call the tower on the correct frequency several miles out (at least 5) and get landing instructions. After you've entered the pattern and landed, the tower will give directions during the landing roll such as: TURN RIGHT NEXT INTERSECTION, CONTACT GROUND CONTROL 121.9 MEGAHERTZ. (Or ground control may be on 121.7 or 121.8 MHz; it depends on the airport.) *You'll stay on tower frequency until clear of the runway,* then will switch to ground control for taxi directions to your destination on the airport. After your business is completed and you are ready to leave, you'll listen to Automatic Terminal Information Service (ATIS) and get the basic information (more about ATIS shortly), then you'll talk to ground control and will be directed to the warmup area at the take-off end of the active runway. You'll hold clear of the runway and make your pre-take-off check. When you're ready for take-off you'll switch to the tower frequency and ask for take-off clearance. If making a right turn (instead of the "normal" left turn) after take-off would be to your advantage, request it.

For simplification and summary of local (tower) and ground control duties: Local control has jurisdiction of aircraft in the process of landing and taking off. This includes aircraft while in the pattern and *on* the active runway. Ground control is used for ground traffic on the airport *other than on the active runway during the take-off or landing process.* The ground controller will be in the tower beside the local controller. (And in some cases the same man may talk to you in both capacities, but on a different frequency, of course.)

3. *Approach Control*— The busier controlled airports have another position called "Approach Control." This may be a radar or nonradar setup. For nonradar setup, the approach controller is in the glassed-in portion of the tower with the other two positions. His primary duty is to coordinate IFR traffic approaching the control zone, but he may coordinate IFR and VFR traffic during marginal VFR conditions, as well as coordinating VFR traffic at busy terminals, even in CAVU (Ceiling and Visibility Unlimited) conditions.

Approach controllers using radar are usually in an IFR room which is located in the tower building but not necessarily in the glassed-in portion. Approach controllers work directly with the tower and their duties are rotated between tower and IFR room positions.

It won't be long until you'll be introduced to the busier airports that expect inbound VFR pilots to contact approach control some distance out (usually 25 miles, but check the *Airport/Facility Directory*). They'll have you switch to local control at some specific point, and of course, you'll switch to ground control after clearing the active runway. In a deal like this it will appear that nobody wants you, the way each operation shoves you off to the next one, but it's all necessary for smooth ground and air traffic flow.

These larger airports provide a VFR Radar Traffic Advisory Service (Terminal Radar Service Area — TRSA) for arriving and departing pilots. Figure 21-12 is part of a sectional chart showing what the TRSA around Huntsville-Madison County Jetport looks like. The foldout chart in the back of this book also has the Huntsville TRSA included.

Note that your position relative to the airport determines what frequency you'd use in contacting approach control when using this service. The line of demarkation is the centerline of the ILS runway (Runway 36, which has a magnetic bearing of 359° but is rounded off to the nearest 10°.

Service in the TRSA (pronounced "tersa") is voluntary as far as the VFR pilot (you) is concerned, but the controllers will assume that you'll want it unless you advise otherwise. You'd let approach control know when arriving and tell ground control as you taxi out that you want *no* participation. If

participating, you'll be under radar surveillance and given vectors to mix with the flow to the primary airport (or you may be vectored to another airport if you so desire).

When arriving, you'd contact approach control on the appropriate frequency in relation to geographical fixes depicted on the TRSA chart or sectional chart before entering. For instance, coming from the northwest, Athens (Alabama) or Epps Airport might be your reference for giving your position and you would call on 118.05 MHz (Appendix B and the legend of the sectional chart in the back of this book).

If you were landing at Decatur (Pryor Field) and didn't want to use TRSA you could stay below 2000 feet MSL (watch out for TV towers!) and proceed in and land.

If you were flying through from northwest to southeast and would proceed through the TRSA (sometimes called Stage III) right over the Huntsville-Madison County Jetport at 5500 MSL, you'd call, say, just northwest of Athens and stay on 118.05 MHz until crossing the dividing line. You'd be asked to change to 125.6 MHz and would work with another controller until he says (when you're out of the TRSA), "Radar service terminated." He would vector you as necessary to avoid the restricted areas.

The service will be discussed further as you plan and fly the cross-country flight in Chapters 24 and 25.

Using TRSA *does not relieve you of the responsibility to avoid other traffic. Also, keep in mind that the radar controller may not know the weather conditions in your vicinity and could vector you into conditions where visual references would be lost.* You are responsible for maintaining visual flight conditions and must notify him of a marginal situation. Remember that when you are solo you are the pilot in command. The final responsibility for safety is *yours*. ATC people and FSS personnel are conscientious, but they are also human and can make mistakes. Don't hesitate to speak up or deviate from their instructions if it looks as if your safety is involved. Keep them posted on your plans, though.

When the weather is less than that required for VFR operations in a control zone, you, as a VFR pilot, may request and be given a clearance to enter, leave, or operate within it. This, of course, depends on traffic and nondelay of IFR operations (Special VFR — FAR 91.107). You'll get a clearance from a tower, or if it is a control zone without a tower, a clearance may be obtained from an FSS, nearest tower, or Air Traffic Control Center. The minimum visibility requirements are 1 mile flight visibility for operations in the control zone and 1 mile ground visibility for take-offs and landings. You'll stay clear of clouds, but remember that you might end up so low that you fracture the FAR concerning clearance from ground objects. Only instrument rated pilots and IFR equipped airplanes can get a Special VFR clearance at night.

Some airports have too much traffic to allow

Special VFR and their control zones are outlined on the sectional chart with a series of "Ts." (See the legend in the sectional chart in the back of this book.)

As a student or low time private pilot the Special VFR clearance may allow you to get legally into an airport as the weather is deteriorating, but to use it to get out in marginal conditions on a VFR flight should be rejected. You could get into worse weather and lose control of the airplane. Wait for better weather before departing; spend that ground time studying for the instrument rating, so that you can safely use more and more of the air traffic control facilities as you get experience.

AUTOMATIC TERMINAL INFORMATION SERVICE (ATIS)

ATIS is the continuous broadcast of recorded noncontrol information for certain high-activity airports. Information such as ceilings, visibility, wind, altimeter settings, instrument approach, and runways in use is continuously broadcast on the voice feature of the VOR located on or near the airport or on a VHF tower frequency. You are expected to tune in ATIS and get the basic information while still some distance out. This will help plan your pattern better. Also listen before taxiing at an ATIS airport.

At the end of each ATIS broadcast the pilot is reminded that the information given was, for example, "INFORMATION DELTA." When the information changes (the wind shifts, etc.), the broadcast data will be given as "INFORMATION ECHO." It's quite possible that it could change between the time you first listened and when you contact the tower. Some airports may update the ATIS every hour even though no significant change has occurred.

Let the *ground control, tower,* or *approach control* (as applicable) know that you have "INFORMATION DELTA" (or the latest information) upon *initial* contact.

Airports having ATIS are listed in the *Airport/Facility Directory*.

UNICOM

Unicom, or aeronautical advisory, is an aid to the pilot operating into smaller airports with no tower. The Unicom frequencies are the "private pilot's frequencies" and you can call into an airport so equipped and get the surface wind, traffic, or other information. You can also call in and get transportation if needed.

Unicom is merely an advisory service by the airport operator. He cannot give you traffic clearances as would be done by a tower.

The FAA indicates that you may use Unicom, however, for ATC information such as a revision of proposed departure time, take-off, arrival and flight plan cancellation time or ATC clearances, provided arrangements for such information have been made between the Unicom licensee and ATC to handle such an arrangement.

The primary Unicom frequencies for airports without a control tower or an FSS are 122.7, 122.8 and 123.0 MHz. Flight schools or operations at airports with a control tower are assigned 122.95 MHz. These frequencies have been assigned to ease the congestion from 122.8 MHz which in earlier days was the only frequency used for uncontrolled airports.

Look at the sectional chart or the applicable Flight Information Publication for that airport for the Unicom frequency. If the airport has *no* radio facilities, it has been suggested that you broadcast your intentions on 122.9 MHz. Be careful, and look around.

MULTICOM

This is a frequency (122.900 MHz) used to provide communications essential to conduct activities being performed by, or directed from, private aircraft. Examples might be ground/air communications pertaining to forest fire fighting, aerial advertising, conservation activities, parachute jumping or ranching and agriculture. Multicom, like Unicom, is not to be used for traffic control. Other assigned Multicom frequencies are 122.850 and 122.925 MHz. *Now, changing the subject . . .*

Figure 21-11 is a popular transceiver (transmitter/receiver) or NAV/COMM (Navigation/Communications) set. In the communications part of the equipment, you would set up the desired frequency that would allow you to transmit *and* receive.

Fig. 21-11. A NAV/COMM set (*King Radio Corp.*)

The console (A) consists of the transceiver set at 123.00 MHz for communications (you'd transmit and receive with Unicom on this setting) and the right half (NAV) set on a VOR frequency of 115.95 MHz for navigating. The NAV receiver here can pick up VOR/LOC (localizer) signals for navigation and approaches. The range is from 108.00 to 117.95 MHz. The localizer is used for instrument approaches (you can use it in good weather too if you want) and utilizes the odd frequencies (tenths) from 108.10 to 111.95 MHz (108.*10*, 108.*15*, 108.*30*, etc.). VORs use the even frequencies in that range (108.*00*, 108.*20*, 108.*25*,

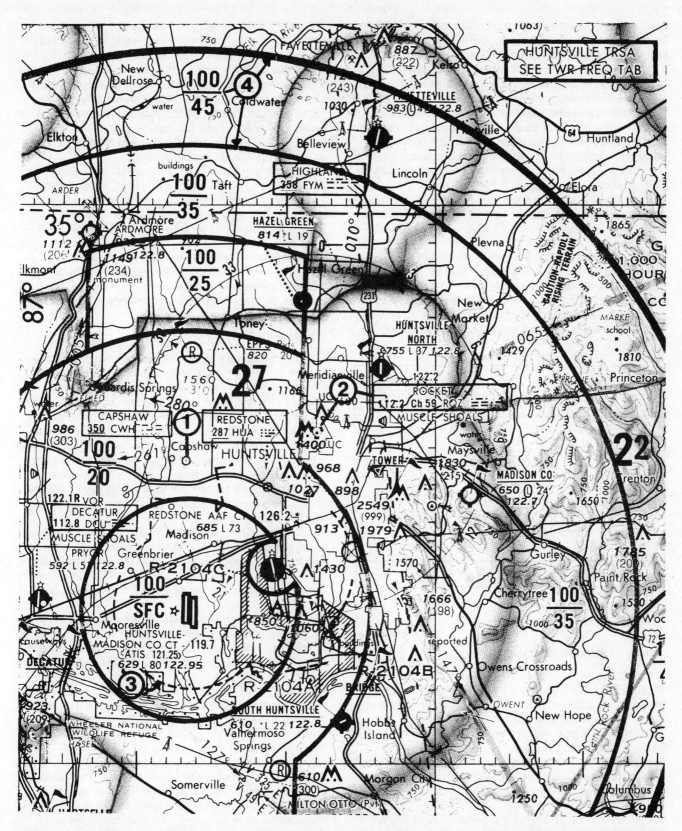

Fig. 21-12. Facilities near Huntsville. (1) The Capshaw radio beacon — identification CWH, frequency 350 kHz. The line under the "350" indicates that there is no voice facility on that frequency. (2) The Rocket VORTAC and frequency box. (3) Airport information for the Huntsville-Madison County Jetport. The tower frequency is 119.7 MHz, Automatic Terminal Information Service (ATIS) is 121.25 MHz, the airport elevation is 629 feet MSL, it has lights (L), the longest runway is 8000 feet long and there's a Unicom on the airport (122.95 MHz). The dashed lines indicated by (3) show the boundary of the control zone. Airport Traffic Areas are not shown on the sectional chart, but as stated earlier an ATA exists when a control tower is in operation. (4) Limits of the 4500- to 10,000-foot segment of the TRSA.

etc.) plus both odd *and* even frequencies from 112.00 to 117.95 MHz.

(B) is a VOR/LOC indicator and (C) is a VOR/LOC indicator with a GS (Glide Slope) needle added. As a student pilot, you will normally use only the vertical needle of this indicator. Note that this is COMM 1 and NAV 1, which would usually be the uppermost set on the instrument panel. (See Fig. 3-1.) The bottom NAV/COMM set is cited as "No. 2." (You may, however, call it "No. 7" if the whim strikes.)

Your instructor will check you out on the NAV/COMM equipment for your airplane.

Figure 21-12 shows the navigation and communications facilities in the vicinity of Huntsville-Madison County (Alabama) Jetport and ties together the subjects covered earlier in this chapter.

Figure 21-13 shows a cross section of the Huntsville TRSA extending from the airport to its north boundary, a distance of a little over 30 nautical miles. The vertical dimensions have been exaggerated for clarity. The TRSA has a maximum height of 10,000 feet (less than 2 nautical miles) and a radius of 30 NM.

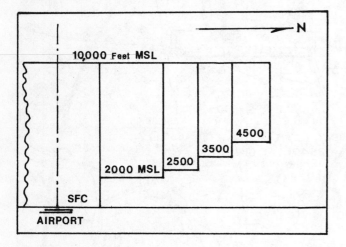

Fig. 21-13. A cross section of the northern sector of the Huntsville TRSA. You are looking west.

VISUAL APPROACH SLOPE INDICATOR (VASI)

VASI is located at some airports to provide a visual light path within the approach zone; it is inclined at an angle of from 2 1/2° to 4° from horizontal. The standard installation of the complete system consists of 12 light-source units, arranged in light bars, with 3 units placed on each side of the runway opposite the 600-foot mark (threshold), and 3 on each side of the runway at the 1300-foot mark. The VASI glide slope reference point is midway between the two points.

Each light unit projects a beam of light having a white color in the upper part and a red color in the lower part. The indications would be:

(A) Above glide slope   white   white
    white   white

(B) On glide slope   red   red
    white   white

(C) Below glide slope   red   red
    red   red

When on the proper glide slope, the airplane is in effect overshooting the bars at the threshold and undershooting the bars farther down. You will see the upper half (white) of the closer bars and the lower half (red) of the far set.

The VASI can normally be seen from 4 to 5 miles out on the final approach.

There are three-bar VASI installations as well as Tricolor types at larger airports. The Tricolor VASI lights have an approximate useful range of 0.5 to 1 mile in daylight and 1 to 5 miles at night.

Figure 21-14 is a summary of airspace limitations and altitudes.

Airplanes flying above 12,500 feet MSL are required to have a 4096 code transponder with Mode C (altitude reporting capabilities). There may be changes in these numbers by the time you read this.

TRANSPONDER

The airplane you are using may have a transponder for use in being more readily identified on radar. Basically, the transponder is a radar "transceiver" that picks up interrogations of the Air Traffic Control radar beacon systems and transmits or "replies." The two modes or operational types of equipment you'll be encountering are "A" — which is a straight reply type — and "C" — which replies and through special, encoding, altimeter equipment allows the ground controller to read off your altitude on his radarscope. Figure 21-15 shows a transponder control panel.

The "IDENT" selection in Figure 21-15 makes an airplane stand out on the controller's radarscope and is used momentarily to identify one target among many ty ATC. The reply lamp ("DIM") flashes when the transponder replies to each interrogation from the ground station.

Primary radar depends on the reflection and return of its impulses; the transponder in the airplane is triggered by these impulses and, in effect, boosts them back for a better target indication on the ground radar.

For VFR flying (not in contact with a radar facility) you would set up 1200 on the transponder and present a clearer target as you fly — for their traffic-avoidance purposes. (They'll see you and warn "their" traffic of your presence.)

For instance, if you were lost but in contact with an FSS or other nonradar FAA facility, they would probably have you switch frequencies to talk to a radar equipped facility which would ask you to "squawk" a certain setting on your transponder. They could readily locate you among the many targets and vector you to an airport.

The emergency code is 7700; if you're in bad trouble in flight, this setting will get the attention of every radar facility in the area. (It's best to talk to the people, but if you can't, 7700 will get you help.) The lost communications code, used primarily for

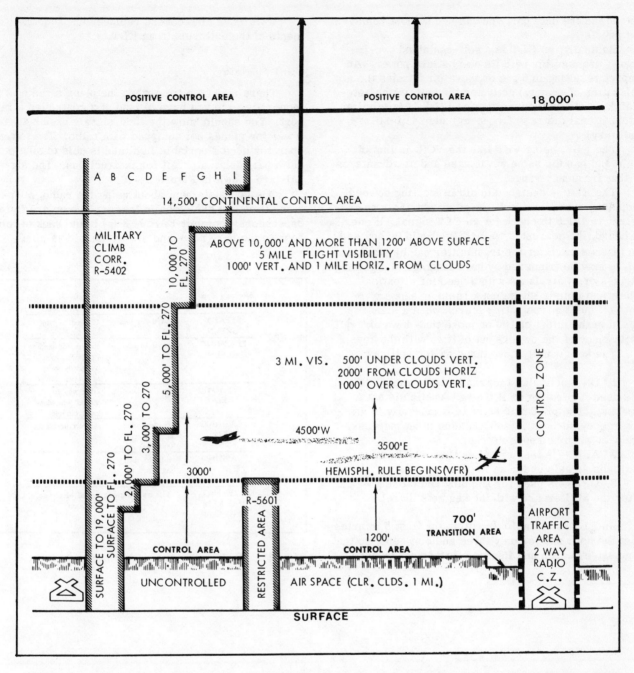

Fig. 21-14. A look at the airspace below 18,000 feet MSL. Note that the transition and control areas begin at 700 feet and 1200 feet *above the ground*. The airport traffic area extends from the surface to 3000 feet *above the ground*. All other altitudes are ASL. Airplanes flying above 12,500 feet MSL are required to have a 4096 code transponder with Mode C (altitude reporting capabilities).

IFR problems, is 7600. There's even a code you'd use if someone is hijacking your Cessna 152, or whatever. Your instructor will no doubt discuss the use of the transponder (if the airplane has one) before you go solo cross-country.

The transponder is "line of sight" like the VOR and DME.

EMERGENCY LOCATOR TRANSMITTER (ELT)

The ELT is required by Federal Aviation Regulations for all aircraft *except* those training within a 50-mile radius of the airport used for that training, flight test aircraft, new aircraft being ferried,

and other special uses listed in FAR 91.52. It's likely that the airplane you are using now has one, and the instructor may point out its location and antenna. (It may be so located in the airplane that the

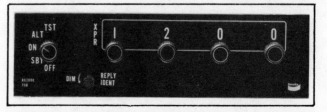

Fig. 21-15. Transponder control panel. (*Bendix Avionics Division*)

antenna is the only part you can see without removing panels.)

Basically, an ELT is a self-contained two-frequency transmitter with its own battery power. An impact resulting in 5 g's or more (or 5 times the acceleration of gravity) activates the unit, which automatically starts transmitting on 121.5 MHz (civilian international distress frequency) and 243.0 MHz (military).

The ELT, being VHF like the VOR, is line of sight and has the same advantages and disadvantages of that frequency range.

The ELT is designed to aid in locating downed airplanes, and pilots in flight often turn their receiver to 121.5 to check for an ELT signal. If one is heard, the nearest FAA facility should be advised so that a search for the transmitter can be started. ELTs may be triggered by hard landings or lightning strikes or in airplanes with a need for attention while just quietly sitting on a ramp or hangar. It sets off quite a frustrating search when a signal is heard in the midst of 100 or more tied-down aircraft (with many of the owners out of town with the keys).

The sets usually have three switch settings:

1. ON — activates the transmitter immediately. It's used for testing or if the "g" function is not working. The pilot may activate it manually in an emergency such as a "soft" landing in an inaccessible spot when he needs rescue.

2. ARM — is the normal setting, which would start the signals under an impact.

3. OFF — is used for shipping and storing — (and after the St. Bernard with the keg gets there).

An ELT is tested *only* within the first 5 minutes past the hour and for only three audio sweeps, so that a massive Search and Rescue effort is not launched.

FAR 91.52 also covers replacement requirements of the batteries in an ELT.

LIGHT SIGNALS

There may be a time when the plane's radio is inoperative and you have to land at a controlled airport. You should know the light signals used by the tower for planes not equipped with radio. The tower operator uses a portable light and is able to single out a particular aircraft for instructions. The signals are shown in Figure 21-16.

One last statement about using the radio, or *any* other time you are alone in the airplane or are flying passengers: commit FAR 91.3 (a) in the back of this book to memory now—and always keep it in mind.

Color and Type of Signal	On the Ground	In Flight
STEADY GREEN	Cleared for take-off	Cleared to land
FLASHING GREEN	Cleared to taxi	Return for landing (to be followed by steady green at proper time)
STEADY RED	Stop	Give way to other aircraft and continue circling
FLASHING RED	Taxi clear of landing area (runway) in use	Airport unsafe-do not land
FLASHING WHITE	Return to starting point on airport	
ALTERNATING RED & GREEN	General Warning Signal—Exercise Extreme Caution	

Fig. 21-16. The light signals used by local control.

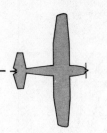

22. *Weather Information*

BACKGROUND

You're well ahead of the student pilots of pre-TV days, as far as weather knowledge is concerned, because you've been seeing the frontal systems and weather patterns on your screen every day. For instance, you know of the existence of high- and low-pressure areas and warm and cold fronts and the effects of circulation, but maybe a little review is in order:

PRESSURE

The standard sea level pressure is 29.92 inches of mercury (abbreviated Hg.). The approximate drop in pressure is about 1 inch of mercury per thousand feet of altitude. (This is valid up to about 10,000 feet; the *decrease* in pressure is less as the altitude increases. In the 18,000- to 20,000-foot levels, for instance, the drop in pressure is only about 0.60 inch per thousand feet.)

The pressure may also be given in millibars, and at standard sea level conditions the value is 1013.2 millibars (a millibar is a pressure based on the metric system). Since the standard pressure in inches of mercury is 29.92, it would follow that 1 inch of mercury pressure is equal to about 34 millibars — if you should need to convert from one to the other system. In the United States the altimeter settings are given in inches of mercury. Although the pressure is also given in millibars on the hourly sequence reports, it is *not* reported on the scheduled weather *broadcast*.

Standard sea level pressure may be given in the following ways: (a) 29.92 inches of mercury; (b) 1013.2 millibars; (c) 14.7 pounds per square inch; or (d) 2116 pounds per square foot.

PRESSURE AREAS

If the pressure stayed the same everywhere, the weather wouldn't be very interesting — and people would have a hard time making conversation.

Figure 22-1 shows the circulation around high- and low-pressure systems in the northern hemisphere. The opposite circulation occurs in the

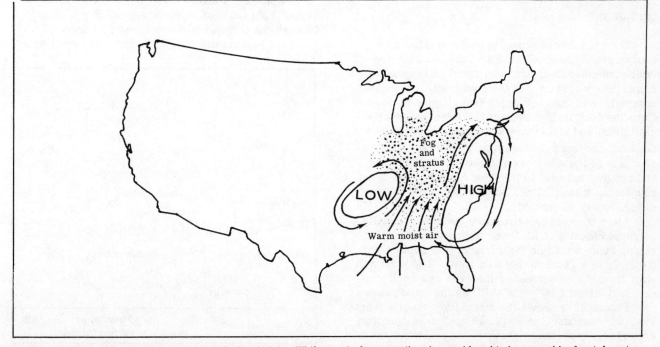

Fig. 22-1. High- and low-pressure areas and circulation. While most of our weather is considered to be caused by frontal systems, circulation can bring warm, moist air into cool areas, causing fog, low stratus, and precipitation. The Coriolis force, a result of the earth's rotation, in the Northern Hemisphere causes deflection of the winds to the right (and finally parallel to the isobars) at altitudes out of surface friction effects. The Coriolis force is directly proportional to the wind speed.

southern hemisphere — the earth's rotation (sometimes called Coriolis Force) causes this.

A high-pressure area *usually* means good weather (except for the circulation problem just covered), and low-pressure *usually* means bad weather, but you'll want to get more information from all possible sources (which is the purpose of the last part of this chapter). An elongated high-pressure area is called a "ridge"; the equivalent low-pressure shape is called a "trough."

FRONTAL SYSTEMS

A front is defined as a "zone of transition between two air masses of different densities."

The National Weather Service publishes charts of observed weather, and Figure 22-2 shows the symbols used to depict the various types of fronts (plus squall lines) on the charts.

You may set up your own memory aids to remember the symbols (cold is blue and sharp, etc.).

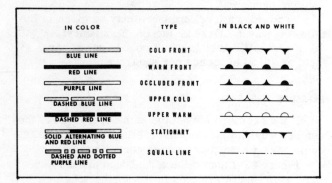

Fig. 22-2. Front symbols used on a weather chart.

COLD FRONT

The cold front is usually characterized by a comparatively narrow weather band and by more violent weather than is associated with the warm front. The worst part of the cold front weather is normally less than 100 miles from beginning to end. Cumulus (vertically developed clouds), heavy precipitation, and turbulence are usually associated with it. Fast-moving cold fronts may have squall lines, or a line of thunderstorms, 50 to 300 miles ahead and roughly parallel to the front. Your move, if encountering a squall line, is to get out of its area as expeditiously as possible.

After the cold front passage there will usually be rapid clearing, with lower temperatures and strong gusty winds on the surface; this applies particularly to a fast-moving cold front. The wind will shift from the southwest or the west to a northwest or north (about a 90° wind shift) as the front passes.

Figure 22-3 shows the circulation about a frontal system. Note that the "typical" system is "pivoting" around a low-pressure system.

Lines joining points of equal pressure are called "isobars." The closer the isobars are together the steeper the pressure gradient and the stronger the

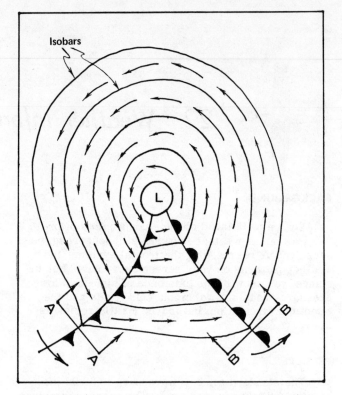

Fig. 22-3. Circulation in the vicinity of a frontal system.

winds in that area. You might keep this in mind when you look at a surface weather chart in a Weather Service Office (WSO).

The cold front moves faster than the warm front associated with the system, which can lead to a situation known as an occlusion (which will be covered later).

Figure 22-4 shows the cross-section of an "average" cold front as it would appear if you sliced through the front as shown by A-A in Figure 22-3. (You are looking the way the arrows are pointing.)

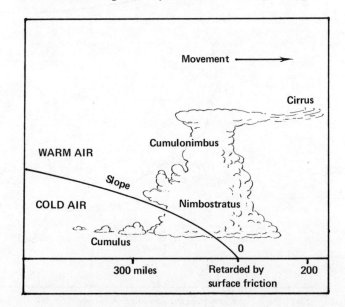

Fig. 22-4. Cross-section of a typical cold front. The slope varies from 1:50 to 1:150 and averages about 1:80.

The average cold front moves at a speed of 15 to 20 K but may under extreme conditions move at 50 K or more. It seems to move at a much higher speed than that if you happen to be in a 90 K trainer trying to outrun it.

WARM FRONT

The warm front usually produces a much wider band of weather consisting of stratus type clouds, with widespread areas of low ceilings, rain, and fog. However, if the warm air is unstable, cumulus type clouds and thunderstorms may be found in the stratus layer. Many an instrument pilot has had unexpected excitement flying through what he thought was going to be stable, smooth air. This, of course, is only of academic interest to you as a student pilot since one of your primary aims is to avoid getting within *any* type cloud.

The warm front usually moves at about one-half the speed of the cold front and this, plus the wider spread weather area, can sometimes mean a number of days when the birds are walking at your airport.

Figure 22-5 shows the cross-section of an "average" warm front as indicated by the slice B-B in Figure 22-3.

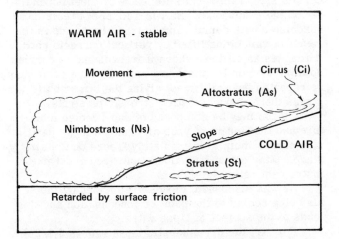

Fig. 22-5. Cross-section of a typical warm front with the warm air stable. The slope of the warm front may vary from 1:50 to 1:200, the average being about 1:100.

While you won't be planning on flying within the clouds, the fall or wintertime warm front may pose problems in addition to low ceilings, as can be seen by Figure 22-6.

You can be flying well below the cloud level and suddenly encounter this problem. It's a very serious situation because ice can cover the windshield (and the entire airplane) in a very short time. A student pilot has no business flying if there is any possibility of freezing rain. (And this also applies for private and commercial pilots.) If you start running into freezing rain, get back out of the area as quickly as possible. You may find that climbing to just below the clouds will keep you in warm enough air so that the rain hasn't started to freeze. Remember, though, that you may have to let back down through the

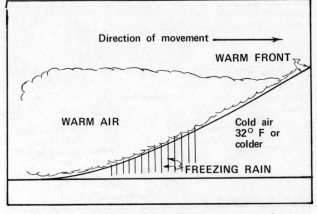

Fig. 22-6. Freezing rain associated with a warm front.

freezing levels for landing, which can be a hazardous operation.

OCCLUDED FRONT

The occluded front generally contains weather of both warm and cold fronts. Since the cold front moves faster than the warm front, it often catches up with it. The occluded front contains all the disadvantages of the two types, with widespread stratus, low ceilings and poor visibilities with build-up, and thunderstorms within the frontal area.

Figure 22-7 shows the occluded front.

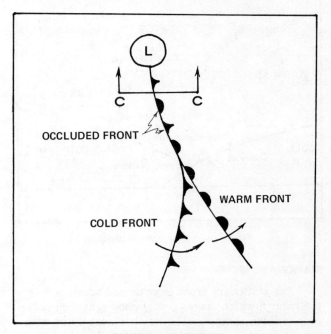

Fig. 22-7. The occluded front.

Figure 22-8 shows the cross-section of an occluded front as indicated by C-C in Figure 22-7. There are two types of occlusions and Figure 22-8 shows the warm type. If the air in front of the system is colder (and denser) than the air behind the cold front overtaking the warm front, it will move up over the cold air as shown. Most of the

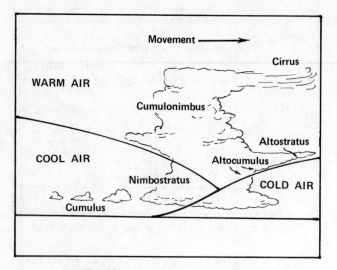

Fig. 22-8. A warm type occlusion.

weather will be found ahead of the surface front.

The cold type occlusion is a situation in which the air behind the cold front is colder than that ahead of the system. It slides under the cool air as shown by Figure 22-9. Most of the weather for this type of occlusion will be found near the surface front.

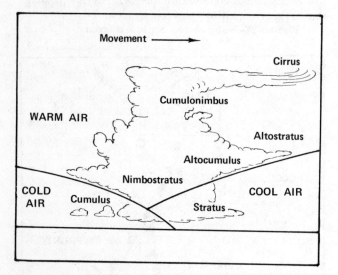

Fig. 22-9. A cold type occlusion.

STATIONARY FRONT

The stationary front is so named because it is stationary, which makes pretty good sense when you stop to think about it. The weather associated with the stationary front is similar to that found in a warm front but usually not as intense. The problem is that the bad weather hangs around until the front moves out or dissipates.

CLOUD TYPES

In discussing the weather indicated on the weather map it would be well to take a general look at cloud types you'll expect to encounter in flying.

Cloud types are broken down into four families: High, middle, and low clouds and clouds with large vertical development. The clouds are further described as to their form and appearance. The puffy or billowy type clouds are "cumulus," the layered types are "stratus."

The term "nimbo" (rain cloud) is added to clouds that would be expected to produce precipitation.

Figure 22-10 shows some representative types of clouds.

Normally, when flying near clouds of stratus type formation, you would expect fairly smooth air. Cumulus clouds by their very nature are the product of air conditions that indicate the presence of vertical currents.

Clouds are composed of minute ice crystals, or water droplets, and are the result of moist air being cooled to the point of condensation. The high clouds (cirrus, cirrostratus, and cirrocumulus) are composed of extremely fine ice crystals. (The biggest puzzle to the layman is that if they are composed of ice — why don't they fall?) For that matter, since the lower clouds are composed of water droplets, why don't they fall also? The answer is, of course, that the moisture is comparatively less dense than the ambient air. When the water droplets become a certain size, rain results (or snow or sleet depending on the conditions). Hail is a form of precipitation associated with cumulonimbus type clouds and is the result of rain being lifted by vertical currents until it reaches an altitude where it freezes and is carried downward again to gain more moisture; the cycle may be repeated several times, giving the larger hailstones their characteristic "layers," or strata.

Clouds may be composed of supercooled moisture and the impact of your airplane on these particles causes them to immediately freeze on the airplane. (Stay out of *any* clouds until you get that instrument rating later.)

As was discussed, clouds are formed by moist air being cooled to the point of condensation and this leads to the subject of lapse rates.

For air, the dry adiabatic lapse rate is 5 1/2° F per thousand feet. (Adiabatic is a process during which no heat is withdrawn or added to the system or body concerned.) The normal lapse rate of "average" air is 3 1/2° F, or 2° C. The moist adiabatic lapse rate is the lapse rate produced by convection in a saturated atmosphere such as within a cumulus cloud. At high temperatures it will be in the vicinity of 4 to 5° F. The dew point lapse rate is about 1° F per thousand feet.

For cumulus type clouds that are formed by surface heating, the base of the clouds may be estimated by the rate at which the dry lapse rate "catches" the dew point. (Dry lapse rate is 5 1/2° F and dew point drop is 1° F per thousand, so the temperature is dropping 4 1/2° faster than the dew point, per thousand feet.) Assume the surface temperature is 76° F and the dew point 58° F, a difference of 18° F: dividing this number by 4 1/2, you find that the temperature and dew point make connections at 4000 feet — the approximate base of

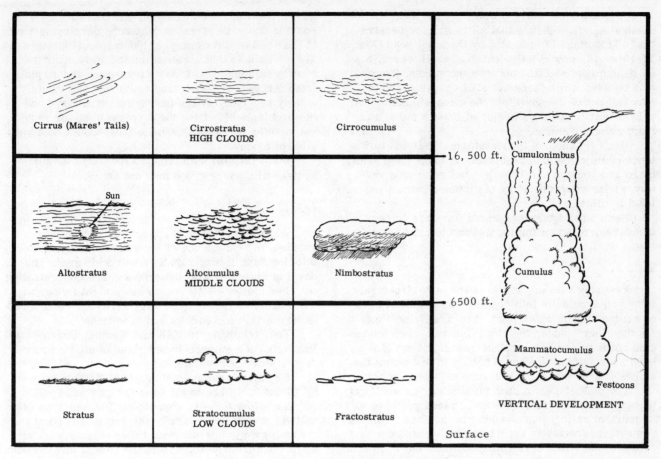

Fig. 22-10. Some typical cloud formations.

the clouds. This only works for the type of cloud formed by surface heating.

HAZARDS TO FLIGHT

Freezing rain and hail were covered earlier briefly, but you'll encounter other weather problems as you gain flying experience.

THUNDERSTORMS

Thunderstorms are a triple threat: (1) They are clouds, so that an inexperienced or noninstrument-rated pilot could lose control because of loss of outside references, but that's usually the least of the problems because of (2) the extreme turbulence that could cause loss of control by even the most experienced instrument pilot, as well as the possibility of the airplane being overstressed and coming apart, and (3) aircraft structural icing and hail-encounters.

The turbulence may also be so great that your head is being jolted so fast and hard that the instruments become difficult or impossible to read. It was once noted that an "average" thunderstorm (whatever that is) was continually releasing the energy of 50 Hiroshima type nuclear weapons. Whether this was ever confirmed is not known, but most people wouldn't like to fly into the energy of *one* Hiroshima type bomb.

Your lifetime project will be to avoid thunderstorms — whether you have an instrument rating or not. They can cause airliners to crash, and smaller aircraft could be pulled apart and *then* crash — the end product being the same.

Take a look at an "average" thunderstorm from start to finish: There are generally three stages, as noted by the book *Aviation Weather*:

1. *Cumulus Stage* — The thunderstorm begins as a cumulus cloud. An updraft is the key part of the thunderstorm. The cumulus may be growing at a rate of 3000 feet per minute and you won't be able to outclimb it to go over the top in a light aircraft.

The water droplets at this stage are small but are lifted past the freezing level, so icing could be a problem. As the raindrops get bigger they fall and the rain creates a cold downdraft coexisting with the updrafts. When this occurs the thunderstorm has entered the second stage.

2. *Mature Stage* — When precipitation starts falling out of the base the mature stage is reached. The downdraft may exceed 2500 feet per minute; it spreads outward at the surface and may be felt there as the "first gust." Meanwhile, updrafts may be moving up at 6000 feet per minute, and the shear area with its turbulence at the edge of these divergent drafts is better imagined than experienced.

All thunderstorm hazards are worse during the mature stage.

171

3. *Dissipating Stage* — Don't get the idea that the dissipating stage means that all is fine for penetration. This stage is indicated by the anvil head (Fig. 22-10) and is now mostly downdrafts. However, since there is no defined line between the stages, the anvil may be seen while there are still updrafts, and hail may fall out of the anvil into the clear air below. A rule of thumb would be to stay at least 5 miles away from a thunderstorm.

Don't fly under a thunderstorm. Hail and turbulence could cause bad problems. It looks clear under there and you can see 15 miles, but go around anyway, giving yourself plenty of distance from it (at least 5 miles).

Remember again that squall lines are lines of thunderstorms, multiplying the problems.

ICING

Freezing rain or drizzle is the only structural icing you should get into "legally" as a student pilot or noninstrument rated pilot. You are flying along "in the clear" (under the clouds) in rain when ice begins collecting on the airplane; you'll get out of it as soon as possible, perhaps climbing to just below the clouds and/or making a 180° turn as noted earlier.

The other types of structural icing you won't get unless you are in the clouds and, unless you have an instrument rating, you shouldn't be in clouds. Maybe you will inadvertently get into a cloud when on a cross-country in deteriorating weather and will be in there as long as it takes to make a 180° turn, but your job won't be to identify what type of ice is being picked up; you'll want to get back out of the cloud as safely and expeditiously as possible (Chapter 15).

As a private pilot, after getting back out and wiping those sweaty palms, you could say to your passenger(s), "We picked up some rime (or clear) ice, back there." This could tend to establish your credentials as a "weather" pro to them, but that's about all.

Clear ice — is formed by large droplets of moisture such as found in rain or cumuliform clouds. It is hard and glossy and difficult to remove. It's the type of ice you'd find in ice cubes — solid.

Rime ice — is formed by small droplets such as found in stratiform clouds or drizzle. There's air trapped in it and its appearance is close to that of the ice forming on the trays or the inside walls of a freezer. It's comparatively easy to remove. You may feel tempted later, when flying IFR, to ask that particularly obnoxious passenger (the one who keeps asking, "Where are we?") to go out and remove it — in flight.

FROST

You've left the airplane tied down in the fall or winter and find very early in the morning that it is covered with a very thin layer of frost. You figure that the weight of the frost is certainly negligible, and it's so extremely thin that there will be no problems aerodynamically, so you load up everybody and

go — for awhile. You find yourself (and airplane) roaring down the street of a housing development off the far end of the runway. (Housing developments are always built in that location immediately after the runway is completed.) After untangling the airplane from fences and playground equipment (fortunately nobody was out yet) and surveying the damage and the problems of getting the airplane back for repair, you wonder if maybe that little frost hasn't cost you a lot of money.

Don't take off with frost on the wings or horizontal tail surfaces; you may not get off.

FOG

While the other hazards are more readily avoided, fog can be one of the greatest dangers to any pilot because it may rapidly cover wide areas and develop while you are airborne and are concentrating on other matters. As you do more night flying, fog will become a factor to be very seriously considered under certain meteorological conditions.

Fog, according to FAA and Weather Service publications, is a surface-based cloud of either water droplets or ice crystals.

Fog may form by cooling air to its dew point or by adding moisture to air near the ground.

Radiation fog — is a shallower fog; one type is called "ground fog." You'll see ground fog from the air as a gray-white sea with taller objects sticking up through it. The top half of the hangar and the wind sock with towers may be quite visible, but the runway and surrounding area are covered. This fog usually occurs at night or in early morning with a clear sky, little or no wind, and a small temperature-dew point spread. The lack of overcast allows the ground to lose heat; the cooler (or cold) ground cools the highly moist air next to it, lowering the temperature to the dew point, and visible moisture is formed.

In addition, nuclei from industrial exhausts hasten the production of fog; an airport in a river bottom or on a lake shore near industrial emissions usually has a higher number of mornings with ground conditions of zero visibility. This fog will usually burn off well before noon on clear days.

Wind may disperse the fog or increase its depth, depending on the velocity.

Radiation fog is formed over land because land cools rapidly as compared to water.

If you are shooting landings and the runway lights begin to have haloes (at night) or the runway or other ground objects start becoming slightly less distinct in outline, you'd better consider terminating the flight early, unless you have a good alternate airport in mind.

Advection fog — is formed when moist air moves over colder ground or water. If you are flying in the west coast area of the United States you are well aware of how "sea fog" can form and move inland at times. Wind may also move fog up into the United States from the Gulf of Mexico during the winter.

These fogs look alike from the air, but advection fog may be found under an overcast, unlike radiation fog. If you ever have to race advection fog to an airport, you'll see how fast it can spread.

Upslope fog — When moist air is moved up a slope, cooling it, this type of fog is formed. The Sewanee, (Tennessee) airport, the point of origin for the example cross-country in this book, is on the edge of a plateau; when warm moist air is moved up the slope under certain wind conditions Sewanee can be fogged in solid on some winter days — the victim of upslope fog.

Ice fog — The temperature has to be very cold for this fog to form because the water vapor sublimates directly to ice. It's mostly an arctic problem but can happen in very cold spots in the United States.

Precipitation fog — You've seen this fog when it's raining, or has been, and the moisture falls into cool air. When you're flying in light rain and look down to see fog forming (particularly in the wooded areas where the trees hold moisture), you'd better plan on getting to an airport. Warm fronts are usually the causes, and widespread areas of very dense fog can be formed in a short while. Also, if you're flying over a layer of scattered clouds, and rain is falling out of an overcast above, you'd better watch for that scattered layer to very soon become broken and then overcast. There's nothing like flying along without a care in the world and looking down to discover that the undercast is nearly total — and you don't have an instrument rating!

A recommended book for you to read on weather theory and Weather Services is *Aviation Weather*, available from the U.S. Government Printing Office. (See the Bibliography in the back of this book.) As you progress in aviation you'll be branching out into areas of weather knowledge that may not apply to you now as a student pilot. Your job will be to assure that you don't stop the learning process. (This will give the male pilot an excellent excuse to keep a close eye on the TV Weather Girl.)

WEATHER INFORMATION SOURCES

The most important things for you to know about weather are where to get information about it and how to understand what's being said about it. You can get the latest forecasts or hourly reports from either the FAA Flight Service Stations or the National Weather Service Offices.

You aren't expected to analyze and forecast the weather. But you must be able to use the services. If you can't read sequence reports or forecasts, all of that expensive weather-watching system will be of small value to you. The people in the Flight Service Stations and Weather Services Offices are always willing to help. They will explain the symbols and will give the weather in everyday language if you request it. You're better off if you know how to read the information yourself, because you can browse through the data at your leisure and compare the various reports. You can then ask more concise and worthwhile questions.

When you contact these agencies, tell them you're a pilot and give them your time of departure, route (if you aren't going direct), destination, and expected time of arrival.

WEATHER SEQUENCES

Weather sequence reports are sent each hour by Teletype and are available at Flight Service Stations and Weather Service Offices (and privately leased Teletypes). Figure 22-11 is a key to an hourly weather report and aviation weather forecasts.

Figure 22-12 shows some actual hourly reports for stations in the state of Tennessee. Normally the reports come out by state, and the stations within the state are listed alphabetically.

The heading in Figure 22-12 (TN 191703) notes that this is the Tennessee group and the reports are released on the 19th of the month at 1703 Zulu time.

Looking at the Chattanooga (CHA) report (arrow):

SA 1655 — Means that this is a standard record report with the time of observation at 1655 Zulu time. Dyersburg (DYR) has a record special (RS) report released at 1657Z which means that the observation met the standards of a *special observation* (which may be put out at other times during the hour as required) in that significant weather changes have occurred.

M 16 OVC — The ceiling is a measured 1600 feet (overcast) *above the surface*.

Broken *or* overcast clouds constitute a ceiling. A thin overcast (-OVC), thin broken (-BKN), partial obscuration (-X), or scattered (SCT) clouds do not. *All* cloud bases in the main body of the sequence are given in feet above the station. Cloud bases are reported to the nearest 100 feet when they are 5000 feet or less above the surface. From 5001 to 10,000 feet they are noted to the nearest 500 feet, and to the nearest 1000 feet above 10,000 feet. As an additional tip for recognizing which of the cloud layers is the ceiling — a letter denoting how the ceiling was determined precedes the height.

3 K — The visibility is 3 statute miles in smoke.

147 — The barometric pressure corrected to sea level is 1014.7 millibars. The standard sea level pressure is 1013.2 mb. This information is of little use to the U.S. pilot (it's used in Europe for altimeter settings) and is omitted in the scheduled weather broadcasts.

/51 — The surface temperature is 51° F.

/45 — The dewpoint is 45° F. If the temperature of this parcel of air were to be lowered to 45° F it would become saturated and visible moisture (usually fog) would form. Watch for fog anytime the temperature and dewpoint are within 4° F of each other. *Be especially alert for this problem during night flying.*

/ØØØØ — The wind is calm. Note that "zeroes" have slashes through them to separate them from "Oh's."

/996 — The altimeter setting is 29.96 inches of mercury (barometric pressure). A rule of thumb is that if the last two digits (96 here) are more than 50

KEY TO AVIATION WEATHER OBSERVATIONS . . . .

LOCATION IDENTIFIER TYPE AND TIME OF REPORT*	SKY AND CEILING	VISIBILITY WEATHER AND OBSTRUCTION TO VISION	SEA-LEVEL PRESSURE	TEMPERATURE AND DEW POINT	WIND	ALTIMETER SETTING	REMARKS AND CODED DATA
MKC SA Ø758	15 SCT M25 OVC	1R-K	132	/58/56	/18Ø7	/993/	RØ4LVR2ØV4Ø

SKY AND CEILING

Sky cover contractions are in ascending order. Figures preceding contractions are heights in hundreds of feet above station. Sky cover contractions are:

CLR Clear: Less than 0.1 sky cover.
SCT Scattered: 0.1 to 0.5 sky cover.
BKN Broken: 0.6 to 0.9 sky cover.
OVC Overcast: More than 0.9 sky cover.

— **Thin** (When prefixed to SCT, BKN, OVC)

—X Partial obscuration: 0.9 or less of sky hidden by precipitation or obstructon to vision (bases at surface.)

X Obscuration: 1.0 sky hidden by precipitation or obstruction to vision (bases at surface.)

Letter preceding height of layer identifies ceiling layer and indicates how ceiling height was obtained. Thus:

E Estimated height
M Measured
W Indefinite

V=Immediately following numerical value, indicates a variable ceiling.

VISIBILITY

Reported in statute miles and fractions. (V=Variable)

WEATHER AND OBSTRUCTION TO VISION SYMBOLS

A	Hail	IC	Ice crystals	S	Snow
BD	Blowing dust	IF	Ice-fog	SG	Snow grains
BN	Blowing sand	IP	Ice pellets	SP	Snow pellets
BS	Blowing snow	IPW	Ice pellet showers	SW	Snow showers
D	Dust	K	Smoke	T	Thunderstorms
F	Fog	L	Drizzle	T+	Severe thunderstorm
GF	Ground fog	R	Rain	ZL	Freezing drizzle
H	Haze	RW	Rain showers	ZR	Freezing rain

Precipitation intensities are indicated thus: — Light; (no sign) Moderate; + Heavy

WIND

Direction in tens of degrees from true north, speed in knots. ØØØØ indicates calm. G indicates gusty. Peak speed of gusts follows G or Q when gusts or squall are reported. The contraction WSHFT followed by GMT time group in remarks indicates windshift and its time of occurrence. (Knots × 1.15=statute mi/hr.)

EXAMPLES: 3627=36Ø Degrees, 27 knots;
3627G40=36Ø Degrees, 27 knots, peak speed in gusts 4Ø knots.

ALTIMETER SETTING

The first figure of the actual altimeter setting is always omitted from the report.

RUNWAY VISUAL RANGE (RVR)

RVR is reported from some stations. Extreme values during 10 minutes prior to observation are given in hundreds of feet. Runway identification precedes RVR report.

PILOT REPORTS (PIREPS)

When available, PIREPS, in fixed-formats are appended to weather observations. The PIREP is desgnated by UA.

DECODED REPORT

Kansas City: Record observation taken at 0758 GMT 15ØØ feet scattered clouds, measured ceiling 25ØØ feet overcast, visibility 1 mile, light rain, smoke, sea-level pressure 1013.2 millibars, temperature 58°F, dewpoint 56°F, wind 18Ø°, 7 knots, altimeter setting 29.93 inches. Runway Ø4 left, visual range 2ØØØ feet variable to 4ØØØ feet.

*TYPE OF REPORT

SA—a scheduled record observation

SP—an unscheduled special observation indicating a significant change in one or more elements

RS—a scheduled record observation that also qualifies as a special observation.

All three types of observations (SA, SP, RS) are followed by a 24 hour-clock-time-group in GMT.

KEY TO AVIATION WEATHER FORECASTS . . . .

TERMINAL FORECASTS contain information for specific airports on expected ceiling, cloud amounts, visibility, weather, and obstructions to vision and surface wind. They are issued 3 times/day and are valid for 24 hours. The last six hours of each forecast are covered by a categorical statement indicating whether VFR, MVFR, IFR or LIFR conditions are expected (L in LIFR and M in MVFR indicate "low" and "marginal"). Terminal forecasts will be written in the following form:

CEILING: Identified by the letter "C"
CLOUD HEIGHTS: In hundreds of feet above the station (ground)
CLOUD LAYERS: Stated in ascending order of height
VISIBILITY: In statute miles but omitted if over 6 miles
WEATHER AND OBSTRUCTION TO VISION: Standard weather and obstruction to vision symbols are used
SURFACE WIND: In tens of degrees and knots; omitted when less than 1Ø

EXAMPLE OF TERMINAL FORECAST

DCA 221Ø1Ø: DCA Forecast 22nd day of month—valid time 1ØZ–1ØZ.
1Ø SCT C18 BKN 5SW–3415G25 OCNL C8 X 1/2SW: Scattered clouds at 1000 feet, ceiling 18ØØ feet broken, visibility 5 miles, light snow showers, surface wind 34Ø degrees 15 knots Gusts to 25 knots. occasional ceiling 8 hundred feet sky obscured, visibility ½ mile in moderate snow showers.
12Z C5Ø BKN 3312G22: At 12Z becoming ceiling 5ØØØ feet broken, surface wind 33Ø degrees 12 knots Gusts to 22.
Ø4Z MVFR CIG: Last 6 hours of FT after Ø4Z marginal VFR due to ceiling.

AREA FORECASTS are 18-hour aviation forecasts plus a 12-hour categorical outlook prepared 2 times/day giving general descriptions of cloud cover, weather and frontal conditions for an area the size of several states. Heights of cloud tops, and icing are referenced ABOVE SEA LEVEL (ASL); ceiling heights, ABOVE GROUND LEVEL (AGL); bases of cloud layers are ASL unless indicated. Each SIGMET or AIRMET affecting an FA area will also serve to amend the Area Forecast.

SIGMET or AIRMET messages broadcast by FAA on NAVAID voice channels warn pilots of potentially hazardous weather, SIGMET concerns severe and extreme conditions of importance to all aircraft, (i.e. icing, turbulence, and duststorms/sandstorms). Convective SIGMETS are issued for thunderstorms by the Severe Storms Forecast Center at Kansas City for the conterminous U.S. AIRMETS concern less severe conditions which may be hazardous to some aircraft or to relatively inexperienced pilots.

WINDS AND TEMPERATURES ALOFT (FD) FORECASTS are 12-hour forecasts of wind direction (nearest 1Ø° true N) and speed (knots) for selected flight levels. Temperatures aloft (°C) are included for all but the 3ØØØ-foot level.

EXAMPLES OF WINDS AND TEMPERATURES ALOFT (FD) FORECASTS:
FD WBC 121745
BASED ON 121200Z DATA
VALID 13000Z FOR USE 1800-0300Z. TEMPS NEG ABV 24000
FT
3000 6000 9000 12000 18000 24000 30000 34000 39000
BOS
3127 3425-07 3420-11 3421-16 3516-27 3512-38 311649 292451 283451
JFK
3026 3327-08 3324-12 3322-16 3120-27 2923-38 284248 285150 285749
At 6000 feet ASL over JFK wind from 330° at 27 knots and temperature minus 8°C.

TWEB (CONTINUOUS TRANSCRIBED WEATHER BROADCAST)—Individual route forecasts covering a 25-nautical-mile zone either side of the route. By requesting a specific route number, detailed en route weather for a 12- or 18-hour period (depending on forecast issuance) plus a synopsis can be obtained.

PILOTS . . . report inflight weather to nearest FSS. The latest surface weather reports are available by phone at the nearest pilot weather briefing office by calling at H+10.

Fig. 22-11. Keys to aviation weather reports and forecasts. As you read this chapter you may have to refer back to this for symbols used in the various reports and forecasts.

```
                    TN 191703
          ←—CHA SA 1655 M16 OVC 3K 147/51/43/0000/996
             CHA 12/012 CHA TOWER 210AGL 4 WEST UNLGTD
             DYR RS 1657 E10 BKN 20 OVC 7 097/63/58/2420/G25/981
          PK WND 2326/35
             DYR 12/006 MXA NDB OTS
          ←— MEM SA 1655 M14 7 114/66/56/2216G25/987/OCNL RINOVC OVHD
          PK WND 2126/38
          !MEM 11/001 HLI TOWER 916 5 EAST UNLGTD
           MEM 12/006 CKM NDB OTS
             MEM 12/024 MEM 9-27 CLSD
           MEM 12/025 MEM RVR 9 OTS
             MEM 12/026 MEM ILS MM 9 OTS

           MEM 12/027 MEM ILS OM 9 OTS
           MEM 12/028 MEM ILS LOC 9 OTS
           MEM 12/029 MEM ILS GS 9 OTS
             MEM 12/047 MEM 17L-35R CLSD 20-2200
             MEM 12/048 MEM RVR 35R OTS
             TRI SA 1654 2 SCT M5 OVC 2R-L-F 158/41/39/0606/998/CIG RGD
```

Fig. 22-12. Actual hourly sequence reports and NOTAMS for Chattanooga, Dyersburg, Memphis, and Tri-Cities, Tennessee.

```
              SA14 191700
    TRI SA 1654 2SCT M5 OVC 2R-L-F 158/41/39/0606/998/CIG RGD
    UA /OV O/TRI 1653 FL DURGC 90/TP PA31 /SK OVC55 57 OVC /TA +4
    CSV SA 1654 W3 X 3/4LF 131/47/47/1605/992
    BNA SA 1653 M9 OVC 11/2L-F 116/50/48/1505/987
    CKV SA 1654 W3X 3/4L-F 48/47/1204/990
    MKL SA 1700 E15 OV6H 100/64/58/2115/983
    PAH SA 1651 W2 X 1/2L-F 090/50/49/1407/980
    BWG SRS 1653 W5X1LF 128/47/46/0605/991/ CIG RGD
    OWB SA 1649 E19 OVC 10 M/M/0908/985
    SDF SA 1655 M40 OVC 5R-F 133/41/39/0805/991
    LOU SA 1653 E50 OVC 4R-F 41/39/0607/993
    LOZ SA 1655 -XE4 BKN 15 OVC 11/2R-F 148/44/44/1804/995 RDGS OBSCD E
    TYS SA 1655 W2X1/2R-F 44/42/0604/996/R22RVR60+
    DKX SA 1655 W2X 3/4L-F 0504/997


    MKL 11/001 M53 RWY LGTS OTS
    MKL 12/003 JKS DME OTS 16-2100
    PAH 11/003 CEY PCL KEY 122.8 5 TIMES ON
    LOU 11/001 FTK ATCT 11-0300 EXCPSAT 13-2100/NAVAIDS UNMON WHEN CLSD
    LOU 12/014 IMS NDB OTS
    LOU 12/020 EWO VOR OTS UNTIL 202000
    LOU 12/022 LOU R3704A ACTV UNTIL 221100
    TYS 11/001 MOR TOWER 200AGL 4 NORTH UNLGTD
    TYS 11/002 MOR 5-23 NOW 5700
```

Fig. 22-13. The local scan stations have the NOTAM information given in a block following the weather information.

put a "2" at the beginning of the numbers. If those digits are less than 50 put a "3" at the beginning of the numbers. If you see a "013," for instance, on the barometric pressure spot on the hourly report, you would add a "3" and know that the altimeter setting is 30.13 inches of mercury.

NOTAMS are placed directly below the station in the listing by states.

The month (12 — December) and the number of the NOTAM for that month (Ø12 — the twelfth issued by Chattanooga in December) indicate that there is an unlighted tower with a height of 210 feet above the ground level 4 miles west of the airport.

Looking at Dyersburg (DYR) weather, you can see that the *ceiling* is an *estimated 1000 broken* with a 2000 foot overcast. The visibility is 7 miles. The wind (242Ø/G25) indicates that it is from 240° true at 20 K with gusts to 25 K. The slash between 2Ø and G25 is a typographical error. The PK WND (peak wind) was from 230° true at 26 K at 35 minutes past the last hour. (The slash is at the proper spot for the peak wind information.)

Checking Memphis (MEM) weather (arrow) an error is found. (This is an actual Teletype report.) The ceiling height is a measured 1400 feet but the type of cloud cover was omitted. Since the M designates it as a ceiling, the cloud cover must either be broken or overcast. The wind is from 220° true at 16 K, gusts to 25 K.

Memphis has a "few" NOTAMS right below the weather. Preceding each NOTAM is an exclamation point (!) to grab your attention. They are not repeated here since once you've seen one, you've seen them all. There's still a NOTAM on an unlighted

tower 5 miles east (the first NOTAM issued the month before — November).

Memphis is having problems here with the RVR (Runway Visual Range) equipment and ILS components, among other things. (OTS means Out of Service.)

The ceiling at Tri-Cities is ragged.

Figure 22-13 shows how the NOTAMS follow the group of stations for a local scan. Tri-Cities has a pilot report (UA) from PA-31 noting the tops are at 9000 feet over that area. There will be more about pilot reports (PIREPS) later in the chapter.

Bowling Green, Kentucky (BWG) started the report as an SA (standard) but it was corrected as an RS (record special).

Some notes: MKL (Jackson, Tennessee) has an overtype problem; it's probably 1500 overcast.

The ceiling is ragged at BWG and the ridges are obscured east of LOZ (London, Kentucky).

At Owensboro, (OWB) the temperature and dew-point are missing (M/M).

Knoxville (TYS, for Tyson Airport) has generally bad weather with an indefinite ceiling (W) 200 feet with obscuration (X), visibility one-half mile in light rain and fog. The runway visual range (RVR) for Runway 22 Right is 6000 plus feet.

You might want to check with your instructor about other information in Figures 22-12 and 22-13.

Figure 22-14 includes two special weather reports that were sent out between the regular hourly sequences.

Little Rock (LIT) sent out a special at 1729Z noting that the weather is a measured 300 feet broken, 500 feet overcast, visibility 1 1/2 miles in drizzle (L) and fog (F). The wind is from 140° at 10 K and the

```
LIT SP 1729 M3 BKN 5 OVC 11/2LF   1410/003/ SFC VSBY 1V2




SGF SP 1735 M2 OVC 7/8L-F 0308/003
```

Fig. 22-14. Special weather reports are sent in addition to the regular hourly reports.

altimeter setting is 30.03 inches of mercury. The surface (SFC) visibility of 1 mile (statute) variable to 2 miles.

Springfield (SGF), Missouri, issued a special report at 1735Z, showing that the weather is a measured 200 feet overcast, visibility 7/8 mile (statute) in light drizzle (L-) and fog (F). The wind is from 030° at 8 knots and the altimeter setting is 30.03 inches of mercury.

WEATHER FORECASTS

TERMINAL FORECASTS

Terminal forecasts are for terminal areas such as Atlanta, St. Louis, Kansas City, and other big airport centers. However, some smaller airports are included as well to give a fuller coverage of the country.

Figure 22-15 shows the terminal forecasts (FTs) for several stations. The bottom part of the illustration will be discussed later.

Looking at Chattanooga (CHA), the number 291515 indicates that the forecast is issued on the 29th of the month and is valid from 1500Z on that date to 1500Z the next day.

Not shown, but the time of issuance here is 1400Z, which starts the valid period of from 1500Z

to 1500Z the next day. Terminal forecasts are issued three times daily at 0940Z, 1440Z, and 2140Z in the East and Central time zones of the United States, and 0940Z, 1540Z, and 2240Z in the Mountain and Pacific zones.

The weather forecast for CHA from the beginning of the valid period to 1800Z is 4000 scattered, ceiling 8000 broken, with the scattered clouds variable to broken. (The ceiling would be 4000 feet if or when *that* layer is broken.) The wind is not mentioned in a terminal forecast if it is expected to be less than 10 K (it's calm in the actual report) and the visibility is omitted from the forecast if it is expected to be more than 6 statute miles. The forecast for that first 3-hour period omitted wind and visibility.

After 1800Z the forecast is for a ceiling of 3000 overcast, wind from 150°T at 12 K with a chance of light rain (R-). Note that visibility information was omitted so it's expected to be more than 6 miles.

After 2100Z the ceiling will be 1500 feet overcast, with 3 miles visibility in light rain, and the wind will be from 150° T at 12 K.

The last 6 hours of a terminal forecast gives a general outlook at the weather. So after 0900Z on the 30th of the month, conditions will be IFR (Instrument Flight Rules) because of the ceiling (CIG) and rain (R). As an example, Paducah (PAH), Bowling Green (BWG), Lexington (LEX), and Standiford Field at Louisville (SDF) are forecast to be marginal VFR

```
CHA 291515 40 SCT C80 BKN SCT V BKN. 18Z C30 OVC 1512 CHC R-.
   21Z C15 OVC 3R- 1512. 09Z IFR CIG R..
PAH 291515 20 SCT C30 OVC SCT VRBL BKN OCNL C10 OVC 2RW/TRW. 09Z
   MVFR CIGS RW..
BWG 291515 30 SCT C100 OVC SCT VRBL BKN FQT C10 OVC 2 RW/TRW. 09Z
   MVFR CIGS RW..
SDF 29 1515 30 SCT C80 OVC 3F SCT VRBL BKN. 18Z C25 BKN 50 OVC 4H
   OCNL C10 OVC 2 RW/TRW. 09Z MVFR CIGS RW..
LEX 291515 30 SCT C100 OVC 3GF. 18Z C30 BKN 100 OVC FQT C10
   OVC 2RW/TRW. 09Z MVFR CIGS RW..
TRI 291515 CLR. 16Z 35 SCT C100 BKN. 19Z C30 BKN 1510 BKN V OVC
   CHC R- LATE AFTN. 09Z IFR CIG R..


HUF FT AMD 1 291010 1215Z 15 SCT C30 OVC 4H. 16Z 8 SCT C20 OVC 5H
   CHC C8 OVC 2R-F. 22Z C8 OVC 1R-F 1510. 04Z IFR CIG R F..
```

Fig. 22-15. Terminal forecasts for several stations and an amended terminal forecast for Terre Haute (HUF).

(MVFR) because of the ceiling and rain showers (RW). If VFR is noted for the last 6 hours of the forecast, the ceiling is expected to be higher than 3000 feet and visibility to be greater than 5 miles. If MVFR is indicated, the ceiling is expected to be between 1000 and 3000 feet and/or visibility 3 to 5 miles. If IFR is noted, the ceiling is expected to be less than 1000 feet and/or visibility less than 3 miles. LIFR (Low IFR) is noted when the ceiling is less than 500 feet and/or visibility is less than one mile.

Note that the general weather trend is expected to be deteriorating as indicated by Figure 22-15. Tri-Cities (TRI) is forecast to be clear (CLR) at the beginning of the forecast period but conditions steadily go downhill. From 1600Z to 1900Z it's forecast to be 3500 scattered, ceiling 10,000 broken, with no problems with wind (less than 10 K) or visibility (more than 6 miles). The wind was actually 4 K and visibility 20 miles at 1700Z.

Check earlier actual weather with the forecasts for those earlier periods when you are in an FSS or WSO, planning for a cross-country flight. Were the forecasts overly optimistic? They may be so *now* as you check them. Many times, if you are able to look at several previous hourly sequences (actual weather), you may see a trend that will help you further in your go or no-go decision.

To err is human and so the *amended* forecast is available. The lower part of Figure 22-15 is from HUF (*Hu*lman *F*ield at Terre Haute) and is a terminal forecast (FT) amendment number one. It's for the forecast on the 29th of the month, the one that is valid at 1000Z on that date to 1000Z the next morning. The amendment was issued at 1215Z. If you had the original HUF forecast you would compare the two. Is it expected to be getting worse than was expected earlier? (This is usually the case.) Be sure to check for amended forecasts and special weather reports when you are planning a cross-country.

AREA FORECAST

The area forecast covers several states and parts of states (Fig. 22-16).

The heading of this *actual* area forecast indicates that it is sent out from New Orleans (MSY) and is a Forecast, Area (FA) issued on the 31st of the month at 0040Z, valid for a period of 18 hours (31-0100Z to 31-1900Z), with an outlook (OTLK) for an additional 12 hours from 1900Z on the 31st, to the first of the month at 0700Z (010700Z). It covers Tennessee, Arkansas, Louisiana, Mississippi, Alabama and Florida west of 85 degrees west longitude, and those coastal waters. The heights are given above mean sea level unless noted.

The forecast is broken down as indicated:
THUNDERSTORMS IMPLY POSSIBLE SEVERE OR GREATER TURBULENCE, SEVERE ICING, AND LOW LEVEL WIND SHEAR.

```
MSY FA 310040
310100Z-311900Z
OTLK 311900Z-010700Z

TN AR LA MS AL FL W OF 85 DEG CSTL WTRS...

HGTS MSL UNLESS NOTED...

TSTMS IMPLY PSBL SVR OR GTR TURBC SVR ICG AND LOW LVL WND
SHEAR...

FLT PRCTN... OVR AR LA ADJ CSTL WTRS FOR EMBDD TSTMS FQTLY
IN BKN LNS AND FEW SVR TSTMS. AR LA ADJ CSTL WTRS FOR TURBC
BLO 7 THSD FT AND LOW-LVL WND SHEAR DUE STG LOW LVL WNDS. E
HLF TN 08Z-14Z FOR LOW CIGS AND LOW VSBYS.

SYNS... A N-S CDFNT IN E OK E TX WL MOV EWD SLOLY DURG PD.
SQLN AHD FNT IN EXTRM W PTNS OF AR LA ADJ CSTL WTRS MOVG E
20 KT.

SIG CLDS AND WX...

AR LA AND ADJ CSTL WTRS...
E OF A HRO-LCH LN CIGS 3 THSD BKN V SCT 50-250 BKN VSBY 5HK
FEW SHWRS /TRW TOPS 330. W OF A HRO-LCH LN CIGS 12 BKN V OVC
LYRD TO 180-250 OVC ABV VSBYS 3-5FSCT EMBDD TRW TOPS 400 FQTLY
IN BKN LNS WITH CIGS BLO 10 VSBYS BLO 3TRW. ALSO FEW SVR TRW
ISOLD TORNADOS. CONDS GRDLY SPRD EWD IN RMDR AREA E OF A HRO-LCH
LN BY 19Z. OTLK... MVFR CIG TRW.

W HLF TN MS AL FL W OF 85 DEG ADJ CSTL WTRS...
 AGL 3 THSD SCT OCNL BKN OCNL VSBYS 5KH. BY 06Z CIGS 12-25 BKN
OCNL SCT 40 VSBYS 3-5KH WITH CONDS LWR IN WDLY SCT RW/TRW W
OF A HOP-PGL LN. FM 10Z-15Z CIGS NR 10 OVC VSBYS NR 3FKH. OTLK...
MVFR CIG.

E HLF TN...
OCNL CIGS 20 BKN V SCT 40. 06Z AGL 10 SCT OCNL BKN VSBYS 3F
LWRG AT 09Z TO CIGS FQTLY BLO 10 VSBYS GENLY BLO 3F. 15Z CIGS
40 BKN 60-250 OVC VSBYS 6H. OTLK... MVFR CIG.

ICG AND FRZLVL... MDT TO SVR MXD ICG IN BLDUPS ABV FRZLVL 100
N SLPG TO 120 S. ADNLY OCNL MDT CLR ICG NW QTR AR ABV 100.

TURBC... SEE FLT PRCTNS.

THIS FA INCORPORATES THE FOLLOWING AIRMETS STILL IN EFFECT...
NONE.
```

Fig. 22-16. Area forecast.

FLIGHT PRECAUTION (FLT PRCTN) . . . Over Arkansas, Louisiana (and) adjacent coastal waters for embedded thunderstorms, frequently in broken lines and a few severe thunderstorms. (Flight precaution) Arkansas, Louisiana and adjacent coastal waters for turbulence below 7000 feet and low level wind shear due (to) strong low level winds. (Flight precaution) for the eastern half of Tennessee, 0800Z to 1400Z, for low ceilings and low visibilities.

SYNOPSIS (SYNS) . . . A north-south cold front in eastern Oklahoma and eastern Texas will move eastward slowly during the period. (There will be) a squall line ahead of the front in (the) extreme west portions of Arkansas, Louisiana (and) adjacent coastal waters, moving east at 20 knots.

SIGNIFICANT CLOUDS AND WEATHER (SIG CLDS AND WX) . . . *Arkansas, Louisiana and adjacent coastal waters* . . . .

East of a Harrison-Lake Charles line ceilings (are forecast to be) 3000 broken variable to scattered, 5000 to 25,000 broken, visibilities 5 miles in haze and smoke with a few showers/thunderstorms and rain showers, tops at 33,000 feet. West of a Harrison-Lake Charles line ceilings (will be) 1200 broken variable to overcast layered 18,000 to 25,000 overcast above. Visibilities will be 3-5 miles in fog. There will be embedded thunderstorms and rain showers with tops at 40,000 feet, frequently in broken lines with ceilings below 1,000 feet, visibilities below 3 miles in thunderstorms and rain showers. Also (there will be) a few severe thunderstorms with rain showers and isolated tornadoes. (*Author's note: Put the airplanes in the storm cellar, Harry.*) The conditions will gradually spread eastward in (the) remainder of the area east of a Harrison-Lake Charles line by 1900Z. OUTLOOK . . . . Marginal VFR because of (low) ceilings and thunderstorms with rain showers.

Western Half of Tennessee, Mississippi, Alabama, Florida west of 85 degrees (west longitude) and adjacent waters . . . .

Above ground level (clouds) will be 3000 scattered, occasionally broken, (with) occasional visibilities 5 miles in smoke and haze. By 0600Z ceilings (will be) 1200 to 2500 broken, occasionally scattered at 4000 feet, visibilities 3 to 5 miles in smoke and haze with conditions lower in widely scattered rain showers and thunderstorms with rain showers west of a Hopkinsville-Pascagoula line. From 1000Z to 1500Z, ceilings (will be) near 1000 overcast, visibilities near 3 miles in fog, smoke and haze. OUTLOOK . . . . Marginal VFR because of (low) ceilings.

Eastern Half of Tennessee . . . .

(There will be) occasional ceilings of 2000 broken variable (to) scattered (at) 4000 feet. (After) 0600Z (AGL) clouds will be at 1000 feet scattered, occasional broken (with) visibilities 3 miles in fog, lowering at 0900Z to ceilings frequently below 1000 feet, visibilities generally below 3 miles in fog. (After) 1500Z ceilings (are forecast to be) 4000 broken, 6000-25,000 overcast, visibilities 6 miles in haze. OUTLOOK . . . . Marginal VFR because of ceilings.

ICING AND FREEZING LEVEL . . . Moderate to severe mixed icing in buildups above freezing level (which is at) 10,000 feet in the north (ern portion) sloping to 12,000 in the south. Additionally, (there will be) occasional moderate clear icing (in the) northwest quarter (of) Arkansas above 10,000 feet.

TURBULENCE . . . See Flight Precaution (in early part of forecast).

This FA incorporates the following Airmets still in effect . . . .

NONE.

You'll see abbreviations in Area Forecasts such as AOB (At Or Below): "ceilings will be AOB fourteen hundred feet."

When you first start reading area forecasts the sentence structure seems that of an ex-Luftwaffe pilot with punctuation problems, but with practice *yu cn rd thm without mch trbl.*

AIRMETS

AIRMETS are advisories concerning weather of such a degree as to be potentially hazardous to inexperienced pilots and/or aircraft of limited equipment, but not necessarily hazardous to more experienced pilots (and more sophisticated equipment). AIRMETS will cover:

Moderate icing
Moderate turbulence
Sustained winds of 30 knots at the surface
Widespread areas of ceilings less than 1000 feet and/or visibilities of less than 3 miles
Extensive mountain obscurement

If the above phenomena are adequately forecast in the FA, an AIRMET will not be issued. Figure 22-17 is an actual AIRMET.

SIGMETS

SIGMETS are advisories concerning significant *met*eorological developments of such severity as to be potentially hazardous to *all* aircraft in flight. SIGMET advisories will cover:

Embedded thunderstorms
Tornadoes
Lines of thunderstorms (squall lines)
Hail 3/4 in. or more
Severe and extreme turbulence
Severe icing
Widespread duststorms/sandstorms lowering visibilities to less than 3 miles

The first four items listed are issued as "Convective SIGMETS" and would be designated as "WST" and "CONVECTIVE SIGMET" would be a part of the heading (not shown in Figure 22-18). The last three items are issued as "Nonconvective SIGMETS". SIGMETS are always to be kept current whether the problems were forecast in the FA or not. Figure 22-18 shows an actual SIGMET.

The AIRMETS and SIGMETS last issued naturally supersede those previous. When you are checking the weather, don't just look at the regularly released information; there may be special reports, revised terminal forecasts, and new SIGMETS or AIRMETS.

```
        MSY WA 291535
        291535-292100

        AIRMET PAPA 3. FLT PRCTN. ARK EXTRM WRN TENN EXTRM NW MISS FOR
        IFR CONDS.
        OVR ARK ANDEXTRM NW MISS CIG BLO 10 VSBY BLO 3R-F SPRDG INTO EXTRM
        WRN TENN AND CONTG PAST 21Z.
```

Fig. 22-17. An AIRMET (WA) issued by New Orleans (MSY) on the 29th of the month at 1535Z and valid for a period on the 29th of from 1535Z to 2100Z. Translated:

AIRMET Papa 3. (The third AIRMET issued since the preceding midnight by New Orleans for a particular phenomenon.)
Flight precautions (for) Arkansas, extreme western Tennessee, extreme northwest Mississippi for IFR conditions.
Over Arkansas and extreme northwest Mississippi ceilings (will be) below 1000 feet, visibility below 3 miles in light rain (R-) and fog (F), spreading into extreme western Tennessee and continuing past 2100Z.

```
        MSY WS 291850
        291850-292300

        SIGMET ECHO 6. FLT PRCTN. EXTRM S ALA NW FLA AND ADJ CSTL WTRS
        FOR TSTMS.
        SCTD EMBEDDED TSTMS TOPS TO 350 OVR ALA S OF MONTGOMERY AND
        NW FLA AND ADJ CSTL WTRS CONTG PAST 23Z.
```

Fig. 22-18. A SIGMET (WS) issued by New Orleans on the 29th at 1850Z. The valid period is from 1850Z to 2300Z.
SIGMET Echo 6. (The 6th SIGMET issued for the New Orleans Echo area since the past midnight.)
Flight precaution (for) extreme southern Alabama, northwest Florida, and adjacent coastal waters for thunderstorms.
Scattered embedded thunderstorms (with) tops to 35,000 (ASL) over Alabama south of Montgomery and (over) northwest Florida and adjacent coastal waters (will be) continuing past 2300Z.

WIND INFORMATION

Figure 22-19 is part of an actual winds aloft forecast. The altitudes given are above mean sea level; some of the western stations may not issue the winds at 3000 or even 6000 feet because of the elevation of the station.

Looking at the forecast winds at Raleigh-Durham (RDU) at 3000 feet you'll see 9900. This means that the wind is forecast to be 5 K or less, or would be read as "light and variable."

At 9000 feet at RDU the wind is forecast to be from 290° true at 24 K (2924) and the temperature is expected to be -4°C (-04).

At 34,000 feet in the RDU area the wind will be from 760° at 10 K and . . . *hold it!* The compass only

```
    FDUS1 KWBC 290540

    DATA BASED ON 290000Z

    VALID 291200Z   FOR USE 0600-1500Z. TEMPS NEG ABV 24000

    FT   3000     6000     9000     12000    18000    24000    30000    34000    39000

    LOU  1715   2116+01   2423-03  2532-08  2647-21  2659-34  258049   258757   257158
    MEM  1526   1630+05   1827+00  1925-06  2240-20  2358-33  237848   248852   247960
    MKC  0707   1205-02   1808-06  2014-10  2119-23  2121-36  222652   232655   24215A
    MOB  1823   1926+06   2027+01  2129-03  2338-17  2349-29  247544   740153   740660
    MSY  2330   2331+09   2334+04  2337-02  2343-16  2352-28  247944   740754   740961
    PIE  0713   1706+10   2316+05  2428-01  2450-14  2462-25  247739   248647   249457
    RDU  9900   2814+00   2924-04  2933-07  2852-19  2772-30  269945   761053   760860
    RIC  3107   2819-03   2928-06  2937-09  2858-20  2780-31  770845   761453   269958
    SGF  0914   1415+01   1717-04  1922-08  2132-22  2241-35  235452   235758   234456
    SHV  2103   2113+06   2118+00  2123-05  2244-20  2259-32  228148   239457   238259
    STL  1413   1816+01   2120-04  2227-08  2336-22  2443-35  245650   246158   24A857
    TLH  1214   1717+07   1918+02  2122-03  2339-16  2453-27  247541   249250   740059
    TRI         2510+01   2720-03  2831-07  2750-20  2667-32  269346   750355   259559
```

Fig. 22-19. Winds aloft forecast (FD), data based on the 29th midnight (0000Z) and valid at 1200Z on that date. It's for use between 0600Z and 1500Z. All temperatures are negative above 24,000 feet (this saves putting in a lot of "minus" signs). All heights are above sea level.

includes 360°, but this is no misprint. When the wind is over 100 K, 50 is added to the direction (this way they can keep the number of digits down to a maximum of six for wind and temperature), and 100 subtracted from the wind value (given as 10 K here). So you would subtract 50 from the 76 which gives a direction of 26 (260° true) and add 100 to the force to get 110 K (10 + 100). The temperature is a cool -53°C at that altitude.

WINDS ALOFT CHARTS

The National Meteorological Center plots and transmits wind data obtained from balloon observations four times daily. This information is sent by Teletype in coded form and facsimile charts to National Weather Service Offices throughout the United States.

The Teletype code is complex and you should ask the Weather Service personnel to help you, rather than try to memorize it.

The winds aloft chart is a map of the continental United States for each particular altitude (or pressure level) of interest with an "arrow, barb and pennant" presentation at selected stations to show the wind direction and velocity and temperature (in degrees of Celsius) for that altitude.

Figure 22-20 shows the "arrow, barb and pennant" idea. Each pennant is 50 K, a full barb is 10 K, a half barb is 5 K. Remember that winds aloft are given in *true* directions and knots.

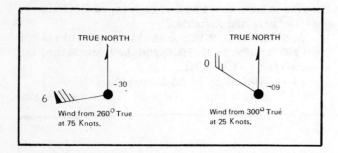

Fig. 22-20. Barb and pennant presentation for the winds aloft chart. The wind is blowing the way the arrow is going. The temperatures are -30° C and -9° C.

The numbers associated with the arrows are the middle digit of the direction from which the wind is coming. The "6" in the left-hand arrow system in Figure 22-20 confirms that the wind is from 260° true. (You could guess by the arrow that it is west-

southwest but now know it's 260°.) The right-hand arrow in the figure has an "0" noting that the wind is from 300° true.

PILOT REPORTS

One of the most valuable sources of information is pilot reports, or PIREPS. These are on-the-spot reports *in the air* and are not forecasts or information based on observations from the ground. Figure 22-21 is an actual PIREP. One way to remember the symbol for pilot reports is that it is an *U*p in the *A*ir (UA) report.

OTHER SERVICES

There are some other weather services available to you:

1. PATWAS — Pilots Automatic Telephone Weather Answering Service. The telephone numbers are listed in the *Airport/Facility Directory*, and by dialing you can get a transcription of current and forecast weather. If you require more specific information, a forecaster is available.

2. *Transcribed Weather Broadcasts* — At certain LF/MF radio facilities throughout the country current weather, winds, forecasts, and PIREPS are transmitted continuously and forecasts are updated every few hours. Check with Flight Service Stations and Weather Service Offices.

3. FLIGHT WATCH.

This service will provide timely weather information *in flight* and is available throughout the conterminous United States along prominent and heavily travelled flyways. You should be able to get the service at 5000 feet above the ground level within 80 miles from an FLIGHT WATCH outlet. Selected Flight Service Stations will provide the service, using remote communications facilities, as necessary. (FLIGHT WATCH is not intended for flight plan filing or position reporting, but for weather information only.)

FLIGHT WATCH will use 122.0 MHz and you would call the particular FSS controlling the FLIGHT WATCH in the area. ("CHATTANOOGA FLIGHT WATCH, THIS IS ZEPHYR SIX FIVE FOUR FOUR TANGO," etc.) If you don't know which FSS controls the service, just call "FLIGHT WATCH" and give your position relative to the nearest VOR, and they will contact you. This service is also known as En-

ROA UA /OV ROA 1409 FL DURGC /TP BE90 /SK OVC /IC RIME / RM TRACE

Fig. 22-21. A pilot report (UA) released by Roanoke (ROA) at 1409Z. The pilot reports after take-off at Roanoke and during the climb that there was a trace of rime (structural) icg, er, icing (Beech 90).

route Flight Advisory Service (EFAS).

4. *Weather Radar*—Some Flight Service Stations located near one of the 90 weather radar stations of the National Weather Service have radar repeaterscopes. You may be able to get inflight information concerning the intensity of precipitation in your area of flight. (As a student pilot you shouldn't be flying into areas of intense precipitation.)

These other services are covered briefly so that you will have an idea of what is available. As you gain experience you'll make more and more use of these aids.

WEATHER CHARTS

SURFACE ANALYSIS CHART

The surface chart shows weather at various stations, and a date-time group (GMT) indicates the time of the observation.

The isobars, pressure systems, and fronts are indicated on the chart as mentioned earlier in the chapter and as shown in Figures 22-2 and 22-3.

This chart is a good first reference when you go to a WSO or FSS as a check of the general layout of the weather. Since weather in the United States moves generally from west to east, you can check fronts or pressure systems to the west of your route

and get a general idea of what might be a factor later.

After you've seen the map, take a look at the sequence reports along the route and compare them with what had been forecast. The presence of a cold or warm front nearly always means some kind of ceiling and visibility restriction, but occasionally "dry" fronts will move through an area. By only looking at the chart you might decide to "cancel because of the front."

Remember that the chart may be 2 or 3 hours out of date before *you* get to it, and you'll have to take the weather movement into consideration.

Figure 22-22 is redrawn from an actual Surface Analysis Chart. The solid line isobars are spaced at 4-millibar intervals, but if the pressure gradient is weak, dashed isobars are put in at 2-millibar intervals to better define the system. A "24" is 1024.0 mb and "92" stands for 992 mb. The Highs and Lows have a two-digit underlined number ("22" means that the pressure at the center is 1022 mb, etc.). Look back at Figure 22-2 for color presentations of fronts and squall lines.

A three-digit number is placed by a frontal system on the chart to show type, intensities, and character of the front. For instance, "453" by a front means that it is a cold front at the surface (4), moderate, little, or no change in intensity (5), with frontal activity increasing (3). These codes are in the Weather Service Offices so don't try to memorize them.

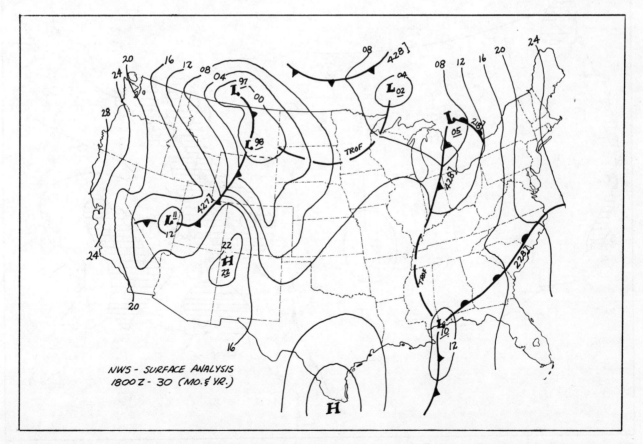

Fig. 22-22. The major value of the Surface Analysis Chart is to give an overall view of fronts and pressure systems. (*Instrument Flight Manual*)

On the chart are "station models" (not included here) showing sky coverage, temperature, dew point, and other information. You'd be better off to get this information on the latest hourly report for a particular station since the map may be several hours old when you see it.

WEATHER DEPICTION CHART

This chart is a good one for getting a good look at restrictions to visibility and low ceilings that would not be actually shown on the Surface Analysis Chart.

"Scalloped" lines are drawn on the chart to form boundaries of areas of MVFR (Marginal VFR) with ceilings between 1000 and 3000 feet and visibilities of 3 to 5 miles. IFR areas are outlined by smooth lines (ceiling less than 1000 feet and/or visibility less than 3 miles. VFR areas are not outlined and consist of ceilings greater than 3000 feet and visibilities greater than 5 miles.

Figure 22-23 is a sample Weather Depiction Chart, showing areas of IFR and MVFR weather. Only a few of the reporting stations are shown for example purposes.

Station (1) is overcast as shown by the solid black circle and the visibility is 5 (statute) miles in smoke (5K). The ceiling is 1400 feet (MVFR).

Station (2) is overcast at 1300 feet with a visibility of 6 miles in smoke (MVFR).

Station (3) has a ceiling of 600 overcast, visibility of 1 mile in smoke, which puts it properly in the IFR boundary.

Station (4) has a broken layer at 10,000 feet and the visibility is *more* than 6 miles, since it is not reported at the station. (Visibility is reported if 6 miles or less.)

Station (5) is clear with a visibility over 6 miles.

Station (6) has scattered clouds at 25,000 feet, visibility more than 6 miles.

RADAR SUMMARY CHART

Figure 22-24 is part of an actual Radar Summary Chart. The shading shows radar echo areas and the contours outline intensities. For instance, over north central Alabama, the intensities are shown building toward the center of the area with tops at 32,000 (320). Bases would be designated with a bar *over* the height value (in hundreds). Note also that

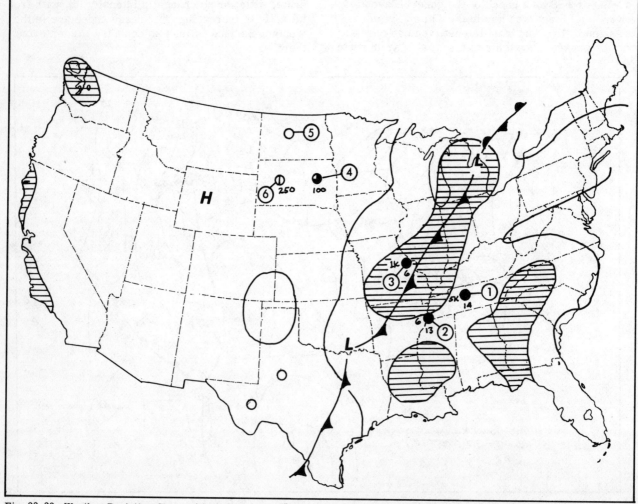

Fig. 22-23. Weather Depiction Chart. (1) Shaded areas — IFR with ceilings less than 1000 feet and/or visibility less than 3 statute miles. (2) Contoured without shading — MVFR areas with ceilings 1000 to 3000 feet and/or visibility 3 to 5 statute miles. (3) No contours — VFR areas with ceilings greater than 3000 feet and visibility greater than 5 miles.

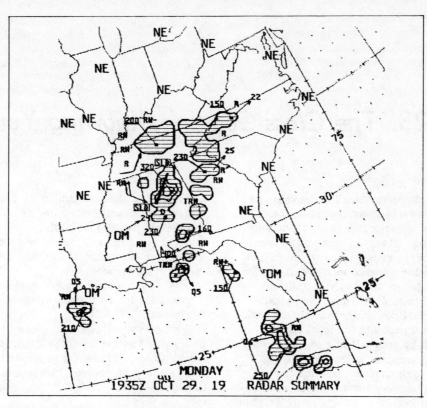

Fig. 22-24. Radar Summary Chart.

there is a squall line in that area as indicated by the solid line. The direction and velocities of movement of areas and lines are shown by pennants (that Alabama line is moving east-southeast at 20 knots).

There is a rain shower area of increasing intensity (RW+) south of the Florida panhandle, with tops at 15,000 feet (150). There is an area of thunderstorms and rain showers (TRW) south of Pensacola moving south (arrow) at 5 knots (05).

NE means "no echoes" and OM indicates that a station is out for maintenance.

There is an area with rain and rain showers (tops at 23,000 feet) moving northeast at 25 knots (arrow) in the Atlanta area.

The Radar Summary Chart is especially valuable in showing intensities and movements of significant precipitation.

WEATHER PROGNOSTIC CHARTS

The low level prognostic chart would be of the most value to you as a student or new private pilot. Like the other charts, the weather areas are superimposed on a map of the United States.

The low level prog is composed of four panels. Two of these are for 12- and 24-hour forecasts of fronts and pressure centers (surface prog). The movement of each pressure center is indicated by an arrow and number showing direction and speed in knots. The surface prog also outlines areas of forecast precipitation (smooth lines) and/or thunderstorms (dashed lines).

The other two panels of the prog chart show *significant weather* forecasts for 12 and 24 hours

with scalloped or smooth lines respectively indicating MVFR or IFR areas of the country.

The weather charts just covered plus actual reports, checked against terminal and area forecasts, will give you a look at the weather from several directions for your cross-country planning.

SUMMARY

Your probable first reaction to this chapter on weather is that it is impossible to know everything about what is available to you as far as weather services are concerned. You don't have to remember that the terminal forecast comes off the Teletype at such and such a time. The majority of professional pilots don't have time to keep up with such information — and it was probably changed last week anyway. You do need to have some idea that sequence reports, winds aloft forecasts, area forecasts, terminal forecasts, and NOTAM summaries *are available* to you through either a National WSO or a FSS. Tell them that you're a (student) pilot and you're planning to fly from A to B, leaving A at such and such a time and expecting to get to B at about so and so. Will they give you the word? The specialists will help every way they can, so don't expect to know weather facilities like those who spend 8 hours a day working at it.

If you are in doubt about the weather before take-off — don't go. If you are in doubt about the weather ahead when you're flying — make a 180° turn before you are also in doubt about the weather *behind* you.

183

Before planning the navigation for the trip you must be introduced to facts about operating the airplane—which will be of particular importance now that you will be making extended flights away from the home airport. On the cross-country you will be more likely to encounter adverse weather, including flying in areas of moderate to severe turbulence, perhaps for extended periods of time. You should know about setting exact power and conserving fuel, a minor or nonexistent problem for local flying.

When you are off by yourself at a strange airport you'll have added responsibility and will have to know more about your airplane systems than is needed at home base where your instructor is available to answer questions.

The following information is both for your present cross-country planning and for future reference. For instance, it's unlikely that you'll have problems with Weight and Balance of the airplane on your solo cross-country. But later, after you get that private certificate and decide to fly on vacation with your family or friends, and their baggage, knowledge of this area of flying will be of vital interest to you.

AIRPLANE PAPERS

In Chapter 3 you noted that the airplane must have certain documents on board at all times. Make sure that these are in the aircraft before you leave the home airport.

(1) The *Registration Certificate* must be current.

(2) The *Airworthiness Certificate* must also be *displayed* so that it can be easily read. Your airplane will have a *Standard Airworthiness Certificate*, because it will meet either "normal" or "utility" airworthiness requirements. (Airplanes can meet both requirements, but this will be covered a little later.) "Acrobatic" and "transport" category airplanes also have a *Standard Airworthiness Certificate*, but it's unlikely that as a student pilot you'll be flying these last two categories.

A *Standard Airworthiness Certificate* is used in aircraft that carry people and property for compensation or hire. Categories other than *Standard* include *Restricted*, *Limited*, and *Experimental*.

(3) The *Airplane Flight Manual*, or *Operations Limitations Form*, must be aboard; the airplane Weight and Balance information (and *Equipment List*)

are a part of these documents. Check to see that the *Major Repair and Alteration Forms* (if any) are with the Weight and Balance information. These forms show major repairs. Their effects on empty weight and center of gravity of the airplane are indicated in the aircraft logbook.

(4) Be sure that an *Aircraft Radio Station License* is aboard if your airplane has transmitting equipment.

Since you will be flying away from the home base, you'd better have the *Aircraft and Engine Logbooks* along. (There's a separate book for the airframe and each engine.) *Make sure that the logbooks are up-to-date.*

AIRPLANE CATEGORIES AND LOAD FACTORS

The airplane you will be flying will be of the normal or utility category, as mentioned in the last section. The primary difference between the two categories is that the normal category airplane normally has "limit load factors" of 3.8 positive g's and 1.52 negative g's, and the utility category airplane has limit load factors of 4.4 positive and 1.76 negative g's. Intentional spins are prohibited for normal category airplanes, but may be done in airplanes in the utility category. (Some airplanes are licensed as being "characteristically incapable of spinning.")

The term "g" is a unit of acceleration based on that of gravity, as was discussed in Chapter 9 in "The Turn." The airplane in straight and level flight and unaccelerated glides and climbs has 1 g acting upon it (and so do you). In the utility category airplane you can create positive acceleration forces up to 4.4 times its weight without exceeding safe limits (*if* the airplane hasn't been previously damaged). If you should encounter an upward gust during your 4.4 g maneuver, the lift is increased even more sharply, and instead of 4.4 g's you may suddenly have a load factor of 6 or 7. Airplanes get bent this way.

Some airplanes are licensed in both categories. At the maximum certificated weight the airplane is in the normal category and must be held to a load factor of 3.8 positive and 1.52 negative g's, or less. At a specified lighter weight it can be flown as a utility category airplane and can safely cope with a load factor of up to 4.4 positive g's (and 1.76 negative g's). This can be seen by an example: An airplane having a maximum certificated weight of 2300 pounds is classed as normal category at that weight; when it is

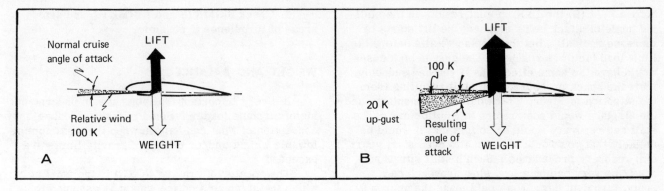

Fig. 23-1. Airfoil showing the effects of a 20 K upward gust on an airplane cruising at 100 K.

flown at a reduced weight of 2000 pounds it can be operated as a utility category airplane. The maximum force acting on the wings would be approximately the same in both cases. At a weight of 2300 pounds a load factor of 3.8 g's (normal category limit) would be 3.8 × 2300 or 8740 pounds. At 2000 pounds a load factor of 4.4 g's (utility category limit) would result in a force of 8800 pounds. Very nearly the same force would be supported by the wings, and 8800 pounds would be the maximum they would be expected to carry without showing signs of permanent deformation. Not all airplanes would work out this close in total force but would have been checked out to sustain the *maximum* force expected from either of the two categories. The wings are not the only structures subject to failure; the horizontal tail or other components might break first if you exceed the limit load factor.

The load factors just mentioned are the *total* g's imposed. You start at 1 g, so only 3.4 g's more are needed to reach the positive limit load factor of 4.4. As far as the negative load factors are concerned, the normal positive 1 g is to the good — you'll have to go farther to get to the negative limit load factor.

Knowing that vertical gusts (up *or* down) can impose g loads on the airplane, you should be aware of several points. Take a look at your airspeed indicator markings and review the discussion of the airspeed indicator in Chapter 3. The green arc is the *normal operating range,* and the lower limit is the flaps-up, power-off stall speed at maximum certificated weight. The upper limit (where it meets the yellow) is called the *maximum structural cruising speed.*

The yellow arc is the caution range, and, of course, the red line speaks for itself. Even if the air is only mildly turbulent, keep the airspeed in the green arc. Although your airplane at normal cruise will be indicating in the green, on letdowns you will have a tendency to let it slip up into the yellow, and the sudden encountering of turbulence at those speeds could result in excessive load factors. Figure 23-1 shows what happens when an up-gust is encountered.

In (A) in Figure 23-1, the airplane is flying in normal cruising flight at a certain required angle of attack. (You wouldn't know the angle but would have the proper cruise power setting and would be maintaining a constant altitude.) In (B) a sharp up-gust of 20 K is encountered. The vector diagram in (B) shows that the angle of attack has been sharply increased and lift is at a much higher value than normal. *A high positive load factor is imposed.* A measure of the load factor is the ratio of lift-to-weight. You remember that in the steep turn at 60° of bank you had to double the lift in order to maintain a constant altitude, which resulted in a load factor of 2.

The airplane would quickly return to the original lift-to-weight ratio of 1 since drag would also rise sharply, but in the meantime the load factor would have already been at work.

Figure 23-2 shows what would happen if the airplane were flying at a much lower airspeed when it encountered the same 20 K upward gust.

You'll note in (A) that angle of attack to maintain this lower airspeed of 70 K is higher. (The lift-to-weight ratio is still 1, or lift equals weight, as

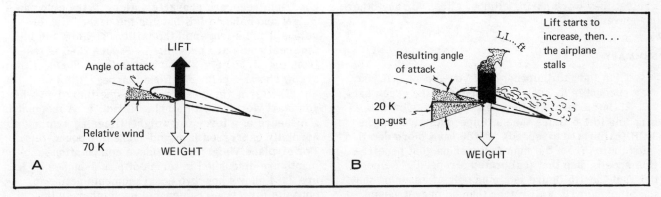

Fig. 23-2. Effects of a 20 K upward gust on the airplane cruising at 70 K.

before.) At (B) the 20 K up-gust results in the stalling angle of attack being reached; the lift starts to increase radically, but the airplane stalls before the limit load factor is reached. The gust in both cases would have the same effect — as if you had suddenly increased back pressure. The stall resulting from the situation in Figure 23-2 would be momentary, and the airplane would soon return to equilibrium. (The stall and recovery would be so fast that it would be unlikely that you would have time to even start your own recovery procedures.) Such a stall situation *would* be very bad on a low, slow approach on a gusty, turbulent day. You would make the approach several knots faster to lower the chances of an inadvertent stall at a critical point. This was also covered in "Gusty Air and Wind Gradients" in Chapter 13. Because of the comparatively low speeds used in the approach, naturally, the stall, rather than high load factors, is the problem to be encountered. At cruise and higher speeds the possibility of overstress is the major factor; as everyone will agree, it's better to have a temporary stalled condition than to overstress the airplane, so in very turbulent air you would slow the airplane to assure that it would stall before this could occur. The speed that divides the stall area from the area of possible overstress is called the "maneuvering speed" and has the designation V_A. The maneuvering speed varies from approximately twice the stall speed, as given by the calibrated stall speed (at maximum certificated weight), to about 1.5 times that figure at minimum flyable weight for most lightplanes. As an all-around figure, when encountering moderate to severe turbulence slow the airplane to indicate 1.5 times the calibrated stall speed *at all weights*. This will mean that the airplane will stall momentarily rather than exceed the limit load factor; it will also mean an easier ride for you. Pilots' ideas of "moderate" and "severe" turbulence vary widely. Avoid such turbulent conditions if possible — check for SIGMETS and AIRMETS before you go.

If you had "maneuver" and "gust" envelope diagrams for your airplane you could pick out a range of speeds within which the airplane would neither stall nor be overstressed by expected maximum gusts, but since these are not normally available you may have to use rules of thumb and stay on the safe side. Vertical gusts don't just affect the airplane in cruise; they work during climbs, glides, or any other maneuvers.

SUMMARY

1. In light turbulence, or if you expect that you may encounter it, keep the airspeed in the green arc.

2. In moderate to severe turbulence slow the airplane to 1.5 times the stall speed as given in the POH (calibrated airspeed). If you have more detailed information from the manufacturer on gust penetration speeds, use that (calibrated airspeed). Remember that the 1.5 figure is aimed only at assuring that the airplane will stall rather than be overstressed. Stalls at low altitudes are dangerous, also.

3. Check SIGMETS and AIRMETS, and avoid areas of turbulence if possible.

WEIGHT AND BALANCE

It's very important that you have an understanding of airplane loading. Some pilots have only a hazy conception of what can happen when the maximum allowable weight and/or center of gravity limits are exceeded.

The "center of gravity" (C.G.) is the point at which the airplane's entire weight is assumed to be concentrated. The manufacturer sets limits on weight *and* the C.G. location so that the airplane will not be in a dangerous condition. Figure 23-3 shows a Weight and Balance Envelope for a two-place trainer certificated in both normal and utility categories. The weight and C.G. must stay within the envelope.

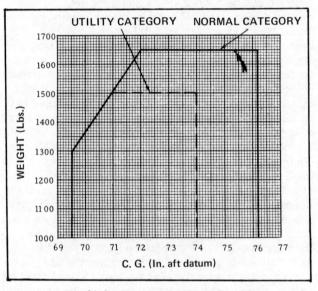

Fig. 23-3. Weight and Balance Envelope.

You see that the airplane has closer limits in both weight *and* rearward C.G. location in the utility category. The less rearward C.G. limit is present because the airplane in the utility category is *not* restricted against intentional spinning. The less rearward C.G. limit assures that the airplane will retain good spin recovery characteristics. If the airplane's weight and balance fall outside the dashed line envelope it is no longer in the utility category and intentional spins are prohibited. Figure 23-3 is taken from the airplane's *Weight and Balance Form*. (The arrow shows a point mentioned on page 188.)

The term "moment" will become important when you start working with airplane loading. A moment is a measure of a force (or weight) times an arm and is normally expressed in pound-inches or pound-feet. For airplane Weight and Balance computations moments are discussed in terms of pound-inches. Figure 23-4 shows how two equal moments acting in opposite directions can cancel each other so that equilibrium exists.

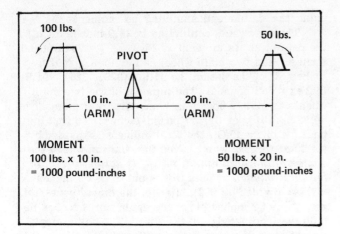

Fig. 23-4. A system of two equal moments.

You've used the principle of moments by using a long pole in levering. (Automobile bumper jacks use this principle.) Figure 23-5 shows the lift and weight moments acting on an airplane in straight and level cruising flight.

The forces and moments must be in balance for equilibrium to exist. A tail-down force normally exists in flight. To simplify matters, rather than establish the moments from the center of gravity, which is the usual case, for this problem they will be measured fore and aft from the center of lift. Assume for now that the lift force is a string holding the airplane "up"; its value will be found later.

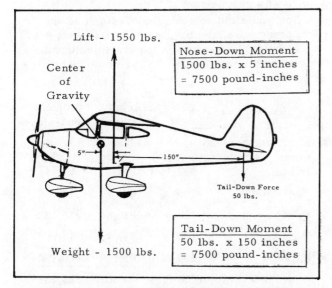

Fig. 23-5. Lift and weight forces and moments acting on an airplane in flight at a particular weight and C.G. position.

The airplane of Figure 23-5 weighs 1500 pounds and the C.G. is 5 inches ahead of the center of lift. This results in a *nose-down* moment of 7500 pound-inches (5 × 1500). To balance this, a moment acting in the opposite direction is required and will be furnished by a tail-down force. The center of "lift" (down acting) of the horizontal tail is 150 inches behind the wing center of lift, so that in order to have an equal *nose-up* moment, a tail-down force of 50

pounds is necessary (50 × 150 = 7500 pound-inches). The airplane nose does not tend to pitch either up or down — the weight and tail-down moments are balanced. This is a simplified approach — there are other moments in existence (the wing has a moment of its own, which was neglected here). The tail-down force varies with C.G. position and/or airspeed.

Earlier in this book it was stated that in straight and level flight lift equals weight. This was done to keep from complicating the issue in the introduction to flight and the Four Fundamentals. The *vertical* forces working on the airplane must be equal. Looking at Figure 23-5, you'll note that the down forces are weight, 1500 pounds, and the tail-down force, 50 pounds. In order to fly straight and level the total up force (lift) must equal these down forces. Hence lift must be 1550 pounds, not 1500 pounds as would be expected from the weight of the airplane. But in flight you don't worry about this. You make the airplane do its job by varying the tail force as necessary to obtain the desired angle of attack — and airspeed. You use trim or wheel pressure as necessary (plus power) to attain the end performance. There are thrust and drag moments existing also in flight, but these are comparatively minor and were neglected for this problem. So, as far as flying the airplane and the g force discussion is concerned, the tail-down force could be considered as weight, and it is important to the stability of the plane.

The position of the C.G. has an effect on the stall speed for a given weight because the higher the tail-down force (as would be required at a forward C.G. position) the greater the total load carried or the more the airplane "weighs." Look at Figure 23-5 and see that if the C.G. is moved far enough forward so that the tail-down force increases to, say, 150 pounds total, the wings would have to support 1650 pounds, not 1550. The stall speed increases as the square root of the "weight" increases (actual or aerodynamic down load, as is the case for the example here). The stall speed marked on the airspeed indicator is based on maximum certificated weight at the most forward C.G. that would give the highest stall speed, a conservative approach.

If you place a lot of weight too far aft, a condition known as "longitudinal instability" could arise. First, look at the correctly loaded airplane; you know that the airplane, as you have flown it to date, has been inherently stable. That is, you can trim it at airspeeds from just above the stall to just below the red line and it tends to stay at that speed. You also know that if you trim it for cruise, for instance, to slow it down requires more and more back pressure as the speed decreases. Conversely to increase the speed above the trimmed speed requires more and more forward pressure. This is the "weigh" it should be.

If you load it so that the center of gravity is too far aft, the required tail-down force decreases. If you move the C.G. to a certain point, the requirement for a tail-down force may disappear completely. In effect, the airplane's nose may be displaced up or down with little or no effort on your part. In extreme

187

cases, if offset by bumpy air, the nose could pitch up (or down) at an increasing rate, and an extremely dangerous situation would be in effect. In short, the airplane would *not* tend to return to its trim speed and would not want to maintain any particular air-speed.

If you observe the rearward C.G. limits as shown on the Weight and Balance Envelope of your airplane you'll avoid this condition.

Notice in Figure 23-3 that there is a forward C.G. limit on the envelope; this is to be observed also. However, just from the general characteristics of most light trainers, this one is sometimes hard to exceed, simply because there's just too little space up front to put baggage and other excess weight. (However, there are always those who will manage to put an anvil or two under the pilot's feet or pull some other unlikely stunt.) The main reason for the forward C.G. limit is that of control, rather than stability. The C.G. may be so far forward that you don't have enough up-elevator to get the nose up to the proper position on landing — and end up bending something.

You'll notice that the airplane's baggage compartment is placarded for maximum weight. This is done for two reasons: (1) To prevent the center of gravity from being moved outside approved limits, which could be the case if the compartment were overloaded, and (2) structural considerations. The baggage compartment floor will be able to take its placarded weight up to the positive limit load factor, but suppose instead of putting in 100 pounds as placarded, you put in *200 pounds*. This would mean that at 3.8 g's *760* pounds would be exerted instead of the 380 pounds it was designed to take. You just might have a new observation window where the baggage compartment floor used to be. *Observe all placards in the airplane.*

RUNNING A WEIGHT AND BALANCE

The next step is to assure yourself that your airplane will stay within approved C.G. limits.

The "datum" is the point from which all measurements are taken for Weight and Balance computations. It may be a point on the airplane or it may be well in front of the airplane. Figure 23-6 shows a high-wing trainer with the datum located 60 inches in front of the wing leading edge. It is standard practice to establish the datum at a fixed distance ahead of a well-defined part of the airplane, or in some cases the front side of the firewall may be used. For trainers so equipped, the reference point is the straight leading edge.

Suppose that the empty weight C.G. is required. This is determined initially at the factory, but may change if equipment is added. In such event it would be duly noted in the logbook by the mechanic who makes the change.

The airplane is weighed in a level attitude with a scale under each wheel. The illustrated airplane's empty weight is a total of the three scale weights, or 982 pounds. The empty weight C.G. is found by using the datum and summing up moments.

The nosewheel centerline is 23.9 inches aft of the datum, so its moment is $23.9 \times 327 = 7815$ pound-inches. The two main wheel centerlines are 91.5 inches aft of the datum, so $91.5 \times (329 + 326) = 91.5$ inches $\times$ 655 pounds. The moment of the two main wheels is 59,932 pound-inches. The total moment is $59,932 + 7815$, or 67,747 pound-inches. To find the position of the C.G., the total moment is divided by the total weight, which gives the position where the *center of the total empty weight is acting to create the total moment.* This works out to be 69 inches (67,747 divided by 982). Hence, the empty center of gravity is 69 inches aft of the datum, or 9 inches behind the leading edge of the wing. The basic empty weight of an airplane includes fixed ballast, unusable fuel, full oil, full engine coolant (naturally not applicable to air-cooled engines), and hydraulic fluid. The unusable fuel for this particular airplane was negligible and did not add any weight to the empty weight "as weighed." If the airplane had not yet been painted at the time of the weighing, the weight of the paint (this may be from 5 to 20 pounds, depending on the size of the airplane), plus unusable fuel (if applicable) would have to be added to get the basic *empty weight* and C.G. This is a favorite subject for questions on the Private Written and the student usually forgets that unusable fuel and full oil are included in the basic empty weight. Item 1 in Figure 23-7 gives the basic empty weight. Included in that item is 3.5 gallons of unusable fuel (the total tank capacity is 26.0 gallons with 22.5 usable).

Now you could compute the effects of adding fuel, pilot, passengers, and baggage. The following would be a computation as given in the example airplane's Weight and Balance Form. The arms would be given on the form.

Item	Weight		Arm (aft of datum)	Moment (pound-inches)
1. Basic empty weight (includes full oil)	982	×	69	67,747
2. Fuel (36 gal.)	216	×	84	18,144
3. Pilot	180	×	81	14,580
4. Passenger	160	×	81	12,960
5. Baggage	100	×	101	10,100
	1638			123,531

Again, dividing the *total moment* (123,531 pound-inches) by the *total weight* (1638 pounds), it is found that the C.G. is located at 75.4 inches aft of the datum. Looking back to Figure 23-3, the Weight and Balance Envelope for this airplane, you see by the dot that the C.G. is within limits for the *normal* category (you have 12 pounds to spare in weight and about 0.8 inch in C.G. range). The airplane as loaded in this problem is outside the utility category envelope, so intentional spins would be prohibited.

You could work out combinations of pilot, fuel,

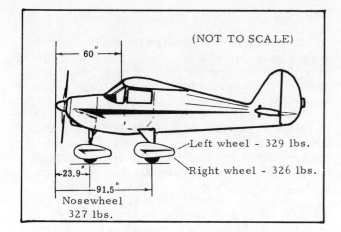

Fig. 23-6. The datum, with weighing point locations and weights. The arms have been rounded off here.

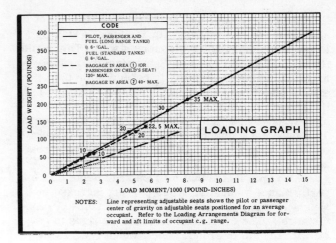

Fig. 23-8. A loading graph.

baggage, and passenger to allow the airplane to be operated in the utility category.

The method used earlier to find the empty weight C.G. is not the shortest way to arrive at the proper answer — the Weight and Balance Form will give simple preset equations to arrive at the answer. The method shown here was done to show the principle. (Also, some of the figures were rounded off for simplicity.)

The FAA considers fuel to weigh 6 pounds per gallon and oil 7 1/2 pounds per gallon. In practice you'd use actual passengers' weights to be accurate. (Naturally, you'd better not be flying nonrated persons until you get that private certificate.)

Other airplanes use a slightly different approach to the Weight and Balance problem. Figures 23-7, 23-8, and 23-9 show the steps as would be applied to a Cessna 150.

The sample problem in Figure 23-7 shows that the loaded airplane weighs 1600 pounds and has a moment of 55,600 pound-inches. This would place it in the envelope, as shown in Figure 23-9.

Note in Figure 23-7 that the total baggage capacity of the airplane is 120 pounds. You can either put it all in Area 1, or 80 pounds in Area 1 and 40 pounds (*its* maximum allowable) in Area 2.

Figure 23-8 shows how the various moments were obtained. The more shallow the slope of the line, the more effect each pound has in increasing the moment. As an example, 100 pounds of baggage in Area 1 furnishes the same moment (6500 pound-inches) as a 167-pound pilot or front-seat passenger.

Don't try to beat the system by overloading the airplane (and having it in a critical aft C.G. condition) and thinking that you'll "just get it a foot or so off the ground and if it doesn't feel right, I'll put it back on." An interesting phenomenon is that an airplane for a given weight and C.G. position is more stable in ground effect; that is, it doesn't want to nose up abruptly as it might up at altitude at a rearward C.G. Ground effect starts to make itself known on approach and landing at a height of about one-half wingspan above the ground and becomes stronger as the airplane descends. The "downwash" from the wing is altered in ground effect; the direction of the

SAMPLE LOADING PROBLEM	SAMPLE AIRPLANE		YOUR AIRPLANE	
	Weight (lbs.)	Moment (lb.-ins. /1000)	Weight (lbs.)	Moment (lb.-ins. /1000)
1. Basic Empty Weight (Use the data pertaining to your airplane as it is presently equipped. Includes unusable fuel and full oil)	1125	36.6		
2. Usable Fuel (At 6 Lbs./Gal.) Standard Tanks (22.5 Gal. Maximum)	135	5.7		
Long Range Tanks (35 Gal. Maximum)				
Reduced Fuel (As limited by maximum weight)				
3. Pilot and Passenger (Station 33 to 41)	340	13.3		
4. Baggage - Area 1 (Or passenger on child's seat) (Station 50 to 76, 120 Lbs. Max.)				
5. Baggage - Area 2 (Station 76 to 94, 40 Lbs. Max.)				
6. TOTAL WEIGHT AND MOMENT	1600	55.6		
7. Locate this point (1600 at 55.6) on the Center of Gravity Moment Envelope, and since this point falls within the envelope, the loading is acceptable.				

Fig. 23-7. A sample loading problem. If the airplane had been weighed at the factory without full oil or unusable fuel, this would have been "added" mathematically to get the basic empty weight of 1125 pounds. (*Cessna Aircraft Co.*)

flow at the horizontal tail is changed and the effect is slightly more of a tendency for the nose to stay lower, or the airplane feels more stable. This could fool a pilot who is *taking off;* the airplane may be marginal as far as stability is concerned in the ground effect but as it moves upward after lift-off the stabilizing influence is lost and the nose rises higher and higher and a stall — and accident — occurs. This problem often occurs when people are leaving on vacation and "need" all that gear in the back seat and baggage compartment.

Also, you'll find that overloading affects take-off performance radically. (A 10 percent increase in weight means a 21 percent increase in take-off run distance.) The overloaded airplane manages to get off with the aid of ground effect, which reduces the induced drag, but is unable to climb more than a few feet. Obstructions at the far end of the runway could mean a hasty end to the flight. With the aid of ground effect the airplane's performance is marginal, and when it starts to move upward the increase in induced drag stops any further climb. Too many accidents are caused by the pilot trying to beat aerodynamic laws.

FUEL AND OIL INFORMATION

When you refuel at a strange airport it will be your responsibility to see that the proper grade of fuel and oil are used.

FUEL

Never use fuel rated below the minimum grade recommended for your airplane. You may go above as a temporary arrangement, but even then, stay as close to the recommended grade as you can. *Never use automotive fuel.*

The numbers are the antiknock quality of the fuel — the higher the number, the better the antiknock qualities. For instance, 80/87: The first number (80) is the minimum antiknock quality of the fuel in the lean mixture, the last (87) is the minimum antiknock quality in the rich mixture.

Grade 80 is not available at some airports in the United States. Some operators are stocking only one grade, 100 Low Lead, for use by airplanes requiring as minimum either 80/87 or the 100/130 grade higher-leaded fuel.

You'll hear aviation fuel referred to as, for instance, grade 80 or grade 100, without the qualifying second figure (80/87). This term use was recommended by the American Society for Testing and Materials (ASTM) for simplification purposes, but the rich and lean antiknock ratings still stand.

The various octanes and performance-numbered fuels contain dyes of different colors to aid in identification.

The colors are valid in the United States, but may not be the same in foreign countries.

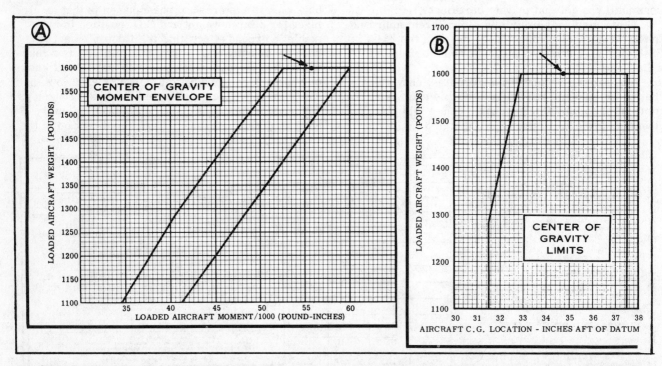

Fig. 23-9. Center of Gravity Moment Envelope and C.G. Limits Envelope for the sample airplane in Figure 23-7. The datum for that airplane is the front face of the firewall. In this arrangement weights rearward of that point have "positive" arms; weights forward would have "negative" arms and this is basically the same idea as that shown in Figure 23-4. The total of the "negative" moments would be subtracted from the total of the "positive" moments to get some answer with the C.G. as (A) a positive moment acting "behind" the datum or (B) the weight and C.G. in inches aft of the datum (firewall) as shown by the arrows in the two envelopes. To find the location of the C.G. divide the total moment (55,600) by the total weight (1600 pounds) as indicated by the arrow (B) to get a position of 34.75 inches aft of the datum.

Grade	Fuel Color
80/87	Red
100LL	Blue
100/130	Green
115/145	Purple

In planning the cross-country, check in the *Airport/Facility Directory* to be sure that at least the minimum rated fuel for your engine is available at any place you intend to refuel.

OIL

The viscosity of oil will be indicated in one of two ways. You are probably most familiar with the SAE (Society of Automotive Engineers) numbers.

SAE Number	Commercial Aviation Number
40	80
50	100
60	120
70	140

Notice that in every case the commercial aviation number is exactly twice the SAE "weight." To get the SAE equivalent, divide the aviation number by two.

Know what type of oil your airplane has been using. You'll hear the terms "detergent" and "nondetergent," but the oil primarily used in airplane engines today is one of two types: (1) *Mineral oil* (called nondetergent) — which is plain oil with no additives and (2) *ashless dispersant* (*AD*) *oil* (often mistakenly called "detergent") — is mineral oil with additives that give better wear qualities and multiviscosity and that also pick up small particles (contamination), keeping them suspended in the oil so that sludge and carbon formations aren't formed. The old detergent oils could wash out carbon if added to an engine that had been using straight mineral oil and cause sludge problems in filters.

Know and add *only* the brand and type of oil the airplane has been using. Some brands or types may not mix, but some oil manufacturers say that adding straight mineral oil to AD oils is normally all right if you feel you really need the oil to get home safely.

CRUISE CONTROL

Probably the term "cruise control" brings to your mind a vision of a vast array of knobs and dials requiring continual monitoring on your part. Cruise control actually means that in cruising flight you know such things as the amount of power being carried and the fuel consumption. This section is based on the premise that your trainer uses a fixed-pitch prop.

Up to now you've probably paid little attention to what power has been carried or the specific fuel consumption, but you have used your instructor's recommendations for tachometer settings for various maneuvers; and, of course, you always checked to make sure you had more than enough fuel to make those local flights. (And if asked the fuel consumption you probably could answer vaguely "five or six gallons an hour, or somewhere in there.")

On extended flights it is vital that you *know* how much fuel you are using and how to plan and conserve fuel if necessary.

Back in Chapter 5 the mixture control was introduced, but it could be that for local flying you haven't been checked out on mixture leaning techniques and have flown the airplane in the full rich setting.

Figure 23-10 is a Time, Fuel, and Distance to Climb tabulation for a particular airplane. Pressure altitudes and standard temperatures are given. Suppose the elevation of your airport is 1000 feet (and the pressure altitude and temperature are standard). You want to depart on a cross-country to cruise at 5500 MSL. Your problem might be worked out like this: You would interpolate between 5000 and 6000 feet and get totals from *sea level* of 10 minutes, 1.45 gallons of fuel (call it 1.5 gallons) and a distance of 11.5 NM (call it 12 NM). However, you're starting from 1000 feet so would subtract those values (2 minutes, 0.2 gallons, and 2 NM) from the 5500 figure and get an answer of *8 minutes, 1.3 gallons, and 10 NM — to climb from your airport at 1000 feet elevation to the cruise level of 5500 MSL.*

TIME, FUEL, AND DISTANCE TO CLIMB

MAXIMUM RATE OF CLIMB

CONDITIONS:
Flaps Up
Full Throttle
Standard Temperature

NOTES:
1. Add 0.8 of a gallon of fuel for engine start, taxi and takeoff allowance.
2. Increase time, fuel and distance by 10% for each 8°C above standard temperature.
3. Distances shown are based on zero wind.

WEIGHT LBS	PRESSURE ALTITUDE FT	TEMP °C	CLIMB SPEED KIAS	RATE OF CLIMB FPM	FROM SEA LEVEL		
					TIME MIN	FUEL USED GALLONS	DISTANCE NM
1600	S.L.	15	68	670	0	0	0
	1000	13	68	630	2	0.2	2
	2000	11	67	590	3	0.5	4
	3000	9	66	550	5	0.7	6
	4000	7	65	510	7	1.0	8
	5000	5	65	470	9	1.3	10
	6000	3	64	425	11	1.6	13
	7000	1	64	385	14	1.9	16
	8000	-1	63	345	17	2.3	19
	9000	-3	63	305	20	2.7	23
	10,000	-5	62	265	23	3.2	27
	11,000	-7	62	220	27	3.7	32
	12,000	-9	61	180	33	4.3	38

Fig. 23-10. Time, Fuel, and Distance to Climb Chart.

Note that for each 8° C above standard for the altitudes, you would add 10 percent to the three values of time, fuel used, and distance.

The distances shown are based on zero wind conditions. Wind would only affect distance (assuming that turbulence isn't hurting your climb performance) since the airplane would require the same amount of time and fuel to get to a certain altitude. Head wind or tailwind components would affect the number of miles covered in that time. (More about that later in the book.)

SETTING POWER

In Chapter 12 you had a brief encounter with cruise control when it was mentioned that airplanes cruised at 75 percent of the rated power or below (65 and 75 percent are the most popular settings and 65 percent is a lot easier on the engine, for only a very small loss in airspeed).

To review some theory of airplane performance: Figure 23-11 shows a performance chart for a light trainer with a fixed-pitch prop.

Point (1) is the top speed of the airplane. For airplanes with unsupercharged engines the *top speed is always found at sea level,* because this is the place where the engine develops its maximum power. As altitude increases the air becomes less dense and power is lost, so that the maximum possible airspeed decreases. (You lose power faster than T.A.S. is gained.)

At Point (2) you'll note that the power has dropped off such that only 75 percent of the sea level power is being developed. Because 75 percent is the

maximum legitimate cruising power setting, you'd get the most true airspeed per horsepower for extended operations at about 7000 feet (standard, or density altitude). If your airplane has a fuel consumption of, say, 7 gallons per hour at 75 percent power, you'll do better at that power by cruising at 7000 feet (115) than at sea level (110). This is, of course, taking winds, ceiling, and other outside factors into consideration.

If you are a believer in the use of 65 percent as a cruise power setting, you can see that Point (3) is best for this setting as far as getting the maximum T.A.S. is concerned. An altitude of 10,000 feet is the highest at which you will be able to develop 65 percent of the sea level power.

Notice that T.A.S. is gained with altitude at 65 and 75 percent — until you run out of throttle. You'll have to open the throttle as you increase altitude to maintain the same percentage of power. (You'll need a higher rpm to get 75 percent at 7000 feet than at sea level.) Obviously, the first thought is that if you are carrying more throttle (rpm) you must be burning more fuel at the higher altitudes. That's where cruise control comes in: Because of the decrease in air density, the mixture can be progressively leaned with altitude increase so that 75 percent power at the higher altitudes results in a no-higher fuel consumption than that same power setting at sea level.

Next comes the question as to how to obtain the various power settings; the *Pilot's Operating Handbook* will help you out here. Figure 23-12 shows a graphical method of setting up power for various altitudes.

If you wanted to carry 70 percent power at 4000 feet it would require 2500 rpm and the airplane would have a T.A.S. as shown (Figs. 23-11 and 23-12).

A careful look at Figure 23-12 shows that a power setting of 2410 rpm is required for 70 percent at sea level, and 2500 rpm at a standard (density) altitude of 4000 feet. This means an increase of 90 rpm, which works out to be approximately 1 percent increase in rpm per thousand feet. For airplanes having rpm settings for cruise at sea level of 2300-2500

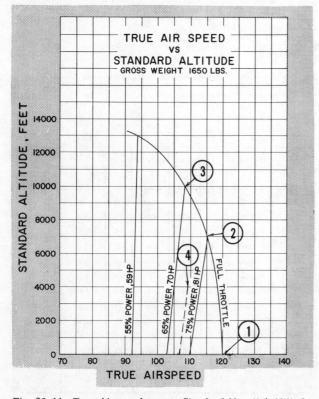

Fig. 23-11. True Airspeed versus Standard (density) Altitude for a light trainer.

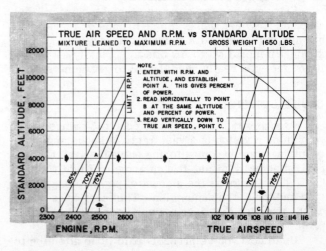

Fig. 23-12. True Airspeed and RPM versus Standard (density) Altitude.

192

rpm you could, as a rule of thumb, add 25 rpm per thousand feet to maintain the sea level percentage of power. As an example, if 70 percent power at sea level requires 2410 rpm you'd be very close to the *Pilot's Operating Handbook* figure for *4000 feet* by adding 100 rpm (4 × 25) to the sea level figure. This comes out to be 2510 rpm, as compared to the 2500 rpm in Figure 23-12. (It's extremely difficult to read a difference of 10 rpm on the tachometer, anyway.) Obviously, it is always better to use the manufacturer's figures, but if you know the sea level rpm for the desired power setting you can get within the ball park for your altitude if you don't have a power setting chart along. You will be limited by the maximum allowable rpm as you reach a certain altitude. (Don't exceed the red line on the tachometer at any time.)

LEANING THE MIXTURE

How do you know your fuel consumption? Figure 23-13 is a fuel consumption graph for the airplane just discussed. The mixture control can make quite a difference in fuel consumption. At 2500 rpm there is a difference of about 1.1 gallons -- in this case you'd burn about 16 percent more fuel in the full rich setting than in best lean. (Non-turbocharged, direct drive engines can normally be leaned at *any* altitude in cruise at 75 percent power and below.)

There are several techniques, some of which include the use of cylinder head temperature gages or even special gages designed specifically for use in leaning. For your present situation, however, the following technique, while not as accurate as some, is simple to use.

After you have reached the desired altitude let the airplane establish the cruise airspeed and set the power. Then slowly move the mixture control aft until the engine begins to roughen slightly. Move the mixture control forward *just enough* to smooth out the engine again.

On the climb-out, the mixture should be full rich until an altitude at which the engine starts to run rough is reached. The air becomes less dense, and less fuel is needed for a proper mixture as you increase altitude. If the engine starts running rough as altitude is gained (it will normally require at least 5000 feet density altitude for this problem to make itself known), lean the mixture until smooth operation occurs. Use a full rich mixture for climbs unless you encounter the just mentioned problem, because engine cooling depends on the mixture setting as well as airflow over the cylinders. Use the *Pilot's Operating Handbooks* for any leaning procedures.

Because of the loss of power involved with an overly rich mixture, at fields of higher elevation you may need to lean to obtain best power for take-off. Do this at full throttle at static run-up. Lean the mixture until maximum rpm occurs. Richen the mixture slightly from this maximum rpm setting to assure proper cooling.

One of the problems you may encounter on one of the solo cross-countries is forgetting to richen the mixture when descending from cruising altitude. You'll probably be so engrossed in getting into the traffic pattern and watching for other airplanes (plus maybe having a little stage fright about going into a controlled field) that the need for richening the mixture on the descent doesn't occur to you. The engine may start running rough — or even quit momentarily — to remind you of this oversight. *Use a checklist.*

Figure 23-14 is a Cruise Performance Chart for a current trainer. You can interpolate between altitudes, horsepower, and temperatures to get the conditions you're flying in. For instance, you're flying at a pressure altitude of 5500 feet and the temperature is 5°C above normal for that altitude. You want to carry 69 percent power and so would go through the following process. You'd start with the standard temperature numbers: At 4000 feet use 69 percent to get a T.A.S. of 100 K and fuel consumption of 5.2 gallons per hour. At 6000 feet (standard temperature) the values are 102 K and 5.2 gallons per hour (again interpolated between 73 and 64 percent brake horsepower).

So the values at 5500 feet would be three-fourths of the difference between 4000 and 6000, or 101.5 K and 5.2 gallons per hour. (Practically speaking, you could get the information for 6000 feet and be very close.) Further checking by interpolation of the effect of the addition of about 5°C above standard would show a very small addition of about 0.4 of a knot.

One point should be brought out: The airplane will use basically the same amount of fuel for, say, 70 percent power at any altitude assuming that the mixture has been leaned properly in each case, but

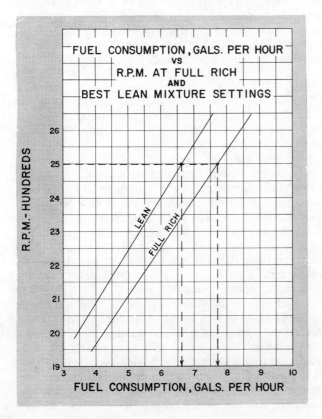

Fig. 23-13. Fuel consumption versus rpm.

the advantage of altitude (once you get there) is that you are getting more miles to the gallon because of increased T.A.S. Take a look under the *standard temperature column* at 65 percent power at 2000 feet and at 8000 feet. At 2000 feet pressure altitude, the T.A.S. is 96 K at a fuel consumption of 4.9 gallons per hour. Interpolating to get 65 percent at 8000 feet, the same fuel consumption (4.9 gph) is found but with a T.A.S. of 101+ K. Note that the chart is given to the nearest knot and one-tenth gallon.

CRUISE PERFORMANCE

CONDITIONS:
1600 Pounds
Recommended Lean Mixture

PRESSURE ALTITUDE	RPM	20°C BELOW STANDARD TEMP			STANDARD TEMPERATURE			20°C ABOVE STANDARD TEMP		
		% BHP	KTAS	GPH	% BHP	KTAS	GPH	% BHP	KTAS	GPH
2000	2650	---	---	---	78	103	5.9	72	102	5.4
	2600	80	102	6.0	73	101	5.5	68	100	5.1
	2500	70	97	5.3	65	96	4.9	60	95	4.6
	2400	62	92	4.7	57	91	4.3	53	91	4.1
	2300	54	87	4.1	50	87	3.9	47	86	3.7
	2200	47	83	3.7	44	82	3.5	42	81	3.3
4000	2700	---	---	---	78	105	5.8	72	104	5.4
	2600	75	101	5.6	69	100	5.2	64	99	4.8
	2500	66	96	5.0	61	95	4.6	57	95	4.3
	2400	58	91	4.4	54	91	4.1	50	90	3.9
	2300	51	87	3.9	48	86	3.7	45	85	3.5
	2200	45	82	3.5	42	81	3.3	40	80	3.2
6000	2750	---	---	---	77	107	5.8	71	105	5.3
	2700	79	105	5.9	73	104	5.4	67	103	5.1
	2600	70	100	5.2	64	99	4.8	60	98	4.5
	2500	62	95	4.7	57	95	4.3	53	94	4.1
	2400	54	91	4.2	51	90	3.9	48	89	3.7
	2300	48	86	3.7	45	85	3.5	42	84	3.4
8000	2700	74	104	5.5	68	103	5.1	63	102	4.8
	2600	65	99	4.9	60	99	4.6	57	98	4.3
	2500	58	95	4.4	54	94	4.1	51	93	3.9
	2400	52	90	4.0	48	89	3.7	45	88	3.5
	2300	46	85	3.6	43	84	3.4	40	82	3.2
10000	2700	69	103	5.2	64	102	4.8	59	102	4.5
	2600	61	99	4.6	57	98	4.3	53	97	4.1
	2500	55	94	4.2	51	93	3.9	48	92	3.7
	2400	49	89	3.8	45	88	3.6	43	87	3.4
12000	2650	61	100	4.6	57	99	4.3	53	98	4.1
	2600	58	98	4.4	54	97	4.1	50	96	3.9
	2500	52	93	4.0	48	92	3.7	45	91	3.5
	2400	46	89	3.6	43	87	3.4	41	84	3.3

Fig. 23-14. Cruise Performance Chart. Note, as mentioned earlier, that the power required for a specific horsepower must be increased by 25 rpm per 1000 feet of altitude. The underlined figures for 54 percent power for 4000, 8000, and 12,000 feet show this (2400, 2500, and 2600 rpm respectively).

Figure 23-15 includes Range and Endurance Profile charts. Note (1) in each chart indicates that the chart allows for the fuel used for engine start, taxi, take-off and climb distance (range profile), and climb time (endurance profile) as would be gotten from the Time, Fuel, and Distance to Climb Chart (Figure 23-10). You could use Figures 23-10 (for climb) and 23-14 (for level cruise) to make your own graphs.

Looking at Figure 23-15 you can see some interesting points:

Range is not so much affected by altitude (at lower altitudes) as is endurance. The range stays constant with altitude until certain altitudes are reached and then decreases with altitude. This is because the time and fuel required to climb to higher altitudes cut down on the total range avail-

able. (The miles covered during the climb are considerably less than those covered in straight and level flight — and at higher fuel consumption.)

Note that endurance is greatest at sea level and starts dropping immediately with altitude increase. Maximum endurance is found at lower altitudes (and at power settings of 40-45 percent power for this airplane (look back at Figure 23-14).

As an example, using the Range Profile you would expect to have a range of 400 NM (including climb) at 7000 feet density altitude (standard pressure and temperature at that altitude) at 55 percent power (94 K T.A.S.) in zero wind. At sea level at 45 percent power you could expect a range of 440 NM at 81 K (T.A.S.).

A point you might notice by checking Figure 23-14 is that the maximum range (miles) for the various altitudes is found at a power setting of around 45 to 50 percent of the rated brake horsepower. Looking back at Figure 12-13 you note that this is the area indicated by Point (2) for maximum range conditions. The thumb rule cited for maximum range was an indicated airspeed of 1.5 times the power-off, flaps-up stall speed. The stall speed for this example airplane (flaps up, etc.) as indicated on the bottom of the green arc on the airspeed is 47 K. Converting the true airspeeds for the various altitudes, you would find that the thumb rule is close to optimum.

Figure 23-16 shows another method of computing Fuel, Time, and Distance to Climb.

The example shows how you would work a problem from an airport of 1100 feet pressure altitude at 8°C temperature for a climb of 3300 feet. A quick way to see how the graph works is to assume that the climb is from sea level to 8000 feet (standard temperatures). You'd see that approximately 2.2+ gallons is used, with 17 minutes and 21 NM (no-wind) required to reach that altitude.

FUEL MANAGEMENT

If your plane has more than one tank, cross-country flying will likely be your introduction to switching tanks in flight.

If your airplane has two fuel tanks, one may be listed as the "main" tank and the other the "auxiliary." The manufacturer in this case will recommend use of the main tank (both may have the same fuel capacity) for take-off and landing and the use of the auxiliary only in level flight. A recommended procedure in this case would be to use the main tank until cruising flight is established, then switch to the other one. This will give you a check as to whether fuel can be gotten from that second tank. There's no law that says you couldn't use most of the fuel in one tank and *then* switch to the other for the first time, *but,* if the system of that second tank has a malfunction and won't feed, you'll have used nearly all of the available fuel and might not have enough left to make it to an airport. If you switch tanks right after cruise is established and the tank does have a malfunction, you can switch back to the good one and

194

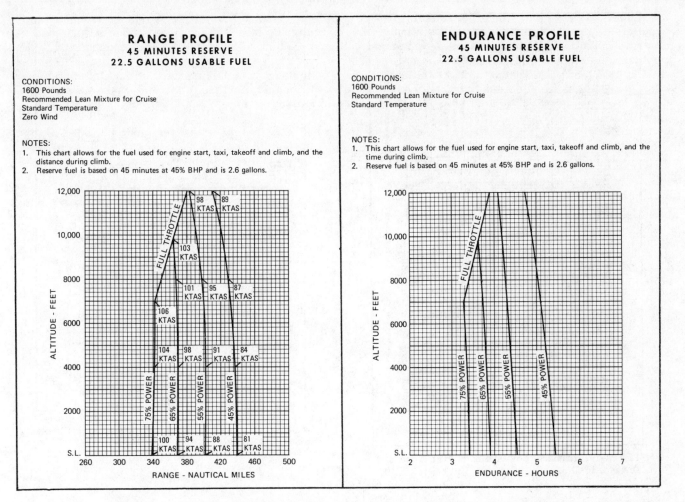

RANGE PROFILE
45 MINUTES RESERVE
22.5 GALLONS USABLE FUEL

CONDITIONS:
1600 Pounds
Recommended Lean Mixture for Cruise
Standard Temperature
Zero Wind

NOTES:
1. This chart allows for the fuel used for engine start, taxi, takeoff and climb, and the distance during climb.
2. Reserve fuel is based on 45 minutes at 45% BHP and is 2.6 gallons.

ENDURANCE PROFILE
45 MINUTES RESERVE
22.5 GALLONS USABLE FUEL

CONDITIONS:
1600 Pounds
Recommended Lean Mixture for Cruise
Standard Temperature

NOTES:
1. This chart allows for the fuel used for engine start, taxi, takeoff and climb, and the time during climb.
2. Reserve fuel is based on 45 minutes at 45% BHP and is 2.6 gallons.

Fig. 23-15. Range and Endurance Profile Charts for the airplane of Figures 23-10 and 23-14.

have sufficient fuel to turn around and get back to the airport.

It's important that the run-up before take-off be done on the tank to be used for take-off. If you make the run-up on one tank and at the last second decide to use another one, run the engine on the new tank for at least a minute at fairly high power settings (at 1500 rpm or above). You might switch to that new tank, immediately start your take-off, and learn the hard way that it won't feed. (Roughly speaking, you'll find that there'll be just enough fuel left in the carburetor to get you to exactly the worst point to have the engine quit.)

Figure 23-17 shows the schematic of a simple fuel system for a current high-wing trainer. The engine is gravity-fed (the tanks are in the wings). The fuel from both tanks simultaneously moves to the fuel shut-off valve which has two positions, OFF and ON.

Figure 23-18 is a fuel system schematic for a current low-wing trainer. Because the fuel tanks in the wings don't give gravity feed, an engine-driven fuel pump must be a part of the system. An electrically driven fuel pump also is installed as a safety standby for take-off and landing, or at any time that the engine-driven pump should fail. This was discussed briefly in Chapter 7. Since a fuel pump is

used, a fuel pressure gage is added to the system. This particular airplane uses fuel from either the left or right tank at a time (you don't have a setting to use both tanks simultaneously). There is also an OFF position on the fuel selector valve.

Figure 23-19 is another low-wing fuel system.

An important factor is the amount of *usable* fuel in the tank. If a tank has a capacity of 20 gallons, yet only 18 gallons are usable, you'll have to do your planning on the basis of 18 gallons, no matter what it says on the tank caps.

Have an idea ahead of time about how long you can expect to run on each tank at the planned power setting. Fuel gages may not always be truthful and also, if they are a part of the electrical system, will go out if that system fails.

SUMMARY

You should be familiar with the following airplane systems before going solo cross-country:

Fuel system — Total capacity; usable fuel; minimum grade of fuel; recommended order of tank usage (if pertinent).

Oil — Proper brand and grade for the engine

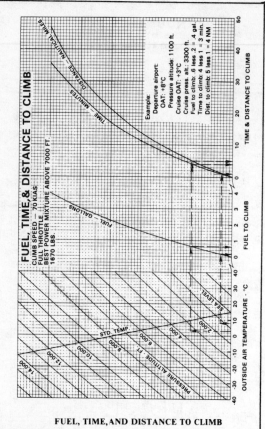

FUEL, TIME, AND DISTANCE TO CLIMB

Fig. 23-16. Graphical presentation of Fuel, Time, and Distance to Climb.

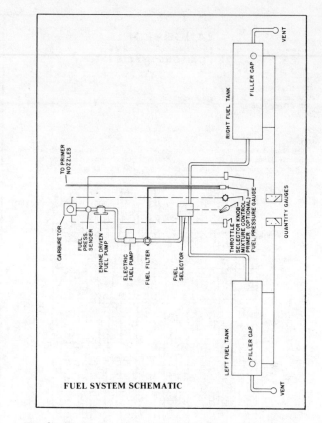

FUEL SYSTEM SCHEMATIC

Fig. 23-18. Fuel system schematic for one current low-wing trainer.

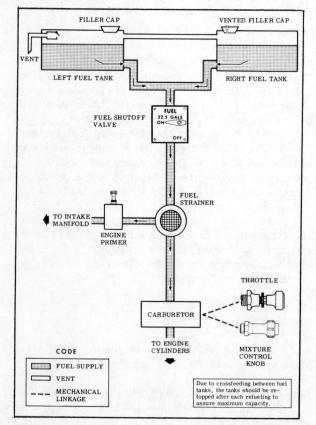

Fig. 23-17. Fuel system schematic for a current high-wing trainer.

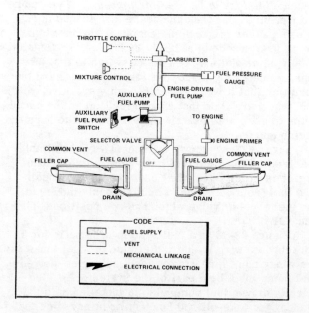

Fig. 23-19. Fuel system for a current low-wing airplane. Note that the fuel level indicators are direct sight reading types rather than electrical.

(ashless dispersant or straight mineral oil).

Electrical — Know the location of the circuit breakers and what other systems would be affected by electrical power loss; battery capacity and location.

Many airplanes are equipped with outlets for use with *external power* sources so that the engine can be started if the battery is dead. Some electrical systems need a certain amount of electrical power to start the process of battery charging again. If the battery is completely dead, and the engine is hand propped (*not* using an external power supply to "energize" the system), the alternator *won't* charge the battery. While the engine will run very well, electrical components (radios, lights, etc.) will still not be available. Check on this concerning your airplane. Don't prop the airplane unless you have had thorough instruction in the art, and a competent operator is in the airplane. Someone can fly to get you, if necessary. Better that, than an accident.

Radios — Ability to transmit and receive on all of the equipment; a knowledge of required frequencies, *plus* light signals used by the tower; how to use the radio to obtain aid in an emergency.

Power plant and cruise control — Engine operating limitations; setting up proper rpm for the power required; fuel consumption at various power settings; use of mixture control; use of carburetor heat.

NOTICE

The performance and system charts shown in this chapter, like performance and navigation charts in the rest of the book, are for example purposes only and are not to be used in an actual flight situation or for flight planning.

24. Navigation Planning

Most student cross-countries are in the form of a triangle, with landings at two strange airports. By the time you are ready for the private flight test you'll have at least 10 hours of solo cross-country (the minimum is also 10 hours for an FAA approved flight school). Each flight will have included a landing at a place more than 50 NM from the original point of departure. One flight must be of at least 300 nautical miles with landings at a minimum of three points, one of which is at least 100 nautical miles from the original departure point.

In accordance with Federal Aviation Regulations, before you will be allowed to fly solo out of the local area you must be familiar with flight planning (plotting courses, estimating times enroute and fuel required, plus obtaining and evaluating weather reports). You'll have had flight instruction in crosswind and simulated short- and soft-field take-offs and landings and slow flight, as well as cross-country navigation by reference to aeronautical charts and to the magnetic compass. You'll also be checked out on emergency situations such as engine failure, loss of flying speed, marginal visibility, deteriorating weather, getting lost, and flying by reference to the instruments. You'll have the word on conforming with air traffic control instructions by radio and lights, and the proper use of two-way radio communications and VFR navigational procedures and techniques.

You should check back to Chapter 21 and be sure that you are familiar with the various air space and clearance-from-clouds requirements.

MAP WORK

Your first cross-country flight will be with your instructor. After you've proved to him on the dual cross-country that you can do the job, he'll endorse your student pilot certificate for solo flights out of the local area. This doesn't mean that you're now free to go anywhere, anytime the whim hits you. He'll supervise all of your solo cross-country planning *and* flying because you aren't a pro just yet. Speaking of planning, there are a few things you should make sure to cover.

The chart in the back of this book is set up for a flight from Franklin County Airport (Sewanee, Tennessee), to Maury County Airport (Columbia-Mount Pleasant, Tennessee), to Huntsville-Madison County Jetport (Alabama), and back to Sewanee. It's intended as an example to cover points that might arise on *your* cross-countries.

Each 10 NM of the route has been marked off to aid in checking distances and enroute times. This probably won't be needed after the first few trips.

1. *Check the Airport/Facility Directory* for the facilities of the airports at which you plan on landing. This material is always more up-to-date than the charts in this matter. Pay particular attention to Teletype NOTAMS, or NOTAMS received on the scheduled weather broadcasts that can be heard on an LF/MF receiver in the airport office (if either a Teletype or LF/MF receiver is available). If you are based at an airport with a Flight Service Station, when you check the weather you can readily get the latest NOTAM information on the airports and radio facilities you'll be using. NOTAM information changes rapidly, so confer with FSS personnel if possible.

Check Appendix B for this information on the airports and facilities to be used.

2. *Check the weather*, present and forecast, for the routes you'll be flying. This means also check the forecast weather for the area of the home airport. You may get off and not be able to get back. (Guys with girl friends in other towns have been known to accidentally overlook this last point, and almost invariably get "weathered in" at one of the towns in question.)

3. *On the chart draw course lines between the airports.* Convert the true courses to magnetic and write this and the distance by each course line on the map. The chart in the back of the book is a *reduced* presentation of this cross-country as drawn on a sectional chart. (Refer to it as you read.)

If the courses lie close to omni "roses" on the chart (the calibrated circles around each VOR station) you can save the step of converting the true course to a magnetic course by laying off a straight edge through the omni rose parallel to the course line and find the magnetic course directly (VOR stations are oriented with magnetic north, you remember).

Always, when planning a cross-country of this type, look over the entire route generally to get familiar with landmarks on the map and to check on possible hazards.

Taking each leg of the example here you might check the following:

Some of the checkpoints of the legs discussed next have been photographed from an airplane flying the route. Carefully compare that checkpoint on the chart with its accompanying photograph. Sometimes railroads or streams are hard to see from the airplane and you should compare different topographical features before jumping to conclusions about the checkpoint. For instance, maybe the town you see down there has a railroad running through but there's no fair sized river west of town. You may want to remove the chart from the back of the book so that you can rotate it to get a better comparison of photos and chart.

LEG 1—SEWANEE TO MAURY COUNTY AIRPORT (4500 FEET MSL)

All of the distances noted on this flight are nautical miles and are rounded off to the nearest mile.

8 miles — You will cross a highway and power line and note that the town of Decherd is about 2 miles to your left and that Woods Reservoir is about 4 miles off to your right.

12 miles — The town of Estill Springs (and bridges) is below and slightly to the right as you cross a part of Tims Ford Reservoir (Fig. 24-1).

Fig. 24-1. A "close-up" view of Estill Springs. The road and railroad run northwest to Tullahoma.

18 miles — There are two inlets of Tims Ford Reservoir just ahead and to the left and the town of Tullahoma and Northern Field are approximately 4 miles to the right.

24 miles — The course crosses a major highway just north of a road junction and the town of Lynchburg with its distillery and storage warehouses is 3 miles to the left (Fig. 24-2).

32 miles — You will cross a major highway 1 mile south of where it is crossed by a transmission line.

41 miles — The route goes directly over the village of Belfast, intersecting a highway and railroad combination, and going on from there to Lewisburg.

46 miles — The town of Lewisburg is below. Outstanding landmarks are (1) a quarry just north and east of town (note the crossed-picks symbol on the chart), (2) a drive-in theater, and (3) the perime-

Fig. 24-2. Approximately 24 miles from Sewanee: The town of Lynchburg is 3 miles down the road to the left (south). The junction of the highways to Shelbyville and Tullahoma is just to the left of course. Note the stream to the west side of the road to Lynchburg and that it crosses just north of town (chart and photo). The secondary road between the highway and the stream is not shown on the sectional chart. Small streams usually can be picked out by the trees along the banks; this one is "open" at the northern portion (at bottom right in photo).

ter highway and airport north of town (arrow). Note the stream running generally north-south through town (Fig. 24-3).

51 miles — You will cross the interstate (I-65) approximately 1 mile north of an intersection. Another intersection can be seen about 3 miles north of course (Fig. 24-4).

56 miles — You will cross a railroad and highway (the highway is merged with the railroad on the chart) about a mile north of Culleoka.

60 miles — A major highway is crossed at the village of McCains (Fig. 24-5). Maury County Airport is in sight 6 miles ahead. The airport is centered in an area of mining. The *Airport/Facility Directory* (Appendix B) indicates that Unicom is available and you should give a call at this point for wind, runway, and traffic information. Note that the main runway is 5-23, which is hard surfaced and 5000 feet long; there is a shorter grass runway. Figure 24-6 shows the airport as seen from about 3 miles out. Note the mining areas.

Check on the layout of the airports you'll be flying into both as a student pilot and in your future flying as well (Fig. 24-7).

When looking at each leg, check the airports that can be used if you need to divert because of weather

Fig. 24-3. Lewisburg, with the quarry on the northeast edge and the airport seen off to the north of town (arrow). The drive-in theater is out of the picture to the right. The railroad runs through the western edge of the town (photo arrow and chart).

Fig. 24-4. An intersection to I-65 and a secondary road 1 mile to the left (south) of the course. Note the stream in the right side of the photo (the secondary road crosses it), also shown on the sectional chart, as it meanders southeast to cross the interstate (arrows). The chart tends to give the impression that the secondary road is offset as it crosses, but, as you can see, this is not the case.

Fig. 24-5. Crossing a highway due south of the city of Columbia, which can be seen off to the right (north) at about 5 miles. The village of McCains is directly below and not seen here. The curves in roads and highways are not shown in great detail on sectional charts, but are general representations. You'll note that the curve shown in the photograph appears to be slightly sharper than that on the chart. Part of this is due to perspective, but the chart cannot follow the sharper, smaller curves exactly.

Fig. 24-6. Approaching Maury County Airport. The town of Mount Pleasant is in the upper left corner of the picture.

or other problems. On this route are Winchester, Tullahoma, Shelbyville, and Lewisburg airports and Lowndes airstrip at Estill Springs, which is grass and 2700 feet long, as indicated by the sectional chart in the back of this book. Arnold AFS could be used in an emergency (it's normally restricted to military traffic except by prior permission), but you could get to either Tullahoma or Winchester more easily during that portion of the trip. For instance, if visibility was sharply restricted when you were south of Tullahoma, you would turn north and fly until you either hit a highway and railroad (in which case you'd turn left to follow them to the city of Tullahoma and the airport), or a highway (alone) running east-west (and you'd turn right to find the airport). Roads and railroads can be "brackets" to funnel you into a town. In other words, don't cross over these references, but use them to bring you to a prechosen point if visibility is down. You can look at the chart before going to see what would be a sure way to get to each of the airports, but more about that in the next chapter.

Be sure to have a good idea beforehand of the relative position of the airport to the town and other prominent landmarks. This is very important for airports having only grass landing areas; they are sometimes very hard to find.

LEG 2—MAURY COUNTY AIRPORT
TO HUNTSVILLE-MADISON COUNTY
JETPORT (5500 FEET MSL)

4 miles on course — A good check to see that you've started right is the quarry that should be one-half mile to your left.

9 miles — The route crosses a secondary road and power line, with a settlement about one-half mile to the left. A secondary road will be to the right, more or less paralleling the course line. A larger

highway will be converging with the course from behind and the left; it's about 4 miles left at this point.

18 miles — You'll cross two streams and a railroad and then intercept a major highway by the village of Riversburg. The city of Pulaski will be in sight 5 miles ahead.

22 miles — The route crosses the eastern edge of Pulaski and will "parallel" the railroad for a few miles. Abernathy Airport will be a little over 2 miles to the right as you pass it (Fig. 24-8). Confirm that this is Pulaski by the road and railroad patterns out of the city. In very poor visibility, if you get off course, it's possible that you might, for instance, confuse Lawrenceburg with Pulaski at first glance. One railroad runs directly through Lawrenceburg, but another skirts the west edge of Pulaski after it passes the airport. An outdoor theater is north of town (on the east side of the highway) at Lawrenceburg. The outdoor movie at Pulaski is west of town.

30 miles — Rivers and stream bends make good checks; look at the system in the vicinity of the 30- to 35-mile distances. There's a railroad with a tunnel off to the right, but it may be hard to see. The railroad is more or less "paralleling" the course and is off to the right (Fig. 24-9).

40 miles — You'll cross the interstate at a curve just north of where the railroad, running from Athens to Ardmore, goes under the highway. Figure 24-10 looks down the railroad to the southwest, shortly after the interstate is crossed.

45 miles — The city of Athens is about 5 miles off to the right of course and you should listen to ATIS (121.25 MHz) and then contact Huntsville approach control on 118.05 MHz with your position information as indicated by the Terminal Radar Service Area (Appendix B or sectional chart legend).

You will be asked to "squawk" a certain

transponder code and probably to *ident*. If your airplane doesn't have a transponder, you'd say so and may be given a turn or turns for identification. You'd then be vectored as necessary to avoid other traffic. You may be cleared straight in, if wind and traffic permit (Fig. 24-11).

Let approach control know if you are changing altitude as this would affect other traffic at your new level. You'll be switched to the tower frequency about 5 miles out and after clearing the active runway will contact ground control for taxiing.

You may be shy about getting taxi directions the first time or two you go into a large airport. An "I'm a stranger here; could you direct me to _____", will always get you the right help.

LEG 3—HUNTSVILLE TO SEWANEE (5500 FEET MSL)

There's a lack of checkpoints on this leg, and you can figure before you even start that about halfway along a leg like this in poor visibility you might decide that you are "lost" and maybe ought to circle to try to find a recognizable check point. *DON'T*. Look at the route; you'll see that the L & N Railroad and road(s) on the left (west) of the course can form one side of a bracket; the railroad and road coming up from the south through Sherwood will be the other side and will be enough to get back to familiar territory. (In other words, in this particular case, if you are "temporarily disoriented with respect to the preplanned route" and off to either side of the course,

Fig. 24-7. After talking to Unicom and entering traffic at Maury County Airport, you are circling and are on the crosswind leg (heading 140°); a 90° turn will be made shortly to get on the downwind leg for Runway 23. (You are looking to the east-northeast here.) Check the layout of an unfamiliar airport as you circle. The wind is across the runway but Unicom has noted that traffic is using Runway 23. Note: This is still the crosswind leg of the pattern, even if the tetrahedron in the photo indicates you're flying "upwind" at this point.

Fig. 24-8. Looking southwest (to the right) at the Pulaski airport (Abernathy Field) from over the city. Compare the sectional chart with the view here. Note on the chart that there is a road fork about a mile north of the airport (arrow), a quarry on the south edge of the airport (the quarry symbol is partially obscured on the chart), and a well-defined stream and a railroad east of the airport.

Fig. 24-10. Over the railroad after crossing the interstate. Athens (Alabama) is 7 miles south-southwest.

flying in a northerly direction up a railroad will take you either to Cowan or Winchester and you can locate yourself, if you haven't already done so on the way.)

Always, in planning a flight by pilotage, look for such brackets. Spend a lot of time looking over sectional charts; you'll be surprised at the amount of information available.

Use the whole sectional chart. (One student cut out the piece of the sectional chart that pertained to his flight but discovered that strong winds had caused him to drift off of his little patch of chart. He had to finally pick a field and land when fuel ran low.) Along these same lines, if one of your routes is close to the edge of the sectional chart, better take along the adjacent chart as well.

Huntsville-Madison County Jetport has Automatic Terminal Information Service (ATIS) so listen (121.25 MHz) before you contact ground control on 121.9 MHz (Appendix B) for taxi instructions. Give your ground location and indicate that you have "Information Delta" (or whatever — see Chapter 21) and will be northeast bound after take-off. Ground control will give instructions such as, "TAXI TO RUNWAY 18 (ONE-EIGHT) LEFT, WIND (FROM) ONE EIGHT ZERO (DEGREES) AT 10 (KNOTS), ALTIMETER (SETTING) 29.97 (INCHES OF MERCURY), DEPARTURE CON-

Fig. 24-9. At 33 miles from Maury County Airport a road and a railroad cross the Elk River 3 miles off to the right (west) of the course. Compare the distinctive bends in the river (photo and chart).

Fig. 24-11. Getting set up for a straight-in approach to Runway 18 Left at Huntsville-Madison County Jetport. It would be best to move over to the left from here in order to have about a 1-mile straightaway to check for wind drift and not angle all the way to the touchdown point.

TROL FREQUENCY 125.6 (MHz). SQUAWK ZERO ONE THREE FOUR." The wind, and the altimeter setting is not given if you indicated that you had received ATIS information. (If you had a transponder you'd squawk as late as feasible prior to the take-off.) If you need to, ask for taxi directions to the runway.

After taxiing to the run-up area (at Runway 18 Left for this example) and completing the run-up, switch to tower frequency (119.7 MHz) and request take-off clearance. Before you're cleared for take-off you first may be told to hold, or taxi into position and hold. After you're airborne and about one-half mile past the end of the runway, the tower will tell you to switch to departure control. (No frequency will be given; you got that earlier, although you may ask, if you forgot.) You'll get a radar vector ("Heading 020") to avoid the Redstone Restricted Area. After clearing the area you'll be told to resume normal navigation and can track to the VOR and thence fly to Sewanee.

The VOR is on top of a knoll, 12 NM from the airport, and you may have flown slightly more than this distance, depending on the radar vectors.

16-17 miles — You'll cross Highway 231 and then pass about 1 mile south of the North Huntsville airport (Fig. 24-12).

24 miles — The town of New Market, Alabama, is directly below. Note that the highway crosses a railroad just south of town and then recrosses it on the north edge.

31 miles — The town of Elora is 3 miles to the left (note the railroad junction). After passing New Market the terrain in this area to the right of course is rugged and rises rapidly from the flatlands, as evidenced by the warning (Fig. 24-13).

36 miles — The course line crosses a secondary road and the town of Huntland is 3 miles to the left. Visibility permitting, you should see that you are "paralleling" a highway (U.S. 64) and a railroad about 3-4 miles to the left (Fig. 24-14).

42 miles — The village of Belvidere is 4 miles to the left. The railroad track is south of the road and swaps sides going through the town. (Historical note: Davy Crockett's first wife, Polly, is buried near Maxwell, just southwest of Belvidere.) You'll likely be seeing Tims Ford Lake and Winchester and Decherd by now.

48 miles — Decherd and Winchester are about 5 miles to the left and Winchester airport is 3 miles to the left (Fig. 24-15).

50 miles — Cowan is 1 mile to the left and the

Fig. 24-12. Just after crossing Highway 231 after passing the VOR enroute to Sewanee (looking south). Note the drive-in theater (arrow) on the east side of the highway and as shown on the sectional chart. The secondary road that forms a "V" with Highway 231 is not shown on the sectional.

204

Fig. 24-13. After passing New Market the terrain ahead and to the right becomes more rugged (looking south-southeast).

town of Sewanee and Franklin County Airport will be in sight (Fig. 24-16). At 5500 feet MSL you can figure on starting the descent at 500 fpm before getting to Cowan, since the traffic pattern at Sewanee is 2800 MSL (elevation 1950) and a descent of 2700 feet, or about 5 1/2 minutes, is required. Don't be letting down in the pattern, so start a little sooner.

Figure 24-17 is a portion of the chart with the checkpoints of Figures 24-1 through 24-16 indicated by the numbers. You're at the point of the indicator and looking in the direction the indicator is pointing.

To continue the general checklist:

4. *Using the expected true airspeed* of your plane, compute the approximate flight time involved in making the trip. (The *Pilot's Operating Handbook* gives the range for your airplane, as well as covering the fuel consumption in gallons per hour.) Always allow yourself at least 45 minutes of fuel reserve — an hour is even better. Your instructor will have some suggestions; also the *Pilot's Operating Handbook* gives the amount of fuel used to climb to particular altitudes (along with recommended airspeeds and resulting climb rates at the various altitudes), as shown in Figures 23-10 and 23-16.

COMPUTING TIME AND FUEL FOR THE LEGS

The trip, as shown on the sample chart, covers a total distance of 66 + 58 + 56 = 180 NM. An estimate of *flying* time at 96 K shows that 1 hour and 52 minutes would be *required just to fly the legs themselves;* another 10 minutes must be allowed at each stop for entering and leaving traffic and takeoff and landing, for a total of 2 hours and 12 minutes. The fuel to be used, based on this quick and dirty look at things, would be 10.8 gallons. It's a good idea to add another 30 percent, giving a final figure of about 14 gallons.

Plan on a minimum of 15 minutes on the ground at Maury County Airport and 30 minutes at a controlled field like Huntsville-Madison County Jetport, or figure the example trip would take a minimum of 2 hours and 57 minutes (call it 3 hours).

Fig. 24-14. The town of Huntland, 3 miles to the left of course. Not much detail here but if you've been keeping up with checkpoints you'll know it's Huntland.

Fig. 24-15. Winchester airport, with the city of Winchester and Tims Ford in the upper left of the photo; Decherd is just past the airport to the north.

Okay, for practice, plan the trip from Sewanee to Columbia-Mount Pleasant to Huntsville and back to Sewanee. You're using the numbers as given as an example in Figure 24-18.

The weather at Nashville, Huntsville, and surrounding areas is clear and 15 miles visibility and forecast to be good VFR for the next 12 hours.

The winds-aloft forecast for the area is:

3-1914 (at 3000 MSL, from 190° true at 14 K)
6-2312
9-2614

Assume standard temperatures.

You'll fly to Columbia-Mount Pleasant at 4500 MSL and to Huntsville and Sewanee at 5500 MSL using 65 percent power. Stops will be made at Columbia-Mount Pleasant and Huntsville.

Work out on a computer the ground speed and true heading for the first leg (true course 288°). It's to be flown at 4500 feet, so you'd split the wind directions and velocities between 3000 and 6000 feet and get an "average" at 4500 feet of 210° true at 13 K.

The wind side of your computer shows that for a T.A.S. of 98 K (65 percent power at 4500 feet at standard temperature – see Figure 24-18), a ground speed of 94 K and a true heading of 281° results. Note on the sectional chart that the 1° E isogonic line crosses the course, so the magnetic heading will be 280°. Looking at Figure 24-18 as the compass card for this trip, you'd see that for this heading you'd add 4°, so the compass heading would be 284°. Note that this is for the cruise part of the flight. If you worked out the climb portion also (Fig. 24-18) you'd find that during the climb at 66 K (average T.A.S. 69 K), the ground speed would be 70 K, the true heading 276°, and the compass heading 280°. (Use the 3000-foot wind as "average.")

Fig. 24-16. Cowan is 1 mile to the left of course. Check the railroad running to the northwest through town. Note the quarry south of town as seen here and as indicated by the crossed picks on the chart.

You'd set this up on the compass and have no worries on the trip. *Nonsense.* You'll find in actual flying, for instance, that (1) the wind was not forecast accurately, (2) the wind has changed, (3) the compass hasn't been swung or the card corrected since Montgolfier's balloon flight, or (4) you added variation or deviation when you should have subtracted — or vice versa. *You'll watch those checkpoints and make heading corrections as necessary.*

The time, fuel, and distance required to climb from Sewanee (assume a 2000-foot elevation) to 4500 feet will be *5 minutes, 0.6 gallons, and 5 NM* (Fig. 24-18 — no wind).

Your ground speed (assuming you take off and immediately head on course) for the first 5 minutes during the climb will be 70 K and you'll cover 6 miles. The cruise part of the trip, or the remaining 60 miles will be at an estimated ground speed of 94 K, so the time required to get there will be (5 + 38) = 43 minutes.

The letdown to Maury County Airport may be made at the same indicated airspeed as you had at cruise and you would reduce the power to get a 500 fpm descent. You'll be letting down from 4500 to 1500 feet (elevation here is 676 and an 800-foot traffic pattern would be used for an altitude of 1476 feet — call it 1500). A 3000-foot descent at 500 fpm would take 6 minutes. Six minutes from your estimated, or recomputed, time of arrival you'll set up the descent. Since the last 6 minutes enroute will

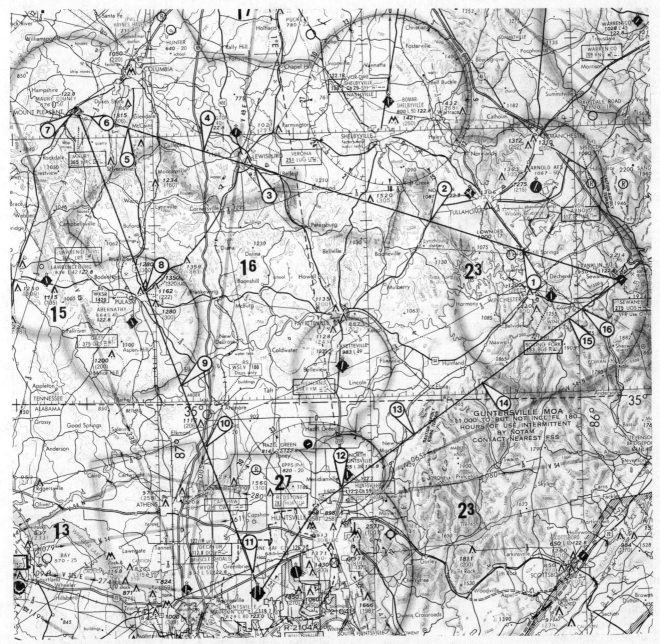

Fig. 24-17. The route, with photographed checkpoints. This is an older sectional chart without the Huntsville TRSA for more clarity of checkpoints. (The old VORTAC name was Huntsville, HSV.) The charts are becoming so cluttered with Air Traffic Control boundaries and frequencies that their primary purpose is being lost.

TIME, FUEL, AND DISTANCE TO CLIMB

MAXIMUM RATE OF CLIMB

CONDITIONS:
Flaps Up
Full Throttle
Standard Temperature

NOTES:
1. Add 0.8 of a gallon of fuel for engine start, taxi and takeoff allowance.
2. Increase time, fuel and distance by 10% for each 8°C above standard temperature.
3. Distances shown are based on zero wind.

CRUISE PERFORMANCE

CONDITIONS:
1600 Pounds
Recommended Lean Mixture

WEIGHT LBS	PRESSURE ALTITUDE FT	TEMP °C	CLIMB SPEED KIAS	RATE OF CLIMB FPM	FROM SEA LEVEL		
					TIME MIN	FUEL USED GALLONS	DISTANCE NM
1600	S.L.	15	68	670	0	0	0
	1000	13	68	630	2	0.2	2
	2000	11	67	590	3	0.5	4
	3000	9	66	550	5	0.7	6
	4000	7	65	510	7	1.0	8
	5000	5	65	470	9	1.3	10
	6000	3	64	425	11	1.6	13
	7000	1	64	385	14	1.9	16
	8000	-1	63	345	17	2.3	19
	9000	-3	63	305	20	2.7	23
	10,000	-5	62	265	23	3.2	27
	11,000	-7	62	220	27	3.7	32
	12,000	-9	61	180	33	4.3	38

PRESSURE ALTITUDE	RPM	20°C BELOW STANDARD TEMP			STANDARD TEMPERATURE			20°C ABOVE STANDARD TEMP		
		% BHP	KTAS	GPH	% BHP	KTAS	GPH	% BHP	KTAS	GPH
2000	2650	- - -	- - -	- - -	78	103	5.9	72	102	5.4
	2600	80	102	6.0	73	101	5.5	68	100	5.1
	2500	70	97	5.3	65	96	4.9	60	95	4.6
	2400	62	92	4.7	57	91	4.3	53	91	4.1
	2300	54	87	4.1	50	87	3.9	47	86	3.7
	2200	47	83	3.7	44	82	3.5	42	81	3.3
4000	2700	- - -	- - -	- - -	78	105	5.8	72	104	5.4
	2600	75	101	5.6	69	100	5.2	64	99	4.8
	2500	66	96	5.0	61	95	4.6	57	95	4.3
	2400	58	91	4.4	54	91	4.1	50	90	3.9
	2300	51	87	3.9	48	86	3.7	45	85	3.5
	2200	45	82	3.5	42	81	3.3	40	80	3.2
6000	2750	- - -	- - -	- - -	77	107	5.8	71	105	5.3
	2700	79	105	5.9	73	104	5.4	67	103	5.1
	2600	70	100	5.2	64	99	4.8	60	98	4.5
	2500	62	95	4.7	57	95	4.3	53	94	4.1
	2400	54	91	4.2	51	90	3.9	48	89	3.7
	2300	48	86	3.7	45	85	3.5	42	84	3.4
8000	2700	74	104	5.5	68	103	5.1	63	102	4.8
	2600	65	99	4.9	60	99	4.6	57	98	4.3
	2500	58	95	4.4	54	94	4.1	51	93	3.9
	2400	52	90	4.0	48	89	3.7	45	88	3.5
	2300	46	85	3.6	43	84	3.4	40	82	3.2
10000	2700	69	103	5.2	64	102	4.8	59	102	4.5
	2600	61	99	4.6	57	98	4.3	54	97	4.1
	2500	55	94	4.2	51	93	3.9	48	92	3.7
	2400	49	89	3.8	45	88	3.6	43	87	3.4
12000	2650	61	100	4.6	57	99	4.3	53	98	4.1
	2600	58	98	4.4	54	97	4.1	50	96	3.9
	2500	52	93	4.0	48	92	3.7	45	91	3.5
	2400	46	89	3.6	43	87	3.4	41	84	3.3

FOR (MAGNETIC)	N	30	60	E	120	150
STEER (COMPASS)	0	26	58	87	118	150
FOR (MAGNETIC)	S	210	240	W	300	330
STEER (COMPASS)	183	214	243	275	303	332

Fig. 24-18. A composite of Figures 19-4, 23-10, and 23-14 for use in planning the sample trip. (Do not use for actual flight planning.) Assume I.A.S. = C.A.S. in the climb.

be at reduced power, the fuel consumption would be slightly less, but to be on the conservative side, assume it to be the same as at cruise.

Fuel to be used then would be the start, taxi, and take-off allowance (0.8 gallon), climb (0.6 gallon), plus the 38 minutes at 4.9 gph (3.1 gallons), which gives a total for the leg of 4.5 gallons. Admittedly, this is carrying calculations pretty far, but later you may want to try out for the U.S. Proficiency Flight Team or, if you're in a college which is a member of the National Intercollegiate Flying Association, such computations could help you to be top pilot in various air meets.

Looking at the Leg from Columbia-Mount Pleasant to Huntsville:

The climb portion will be from 676 feet to 5500 feet for this leg (you might want to use 3500 feet as a cruising altitude in an actual situation for a short trip like this). A quick estimate would be to assume a climb from 500 feet to 5500 feet. Interpolating in Figure 24-18 between sea level and 1000 feet, you'd need 1 minute, 0.1 gallon of fuel, and 1 NM. You'd then subtract this from the result of the interpolation between 5000 and 6000 feet which is 10 minutes, 1.5 gallons (rounded off), and 12 miles. The difference would be 9 minutes, 1.4 gallons of fuel, and 11 miles (no wind).

The wind at 5500 could be interpolated (and rounded off) to be from 225° at 12 K; you would use that for your computer numbers. Using the 6000-foot wind would be accurate enough since there is only a 500-foot difference. Again, the time required to climb and the fuel used would not be affected by wind (except for turbulence, which might cut down performance), but the distance would be, so working it out on the computer:

Wind — 190° true at 14 K (average wind in the climb)
True course — 160°
T.A.S. (average in climb — see Figure 24-18) for an I.A.S. of 66 K — 69 K
Ground speed in climb — 57 K
True heading — 166°
Magnetic heading — 165°
Compass heading — 167° (Fig. 24-18)

The time required to climb has already been found to be 9 minutes, which at 56 K would be found on the computer to cover 8.6 NM (call it 9 miles).

The level and descent portion of the trip would cover 49 NM, so by looking at the cruise performance chart (Fig. 24-18), you'd interpolate to find that at 5500 feet (standard temperature) at 65 percent power the T.A.S. would be 99 K (rounded off).

Working the last 49 miles at 99 K T.A.S. (and not worrying about computing the average T.A.S. and ground speed in the descent), the wind is interpolated to be 225° true at 12 K, the computer indicates that the true heading is 166° (compass heading is 167°), and the ground speed is 93 K.

The time required to fly the 49 NM leg is 32 minutes and the fuel used will be 2.6 gallons (again rounded off). The total fuel and time required for this leg will be:

Start, taxi, take-off — 0.8 gallon
Climb — 1.4 gallons and 9 minutes
Level — 2.6 gallons and 32 minutes
Total — 4.8 gallons and 41 minutes.

Huntsville to Sewanee:

Altitude to be flown — 5500 feet MSL.
Winds aloft — 225° true at 12 K at 5500 feet (The winds may have changed during the first part of the trip but assume that this is a still correct interpolation.)
Average wind in the climb — 190° true at 14 K
Climb — no-wind climb information in Figure 24-18 from 500 feet MSL to 5500 feet is the same as for the last leg

Count on 9 minutes in the climb at an average T.A.S. of 69 K and a fuel consumption of 1.4 gallons. The ground speed and true heading, after using the computer, turns out to be 81 K and 041° respectively. The magnetic heading will be 040° and the compass heading 037° (Fig. 24-18). The distance covered in the 9 minutes of climb at 81 K is 12 NM.

T.A.S. at 5500 — 99 K at 65 percent power
True course (climb) to VOR — 036°; VOR to Sewanee — 056°
Compass heading for cruise — 055°
Ground speed — 111 K

Time and fuel required to fly 44 miles will be

23.8 minutes (24 minutes) and 2.0 gallons of fuel.

This leg will require 0.8 gallon for start, taxi, and take-off; 1.4 gallons for climb; and 2.0 gallons for cruise, or a total of 4.2 gallons and a time of 33+ minutes. The flight log shows a total of 34 minutes, the result of rounding off to the nearest minute the time between each checkpoint.

The total flying time and fuel required for the three legs: 1 hour and 58 minutes and 13.5 gallons.

The climb takes more fuel than generally considered. For instance, looking at the climb chart portion of Figure 24-18, you'd see that to climb from sea level to 6000 feet would require 11 minutes and 1.6 gallons of fuel. To fly at 6000 feet at 65 percent power for 11 minutes — at 4.9 gph — would require 0.9 gallon. The climb fuel consumption is, for that example, nearly twice as much as for cruise consumption at 65 percent. The relative amount of fuel used in the climb part of a trip depends on a ratio of climb to cruise for that trip. The example here had short legs at comparatively high altitudes (maybe *too* high for a practical application in smooth air, but it gave more time for example purposes).

As noted earlier, you normally won't go into such detail on a short pilotage flight but, with experience in a particular airplane, will be able to estimate the fuel and time required to climb to various altitudes and the fuel consumption at, say, 65 and 75 percent power.

As a rule of thumb, for cruise (leaned) fuel consumption for airplanes with fixed-pitch props, multiply the actual brake horsepower being used (at 65 percent power in a 100 hp engine, used in the example, you'd be using 65 hp) by 0.075 to get gallons of fuel per hour being consumed. Multiplying 0.075 by 65 would give a number of 4.875 gph, which is "pretty close" to the 4.9 gph cruise consumption found on the chart (Fig. 24-18). Of course you will have some different horsepower engines to deal with — now or later — for example, one rated at 150 hp. If you wanted to find the gallons per hour consumed at 65 percent power (leaned) in this engine, you'd multiply 150 by 0.65 to find the number of horsepower (which works out to be 97.5 — call it 98 hp) and multiply this by the constant *0.075* to get 7.35 gph at cruise (call it 7.4 gph). You'll find that this works out close to the *Pilot's Operating Handbook*s for most light aircraft reciprocating engines.

FLIGHT LOG

In making up the flight log and planning the flight, remember to take into consideration the rule that on *magnetic courses* of 0° through 179° inclusive, the airplane is to fly at an odd altitude plus 500 feet (3500, 5500, etc.) and on *magnetic courses* of 180° through 359° inclusive, even altitudes plus 500 feet (4500, 6500, etc.). *Although this must be followed if the airplane is flying 3000 feet or more above the surface, it may be used at lower altitudes.*

If you have made wind triangles or used the wind side of your computer, the *original* time estimates will be based on estimated ground speed; otherwise use your cruise T.A.S. During the flight the actual ground speed as checked on the computer will generally vary slightly because of changing wind velocities, as well as the fact that you will probably round off the time (minutes) between checkpoints.

Flight logs are printed on the back of FAA Flight Plan Forms.

Figure 24-19 is the flight log for the trip. The distances are between checkpoints and also the cumulation for each leg. ETE is the estimated time enroute and ATE is the actual time enroute. You'll work out the estimated ground speed (EST GS) before leaving. AGS is actual ground speed.

AIRCRAFT N 9880J	WEATHER	Reported HSV CLR 15 1810			WINDS	
DATE June 29, 19—		Forecast CLR 1810			3-1914	
PILOT S.G. Dickson	Time 1115 CST	Reported BNA CLR 15			6-2312	
		Forecast 30 SCT 2215			9-2614	

CHECK POINT	TC	MC	TAS	TH	MH	CH	DIST. Rmdr.	EST. GS	ETE	EST. FUEL	TIME OVER	ATE	AGS	Notes, T.O.Time, Alt., Actual Fuel Used, etc.
ROAD & POWER LINE	288°	287°	69/98	276/281	275/280	280/284	8/58	70/94	6	1.5				FUEL INCLUDES TAXI, T.O. CLIMB, SHORT CRUISE (0.1)
ESTILL SPRINGS			98	281°	280°	284°	4/54	94	3					T.O. TIME _____
ROAD/ LYNCHBURG							12/42		8					
BELFAST							18/24		11					
McCAINS							18/6		11					
MAURY CO. AIRPORT							6/0		4	3.0				TOTAL CRUISE FUEL 3.1 TAXI, T.O. AND CLIMB 1.4
									43	4.5				TOTAL MINUTES AND GALLONS - LEG 1
ROAD & POWER LINE	160°	159°	69	166°	165°	167°	9/49	57	9	2.2				FUEL INCLUDES TAXI, T.O., & CLIMB - 2.2 GALLONS
RIVERSBURG			99	166°	165°	167°	9/40	93	6					T.O. TIME
INTERSTATE (CROSS)							22/18		14					
4 LANE HWY (CROSS)							10/8		7					
MADISON COUNTY AIRPORT							8/0		5	2.6				TOTAL CRUISE FUEL 2.6 GALLONS
									41	4.8				TOTAL MINUTES AND GALLONS - LEG 2
HUNTSVILLE VOR	036°	035°	69	041°	040°	037°	12/44	81	9	2.2				FUEL INCLUDES TAXI, T.O. AND CLIMB - 2.2 GALLONS
N. HSV AIRPORT	056°	055°	99	057°	056°	054°	5/39	111	3					T.O. TIME _____
NEW MARKET							7/32		4					
ELORA							7/25		4					
HUNTLAND							5/20		3					
COWAN							14/6		8					
FRANKLIN COUNTY AIRPORT							6/0		3	2.0				CRUISE FUEL 2.0 GALLONS
									34	4.2				TOTAL MINUTES AND GALLONS - LEG 3
									1:58	13.5				TOTAL TIME AND GALLONS-ALL 3 LEGS

NOTAMS/Airspace Restrictions
R 2104A To 30,000
R 2104B To 2400

COMM/NAV Frequencies
MAURY COUNTY - 122.8 MHz, NDB 365 kHz-PBC
HSV- APPROACH (FROM MAURY CO.) 118.05
TOWER - 119.7, GROUND - 121.9
VOR - RQZ 112.2, DEPARTURE - 125.6

Fig. 24-19. A flight log for the three legs of the sample cross-country. Minutes have been rounded off and time for climb has been added at the first part of each leg. Later you won't use so many checkpoints on the flight log (but will still keep up with all of the checkpoints). Sometimes it's pretty discouraging to work out a complex and lengthy flight log only to discover that the wind information was all wet and your estimated ground speeds and estimated headings have no resemblance to what you have during the flight. The big idea is to follow that line on the map. Anyway, making out a flight log is a good way to insure that you've checked the route and is an aid in getting ready for the private written examination. Too many students make a flight log and blindly follow the headings computed (with sometimes interesting results).

DEPARTMENT OF TRANSPORTATION FEDERAL AVIATION ADMINISTRATION **FLIGHT PLAN**	CIVIL AIRCRAFT PILOTS. FAR Part 91 requires you file an IFR flight plan to operate under instrument flight rules in controlled airspace. Failure to file could result in a civil penalty not to exceed $1,000 for each violation (Section 901 of the Federal Aviation Act of 1958, as amended). Filing of a VFR flight plan is recommended as a good operating practice. See also Part 99 for requirements concerning DVFR flight plans.						

1. TYPE	2. AIRCRAFT IDENTIFICATION	3. AIRCRAFT TYPE/ SPECIAL EQUIPMENT	4. TRUE AIRSPEED	5. DEPARTURE POINT	6. DEPARTURE TIME		7. CRUISING ALTITUDE
☒ VFR / IFR / DVFR	N9880J	C-150/X	99 KTS	HUNTSVILLE - MADISON CO. JETPORT	PROPOSED (Z) 1545	ACTUAL (Z)	5500

8. ROUTE OF FLIGHT

DIRECT HUNTSVILLE VOR, DIRECT

9. DESTINATION (Name of airport and city) FRANKLIN CO. AIRPORT SEWANEE, TN	10. EST. TIME ENROUTE HOURS 0 / MINUTES 34	11. REMARKS —

12. FUEL ON BOARD HOURS 2 / MINUTES 40	13. ALTERNATE AIRPORT(S) —	14. PILOT'S NAME, ADDRESS & TELEPHONE NUMBER & AIRCRAFT HOME BASE STEWART G. DICKSON SEWANEE, TN (615)598-5318 (FRANKLIN CO. AIRPORT)	15. NUMBER ABOARD 1

16. COLOR OF AIRCRAFT RED, WHITE & BLUE	CLOSE VFR FLIGHT PLAN WITH CROSSVILLE FSS ON ARRIVAL

Fig. 24-20. VFR flight plan from Huntsville, Alabama, to Sewanee, Tennessee. The back of the flight plan has a flight log form and preflight checklist.

FILING A FLIGHT PLAN

The following are the types of flight plans available to the pilot:

VFR — A VFR flight plan, like the other types of flight plans, is filed with the nearest Flight Service Station in person or by phone. (Filing a flight plan by radio is frowned upon because it ties up needed frequencies, but can be done.) The VFR flight plan is the simplest; basically, you follow these steps when filing:

You file the flight plan with a Flight Service Station using the format as shown in Figure 24-20. It will be held by the FSS for 1 hour after the proposed departure time unless (1) the actual departure time is received; (2) a revised proposed departure time is received; or (3) at the time of filing, the FSS is informed that the proposed departure time will be met but the actual time cannot be given because of inadequate communications (assumed departures).

The "X" following the aircraft type (C-150/X) indicates that your airplane has no transponder. *Basic Flight Information and ATC Procedures* has a listing of letters used to show special equipment (or lack thereof) on board when filing a flight plan.

The VFR flight plan does not require such information as altitude changes enroute or alternate airports. You can use the remarks section of the flight plan for pertinent information such as "will close by phone after landing at Sewanee" or other data; you may use this space to list the names of your passengers after you get the private certificate. Closing a flight plan by radio is perfectly acceptable because it only requires a short transmission. (More

about this in the next chapter.) If you have no vital information for the remarks section you may want to use this space to write some stirring line such as "Don't give up the airplane."

If your flight is terminated before reaching the destination, be sure to contact the nearest Flight Service Station and have them pass this information to the FSS responsible for the destination airport. If a flight plan is not closed within one-half hour of the estimated time of arrival, queries are sent to determine the location of the aircraft. If this and further checking down the line fail to locate the aircraft, search and rescue people are alerted 1 1/2 hours after your ETA. (And if you want to get into a real jam, just be the guy who gets Search and Rescue alerted by forgetting to close a flight plan!)

If it looks like headwinds or other factors are going to result in a delay in arriving at your destination, you'd better get on the radio and tell the nearest FSS to pass this information along.

DVFR — The DVFR flight plan is necessary if you are going to fly in an ADIZ (Air Defense Identification Zone). It is a little different from the first mentioned, in that filing in the air is not just frowned upon, but doing so is to invite possible interception for positive identification. (This is an interesting experience, to say the least.) If you look suspicious the interceptors could go further, but it's mighty hard to look suspicious in a trainer that cruises at 90 K or so, although perhaps looking at the interceptor pilots with a dark scowl or wearing a false red beard would help. If you are operating solely over the continental United States this type of flight plan is not going to be a problem for you. The *Basic Flight Information and ATC Procedures* gives details on procedures for filing and flying a DVFR flight plan.

IFR -- The IFR flight plan is not for you yet and won't be covered here. Later as you work on the instrument rating you will be checked out on the procedures of filing and flying an IFR flight plan.

SUMMARY

Be sure before you go that you have the proper charts, flight log, simple computer, a protractor or plotter (preferably with a straight edge ruler as a part of it), a pencil, note paper, and a watch (if the airplane doesn't have a reliable clock).

In your flight planning remember that FAR Part 91 requires that there be enough fuel to fly to the first point of intended landing and assuming normal cruising speed — during the day, to fly after that for at least 30 minutes; or at night, to fly, after reaching the first point of intended landing, at normal cruising speed for at least 45 minutes. It would be well for you as a student pilot to plan on having at least twice this amount of time.

So much for the navigation planning; now you'll fly the cross-country.

25. Flying the Cross-Country

DEPARTURE

You've planned the trip and checked the weather and the plane. You know how to operate the radios, know the light signals, and have checked the destination airports, so there's nothing left to do but go.

There are two ways to get established on course:

1. You may leave traffic and turn on course.
2. You may climb to altitude and fly back over the airport on course.

The first method is most commonly used, but you must realize that you'll be slightly off course in the beginning of the trip. Students generally have the most trouble at the first checkpoint. They have not had time to set up a heading. Use the compass (and heading indicator) as a reference to get you headed in the right direction. Set the heading indicator with the magnetic compass *at least once* during each leg (Fig. 25-1). There may not be winds-aloft information available, so fly the first few miles of the course with an estimated drift correction held. As soon as the first couple of checkpoints are passed you will have some idea of the amount of correction needed.

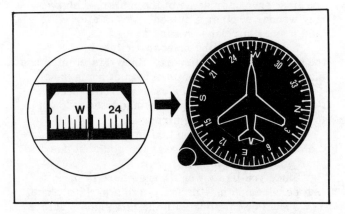

Fig. 25-1. Set your heading indicator with the magnetic compass *at least once* on each leg of the cross-country (every 15 minutes would be a good interval). Students have set the heading indicator before leaving the home airport and *not* compared it with the magnetic compass further during the flight. After a couple of landings and engine shutdowns at other airports (the H/I may be well off because of this), the homeward bound leg is often very interesting, and gives the student experience in using orientation, or lost aircraft, procedures.

ENROUTE

After take-off, if you've filed a flight plan and have a radio, let the FSS know of your take-off time (and write it on your log). Once you have leveled off and established the cruise power setting — making sure that you are at the proper altitude for your course if above 3000 feet above the surface — switch tanks, if applicable, and lean the mixture.

When you are established on course and the first checkpoint is where it is supposed to be, note the compass heading.

Hold the map so the course line on the map is parallel to the course you're flying in the airplane (Fig. 25-2). This way the towns will lie in their proper places. Sure, you have to read the names of towns upside down if you're headed south, but this is better than getting a checkpoint's relative position fouled up when you try to turn the map around in your mind.

As you come to each checkpoint, look on the map to see how far it is from the course line. If you're more than a mile off course, better make a correction, because you'll probably be even farther off course by the time you get to the next checkpoint. *Keep up with the checkpoints.* Run a ground speed check when you get to the prechosen checkpoint.

If there are scattered or broken clouds near your altitude you can get a rough idea of the wind direction and velocity by observing the movement of the cloud shadows on the ground.

Watch your altitude and heading. (Airplanes sometimes ease off heading while you're checking the map.)

Don't bury your head in the cockpit; keep an eye (or two) out for other airplanes.

Be sure to check the engine instruments at least every 5 minutes (checking more often is a lot better). See each time if the fuel gage is showing about the right reading for the time you've been flying.

If you have a radio, listen to the transcribed weather broadcasts for your area of operation. Reset your altimeter to that of the nearest FSS to you.

If you decide to make a position report enroute, use the PTA (*Position, Time,* and *Altitude*) system. Tell them what kind of flight plan you're on and from *where* to *where*. For instance you might call an FSS as follows:

Fig. 25-2. Hold the map so that the course line on it is parallel to the course you are flying.

You: "JONESVILLE RADIO, THIS IS CESSNA 9880 JULIET, STUDENT PILOT, LISTENING JONESVILLE VOR, OVER."

After Jonesville Radio has acknowledged your call you might say the following:

You: "CESSNA 80 (EIGHT ZERO) JULIET, (POSITION) GEORGETOWN AT (TIME) THREE TWO, (ALTITUDE) FOUR THOUSAND FIVE HUNDRED (4500 feet), VFR FLIGHT PLAN FROM PALMYRA TO CUMBERLAND CITY, OVER."

Jonesville Radio will acknowledge and give you the altimeter setting, as well as any other information which they feel would be of assistance.

You'll want to contact the nearest FSS if you're on a flight plan and decide to change your destination or return to the point of departure.

DESTINATION AIRPORT

To the student on his first cross-country, the new airports are strange indeed. It seems that the sky is filled with planes, and at noncontrolled fields the airport personnel seem to have hidden the wind indicator. The wind indicator will be in a hard place to spot — not put in a clear place like your airport's indicators are. (Of course, the students going into your airport have the same thought.)

Start the letdown some distance out so you won't be diving into the traffic pattern. If you have a mixture control don't forget to richen the mixture. Use your prelanding checklist. If the field has a tower give a call about 15 miles out or as indicated in the A/F Directory (Chapter 20). If the field has a Flight Service Station, the personnel can only give information such as surface wind and altimeter setting and known traffic. You should contact the FSS for Airport Advisory Service (AAS) 15 miles out. (Unicom can be used also.)

Airport advisories also provide Notices to Airmen, airport taxi route, and traffic patterns. When

you're ready to taxi at an airport having AAS you should call the Flight Service Station and let them know your intentions. (Give your aircraft number, type, location of the airport, and type of flight plan, if any.) They'll give you the recommended runway and other necessary information. AAS is not mandatory and no traffic control is exercised, but you should take advantage of this service whenever possible. (The frequency 123.6 MHz is first choice for AAS, but you may use any of the other FSS frequency combinations, if you choose.)

Check the field elevation on the chart. Add the traffic pattern altitude you want to fly to this and use the result as your indicated altitude around the airport.

Figure 25-3 shows some types of runways you may see on your trips into larger airports. When you first encounter some of the markings shown, you may wonder whether a student pilot is allowed to land a small airplane on such areas.

It's an interesting point that pilots tend to be too high at a strange airport. Keep this in mind and make a slightly wider pattern than at home base.

Look the airport over as you circle. See how the taxiways are laid out. It's mighty easy to get lost on the ground at big airports.

After landing, as you taxi in to the ramp, locate the parking areas. If there is the slightest doubt in your mind about fuel — *gas up.*

Since you likely won't know where to park, a line serviceman may direct you to a parking place. You should be familiar with the taxi signals before going on the cross-country (Fig. 25-4). The taxi director does *not* have to stand directly in front of the airplane to direct it, but may stand well to one side. He'll point to the wheel that needs braking and put you in the proper spot. Follow his directions; he has a reason for putting you in a parking place, even if you don't see his point as you taxi in. Park there and discuss it with him after the engine shutdown if you want another spot. Most student pilots don't give taxi directors trouble. It's the more experienced pilots who tend to argue — while the engine (and prop) is running in a congested area. Some operations ask on Unicom, while you are still in the air, if you will need service, so that they'll know where to park you.

Tie the plane down. Don't go off and leave it untied, for several reasons: (1) Even if the wind is calm, it could pick up suddenly. (2) In the summer, quite often dust devils, or whirligigs as they are sometimes called, suddenly move across the airport ramp. Some are strong enough to pick up a lightplane. (3) Propwash from other planes, particularly from big planes, can move your plane into other planes or into the side of the hangar.

Take your logbook on solo cross-countries and have somebody sign it, attesting that you were at that airport.

Don't forget to close your flight plan. Sometimes you'll find it more convenient to contact the FSS and close it just after making the initial call to the tower. Or you may prefer to wait until you are on the ground and close it by phone.

It's an outside chance, but it has happened that pilots have closed their flight plans well before reaching their destination and had engine problems before contacting the tower (or landing at an uncontrolled airport), and search and rescue was delayed. You'll want to give yourself and your passengers the best protection, so you could cancel with the nearest FSS *after* initially contacting approach control or the tower, getting their permission to leave the tower frequency for a minute or so. If you had problems, approach control or the tower would wonder why you didn't call back or show up and could get things moving faster to find you. The tower will not automatically close your flight plan.

If you are on a solo cross-country and something happens that will delay you at an airport for a length of time (say, 30 minutes or more) also call

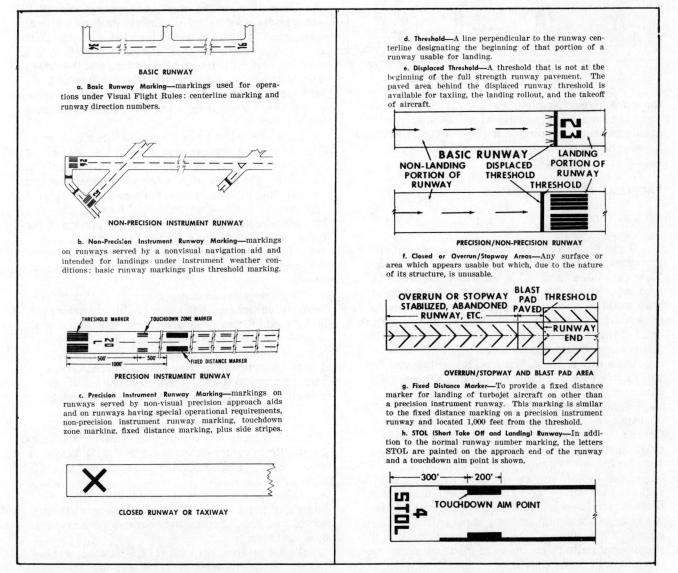

Fig. 25-3. Runway markings as published in the *Basic Flight Information and ATC Procedures Manual*. This illustration is not so much an item for you to memorize, but for reference if an AIM isn't available. While the fixed distance marker (g) is of little interest to you now, the symbol for a *closed* runway or taxiway could be. The precision instrument runway is one of parallel runways (20 Left).

Fig. 25-4. Taxi director signals.

the home airport and let them know what's happening. They have figured approximately when you should get home, allowing for time on the ground and average flight time, so don't make them have to call to find out what happened.

PROBLEMS AND EMERGENCIES

GETTING LOST

If you encounter a problem it will be most likely that of getting off course and/or losing checkpoints. The expression "and/or" is used because students (and experienced pilots) sometimes lose checkpoints even while *on course*. This is particularly true on those parts of the trip where checkpoints are sparse or visibility is somewhat restricted. Being at a low altitude aggravates the problem.

When this happens, don't start circling or heading off into what you think might be the "new" right direction. Maintain the compass heading that you were doing okay with earlier and try to identify other checkpoints. Pilots have missed a checkpoint and figured they were lost, but by continuing on their original heading found they were right on course, and checkpoints began to show up again.

If you are off course *and know it*, take a cut that will get you back to the course line at the next checkpoint (watch for it). Later when you have more experience you won't be so hasty about getting back on course, but for now it's best that you get back to the preplanned route fairly soon (or else you might continue to drift farther off).

For the sake of argument, let's say that you've been flying for a long time and nothing looks as it should. You should have reached the destination air-

port several minutes ago, and because of low visibility you believe (and your ground speed estimates tend to confirm this) that you have missed it. It wouldn't be wise to continue blindly on, but you would set up definite means of locating yourself. First you'd climb, if the ceiling permits, to be able to see farther and to get better radio reception.

If the destination airport has an associated VOR and you have a working omni receiver in the airplane, your problem is a small one. You'd look at the sectional chart (better yet, the *Airport/Facility Directory*) and get the VOR frequency. You'd turn on the set, *identify the station*, and rotate the Omni Bearing Selector (OBS) until the needle was centered and the TO-FROM indicator showed TO. Then you'd track into the station using the OBS indicator as the base course.

If the destination airport doesn't have an associated VOR, your omni receiver can still help locate you. Look on the sectional chart and pick a couple of VOR stations in the *area* in which you are. Pick some fairly outstanding landmark, such as a river bend, road fork, or railroad junction, and stay near it. Tune in one of the VOR stations, *identify it*, and turn the OBS until the needle centers and the TO-FROM indicator says FROM. Draw a line on the map from the chosen VOR along the bearing indicated on the OBS. Then tune in the other VOR and repeat the procedure.

You are in the *area* where the lines intersect. The term *area*, rather than *point*, is used because both your omni set and the VORs may be slightly inaccurate. Find that outstanding checkpoint that you are circling by looking in the area of the intersecting lines on the map. This method of locating yourself by cross-bearings is particularly interesting in turbulent air, and you may rest assured that at some time during the process you will drop (a) the pencil, (b) the straight-edge, (c) the map, or (d) all three at once.

Suppose you are on the Sewanee to Columbia-Mount Pleasant leg with the visibility deteriorated and you don't know where you are. You've made a couple of corrections and suspect that you may be south of course but aren't sure at all anymore. There's a very small town with a railroad track running north and south through it just ahead and you circle it as you work out the cross-bearings.

1. You set up the Shelbyville VOR (109.0, SYI) on your receiver and *identify it*. Turn the OBS until the needle is centered and the TO-FROM indicator says FROM. You see that you are on the 243 radial of SYI.

Continuing to circle the small town, you note that there is a two-lane highway running north and south, just west of town, but continue your cross-bearing check.

2. Set up Graham VOR (111.6-GHM) and *identify it*. With the needle centered and the TO-FROM indicator reading FROM you see that you are on the 142 radial of Graham. The *precise* line intersection of the two bearings shows that you are over

the town of Bufords (and have an extraordinarily accurate VOR receiver in this example).

Now that you have located yourself, you note that the visibility is worse now to the south and east and your best move is to go on to Maury County Airport rather than try to find the Lawrenceburg or Pulaski airports.

OK, the visibility is poor and you don't have an ADF. How would be the best way to get there? If you fly directly for it, there's a possibility that you might pass to the left or right of the airport and miss it. (And after deciding you had missed it — were you to the right or the left?)

Shown in Figure 25-5 are two ways of getting to Maury County Airport. Regardless of the great ac-

curacy of dead reckoning and other types of navigation as indicated by novels and movies, roads and railroads are still very good ways in a pinch to get to a point. Notice that using route (A) you are going to intercept the highway well south of the airport — and will *know* which way to turn. You'll turn right, staying on the right side of the highway. It is an unwritten rule that airplanes following a highway always stay to the *right*. This makes it easier to see the highway from the left seat and, if everybody stays on the right, there will be less chance of mid-air collisions. You would follow the highway north and call Unicom about 5 miles out.

Route (B) is another possibility. In this one you are staying over the original highway, following it

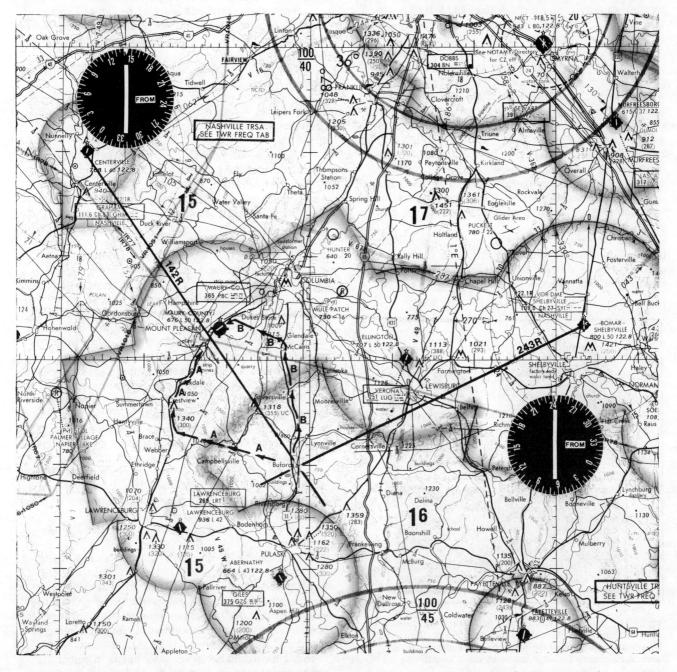

Fig. 25-5. Using VOR cross-bearings to help locate yourself. Watch for that 300 foot (AGL) tower on route A.

north and turning to intercept the "airport highway" *well north* of the airport. You would then follow that highway south to the airport, calling Unicom about 5 miles out. Following a highway if you are caught in bad weather is one way of getting to a safe place. Note the relationship of railroads and highways to each other if they are running side by side. Make sure that, for instance, the railroad is west (or east, etc.) of the highway as it should be. (You may be following the wrong highway.) Look for good checkpoints along the highway such as bridges, power line crossings, and other references. Watch for television or radio towers as shown on the chart.

Best of all, when you check the weather before the flight, if it looks like it will be deteriorating, don't go. It's better to be sitting in an airport office wondering why you *didn't* go than to be flying with a tense stomach in rapidly decreasing visibility — wishing you were back in the airport office.

Assume for this example that the radio beacon is on the airport, so getting back to your imaginary problem with Maury County Airport, if you have an ADF on board, you may tune in the radio beacon, *identify it,* and *home* into the airport (Fig. 25-6). (You'll probably have a curving path because of wind, as indicated by Figure 21-3, but that's alright.) You could also use the ADF to help you in the highway-following process as discussed earlier. In the (B) route you could follow the highway north from Bufords until the ADF needle points well behind the left wing, and then make your turn west to intercept the "airport's highway."

You may have to divert to an alternate airport because of weather or engine problems (such engine problems to be discussed shortly) and should have a good idea of the procedure before going on a solo

cross-country. Your instructor, or the check pilot, may require that you leave the preplanned route for another airport on a dual flight, or the check ride.

You should pinpoint your present position, if possible, and estimate the heading (check the time), and then further work out heading and distances with a plotter — enroute.

Figure 25-7 shows that a nearby VOR can be an aid in finding an alternate airport in poor visibility. You could find the radial that the airport is on, fly over to that radial, and fly — from TO or FROM the station (as applicable) — to get to the airport. Remember to look on both sides as well as straight ahead when looking for the airport. You may not have set up the exact radial and also your VOR receiver could be a couple of degrees off.

Suppose nothing has worked so far and you still have no idea of your location: Better make up your mind to get help before things get too far out of hand and you run out of fuel.

The FAA suggests the use of the "FOUR Cs" in such a situation:

Confess — Admit to yourself that you have a problem and *confess* it to the nearest ground station.

Climb — Altitude enables you to see farther and makes for better communications.

Communicate — You have a complex system of emergency aid no farther away than your microphone. Use 121.5 MHz if the other frequencies don't get any results. For instance, you can get an emergency steer by VHF/DF (VHF Direction Finding) by letting ground stations know of your problem.

By transmitting a steady tone (say "ahhhh") for 10 to 20 seconds after being told to "transmit for homing" by the DF facility, a bearing can be obtained on your airplane in a short while. To get this service, contact the nearest (or what you think is the nearest) FSS or tower and they will relay your request immediately to the nearest DF facility. Don't try to memorize the procedure; just call the nearest FAA facility and they will give instructions.

Radar may also give you a hand. After you've called for help the nearest radar facility may pick you up. The FSS or tower may have you switch to another frequency for radar help and you'll be requested to make various turns for radar identification or set up a particular transponder code, if you have the equipment. They will then vector you to an airport and will probably keep an eye on you to keep you on the straight and narrow.

Comply — Do what you're told by the aiding facilities.

Conserve — This a fifth "C" that is also very important. *Conserve fuel!* You'll be needing it. Don't grind around aimlessly at 75 percent power and rich mixtures when you could be using half the gas. For a situation where maximum endurance is needed (you are in communication and are being located and want to stay aloft as long as possible) a thumb rule would be to set up a speed of about 1.2 times the flaps-up, power-off stall speed as shown

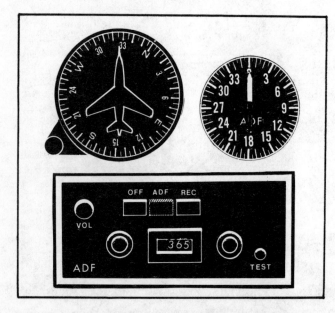

Fig. 25-6. Using the ADF to home into Maury County Airport after locating yourself over the town of Bufords. You could home into the station at the airport by changing the heading as necessary to keep the ADF needle on the 0° position in the indicator.

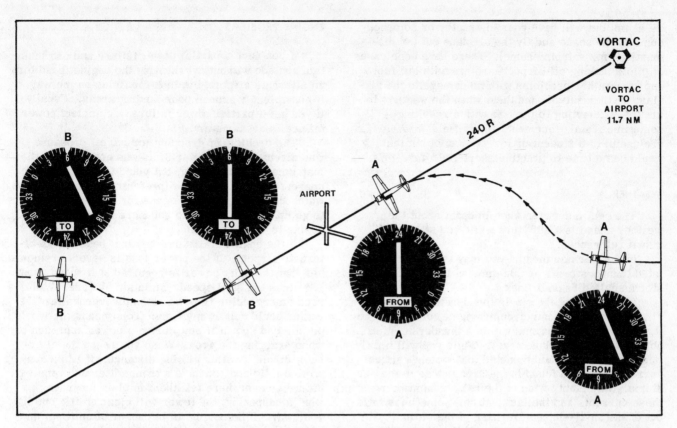

Fig. 25-7. Using a VOR to help find an airport which for the example is on the 240 radial of the VORTAC. The pilot of airplane *A* would set up 240 – FROM on his VOR receiver, and turn toward the radial and fly until the needle is centered. He would set up a heading to keep the needle centered and "fly the radial" to the airport. The pilot of airplane *B* would set 060 – TO on his VOR receiver and fly over to the radial, keeping the needle centered as he looks for the airport. Both pilots would keep their eyes out of the cockpit, with only an occasional glance at the VOR receiver and heading indicator. DME equipment in the airplane would make it easier, too.

on the bottom of the green arc on the airspeed indicator, then adjust your power to maintain a constant altitude and lean the mixture. If your airplane is shown on the airspeed indicator as stalling at 50 K (flaps up) the maximum endurance speed would be at about 60 K. This would roughly give the most *time* per *gallon*.

For maximum range — *miles* per *gallon* — another thumb rule is to set up an airspeed of 1.5 times the figure as given at the bottom of the green arc on the airspeed. (The plane stalls at 50; 1.5 × 50 = 75 K for maximum distance per gallon.) This would be important over bad terrain or water when it is questionable whether or not you have the fuel left to get back to decent terrain. (Lean the mixture.)

Airplanes manufactured in 1976 and after have the airspeed indicators marked in knots and *indicated* airspeeds. The older airspeed indicators were marked in *calibrated* (or corrected indicated) airspeeds and that's what these rules of thumb are based on. For the newer airplanes you would check Part 5 of the *Pilot's Operating Handbook* and get the calibrated airspeed for the bottom of the green arc and multiply *that* number by the 1.5, or 1.2, as just given. You then might have to reconvert from the calibrated number you got by the multiplication back to indicated airspeed for more accurate flying.

Cool, keeping of — This sixth "C" is probably

the most important of all of the items listed. *Take it easy.* If you have to, you can follow a road or railroad to a town and try to recognize it from the chart by landmarks such as race tracks, factories, and road and railroad complexes. *Many towns of any size have air markers, with the name of the town and a pointer to the nearest airport, on the roof of a large building.* One student with a great opinion of the accuracy of VOR cross-bearings, argued with his instructor: "That couldn't be Sewanee, the VOR bearings show us to be 5 miles north of there." (He was looking at Sewanee prominently displayed in yellow on the roof of one of the buildings.) This goes back to the idea that a VOR cross-bearing is a good check of the *area* you are in. *Do not blindly depend on your navigation equipment when supposedly flying a cross-country by pilotage.*

All right, so you haven't been able to contact anybody; the ceiling is too low to pick up any help on the radio, or you have no radio and fuel is about gone. You'll have to make the decision to land the airplane before the engine quits from fuel starvation and you have no choice of fields. This is where dragging the area is a useful maneuver. You'll pick the most likely looking field in the area and look it over. You've had practice is short- and soft-field landings, so do what is necessary — then get to a phone.

Probably it's unnecessary to note that once you've made an off-airport landing, you *do not* take off again, but will have your instructor or somebody come to the scene and fly the airplane out (or dismantle it for shipping home). There have been cases of pilots making off-airport landings with low fuel and/or weather problems with no damage to the airplane or themselves, and then, when the weather improved, attempting to take off with a resulting — sometimes fatal — accident. Short-field *landings* are useful to a student or low-time pilot but that would be no time to practice short-field *take-offs*.

WEATHER

The best maneuver when in doubt about the weather ahead is a 180° turn while you still have visual references.

In the warmer months you may encounter isolated thunderstorms or fast-moving lines of thunderstorms called "squall lines."

In the case of the single thunderstorm (cumulonimbus cloud) you can circumnavigate, or fly around it. The vertical currents within a thunderstorm are able to tear an airplane apart. While you will not fly into the cell, it should be noted that violent vertical currents are also found in the areas close to the storm. Stay plenty wide of the cell, remembering these currents and the fact that hail sometimes falls out of the anvil-shaped overhang of the cloud.

If you are blocked by a squall line that is too long to fly around, there's nothing to do but go back.

Occasionally a squall line will have a break, through which the sun can be seen shining brightly on the other side. This is one version of what is known as a "sucker hole." If, in trying to go through the gap, the turbulence doesn't get you, the closing of the hole will probably do the trick.

In winter, snow and snow showers will be a problem. Visibility goes to nothing in snow, and snow areas can spread rapidly.

When the visibility is well down and you are flying a strange area, don't bore along at full cruise, but slow the airplane down. While this isn't as critical now in the comparatively slow trainer you're flying, later, when you are flying that fast retractable, it could make quite a difference. The radius of turn of an airplane for a given bank angle is a function of the *square* of the velocity, so if you are traveling twice as fast as you need to be, when you see that ridge suddenly appear, your radius of turn will be four times as great. This doesn't mean you'd put the airplane right on the edge of a stall, but you would reduce airspeed to a value that would still give you safe control but would not maintain full-out cruise. Trying to remain VFR while the ceiling and visibility are getting below VFR minimums is an exotic form of Russian roulette.

If you are approaching for a landing and there's a thunderstorm in the near area, be prepared for very strong and shifting winds. Sometimes the thunderstorm may beat you to the airport. Usually they move on in a few minutes, but you will have to make the decision to wait it out or go on to another airport.

ENGINE PROBLEMS

If you have a partial power failure and can maintain altitude without overheating the engine, head for an alternate airport, but look for fields on the way. If possible, fly around poor landing areas. Usually if you get a partial power failure, a complete power failure is not far away.

The problem of dropping (or no) oil pressure was discussed in Chapter 3; as was noted there, the instrument can be wrong, but you'd turn toward the nearest good landing area (preferably an airport) and watch the oil temperature gage for a rise. If it starts to go up, reduce power to get more time from the engine to make that field.

If the engine starts overheating, head for an alternate airport. If the power loss is severe, remember that the least power is required at a speed about 1.2 times the stall speed. Maintain altitude. With such emergencies as power loss or overheating, the engine could quit at any time. This means that you'd be in a bad spot if it quit during a power approach or when dragging the area. When you reach the alternate, circle it within gliding distance. If it's a controlled field and you have a transmitter and receiver, before you get there tell them in plain language what's happening; the tower will clear traffic out of your way. If the engine is in danger of quitting, an emergency situation exists and you will have the right of way. For noncontrolled fields keep your eyes open and land. (Contact Unicom, if available.)

Carburetor ice (discussed in Chapter 4) may ease in while you're looking for checkpoints or have your attention diverted from engine operations. If the rpm (on a fixed-pitch prop) starts creeping back you'd better check on this. If you're using a constant speed prop, the best indication of carburetor ice is a decrease in manifold pressure — if you are at a constant altitude and haven't moved the throttle. Follow your instructor's recommendations on use of carburetor heat (full or partial heat).

You may inadvertently fly into such heavy rain sometime that in addition to the expected visibility problems, the rain may partially block the carburetor intake screen and the engine will lose much of its power. Use carburetor heat or alternate air. Talk to your instructor and check the *Pilot's Operating Handbook* for recommendations for *your* airplane.

Engine fires in flight are very rare, and while you'll follow the instructions of your particular *Pilot's Operating Handbook* and/or instructor, generally you'll want to shut off fuel controls (mixture and fuel selector) and sources of sparks (ignition and master switches). This naturally would mean a forced landing, but that is not *immediately* the big problem. Sometimes the fire can be put out by diving. After the fire is out you can keep your mind occupied with picking a field (Chapters 11 and 18).

You may be so absorbed in navigation that you run a tank dry enroute. The sudden silence will certainly grab your attention and for a couple of seconds your mind will be blank. Throttle back and switch to the fuller tank and then reset power after the engine is running properly again. (It will take about 5 minutes after operations are normal for *you* to settle down again.) If you have been so remiss as to have flown out *all* of your fuel and have no other tank to switch to, you can get practice in picking a field (Chapters 11 and 18).

ELECTRICAL PROBLEMS

Your instructor will go over possible electrical problems on the cross-country (or local flights, for that matter). If you smell burning insulation, better turn off the electrical master switch. If you don't need radios, etc., leave the switch off for the rest of the flight. If things are tight and you need radios and/or other electrical equipment, you might turn off the master switch to stop the immediate problem (kill the electrical system), and then turn off all the radios and other equipment. Open cabin ventilators to get rid of residual smells or smoke. One method of isolating the troublemaker is to turn the master switch back ON, and turn ON the individual systems one by one, until you smell the culprit. Of course, what you will do in such a situation will actually depend on your airplane's electrical system and your instructor's recommendations, based on your hours of experience. He may prefer to have you turn the master switch OFF and leave it that way and land at an airport as soon as practicable in case of "funny smells." (Remember that the electrical system has nothing to do with *keeping* the engine running; it only furnishes the power for starting.)

There have been cases of a popped circuit breaker, or of inadvertently turning the master switch OFF ("somebody's" knee hit it), and the pilot looks up to see the fuel gages on *empty*. This usually happens over water or the worst terrain in a 700-mile radius. Pilots have landed or ditched airplanes, thinking that there must have been a sudden and complete fuel leak because they should have had 2 (or 3, etc.) hours of fuel left at the expected consumption. This is not to say that a fuel leak should not be considered, but you might first check the master switch and circuit breaker(s) or fuses before landing in a strange place. If the master switch and circuit breaker(s) are okay (and the fuel gages still indicate empty), a turn toward better terrain and airports should be in order.

Take a look at Figure 3-25 in this book, or Figure 3-C in *Student Pilot's Study Guide*. Note that the oil *temperature* gage for that airplane has a circuit breaker. People generally don't get as excited about *no* oil *temperature* as they do about an indication of *no* fuel (understandably).

Probably after reading this section you're wondering if the cross-country flight will be nothing less than a hazardous operation. That isn't the case at all; it's highly unlikely that you will ever have a real problem on the cross-country. You may have to avoid bad weather or may find yourself off course temporarily, but you can minimize the chances of trouble by *careful preflight planning*. The flight is usually a success or failure before leaving the ground. The cross-country is just like the rest of flying — *a matter of headwork*.

26. Introduction to Night Flying

BACKGROUND

You will probably face your first session of night flying with some trepidation, but will find that once you get started, it can be even more enjoyable than daytime operations. It will increase your confidence in your daytime flying, too.

Usually the air is smoother, and you can see cities and towns at greater distances because of their lights. You'll also be able to see more airborne traffic for this same reason.

There's one factor that you will likely encounter, and that is *Zilch's Law*. Zilch's Law basically states that as you get out of gliding range of the airport at night, the engine starts running rough. Zilch's Law is also applicable in the daytime when flying over mountainous terrain or well out over the water (in a land plane). "The roughness of the engine is directly proportional to the *square* of the roughness of the terrain and the *cube* of the pilot's imagination." This phenomenon is also known as *automatic rough* (Fig. 26-1).

You'll get three hours of dual instruction including at least 10 take-offs and landings. If you don't get this night dual, your private certificate will have a limitation, "Night Flying Prohibited" on it. Even if you never plan to fly at night on your own it would be well to get the instruction cited. The instructor

will probably have you fly in the local area at a good altitude before having you come back into the pattern for the dual take-offs and landings.

CONES AND RODS

Owls and cats — and other night predators — do better than people at night because their eyes are designed for it.

The retina, or layer of cellular structure at the back of the eyeball, electrochemically converts the light of the optical image into nervous impulses flowing to the brain. This conversion takes place in light-sensitive cells (millions of them), which are of two distinct types: (1) The rods, highly sensitive, activated by a minimum of light intensity, enable only black and white (but no color) perception and are mostly useful for night vision. (2) The cones, considerably less light sensitive than the rods, require higher light intensities to get activated, enable color perception as well as black and white, and are mostly useful for daylight vision.

The human retina contains both types of cells, the animal retina only rods. A bull gets excited by the movements of the bullfighter's muleta, not by its red color, which he is unable to perceive.

Your top visual acuity occurs by focusing your eyes on an object, in which case its optical image is projected on a tiny portion of the retina called the *fovea*. Foveas are very useful for the details needed in, say, "girl watching."

You will never make out visual details at night as well as by daylight because the human fovea contains exclusively the less sensitive color-distinguishing cones and in the dark becomes much less sensitive than the rest of the retina, which contains only rods. The resulting differences in the visual perception can, in principle, be illustrated in Figure 26-2, which shows an identical scene visualized by the human eye by daylight and at night. Owls, cats, etc., don't have this kind of visual problem (they have other visual problems). Their retinas, containing only rods, are uniformly relatively highly sensitive in the dark.

Figure 26-3 gives an idea of the physical makeup of the human eye. The light reflected from the objects in your visual field enters the eyeball; the amount of that light let in is constantly being adjusted by the changes in diameter of the iris (which is comparable to the diaphragm of a camera). The

Fig. 26-1. Zilch's Law makes the engine run rough and "sound funny" over bad terrain or when out of gliding distance of the airport at night. This phenomenon starts to make itself known when darkness approaches and you are still some distance from the airport.

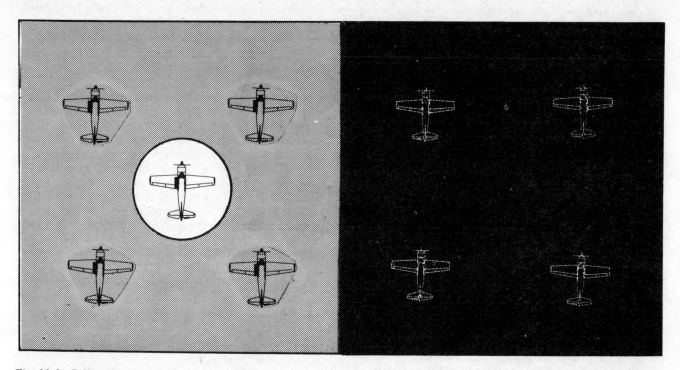

Fig. 26-2. Different views of a flight of five airplanes as seen by day and night. The vision is focused in the center of the formation in both cases. At night a blind spot exists in the center, and in order to see that airplane, you would focus on one of the outer airplanes. *Scan* at night.

light rays go through the optical media (lens, etc.), form an optical image of those objects, and project it on the retina (which is comparable to the film in a camera).

The optical nerves of both eyes are interconnected in a crossover and transmit the light-generated impulses to the optical centers in the brain.

The final visual perception results from interactions between the transferred image from the retina and the activity of the optical brain centers and is therefore different from the real optical image. In other words, the eyes can lie to you about what's really going on. You could have an eye disease characterized by a blind sector in the retina and not be aware of it. The brain simply fills in what it feels should be there. A blind spot exists in the normal eye where the optical nerve leaves the retina; you can find it in your own eye by the following experiment: Figure 26-4 is a section from this book with a cross and large dot marked in it. Hold the figure approximately 6 inches from your eyes — eyes perpendicular to the page — and focus with your right eye on the cross. When you cover or close your left eye the dot will disappear because its image will fall on that eye's blind spot. You may have to adjust the distance from your eye to the figure. The experiment can be repeated with the left eye (right eye closed) focusing on the dot. You'll get the impression that you can see the printing that's covered by the dot or cross because the brain "fills it in." Think about that when you stare fixedly from the airplane (day or night). Another airplane might be in your blind spot and the brain fills in background details (horizon or blue sky) because it can't "see" that area and assumes that it's landscape like the rest.

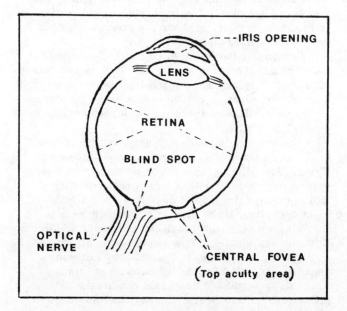

Fig. 26-3. A look at the human eye.

There's one factor that you will likely encounter, and that is *Zilch's Law*. Zilch's Law basically states that as you get out of gliding range of the airport at night, the engine starts running rough. Zilch's Law is also applicable in the daytime when flying over mountainous terrain or well out over the water (in a land plane). "The roughness of the engine is directly proportional to the *square* of the roughness of the terrain, and the *cube* of the pilot's imagination." This phenomenon is also known as

Fig. 26-4. A test for checking the blind spot in each eye.

Of course, using two eyes tends to cover possible blind spots and the idea of two-eye *scanning* is even better . . . day or night.

You'll never be able to see as well at night as in the day and Figure 26-2 is merely given to show the comparative areas of coverage.

The shift from cones to rods is gradual; as the light decreases, more and more of the rods take over. The rods require a certain period of adaptation to the dark. That's why you sat on the fat lady's lap that time in the movie theater — your eyes weren't dark-adapted.

It takes about 30 minutes to become night-adapted. The rods are not as sensitive to red lights, so night fighter pilots are briefed in a room with red lights or wear red-lensed goggles before a flight.

Adaptation to the dark actually occurs in two steps: (1) A first rise in sensitivity, due to the cones, is completed in 4 to 5 minutes. (2) The second rise is due to rods and is completed in 40 minutes, making a *total* time of about 45 minutes. But, as was noted, you'll be about as dark adapted as is practical after a total time of 30 minutes. That last 15 of the 45 minutes raises adaptation only a little.

While a theoretical look at the eyes' reactions to darkness might warrant the program of red lighting just mentioned (as well as having all cockpit and instrument lights red), for practical purposes in civil aviation, white lighting is used in many of the newer airplanes.

If you are night-adapted, a bright flash of white light will ruin your careful work, and the whole adaptation procedure has to begin again.

It's impractical and unnecessary for you to wear red goggles for 30 minutes before the flight, but you should have an idea of what to do for night vision:

1. Avoid *brilliant* white lighting before flying, if possible.
2. Under normal flying conditions keep the instrument and cockpit lighting as low as practicable.
3. If you are over a brightly lighted city or other bright outside lights, turn the instrument lights up in intensity.
4. When looking for objects at night, scan, don't stare. Remember that center blind spot.
5. *Always* carry a flashlight when night flying. It can be very difficult to fly while holding a cigarette lighter or matches to check the instruments. Older instruments had luminous paint on the numbers and hands that could be "excited" by shining a flashlight on each instrument for a few seconds. The flashlight could be turned off and the hands and numbers would continue to glow for several minutes. This was helpful when cockpit lighting was lost. On the downwind leg the instruments could be "energized." You wouldn't need the flashlight any more and would have both hands free for the rest of the approach and landing. You might order a Cyalume, a "cold" lightstick that can be stored in the map compartment until needed. It can be taken out of its wrapper and energized by bending it and shaking it, then it gives several hours of constant light for chart or instrument reading.

Since the light is "cold" it can be put in a pocket or back in the compartment when light is not needed.
6. Don't stare at the instruments; it tires your eyes quickly.

Oxygen helps night vision but it's doubtful that you would have it or want to use it. Alcohol and tobacco hurt night vision. If you were a night fighter, you could set up a daily routine (including a diet to insure that there is sufficient vitamin A in your system) to help improve your night vision, and all of your cockpit lighting would be red, including your flashlight lens. (If you need to convert your flashlight to a red light type, a round piece of red cellophane placed inside the lens is an inexpensive way.)

AIRPLANE LIGHTING

Following are requirements for night lighting and equipment, in addition to the required equipment discussed in Chapter 3:

1. Approved position lights.
2. An approved aviation red or aviation white anticollision light system.
3. If the aircraft is operated for hire, one electric landing light.
4. An adequate source of electrical energy for all installed electrical and radio equipment.
5. One spare set of fuses, or three spare fuses of each kind required.

The airplane's navigation (or position) lights, like a lot of other aviation equipment and terminology, are arranged similarly to those of ships. The lighting arrangement (red light on the left wing, green on the right, and white light on the tail) can tell you approximately what that other airplane is doing.

Suppose that you see the red and green wing lights of an airplane dead ahead and on your altitude. Is he coming or going? One clue that he's moving toward you is the fact that the white taillight is very dim or not showing. The final touch would be if the red light is on your right and the green is on your left — he's headed your way!

Remember the term, "Red Right, Returning," meaning that when you see the red and green lights of another airplane and the red light is on the right, the other airplane is headed toward you — not necessarily on a collision course but at least in your general direction.

The airplane's position lights must be on *any time the airplane moves after sunset* — taxiing or flying. Also, the lights must be on if the airplane is parked or moved to within dangerous proximity of that portion of the airport used for, or available to, night operation, if the area is not well lighted.

The red rotating beacon (or a white anticollision light, as applicable) is now required for all airplanes flying at night. (It was *not* mandatory for many years.) The anticollision light can be seen many miles away in good atmospheric conditions. Many pilots turn on this light in the daytime also when visibility is down.

The landing light is a great aid but not as necessarily vital to night operation on a lighted field as you might think. If you find yourself at night with the landing light on the blink, you'll still have no trouble at all making a good landing by watching the runway lights and using a little power in the landing.

Don't fly without adequate cockpit lighting. If you fly into hazy conditions, it's possible that you may lose all visual references and have to go on instruments to get out of that area. You may also fly into clouds or fog before realizing it. You'd be in pretty sad shape if you couldn't see the instruments.

If you inadvertently get on solid instruments, turn off the anticollision light. The "flashing" effect as it rotates can lead to disorientation. After you've completed the 180° turn and are back out in VFR conditions, turn it on as you go back home.

AIRPORT LIGHTING

One of the toughest parts of night flying, going into or out of a strange, large airport, is the taxiing. This is especially rough if you haven't been there in the daytime. Even a familiar airport is strange the first time you try to taxi at night. The only thing to do is to get help from ground control if it's available. Otherwise just take it slow and easy until you find your destination on the field. One private pilot, on his first night taxi, was too proud to ask directions and managed to taxi out the airport gate and onto the freeway. He was last seen taxiing at 60 miles an hour, trying to keep from being run over by traffic (auto type). He didn't know that taxiway lights are blue. Figure 26-5 shows taxiway and runway lighting. Some bigger airports have small lights imbedded in the taxiway for guidance.

The runway edge lights are white lights of controlled brightness and are usually at the lowest brightness compatible with atmospheric conditions. The runway lights in some airports may be nearly flush with the runway; others may be on stands a foot or two high. The lights marking the ends of the runway are green (Fig. 26.5). Some runway end

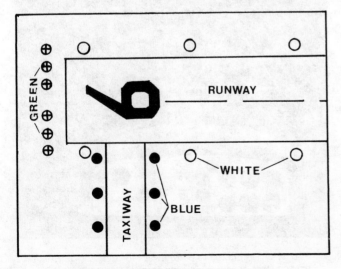

Fig. 26-5. Taxiway and runway lighting.

lights are red on the runway side to warn pilots on the roll-out that The End Is Near.

Airport beacons flash alternating green and white. This is because they are rotating and have the different-colored lights on opposite sides of the beacon head. The following should be noted:

1. Civilian airport beacons — green — white — green, etc.
2. Military airport beacons — green — white — white — green, etc.

The military airport beacon has a dual-peaked white flash between the green flashes to differentiate it from the civilian. Remember this because the beacons can be seen from a great distance and are used to help the pilot locate the airport at night. It would cause plenty of excitement if you were talking to a civilian tower and landed at a nearby SAC base by mistake.

If an airport beacon is on during the day in a control zone, it means that the weather conditions at the airport are less than 3 miles visibility and/or 1000 feet of ceiling. It's no longer VFR.

All dangerous obstructions near the airport are marked by red lights. High-intensity flashing white lights are beginning to be used to identify tall structures (chimneys, etc.) and overhead structures of transmission lines going across rivers, gorges, etc.

TIPS FOR NIGHT FLYING

You might consider the following when you are about to start night flying:

STARTING

Be doubly careful in starting at night. The darkness could result in your starting the engine when someone was in the propeller arc. Turn on the position lights before starting. Granted, this won't help the battery, but it will serve to warn people on the ramp that you are going to start. If other airplanes' engines are running up close-by, no one can hear your "CLEAR." Keep all other equipment off while starting, particularly the taxi and landing lights and radios. If you can possibly work it, have a man standing outside as you start. If it's all clear, he'll give you a signal which consists of moving one of the wands or flashlights in a rotary motion and pointing to the engine to be started with the other wand. (In your case, at this stage, he'll be pointing to *the only* engine.)

TAXIING

After the engine or engines are started, turn on other needed equipment but leave the taxi or landing lights off until you are released by the taxi director. The taxi signals shown in Figure 25-4 still apply at night. The director will hold a lighted wand or flashlight in each hand.

A signal normally used at night but not shown in Figure 25-4 is crossed wands or flashlights, meaning "stop" or "hold brakes."

Taxi slowly at all times and very slowly in congested areas at night. You'll find that judgment of distances is harder when you first start night operations. Your visibility is limited to the area covered by the taxi light and you don't want to have to suddenly apply brakes while moving at a high speed.

RUN-UP

Once you have reached the run-up position and have stopped, turn the taxi or landing lights off to conserve electrical power. Turn off the strobes to avoid distracting other pilots. Use a flashlight to check controls and switches not readily seen by normal instrument or cockpit lighting. Make a pretakeoff check carefully, as you should always do — day or night.

When you are ready to go, call the tower — or if you have no transmitter, turn on the landing light and turn toward the tower. Airplanes with no transmitters may acknowledge tower instructions by blinking the position or landing lights. If you are at a nontower airport, clear the area carefully before taxiing out onto the runway. Make sure the cockpit lighting is at the proper level and that the navigation lights and strobes or rotating beacon are on.

TAKE-OFF

You will normally use the landing light(s) during the take-off roll, but the instructor will probably have you make several take-offs and landings without it during one or more of the dual sessions. You'll find that the runway edge lights and the landing light will be more than sufficient to help you keep the airplane straight. Don't just stare into the area illuminated by the landing lights. Scan ahead, using the runway edge lights as well. Your first feeling will be that of a great deal of speed because of your tendency to pick references somewhat closer than during daytime take-offs. Because of this, make sure that you have reached a safe take-off speed before lifting off — don't try any short- or soft-field take-off techniques for the first few times. Actually, only in an emergency would you attempt taking off from a very short or soft field at night.

Retract the gear (if applicable) when you are definitely airborne and can no longer land on the runway ahead. Establish a normal climb and turn off the landing light(s). Turn off the boost pump (if applicable) at a safe altitude.

AIRWORK

You'll find that you are referring more to the flight instruments at night than in the daytime because of the occasional lack of a definite horizon in sparsely populated areas.

On a hazy night with few scattered lights, the ground lights may appear as a continuation of the stars and you could talk yourself into a good case of disorientation. If you're in doubt, rely on the instruments.

You may have a tendency to fumble for controls in the cockpit at first. It's wise to spend extra time

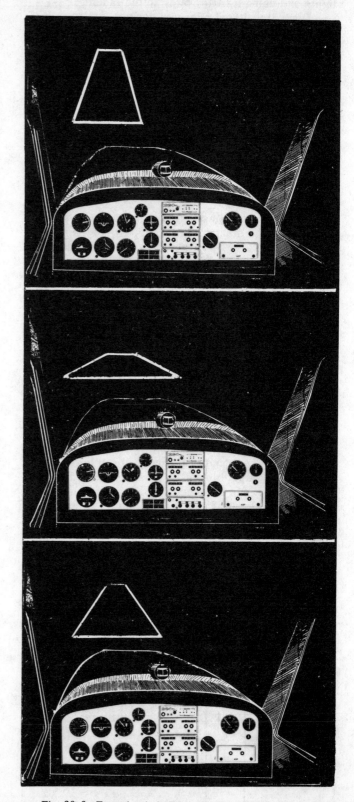

Fig. 26-6. From top to bottom: a too-high, too-low, and proper final approach as seen from the cockpit.

Fig. 26-7. On your first night landing, things will seem to be moving much more rapidly than in the daytime.

sitting on the ground in the cockpit until you can find any control blindfolded. At night you may suddenly encounter instrument conditions. Make a 180° turn as discussed in Chapter 15.

APPROACH AND LANDING

The landing checklist should be carefully followed, taking even more time than in daylight, to insure you make no mistakes.

Make the downwind leg farther from the runway than in the daytime. Plan on a wider, more leisurely pattern. Since judging distances also is more difficult, plan on a pattern that requires the use of power *all* the way around. Figure 26-6 shows three views of the lighted runway after turning final.

Turn the landing lights on after turning onto final. You will notice that if the night is hazy, your visibility will be less during the early part of the final approach with the landing lights on, but will improve as you get to the round-off height. When you are using landing lights, the landing technique should be very close to that used in daytime landings (power-off). If the landing lights are not used, make the touchdown still carrying some power. Those first few landings seem to be a speeded up process. Figure 26-7 shows how that first night landing might seem to you.

The common tendency is to carry too much airspeed on night landings; watch for it.

The landing light is important, but the amount of light reflected varies with the atmospheric conditions for a particular runway and will vary from airport to airport. The runway lights may be the essential reference.

Your instructor will probably have you shoot take-offs and landings without the landing lights and may also have you shoot one or two without cockpit lighting so that you can see the difficulty of handling a flashlight and flying the airplane. He will also review emergency procedures such as partial power loss or total engine failure, and electrical problems with special attention to your particular airplane and local terrain.

SUMMARY

You'll find that after the slight confusion of the first flight has passed, you'll be sold on night flying and Zilch's Law won't be such a big factor. If you get caught away from the airport after dark it won't be a crisis situation after you've had instruction. Night flying is like everything else: familiarity and experience ease your worry.

27. The Written Test

BACKGROUND

The purpose of your flight and ground instruction is to make you an efficient and safe pilot, *not* to specifically prepare you for passing tests. However, in order to use all of that good training and to fly passengers to those vacation spots you have in mind, you'll have to pass the written and flight tests.

Before going up for the flight test you'll have to have passed the FAA written test with a score of 70 percent or better. Some people sweat the written more than the flight test, particularly if they've been out of school and haven't taken any examinations for more years than they'd like to remember. As often happens, however, they have better self-discipline than recent high school or college graduates (applying their studying time better) and they do better on the written test than expected. This doesn't ease that initial nervousness when sitting down face to face with a blank answer sheet.

The purpose of this chapter is to give some ideas for review and preparation and to make your encounter with the written test a less traumatic experience.

HOME STUDY

You may not have an opportunity to attend a formal ground school or you may prefer to study on your own; either is a legitimate way to get ready for the written test. However, you'll want to get some advice from your instructor on areas to study. He can then review your work and make a written statement that you have successfully completed the required study, so that you can take the written test. Your instructor will suggest sections of the Federal Aviation Regulations (Parts 61, 91, and NTSB 830) to study. You will find these reproduced at the back of this book.

REVIEW

Following is a list of chapters with suggestions for home study which apply especially to the written test:

Chapter 2 — Know the Four Forces and how they work. Remember that lift doesn't make the airplane climb, but that the axis of reference is the airplane's flight path and the Forces are measured parallel and perpendicular to the flight path. Make sure that you know how the trim tabs move to get the required control (elevator, etc.) reaction.

Chapter 3 — Review the actions of the various flight instruments, noting what could cause erroneous indications. (Know the various types of airspeeds and altitudes.) Be sure that you know what airplane paper must be *displayed* and whether the logbooks must be kept in the airplane at all times. Know the requirements for 100-hour and annual inspections.

Chapter 4 — Know *why* you check the various items in the preflight check. It will make it much easier to remember. In fact, in all of your ground instruction study, try to tie all of the information with your experiences in the airplane. You should be getting ready for the written test as you fly — don't wait and cram just before the test. It's best to take the FAA written test after you've had at least one solo cross-country and had a chance to pin down in your mind that area of the training, because many of the questions are based on a typical cross-country trip.

Chapter 5 — Review the mixture control, general starting and shutdown, and procedures for cold or hot engines or different outside air temperatures. Remember that the airplane should not be hand propped by anyone who has not had proper instruction in the art; there must be a competent operator inside the airplane during this effort.

Chapter 6 — You may run into a question on the FAA written about how the controls should be held when taxiing in winds from various directions relative to the airplane. Confirm that you know the various airport wind indicators and can read them properly (and know what indicates a right-hand traffic pattern).

Chapter 7 — Here in the pretake-off or cockpit check, know *why* items are checked. (What are you looking for in the mag check or carb heat check, etc.?)

Chapter 8 — Know the three axes of the airplane and how the flight controls (and trim) work.

Chapter 9 — Know the Four Fundamentals, and the effects of bank on the stall speeds. Understand torque and the forces and moments that operate on the airplane at lower airspeeds and higher power settings.

Chapter 12 — The stall is a function of angle of attack, *not* airspeed, although the calibrated airspeed at the stall depends directly on the square root of the weight of the airplane. Know the effects of flaps and power on the stall speed (C.A.S.) at a given weight. For light general aviation trainers, altitude has no effect on the indicated airspeed (C.A.S.) at the stall if flaps, weight, power used, and bank angle are the same. Check Figure 12-13 for a review of power required in relation to I.A.S.

Chapter 13 — Check with your instructor about the maximum allowable crosswind component for your airplane and also get the word on avoiding wake turbulence. If the *Pilot's Operating Handbook* has a crosswind chart, you should review its use.

Chapter 14 — Know the effects of bank on the stall speed (C.A.S.).

Chapter 15 — Be able to look at diagrams of flight instruments and describe what actions the airplane is taking (Figs. 15-1, 15-3, 15-4, 15-5, and 15-12).

Chapter 16 — Note that in turns around a point and eights around pylons, the angle of bank, as in S-turns across the road, is proportional to the ground speed. Be able to look at any diagram of these maneuvers (with wind direction shown) and pick the point of steepest or shallowest bank.

Chapter 17 — Look over Figures 17-10, 17-11, 17-12, 17-13, and 17-14 to make sure you can use the different types of take-off and landing performance charts. Review the atmospheric factors that affect the performance (e.g., moist air, if factors of temperatures and pressure are equal, gives *poorer* performance than dry air). Temperature changes affect the density altitude more than pressure changes.

Chapter 18 — Know the significance of charts such as Figure 18-4.

Chapter 19 — Review this chapter thoroughly and be able to work from true to magnetic to compass directions and back, using isogonic lines and a compass correction card (Fig. 19-4). When working from C.A.S. to I.A.S. on an airspeed correction table, you may have a tendency to add when you need to subtract, and vice versa (check Fig. 19-6). You may want to have your instructor give you some sample problems in "different approaches." For example, he may give you the pressure altitude and density altitude and require you to find the outside air temperature. In other words, pin down your knowledge and use of the computer.

When measuring courses with the plotter, double check the figures you get. You might measure a number of courses between points on your sectional chart and ask the instructor to confirm their accuracy.

Chapter 20 — Sit down one evening for a few minutes with your sectional chart and look it over for symbols you might not have encountered on your cross-country planning.

You'll be expected to be able to use the *AIM — Basic Flight Information and ATC Procedures* and the *Airport/Facility Directory* on the written *and* the flight test, so you should review all parts (available at the airport). (Maybe you could borrow them overnight for some home study.) You won't be expected to memorize any of the *AIM,* but a fairly brief review of what information is available and how to use the *Airport/Facility Directory* could save you some fumbling around during the written test. (Such information is furnished with the written but it's better if you've looked it over again just before taking the test.)

Chapter 21 — Review the uses of the VOR and ADF and their advantages and limitations. One question sometimes used on the written test includes a diagram showing several airplanes at various positions around a VOR station, and you are required to match the proper VOR received indication with the airplane at a particular position. (One hint is to "turn" the airplane in your mind to the OBS given and see whether the needle is pointed toward the selected radial.) Your instructor will want to review this with you.

Figures 21-10 and 21-14 would be good study items, and the information therein should be compared with the indications on the sectional chart (Figs. 21-12 and 21-13) to get a "top view" as well.

Know the basics of ATIS and VASI.

Chapter 22 — Confirm the circulation around low and high pressure areas, the symbols, and weather associated with warm, cold, occluded, and stationary fronts. Be able to read hourly reports, forecasts, and wind information. (Brush up on converting local time to GMT and back.) Know what weather information services are available to the pilot.

Chapter 23 — Know the significance of maneuvering speeds and the effects of turbulence on the airplane. Brush up on the steps of running a weight and balance calculation and remember that the *basic* empty weight includes full operating fluids and unusable fuel and full oil. Be able to use both types of cruise charts as shown by Figures 23-12 and 23-14.

Chapter 24 — Go over in your mind the steps involved in navigation planning, including filling out a flight log and filing a VFR flight plan. Ask your instructor to review with you the procedure for reporting an accident or an overdue aircraft.

Chapter 25 — Fly one of your own cross-countries again in your mind and think of the items you had to consider on the trip, including (as applicable) taxi director signals and runway markings, as you review this chapter.

Take another look at procedures used in helping to locate yourself by use of VOR crossbearings and what FAA ground facilities are available to help.

Chapter 26 — Hit this chapter for aircraft and airport lighting and the physiological aspects of night vision.

Check Appendix C for "Medical Facts for Pilots" taken from the *AIM — Basic Flight Information and ATC Procedures.* There will be questions on the written test about these subjects; as a pilot you should be aware of the factors discussed.

WRITTEN TEST

At the end of this chapter is a sample test of 60 questions based on the general knowledge required to pass the FAA written test for the private certificate. These questions are intended to act as a further review of the material you've studied and to give you some experience with multiple choice answers as found on the FAA written test. In the back of this book there is a sample written test application and answer sheet so that you can see what you'll be using when taking the written. Tear out and use the answer sheet to mark the answers on the sample quiz. (Use the first 60 answer spaces.) The answers and explanations are included later in the book but should be saved for checking your grade. Your instructor may want to keep the answer sheet in his file to affirm that you've successfully completed home study and his briefing. He'll probably put your name and the date on a blank part of the answer sheet when he enters it in his file.

When you're taking the test (the sample *and* the FAA one) be careful about how you mark the answers and make sure that the number of the answer coincides with the number of the question. It seems very simple now, but under pressure of time you might start marking *across* the columns instead of *down* as indicated.

Be sure that you follow the instructions concerning the selection of questions. The Question Selection Sheet should be carefully checked so that you answer the proper 60 questions out of the 600. (A sample is included — later in this book — on the back of the Airman Written Test Application.)

A form is included in the back of the book for your instructor (ground or flight) to complete when he is satisfied you are ready to take the written test. You can take this to the FAA office when applying to take the written test.

The check pilot on the flight test will look at your grade and likely quiz you especially in those areas you had some trouble with on the written.

If you make a grade less than 70 on the FAA written, your instructor will give you the word on what to do about retaking the test. But, if you study as you go and ask questions about matters that aren't clear, you'll do fine. The evening before you take the FAA written do a short review of the material and then get a good night's sleep.

One consolation: When you walk into the test room you'll probably see several other people whose stomach butterflies are even more active than yours.

SOME POINTS TO PONDER ABOUT THE WRITTEN TEST

While in the following sample questions you'll find some humor to make a point and help you to remember, the FAA written examinations are dead serious in approach. Check the official word on what you can expect concerning the FAA written examination. If you miss more than 15 of these questions you had better do some more reviewing.

Good luck on your written and flight tests, and

with your future flying. *Here's some advice from the FAA about the written:*

Years ago in the early days of aviation the private pilot was concerned primarily with flights in the vicinity of the local airport. Today, however, the area of operation is virtually unlimited for the private pilot who participates in extended personal or business flights. Consequently, today's private pilot often encounters various conditions over unfamiliar terrain, which requires adequate knowledge of weather, air traffic rules, and principles of flight to safely cope with normally anticipated situations and to safely and efficiently proceed to the destination.

FAA written tests are developed to require the ability to use aeronautical knowledge in practical situations.

An applicant for a private pilot certificate is required to have received and logged ground instruction from an authorized ground or flight instructor, or present evidence showing satisfactory completion of a course of instruction or home study, in specific aeronautical subjects. Those subjects are outlined in this study guide. To ensure that adequate knowledge of those subjects has been acquired, applicants are required to pass the FAA Private Pilot Airplane Written Test.

As a convenience to the prospective private pilot, portions of the Federal Aviation Regulations concerning general eligibility and aeronautical knowledge requirements for the private pilot certificate are included in this guide.

All test questions in the Private Pilot Written Test are the objective, multiple-choice type and can be answered by the selection of a single answer. This type of test conserves the applicant's time when taking the test, permits greater coverage of subject matter, reduces the time required for scoring, and eliminates subjective judgment in determining grades.

Each item is independent of other test items. That is, a correct answer to one test item does not depend upon, nor influence, the correct answer to another item.

The Private Pilot Airplane Written Test contains 60 test items; 4 hours are allowed for completing the test. The equipment needed for taking the test includes a protractor or plotter and a navigation type computer. The applicant may also use electronic or mechanical calculators subject to the following limitations: (1) prior to, and on completion of the test, the test monitor will instruct the applicant to actuate the "ON/OFF" switch, observing this action, to ensure erasure of any data stored in memory circuits; (2) tape printout of data must be surrendered to the test monitor if the calculator incorporates this design feature; and (3) the applicant is not permitted to use any material containing instructions related to operation of the calculator during the written test. Textbooks or notes are forbidden. The office administering the test will furnish paper and special pencils.

Communication between individuals through the use of written words is a complicated process. Consequently, considerable effort is expended to write each test item in a clear, precise manner. Applicants should carefully read the information and instructions given with the tests, as well as the test items.

Remember the following when taking the written test:

1. There are no "trick" questions. Each statement means exactly what it says. Do not look for hidden meanings. The statement does not concern exceptions to the rule, but refers to the general rule.

2. Carefully read the entire test item before selecting an answer. Skimming and hasty assumptions can lead to a completely erroneous approach to the problem because of failure to consider vital words. Examine and analyze the list of alternative responses, then select the one that answers the question or completes the statement correctly.

3. Only one of the answers given is completely correct. The others may be the result of using incorrect procedures to solve problems, common misconceptions, or insufficient knowledge of the subject. Consequently, many of the incorrect answers may appear to be correct to those persons whose knowledge is deficient. If the subject matter is adequately understood, the questions should not be difficult to answer correctly.

4. If considerable difficulty is experienced with a particular test item, do not spend too much time on it, but continue with other items you consider to be less difficult. When all of the easier items are completed, go back and complete those items that were found to be more difficult. This procedure will enable you to use the available time to maximum advantage.

5. In solving problems that require computations or the use of a plotter and computer, select the answer that most nearly agrees with the calculated result. Due to slight differences in navigation computers and small errors that may exist in the measurement of distances, true courses, etc., it is possible that an exact agreement with available answers will not occur. Sufficient spread is provided between right and wrong answers, however, so that selection of the answer more nearly that of the calculated result will be the correct choice, *provided* correct technique and reasonable care were used in making computations.

When the test was constructed, various types of navigation computers were used to solve the problems. The correct answer is an average of the results produced by these computers; therefore, any of the several types of computers authorized by the FAA for use on written tests should prove satisfactory.

Applicants may find that certain test questions involving regulations, ATC procedures, etc., are outdated by very recent changes. In these instances, applicants are *given credit* for the test item during the period that it takes to distribute a revised question.

To become familiar with the procedures and materials used for taking the FAA Private Pilot Airplane Written Test, samples of the actual General

Instructions, Written Test Application, Question Selection Sheet, and answer sheet are provided in this guide.

After completing the test, your answer sheet is forwarded to the Federal Aviation Administration, Aeronautical Center in Oklahoma City, for scoring by electronic computers (ADP). Shortly thereafter, you will receive an Airman Written Test Report, which not only includes the grade but also lists the subject areas in which test items were answered incorrectly.

When reporting for the written test, be prepared to present to the person administering the test proof of your eligibility to take the test, as well as documentary evidence of your identity. Additionally, you should plan your arrival to allow sufficient time to complete the test.

STUDENT PILOT'S FLIGHT MANUAL WRITTEN EXAMINATION

1. The angle of attack:
    1. Is the angle between the relative wind and the chord line of the airfoil.
    2. Is the angle between the horizon and the longitudinal axis of the airplane.
    3. Is that fixed angle between the longitudinal axis and the wing chord line.
    4. None of the above.
2. A 2000 pound airplane flying at 100 K is producing 2000 pounds of lift and is maintaining straight and level unaccelerated flight. Assuming no change in its weight and disregarding taildown forces (discussed in the latter part of this book), in balanced straight and level flight at 200 K it would need to produce:
    1. 4000 pounds of lift   3. 2000 pounds of lift
    2. 8000 pounds of lift   4. 1000 pounds of lift
3. The following forces or moments contribute to torque effects at one time or another:
    A. Rotating slipstream
    B. P-factor, or asymmetric disk loading
    C. Coriolis effect caused by the latitude and longitude of the airplane's position
    D. Opposite and equal reaction
    E. Gyroscopic precession
    F. A crosswind in flight
        1. ABDE   3. ABDF
        2. ACDE   4. ABD
4. Standard sea level values for atmospheric pressure and temperature are:
    1. 29.92 inches of mercury and 15°F
    2. 29.92 inches of mercury and 59°F
    3. 29.92 centimeters of mercury and 59°F
    4. None of the above
5. Flying in very fine visual conditions from an area of comparatively low pressure (altimeter setting 29.52 inches of mercury) to an airport of higher pressure (30.12 inches of mercury) you don't reset your altimeter before landing. As you taxi up to the gas pump you discover to your

surprise that *according to your altimeter:*

1. You are still about 600 feet *above* the airport and shouldn't step out of the airplane.
2. You are at 2720 feet because that number was mentioned in Figure 3-3 in this book.
3. You are about 600 feet *below* that airport elevation.
4. It doesn't matter since you weren't flying on an instrument flight plan and could see obstructions, anyway.

6. The normal temperature lapse rate per thousand feet is approximately:
   1. $3\ 1/2^\circ$C or 2°F
   2. 2°C or $3\ 1/2^\circ$F
   3. 15°C
   4. 15°F

7. A standard rate turn (3° per second) at 130 K T.A.S., according to the rule of thumb given in this book, would require a bank of approximately:
   1. 30°
   2. 10°
   3. 15°
   4. 20°

8. If the battery *and* alternator systems fail completely in flight, what effect will it have on operations?
   A. The engine will stop immediately since no electrical power is available.
   B. The engine will continue running exactly as before.
   C. The electrically powered instruments will not be available (fuel gages and others).
   D. The engine will lose power in that case because of the loss of efficiency due to a cooler spark.
   E. The communications and navigation equipment will be out of operation.
      1. ABD
      2. ACD
      3. BCE
      4. BCD

9. Which of the following documents must be up to date and *in* the airplane at all times when it is being operated?
   A. Certificate of Registration
   B. Certificate of Airworthiness
   C. Airplane logbooks
   D. *Airplane Flight Manual* or an equivalent form of information
      1. ABC
      2. ABD
      3. BCD
      4. ACD

10. An airplane being owned and flown as a "private vehicle" has an annual inspection completed and signed off on June 17, 1983. If the airplane is to legally continue flying, the next annual will be due by:
    1. June 16, 1984
    2. June 17, 1984
    3. July 1, 1984
    4. June 1, 1984

11. As a student pilot, in the process of checking the engine compartment, you discover that one of the magnetos is loose. You should:
    1. Complete the inspection and fly; that's why the airplane has two magnetos.
    2. Call an instructor or mechanic over to check it.
    3. Fasten the cowling and quietly leave the airport in disgust.
    4. Call Henry Schmotz and/or Oswald Zilch long distance (collect) to see what *they* think.

12. In a preflight check of a particular airplane you find that the ground wire, which can be readily seen, is disconnected from one of the magnetos. Which one of the following statements is applicable to the situation?
    1. The engine will not start until the ground wire is refastened.
    2. The ground wire has no effect at this point because the airplane is touching the surface and forms its own electrical ground.
    3. The engine can be started but only the mag with the still-attached ground wire will be working.
    4. That magneto is "hot" as long as the wire is off. A dangerous situation exists.

13. In Figure 6-3 assume that runway 31 (which is *exactly* lined up 310° magnetic) has a right-hand traffic pattern and the wind is very light and right down the runway. Your heading on the base leg to that runway (just *before* making an exact 90° right turn to line up with the runway centerline) would be:
    1. 220° magnetic
    2. 200° true
    3. 040° magnetic
    4. 040° true

14. You are taxiing a tricycle-gear airplane in a strong tailwind from the left rear; the controls should be held as follows:
    1. Control wheel back, right aileron (wheel turned to the right), and rudder as necessary to keep the airplane straight.
    2. Control wheel forward, left aileron, and left rudder.
    3. Control wheel forward, right aileron, and rudder as necessary to keep it straight.
    4. Control wheel forward, right aileron, and full left rudder.

15. When checking the aileron movements in a pre-take-off check you turn the control wheel to the left and note that the left aileron goes down and the right aileron goes up. This is:
    1. Normal.
    2. Backward, but you can remember to reverse the wheel movement for turns during the flight.
    3. Abnormal, and the airplane should be immediately taxied back to the hangar and grounded until repaired.
    4. The question is immaterial since the only reason for moving the controls during this check is to see that they move freely, not to see which way they move.

16. During the magneto check you find that there is a 75 rpm drop on "right" but there is no rpm drop when the switch is on the "left" magneto position. Such a reaction is probably due to:
    1. A very efficient left magneto.
    2. The left magneto is not grounded.
    3. The right magneto is not grounded.
    4. A defective alternator.

17. During the carburetor heat check at 1800 rpm, you pull the heat on and leave it on. There's a drop of about 100 rpm and then, after a few seconds, it picks quickly up to *1900* rpm without the throttle being moved. This is probably an

indication that:

1. Carburetor ice was present before the heat was pulled on.
2. Carburetor heat increased the efficiency of the engine.
3. The engine had warmed up.
4. Nothing of significance has occurred.

18. An airplane stalls wings-level at a calibrated airspeed of 60 K at a certain weight. In a 60° banked level turn at the same weight, the stall speed would be approximately (calibrated airspeed):
    1. 60 K
    3. 85 K
    2. 120 K
    4. 65 K

19. Refer to Figure 12-13. You are flying at Point (5) in that figure, *carrying full power* about 100 feet above the ocean. (Never mind how you got yourself in this position.) There is an island ridge well ahead that is about 200 feet higher than the altitude you are barely maintaining. To climb over that island you would need to:
    1. Ease the nose up a couple of degrees farther.
    2. Ease the nose over to about the airspeed at Point (3), keeping full power on.
    3. Ease the nose over to Point (3), throttling back to about 45 brake horsepower. (Assume that you know the rpm required for 45 brake horse-power.)
    4. Ease the nose up, reducing power to about 45 horsepower.

20. If, in an accelerated stall, you stall the airplane at a calibrated airspeed of 100 K (its normal 1-g stall calibrated airspeed is 50 K at that weight and configuration) a load factor of _____ g's would result.
    1. 4
    3. 1
    2. 2
    4. 3

21. Select the correction to be done first in a recovery from a power-on spiral, using the partial or emergency panel instruments (disregard any power changes for this question):
    1. Decrease back pressure.
    2. Increase back pressure.
    3. Center the needle and ball, or turn coordinator.
    4. None of the above.

22. From clear conditions you "inadvertently" fly into instrument conditions while on a magnetic heading of 250°. After some weaving around, control is regained on a magnetic heading of 340°. For the shortest way out of the weather you should turn:
    1. Left to a heading of 250°
    2. Left to a heading of 160°
    3. Right to a heading of 160°
    4. Right to a heading of 070°

23. Assume that back in Figure 16-3 the wind is from 090° at 40 K instead of from 360° at 40 K. the airplane is still flying around the point in a left turn as shown and, under the new wind conditions cited, the position at which the steepest bank is required is now (use the numbers as given in the illustration):

1. Point (3)
3. Point (7)
2. Point (1)
4. Point (5)

24. The rate of climb of an airplane climbing directly into a strong wind will be _____ than (as) when it is climbing downwind (assume no turbulence).
    1. Greater
    3. Much greater
    2. The same
    4. Less

25. You are preparing to take off at an airport at a pressure altitude of 2000 feet, and note that the outside air temperature gage indicates +75°F (24°C). The density altitude is approximately:
    1. 2000 feet
    3. 5500 feet
    2. 3500 feet
    4. 1500 feet

26. In planning a cross-country flight you have available the following information if you need it: True course – 170°, variation 4°W, wind from 260° true at 17 K, true airspeed – 100 K. The magnetic course is:
    1. 166°
    3. 164°
    2. 160°
    4. 174°

27. Refer to Figure 19-4. Your computed *true heading* for a cross-country is 282° and the variation is 3°W. Your *compass heading* would be:
    1. 279°
    3. 293°
    2. 289°
    4. 281°

28. Your airplane uses 8.4 gallons per hour at the *cruise* setting you have been using on a particular cross-country. The usable fuel available when you leveled off at cruise 2 hours and 14 minutes ago was 31.5 gallons. Assuming that 45 minutes of fuel reserve at cruise airspeed will be retained, you should at this point be able to fly on for a period of _____ before landing.
    1. 46 minutes
    3. 56 minutes
    2. 34 minutes
    4. 39 minutes

29. The length of the runway at Sewanee-Franklin County Airport is (check Appendix B):
    1. 3300 feet and has a runway 1
    2. 1950 feet
    3. 3300 feet and has one physical runway
    4. 4000 feet

30. Select the one description that fits Airport Traffic Area dimensions.
    1. Extends from the surface to 14,500 feet MSL and is 5 statute miles in diameter.
    2. Extends from the surface to 3000 feet MSL and has a 5 NM radius from the geographical center of the airport.
    3. Extends from the surface up to but not including 3000 feet above the surface and has a horizontal radius of 5 statute miles from the geographical center of the airport.
    4. Extends from the surface up to but not including 1200 feet above the surface and has a radius of 5 statute miles.

31. Choose from the following the items which characterize a typical cold front.
    A. Comparatively narrow weather band
    B. Widespread low ceilings and poor visibilities
    C. Stratus type clouds
    D. Often violent weather with build-ups
    E. Rapid clearing following its passage

F. Gusty winds after passage
   1. ABDG   3. ACEF
   2. ADEF   4. BDEF

Refer to Figure 22-13 for questions 32 through 34.

32. The ceiling at Standiford Field (SDF) is:
    1. Measured 400 overcast
    2. Measured 4000 overcast
    3. Estimated 1900 overcast
    4. None of the above
33. The surface wind at Jackson-McKellar Field (MKL) is:
    1. From 021° true at 15 K
    2. From 211° true at 15 mph
    3. From 210° true at 15 K
    4. From 210° magnetic at 15 K
34. The visibility at Nashville (BNA) is:
    1. Eleven miles in light drizzle and fog
    2. One-half mile in drizzle and fog
    3. Two miles in drizzle and fog
    4. One and one-half miles in light drizzle and fog

Refer to Figure 22-15 for questions 35 through 37.

35. At 1100 CST on the 29th the visibility at Standiford (SDF) is forecast to be:
    1. 3 statute miles in fog
    2. 3 nautical miles in fog
    3. 4 nautical miles in fog
    4. 4 statute miles in hail
36. Which stations predict that at some part of the forecast period frequently the weather will be a ceiling of 1000 feet overcast and two miles in rain showers and thundershowers?
    1. PAH and SDF   3. TRI and CHA
    2. LEX and BWG   4. None of the above
37. HUF at 1800 CST (amended forecast) forecasts a visibility of:
    1. 1 statute mile in light rain and fog
    2. 1 statute mile in rain and light fog
    3. 5 statute miles in hail
    4. 1 nautical mile in rain showers and fog

Questions 38 and 39 are based on Figure 22-19.

38. Which of the stations shown has a wind of over 100 K at the lowest altitude?
    1. RIC (Richmond)   3. MOB (Mobile)
    2. MSY (New Orleans)   4. TRI (Tri-Cities)
39. The temperature at 34,000 feet at SHV (Shreveport) is:
    1. -57° F   3. -57° C
    2. +57° C   4. -45° C
40. For this question refer to Figure 22-16, *Area forecast.* In the "Arkansas, Louisiana and adjacent coastal waters" portion of the FA the restrictions to vision are:
    A. Fog
    B. Hail
    C. Smoke
    D. Haze
    E. Thunderstorms and rain showers
    1. ABCE
    2. ABE
    3. BCDE
    4. ACDE
41. When checking a winds aloft forecast you read for the altitude you plan to fly — "3333-Ø7." You decipher it to mean the following:
    1. The wind is forecast to be light and variable at that altitude.
    2. The wind is forecast to be from 330° magnetic at 33 K and the temperature, -7° C.
    3. The wind is forecast to be from 330° true at 33 mph and the temperature will be -7° C.
    4. The wind is forecast to be from 330° true at 38 mph and the temperature, -7° C.

Following are some numbers for the airplane you are going to take on a cross-country (questions 42 and 43):

Maximum certificated weight	2300 pounds
Basic empty weight	1439 pounds
Total fuel capacity	40 gallons
Unusable fuel	2 gallons
Maximum allowed baggage (compartment)	100 pounds
Pilot's weight	168 pounds
First passenger's weight	170 pounds
Second passenger's weight	140 pounds

42. You will fly the airplane with full fuel. Based on the figures given for the airplane's empty and max certificated weights and the three people's weights and other information given above, you can plan on carrying the following maximum weight of baggage in the baggage compartment on the flight:
    1. 155 pounds   3. 100 pounds
    2. 143 pounds   4. 167 pounds
43. The airplane, if loaded with full fuel, the three people as listed, plus 100 pounds of baggage, would be _____ pounds under the maximum certificated weight:
    1. 55   3. 67
    2. 43   4. None of the above
44. Your airplane normally uses grade 80 fuel and after landing at an airport for refueling you find that the operator has only grade 100 and 115/145. However, there is a service station across the road which, as far as you can tell, has a grade of fuel slightly above 80/87 octane. Your best choice in this case would be to:
    1. Use grade 100 for this refueling but go back to using grade 80 as soon as possible.
    2. Use the 115/145 and for once give the airplane a real boost.
    3. Fill up with the automotive fuel, since you feel

that it's closest in octane to what you've been using.

4. Fly to another airport to get grade 80 fuel, even if it means a no-reserve situation getting there.

45. Refer to Figure 24-18 (the tabulated cruise performance chart). If you were cruising at 2550 rpm at the pressure altitude of 6000 feet (standard temperature) you would be using _____ % of the total brake horsepower and the airspeed indicator would be showing _____:
   (Hint: Figure 19-6 is an airspeed correction table for this airplane.)
   1. 57% power and 95 K
   2. 61% power and 97 K
   3. 64% power and 99 K
   4. 61% power and 88 K

46. You have become lost after passing Pulaski for Huntsville (use the sectional chart) and believe you might be well east of your course. Circling over a small town on a crossroads, you tune in the Muscle Shoals VOR, identify it and find that when the needle is centered and the TO-FROM indicator reads FROM, the OBS reads 061. Setting up Huntsville (Rocket) VOR you note that the OBS indicates 339 when the needle is centered and the TO-FROM indicator shows FROM. The town you are most likely to be over is:
   1. Ardmore   3. Lincoln
   2. Taft   4. New Dellrose

(Note: The chart in the back is a smaller scale; you may have to take a little time here setting up the bearings.)

47. At about the 30-mile point (you think) on the flight from Huntsville to Sewanee the weather is starting to deteriorate from the south; Huntsville is now barely VFR. You are over the mountains and aren't at all sure of your position. Assuming that Sewanee would have good weather for another 30 minutes, the safest move would be (refer to the chart in the back of the book):
   1. Continue on the original heading and by dead reckoning hope to locate yourself near Sewanee.
   2. Turn south to hit the railroad and road combination that runs through Scottsboro and then fly the railroad up through Anderson and Sherwood to Sewanee.
   3. Turn north to hit the railroad that runs through New Market, Elora, and Huntland, following it to Winchester and then turn to Sewanee (following the highway if necessary from Winchester to the Sewanee Airport).
   4. Reverse course and try to locate yourself for a return to Huntsville.

48. On final approach to an airport having VASI (Visual Approach Slope Indicator) you note that the lights indicate as shown here:
          red   red
          white   white
   1. Your airplane is dangerously low. Add power.

2. Your airplane is too high, the angle of descent must be increased or a go-around may be needed.
3. Your airplane is on the proper approach slope.
4. None of the above answers apply to the light arrangement as given.

49. Just before opening the throttle to take off on a two-hour night cross-country you realize that you left your flashlight by the gas pump after finishing the preflight check. Your move would be:
   1. To continue the take-off and the flight, since the particular airplane you are in has never had any electrical problems.
   2. Taxi back immediately in the safest and most expeditious manner to get the flashlight.
   3. Continue the flight but definitely plan on getting a flashlight at the destination airport.
   4. Since it is one of the brightest moonlit nights you've seen lately here at Jonesville Airport, you would be able to read the instrument panel without *any* lights if necessary.

50. Lights marking the edges of taxiways are:
   1. Red   3. Chartreuse
   2. White   4. Blue

51. Drugs that have been associated with aircraft accidents in the past include:
   1. Antihistamines   3. Tranquilizers
   2. Reducing drugs   4. All of the above

52. If you are getting symptoms of carbon monoxide while in flight you should shut off any heaters, open the air ventilators, descend to lower altitudes, and
   1. Slow down your breathing rate.
   2. Speed up your breathing rate.
   3. Breathe into a paper bag.
   4. Land at the nearest airfield.

53. You find that someone left the electrical master switch on overnight in the light training airplane you are about to fly and the battery is dead. The airplane has a normal alternator/battery system and you get a competent person to hand-crank the airplane (with you in the cockpit). Which of the following statements covers the most likely result of this action?
   1. The engine won't start because the battery is dead and cannot furnish electrical power to the plugs.
   2. The engine will start and run well but the electrical equipment (radios, etc.) will not be usable.
   3. The engine will start and the battery will start charging the alternator immediately.
   4. The engine won't start because the starter cannot be energized.

54. You are up practicing stalls solo and after the stall break a wing drops rapidly and rotation starts. The nose is down but the airspeed is low and even though you are holding the control wheel full aft, the nose won't come up. The best *initial* procedure in this case is to:
   1. Close the throttle, neutralize the ailerons, apply full rudder against the rotation, followed

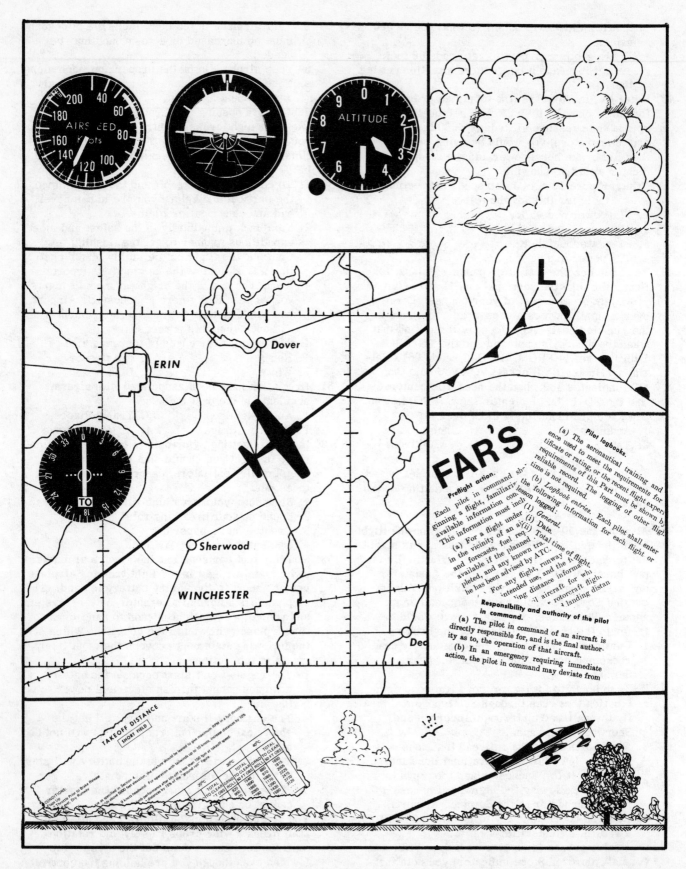

Fig. 27.1. A good written test should have information that applies to flying an airplane. Too many students and flight instructors tend to look at it as a separate obstacle to be overcome and neglect to use it to gain practical knowledge of flying. ("That's out of the way; now we can get on with training.")

by forward movement of the control wheel.
2. Open the throttle, use full aileron against the rotation, and hold the wheel back to continue trying to bring the nose up.
3. Open the throttle, apply rudder and aileron in the direction of rotation.
4. Leave the throttle at the same setting, hold the control wheel back, and use aileron opposite to the rotation.

55. The maximum structural cruising speed (V_{NO}) is shown on the airspeed indicator:
1. At the point where the white arc meets the green arc.
2. At the highest speed shown by the yellow arc.
3. At the highest value of airspeed indicated by the green arc.
4. Is not shown because it varies with airplane weight.

56. A transition area extends:
1. From the surface to 700 feet above the surface.
2. From the surface to 1200 feet above the surface.
3. From 700 feet above the surface upward.
4. From 1200 feet above the surface upward.

57. Above 10,000 feet MSL and more than 1200 feet above the surface the visibility and cloud clearance minimums are:
1. 3 miles flight visibility, 1000 feet vertical and 1 mile horizontal from the clouds.
2. 5 miles flight visibility, 1000 feet vertical and 1 mile horizontal from clouds.
3. 3 miles flight visibility and cloud clearance, 500 feet under, 1000 feet over (vertically), and

2000 feet horizontally.
4. None of the above.

58. You are flying at a T.A.S. of 120 K on a true course of 280° with the wind from 230° true at 30 K. You would expect the following:
1. You would make a wind correction to the right and have a ground speed less than the true airspeed.
2. You would make a wind correction to the left and have a ground speed greater than the true airspeed.
3. You would make a wind correction to the right and have a ground speed greater than the true airspeed.
4. You would make a wind correction to the left and have a ground speed less than the true airspeed.

59. Which of the following instruments is not required to be in the airplane for day VFR operations?
1. Turn and slip indicator
2. Magnetic direction indicator
3. Oil pressure gage for each engine
4. Tachometer for each engine

60. You are a private pilot who had a Biennial Flight Review on October 13, 1982. In order to continue to be legal to fly as pilot in command you would have to have a BFR before:
1. November 1, 1984
2. October 13, 1984
3. October 13, 1983
4. November 1, 1983

28. *The Flight Test*

After you've passed the written test you'll fly more dual and solo flights to review any particular problems and bring your skill up to private pilot level. As was noted in the last chapter, you should take the written test sometime *after* the first solo cross-country so that you'll have the procedures well in mind; but allow a few days and some flying time after getting your passing grade back before taking the flight test.

Figure 28-1 is a recommended checklist to use when going to take the flight (practical) test; it wouldn't look too well, for instance, if the examiner (check pilot) found that the airplane was lacking

---

APPLICANT'S FLIGHT TEST CHECKLIST
(Suggested)

**APPOINTMENT WITH INSPECTOR
OR EXAMINER:** Name _____

Time/Date _____

**ACCEPTABLE AIRPLANE WITH
DUAL CONTROLS**
  View-limiting device
  Aircraft Documents:
    Airworthiness Certificate
    Registration Certificate
    Operating Limitations
  Aircraft Maintenance Records:
    Airworthiness Inspections
  FCC Station License

PERSONAL EQUIPMENT
  Current Aeronautical Charts
  Computer and Plotter
  Flight Plan Form
  Flight Logs
  Current AIM

PERSONAL RECORDS
  Pilot Certificate
  Medical Certificate
  Signed Recommendation
  Written Test Results
  Logbook
  Notice of Disapproval (if applicable)
  Approved School Graduation Certificate
    (if applicable)
  FCC Radiotelephone Operator Permit
  Examiner's Fee (if applicable)

Fig. 28-1.

---

required papers.

Following are areas of knowledge necessary for you to safely perform the privileges of a private pilot. (The chapter numbers in parentheses after the various procedures/maneuvers are *Student Pilot's Flight Manual* [SPFM] and *Student Pilot's Study Guide* [SPFG] references.)

SOME IDEAS TO CONSIDER

You may encounter the term *Areas of Operation* in the flight test. *Areas of Operation* are phases of flight arranged in a logical sequence within the guide. They begin with the flight's preparation and end with its conclusion. The examiner, however, may conduct the practical test in any sequence that results in a complete and efficient test.

You most likely won't be tested on every procedure and maneuver within each Area of Operation but only on those considered necessary by the examiner to determine your competence in each pilot operation. Certain demonstrations may be impractical (for example, night flying), so your knowledge may be checked by oral testing.

TASKS are procedures and maneuvers appropriate to an *Area of Operation. Preflight Preparation*, for example, is an *Area of Operation;* one TASK in that area would be an explanation of the Certificates and Documents pertaining to you *and* the airplane.

Consistently exceeding the tolerances noted before taking corrective action will be considered unsatisfactory. Any procedure, or lack thereof, that requires the examiner to take over will be disqualifying. If, during the flight test, you don't clear the flight area adequately, you could be failed. (A midair collision can certainly spoil a flight test — or any flight.)

The examiner will be looking for safe performance as a pilot; you won't be expected to fly like an ace, but the main thing is to use good clearing procedures, checklists, and other techniques and aids in avoiding accidents and incidents. There also will be emphasis on coping with spatial disorientation and wake turbulence hazards.

You'd better know the meaning and significance of airplane performance speeds, including:

V_{SO} — the stalling speed or minimum steady flight speed in landing configuration.

V_Y — the speed for the best rate of climb.
V_X — the speed for the best angle of climb.
V_A — the design and maneuvering speed.
V_{NE} — the never exceed speed.

GENERAL PROCEDURES FOR FLIGHT TESTS

The ability of an applicant for a private or commercial pilot certificate, or for an aircraft or instrument rating on that certificate, to perform the required pilot operations is based on the following:

1. Executing procedures and maneuvers within the aircraft's performance capabilities and limitations, including use of the aircraft's systems.
2. Executing emergency procedures and maneuvers appropriate to the aircraft.
3. Piloting the aircraft with smoothness and accuracy.
4. Exercising judgment.
5. Applying aeronautical knowledge.
6. Showing mastery of the aircraft, with the successful outcome of a procedure or maneuver never seriously in doubt.

If you fail any of the required TASKS you fail the flight test. The examiner or you may discontinue the test at any time when the failure of a required TASK makes you ineligible for the certificate or rating sought. If the test is discontinued you are entitled to credit for only those pilot operations, or TASKS, that you have successfully performed. At the discretion of the examiner any TASK may be reevaluated, including those previously passed.

As an applicant for the private pilot flight test you are required by the Federal Aviation Regulations to have (1) passed the appropriate private pilot written test within 24 calendar months before the date you take the flight test, (2) the applicable instruction and aeronautical experience prescribed for a private pilot certificate, (3) a first, second, or third class medical certificate issued within the past 24 months, (4) reached at least 17 years of age, and (5) a written statement from an appropriately certificated flight instructor certifying that he has given you flight instruction in preparation for the flight test within 60 days preceding the date of application and finds you competent to pass the test and to have a satisfactory knowledge of the subject areas in which you were shown to be deficient by the airman written test report.

You are required to provide an airworthy airplane for the flight test. This airplane must be capable of, and its operating limitations must not prohibit, the pilot operations required in the test. The following equipment is needed for the pilot operations required for the private pilot flight test:

1. A two-way radio suitable for voice communications with aeronautical ground stations.

2. A radio receiver that can be utilized for available radio navigation facilities (may be the same radio used for communications).
3. Appropriate flight instruments for the control of the airplane during instrument conditions. Appropriate flight instruments are considered to be those required by FAR Part 91 for flight under instrument flight rules.
4. Engine and flight controls that are easily reached and operated in a normal manner by both pilots.
5. A suitable view-limiting device, easy to install and remove in flight, for simulating instrument flight conditions.
6. Operating instructions and limitations. You should have an appropriate checklist, a *Pilot's Operating Handbook* (POH), or, if required for the airplane used, an FAA approved Airplane Flight Manual. Any operating limitations or other published recommendations of the manufacturer that are applicable to the specific airplane will be observed.

USE OF DISTRACTIONS DURING PRACTICAL TESTS

It's been noted that many accidents occur when the pilot's attention is distracted during various phases of flight. Many accidents have resulted from engine failure during take-offs and landings under conditions in which safe flight would have been possible had the distracted pilot not used improper techniques.

Distractions that have been found to cause problems are:

1. Preoccupation with situations inside or outside the cockpit.
2. Maneuvering to avoid other traffic.
3. Maneuvering to clear obstacles during take-offs, climbs, approaches, or landings.

The examiner will provide realistic distractions during the practical (flight) test, which could include:

1. Simulating engine failure.
2. Simulating radio tuning and transmissions.
3. Identifying a field suitable for emergency landings.
4. Identifying features or objects on the ground.
5. Reading the outside air temperature gage.
6. Removing objects from the glove compartment or map case. (This could start an avalanche of objects you didn't even know were in there, including the ham sandwich that you misplaced while on that cross-country flight last month.)

A good question on the oral part of the test is, Does this particular airplane require a propeller spinner to be legal to fly? In some cases the spinner is required to smooth airflow into the cowling for cooling, and the airplane has been flight tested and is certificated *on that basis*. It's possible that without the spinner the engine could run hot. Look at the

Equipment List in the *Pilot's Operating Handbook* or pertinent airplane papers to see if the letter designating required equipment is by the spinner listing.

Take time to go through the POH well beforehand so that you'll at least know where to look for information.

PREFLIGHT PREPARATIONS

Certificates and Documents. You may be required to present your pilot and medical certificates and locate and explain the airplane's papers and other records (Chapter 3).

Obtaining Weather Information. You'll need to obtain and be able to read and analyze weather charts and forecasts, surface weather reports, winds aloft forecasts and reports, pilot weather reports, SIGMETS, AIRMETS, and Notices to Airmen. You'll check the proper weather and understand its significance to a particular flight. You'll make a sound GO/NO-GO decision based on the available weather information (Chapter 22).

Determining Performance and Limitations. You may be orally quizzed on performance capabilities, approved operating procedures, and limitations of your airplane. Know the power settings, placarded speeds, and fuel and oil requirements. You may be asked to demonstrate the application of the approved weight and balance data for your airplane to determine that the weight and C.G. locations are within limits for various passenger, fuel, and/or baggage combinations. Use the manufacturer's charts and graphs. (Review Chapter 23.)

Know what could happen if you exceed various limitations, such as loading, so that the C.G. is out of the envelope? What are the effects of frost or ice on the airplane's take-off performance? (See Chapter 22; review Chapters 17 and 23 also.)

Cross-Country Flight Planning. You'll be expected to plan, within 30 minutes, a VFR cross-country flight of a duration near the maximum range of the airplane, including reserve fuel. You'd better be sure that your sectional chart(s) and Airport/Facility Directory are up to date and pertain to the route and airports. Plot your course(s) and double-check for fuel stops, if necessary; be sure that these stops have the proper fuel for your airplane. Your checkpoints should be prominent and useful in navigating the trip. Compute the flight time, headings, and fuel requirements, and don't forget a reserve! Check for VORs or NDBs that can be used on the flight, and check the route carefully so that you don't fly through a Prohibited Area or a less restrictive but still hazardous one. Check obstructions enroute. You'll choose airports that can be used as alternates and check their facilities also. You'll be expected to complete a navigation log and file a VFR flight plan.

GROUND OPERATIONS

Visual Inspection. Be able to explain *why* you are checking various items on the airplane. Use the checklist in going around it. You'll be expected to determine that the airplane is in condition for safe flight; if you try to take the airplane when one wing is lying flat on the ground, certain questions (and eyebrows) might be raised. Know the colors of the various fuel grades and the grade and type of fuel and oil used (and also be able to find all fuel and oil filler points). Know where the battery and other components are located. Check for fuel contamination and be able to explain what you are looking for and when it is most likely to occur. Know capacities of fuel and oil tanks and where to look for leaks in these systems. (This also goes for the hydraulic and brake systems.) Check and explain the flight controls and look at the balance weights on the rudder, elevator, and ailerons, as applicable. (You should know by now that in normal operations when one aileron goes up, the other goes down.) Check for structural damage (hangar rash) as you go around, and for Pete's sake, don't try to taxi off with the airplane tied down, control lock(s) in place, or chocks under the wheels. Again, you should know that ice and frost are detrimental to take-off operations. See to the security of baggage, cargo, and equipment. You are acting as pilot-in-command and will be checked on your judgment of the airplane's readiness to fly safely (Chapters 4 and 23).

Cockpit Management. You are to have an adequate knowledge of cockpit management and be able to explain the related safety factors. In other words, you'll be expected to organize your material and equipment in a manner that makes them readily available. (Taking off with the charts and other navigation equipment well out of reach in the far corner of the baggage compartment could cost you several points.) Make sure that the safety belts and harnesses are fastened (with you and the examiner *inside* them). Your seat should be adjusted — and locked — in the proper position. Be sure that the controls are free and have full and proper movement. Since the examiner is a "passenger," you should brief him (and any others on board) on the use of the belts and any emergency procedures (Chapter 4).

Starting the Engine. You'll be expected to explain the starting procedures, including starting under various conditions. *Use the checklist — all items —* for prestart, start, and poststart procedures. You'll be expected to be safe, with emphasis on (1) positioning the airplane to avoid creating hazards (don't blast people or airplanes behind you), (2) making sure that the propeller area is clear, (3) assuring that the engine controls are properly adjusted (for instance, a wide open throttle with a cold engine, a mixture left in idle cutoff, or a fuel selector OFF could cause problems). Set (or better yet, *hold*) the brakes before, during, and after start, and don't let the airplane *inadvertently* move after the start. *Don't* let the engine roar up after the start; keep the rpm under control. Check the engine instruments after the start. (Read Chapter 5 — *now*, not while starting the engine on the check flight.)

Taxiing. You'll be expected to explain and use safe taxi procedures. Check the brakes for effectiveness as you move out of the parking spot. You'll be

240

checked on safe ground operations, your use of brakes and power to control taxi speeds, and proper positioning of the flight controls for the existing wind conditions. You'll be expected to be aware of ground hazards and comply with taxi procedures and instructions (Fig. 25-4). (Review Chapter 6.) (As one applicant said to the check pilot after sideswiping two airplanes, nearly running over a flight instructor, and ending up with the airplane's nose sticking into the flight office: "I suppose this means that I've flunked the surface operations part of the test.")

Don't abuse the brakes by carrying too much power and then using them to keep the speed down.

Pretake-off Check. Review Chapter 7 of SPFM and SPSG. On the flight test, as anytime, you should be able to explain the reasons for checking the items. Make the run-up so as to not create a hazard. *Don't* stick your head down in the cockpit and keep it there; divide your attention. Touch each control or switch as you *follow the checklist*, and call out each item as you check it. Give the instrument reading, if applicable, after checking it on the list. Make sure, again as always, that the airplane is in a safe operating condition, emphasizing (1) flight controls and instruments, (2) engines and propeller operation, (3) seats adjusted and locked, (4) belts and harnesses fastened, and (5) doors and windows secured. If there is any discrepancy you'll have to determine if the airplane is safe for flight or requires maintenance. Know the take-off performance — airspeeds and take-off distances (Chapter 17) — and be able to describe take-off emergency procedures (Chapter 13). You'll handle the take-off and departure clearances and will note the take-off time.

AIRPORT AND TRAFFIC PATTERN OPERATIONS

Radio Communication and ATC Light Signals. Be at ease using the radio, which includes knowing pertinent frequencies. Be able to use ATIS; the Airport Advisory Service (with Flight Service Stations); local approach and departure controls; and Unicom as necessary (Chapter 21). You may be required to recognize and comply with ATC light signals (see Fig. 21-16). Make sure you comply with traffic procedures and instructions.

Traffic Pattern Operations. You'll be expected to explain traffic pattern procedures at controlled and noncontrolled airports. You'll be expected to follow prescribed traffic patterns, using proper arrival and departure procedures. Watch your wind drift corrections, spacing with other aircraft and altitudes, airspeeds, and ground traffic. Better hold altitudes within ± 100 feet and airspeeds within ± 10 K of those required. Prompt corrections will be expected.

You are to maintain orientation with the runway in use, perform the prelanding cockpit check on the downwind leg, and have a final approach leg of at least 1/4 mile (Chapter 13).

Airport and Runway Marking and Lighting. Re-

view Chapters 25 and 26 of SPFM and SPSG for markings and lighting aids.

TAKE-OFFS AND CLIMBS

Normal Take-off and Climb. Be able to describe the elements of a normal take-off and climb, including airspeeds, configurations, and emergency procedures. The examiner will watch for safe operations in normally anticipated conditions. Align the airplane on the runway centerline and open the throttle *smoothly* to max power — don't ram it open. Check the engine instruments as the run commences and watch your directional control. Rotate at the POH recommended speed and establish the pitch attitude for $V_Y \pm 5$ knots during the climb. Retract the flaps (and gear, if applicable) at a safe point and altitude. (Keep the landing gear extended until you can no longer land on the runway.) *Use* the take-off power until at a safe altitude and don't forget to maintain a straight track on the climb-out (Chapter 13).

Crosswind Take-off and Climb. Know and be able to explain the elements of a crosswind take-off and climb, including airspeeds, configurations, and emergency procedures. As in the case of normal take-offs, apply power smoothly after you are well lined up on the centerline. Use full aileron deflection (in the proper direction) and check the engine instruments as the take-off run starts. Stay on the centerline and adjust the aileron deflection pressure as the run progresses. Again, you'll rotate at the POH recommended speed and maintain $V_Y \pm 5$ knots. Get the gear and flaps up as applicable at a safe point and altitude during the climb. Maintain the take-off power to a safe maneuvering altitude and don't drift over into the next county during the straight portion of the climb-out. You'll be judged on power application, smoothness, and wind drift correction (make sure the airplane doesn't skip and drift during the take-off and climb — keep it on the centerline). (Review Chapter 13.)

Short-field Take-off and Climb. Know and be able to describe the procedure and the expected performance for the existing conditions. Review Chapter 17 and the POH for your airplane to be able to use the Take-off Performance Charts. Select the proper wing flap setting, line up with the centerline, and smoothly apply power. Keep your directional control. (Taking off *across* the runway won't cut it.) Set up the proper pitch attitude to get the best acceleration and rotate the airplane at the recommended airspeed. Accelerate to V_X and maintain it within +5 and -0 knots until at least 50 feet above the surface or until the "obstacle" is cleared; then assume V_Y. Don't suddenly pull up the flaps and settle back in, but retract them and the landing gear at a safe point and altitude, as noted in the earlier take-off procedures. Keep that full power on until the "obstacle" is cleared and check back occasionally during the straight part of the climb-out to see that you are tracking along the extended runway centerline. Airspeed control is a big factor; you should maintain $V_Y \pm 5$ knots (Chapter 17).

Soft-field Take-off and Climb. You should be able to describe the elements and possible emergency situations of the soft-field take-off and climb, noting that attempting to climb at airspeeds of less than V_X can be fraught with peril. Select the proper flap setting and keep rolling as you turn onto the take-off surface, but don't make a full-power, hairy, tire-ruining turn onto the runway. Set the pitch attitude to get the weight off the wheels as soon as possible and — here's where problems might occur at that slow speed and blocked forward view — maintain directional control. If obstructions are a problem, maintain V_X +5 and -0 until you've cleared them. Lift off at the lowest possible airspeed and use ground effect to help acceleration. The same rules apply concerning when to retract flaps (and gear) and tracking straight after take-off (Chapter 17).

CROSS-COUNTRY FLYING

Piloting and Dead Reckoning. You'll give the examiner the straight information on piloting and dead reckoning techniques and procedures. You'll demonstrate that you are able to follow the preplanned course solely by reference to landmarks and identify these landmarks by relating the surface features to chart symbols.

You also must be able to navigate by means of precomputed headings, ground speed, and elapsed time and *combine* pilotage and dead reckoning with a verification of the airplane's position within 3 nautical miles at all times. You're expected to hit enroute checkpoints within 5 minutes of the initial or revised ETA and make your destination within 10 minutes of the ETA. Keep up with the remaining fuel at all times. Make corrections for differences between preflight ground speed and heading calculations and those determined enroute (and record them). Keep your altitude within ± 200 feet. You'd better use the appropriate power setting for the desired airspeed and maintain the desired heading within $\pm 10°$. Use those climb, cruise, and descent checklists. Don't get lost (Chapters 23 and 25).

Radio Navigation. Be able to explain radio navigation equipment, procedures, and limitations. You'll likely be required to select, tune, and identify the desired radio facility and locate the airplane's position relative to that facility. Better practice up on using VOR and NDB facilities and be able to intercept or track a given radial or bearing. Know how to locate the airplane's position using cross bearings (see Figure 25-5). Recognize station passage and/or be able to describe it. Check with your flight instructor to find out the best method of recognizing signal loss and how best to regain the signal, as applied to the equipment you're using. While you're doing the radio navigation, stay within ± 200 feet of the altitude chosen and keep the desired airspeed within ± 5 knots. Read Chapters 21 and 25 again.

Diversion to Alternate. The examiner will want to see how you can cope with having to change your plans during the flight. You'll be expected to recognize the conditions requiring a diversion (such as unexpected headwinds, lowering ceilings and visibilities, or other factors). At the examiner's prompting you'll select an alternate and route and proceed to it promptly. Make a reasonable estimate of heading, ground speed, arrival time, and fuel required to get there. Use pilotage, dead reckoning, or radio navigation aids to get there and keep the altitude to ± 200 feet and airspeed to ± 5 knots during the sashay off the preplanned course (Chapter 25).

Lost Procedures. Make sure that you know and can explain lost procedures, including the following items:

1. Maintaining the original or appropriate heading, identifying landmarks, and climbing if necessary. (See Chapter 25, Problems and Emergencies.)
2. Rechecking the calculations. ("Ah, Igor, it's really 110 knots ground speed—not 1100!")
3. Proceeding to and identifying the nearest concentration of prominent landmarks. ("Is that the Atlantic or the Pacific Ocean over there?")
4. Using available radio navigation aids for contacting an appropriate facility for assistance. ("Jonesville Radio, I'd like a *practice* VHF/DF steer.")
5. Planning a precautionary landing if deteriorating visibility and/or fuel exhaustion is imminent. Use your skills at dragging the area and short- and soft-field landings. (One pilot inadvertently made a precautionary landing in the middle of a nudist colony in 1975 and has not yet gotten over it.)

You'll be expected to select the best course of action when given a lost situation. (See Chapter 17, Dragging the Area, and take another good look at Chapter 25.)

EMERGENCY FLYING BY REFERENCE TO INSTRUMENTS

Straight and Level Flight. Know *why* you are looking at the various instruments in your scan and how you control the airplane when flying by reference to instruments. (It's exactly the same as when using outside references.) Your control application should be smooth, timely, and coordinated; if the ball in the T/C or T/S leaves the cockpit, you may be in a little trouble. You are to maintain straight and level flight for at least 3 minutes, keeping the heading within $\pm 15°$, the assigned altitude within ± 100 feet, and the desired airspeed within ± 10 knots. Use all flight instruments available (Chapter 15).

Straight Constant Airspeed Climbs. You should be able to explain what you are doing and what makes the airplane climb. Establish the climb pitch attitude and power setting on an assigned heading. Fly smoothly and with coordination. The heading must be maintained within $\pm 15°$ (watch that "torque" effect) and airspeed within ±10 knots, and you are to level off within ±200 feet of the desired altitude (Chapter 15).

Constant Airspeed Descents. Again, know what you're doing and be able to talk about it. Set up the airspeed and power (see Chapter 15 for some suggestions) for about a 500 fpm descent and be smooth and coordinated. Heading should be kept within ±15° and airspeed limits within ±10 knots; be sure to level off within 200 feet of the desired altitude.

Turns to Headings. Know the background of what you propose to do. Use standard rate turns and don't make the examiner sick with your control roughness. Keep the altitude within ±200 feet and airspeed ±10 knots, don't exceed 25° bank altitude at any time, and roll out within ±20° of the desired heading (Chapter 15).

Critical Flight Attitudes. You'll demonstrate here that you have the background to cope with the situation when it's necessary to recover from a nonstandard flight situation. You're to recognize the critical attitudes promptly; interpret the instruments; and recover by prompt, smooth, coordinated controls, applied in the proper sequence. If you bend something, go too fast, spin the airplane, and/or make the examiner's voice rise a couple of octaves as he says, "I've got it," you aren't doing a satisfactory job of flying (Chapter 15).

Radio and Radar Navigation. Know your radio navigation and be aware of the radar services available. Check on your local sectional chart legend (control tower frequencies) to see what facilities have ASR (Airport Surveillance Radar) or TRSA (called STAGE III SVC in the A/FD). You'll be expected to fly by reference to instruments while tuning and identifying the appropriate facility, following verbal or radio navigation guidance, and determining the minimum safe altitude. Maintain altitude within ±200 feet and heading within ±15° (Chapters 21 and 25).

FLIGHT AT CRITICALLY SLOW AIRSPEEDS

Full Stalls — Power Off. These are basically the *approach to landing stalls* covered back in Chapter 12, but you might want to review Chapter 14 also. You'll be expected to explain the aerodynamics of the full stall and know the flight situations that result in power-off full stalls, including the proper recovery procedures and hazards of stalling during slips and skids. Recover above 1500 feet AGL. Set up the normal approach or landing configuration and airspeed with the throttle closed or at a reduced power setting. Establish a straight glide or a gliding turn of 30° (±10°) in coordinated flight. Maintain good coordination, establish a landing pitch attitude, and keep it there to induce a full stall. You will be expected to recognize the indications of a full stall and promptly recover by decreasing the angle of attack, leveling the wings, and advancing the power to the maximum allowable. Retract the flaps and landing gear (if retractable) and establish straight and level flight or a climb. Don't get a secondary

stall, build up excessive airspeed, lose excessive altitude, spin, or get below 1500 AGL at any time.

Full Stalls — Power On. The examiner will want to know that you understand the principles of these stalls and what can contribute to aggravating them (slips and skids), and he'll look at your recovery effectiveness. Again, don't get below 1500 AGL at any time during the demonstration. Basically these stalls are the *take-off and departure stalls* covered in Chapter 12. You'll set the airplane up in the take-off or normal climb configuration and establish the take-off or climb airspeed before applying take-off or climb power. (You may have to use reduced power to avoid excessive pitch-up during the entry but then apply more power as things progress.) You'll smoothly set up and maintain a pitch attitude that will induce a full stall in both wings-level and 20° (±10°) banks. "Torque" may tend to skid and turn the airplane to the left, and watch your coordination during the entry. You'll increase elevator (stabilator) back pressure smoothly until the stall occurs, as indicated by (1) a sudden loss of control effectiveness (you run out of pitch control) or (2) uncontrollable pitching.

The required recovery will be to reduce the angle of attack promptly and positively, level the wings, and regain normal flight attitude with coordinated use of flight and power controls. (*Always* use full power in recovering from stalls unless the examiner asks for a power-off recovery as a demonstration of your knowledge that reducing the angle of attack is the main action in stall recovery; remember that the use of power reduces the altitude loss.) After recovery, clean up the airplane and establish straight and level flight or climb. Again, if the examiner has to take over to keep you from spinning or having other problems, such as going below 1500 feet AGL, or if you get a secondary stall during recovery, it will be disqualifying (Chapters 12 and 14).

Imminent Stalls — Power On or Power Off. Tell and show the examiner that you are aware of the situation in imminent stalls. The same ideas apply here as for the full stalls (power on and power off) concerning entries, configurations, banked or wings-level attitude, minimum altitude, and possible problems. The difference here is that you recover at the *first indication* of buffeting or decay of control effectiveness by increasing power and reducing the angle of attack to resume the initial flight maneuver (Chapters 12 and 14).

Maneuvering at Minimum Controllable Airspeed (Slow Flight). Know the background of this requirement and *why* it is an important part of flight training. Stay above 1500 feet AGL. You'll establish and maintain an airspeed at which any further increase in angle of attack resulting from an increase in load factor or reduction in power would result in an immediate stall while

1. in coordinated straight and turning flight in various configurations and bank angles and
2. in coordinated departure climbs and landing approach descents in various configurations.

You'll maintain the desired altitude within ±100 feet when a constant altitude is specified, and level off from climbs and descents within ±100 feet. Your heading during straight flight must be maintained within ±10° of that designated. Your bank angle must be held to within ±10° of that specified in coordinated flight. Keep that airspeed within +5 and -0 knots during the process and if buffet occurs recover immediately (Chapter 12).

TURN MANEUVERS

Constant Altitude Turns. Review this maneuver in Chapter 10. (It's called "Steep Turns" there.) Be able to explain the requirements involved, including increased load factors, power addition, and other elements. Stay above 1500 feet AGL. You'll establish airspeed below the airplane's maneuvering speed (V_A) and set up a bank angle of 40° to 50°, maintaining coordinated flight. Divide your attention between airplane control and orientation and roll out within ±20° of the desired heading. Keep the altitude within ±200 feet.

FLIGHT MANEUVERING BY REFERENCE TO GROUND OBJECTS

Rectangular Course. Know the principles of wind drift correction in straight and turning flight and the tie-in between the rectangular course and airport traffic patterns. You'll have to pick the field or fields, set up the maneuver, and enter at the proper distance from the boundary at 600-1000 feet AGL. (No, you aren't allowed to fly up and down between those altitudes; keep the altitude within ±100 feet of that selected.) Keep your flight path parallel to the sides and be prepared to fly it with both left or right turns. You'll be expected to be able to divide your attention between airplane control and the ground track. Check your coordination.

Avoid excessive maneuvering (keep the bank angle to a maximum of 45° and airspeed to ±10 knots) and stay above the minimum legal altitude for local obstructions. Watch for other airplanes (Chapter 10).

S-Turns across a Road. Be able to expound on the principles of this maneuver. Select a long, straight reference perpendicular to the wind and fly it at a selected altitude of 600-1000 feet AGL. Keep the turns of constant radius (see Fig. 10-7), divide your attention between airplane control and the ground, and keep the maneuver coordinated. Reverse the turns directly over the reference line and keep the altitude within ±100 feet of that selected. The airspeed should stay within ±10 knots of that desired; don't exceed a bank of 45°. Keep it legal as far as obstructions are concerned and don't have a mid-air.

Turns about a Point. Pick the point promptly and enter, checking your heading by the heading indicator or a geographic reference. While the practical test guide doesn't require a specific number of turns,

the examiner could ask for such, so you'd better get in the habit of knowing where you are during practice sessions. As Chapter 16 notes, be prepared to do the turns in either direction. The altitude, airspeed, and max bank limitations are the same as for the S-turns just covered (Chapter 16).

Constant Radius Descending Turns. You should be able to maintain constant radius turns while descending. (This is particularly important when making a simulated— or real— high altitude emergency because you need to stay over that good field that you picked.) You should keep the airspeed within ±15 knots while doing these maneuvers (Spirals, Chapter 16).

NIGHT FLIGHT OPERATIONS

Preparation and Equipment. You may be asked how you would go about preparing for a local or cross-country night flight. You should be able to answer questions on airport lighting and the airplane lights and their operation. Be sure to know what equipment you'd need— a flashlight or other backup would be essential. Weather factors are particularly pertinent to night flight (such as the relationship of temperature and dew point and the possibility of ground fog forming during night flights). You should be aware of the possible need for reference to the flight instruments (1) over unlighted areas and (2) if actual instrument conditions are unexpectedly encountered. Understand the factors affecting night vision. If you don't meet night flying experience requirements this area won't be evaluated and your certificate will bear the limitation "Night Flying Prohibited" (Chapter 26).

Pilot Operation. If the demonstration of night flight is impracticable your competency may be determined by oral testing. If night navigation is required by the examiner you will follow procedures similar to those described earlier under "Cross-Country Flying." Be aware of night flying procedures, including safety precautions and emergency action. *Use a checklist.* You should be sharp at explaining (and demonstrating, if required) the starting, taxiing, and pretake-off check. You'll use good operating practices for night take-off, climb, approach, and landing. Don't forget your flashlight (Chapter 26).

EMERGENCY OPERATIONS

Emergency Approach and Landing (Simulated). Know the best glide speed and configuration and select a suitable landing area within gliding distance. Use preplanning and follow a flight pattern to the selected landing area, considering altitude, wind, terrain obstructions, and other factors. Refer to Chapter 16, Spirals, and to Chapter 18. *Use the checklist* and also try to determine the reason for the malfunction. And above all, *maintain control* of the airplane while you're scrambling around looking for the cause.

Systems and Equipment Malfunctions. Be able to explain causes, indications, and pilot actions for various systems and equipment malfunctions and take appropriate action for simulated emergencies, such as

1. Partial power loss (Chapter 25)
2. Rough-running engine (Chapter 25)
3. Carburetor or induction icing (Chapters 4, 11, 23, and 25)
4. Fuel starvation (Chapters 11, 18, 23, and 25)
5. Engine compartment fire (Chapters 5 and 25)
6. Electrical system malfunction (Chapters 3 and 25)
7. Gear of flap malfunction (Chapter 3, Electrical System, and Chapter 13, Flaps)
8. Door opening in flight (Chapter 7)
9. Trim inoperative (Read Chapter 8 for the purposes of trim.)

Look up in the POH each item listed here and go over the proper procedures for your airplane with your instructor.

APPROACHES AND LANDINGS

Normal Approach and Landing. Know what elements affect a normal approach and landing, including airspeed and configuration. Keep a good straight track on final at the proper approach and landing configuration and power, maintaining the recommended airspeed within ±5 knots. You'll be expected to make smooth, timely, and correct control application during the final approach and during the transition to landing. You should touch down smoothly on the main gear (tricycle gear) or three point (tailwheel landing gear) at the approximate stalling speed, beyond and within 500 feet of a specified spot, with no appreciable drift and the longitudinal axis aligned on the runway centerline. Maintain directional control during the roll-out. It's possible that you could be asked to make full-flap, half-flap, or no-flap landings (Chapter 13).

Forward Slips to Landing. You should have a good grasp of the principles involved and be aware of technique, limitations, and effect on the airspeed indicator. Be aware of any manufacturer's limitations on slips with flaps. You are to demonstrate a forward slip at a point from which a landing can be made in a desired area, using the recommended configuration. Keep the airplane's track straight with the runway and maintain an airspeed that results in little or no floating during the landing. The requirements for touchdown point and directional control are the same as for the normal landing just cited (Chapter 13).

Go-Around from a Balked Landing. You may have to demonstrate the procedure for go-around on an approach (balked landing). You'll be expected to make a timely decision, fly the recommended airspeeds, and cope with any undesirable pitch and yaw tendency (keep up with the trim requirements). Apply take-off power, attain the proper pitch attitude (airspeed), and retract the flaps as recommended at a safe altitude. If the airplane has retractable gear,

pull it up after a rate of climb has been established and you can't land on the remaining runway. Trim the airplane and climb at $V_Y \pm 5$ knots and track a good traffic pattern for the next landing (Chapter 13).

Crosswind Approach and Landing. You'll show adequate knowledge by explaining crosswind approach and landing techniques, limitations, and recognition of excessive crosswind. You'll be expected to establish the approach and landing configuration and power and to maintain a straight track on final. Keep the airspeed to within ±5 knots and make smooth, timely, and correct control application through the approach to landing attitude. The airplane is to touch down smoothly (it says here) on the upwind main gear (tricycle gear), or upwind main gear and tailwheel at approximately the stalling speed, beyond and within 500 feet of a specified point, with no appreciable drift and the longitudinal axis aligned on the runway centerline. Maintain directional control after touchdown, increasing aileron deflection into the wind as necessary. If a crosswind doesn't exist you'll be questioned orally about the subject (Chapter 13).

Short-field Approach and Landing. You'll be expected to explain short-field approach and landing procedures, including airspeeds, configurations, and performance data. You'll evaluate obstructions, landing surface, and wind condition and select the touchdown and go-around points. You are to keep the airspeed within ±5 knots of that recommended and maintain precise control of the descent rate along the extended runway centerline. There should be little or no float, and you should touch down beyond and within 200 feet of a specified point, lined up with the runway centerline with no appreciable drift. Keep the airplane directionally straight. Brake as necessary to stop in the shortest distance consistent with safety (no squared-off tires, please). Holding the control wheel or stick full back while braking and upping the flaps (*not the gear*) will give most efficient braking (Chapter 17).

Soft-field Approach and Landing. Know airspeeds, configurations, and operations on various surfaces. Check out the obstructions, landing surface, and wind condition and establish the recommended soft-field approach and landing configuration and airspeed (within ±5 knots of that recommended). Keep it lined up on final; touch down with a minimum descent rate and ground speed with no appreciable drift and the airplane lined up with the runway centerline. Maintain directional control after touchdown and maintain sufficient speed to taxi on a soft surface (Chapter 17).

CHECKITIS

Checkitis is a mysterious disease that strikes just before a flight test. The victims are usually of at least average intelligence, but as soon as this malady hits, they are lucky to remember their own names. It is characterized by shaking knees, a knotted stomach, sweating, and loss of memory. You may not get checkitis — if this is the case, you're one of the chosen few.

The examiner probably has had it himself and will make allowances. The good thing about checkitis is that as soon as you get busy in the flight test, its symptoms lessen or fade completely. The best insurance against it is to know what you're doing beforehand. If you don't do too well on the oral, it may hurt the entire flight because of added nervousness. Learn all you can about the plane and flying in general and then don't worry about checkitis.

Fig. 28-2. As is shown here, the check pilot is just an ordinary human being like yourself. He has no ax to grind.

THE AIRPLANE NUMBERS

AIRPLANE PAPERS AND LOGBOOKS

1. Logbooks

    Date of last annual inspection: _____ .

    Date of last 100-hour inspection: _____ .

    Next 100-hour inspection due (tachometer reading): _____ hours.

2. Airworthiness Certificate — Standard:

    Issued to (number of airplane) _____ .

3. Certificate of Registration:

    Issued to (name) _____ on (date) _____ .

4. Operational Limitations:

    Up-to-date? _____ .

5. Aircraft Radio Station License:

    Issued for _____ , _____ , _____ . (List transmitting equipment.)

6. Weight and Balance Form:

    Is it up-to-date, or has a Major Repair and Alteration Form superseded it?)

    Latest information on equipment list and empty weight (date): _____ .

AIRPLANE STATISTICS

1. Basic Empty Weight: _____ pounds.

2. Empty Weight Center of Gravity: _____ inches aft of datum; or Empty Weight Moment: _____ pound inches.

3. Maximum Certificated (Gross) Weight — Normal category: _____ pounds; Utility category: _____ pounds. (Either or both may apply.)

4. Fuel and Oil:

    Fuel — Total capacity: _____ gallons; usable: _____ gallons. (Fuel weighs 6 pounds per gallon.)

    Oil — Total capacity: _____ quarts; minimum for flight: _____ quarts. (Oil weighs 7 1/2 pounds per gallon.)

    Brand name and viscosity — Winter: _____ ; Summer: _____ .

5. Baggage — Maximum weight: _____ pounds.

PERFORMANCE

(All figures for maximum certificated weight)

1. Range: At __65__ % power, _____ NM, _____ gallons per hour.

    Max range: At _____ % power, _____ K, _____ NM.

2. Rate of Climb at sea level: _____ feet per minute.

    Best rate-of-climb speed: _____ K at sea level.

    Max angle-of-climb speed: _____ K at sea level, _____ ° flaps.

3. Take-off Distance at sea level (run): _____ feet. Total distance over 50-foot obstacle: _____ feet.

4. Landing Roll: _____ feet. Total distance over 50-foot obstacle: _____ feet (sea level).

5. Service Ceiling: _____ feet. (The service ceiling is the altitude at which the airplane's maximum rate of climb is 100 feet per minute.)

MANEUVERS

1. Slow Flight: _____ K (clean). $20°$ to $30°$ banked turns, climbs and glides, cruise and landing configurations.

2. Take-off and Departure Stalls: Slow to _____ K, then apply climb power (a) straight ahead and (b) $15°$-$20°$ banked turns.

3. Approach to Landing Stalls: Start at _____ K and full flaps. Slow to stall. Gliding turns ($20°$ to $30°$ banks) and straight ahead (trim set).

4. Accelerated Stalls:

    (a) Cruise configuration: No flaps, $45°$ bank, _____ rpm, slow to _____ K (bottom of green arc plus 10 K).

CLEAR THE AREA BEFORE DOING STALLS.

5. Emergency Flying by Reference to Instruments:

    Climbs: Full power and best rate of climb speed: _____ K.

    Descents: At _____ K and _____ rpm (to give approximately 500 fpm descent).

6. Turns Around a Point and Other Ground Reference Maneuvers: Note heading of entry. Altitude for maneuver: _____ feet MSL, or _____ feet above the local surface.

7. Short-field Take-off: Flap setting: _____ $°$; climb speed to clear obstacle: _____ K. (This speed is the max angle-of-climb speed.)

8. Short-field Landing: Flap setting (usually full flaps): _____ $°$; approach speed: _____ K.

9. Soft- or Rough-field Take-off: Flap setting: _____ $°$.

10. Soft-field Landings: Flap setting: _____ $°$; approach speed: _____ K.

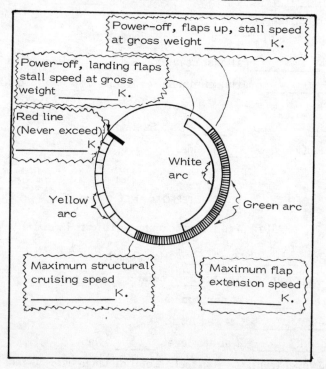

Fig. 28-3. Important airspeeds.

DEPARTMENT OF TRANSPORTATION — FEDERAL AVIATION ADMINISTRATION
AIRMAN WRITTEN TEST APPLICATION

DATE OF TEST	TITLE OF TEST	TEST NO.
MONTH DAY YEAR 07 12 79	*PRIVATE PILOT- AIRPLANE*	

PLEASE PRINT ONE LETTER IN EACH SPACE—LEAVE A BLANK SPACE AFTER EACH NAME

NAME (LAST, FIRST, MIDDLE)	DATE OF BIRTH
DOE JOHN ROCHESTER	MONTH 09 DAY 27 YEAR 29

MAILING ADDRESS   NO. AND STREET, APT. #, P.O. BOX, OR RURAL ROUTE
1427 SIXTH AVENUE

CITY, TOWN OR POST OFFICE AND STATE	ZIP CODE	DESCRIPTION			
SEWANEE TENNESSEE	37375	HEIGHT 72"	WEIGHT 190	HAIR BROWN	EYES BLUE

BIRTHPLACE (City and State, or foreign country) SEWANEE TENNESSEE	CITIZENSHIP U.S.A.	SOCIAL SECURITY NO. 123456789	IF A SOCIAL SECURITY NUMBER HAS NEVER BEEN ISSUED CHECK THIS BLOCK → ☐

Is this a retest? ☒ No ☐ Yes, date of last test ____   Have you taken or are you taking an FAA approved course for this test? ☒ No ☐ Yes *(If "yes" give details below)*

Graduation date: ____   NAME OF SCHOOL ____   CITY AND STATE ____

CERTIFICATION: I CERTIFY that all of the statements made in this application are true, complete, and correct to the best of my knowledge and belief and are made in good faith. Signature *John R. Doe*

— DO NOT WRITE IN THIS BLOCK — FOR USE OF FAA OFFICE ONLY —

Applicant's identity established by:

CARD A				CARD B		FIELD OFFICE DESIGNATION
CATEGORY	TEST NUMBER	TAKE NO.	SECTIONS 1 2 3 4 5 6 7	EXPIRATION MONTH DAY YEAR	CERTIFICATED SCHOOL NUMBER	MECH EXP DATE BY SECTION 1 2 3	ID

SIGNATURE of FAA Representative

INSTRUCTIONS FOR MARKING THE ANSWER SHEET. Completely darken only one circle for each question. DO NOT USE (X) OR (✓). Use black lead pencil furnished by examiner. To make corrections, open answer sheet so erasure marks will not show on page 2. Then erase incorrect response on page 4. On page 2 (copy) mark the incorrect response with a slash (/). Questions are arranged in VERTICAL sequence as indicated by the arrows.

1 ①②③④ 23 ①②③④ 45 ①②③④ 67 ①②③④ 89 ①②③④ 111 ①②③④ 133 ①②③④
2 ①②③④ 24 ①②③④ 46 ①②③④ 68 ①②③④ 90 ①②③④ 112 ①②③④ 134 ①②③④
3 ①②③④ 25 ①②③④ 47 ①②③④ 69 ①②③④ 91 ①②③④ 113 ①②③④ 135 ①②③④
4 ①②③④ 26 ①②③④ 48 ①②③④ 70 ①②③④ 92 ①②③④ 114 ①②③④ 136 ①②③④
5 ①②③④ 27 ①②③④ 49 ①②③④ 71 ①②③④ 93 ①②③④ 115 ①②③④ 137 ①②③④
6 ①②③④ 28 ①②③④ 50 ①②③④ 72 ①②③④ 94 ①②③④ 116 ①②③④ 138 ①②③④
7 ①②③④ 29 ①②③④ 51 ①②③④ 73 ①②③④ 95 ①②③④ 117 ①②③④ 139 ①②③④
8 ①②③④ 30 ①②③④ 52 ①②③④ 74 ①②③④ 96 ①②③④ 118 ①②③④ 140 ①②③④
9 ①②③④ 31 ①②③④ 53 ①②③④ 75 ①②③④ 97 ①②③④ 119 ①②③④ 141 ①②③④
10 ①②③④ 32 ①②③④ 54 ①②③④ 76 ①②③④ 98 ①②③④ 120 ①②③④ 142 ①②③④
11 ①②③④ 33 ①②③④ 55 ①②③④ 77 ①②③④ 99 ①②③④ 121 ①②③④ 143 ①②③④
12 ①②③④ 34 ①②③④ 56 ①②③④ 78 ①②③④ 100 ①②③④ 122 ①②③④ 144 ①②③④
13 ①②③④ 35 ①②③④ 57 ①②③④ 79 ①②③④ 101 ①②③④ 123 ①②③④ 145 ①②③④
14 ①②③④ 36 ①②③④ 58 ①②③④ 80 ①②③④ 102 ①②③④ 124 ①②③④ 146 ①②③④
15 ①②③④ 37 ①②③④ 59 ①②③④ 81 ①②③④ 103 ①②③④ 125 ①②③④ 147 ①②③④
16 ①②③④ 38 ①②③④ 60 ①②③④ 82 ①②③④ 104 ①②③④ 126 ①②③④ 148 ①②③④
17 ①②③④ 39 ①②③④ 61 ①②③④ 83 ①②③④ 105 ①②③④ 127 ①②③④ 149 ①②③④
18 ①②③④ 40 ①②③④ 62 ①②③④ 84 ①②③④ 106 ①②③④ 128 ①②③④ 150 ①②③④
19 ①②③④ 41 ①②③④ 63 (THIS IS A SAMPLE FORMAT OF AN FAA 129 ①②③④
20 ①②③④ 42 ①②③④ 64 (PRIVATE PILOT WRITTEN TEST ANSWER 130 ①②③④
     SHEET, WITH ALL QUESTIONS CREATED)
     SOLELY BY THE AUTHOR.
21 ①②③④ 43 ①②③④ 65 ①②③④ 87 ①②③④ 109 ①②③④ 131 ①②③④
22 ①②③④ 44 ①②③④ 66 ①②③④ 88 ①②③④ 110 ①②③④ 132 ①②③④

Tear here

TITLE	SELECTION NO.
PRIVATE PILOT - AIRPLANE	238246

NAME _____

NOTE: MARKING ON THIS SHEET IS PERMITTED.

On Answer Sheet For Item No.	Answer Question Number	On Answer Sheet For Item No.	Answer Question Number	On Answer Sheet For Item No.	Answer Question Number
1	201	21	414	41	597
2	214	22	420	42	602
3	220	23	425	43	620
4	226	24	433	44	626
5	229	25	440	45	634
6	236	26	456	46	641
7	241	27	462	47	663
8	253	28	470	48	665
9	258	29	478	49	676
10	262	30	481	50	690
11	274	31	484	51	704
12	285	32	498	52	714
13	288	33	501	53	735
14	309	34	506	54	755
15	318	35	515	55	765
16	366	36	522	56	774
17	376	37	528	57	777
18	382	38	534	58	781
19	392	39	552	59	789
20	403	40	560	60	793

Sample

Tear here

Appendix A

(From *Airman's Information Manual*)

WAKE TURBULENCE

GENERAL

Every airplane generates a wake while in flight. Initially, when pilots encountered this wake in flight, the disturbance was attributed to "prop wash." It is known, however, that this disturbance is caused by a pair of counter rotating vortices trailing from the wing tips. The vortices from large aircraft pose problems to encountering aircraft. For instance, the wake of these aircraft can impose rolling moments exceeding the roll control capability of some aircraft. Further, turbulence generated within the vortices can damage aircraft components and equipment if encountered at close range. The pilot must learn to envision the location of the vortex wake generated by large aircraft and adjust his flight path accordingly.

During ground operations, jet engine blast (thrust stream turbulence) can cause damage and upsets if encountered at close range. Exhaust velocity versus distance studies at various thrust levels have shown a need for light aircraft to maintain an adequate separation during ground operations. Below are examples of the distance requirements to avoid exhaust velocities of greater than 25 mph:

25 MPH VELOCITY	B-727	DC-8	DC-10
Takeoff Thrust	550 Ft.	700 Ft.	2100 Ft.
Breakaway Thrust	200 Ft.	400 Ft.	850 Ft.
Idle Thrust	150 Ft.	35 Ft.	350 Ft.

Engine exhaust velocities generated by large jet aircraft during initial takeoff roll and the drifting of the turbulence in relation to the crosswind component dictate the desireability of lighter aircraft awaiting takeoff to hold well back of the runway edge of taxiway hold line; also, the desirability of aligning the aircraft to face the possible jet engine blast movement. Additionally, in the course of running up engines and taxiing on the ground, pilots of large aircraft in particular should consider the effects of their jet blasts on other aircraft.

The FAA has established new standards for the location of taxiway hold lines at airports served by air carriers as follows:

Taxiway holding lines will be established at 100 feet from the edge of the runway, except at locations where "heavy jets" will be operating, the taxiway holding line markings will be established at 150 feet. (The "heavy" category can include some B-707 and DC-8 type aircraft.)

VORTEX GENERATION

Lift is generated by the creation of a pressure differential over the wing surface. The lowest pressure occurs over the upper wing surface and the highest pressure under the wing. This pressure differential triggers the roll up of the airflow aft of the wing resulting in swirling air masses trailing downstream of the wing tips. After the roll up is completed, the wake consists of two counter rotating cylindrical vortices.

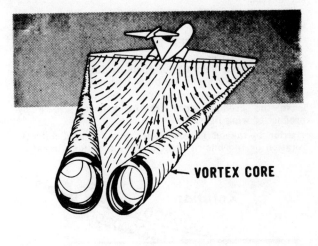

Figure 4–4

VORTEX STRENGTH

1. The strength of the vortex is governed by the weight, speed, and shape of the wing of the generating aircraft. The vortex characteristics of any given aircraft can also be changed by extension of flaps or other wing configuring devices as well as by change in speed. However, as the basic factor is weight, the vortex strength increases proportionately. During a recent test, peak vortex tangential velocities were recorded at 224 feet per second, or about 133 knots. The greatest vortex strength occurs when the generating aircraft is HEAVY—CLEAN—SLOW.

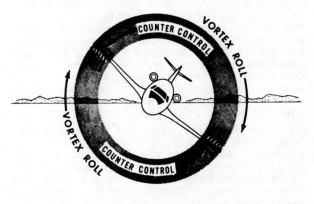

Figure 4–5

2. **Induced Roll.** In rare instances a wake encounter could cause in flight structural damage of catastrophic proportions. However, the usual hazard is associated with induced rolling moments which can exceed the rolling capability of the encountering aircraft. In flight experiments, aircraft have been intentionally flown directly up trailing vortex cores of large aircraft. It was shown that the capability of an aircraft to counteract the roll imposed by the wake vortex primar-

ily depends on the wing span and counter control responsiveness of the encountering aircraft.

Counter control is usually effective and induced roll minimal in cases where the wing span and ailerons of the encountering aircraft extend beyond the rotational flow field of the vortex. It is more difficult for aircraft with short wing span (relative to the generating aircraft) to counter the imposed roll induced by vortex flow. Pilots of short span aircraft, even of the high performance type, must be especially alert to vortex encounters.

The wake of large aircraft requires the respect of all pilots.

VORTEX BEHAVIOR

Trailing vortices have certain behavioral characteristics which can help a pilot visualize the wake location and thereby take avoidance precautions.

1. Vortices are generated from the moment aircraft leave the ground, since trailing vortices are a byproduct of wing lift.

Prior to takeoff or touchdown pilots should note the rotation or touchdown point of the preceding aircraft.

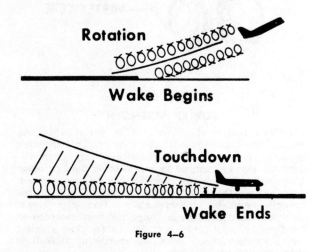

Figure 4—6

2. The vortex circulation is outward, upward and around the wing tips when viewed from either ahead or behind the aircraft. Tests with large aircraft have shown that the vortex flow field, in a plane cutting thru the wake at any point downstream, covers an area about 2 wing spans in width and one wing span in depth. The vortices remain so spaced (about a wing span apart) even drifting with the wind, at altitudes greater than a wing span from the ground. In view of this, if persistent vortex turbulence is encountered, a slight change of altitude and lateral position (preferably upwind) will provide a flight path clear of the turbulence.

3. Flight tests have shown that the vortices from large aircraft sink at a rate of about 400 to 500 feet per minute. They tend to level off at a distance about 900 feet below the flight path of the generating aircraft. Vortex strength diminishes with time and distance behind the generating aircraft. Atmospheric turbulence hastens breakup.

Pilots should fly at or above the large aircraft's flight path, altering course as necessary to avoid the area behind and below the generating aircraft.

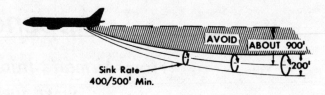

Figure 4—7

4. When the vortices of large aircraft sink close to the ground (within about 200 feet), they tend to move laterally over the ground at a speed of about 5 knots.

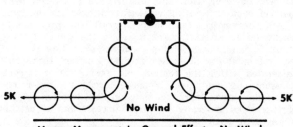

Figure 4—8

A crosswind will decrease the lateral movement of the upwind vortex and increase the movement of the downwind vortex. Thus a light wind of 3 to 7 knots could result in the upwind vortex remaining in the touchdown zone for a period of time and hasten the drift of the downwind vortex toward another runway. Similarly, a tailwind condition can move the vortices of the preceding aircraft forward into the touchdown zone.

THE LIGHT QUARTERING TAILWIND REQUIRES MAXIMUM CAUTION.

Pilots should be alert to large aircraft upwind from their approach and takeoff flight paths.

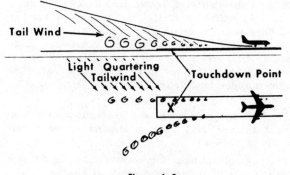

Figure 4—9

OPERATIONS PROBLEM AREAS

1. A wake encounter is not necessarily hazardous. It can be one or more jolts with varying severity depending upon the direction of the encounter, distance from the generating aircraft, and point of vortex encounter. The probability of induced roll increases when the encountering aircraft's heading is generally aligned with the vortex trail or flight path of the generating aircraft.

AVOID THE AREA BELOW AND BEHIND THE GENERATING AIRCRAFT, ESPECIALLY AT LOW ALTITUDE WHERE EVEN A MOMENTARY WAKE ENCOUNTER COULD BE HAZARDOUS.

Pilots should be particularly alert in calm wind conditions and situations where the vortices could:

a. Remain in the touchdown area.

b. Drift from aircraft operating on a nearby runway.

c. Sink into takeoff or landing path from a crossing runway.

d. Sink into the traffic patterns from other airport operations.

e. Sink into the flight path of VFR flights operating at the hemispheric altitude 500 feet below.

2. Pilots of all aircraft should visualize the location of the vortex trail behind large aircraft and use proper vortex avoidance procedures to achieve safe operation. It is equally important that pilots of large aircraft plan or adjust their flight paths to minimize vortex exposure to other aircraft.

VORTEX AVOIDANCE PROCEDURES

1. *GENERAL.* Under certain conditions, airport traffic controllers apply procedures for separating aircraft from heavy jet aircraft. The controllers will also provide VFR aircraft, with whom they are in communication and which in the tower's opinion may be adversely affected by wake turbulence from a large aircraft, the position, altitude and direction of flight of the large aircraft followed by the phrase "CAUTION—WAKE TURBULENCE." WHETHER OR NOT A WARNING HAS BEEN GIVEN, HOWEVER, THE PILOT IS EXPECTED TO ADJUST HIS OPERATIONS AND FLIGHT PATH AS NECESSARY TO PRECLUDE SERIOUS WAKE ENCOUNTERS.

2. The following vortex avoidance procedures are recommended for the various situations:

a. Landing behind a large aircraft—same runway: Stay at or above the large aircraft's final approach flight path—note his touchdown point—land beyond it.

b. Landing behind a large aircraft—when parallel runway is closer than 2,500 feet: Consider possible drift to your runway. Stay at or above the large aircraft's final approach flight path—note his touchdown point.

c. Landing behind a large aircraft—crossing runway: Cross above the large aircraft's flight path.

d. Landing behind a departing large aircraft—same runway: Note large aircraft's rotation point—land well prior to rotation point.

e. Landing behind a departing large aircraft—crossing runway: Note large aircraft's rotation point—if past the intersection—continue the approach—land prior to the intersection. If large aircraft rotates prior to the intersection, avoid flight below the large aircraft's flight path. Abandon the approach unless a landing is assured well before reaching the intersection.

f. Departing behind a large aircraft: Note large aircraft's rotation point—rotate prior to large aircraft's rotation point—continue climb above and stay upwind of the large aircraft's climb path until turning clear of his wake. Avoid subsequent headings which will cross below and behind a large aircraft. Be alert for any critical takeoff situation which could lead to a vortex encounter.

g. Intersection takeoffs—same runway: Be alert to adjacent large aircraft operations particularly upwind of your runway. If intersection takeoff clearance is received, avoid subsequent heading which will cross below a large aircraft's path.

h. Departing or landing after a large aircraft executing a low missed approach or touch-and-go landing: Because vortices settle and move laterally near the ground, the vortex hazard may exist along the runway and in your flight path after a large aircraft has executed a low missed approach or a touch-and-go landing, particularly in light quartering wind conditions. You should assure that an interval of at least 2 minutes has elapsed before your takeoff or landing.

i. Enroute VFR—(thousand-foot altitude plus 500 feet). Avoid flight below and behind a large aircraft's path. If a large aircraft is observed above on the same track (meeting or overtaking) adjust your position laterally, preferably upwind.

HELICOPTERS

A hovering helicopter generates a downwash from its main rotor(s) similar to the prop blast of a conventional aircraft. However, in forward flight, this energy is transformed into a pair of trailing vortices similar to wing-tip vortices of fixed wing aircraft. Pilots of small aircraft should avoid the vortices as well as the downwash.

PILOT RESPONSIBILITY

1. Government and industry groups are making concerted efforts to minimize or eliminate the hazards of trailing vortices. However, the flight disciplines necessary to assure vortex avoidance during VFR operations must be exercised by the pilot. Vortex visualization and avoidance procedures should be exercised by the pilot using the same degree of concern as in collision avoidance.

Wake turbulence may be encountered by aircraft in flight as well as when operating on the airport movement area. (See wake turbulence definition under glossary of aeronautical terms).

2. Pilots are reminded that in operations conducted behind all aircraft, acceptance from ATC of:

a. Traffic information, or

b. Instructions to follow an aircraft, or

c. The acceptance of a visual approach clearance, is an acknowledgment that the pilot will ensure safe takeoff and landing intervals and accepts the responsibility of providing his own wake turbulence separation.

AIR TRAFFIC WAKE TURBULENCE SEPARATIONS

Air traffic controllers are required to apply specific separation intervals for aircraft operating behind a heavy jet because of the possible effects of wake turbulence.

1. The following separation is applied to aircraft operating directly behind a heavy jet at the same altitude or directly behind and less than 1,000 feet below:

a. Heavy jet behind another heavy jet—4 miles.

b. Small/Large aircraft behind a heavy jet—5 miles.

In addition, controllers provide a 6-mile separation for small aircraft landing behind a heavy jet and a 4-mile separation for small aircraft landing behind a large aircraft. This extra mile of separation is required at the time the preceding aircraft is over the landing threshold. (See Heavy, Large, Small definitions in the Pilot/Controller Glossary under *Aircraft Classes.*)

2. Aircraft departing behind heavy jets are provided two minutes or the appropriate 4 or 5 mile radar separation. Controllers may disregard the separation if the pilot of a departing aircraft initiates a request to deviate from the separation requirement and indicates acceptance of responsibility for maneuvering his aircraft so as to avoid the possible wake turbulence hazard. However, occasions will arise when the controller must still hold the aircraft in order to provide separation required for other than wake turbulence purposes.

Appendix B

(From Airport/Facility Directory)

DIRECTORY LEGEND
SAMPLE

① ③ ④ ⑤ ⑥ ⑦

CITY NAME
§ AIRPORT NAME (ORL) 2.6 E GMT−5(−4DT) 28°32'43"N 81°20'10"W JACKSONVILLE
113 B S4 FUEL 100, JET A OX 1, 2, 3 TPA—1000(800) AOE CFR Index A Not insp. H-4G, L-19C

② ⑨ ⑩ ⑪ ⑫ ⑬ ⑭ ⑮ ⑯ ⑰ ⑧
IAP

⑱ ► RWY 07-25: H6000X150 (ASPH) S-90, D-160, DT-300 HIRL
RWY 07: ALSF1. Trees. RWY 25: REIL. Rgt tfc.
RWY 13-31: H4620X100 (ASPH) HIRL
RWY 13: VASI—GA 3.3° TCH 89'. Pole. RWY 31: VASI—GA 3.1° TCH 36'. Tree. Rgt tfc.
⑲ AIRPORT REMARKS: Attended 1200-0300Z‡. LLWSAS. Acft 100,000 lbs or over ctc Director of Aviation for approval (305) 894-9831. Fee for all airline charters, travel clubs and certain revenue producing acft.
⑳ COMMUNICATIONS: ATIS 127.25 UNICOM 123.0
NAME FSS (ORL) on fld 123.65 122.65 122.2 122.1R 112.2T (305) 894-0861
Ⓡ NAME APP CON 124.8 (337°-179°) 120.15 (180°-336°)
TOWER 118.7 GND CON 121.7 CLNC DEL 125.55 PRE TAXI CLNC 125.5
Ⓡ DEP CON 124.8 (337°-179°) 120.15 (180°-336°)
STAGE I SVC ctc ORLANDO APP CON
㉑ RADIO AIDS TO NAVIGATION: VHF/DF ctc PHOENIX FSS
NAME (H) VORTAC 112.2 ORL Chan 59 28°32'33"N 81°20'07"W at fld. 1110/8E
VOR unusable 050-060° beyond 5000'
HERNY NDB (LOM) 221 OR 28°30'24"N 81°26'03"W 067° 5.4 NM to fld.
ILS 109.9 I-ORL Rwy 07. LOM HERNY NDB
ASR/PAR
㉒ COMM/NAVAID REMARKS: Emerg frequency 121.5 not available at tower.

TENNESSEE

SEWANEE
FRANKLIN CO (UOS) .9 E GMT−6(−5DT) 35°12'14"N 85°53'55"W ATLANTA
1950 B S2 FUEL 80, 100 L-14H
RWY 06-24: H3300X50 (ASPH) S-20 LIRL.
RWY 06: REIL. VASI—GA 3.5° TCH 28'. Trees. RWY 24: REIL. VASI. Trees.
AIRPORT REMARKS: Attended irregularly. O/T call (615) 598-5766. Sporadic crosswinds and turbulence.
COMMUNICATIONS: UNICOM 122.8
CROSSVILLE FSS (CSV) Toll free call dial 1-800-262-6787.
RADIO AIDS TO NAVIGATION:
SHELBYVILLE (L) VOR/DME 127°/34.1 NM
SEWANEE NDB (MHW) 275 UOS 35°12'15"N 85°53'45"W at fld
VFR use only

COLUMBIA-MT PLEASANT
§ MAURY CO (MRC) 1.7 NE GMT−6(−5DT) 35°33'15"N 87°11'00"W ATLANTA
676 B S4 FUEL 80, 100, JET A H-4G, L-14C
RWY 05-23: H5000X75 (ASPH) S-30, D-45, DT-70 MIRL IAP
RWY 05: REIL, VASI. Trees. RWY 23: VASI. ODAL. Trees.
RWY 17-35: 2500X300 (TURF)
RWY 17: P-line. RWY 35: Trees.
AIRPORT REMARKS: Attended 1400Z‡-dark. After hrs call (615) 388-8769. For ODALS key 122.8 5 times for low intensity, 3 times for high, 7 times for off.
COMMUNICATIONS: UNICOM 122.8
NASHVILLE FSS (BNA) Toll Free call dial 1-800-342-5802.
GRAHAM LRCO 122.1R 111.6T (NASHVILLE FSS).
Ⓡ MEMPHIS APP/DEP CON 125.85
RADIO AIDS TO NAVIGATION:
GRAHAM (L) VORTAC 111.6 GHM Chan 53 35°50'02"N 87°27'06"W 139° 21.2 NM to fld. 765/03E
NDB (MHW) 365 PBC 35°36'30"N 87°05'29"W 231° 5 NM to fld
SDF 108.7 I MRC Rwy 23

ALABAMA

§ **HUNTSVILLE-MADISON CO JETPORT-CARL T. JONES FLD** (HSV) 8.7 SW ATLANTA
GMT−6(−5DT) 34°38'34"N 86°46'32"W H-4G, L-14H
629 B S4 FUEL 100LL, JET A OX 1, 2, 3, 4 CFR Index C IAP
RWY 18-36L: H8000X150 (ASPH-CONC) S-130, D-160, DT-250 HIRL
RWY 18R: ALSF1. Rgt tfc. RWY 36L: MALSR
RWY 18L-36R: H8000X150 (ASPH) S-90, D-108, DT-170 HIRL
RWY 36R: Rgt tfc.
AIRPORT REMARKS: Attended continuously. Migratory birds Oct 1 to Mar 15, wildlife refuge South and West of arpt.
COMMUNICATIONS: ATIS 121.25 UNICOM 122.95
MUSCLE SHOALS FSS (MSL) Toll free call dial 1-800-942-3162 NOTAM FILE HSV
DECATUR LRCO 122.1R, 112.8T (MUSCLE SHOALS FSS)
ROCKET RCO 122.2 112.2T (MUSCLE SHOALS FSS)
Ⓡ APP CON 125.6 (359°-179°) 118.05 (180°-358°)
TOWER 119.7 GND CON 121.9 CLNC DEL 120.35
Ⓡ DEP CON 125.6 (359°-179°) 118.05 (180°-358°) 120.35
STAGE III SVC ctc APP CON
RADIO AIDS TO NAVIGATION:
ROCKET (L) VORTAC 215°/11.6 NM
DECATUR (L) VOR 112.8 DCU 34°38'54"N 86°56'22"W 090° 7.8 NM to fld
CAPSHAW NDB (MHW) 350 CWH 34°46'25"N 86°46'44"W 180° 7.3 NM to fld
ILS 109.3 I-HSV Rwy 18R
ILS 110.7 I-ELL Rwy 36L
ASR

DIRECTORY LEGEND

LEGEND

This Directory is an alphabetical listing of data on record with the FAA on all airports that are open to the public, associated terminal control facilities, air route traffic control centers and radio aids to navigation within the conterminous United States, Puerto Rico and the Virgin Islands. Airports are listed alphabetically by associated city name and cross referenced by airport name. Facilities associated with an airport, but with a different name, are listed individually under their own name, as well as under the airport with which they are associated.

The listing of an airport in this directory merely indicates the airport operator's willingness to accommodate transient aircraft, and does not represent that the facility conforms with any Federal or local standards, or that it has been approved for use on the part of the general public.

The information on obstructions is taken from reports submitted to the FAA. It has not been verified in all cases. Pilots are cautioned that objects not indicated in this tabulation (or on charts) may exist which can create a hazard to flight operation.

Detailed specifics concerning services and facilities tabulated within this directory are contained in Airman's Information Manual, Basic Flight Information and ATC Procedures.

The legend items that follow explain in detail the contents of this Directory and are keyed to the circled numbers on the sample on the preceding page.

① CITY/AIRPORT NAME
Airports and facilities in this directory are listed alphabetically by associated city and state. Where the city name is different from the airport name the city name will appear on the line above the airport name. Airports with the same associated city name will be listed alphabetically by airport name and will be separated by a dashed rule line. All others will be separated by a solid rule line.

② NOTAM SERVICE
§—NOTAM "D" (Distant teletype dissemination) and NOTAM "L" (Local dissemination) service is provided for airport. Absence of annotation § indicates NOTAM "L" (Local dissemination) only is provided for airport. See AIM. Basic Flight Information and ATC Procedures for detailed description of NOTAM.

③ LOCATION IDENTIFIER
A three or four character code assigned to airports. These identifiers are used by ATC in lieu of the airport name in flight plans, flight strips and other written records and computer operations.

④ AIRPORT LOCATION
Airport location is expressed as distance and direction from the center of the associated city in nautical miles and cardinal points, i.e., 3.5 NE.

⑤ TIME CONVERSION
Hours of operation of all facilities are expressed in Greenwich Mean Time (GMT) and shown as "Z" time. The directory indicates the number of hours to be subtracted from GMT to obtain local standard time and local daylight saving time GMT−5(−4DT). The symbol ‡ indicates that during periods of Daylight Saving Time effective hours will be one hour earlier than shown. In those areas where daylight saving time is not observed that (−4DT) and ‡ will not be shown. All states observe daylight savings time except Arizona and that portion of Indiana in the Eastern Time Zone and Puerto Rico and the Virgin Islands.

⑥ GEOGRAPHIC POSITION OF AIRPORT

⑦ CHARTS
The Sectional Chart and Low and High Altitude Enroute Chart and panel on which the airport or facility is located.

⑧ INSTRUMENT APPROACH PROCEDURES
IAP indicates an airport for which a prescribed (Public Use) FAA Instrument Approach Procedure has been published.

⑨ ELEVATION
Elevation is given in feet above mean sea level and is the highest point on the landing surface. When elevation is sea level it will be indicated as (00). When elevation is below sea level a minus (−) sign will precede the figure.

⑩ ROTATING LIGHT BEACON
B indicates rotating beacon is available. Rotating beacons operate dusk to dawn unless otherwise indicated in AIRPORT REMARKS.

⑪ SERVICING
S1: Minor airframe repairs.
S2: Minor airframe and minor powerplant repairs.
S3: Major airframe and minor powerplant repairs.
S4: Major airframe and major powerplant repairs.

⑫ FUEL

CODE	FUEL	PRODUCT
80	Grade 80 gasoline (Red)	
100	Grade 100 gasoline (Green)	
100LL	Grade 100LL gasoline (low lead) (Blue)	
115	Grade 115 gasoline	
A	Jet A—Kerosene freeze point—40° C.	
A1	Jet A-1—Kerosene, freeze point—50° C.	
A1+	Jet A-1—Kerosene with icing inhibitor, freeze point—50° C.	
B	Jet B—Wide-cut turbine fuel, freeze point—50° C.	
B+	Jet B—Wide-cut turbine fuel with icing inhibitor, freeze point—50° C.	

⑬ OXYGEN
OX 1 High Pressure
OX 2 Low Pressure
OX 3 High Pressure—Replacement Bottles
OX 4 Low Pressure—Replacement Bottles

⑭ TRAFFIC PATTERN ALTITUDE
Traffic Pattern Altitude (TPA)—The first figure shown is TPA above mean sea level. The second figure in parentheses is TPA above airport elevation.

DIRECTORY LEGEND

(15) **AIRPORT OF ENTRY AND LANDING RIGHTS AIRPORTS**

AOE—Airport of Entry—A customs Airport of Entry where permission from U.S. Customs is not required, however, at least one hour advance notice of arrival must be furnished.

LRA—Landing Rights Airport—Application for permission to land must be submitted in advance to U.S. Customs. At least one hour advance notice of arrival must be furnished.

NOTE: Advance notice of arrival at both an AOE and LRA airport may be included in the flight plan when filed in Canada or Mexico, where Flight Notification Service (ADCUS) is available the airport remark will indicate this service. This notice will also be treated as an application for permission to land in the case of an LRA. Although advance notice of arrival may be relayed to Customs through Mexico, Canadian, and U.S. Communications facilities by flight plan, the aircraft operator is solely responsible for insuring that Customs receives the notification. (See Customs, Immigration and Naturalization, Public Health and Agriculture Department requirements in the International Flight Information Manual for further details.)

(16) **CERTIFICATED AIRPORT (FAR 139)**

Airports serving Civil Aeronautics Board certified carriers and certified under FAR, Part 139, are indicated by the CFR index; i.e., CFR Index A, which relates to the availability of crash, fire, rescue equipment.

FAR–PART 139 CERTIFICATED AIRPORTS
INDICES AND FIRE FIGHTING AND RESCUE EQUIPMENT REQUIREMENTS

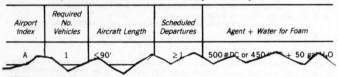

Airport Index	Required No. Vehicles	Aircraft Length	Scheduled Departures	Agent + Water for Foam
A	1	<90'	≥1	500#DC or 450# DC + 50 gal H₂O

(17) **FAA INSPECTION**

All airports not inspected by FAA will be identified by the note: Not insp. This indicates that the airport information has been provided by the owner or operator of the field.

(18) **RUNWAY DATA**

Runway information is shown on two lines. That information common to the entire runway is shown on the first line while information concerning the runway ends are shown on the second or following line. Lengthy information will be placed in the Airport Remarks.

Runway direction, surface, length, width, weight bearing capacity, lighting, gradient (when gradient exceeds 0.3 percent) and appropriate remarks are shown for each runway. Direction, length, width, lighting and remarks are shown for sealanes. The full dimensions of helipads are shown, i.e., 50X150.

RUNWAY SURFACE AND LENGTH

Runway lengths prefixed by the letter "H" indicate that the runways are hard surfaced (concrete, asphalt). If the runway length is not prefixed, the surface is sod, clay, etc. The runway surface composition is indicated in parentheses after runway length as follows:

(AFSC)—Aggregate friction seal coat	(GRVD)—Grooved	(TURF)—Turf
(ASPH)—Asphalt	(GRVL)—Gravel, or cinders	(TRTD)—Treated
(CONC)—Concrete	(PFC)—Porous friction courses	(WC)—Wire combed
(DIRT)—Dirt	(RFSC)—Rubberized friction seal coat	

RUNWAY WEIGHT BEARING CAPACITY

Runway strength data shown in this publication is derived from available information and is a realistic estimate of capability at an average level of activity. It is not intended as a maximum allowable weight or as an operating limitation. Many airport pavements are capable of supporting limited operations with gross weights of 25-50% in excess of the published figures. Permissible operating weights, insofar as runway strengths are concerned, are a matter of agreement between the owner and user. When desiring to operate into any airport at weights in excess of those published in the publication, users should contact the airport management for permission. Add 000 to figure following S, D, DT, DDT and MAX for gross weight capacity:

S—Runway weight bearing capacity for aircraft with single-wheel type landing gear, (DC-3), etc.
D—Runway weight bearing capacity for aircraft with dual-wheel type landing gear, (DC-6), etc.
DT—Runway weight bearing capacity for aircraft with dual-tandem type landing gear, (707), etc.
DDT—Runway weight bearing capacity for aircraft with double dual-tandem type landing gear, (747), etc.

Quadricycle and dual-tandem are considered virtually equal for runway weight bearing consideration, as are single-tandem and dual-wheel.

Omission of weight bearing capacity indicates information unknown.

RUNWAY LIGHTING

Lights are in operation sunset to sunrise. Lighting available by prior arrangement only or operating part of the night only and/or pilot controlled and with specific operating hours are indicated under airport remarks. Since obstructions are usually lighted, obstruction lighting is not included in this code. Unlighted obstructions on or surrounding an airport will be noted in airport remarks.

Temporary, emergency or limited runway edge lighting such as flares, smudge pots, lanterns or portable runway lights will also be shown in airport remarks.

Types of lighting are shown with the runway or runway end they serve.

LIRL—Low Intensity Runway Lights	SALS—Short Approach Lighting System.
MIRL—Medium Intensity Runway Lights	SALSF—Short Approach Lighting System with Sequenced Flashing Lights.
HIRL—High Intensity Runway Lights	SSALS—Simplified Short Approach Lighting System.
REIL—Runway End Identifier Lights	SSALF—Simplified Short Approach Lighting System with Sequenced Flashing Lights.
CL—Centerline Lights	
TDZ—Touchdown Zone Lights	SSALR—Simplified Short Approach Lighting System with Runway Alignment Indicator Lights.
ODALS—Omni Directional Approach Lighting System.	
AF OVRN—Air Force Overrun 1000' Standard Approach Lighting System.	ALSFI—High Intensity Approach Lighting System with Sequenced Flashing Lights, Category I, Configuration.
LDIN—Lead-In Lighting System.	
MALS—Medium Intensity Approach Lighting System.	ALSF2—High Intensity Approach Lighting System with Sequenced Flashing Lights, Category II, Configuration.
MALSF—Medium Intensity Approach Lighting System with Sequenced Flashing Lights.	
MALSR—Medium Intensity Approach Lighting System with Runway Alignment Indicator Lights.	VASI—Visual Approach Slope Indicator System.

VASI approach slope angle and threshold crossing height will be shown when available, i.e. GA 3.5° TCH 37.0'.

RUNWAY GRADIENT

Runway gradient will be shown only when it is 0.3 percent or more. When available the direction of slope upward will be indicated, i.e., 0.5% up NW.

RUNWAY END DATA

Lighting systems such as VASI, MALSR, REIL; obstructions; displaced thresholds will be shown on the specific runway end. "Rgt tfc"—Right traffic indicates right turns should be made on landing and takeoff for specified runway end.

(19) **AIRPORT REMARKS**

LLWSAS—Indicates a Low Level Wind Shear Alert System consisting of a centerfield and several field perimeter anemometers is installed.

Landing Fee indicates landing charges for private or non-revenue producing aircraft, in addition, fees may be charged for planes that remain over a couple of hours and buy no services, or at major airline terminals for all aircraft.

Remarks—Data is confined to operational items affecting the status and usability of the airport.

(20) **COMMUNICATIONS**

Communications will be listed in sequence in the order shown below:

Automatic Terminal Information Service (ATIS) and Private Aeronautical Stations (UNICOM) along with their frequency is shown, where available, on the line following the heading "COMMUNICATIONS". Whenever a second UNICOM frequency is shown in parenthesis, it represents a proposed change to the current frequency with an uncertain date of change. If unable to contact the ground station on the regularly published UNICOM frequency, attempt to establish communications on the frequency shown in parenthesis.

Flight Service Station (FSS) information. The associated FSS will be shown followed by the identifier and information concerning availability of telephone service, e.g. Direct Line (DL), Local Call (LC), etc. Where the airport NOTAM File identifier is different than the associated FSS it will be shown as "NOTAM FILE IAD." Where the FSS is located on the field it will be indicated as "on arpt" following the identifier. Frequencies available will follow. The FSS telephone number will follow along with any significant operational information. FSS's whose name is not the same as the airport on which located will also be listed in the normal alphabetical name listing for the state in which located. Limited Remote Communication Outlet (LRCO) or Remote Communications Outlet (RCO) providing service to the airport followed by the frequency and name of the Controlling FSS.

FSS's and CS/Ts provide information on airport conditions, radio aids and other facilities, and process flight plans. Airport Advisory Service is provided at the pilot's request on 123.6 or 123.65 by FSS's located at non-tower airports or when the tower is not in operation. (See AIM, ADVISORIES AT NON TOWER AIRPORTS.)

Aviation weather briefing service is provided by FSS's and CS/T's: however, CS/T personnel are not certified weather briefers and therefore provide only factual data from weather reports and forecasts. Flight and weather briefing services are also available by calling the telephone numbers listed.

Limited Remote Communications Outlet (LRCO)—Unmanned air/ground communications facility, which may be associated with a VOR. These outlets have receive-only capability and rely on a VOR or a remote transmitter for full capability.

Remote Communications Outlet (RCO)—An unmanned air/ground communications facility, remotely controlled and providing UHF or VHF communications capability to extend the service range of an FSS or C/ST.

Civil Communications Frequencies—Civil communications frequencies used in the FSS air/ground system are now operated simplex on 122.0, 122.2, 122.3, 122.4, 122.6, 123.6; emergency 121.5; plus receive-only on 122.05, 122.1, 122.15, and 123.6.

    a. 122.0 is assigned as the Enroute Flight Advisory Service channel at selected FSS's.

    b. 122.2 is assigned to all FSS's as a common enroute simplex service.

    c. 123.6 is assigned as the airport advisory channel at non-tower FSS locations, however, it is still in commission at some FSS's collocated with towers to provide part time Airport Advisory Service.

    d. 122.1 is the primary receive-only frequency at VOR's. 122.05, 122.15 and 123.6 are assigned at selected VOR's meeting certain criteria.

    e. Some FSS's are assigned 50 kHz channels for simplex operation in the 122-123 MHz band (e.g. 122.35). Pilots using the FSS A/G system should refer to this directory or appropriate charts to determine frequencies available at the FSS or remoted facility through which they wish to communicate.

Part time FSS hours of operation are shown in remarks under facility name.

   Emergency frequency 121.5 is available at all Flight Service Stations, Towers, Approach Control and RADAR facilities, unless indicated as not available.

Frequencies published followed by the letter "T" or "R", indicate that the facility will only transmit or receive respectively on that frequency. All radio aids to navigation frequencies are transmit only.

TERMINAL SERVICES

ATIS—A continuous broadcast of recorded non-control information in selected areas of high activity.

UNICOM—A non-government air/ground radio communications facility utilized to provide general airport advisory service.

APP CON—Approach Control. The symbol Ⓡ indicates radar approach control.

TOWER—Control tower

GND CON—Ground Control

DEP CON—Departure Control. The symbol Ⓡ indicates radar departure control.

CLNC DEL—Clearance Delivery.

PRE TAXI CLNC—Pre taxi clearance

VFR ADVSY SVC—VFR Advisory Service. Service provided by Non-Radar Approach Control.

STAGE I SVC—Radar Advisory Service for VFR aircraft

STAGE II SVC—Radar Advisory and Sequencing Service for VFR aircraft

STAGE III SVC—Radar Sequencing and Separation Service for participating VFR Aircraft within a Terminal Radar Service Area (TRSA)

TCA—Radar Sequencing and Separation Service for all aircraft in a Terminal Control Area (TCA)

TOWER, APP CON and DEP CON RADIO CALL will be the same as the airport name unless indicated otherwise.

(21) RADIO AIDS TO NAVIGATION

The Airport Facility Directory lists by facility name all Radio Aids to Navigation, except Military TACANS, that appear on National Ocean Survey Visual or IFR Aeronautical Charts and those upon which the FAA has approved an Instrument Approach Procedure.

All VOR, VORTAC and ILS equipment in the National Airspace System has an automatic monitoring and shutdown feature in the event of malfunction. Unmonitored, as used in this publication for any navigational aid, means that FSS or tower personnel cannot observe the malfunction or shutdown signal.

NAVAID information is tabulated as indicated in the following sample:

```
              TWEB   TACAN/DME Channel   Geographical Position                    Site Elevation

NAME (L) ABVORTAC 117.5  ■ ABE   Chan 122   40°43'36"N 75°27'18"W    180° 4.1 NM to fld. 1110/8E

          Class    Frequency   Identifier      Bearing and distance              Magnetic Variation
                                                facility to airport


              VOR unusable 020°-060° beyond 26 NM below 3500'

          Restrictions within the normal altitude/range of the navigational aid.

NAME BVORTAC   300°/36 NM


      Bearing and distance from
      VORTAC or VOR/DME
      facility to airport
```

ASR/PAR—Indicates that Surveillance (ASR) or Precision (PAR) radar instrument approach minimums are published in U.S. Government Instrument Approach Procedures.

RADIO CLASS DESIGNATIONS

Identification of VOR/VORTAC/TACAN Stations by Class (Operational Limitations):

Normal Usable Altitudes and Radius Distances

Class	Altitudes	Distance (miles)
(T)	12,000' and below	25
(L)	Below 18,000'	40
(H)	Below 18,000'	40
(H)	Within the Conterminous 48 States only, between 14,500' and 17,999'	100
(H)	18,000' FL 450	130
(H)	Above FL 450	100

(H) = High   (L) = Low   (T) = Terminal

NOTE: An (H) facility is capable of providing (L) and (T) service volume and an (L) facility additionally provides (T) service volume.

The term VOR is, operationally, a general term covering the VHF omnidirectional bearing type of facility without regard to the fact that the power, the frequency protected service volume, the equipment configuration, and operational requirements may vary between facilities at different locations.

AB	Automatic Weather Broadcast (also shown with ■ following frequency.)
DF	Direction Finding Service.
DME	UHF standard (TACAN compatible) distance measuring equipment.
H	Non-directional radio beacon (homing), power 50 watts to less than 2,000 watts (50 NM at all altitudes).
HH	Non-directional radio beacon (homing), power 2,000 watts or more (75 NM at all altitudes).
H-SAB	Non-directional radio beacons providing automatic transcribed weather service.
ILS	Instrument Landing System (voice, where available, on localizer channel).
LDA	Localizer Directional Aid.
LMM	Compass locator station when installed at middle marker site (15 NM at all altitudes).
LOM	Compass locator station when installed at outer marker site (15 NM at all altitudes).
MH	Non-directional radio beacon (homing) power less than 50 watts (25 NM at all altitudes).
S	Simultaneous range homing signal and/or voice.
SABH	Non-directional radio beacon not authorized for IFR or ATC. Provides automatic weather broadcasts.
SDF	Simplified Direction Facility.
TACAN	UHF navigational facility-omnidirectional course and distance information.
VOR	VHF navigational facility-omnidirectional course only.
VOR/DME	Collocated VOR navigational facility and UHF standard distance measuring equipment.
VORTAC	Collocated VOR and TACAN navigational facilities.
W	Without voice on radio facility frequency.
Z	VHF station location marker at a LF radio facility.

FREQUENCY PAIRING PLAN

The following is a list of paired VOR/ILS VHF frequencies with TACAN Channels:

Frequency MHz	Channel	Frequency MHz	Channel	Frequency MHz	Channel	Frequency MHz	Channel
108.0	17	110.5	42	113.0	77	115.5	102
108.1	18	110.6	43	113.1	78	115.6	103
108.2	19	110.7	44	113.2	79	115.7	104
108.3	20	110.8	45	113.3	80	115.8	105
108.4	21	110.9	46	113.4	81	115.9	106
108.5	22	111.0	47	113.5	82	116.0	107
108.6	23	111.1	48	113.6	83	116.1	108
108.7	24	111.2	49	113.7	84	116.2	109
108.8	25	111.3	50	113.8	85	116.3	110
108.9	26	111.4	51	113.9	86	116.4	111
109.0	27	111.5	52	114.0	87	116.5	112
109.1	28	111.6	53	114.1	88	116.6	113
109.2	29	111.7	54	114.2	89	116.7	114
109.3	30	111.8	55	114.3	90	116.8	115
109.4	31	111.9	56	114.4	91	116.9	116
109.5	32	112.0	57	114.5	92	117.0	117
109.6	33	112.1	58	114.6	93	117.1	118
109.7	34	112.2	59	114.7	94	117.2	119
109.8	35	112.3	70	114.8	95	117.3	120
109.9	36	112.4	71	114.9	96	117.4	121
110.0	37	112.5	72	115.0	97	117.5	122
110.1	38	112.6	73	115.1	98	117.6	123
110.2	39	112.7	74	115.2	99	117.7	124
110.3	40	112.8	75	115.3	100	117.8	125
110.4	41	112.9	76	115.4	101	117.9	126

(22) COMM/NAVAID REMARKS:

Pertinent remarks concerning communications and NAVAIDS.

NOTES

Appendix C
(From *Airman's Information Manual*)

MEDICAL FACTS FOR PILOTS

GENERAL

Just as your aircraft is required to undergo regular checks and maintenance, you are also required to undergo regular medical examinations to ensure your fitness to fly. The physical standards you are required to meet are minimum standards. You do not have to be a superman to fly. Many defects can be compensated for, as, for example, wearing glasses for visual defects. You may be required to demonstrate by a medical flight test that you can compensate for any other defects of potential significance to flight safety.

Student pilots should visit a Designated Aviation Medical Examiner and determine if they meet the standards before spending much money taking flying instructions.

It should be recalled that humans are essentially earthbound creatures. However, if we are aware of certain aeromedical factors, and pay attention to these, we can leave the earth and fly safely. What follows will not be one hard comprehensive lesson in aviation medicine. It will point out the more important factors with which you should be familiar prior to flying.

Modern industry's record in providing reliable equipment is very good. When the pilot enters the aircraft, he becomes an integral part of the man-machine system. He is just as essential to a successful flight as the control surfaces. The pilot himself has the sole responsibility for determining his reliability prior to entering the cockpit for flight.

While piloting an aircraft, an individual should be free of conditions which are harmful to alertness, ability to make correct decisions, and rapid reaction times. Persons with conditions which may produce sudden incapacitation, such as epilepsy, serious heart trouble, uncontrolled diabetes mellitus or diabetes mellitus requiring hypoglycemis agents, certain sicle cell disorders and other conditions hazardous to flight, cannot be medically certified according to the Federal Aviation Regulations. Conditions such as acute infections, anemias, and peptic ulcers are temporarily disqualifying. Consult your Aviation Medical Examiner when in doubt about any aspect of your health status, just as you would consult a licensed aviation mechanic when in doubt about the engine status. Specific aeromedical factors are herein explained. For additional information on these or other aeromedical flight factors, write to: The Federal Air Surgeon, Federal Aviation Administration, Washington, D.C. 20591.

FATIGUE

Fatigue generally slows reaction times and causes foolish errors due to inattention. In addition to the most common cause of fatigue, insufficient rest and loss of sleep, the pressures of business, financial worries and family problems, can be important contributing factors. If your fatigue is marked prior to a given flight, don't fly. To prevent fatigue effects during long flights, keep active with respect to making ground checks, radionavigation position plotting, and remaining mentally active.

HYPOXIA

Hypoxia in simple terms is a lack of sufficient oxygen to keep the brain and other body tissues functioning properly. Wide individual variation occurs with respect to susceptibility to hypoxia. In addition to progressively insufficient oxygen at higher altitudes, anything interfering with the blood's ability to carry oxygen can contribute to hypoxia (anemias, carbon monoxide, and certain drugs). Also, alcohol and various drugs decrease the brain's tolerance to hypoxia.

Your body has no built in alarm system to let you know when you are not getting enough oxygen. It is impossible to predict when or where hypoxia will occur during a given flight, or how it will manifest itself.

A major early symptom of hypoxia is an increased sense of well-being (referred to as euphoria). This progresses to slow reactions, impaired thinking ability, unusual fatigue, and dull headache feeling.

The symptoms are slow but progressive, insidious in onset, and are most marked at altitudes starting above ten thousand feet. Night vision, however, can be impaired starting at altitudes lower that ten thousand feet. Heavy smokers may also experience early symptoms of hypoxia at altitudes lower than is so with non-smokers.

If you observe the general rule of not flying above ten thousand feet without supplemental oxygen, you will not get into trouble.

FAR 91.32—Supplemental Oxygen includes: When operating at cabin pressure altitudes above 12,500 feet (MSL) up to and including 14,000 feet (MSL), it is required that the minimum flight crew be provided with and use supplemental oxygen for that part of the flight at those altitudes that is of more than 30 minutes duration. Additionally, this FAR requires that, when operating above 14,000 feet (MSL) the minimum flight crew be provided with and use supplemental oxygen for the entire flight time at those altitudes; and at cabin pressure altitudes above 15,000 feet (MSL) each occupant of the aircraft be provided with supplemental oxygen. It is recommended that pilots review all of the requirements of FAR 91.32 and the information in Advisory Circular, AC 91–8A, Use of Oxygen By General Aviation Pilot /Passengers.

HYPERVENTILATION

Hyperventilation, or over breathing, is a disturbance of respiration that may occur in individuals as a result of emotional tension or anxiety. Under conditions of emotional stress, fright or pain, breathing rate may increase, causing increase lung ventilation, although the carbon dioxide out of the body cells does not increase. As a result, carbon dioxide is "washed out" of the blood. The most common symptoms of hyperventilation are: dizziness; hot and cold sensations; tingling of the hands, legs and feet; tetany; nausea; sleepiness; and finally unconsciousness.

Should symptoms occur which cannot definitely be identified as either hypoxia or hyperventilation, the following steps should be taken:

1. Check your oxygen equipment and put the regulator auto-mix level on 100% oxygen (demand or pressure

demand system). Continuously flow-check oxygen supply and flow mechanism.

2. After three or four deep breaths of oxygen, the symptoms should improve markedly, if the condition was hypoxia (recovery from hypoxia is rapid).

3. If the symptoms persist, consciously slow your breathing rate until symptoms clear and then resume normal breathing rate. Breathing can be slowed by breathing into a bag, or talking loud.

ALCOHOL

Common sense and scientific evidence dictate that you not fly as a crewmember while under the influence of alcohol. Even small amounts of alcohol in the human system can adversely affect judgment and decision-making abilities. Because of this, FAR 91.11 (Liquor and Drugs) is amended to include: "(a) No person may act as a crewmember—(1) *Within 8 hours after the consumption of any alcoholic beverage;*".

Tests have shown that an increase in altitude increases the adverse effect/influence of alcohol. These tests indicate that as a general rule *2 ounces of alcohol at 15,000 feet produces the same adverse effects as 6 ounces at sea level.* In other words, the higher you get, "the higher you get!"

Your body metabolizes alcohol at a fixed rate, and no amount of coffee or other medication will alter this rate. An excellent rule is to allow 24 hours between the last drink and takeoff time. By all means, do not fly with a hangover, or a "masked hangover" (symptoms masked by aspirin or other medications).

DRUGS

Self-medication or taking medicine in any form when you are flying can be extremely hazardous. Even simple home or over-the-counter remedies and drugs such as aspirin, antihistamines, cold tablet, cough mixtures, laxatives, tranquilizers and appetite suppressors may seriously impair the judgment and coordination needed while flying. The safest rule is to take no medicine while flying except on the advice of your Aviation Medical Examiner. It should also be remembered that the condition for which the drug is required may of itself be very hazardous to flying even when the symptoms are suppressed by the drug.

Certain specific drugs which have been associated with aircraft accidents in the recent past are: *Antihistamines* (widely prescribed for hay fever and other allergies); *Tranquillizers* (prescribed for nervous conditions, hypertension, and other conditions); *Reducing Drugs* (amphetamines and other appetite suppressing drugs can produce sensations of well-being which have an adverse affect on judgement); *Barbiturates, Nerve tonics or pills* (prescribed for digestive and other disorders, barbiturates produce a marked suppression on mental alertness).

VERTIGO

The word itself is hard to define. To earthbound individuals it usually means dizziness or swimming of the head. To a pilot it means, in simple terms, that he doesn't know which end is up. In fact, vertigo during flight can have very fatal consequences.

On the ground we know which way is up through the combined use of three senses:

1. Vision—We can *see* where we are in relation to fixed objects.

2. Pressure—Gravitational pull on muscles and joints tells us which way is down.

3. Special Parts in Our Inner Ear—The otoliths tell us which way is down by gravitational pull. It should be noted that accelerations of the body are detected by the fluid in the semi-circular canals of the inner ear, and this tells us when we change position. However, in the absence of a visual reference, such as flying into a cloud or overcast, the accelerations can be confusing, especially since their forces can be misinterpreted as gravitational pulls on the muscles and otoliths. The result is often disorientation and vertigo (or dizziness).

All pilots should have an instructor pilot produce maneuvers which will produce the sensation of vertigo. Once experienced, later unanticipated incidents of vertigo can be overcome. Closing the eyes for a second or two may help, as will watching the flight instruments, believing them, and controlling the airplane in accordance with the information presented on the instruments. All pilots should obtain the minimum training recommended by the FAA for attitude control of aircraft solely by reference to the gyroscopic instruments.

Pilots are susceptible to experiencing vertigo at night, and in any flight condition when outside visibility is reduced to the point that the horizon is obscured. An additional type of vertigo is known as *flicker vertigo*. Light, flickering at certain frequencies, from four to twenty times per second, can produce unpleasant and dangerous reactions in some persons. These reactions may include nausea, dizziness, unconsciouness, or even reactions similar to epileptic seizures. In a single engine propeller airplane, heading into the sun, the propeller may cut the sun to give this flashing effect, particularly during landings when the engine is throttled back. These undersirable effects may be avoided by not staring directly through the prop for more than a moment, and by making frequent but small changes in RPM. The flickering light traversing helicopter blades has been known to cause this difficulty, as has the bounce-back from rotating beacons on aircraft which have penetrated clouds.

CARBON MONOXIDE

Carbon monoxide is a colorless, odorless, tasteless product of an internal combustion engine and is always present in exhaust fumes. Even minute quantities of carbon monoxide breathed over a long period of time, may lead to dire consequences.

For biochemical reasons, carbon monoxoide has a greater ability to combine with the hemoglobin of the blood than oxygen. Furthermore, once carbon monoxide is absorbed in the blood, it sticks "like glue" to the hemoglobin and actually prevents the oxygen from attaching to the hemoglobin.

Most heaters in light aircraft work by air flowing over the manifold. If you have to use the heater, be wary if you smell exhaust fumes. The onset of symptoms is insidious, with "blurred thinking", a possible feeling of uneasiness, and subsequent dizziness. Later, headache occurs. Immediately shut off the heater, open the air ventilators, descend to lower altitudes and land at the nearest airfield. Consult an Aviation Medical Examiner. It may take several days to fully recover and clear the body of the carbon monoxide.

VISION

On the ground, reduced or impaired vision can sometimes be dangerous depending on where you are and what you are doing. In flying it is always dangerous.

On the ground or in the air, a number of factors such as hypoxia, carbon monoxide, alcohol, drugs, fatigue, or even bright sunlight can affect your vision. In the air these effects are critical.

Some good specific rules are: make use of sunglasses on bright days to avoid eye fatigue; during night flights use red covers on the flashlights to avoid destroying any dark adaption; remember that drugs, alcohol, heavy smoking and the other factors mentioned above, have early effects on visual acuity.

MIDDLE EAR DISCOMFORT OR PAIN

Certian persons (whether pilots or passengers) have difficulty balancing the air loads on the ear drum while descending. This is particularly troublsome if a head cold or throat inflammation keeps the eustacian tube from opening properly. If this trouble occurs during descent, try swallowing, yawning, or holding the nose and mouth shut and forcibly exhaling. If no relief occurs, climb back up a few thousand feet to relieve the pressure on the outer drum. Then descend again, using these measures. A more gradual descent may be tried, and it may be necessary to go through several climbs and descents to "stair step" down. If a nasal inhaler is available, it may afford relief. If trouble persists several hours after landing, consult your Aviation Medical Examiner.

NOTE.—If you find yourself airborne with a head cold, you may possibly avoid trouble by using an inhaler kept as part of the flight kit.

PANIC

The development of panic in inexperienced pilots is a process which can get into a vicious circle with itself and lead to unwise and precipitous action. If lost, or in some other predicament, forcibly take stock of yourself, and do not allow panic to mushroom. Panic can be controlled. Remember, *Prevent Panic to Think Straight*. Fear is a normal protective reaction, and occurs in normal individuals. Fear progression to panic is an abnormal development.

SCUBA DIVING

You may use your plane to fly to a sea resort or lake for a day's SCUBA diving, and then fly home, all within a few hours' time. This can be dangerous, particularly if you have been diving to depths for any length of time.

Under the increased pressure of the water, excess nitrogen is absorbed into your system. If sufficient time has not elapsed prior to takeoff for your system to rid itself of this excess gas, you may experience the bends at altitude under 10,000 feet where most light planes fly. It is recommended that 24 hours elapse between completion of a dive and takeoff in an aircraft.

261

Bibliography and Recommended Reading

Airman's Information Manual. Washington, D.C., USGPO.

Aviation Weather. Washington, D.C., USGPO, 1975.

Aviation Weather Services. Washington, D.C., USGPO, 1979.

Flight Training Handbook. Washington, D.C., USGPO, 1980.

Kershner, William K., *Advanced Pilot's Flight Manual*, 4th ed. Ames, Iowa State University Press, 1976.

Langewiesche, Wolfgang, *Stick and Rudder*. New York, McGraw-Hill, 1944.

Pilot's Handbook of Aeronautical Knowledge. Washington, D.C., USGPO, 1980.

Student Pilot's Guide. Washington, D.C., USGPO.

Information received from companies and *Pilot's Operating Handbooks* referred to:

Bendix Avionics Division, Ft. Lauderdale, Fla., TPR-2060.

Cessna Aircraft Co., Wichita, Kans. *Pilot's Operating Handbook* for Cessna 150, 152, 172.

King Radio Corp., Olathe, Kans., KX 170B, KI 208, KI 209.

National Aeronautical Corp. (NARCO), Fort Washington, Pa. ADF equipment information.

Safetech Inc., Newtown, Pa. Information on E-6B Model FDF-57-B computers.

Index

NOTES

ANSWERS

1. (1.)
2. (3.)
3. (1.)
4. (2.)
5. (3.) Flying from a low to a high the altimeter will read low. The atmospheric pressure is 0.60 of an inch of mercury higher at your destination airport and 1 inch of mercury pressure variation equals about 1000 feet of change in altimeter reading. So, the variation of 0.60 inch of mercury would equal 600 feet and your altimeter would read 600 feet lower than the airport elevation. Answer (4) was put in to make the point that you might try to fly the traffic pattern altitude by referring to your altimeter and being 600 feet off in an 800-foot pattern could cause confusion — you would be wondering what was wrong and could get flustered at the strange airport. (Pilots have done it!)
6. (2.)
7. (4.)
8. (3.)
9. (2.) The logbooks must be available for inspection but are not *required to be in* the airplane. Most owners keep them there. You might review this in Chapter 2.
10. (3.)
11. (2.) The answer (1) would be asking for trouble. Answer (3) would be bad because some other pilot might not catch it and have problems in flight. Answer (4) would be incorrect because those two characters have unlisted numbers.
12. (4.)
13. (1.)
14. (3.)
15. (3.) Tell somebody; don't leave the airport quietly in disgust.
16. (3.) The right magneto is not "grounded out" but is still working so that when "left" is selected, *both* magnetos are still in operation.
17. (1.) The carburetor heat cleaned out ice that had accumulated during the taxi and initial part of the pretake-off check.
18. (3.) See Figures 9-4 and 9-5.
19. (2.) When you ease the nose over and reach the airspeed indicated by point (3) in Figure 12-13, you'll note that 45 brake horsepower is required to maintain a constant altitude there. Since you are still carrying 100 horsepower (full power) this will give you the best climb of the choices offered.
20. (1.) 4 g's. The airplane is stalled at twice its 1 g stall speed; $(2)^2 = 4$ g's.
21. (3.)
22. (4.) The reciprocal of your original heading is $070°$ and from $340°$ a *right* turn is the shortest way to that heading.
23. (3.)
24. (2.) Rate of climb is not affected by the direction of the wind relative to the airplane's path.
25. (2.) The standard temperature for 2000 feet altitude would be 52°F or 11°C. The current temperature is 75°F, or 23°F above standard for that altitude. Each 15°F above normal adds another 1000 feet to the density altitude, so the airplane is "raised" about 1500 feet, to 3500 feet density altitude. Using Celsius, the temperature is 13°C above normal, and assuming that for each 8 1/2°C the density altitude increases 1000 feet, the same 1500 feet is added to the pressure altitude. (Or use your computer.)
26. (4.) Again, read the question carefully and don't feel that you're always required to use all information.
27. (2.) The magnetic heading is $(282 + 3) = 285°$. This is exactly between the numbers given in Figure 19-4 for *West* (add 5°) and 300° (add 3°). You would interpolate and add 4° to the magnetic heading to get a compass heading of 289°.
28. (1.)
29. (3.)
30. (3.)
31. (2.)
32. (2.)
33. (3.)
34. (4.)
35. (1.)
36. (2.)
37. (1.)
38. (1.) At 30,000 feet ASL.
39. (3.)
40. (4.)
41. (4.) This question was taken from a sample FAA written examination (only the numbers were changed). This one requires that you convert from knots to mph to get the correct answer, and if the question — and answers — aren't carefully read, you would most likely answer (3).
42. (3.) The maximum baggage allowed in the baggage compartment is 100 pounds, no matter if you have overall weight to spare. This question was inserted to again affirm that such limits must be observed.
43. (1.) The 2 gallons of unusable fuel were included in the basic empty weight of 1439 pounds so that the weight of full fuel (38 gallons) would be 228 pounds, not 240 as might be expected.
44. (1.)
45. (4.) Using a computer you would get a calibrated airspeed of 89 K. Converting this to I.A.S. (the nearest C.A.S. given is for 91 K in Fig. 19-6), you would subtract 1 K from the C.A.S. to obtain the figure of 88 K.
46. (2.)
47. (3.) Use your "bracket" (the railroad). By turning north you are leaving the bad weather and are also getting to better terrain with more check points.

Tear here

48. (3.)
49. (2.) While it might seem that (4) would be a reasonable answer, the night might not be so bright due to an overcast on some part of the cross-country.
50. (4.)
51. (4.)
52. (4.)
53. (2.)

54. (1.)
55. (3.) See Figure 3-26.
56. (3.) See Figure 21-13.
57. (2.) See Figure 21-13.
58. (4.)
59. (1.) (FAR 91.33)
60. (2.) The BFR is valid for 24 months *to the day*, not until the end of the month.

Tear here

INSTRUCTOR CERTIFICATION FORMS

Name _____

Grade on Sample Written Test _____ %

    I certify that I have reviewed the completion of an aviation home study course of the above individual for the private pilot's written test and find that he has satisfactorily completed the course.

Name _____

CFI or GI number _____

Expiration Date _____

Date _____

    I have given (MR./MS.) _____ the required flight instruction within the preceding 60 days, including a review of the subject areas found to be deficient on his/her airmen's written test, and find his/her performance satisfactory to apply for a private pilot certificate.

Signed _____

CFI Number _____ Expires _____

Federal Aviation Regulations

Following are parts of FAR 61 and 91 and National Transportation Safety Board Procedural Regulations Part 830. You'll find gaps in the FAR numbers because, at this stage of your flying career, knowledge of the Regulations pertaining to operations, for instance, above 18,000 feet (or the requirements for becoming a flight instructor) is not necessary for you to become a safe and legal private pilot. The Regulations included are those that will affect you as a new private pilot who will be flying airplanes (not balloons, gliders, or rotorcraft). Later you'll be interested in requirements for the commercial pilot and/or high altitude or turbine-powered aircraft and should be familiar with them as you move on.

If you are using this book as a reference in getting ready for a Biennial Review, be sure to get a good look at Part 91. You'll be quizzed on this in the oral. (Figure 21-14 is a good review for airspace limits.)

These regulations are valid at the time of printing. Amendments are being made continually, so to remain current you should subscribe to these Parts from the U.S. Government Printing Office.

Part 61 — Certification: Pilots and Flight Instructors

Subpart A — General

§ 61.1 Applicability

(a) This Part prescribes the requirements for issuing pilot and flight instructor certificates and ratings, the conditions under which those certificates and ratings are necessary, and the privileges and limitations of those certificates and ratings.

§ 61.3 Requirements for certificates, rating, and authorizations.

(a) *Pilot certificate.* No person may act as pilot in command or in any other capacity as a required pilot flight crewmember of a civil aircraft of United States registry unless he has in his personal possession a current pilot certificate issued to him under this Part. However, when the aircraft is operated within a foreign country a current pilot license issued by the country in which the aircraft is operated may be used.

(c) *Medical certificate.* Except for free balloon pilots piloting balloons and glider pilots piloting gliders, no person may act as pilot in command or in any other capacity as a required pilot flight crewmember of an aircraft under a certificate issued to him under this Part, unless he has in his personal possession an appropriate current medical certificate issued under Part 67 of this chapter. However, when the aircraft is operated within a foreign country with a current pilot license issued by that country, evidence of current medical qualification for that license, issued by that country, may be used. In the case of a pilot certificate issued on the basis of a foreign pilot license under § 61.75, evidence of current medical qualification accepted for the issue of that license is used in place of a medical certificate.

(h) *Inspection of certificate.* Each person who holds a pilot certificate, flight instructor certificate, medical certificate, authorization, or license required by this Part shall present it for inspection upon the request of the Administrator, an authorized representative of the National Transportation Safety Board, or any Federal, State or local law enforcement officer.

§ 61.5. Certificates and ratings issued under this Part.

(a) The following certificates are issued under this Part:

(1) Pilot certificates:

(i) Student pilot.

(ii) Private pilot.

(iii) Commercial pilot.

(iv) Airline transport pilot.

(2) Flight instructor certificates.

(b) The following ratings are placed on pilot certificates (other than student pilot) where applicable:

(1) Aircraft category ratings:

(i) Airplane

(ii) Rotorcraft.

(iii) Glider.

(iv) Lighter-than-air.

(2) Airplane class ratings:

(i) Single-engine land.

(ii) Multiengine land.

(iii) Single-engine sea.

(iv) Multiengine sea.

(3) Rotorcraft class ratings:

(i) Helicopter.

(ii) Gyroplane.

(4) Lighter-than-air class ratings:

(i) Airship.

(ii) Free balloon.

(5) Aircraft ratings are listed in Advisory Circular 61-1 entitled "Aircraft Type Ratings." This list includes ratings for the following:

(i) Large aircraft, other than lighter-than-air.

(ii) Small turbojet-powered airplanes.

(iii) Small helicopters for operations requiring an airline transport pilot certificate.

(iv) Other aircraft type ratings specified by the Administrator through aircraft type certificate procedures.

(6) Instrument ratings (on private and commercial pilot certificates only):

(i) Instrument — airplanes.

(ii) Instrument — helicopter.

§ 61.13 Application and qualification.

(a) Application for a certificate and rating, or for an additional rating under this Part is made on a form and in a manner prescribed by the Administrator.

(b) An applicant who meets the requirements of this Part is entitled to an appropriate pilot certificate with aircraft ratings. Additional aircraft category, class, type and other ratings, for which the applicant is qualified, are added to his certificate. However, the Administrator may refuse to issue certificates to persons who are not citizens of the United States and who do not reside in the United States.

(c) An applicant who cannot comply with all of the flight proficiency requirements prescribed by this Part because the aircraft used by him for his flight training or flight test is characteristically incapable of performing a required pilot operation, but who meets all other requirements for the certificate or rating sought, is issued the certificate or rating with appropriate limitations.

(d) An applicant for a pilot certificate who holds a medical certificate under § 67.19 of this chapter with special limitations on it, but who meets all other requirements for that pilot certificate, is issued a pilot certificate containing such operating limitations as the Administrator determines are necessary because of the applicant's medical deficiency.

§ 61.15 Carriage of narcotic drugs, marihuana, and depressant or stimulant drugs or substances.

(a) No person who is convicted of violating any Federal statute relating to the manufacture, sale, disposition, possession, transportation, or importation of narcotic drugs, marihuana, or depressant or stimulant drugs or substances, is eligible for any certificate or rating issued under this Part for a period of 1 year after the date of final conviction.

(b) No person who commits an act prohibited by § 91.12(a) of this chapter is eligible for any certificate or rating issued under this Part for a period of 1 year after the date of that act.

(c) Any conviction specified in paragraph (a) of this section or the commission of the act referenced in paragraph (b) of this section, is grounds for suspending or revoking any certificate or rating issued under this part.

§ 61.19 Duration of pilot and flight instructor certificates.

(a) *General.* The holder of a certificate with an expiration date may not, after that date, exercise the privileges of that certificate.

(b) *Student pilot certificate.* A student pilot certificate expires at the end of the 24th month after the month in which it is issued.

(c) *Other pilot certificates.* Any pilot certificate (other than a student pilot certificate) issued under this Part is issued without a specific expiration date. However, the holder of a pilot certificate issued on the basis of a foreign pilot license may exercise the privileges of that certificate only while the foreign pilot license on which that certificate is based is effective.

(d) *Flight instructor certificate.* A flight instructor certificate —

(1) Is effective only while the holder has a current pilot certificate and a medical certificate appropriate to the pilot privileges being exercised; and

(2) Expires at the end of the 24th month after the month in which it was last issued or renewed.

(e) *Surrender, suspension, or revocation.* Any pilot certificate or flight instructor certificate issued under this Part ceases to be effective if it is surrendered, suspended, or revoked.

(f) *Return of certificate.* The holder of any certificate issued under this Part that is suspended or revoked shall, upon the Administrator's request, return it to the Administrator.

§ 61.23 Duration of medical certificates.

(a) A first-class medical certificate expires at the end of the last day of —

(1) The sixth month after the month of the date of examination shown on the certificate, for operations requiring an airline transport pilot certificate;

(2) The 12th month after the month of the date of examination shown on the certificate, for operations requiring only a commercial pilot certificate; and

(3) The 24th month after the month of the date of examination shown on the certificate, for operations requiring only a private or student pilot certificate.

(b) A second-class medical certificate expires at the end of the last day of —

(1) The 12th month after the month of the date of examination shown on the certificate, for operations requiring a commercial pilot certificate; and

(2) The 24th month after the month of the date of examination shown on the certificate, for operations requiring only a private or student pilot certificate.

(c) A third-class medical certificate expires at the end of the last day of the 24th month after the month of the date of examination shown on the certificate, for operations requiring a private or student pilot certificate.

§ 61.31 General limitations.

(a) *Type ratings required.* A person may not act as pilot in command of any of the following aircraft unless he holds a type rating for that aircraft:

(1) A large aircraft (except lighter-than-air.

(2) A helicopter, for operations requiring an airline transport pilot certificate.

(3) A turbojet powered airplane.

(4) Other aircraft specified by the Administrator through aircraft type certificate procedures.

(d) *Category and class rating: other operations.* No person may act as pilot in command of an aircraft in solo flight in operations not subject to paragraph (c) of this section, unless he meets at least one of the following:

(1) He holds a category and class rating appropriate to that aircraft.

(2) He has received flight instruction in the pilot operations required by this part, appropriate to the category and class of aircraft for first solo, given to him by a certificated flight instructor who found him competent to solo that category and class of aircraft and has so endorsed his pilot logbook.

(3) He has soloed and logged pilot-in-command time in that category and class of aircraft before November 1, 1973.

(e) *High performance airplanes.* A person holding a private or commercial pilot certificate may not act as pilot in command of an airplane that has more than 200 horsepower, or that has a retractable landing gear, flaps, and a controllable propeller, unless he has received flight instruction from an authorized flight instructor who has certified in his logbook that he is competent to pilot an airplane that has more than 200 horsepower, or that has a retractable landing gear, flaps, and a controllable propeller, as the case may be. However, this instruction is not required if he has logged flight time as pilot in command in high performance airplanes before November 1, 1973.

(f) *Exception.* This section does not require a class rating for gliders, or category and class ratings for aircraft that are not type certificated as airplanes, rotorcraft, or lighter-than-air aircraft. In addition, the rating limitations of this section do not apply to —

(1) The holder of a student pilot certificate;

(2) The holder of a pilot certificate when operating an aircraft under the authority of an experimental or provisional type certificate:

(3) An applicant when taking a flight test given by the Administrator; or

(4) The holder of a pilot certificate with a lighter-than-air category rating when operating a hot air balloon without an airborne heater.

§ 61.33 Tests: general procedure.

Tests prescribed by or under this Part are given at times and places, and by persons, designated by the Administrator.

§ 61.35 Written test: prerequisites and passing grades.

(a) An applicant for a written test must —

(1) Show that he has satisfactorily completed the ground instruction or home study course required by this part for the certificate or rating sought;

(2) Present as personal identification an airman certificate, driver's license, or other official document; and

(3) Present a birth certificate ot other official document showing that he meets the age requirement prescribed in this Part for the certificate sought not later than 2 years from the date of application for the test.

(b) The minimum passing grade is specified by the Administrator on each written test sheet or booklet furnished to the applicant.

This section does not apply to the written test for an airline transport pilot certificate or a rating associated with that certificate.

§ 61.37 Written tests: cheating or other unauthorized conduct.

(a) Except as authorized by the Administrator, no person may —

(1) Copy, or intentionally remove, a written test under this Part;

(2) Give to another, or receive from another, any part or copy of that test;

(3) Give help on that test to, or receive help on that test from, any person during the period that test is being given;

(4) Take any part of that test in behalf of another person;

(5) Use any material or aid during the period that test is being given; or

(6) Intentionally cause, assist, or participate in any act prohibited by this paragraph.

(b) No person whom the Administrator finds to have committed an act prohibited by paragraph (a) of this section is eligible for any airman or ground instructor certificate or rating, or to take any test therefor, under this chapter for a period of one year after the date of that act. In addition, the commission of that act is a basis for suspending or revoking any airman or ground instructor certificate or rating held by that person.

§ 61.39 Prerequisites for flight tests.
(Check Chapter 28 for the word on this.)

§ 61.43 Flight tests: general procedures.

Chapter 28 goes into detail on the general procedures as required by this section of the FAR's. You might review it at this point of study.

§ 61.45 Flight tests: required aircraft and equipment.

Chapter 28 also covers these requirements.

§ 61.49 Retesting after failure.

An applicant for a written or flight test who fails that test may not apply for retesting until after 30 days after the date he failed the test. However, in the case of his first failure he may apply for retesting before the 30 days have expired upon presenting a written statement from an authorized instructor certifying that he has given flight or ground instruction as appropriate to the applicant and finds him competent to pass the test.

§ 61.51 Pilot logbooks.

(a) The aeronautical training and experience used to meet the requirements for a certificate or rating, or the recent flight experience requirements of this Part must be shown by a reliable record. The logging of other flight time is not required.

(b) *Logbook entries.* Each pilot shall enter the following information for each flight or lesson logged:

(1) *General.*

(i) Date.

(ii) Total time of flight.

(iii) Place, or points of departure and arrival.

(iv) Type and identification of aircraft.

(2) *Type of pilot experience or training.*

(i) Pilot in command or solo.

(ii) Second in command.

(iii) Flight instruction received from an authorized flight instructor.

(iv) Instrument flight instruction from an authorized flight instructor.

(v) Pilot ground trainer instruction.

(vi) Participating crew (lighter-than-air).

(vii) Other pilot time.

(3) *Conditions of flight.*

(i) Day or night.

(ii) Actual instrument.

(iii) Simulated instrument conditions.

(c) *Logging of pilot time.*

(1) *Solo flight time.* A pilot may log as solo flight time only that flight time when he is the sole occupant of the aircraft. However, a student pilot may also log as solo flight time that time during which he acts as the pilot in command of an airship requiring more than one flight crewmember.

(2) *Pilot-in-command flight time.*

(i) A private or commercial pilot may log as pilot in command time only that flight time during which he is the sole manipulator of the controls of an aircraft for which he is rated, or when he is the sole occupant of the aircraft, or when he acts as pilot in command of an aircraft on which more than one pilot is required under the type certification of the aircraft, or the regulations under which the flight is conducted.

(ii) An airline transport pilot may log as pilot in command time all of the flight time during which he acts as pilot in command.

(iii) A certificated flight instructor may log as pilot in command time all flight time during which he acts as a flight instructor.

(3) *Second-in-command flight time.* A pilot may log as second in command time all flight time during which he acts as second in command of an aircraft on which more than one pilot is required under the type certification of the aircraft, or the regulations under which the flight is conducted.

(4) *Instrument flight time.* A pilot may log as instrument flight time only that time during which he operates the aircraft solely by reference to instruments, under actual or simulated instrument flight conditions.

Each entry must include the place and type of each instrument approach completed, and the name of the safety pilot for each simulated instrument flight. An instrument flight instructor may log as instrument time that time during which he acts as instrument flight instructor in actual instrument weather conditions.

(5) *Instruction time.* All time logged as flight instruction, instrument flight instruction, pilot ground trainer instruction, or ground instruction time must be certified by the appropriately rated and certificated instructor from whom it was received.

(d) *Presentation of logbook.*

(1) A pilot must present his logbook (or other record required by this section) for inspection upon reasonable request by the Administrator, an authorized representative of the National Transportation Safety Board, or any State or local law enforcement officer.

(2) A student pilot must carry his logbook (or other record required by this section) with him on all solo cross-country flights, as evidence of the required instructor clearances and endorsements.

§ 61.53 Operations during medical deficiency.

No person may act as pilot in command, or in any other capacity as a required pilot flight crewmember while he has a known medical deficiency, or increase of a known medical deficiency, that would make him unable to meet the requirements for his current medical certificate.

§ 61.57 Recent flight experience: pilot in command.

(a) *Flight review.* No person may act as pilot in command of an aircraft unless, within the preceding 24 months, he has—

(1) Accomplished a flight review given to him, in an aircraft for which he is rated, by an appropriately certificated instructor or other person designated by the Administrator; and

(2) Had his log book endorsed by the person who gave him the review certifying that he has satisfactorily accomplished the flight review.

However, a person who has, within the preceding 24 months, satisfactorily completed a pilot proficiency check conducted by the FAA, an approved pilot check airman or a U.S. Armed Force for a pilot certificate, rating or operating privilege, need not accomplish the flight review required by this section.

(b) *Meaning of flight review.* As used in this section, a flight review consists of—

(1) A review of the current general operating and flight rules of Part 91 of this chapter; and

(2) A review of those maneuvers and procedures which in the discretion of the person giving the review are necessary for the pilot to demonstrate that he can safely exercise the privileges of his pilot certificate.

(c) *General experience.* No person may act as pilot in command of an aircraft carrying passengers, nor of an aircraft certificated for more than one required pilot flight crewmember, unless within the preceding 90 days, he has made three takeoffs and three landings as the sole manipulator of the flight controls in an aircraft of the same category and class and, if a type rating is required, of the same type. If the aircraft is a tailwheel airplane, the landings must have been made to a full stop in a tailwheel airplane. For the purpose of meeting the requirements of the paragraph a person may act as pilot in command of a flight under day VFR or day IFR if no persons or property other than as necessary for his compliance thereunder, are carried. This paragraph does not apply to operations requiring an airline transport pilot certificate, or to operations conducted under Part 135 of this chapter.

(d) *Night experience.* No person may act as pilot in command of an aircraft carrying passengers during the period beginning 1 hour after sunset and ending 1 hour before sunrise (as published in the American Air Almanac) unless, within the preceding 90 days, he has made at least three takeoffs and three landings to a full stop during that period in the category and class of aircraft to be used. This paragraph does not apply to operations requiring an airline transport pilot certificate.

(e) *Instrument.*

(1) *Recent IFR experience.* No pilot may act as pilot in command under IFR, nor in weather conditions less than the minimums prescribed for VFR, unless he has, within the past 6 months—

(i) In the case of an aircraft other than a glider, logged at least 6 hours of instrument time under actual or simulated IFR conditions, at least 3 of which were in flight in the category of aircraft involved, including at least 6 instrument approaches, or passed an instrument competency check in the category of aircraft involved.

(ii) In the case of a glider, logged at least 3 hours of instrument time, at least half of which were in a glider or an airplane. If a passenger is carried in the glider, at least 3 hours of instrument flight time must have been in gliders.

(2) *Instrument competency check.* A pilot who does not meet the recent instrument experience requirements of subparagraph (e) (1) of this paragraph during the prescribed time or 6 months thereafter may not serve as pilot in command under IFR, nor in weather conditions less than the minimums prescribed for VFR, until he passes an instrument competency check in the category of aircraft involved, given by an FAA inspector, a member of an armed force in the United States authorized to conduct flight tests, an FAA-approved check pilot, or a certificated instrument flight instructor. The Administrator may authorize the conduct of part or all of this check in a pilot ground trainer equipped for instruments or an aircraft simulator.

§ 61.59 Falsification, reproduction or alteration of applications, certificates, logbooks, reports, or records.

(a) No person may make or cause to be made—

(1) Any fraudulent or intentionally false statement on any application for a certificate, rating, or duplicate thereof, issued under this Part;

(2) Any fraudulent or intentionally false entry in any logbook, record, or report that is required to be kept, made, or used, to show compliance with any requirement for the issuance, or exercise of the privileges, or any certificate or rating under this Part;

(3) Any reproduction, for fraudulent purpose, of any certificate or rating under this Part; or

(4) Any alteration of any certificate or rating under this Part.

(b) The commission by any person of an act prohibited under paragraph (a) of this section is a basis for suspending or revoking any airman or ground instructor certificate or rating held by that person.

§ 61.60 Change of address.

The holder of a pilot or flight instructor certificate who has made a change in his permanent mailing address may not after 30 days from the date he moved, exercise the privileges of his certificate unless he has notified in writing the Department of Transportation, Federal Aviation Administration, Airman Certification Branch, Box 25082, Oklahoma City, Oklahoma 73125, of his new address.

Subpart C – Student Pilots

§ 61.81 Applicability

This subpart prescribes the requirements for the issuance of student pilot certificates, the conditions under which those certificates are necessary, and the general operating rules for the holders of those certificates.

§ 61.83 Eligibility requirements: general.

To be eligible for a student pilot certificate, a person must—

(a) Be at least 16 years of age, or at least 14 years of age for a student pilot certificate limited to the operation of a glider or free balloon;

(b) Be able to read, speak, and understand the English language, or have such operating limitations placed on his pilot certificate as are necessary for the safe operation of aircraft, to be removed when he shows that he can read, speak, and understand the English language; and

(c) Hold at least a current third-class medical certificate issued under Part 67 of this chapter, or, in the case of glider or free balloon operations, certify that he has no known medical defect that makes him unable to pilot a glider or a free balloon.

§ 61.85 Application.

An application for a student pilot certificate is made on a form and in a manner provided by the Administrator and is submitted to—

(a) A designated aviation medical examiner when applying for an FAA medical certificate; or

(b) An FAA operations inspector or designated pilot examiner, accompanied by a current FAA medical certificate, or in the case of an application for a glider or free balloon pilot certificate it may be accompanied by a certification by the applicant that he has no known medical defect that makes him unable to pilot a glider or free balloon.

§ 61.87 Requirements for solo flight.

(a) *General.* A student pilot may not operate an aircraft in solo flight until he has complied with the requirements of this section. As used in this subpart the term solo flight means that flight time during which a student pilot is the sole occupant of the aircraft, or that flight time during which he acts as pilot in command of an airship requiring more than one flight crewmember.

(b) *Aeronautical knowledge.* He must have demonstrated to an authorized instructor that he is familiar with the flight rules of Part 91 of this chapter which are pertinent to student solo flights.

(c) *Flight proficiency training.* He must have received ground and flight instruction in at least the following procedures and operations:

(1) *In airplanes.*

(i) Flight preparations procedures, including preflight inspection and powerplant operation;

(ii) Ground maneuvering and runups;

(iii) Straight and level flight, climbs, turns, and descents;

(iv) Flight at minimum controllable airspeeds, and stall recognition and recovery;

(v) Normal takeoffs and landings;

(vi) Airport traffic patterns, including collision avoidance precautions and wake turbulence; and

(vii) Emergencies, including elementary emergency landings.

Instruction must be given by a flight instructor who is authorized to give instruction in airplanes.

(d) *Flight instructor endorsements.* A student pilot may not operate an aircraft in solo flight unless his student pilot certificate is endorsed, and unless within the preceding 90 days his pilot logbook has been endorsed, by an authorized flight instructor who—

(1) Has given him instruction in the make and model of aircraft in which the solo flight is made;

(2) Finds that he has met the requirements of this section; and

(3) Finds that he is competent to make a safe solo flight in that aircraft.

§ 61.89 General limitations.

(a) A student pilot may not act as pilot in command of an aircraft—

(1) That is carrying a passenger;

(2) That is carrying property for compensation or hire;

(3) For compensation or hire;

(4) In furtherance of a business; or

(5) On an international flight, except that a student pilot may make solo training flights from Haines, Gustavus, or Juneau, Alaska, to White Horse, Yukon, Canada, and return, over the province of British Columbia.

(b) A student pilot may not act as a required pilot flight crewmember on any aircraft for which more than one pilot is required, except when receiving flight instruction from an authorized flight instructor on board an airship and no person other than a required flight crewmember is carried on the aircraft.

§ 61.93 Cross-country flight requirements.

(a) *General.* A student pilot may not operate an aircraft in a solo cross-country flight, nor may he, except in an emergency, make a solo flight landing at any point other than the airport of takeoff, until he meets the requirements prescribed in this section. However, an authorized flight instructor may allow a student pilot to practice solo landings and takeoffs at another airport within 25 nautical miles from the airport at which the student pilot receives instruction if he finds that the student pilot is competent to make those landings and takeoffs. As used in this section the term cross-country flight means a flight beyond a radius of 25 nautical miles from the point of takeoff.

(b) *Flight training.* A student pilot must receive instruction from an authorized instructor in at least the following pilot operations pertinent to the aircraft to be operated in a solo cross-country flight:

(1) For solo cross-country in airplanes—

(i) The use of aeronautical charts, pilotage, and elementary dead reckoning using the magnetic compass;

(ii) The use of radio for VFR navigation, and for two-way communication;

(iii) Control of an airplane by reference to flight instruments;

(iv) Short field and soft field procedures, and crosswind takeoffs and landings;

(v) Recognition of critical weather situations, estimating visibility while in flight, and the procurement and use of aeronautical weather reports and forecasts; and

(vi) Cross-country emergency procedures.

(c) *Flight instructor endorsements.* A student pilot must have the following endorsements from an authorized flight instructor:

(1) An endorsement on his student pilot certificate stating that he has received instruction in solo cross-country flying and the applicable training requirements of this section, and is competent to make cross-country solo flights in the category of aircraft involved.

(2) An endorsement in his pilot logbook that the instructor has reviewed the preflight planning and preparation for each solo cross-country flight, and he is prepared to make the flight safely under the known circumstances and the conditions listed by the instructor in the logbook. The instructor may also endorse the logbook for repeated solo cross-country flights under stipulated conditions over a course not more than 50 nautical miles from the point of departure if he has given the student flight instruction in both directions over the route, including takeoffs and landings at the airports to be used.

Subpart D – Private Pilots

§ 61.101 Applicability.

This subpart prescribes the requirements for the issuance of private pilot certificates and ratings, the conditions under which those certificates and ratings are necessary, and the general operating rules for the holders of those certificates and ratings.

§ 61.103 Eligibility requirements: general.

To be eligible for a private pilot certificate, a person must—

(a) Be at least 17 years of age, except that a private pilot certificate with a free balloon or a glider rating only may be issued to a qualified applicant who is at least 16 years of age;

(b) Be able to read, speak, and understand the English language, or have such operating limitations placed on his pilot certificate as are necessary for the safe operation of aircraft, to be removed when he shows that he can read, speak, and understand the English language;

(c) Hold at least a current third-class medical certificate issued under Part 67 of this chapter, or, in the case of a glider or free balloon rating, certify that he has no known medical defect that makes him unable to pilot a glider or free balloon, as appropriate;

(d) Pass a written test on the subject areas on which instruction or home study is required by § 61.105;

(e) Pass an oral and flight test on procedures and maneuvers selected by an FAA inspector or examiner to determine the applicant's competency in the flight operations on which instruction is required by the flight proficiency provisions of § 61.107; and

(f) Comply with the sections of this Part that apply to the rating he seeks.

§ 61.105 Aeronautical knowledge.

An applicant for a private pilot certificate must have logged ground instruction from an authorized instructor, or must present evidence showing that he has satisfactorily completed a course of instruction or home study in at least the following areas of aeronautical knowledge appropriate to the category of aircraft for which a rating is sought.

(a) *Airplanes.*

(1) The Federal Aviation Regulations applicable to private pilot privileges, limitations, and flight operations, accident reporting requirements of the National Transportation Safety Board, and the use of the "Airman's Information Manual" and the FAA Advisory Circulars;

(2) VFR navigation, using pilotage, dead reckoning, and radio aids;

(3) The recognition of critical weather situations from the ground and in flight and the procurement and use of aeronautical weather reports and forecasts; and

(4) The safe and efficient operation of airplanes, including high density airport operations, collision avoidance precautions, and radio communication procedures.

§ 61.107 Flight proficiency.

Check Chapter 28 for general requirements for flight proficiency (that is, the listing of the basic knowledge and maneuvers required on the private flight test).

§ 61.109 Airplane rating: aeronautical experience.

An applicant for a private pilot certificate with an airplane rating must have had at least a total of 40 hours of flight instruction and solo flight time which must include the following:

(a) 20 hours of flight instruction from an authorized flight instructor, including at least—

(1) Three hours of cross-country;

(2) Three hours at night, including 10 takeoffs and landings for applicants seeking night flying privileges; and

(3) Three hours in airplanes in preparation for the private pilot flight test within 60 days prior to that test.

An applicant who does not meet the night flying requirement in paragraph (a)(2) is issued a private pilot certificate bearing the limitation "Night flying prohibited." This limitation may be removed if the holder of the certificate shows that he has met the requirements of paragraph (a)(2).

(b) Twenty hours of solo flight time, including at least—

(1) Ten hours in airplanes;

(2) Ten hours of cross-country flights, each flight with a landing at a point more than 50 nautical miles from the original departure point. One flight must be of at least 300 nautical miles with landings at a minimum of 3 points, one of which is at least 100 nautical miles from the original departure point.

(3) Three solo takeoffs and landings to a full stop at an airport with an operating control tower;

§ 61.118 Private pilot privileges and limitations: pilot in command.

Except as provided in paragraphs (a) through (d) of this section, a private pilot may not act as pilot in command of an aircraft that is carrying passengers or property for compensation or hire; nor may he, for compensation or hire, act as pilot in command of an aircraft.

(a) A private pilot may, for compensation or hire, act as pilot in command of an aircraft in connection with any business or employment if the flight is only incidental to that business or employment and the aircraft does not carry passengers or property for compensation or hire.

(b) A private pilot may share the operating expenses of a flight with his passengers.

(c) A private pilot who is an aircraft salesman and who has at least 200 hours of logged flight time may demonstrate an aircraft in flight to a prospective buyer.

(d) A private pilot may act as pilot in command of an aircraft used in a passenger-carrying airlift sponsored by a charitable organization, and for which the passengers make a donation to the organization, if—

(1) The sponsor of the airlift notifies the FAA General Aviation District Office having jurisdiction over the area concerned, at least 7 days before the flight, and furnishes any essential information that the office requests;

(2) The flight is conducted from a public airport adequate for the aircraft used, or from another airport that has been approved for the operation by an FAA inspector;

(3) He has logged at least 200 hours of flight time;

(4) No acrobatic or formation flights are conducted;

(5) Each aircraft used is certificated in the standard category and complies with the 100-hour inspection requirement of § 91.169 of this chapter; and

(6) The flight is made under VFR during the day.

For the purpose of paragraph (d) of this section, a "charitable organization" means an organization listed in Publication No. 78 of the Department of the Treasury called the "Cumulative List of Organizations described in section 170(c) of the Internal Revenue Code of 1954," as amended from time to time by published supplemental lists.

Part 91—General Operating and Flight Rules

Subpart A—General

§ 91.1 Applicability

(a) Except as provided in paragraph (b) of this section, this Part prescribes rules governing the operation of aircraft (other than moored balloons, kites, unmanned rockets, and unmanned free balloons) within the United States.

§ 91.3 Responsibility and authority of the pilot in command.

(a) The pilot in command of an aircraft is directly responsible for, and is the final authority as to, the operation of that aircraft.

(b) In an emergency requiring immediate action, the pilot in command may deviate from any rule of this subpart, or of Subpart B to the extent required to meet that emergency.

(c) Each pilot in command who deviates from a rule under paragraph (b) of this section shall, upon the request of the Administrator, send a written report of that deviation to the Administrator.

§ 91.4 Pilot in command of aircraft requiring more than one required pilot.

No person may operate an aircraft that is type certificated for more than one required pilot flight crewmember unless the pilot flight crew consists of a pilot in command who meets the requirements of § 61.58 of this chapter.

§ 91.5 Preflight action.

Each pilot in command shall, before beginning a flight, familiarize himself with all available information concerning that flight. This information must include:

(a) For a flight under IFR or a flight not in the vicinity of an airport, weather reports and forecasts, fuel requirements, alternatives available if the planned flight cannot be completed, and any known traffic delays of which he has been advised by ATC.

(b) For any flight, runway lengths at airports of intended use, and the following takeoff and landing distance information:

(1) For civil aircraft for which an approved airplane or rotorcraft flight manual containing takeoff and landing distance data is required, the takeoff and landing distance data contained therein; and

(2) For civil aircraft other than those specified in subparagraph (1) of this paragraph, other reliable information appropriate to the aircraft, relating to aircraft performance under expected values of airport elevation and runway slope, aircraft gross weight, and wind and temperature.

§ 91.9 Careless or reckless operation.

No person may operate an aircraft in a careless or reckless manner so as to endanger the life or property of another.

§ 91.10 Careless or reckless operation other than for the purpose of air navigation.

No person may operate an aircraft other than for the purpose of air navigation, on any part of the surface of an airport used by aircraft for air commerce (including areas used by those aircraft for receiving or discharging persons or cargo), in a careless or reckless manner so as to endanger the life or property of another.

§ 91.11 Liquor and drugs.

(a) No person may act as a crewmember of a civil aircraft—

(1) Within 8 hours after the consumption of any alcoholic beverage;

(2) While under the influence of alcohol; or

(3) While using any drug that affects his faculties in any way contrary to safety.

(b) Except in an emergency, no pilot of a civil aircraft may allow a person who is obviously under the influence of intoxicating liquors or drugs (except a medical patient under proper care) to be carried in that aircraft.

§ 91.12 Carriage of narcotic drugs, marihuana, and depressant or stimulant drugs or substances.

(a) Except as provided in paragraph (b) of this section, no person may operate a civil aircraft within the United States with knowledge that narcotic drugs, marihuana, and depressant or stimulant drugs or substances as defined in Federal or State statutes are carried in the aircraft.

(b) Paragraph (a) of this section does not apply to any carriage of narcotic drugs, marihuana, and depressant or stimulant drugs or substances authorized by or under any Federal or State statute or by any Federal or State agency.

§ 91.13 Dropping objects.

No pilot in command of a civil aircraft may allow any object to be dropped from that aircraft in flight that creates a hazard to persons or property. However, this section does not prohibit the dropping of any object if reasonable precautions are taken to avoid injury or damage to persons or property.

§ 91.14 Use of safety belts.

(a) Unless otherwise authorized by the Administrator—

(1) No pilot may take off a U.S. registered civil aircraft (except a free balloon that incorporates a basket or gondola and an airship) unless the pilot in command of that aircraft ensures that each person on board is briefed on how to fasten and unfasten that person's safety belt.

(2) No pilot may take off or land a U.S. registered civil aircraft (except free balloons that incorporate baskets or gondolas and airships) unless the pilot in command of that aircraft ensures that each person on board has been notified to fasten his safety belt.

(3) During the takeoff and landing of U.S. registered civil aircraft (except free balloons that incorporate baskets or gondolas and airships), each person on board that aircraft must occupy a seat or berth with a safety belt properly secured about him. However, a person who has not reached his second birthday may be held by an adult who is occupying a seat or berth, and a person on board for the purpose of engaging in sport parachuting may use the floor of the aircraft as a seat.

(b) This section does not apply to operations conducted under Part 121, 123, or 127 of this chapter. Paragraph (a)(3) of this section does not apply to persons subject to § 91.7.

§ 91.15 Parachutes and parachuting.

(a) No pilot of a civil aircraft may allow a parachute that is available for emergency use to be carried in that aircraft unless it is an approved type and—

(1) If a chair type (canopy in back), it has been packed by a certificated and appropriately rated parachute rigger within the preceding 120 days;

(b) Except in an emergency, no pilot in command may allow, and no person may make, a parachute jump from an aircraft within the United States except in accordance with Part 105.

(c) Unless each occupant of the aircraft is wearing an approved parachute, no pilot of a civil aircraft, carrying any person (other than a crewmember) may execute any intentional maneuver that exceeds—

(1) A bank of 60 degrees relative to the horizon: or

(2) A nose-up or nose-down attitude of 30 degrees relative to the horizon.

(d) Paragraph (c) of this section does not apply to—

(1) Flight tests for pilot certification or rating; or

(2) Spins and other flight maneuvers required by the regulations for any certificate or rating when given by—

(i) A certificated flight instructor; or

(ii) An airline transport pilot instructing in accordance with § 61.169.

§ 91.21 Flight instruction; simulated instrument flight and certain flight tests.

(a) No person may operate a civil aircraft that is being used for flight instruction unless that aircraft has fully functioning dual controls.

(b) No person may operate a civil aircraft in simulated instrument flight unless—

(1) An appropriately rated pilot occupies the other control seat as safety pilot;

(2) The safety pilot has adequate vision forward and to each side of the aircraft, or a competent observer in the aircraft adequately supplements the vision of the safety pilot; and

(3) Except in the case of a lighter-than-air aircraft, that aircraft is equipped with functioning dual controls.

(c) No person may operate a civil aircraft that is being used for a flight test for an airline transport pilot certificate or a class or type rating on that certificate, or for a Federal Aviation Regulation Part 121 proficiency flight test, unless the pilot seated at the controls, other than the pilot being checked, is fully qualified to act as pilot in command of the aircraft.

§ 91.22 Fuel requirements for flight under VFR.

(a) No person may begin a flight in an airplane under VFR unless (considering wind and forecast weather conditions) there is enough fuel to fly to the first point of intended landing and, assuming normal cruising speed—

(1) During the day, to fly after that for at least 30 minutes; or

(2) At night, to fly after that for at least 45 minutes.

§ 91.27 Civil aircraft: certifications required.

(a) Except as provided in § 91.28, no person may operate a civil aircraft unless it has within it the following:

(1) An appropriate and current airworthiness certificate. Each U.S. airworthiness certificate used to comply with this subparagraph (except a special flight permit, a copy of the applicable operations specifications issued under § 21.197(c) of this chapter, appropriate sections of the air carrier manual required by Parts 121 and 127 of this chapter containing that portion of the operations specifications issued under § 21.197(c), or an authorization under § 91.45), must have on it the registration number assigned to the aircraft under Part 47 of this chapter. However, the airworthiness certificate need not have on it an assigned special identification number before 10 days after that number is first affixed to the aircraft. A revised airworthiness certificate having on it an assigned special identification number, that has been affixed to an aircraft, may only be obtained upon application to an FAA Flight Standards District Office.

(2) A registration certificate issued to its owner.

(b) No person may operate a civil aircraft unless the airworthiness certificate required by paragraph (a) of this section or a special flight authorization issued under § 91.28 is displayed at the cabin or cockpit entrance so that it is legible to passengers or crew.

§ 91.29 Civil aircraft airworthiness.

(a) No person may operate a civil aircraft unless it is in an airworthy condition.

(b) The pilot in command of a civil aircraft is responsible for determining whether that aircraft is in condition for safe flight. He shall discontinue the flight when unairworthy mechanical or structural conditions occur.

§ 91.31 Civil aircraft operating limitations and marking requirements.

(a) Except as provided in paragraph (d) of this section, no person may operate a civil aircraft without compliance with the operating limitations for that aircraft prescribed by the certificating authority of the country of registry.

(b) No person may operate a U.S. registered civil aircraft unless there is available in the aircraft a current Airplane or Rotorcraft Flight Manual, approved manual material, markings, and placards, or any combination thereof, containing each operating limitation prescribed for the aircraft by the Administrator, including the following:

(1) Powerplant (e.g., r.p.m., manifold pressure, gas temperature, etc.).

(2) Airspeeds (e.g., normal operating speed, flaps extended speed, etc.).

(3) Aircraft weight, center of gravity, and weight distribution, including the composition of the useful load in those combinations and ranges intended to insure that the weight and center of gravity position will remain within approved limits (e.g., combinations and ranges of crew, oil, fuel, and baggage).

(4) Minimum flight crew.

(5) Kinds of operation.

(6) Maximum operating altitude.

(7) Maneuvering flight load factors.

(8) Rotor speed (for rotorcraft).

(9) Limiting height-speed envelope (for rotorcraft).

§ 91.32 Supplemental oxygen.

(a) *General.* No person may operate a civil aircraft of U.S. registry—

(1) At cabin pressure altitudes above 12,500 feet (MSL) up to and including 14,000 feet (MSL), unless the required minimum flight crew is provided with and uses supplemental oxygen for that part of the flight at those altitudes that is of more than 30 minutes duration.

(2) At cabin pressure altitudes above 14,000 feet (MSL), unless the required minimum flight crew is provided with and uses supplemental oxygen during the entire flight time at those altitudes; and

(3) At cabin pressure altitudes above 15,000 feet (MSL), unless each occupant of the aircraft is provided with supplemental oxygen.

§ 91.33 Powered civil aircraft with standard category U.S. airworthiness certificates; instrument and equipment requirements.

(a) *General.* Except as provided in paragraphs (c)(3) and (e) of this section, no person may operate a powered civil aircraft with a standard category U.S. airworthiness certificate in any operation described in paragraphs (b) through (f) of this section unless that aircraft contains the instruments and equipment specified in those paragraphs (or FAA approved equivalents) for that type of operation, and those instruments and items of equipment are in operable condition.

(b) *Visual flight rules (day).* For VFR flight during the day the following instruments and equipment are required:

(1) Airspeed indicator.

(2) Altimeter.

(3) Magnetic direction indicator.

(4) Tachometer for each engine.

(5) Oil pressure gauge for each engine using pressure system.

(6) Temperature gauge for each liquid-cooled engine.

(7) Oil temperature gauge for each air-cooled engine.

(8) Manifold pressure gauge for each altitude engine.

(9) Fuel gauge indicating the quantity of fuel in each tank.

(10) Landing gear position indicator, if the aircraft has a retractable landing gear.

(11) If the aircraft is operated for hire over water and beyond power-off gliding distance from shore, approved flotation gear readily available to each occupant, and at least one pyrotechnic signaling device.

(12) Except as to airships, an approved safety belt for all occupants who have reached their second birthday. After December 4, 1981, each safety belt must be equipped with an approved metal to metal latching device. The rated strength of each safety belt shall not be less than that corresponding with the ultimate load factors specified in the current applicable aircraft airworthiness requirements considering the dimensional characteristics of the safety belt installation for the specific seat or berth arrangement. The webbing of each safety belt shall be replaced as required by the Administrator.

(13) For small civil airplanes manufactured after July 18, 1978, an approved shoulder harness for each front seat. The shoulder harness must be designed to protect the occupant from serious head injury when the occupant experiences the ultimate inertia forces specified in § 23.561(b)(2) of this chapter. Each shoulder harness installed at a flight crewmember station must permit the crewmember, when seated and with his safety belt and shoulder harness fastened, to perform all functions necessary for flight operations. For purposes of this paragraph—

(i) The date of manufacture of an airplane is the date the inspection acceptance records reflect that the airplane is complete and meets the FAA Approved Type Design Data; and

(ii) A front seat is a seat located at a flight crewmember station or any seat located alongside such a seat.

(c) *Visual flight rules (night).* For VFR flight at night the following instruments and equipment are required:

(1) Instruments and equipment specified in paragraph (b) of this section.

(2) Approved position lights.

(3) An approved aviation red or aviation white anticollision light system on all large aircraft, on all small aircraft when required by the aircraft's airworthiness certificate, and on all other small aircraft after August 11, 1972. Anticollision light systems initially installed after August 11, 1971, on aircraft for which a type certificate was issued or applied for before August 11, 1971, must at least meet the anticollision light standards of Parts 23, 25, 27, or 29, as applicable, that were in effect on August 10, 1971, except that the color may be either aviation red or aviation white. In the event of failure of any light of the anticollision light system, operations with the aircraft may be continued to a stop where repairs or replacement can be made.

(4) If the aircraft is operated for hire, one electric landing light.

(5) An adequate source of electrical energy for all installed electrical and radio equipment.

(6) One spare set of fuses, or three spare fuses of each kind required.

(d) *Instrument flight rules.* For IFR flight the following instruments and equipment are required:

(1) Instruments and equipment specified in paragraph (b) of this section and for night flight, instruments and equipment specified in paragraph (c) of this section.

(2) Two-way radio communications system and navigational equipment appropriate to the ground facilities to be used.

(3) Gyroscopic rate-of-turn indicator, except on large aircraft with a third attitude instrument system usable through flight at-

titudes of 360° of pitch and roll and installed in accordance with § 121.305(j) of this title.

(4) Slip-skid indicator.

(5) Sensitive altimeter adjustable for barometric pressure.

(6) Clock with sweep-second hand.

(7) Generator of adequate capacity.

(8) Gyroscopic bank and pitch indicator (artificial horizon).

(9) Gyroscopic direction indicator (directional gyro or equivalent).

§91.52 Emergency locator transmitters.

Rather than go into detail about the various requirements for having an ELT installed, as a student or private pilot you should check that any airplane you rent (or borrow) has an ELT as required and that it is "ON." This section of the FAR's gives all requirements (including airline operations) for ELT's.

Subpart B – Flight Rules

GENERAL

§ 91.61 Applicability.

This subpart prescribes flight rules governing the operation of aircraft within the United States.

§91.623 Waivers.

(a) The Administrator may issue a certificate of waiver authorizing the operation of aircraft in deviation of any rule of this subpart if he finds that the proposed operation can be safely conducted under the terms of that certificate of waiver.

(b) An application for a certificate of waiver under this section is made on a form and in a manner prescribed by the Administrator and may be submitted to any FAA office.

(c) A certificate of waiver is effective as specified in that certificate.

§ 91.65 Operating near other aircraft.

(a) No person may operate an aircraft so close to another aircraft as to create a collision hazard.

(b) No person may operate an aircraft in formation flight except by arrangement with the pilot in command of each aircraft in the formation.

(c) No person may operate an aircraft, carrying passengers for hire, in formation flight.

(d) Unless otherwise authorized by ATC, no person operating an aircraft may operate his aircraft in accordance with any clearance or instruction that has been issued to the pilot of another aircraft for radar Air Traffic Control purposes.

§ 91.67 Right-of-way rules; except water operations.

(a) *General.* When weather conditions permit, regardless of whether an operation is conducted under Instrument Flight Rules or Visual Flight Rules, vigilance shall be maintained by each person operating an aircraft so as to see and avoid other aircraft in compliance with this section. When a rule of this section gives another aircraft the right of way, he shall give way to that aircraft and may not pass over, under, or ahead of it, unless well clear.

(b) *In distress.* An aircraft in distress has the right of way over all other air traffic.

(c) *Converging.* When aircraft of the same category are converging at approximately the same altitude (except head-on, or nearly so) the aircraft to the other's right has the right of way. If the aircraft are of different categories –

(1) A balloon has the right of way over any other category of aircraft;

(2) A glider has the right of way over an airship, airplane or rotorcraft; and

(3) An airship has the right of way over an airplane or rotorcraft.

However, an aircraft towing or refueling other aircraft has the right of way over all other engine-driven aircraft.

(d) *Approaching head-on.* When aircraft are approaching each other head-on, or nearly so, each pilot of each aircraft shall alter course to the right.

(3) *Overtaking.* Each aircraft that is being overtaken has the right of way and each pilot of an overtaking aircraft shall alter course to the right to pass well clear.

(f) *Landing.* Aircraft, while on final approach to land, or while landing, have the right of way over other aircraft in flight or operating on the surface. When two or more aircraft are approaching an airport for the purpose of landing, the aircraft at the lower altitude has the right of way, but it shall not take advantage of this rule to cut in front of another which in on final approach to land, or to overtake that aircraft.

(g) *Inapplicability.* This section does not apply to the operation of an aircraft on water.

§ 91.70 Aircraft speed.

(a) Unless otherwise authorized by the Administrator, no person may operate an aircraft below 10,000 feet MSL at an indicated airspeed of more than 250 knots (288 m.p.h.).

(b) Unless otherwise authorized or required by ATC, no person may operate an aircraft within an airport traffic area at an indicated airspeed of more than –

(1) In the case of a reciprocating engine aircraft, 156 knots (180 m.p.h.); or

(2) In the case of a turbine-powered aircraft, 200 knots (230 m.p.h.).

Paragraph (b) does not apply to any operations within a Terminal Control Area. Such operations shall comply with paragraph (a) of this section.

(c) No person may operate aircraft in the airspace beneath the lateral limits of any terminal control area at an indicated airspeed of more than 200 knots (230 m.p.h.).

However, if the minimum safe airspeed for any particular operation is greater than the maximum speed prescribed in this section, the aircraft may be operated at that minimum speed.

§ 91.71 Acrobatic flight.

No person may operate an aircraft in acrobatic flight –

(a) Over any congested area of a city, town, or settlement;

(b) Over an open air assembly of persons;

(c) Within a control zone or Federal airway;

(d) Below an altitude of 1,500 feet above the surface; or

(e) When flight visibility is less than three miles.

For the purposes of this section, acrobatic flight means an intentional maneuver involving an abrupt change in an aircraft's attitude, an abnormal attitude, or abnormal acceleration, not necessary for normal flight.

§ 91.73 Aircraft lights.

No person may, during the period from sunset to sunrise (or, in Alaska, during the period a prominent unlighted object cannot be seen from a distance of three statute miles or the sun is more than six degrees below the horizon) –

(a) Operate an aircraft unless it has lighted position lights;

(b) Park or move an aircraft in, or in dangerous proximity to, a night flight operations area of an airport unless the aircraft –

(1) Is clearly illuminated;

(2) Has lighted position lights; or

(3) Is in an area which is marked by obstruction lights

(d) Operate an aircraft, required by § 91.33(c)(3) to be equipped with an anticollision light system, unless it has approved and lighted aviation red or aviation white anticollision lights. However, the anticollision lights need not be lighted when the pilot in command determines that, because of operating conditions, it would be in the interest of safety to turn the lights off.

§ 91.75 Compliance with ATC clearances and instructions.

(a) When an ATC clearance has been obtained, no pilot in command may deviate from that clearance, except in an emergency, unless he obtains an amended clearance. However, except in positive controlled airspace, this paragraph does not prohibit him from cancelling an IFR flight plan if he is operating in VFR weather conditions.

(b) Except in an emergency, no person may, in an area in which air traffic control is exercised, operate an aircraft contrary to an ATC instruction.

(c) Each pilot in command who deviates, in an emergency, from an ATC clearance or instruction shall notify ATC of that deviation as soon as possible.

(d) Each pilot in command who (though not deviating from a rule of this subpart) is given priority by ATC in an emergency, shall, if requested by ATC, submit a detailed report of that emergency within 48 hours to the chief of that ATC facility.

§ 91.77 ATC light signals.

(See Fig. 21-16)

§ 91.79 Minimum safe altitudes; general.

Except when necessary for takeoff or landing, no person may operate an aircraft below the following altitudes:

(a) *Anywhere.* An altitude allowing, if a power unit fails, an emergency landing without undue hazard to persons or property on the surface.

(b) *Over congested areas.* Over any congested area of a city, town, or settlement, or over any open air assembly of persons, an altitude of 1,000 feet above the highest obstacle within a horizontal radius of 2,000 feet of the aircraft.

(c) *Over other than congested areas.* An altitude of 500 feet above the surface, except over open water or sparsely populated areas. In that case, the aircraft may not be operated closer than 500 feet to any person, vessel, vehicle, or structure.

§ 91.81 Altimeter settings.

(a) Each person operating an aircraft shall maintain the cruising altitude or flight level of that aircraft, as the case may be, by reference to an altimeter that is set, when operating –

(1) Below 18,000 feet MSL, to –

(i) The current reported altimeter setting of a station along the route and within 100 nautical miles of the aircraft;

(ii) If there is no station within the area prescribed in subdivision (i) of this subparagraph, the current reported altimeter setting of an appropriate available station; or

(iii) In the case of an aircraft not equipped with a radio, the elevation of the departure airport or an appropriate altimeter setting available before departure;

§ 91.83 Flight plan; information required.

(a) Unless otherwise authorized by ATC, each person filing an IFR or VFR flight plan shall include in it the following information:

(1) The aircraft identification number and, if necessary, its radio call sign.

(2) The type of the aircraft or, in the case of a formation flight, the type of each aircraft and the number of aircraft, in the formation.

(3) The full name and address of the pilot in command or, in the case of a formation flight, the formation commander.

(4) The point and proposed time of departure.

(5) The proposed route, cruising altitude (or flight level), and true airspeed at that altitude.

(6) The point of first intended landing and the estimated elapsed time until over that point.

(7) The radio frequencies to be used.

(8) The amount of fuel on board (in hours).

(9) In the case of an IFR flight plan, an alternate airport, except as provided in paragraph (b) of this section.

(10) In the case of an international flight, the number of persons in the aircraft.

(11) Any other information the pilot in command or ATC believes is necessary for ATC purposes.

When a flight plan has been filed, the pilot in command, upon cancelling or completing the flight under the flight plan, shall notify the nearest FAA Flight Service Station or ATC facility.

§ 91.85 Operating on or in the vicinity of an airport; general rules.

(a) Unless otherwise required by Part 93 of this chapter, each person operating an aircraft on or in the vicinity of an airport shall comply with the requirements of this section and of §§ 91.87 and 91.89.

(b) Unless otherwise authorized or required by ATC, no person may operate an aircraft within an airport traffic area except for the purpose of landing at, or taking off from, an airport within that area. ATC authorizations may be given as individual approval of specific operations or may be contained in written agreements between airport users and the tower concerned.

§ 91.87 Operation at airports with operating control towers.

(a) *General.* Unless otherwise authorized or required by ATC, each person operating an aircraft to, from, or on an airport with an operating control tower shall comply with the applicable provisions of this section.

(b) *Communications with control towers operated by the United States.* No person may, within an airport traffic area, operate an aircraft to, from, or on an airport having a control tower operated by the United States unless two-way radio communications are maintained between that aircraft and the control tower. However, if the aircraft radio fails in flight, he may operate that aircraft and land if weather conditions are at or above basic VFR weather minimums, he maintains visual contact with the tower, and he receives a clearance to land. If the aircraft radio fails while in flight under IFR, he must comply with § 91.127.

(c) *Communications with other control towers.* No person may, within an airport traffic area, operate an aircraft to, from, or on an airport having a control tower that is operated by any person other than the United States unless –

(1) If that aircraft's radio equipment so allows, two-way radio communications are maintained between the aircraft and the tower; or

(2) If that aircraft's radio equipment allows only reception from the tower, the pilot has the tower's frequency monitored.

(d) *Minimum altitudes.* When operating to an airport with an operating control tower, each pilot of –

(2) A turbine-powered airplane or a large airplane approaching to land on a runway being served by an ILS, shall, if the airplane is ILS equipped, fly that airplane at an altitude at or above the glide slope between the outer marker (or the point of interception with the glide slope, if compliance with the applicable distance from clouds criteria requires interception closer in) and the middle marker; and,

(3) An airplane approaching to land on a runway served by a visual approach slope indicator shall maintain an altitude at or above the glide slope until a lower altitude is necessary for a safe landing.

However, subparagraphs (2) and (3) of this paragraph do not prohibit normal bracketing maneuvers above or below the glide slope that are conducted for the purpose of remaining on the glide slope.

(e) *Approaches.* When approaching to land at an airport with an operating control tower, each pilot of –

(1) An airplane, shall circle the airport to the left; and

(2) A helicopter, shall avoid the flow of fixed-wing aircraft.

(f) *Departure.* No person may operate an aircraft taking off from an airport with an operating control tower except in compliance with the following:

(1) Each pilot shall comply with any departure procedures established for that airport by the FAA.

(h) *Clearances required.* No pilot may, at an airport with an operating control tower, taxi an aircraft on a runway, or take off or land an aircraft, unless he has received an appropriate clearance from ATC. A clearance to "taxi to" the runway is a clearance to cross all intersecting runways but is not a clearance to "taxi on" the assigned runway.

§ 91.89 Operation of airports without control towers.

(a) Each person operating an aircraft to or from an airport without an operating control towers shall –

(1) In the case of an airplane approaching to land, make all turns of that airplane to the left unless the airport displays approved light signals or visual markings indicating that turns should be made to the right, in which case the pilot shall make all turns to the right;

(2) In the case of a helicopter approaching to land, avoid the flow of fixed-wing aircraft; and

(3) In the case of an aircraft departing the airport, comply with any FAA traffic pattern for that airport.

§ 91.91 Temporary flight restrictions.

(a) Whenever the Administrator determines it to be necesssary in order to prevent an unsafe congestion of sight-seeing aircraft above an incident or event which may generate a high degree of public interest, or to provide a safe environment for the operation of disaster relief aircraft, a Notice to Airmen will be issued designating an area within which temporary flight restrictions apply.

(b) When a Notice to Airmen has been issued under this section, no person may operate an aircraft within the designated area unless –

(1) That aircraft is participating in disaster relief activities and is being operated under the direction of the agency responsible for relief activities;

(2) That aircraft is being operated to or from an airport within the area and is operated so as not to hamper or endanger relief activities;

(3) That operation is specifically authorized under an IFR ATC clearance;

(4) VFR flight around or above the area is impracticable due to weather, terrain, or other considerations, prior notice is given to the Air Traffic Service facility specified in the Notice to Airmen, and en route operation through the area is conducted so as not to hamper or endanger relief activities; or

(5) That aircraft is carrying properly accredited news representatives, or persons on official business concerning the incident or event which generated the issuance of the Notice to Airmen; the operation is conducted in accordance with § 91.79 of this chapter; the operation is conducted above the altitudes being used by relief aircraft unless otherwise authorized by the agency responsible for relief activities; and further, in connection with this type of operation, prior to entering the area the operator has filed with the Air Traffic Service facility specified in the Notice to Airmen a flight plan that includes the following information:

(i) aircraft identification, type and color.

(ii) Radio communications frequencies to be used.

(iii) Proposed times of entry and exit of the designated area.

(iv) Name of news media or purpose of flight.

(v) Any other information deemed necessary by ATC.

§ 91.93 Flight test areas.

No person may flight test an aircraft except over open water, or sparsely populated areas, having light air traffic.

§ 91.95 Restricted and prohibited areas.

(a) No person may operate an aircraft within a restricted area (designated in Part 73) contrary to the restrictions imposed, or within a prohibited area, unless he has the permission of the using or controlling agency, as appropriate.

(b) Each person conducting, within a restricted area, an aircraft operation (approved by the using agency) that creates the same hazards as the operations for which the restricted area was designated, may deviate from the rules of this subpart that are not compatible with his operation of the aircraft.

§ 91.104 Flight restrictions in the proximity of the Presidential and other parties.

No person may operate an aircraft over or in the vicinity of any area to be visited or traveled by the President, the Vice President, or other public figures contrary to the restrictions established by the Administrator and published in a Notice to Airmen (NOTAM).

VISUAL FLIGHT RULES

§ 91.105 Basic VFR weather minimums.

(a) Except as provided in § 91.107, no person may operate an aircraft under VFR when the flight visibility is less, or at a distance from clouds that is less, than that prescribed for the corresponding altitude in the following table:

In addition, he shall ensure that maintenance personnel make appropriate entries in the aircraft and maintenance records indicating the aircraft has been approved for return to service.

Altitude	Flight visibility	Distance from clouds
1,200 feet or less above the surface (regardless of MSL altitude)—		
Within controlled airspace _____	3 statute miles _____	500 feet below. 1,000 feet above. 2,000 feet horizontal.
Outside controlled airspace _____	1 statute mile except as provided in § 91.105 (b).	Clear of clouds.
More than 1,200 feet above the surface but less than 10,000 feet MSL—		
Within controlled airspace _____	3 statute miles _____	500 feet below. 1,000 feet above. 2,000 feet horizontal.
Outside controlled airspace _____	1 statue mile _____	500 feet below. 1,000 feet above. 2,000 feet horizontal.
More than 1,200 feet above the surface and at or above 10,000 feet MSL.	5 statute miles _____	1,000 feet below. 1,000 feet above. 1 mile horizontal.

(b) When the visibility is less than one mile, a helicopter may be operated outside controlled airspace at 1,200 feet or less above the surface if operated at a speed that allows the pilot adequate opportunity to see any air traffic or other obstruction in time to avoid a collision.

(c) Except as provided in § 91.107, no person may operate an aircraft, under VFR, within a control zone beneath the ceiling when the ceiling is less than 1,000 feet.

(d) Except as provided in § 91.107, no person may take off or land an aircraft, or enter the traffic pattern of an airport, under VFR, within a control zone—

(1) Unless ground visibility at that airport is at least 3 statute miles; or

(2) If ground visibility is not reported at that airport, unless flight visibility during landing or take off, or while operating in the traffic pattern, is at least 3 statute miles.

(e) For the purposes of this section an aircraft operating at the base altitude of a transition area or control area is considered to be within the airspace directly below that area.

§ 91.107 Special VFR weather minimums.

(a) Except as provided in § 93.113, when a person has received an appropriate ATC clearance, the special weather minimums of this section instead of those contained in § 91.105 apply to the operation of an aircraft by that person in a control zone under VFR.

(b) No person may operate an aircraft in a control zone under VFR except clear of clouds.

(c) No person may operate an aircraft (other than a helicopter) in a control zone under VFR unless flight visibility is at least 1 statute mile.

(d) No person may take off or land an aircraft (other than a helicopter) at any airport in a control zone under VFR—

(1) Unless ground visibility at that airport is at least 1 statute mile; or

(2) If ground visibility is not reported at that airport, unless flight visibility during landing or takeoff is at least 1 statute mile.

(e) No person may operate an aircraft (other than a helicopter) in a control zone under the special weather minimums of this section, between sunset and sunrise (or in Alaska, when the sun is more than six degrees below the horizon) unless—

(1) That person meets the applicable requirements for instrument flight under Part 61 of this chapter; and

(2) The aircraft is equipped as required in § 91.33(d).

§ 91.109 VFR cruising altitude or flight level.

Except while holding in a holding pattern of 2 minutes or less, or while turning, each person operating an aircraft under VFR in level cruising flight at an altitude of more than 3,000 feet above the surface shall maintain the appropriate altitude prescribed below:

(a) When operating below 18,000 feet MSL and—

(1) On a magnetic course of zero degrees through 179 degrees, any odd thousand foot MSL altitude +500 feet (such as 3,500, 5,500, or 7,500); or

(2) On a magnetic course of 180 degrees through 359 degrees, any even thousand foot MSL altitude +500 feet (such as 4,500, 6,500, or 8,500).

Subpart C—Maintenance, Preventive Maintenance, and Alterations

§ 91.163 General.

(a) The owner or operator of an aircraft is primarily responsible for maintaining that aircraft in an airworthy condition, including compliance with Part 39 of this chapter.

(b) No person may perform maintenance, preventive maintenance, or alterations on an aircraft other than as prescribed in this subpart and other applicable regulations, including Part 43.

§ 91.165 Maintenance required.

Each owner or operator of an aircraft shall have that aircraft inspected as prescribed in Subpart D or § 91.169 of this Part, as appropriate, and § 91.170 of this Part and shall, between required inspections, have defects repaired as prescribed in Part 43 of this chapter.

§ 91.167 Carrying persons other than crewmembers after repairs or alterations.

(a) No person may carry any person (other than crewmembers) in an aircraft that has been repaired or altered in a manner that may have appreciably changed its flight characteristics, or substantially affected its operation in flight, until it has been approved for return to service in accordance with Part 43 and an appropriately rated pilot, with at least a private pilot's certificate, flies the aircraft, makes an operational check of the repaired or altered part, and logs the flight in the aircraft's records.

(b) Paragraph (a) of this section does not require that the aircraft be flown if ground tests or inspections, or both, show conclusively that the repair or alteration has not appreciably changed the flight characteristics, or substantially affected the flight operation of the aircraft.

§ 91.169 Inspections.

(a) Except as provided in paragraph (c) of this section, no person may operate an aircraft unless, within the preceding 12 calendar months, it has had—

(1) An annual inspection in accordance with Part 43 of this chapter and has been approved for return to service by a person authorized by § 43.7 of this chapter; or

(2) An inspection for the issue of an airworthiness certificate.

No inspection performed under paragraph (b) of the section may be substituted for any inspection required by this paragraph unless it is performed by a person authorized to perform annual inspections, and is entered as an "annual" inspection in the required maintenance records.

(b) Except as provided in paragraph (c) of this section, no person may operate an aircraft carrying any person (other than a crewmember) for hire, and no person may give flight instruction for hire in an aircraft which that person provides, unless within the preceding 100 hours of time in service it has received an annual or 100-hour inspection and been approved for return to service in accordance with Part 43 of this chapter, or received an inspection for the issuance of an airworthiness certificate in accordance with Part 21 of this chapter. The 100-hour limitation may be exceeded by not more than 10 hours if necessary to reach a place at which the inspection can be done. The excess time, however, is included in computing the next 100 hours of time in service.

(c) Paragraphs (a) and (b) of this section do not apply to—

(1) Any aircraft for which its registered owner or operator complies with the progressive inspection requirements of § 91.171 and Part 43 of this chapter;

(2) An aircraft that carries a special flight permit or a current experimental or provisional certificate;

(3) Any airplane operated by an air travel club that is inspected in accordance with Part 123 of this chapter and the operator's manual and operations specifications; or

(4) An aircraft inspected in accordance with an approved aircraft inspection program under Part 135 of this chapter and so identified by the registration number in the operations specifications of the certificate holder having the approved inspection program.

(5) Any large airplane, or a turbojet- or turbopropeller-powered multiengine airplane, that is inspected in accordance with an inspection program authorized under Subpart D of this Part.

§ 91.173 Maintenance records.

(a) Except for work performed in accordance with §§ 91.170 and 91.177, each registered owner or operator shall keep the following records for the periods specified in paragraph (b) of this section:

(1) Records of the maintenance and alteration, and records of the 100-hour, annual, progressive, and other required or approved inspections, as appropriate, for each aircraft (including the airframe) and each engine, propeller, rotor, and appliance of an aircraft. The records must include—

(i) A description (or reference to data acceptable to the Administrator) of the work performed;

(ii) The date of completion of the work performed; and

(iii) The signature and certificate number of the person approving the aircraft for return to service.

(2) Records containing the following information:

(i) The total time in service of the airframe.

(ii) The current status of life-limited parts of each airframe, engine, propeller, rotor, and appliance.

(iii) The time since last overhaul of all items installed on the aircraft which are required to be overhauled on a specified time basis.

(iv) The identification of the current inspection status of the aircraft, including the times since the last inspections required by the inspection program under which the aircraft and its appliances are maintained.

(v) The current status of applicable airworthiness directives (AD), including the method of compliance.

(vi) A list of current major alterations to each airframe engine, propeller, rotor, and compliance.

(b) The owner or operator shall retain the records required to be kept by this section for the following periods:

(1) The records specified in paragraph (a)(1) of this section shall be retained until the work is repeated or superseded by other work or for one year after the work is performed.

(2) The records specified in paragraph (a)(2) of this section shall be retained and transferred with the aircraft at the time the aircraft is sold.

(3) A list of defects furnished to a registered owner or operator under § 43.9 of this chapter, shall be retained until the defects are repaired and the aircraft is approved for return to service.

(c) The owner or operator shall make all maintenance records required to be kept by this section available for inspection by the Administrator or any authorized representative of the National Transportation Safety Board (NTSB).

§ 91.174 Transfer of maintenance records.

Any owner or operator who sells a U.S. registered aircraft shall transfer to the purchaser, at the time of sale, the following records of that aircraft, in plain language form or in coded form at the election of the purchaser, if the coded form provides for the preservation and retrieval of information in a manner acceptable to the Administrator:

(a) The records specified in § 91.173(a)(2).

(b) The records specified in § 91.173(a)(1) which are not included in the records covered by paragraph (a) of this section, except that the purchaser may permit the seller to keep physical custody of such records. However, custody of records in the seller does not relieve the purchaser of his responsibility under § 91.173(c), to make the records available for inspection by the Administrator or any authorized representative of the National Transportation Safety Board (NTSB).

PART 830—RULES PERTAINING TO THE NOTIFICATION AND REPORTING OF AIRCRAFT ACCIDENTS OR INCIDENTS AND OVERDUE AIRCRAFT, AND PRESERVATION OF AIRCRAFT WRECKAGE, MAIL, CARGO, AND RECORDS

AUTHORITY: Title VII, Federal Aviation Act of 1958, as amended, 72 Stat. 781, as amended by 76 Stat. 921 (49 U.S.C. 1441 et seq.), and the Independent Safety Board Act of 1974, Pub. L. 93-633, 88 Stat. 2166 (49 U.S.C. 1901 et seq.).

SOURCE: 40 FR 30249, July 17, 1975, unless otherwise noted.

Subpart A—General

§ 830.1   Applicability.

This part contains rules pertaining to:

(a) Providing notice of and reporting, aircraft accidents and incidents and certain other occurrences in the operation of aircraft when they involve civil aircraft of the United States wherever they occur, or foreign civil aircraft when such events occur in the United States, its territories or possessions.

(b) Preservation of aircraft wreckage, mail, cargo, and records involving all civil aircraft in the United States, its territories or possessions.

§ 830.2   Definitions.

As used in this part the following words or phrases are defined as follows:

"Aircraft accident" means an occurrence associated with the operation of an aircraft which takes place between the time any person boards the aircraft with the intention of flight until such time as all such persons have disembarked, and in which any person suffers death or serious injury as a result of being in or upon the aircraft or by direct contact with the aircraft or anything attached thereto, or in which the aircraft receives substantial damage.

"Fatal injury" means any injury which results in death within 7 days of the accident.

"Operator" means any person who causes or authorizes the operation of an aircraft, such as the owner, lessee, or bailee of an aircraft.

"Serious injury" means any injury which (1) requires hospitalization for more than 48 hours, commencing within 7 days from the date the injury was received; (2) results in a fracture of any bone (except simple fractures of fingers, toes, or nose); (3) involves lacerations which cause severe hemorrhages, nerve, muscle, or tendon damage; (4) involves injury to any internal organ; or (5) involves second- or third-degree burns, or any burns affecting more than 5 percent of the body surface.

"Substantial damage":

(1) Except as provided in subparagraph (2) of this paragraph, substantial damage means damage or structural failure which adversely affects the structural strength, performance, or flight characteristics of the aircraft, and which would normally require major repair or replacement of the affected component.

(2) Engine failure, damage limited to an engine, bent fairings or cowling, dented skin, small punctured holes in the skin or fabric, ground damage to rotor or propeller blades, damage to landing gear, wheels, tires, flaps, engine accessories, brakes, or wingtips are not considered "substantial damage" for the purpose of this part.

Subpart B—Initial Notification of Aircraft Accidents, Incidents, and Overdue Aircraft

§ 830.5   Immediate notification.

The operator of an aircraft shall immediately, and by the most expeditious means available, notify the nearest National Transportation Safety Board (Board), field office [1] when:

(a) An aircraft accident or any of the following listed incidents occur:

(1) Flight control system malfunction or failure;

(2) Inability of any required flight crewmember to perform his normal flight duties as a result of injury or illness;

(3) Turbine engine rotor failures excluding compressor blades and turbine buckets;

(4) In-flight fire; or

(5) Aircraft collide in flight.

(b) An aircraft is overdue and is believed to have been involved in an accident.

[40 FR 30249, July 17, 1975, as amended at 41 FR 39758, Sept. 16, 1976]

§ 830.6   Information to be given in notification.

The notification required in § 830.5 shall contain the following information, if available:

(a) Type, nationality, and registration marks of the aircraft;

(b) Name of owner, and operator of the aircraft;

(c) Name of the pilot-in-command;

(d) Date and time of the accident;

(e) Last point of departure and point of intended landing of the aircraft;

(f) Position of the aircraft with reference to some easily defined geographical point;

(g) Number of persons aboard, number killed, and number seriously injured;

(h) Nature of the accident, the weather and the extent of damage to the aircraft, so far as is known; and

(i) A description of any explosives, radioactive materials, or other dangerous articles carried.

Subpart C—Preservation of Aircraft Wreckage, Mail, Cargo, and Records

§ 830.10   Preservation of aircraft wreckage, mail, cargo, and records.

(a) The operator of an aircraft is responsible for preserving to the extent

---

[1] The National Transportation Safety Board field offices are listed under U.S. Government in the telephone directories in the following cities: Anchorage, Alaska; Chicago, Ill.; Denver, Colo.; Fort Worth, Tex.; Kansas City, Mo.; Los Angeles, Calif.; Miami, Fla.; New York, N.Y.; Oakland, Calif.; Seattle, Wash.; Washington, D.C.

possible any aircraft wreckage, cargo, and mail aboard the aircraft, and all records, including tapes of flight recorders and voice recorders, pertaining to the operation and maintenance of the aircraft and to the airmen involved in an accident or incident for which notification must be given until the Board takes custody thereof or a release is granted pursuant to § 831.17.

(b) Prior to the time the Board or its authorized representative takes custody of aircraft wreckage, mail, or cargo, such wreckage, mail, or cargo may not be disturbed or moved except to the extent necessary:

(1) To remove persons injured or trapped;

(2) To protect the wreckage from further damage; or

(3) To protect the public from injury.

(c) Where it is necessary to disturb or move aircraft wreckage, mail or cargo, sketches, descriptive notes, and photographs shall be made, if possible, of the accident locale including original position and condition of the wreckage and any significant impact marks.

(d) The operator of an aircraft involved in an accident or incident as defined in this part, shall retain all records and reports, including all internal documents and memoranda dealing with the accident or incident, until authorized by the Board to the contrary.

Subpart D—Reporting of Aircraft Accidents, Incidents, and Overdue Aircraft

§ 830.15 Reports and statements to be filed.

(a) *Reports.* The operator of an aircraft shall file a report as provided in paragraph (c) of this section on Board Form 6120.1 or Board Form 6120.2 [2] within 10 days after an accident, or after 7 days if an overdue aircraft is still missing. A report on an incident for which notification is required by § 830.5(a) shall be filed only as requested by an authorized representative of the Board.

(b) *Crewmember statement.* Each crewmember, if physically able at the time the report is submitted, shall attach thereto a statement setting forth the facts, conditions, and circumstances relating to the accident or incident as they appear to him to the best of his knowledge and belief. If the crewmember is incapacitated, he shall submit the statement as soon as he is physically able.

(c) *Where to file the reports.* The operator of an aircraft shall file with the field office of the Board nearest the accident or incident any report required by this section.

NOTE: The reporting and recordkeeping requirements contained herein have been approved by the Office of Management and Budget in accordance with the Federal Reports Act of 1942.

---

[2] Forms are obtainable from the Board field offices (see footnote 1), the National Transportation Safety Board, Washington, D.C. 20594, and the Federal Aviation Administration, Flight Standards District Office.

NOTES

NOTES

NOTES

NOTES

NOTES

NOTES